COMPUTER CURRENTS

Navigating Tomorrow's Technology

COMPUTER CURRENTS

Navigating Tomorrow's Technology

GEORGE BEEKMAN

The Benjamin/Cummings Publishing Co., Inc.

Redwood City, California • Menlo Park, California
Reading, Massachusetts • New York • Don Mills, Ontario
Wokingham, U.K. • Amsterdam • Bonn
Singapore • Tokyo • Madrid • San Juan

Sponsoring Editor - **Maureen A. Allaire**
Senior Acquistions Editor - **Michelle Baxter**
Developmental Editor - **Jamie Spencer**
Production Editor - **Jean Lake**
Editorial Assistant - **MaryLynne Wrye**
Art and Design Manager - **Michele Carter**
Cover Art - **© Robert Stein**
Cover Designer - **Ark Stein**
Text Designer - **John Martucci**
Illustrations - **Illustrious, Inc.**
Photo Editors - **Cecilia Mills, Kelli d'Angona West**
Photo Researchers - **Sarah Bendersky, PhotoSynthesis**
Copy Editor - **Barbara Conway**
Desktop Composition - **Bookman Productions**
Film - **Color Tech**
Printing and Binding - **R. R. Donnelley & Sons Company**

Library of Congress Cataloging-in-Publication Data

Beekman, George.
Computer currents / George Beekman.
p. cm.
Includes bibliographical references and index.
ISBN 0-8053-2448-8. — ISBN 0-8053-2454-2
1. Computers. 2. Computer software. I. Title.
QA76.5.B3653 1993
004—dc20 93-36698
CIP

SE ISBN 0-8053-2448-8
IE ISBN 0-8053-2454-2

2 3 4 5 6 7 8 9 10 - DO - 97 96 95 94

The Benjamin/Cummings Publishing Company, Inc.
390 Bridge Parkway
Redwood City, CA 94065

To my children, Ben and Johanna,
and to all children and young adults.

The promise of the future lies not in technology but in you.

Lead Your Students Into the Future With an Outstanding Instructional Support System

Instructor's Edition You'll have course and lecture organization at your fingertips with the instructor's version of the student text, written by George Beekman and Shelly Langman. In a special section found at the end of the book, this important resource includes teaching tips, teaching extras, in-class exercises, and answers to review and discussion questions. (32454-2)

Instructor's Manual Supplement your lecture material with this useful manual written by George Beekman and Shelly Langman that extends the information in both the text and the *Instructor's Edition* with behavioral objectives, chapter overview, key terms, outline, and transparency masters. (32452-6)

Printed Test Bank Written by Karen Forcht and George Beekman, the test bank contains approximately 1500 items, including multiple choice, true/false, matching, completion, and situational essay questions. (32457-7)

Electronic Transparencies Prepared by George Beekman, these innovative "animated" transparencies integrate information from the text into a format that you can manipulate, print as handouts, make into transparencies, or display directly from a computer for use in lectures. Available for the Macintosh (32462-3), IBM (32463-1), and PS/2 (32456-9).

Computerized Test Bank This software provides the same test items as the printed test bank and allows you to edit questions and generate multiple test forms. Available for the Macintosh (32458-5), IBM (32461-5), and PS/2 (32459-3).

Color Transparency Acetates This collection of full-color acetates provides you with excellent visual support in your lectures, bringing the art, diagrams, and application screens from the text to your classroom. (32449-6)

***How Computers Work* CD-ROM Package** Bring the exciting world of computers to life with this CD-ROM package for the Macintosh. For use in either lecture or lab, this completely interactive tool lets you expand on the text while examining the past, present, and future of desktop computing. This package also includes sample versions of popular software programs, an easy-to-use LOGO programming activity, an illustrated look at input and output, and more.

***ComputerWorks* CD-ROM or Software for the PC** Let your students explore the world of computers with this interactive package for the PC. Colorful animated graphics are combined with text to illustrate the inner workings of computer components, chart the evolution of computer technology, and examine related topics, such as artificial intelligence, virtual reality, and multimedia. *ComputerWorks* also features detailed lesson plans, challenging quizzes, and an advanced interactive interface that allows students to take notes on-line, export text and graphics, and print customized reports.

Videos Benjamin/Cummings offers videotapes from our library of commercially produced videos to qualified adopters. This valuable resource is an excellent way to enhance your lectures. Contact your Benjamin/Cummings sales representative for details.

The Machine That Changed the World This award-winning PBS series highlights the 50-year revolution in computing and its profound and unexpected impact on society. The videos chart the course of information technology from data processing to personal computers to the world of virtual reality.

Annenberg Video Series Give your students a comprehensive overview of the computer with this excellent series. Dozens of computer experts, including Grace M. Hopper, Isaac Asimov, and Michael Crichton, place textbook knowledge in a real-world setting.

How Computers Work: A Journey Into the Walk-Through Computer™ An entertaining and educational trip through The Computer Museum's one-of-a-kind working model of a desktop computer.

State of the Art of Computer Animation This collection of computer animation shows works ranging from flights of fancy to realistic simulations to never-seen-before commercials.

University Gradebook A complete recordkeeping system available for the IBM PC and compatibles. (32268-X)

The SELECT System for Custom Publishing

Create a text that fits your course needs exactly with the SELECT System, Benjamin/Cummings' innovative custom publishing program. With SELECT, you can build a custom edition of *Computer Currents* by combining the text with one or more hands-on application modules. Or you can combine the modules with each other to create a custom-bound lab manual.

Written for the beginning student, all of the application modules follow a consistent, pedagogically sound format. The modules include a brief introduction to key concepts plus six to nine increasingly challenging projects. Most modules are 128 to 180 pages in length. Modules for integrated packages are approximately 400 pages in length.

To better provide you with information about pricing, ISBN numbers, and ordering, Benjamin/Cummings offers the SELECT Hotline, a toll-free information line dedicated to answering your questions about custom publishing. Just call 800/854-2595 between 8:30 and 4:30 Pacific time.

Lotus 1-2-3 Software

Teach your students the world's leading business productivity software with "Basic" Lotus 1-2-3 for Students. This affordably priced, fully functional application contains a full-sized spreadsheet and is compatible with the professional version of Lotus 1-2-3, Release 2.2.

Benjamin/Cummings also offers student edition software with tutorial guides for Lotus 1-2-3, Releases 2.2 and 2.3. If you would like more information, contact your local sales representative.

The ATI *Teach Me* Tutorials for Hands-On Instruction

Imagine teaching Lotus 1-2-3, dBASE, or any other program without access to the software. American Training International's (ATI) unique *Teach Me* series helps your students learn popular software packages quickly, easily, and effectively. Created by an educator, this affordable series provides computer-based training in a pedagogical framework that reinforces learning with review material, objectives, and immediate feedback. Offered exclusively from Benjamin/Cummings, this outstanding tutorial software features self-contained training programs, split-screen tutorials, and self-paced learning.

ATI's broad spectrum of training programs provides the latest versions of popular software packages such as dBASE IV Version 1.5, Lotus 1-2-3, Releases 2.2 and 2.4, WordPerfect 5.1, Windows 3.1, and MS DOS 5.0. Programs are available individually for complete instruction in a package or in a multipack that offers broad coverage for survey classes.

For more information and a complete list of the packages available, please contact your Benjamin/Cummings sales representative or call 800/552-2499.

Brief Table of Contents

PART ONE

Approaching Computers
Hardware and Software Fundamentals 1

PART TWO

Using Computers
Essential Applications 61

PART THREE

Mastering Computers

PART FOUR

Living with Computers

Detailed Table of Contents

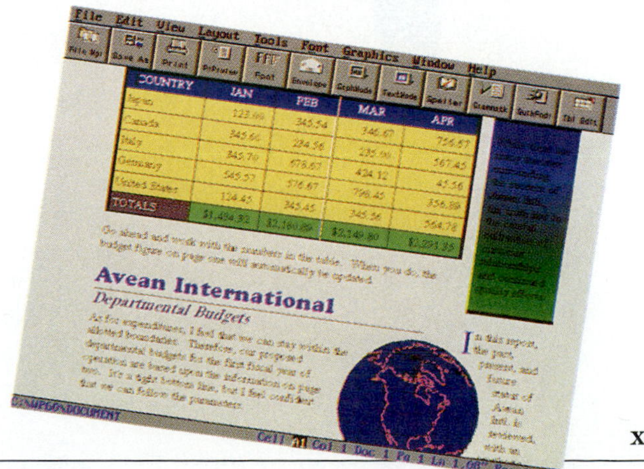

File Edit View Layout Tools Font Graphics Window Help
COUNTRY JAN FEB MAR APR
TOTALS
Avean International
Departmental Budgets

PART TWO

Using Computers

"It is not in the stars to hold our destiny but in ourselves."
Shakespeare
Environmental Science: Action for a Sustainable Future
Fourth Edition
by Daniel D. Chiras

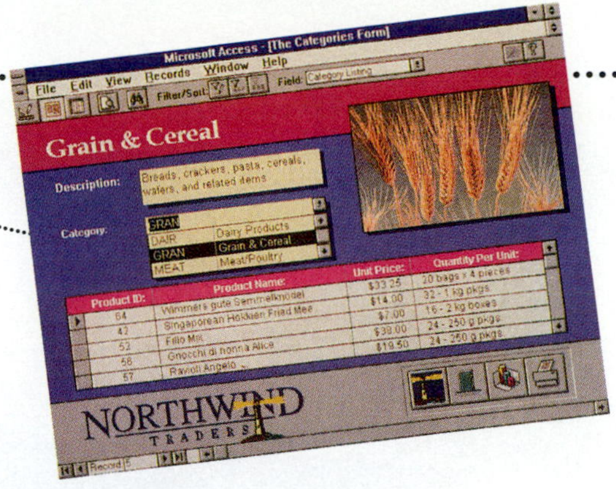

CHAPTER 5

Calculation, Visualization, and Simulation 84

CHAPTER 6

Database Applications and Implications 104

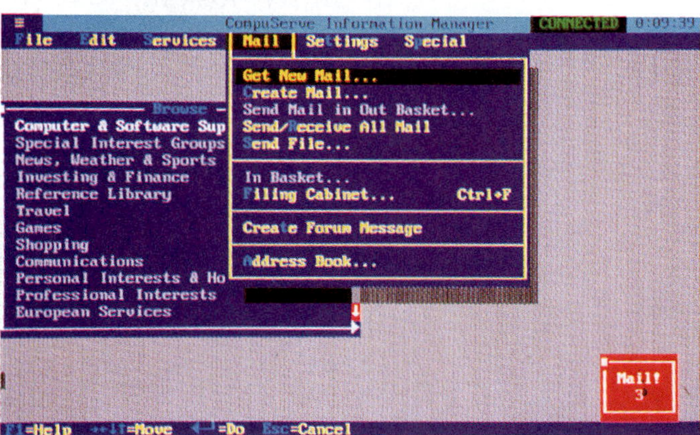

CompuServe Information Manager
CONNECTED 0:09:39
Mail
Get New Mail...
Send Mail in Out Basket...
Computer & Software Sup
Special Interest Groups
News, Weather & Sports
Investing & Finance
Reference Library
Travel
Games
Shopping
Communications
Personal Interests & Ho
Professional Interests
European Services
In Basket...
Ctrl+F
Create Forum Message
Mail!
3

PART THREE

Mastering Computers

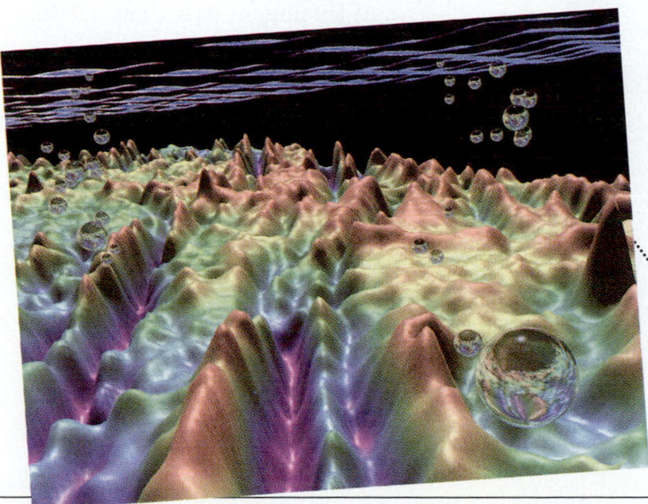

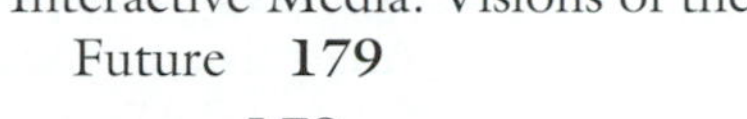

PART FOUR

Living with Computers

Into the Information Age 233

Even if you're on the right track, you'll get run over if you just sit on it.

—— *Pat Koppman*

In the world of computers and information technology, it sometimes seems like change is the only constant. Every day brings news of smaller computers, faster processors, larger networks, and smarter software. And as we think up new ways to put computer technology to work, our world becomes evermore computerized. In less than a human lifetime, the computer has transformed virtually every facet of our society—and the transformation is just beginning. The pace of the computer revolution has become so explosive that farfetched predictions routinely come true.

This headlong rush into the high-tech future poses a formidable challenge to educators: How do we provide timely information on a subject about which last year's news seems antiquated? How can we be sure that a freshman-level Introduction to Computers class won't seem like a History of Computers class by the time those freshmen graduate? How do we design courses that provide students with practical, expansive, lasting knowledge about computers and information technology?

It's no longer enough to teach students the fundamentals of programming in assembly language or BASIC and call them "computer literate." Nor can we assume that students who know WordStar and VisiCalc keystrokes are properly equipped to survive and prosper in the computer age. In fact, any hands-on experience is likely to have a short shelf life unless it's accompanied by material that provides a broader context.

Computer Currents presents computers and information technology on three levels:

- Explanations: *Computer Currents* clearly explains what a computer is and what it can (and can't) do.
- Applications: *Computer Currents* clearly illustrates how computers can be used as practical tools to accomplish a wide variety of tasks and solve a wide variety of problems.
- Implications: *Computer Currents* puts computers in a human context, illustrating how computers affect our lives, our world, and our future.

Who Is This Book For?

Computer Currents: Navigating Tomorrow's Technology is especially written for the introductory computer class for college freshmen, majors and nonmajors. A growing number of computer science departments are developing courses for nonmajors. Business departments are increasingly finding that their introductory computing classes are popular with majors and nonmajors alike. *Computer Currents: Navigating Tomorrow's Technology* is designed for these classes.

Most introductory computer courses are divided into lecture and lab sections. In some courses the labs cover computer applications like Microsoft Excel, WordPerfect, and LotusWorks; in others the labs cover programming with BASIC, Pascal, or HyperCard; still others cover both. Since this book focuses on the concepts covered in lecture, it can be used in any of these classes. There are dozens of books covering applications and programming languages that can be used for the lab segment of this course. The Benjamin/Cummings SELECT System includes hands-on modules covering many of the most popular applications and programming languages. These modules may be purchased separately or bound together with *Computer Currents* in a custom book.

Computer Currents: Navigating Tomorrow's Technology is also ideal for many introductory computer science classes, discipline-specific computer courses offered through other departments, high school courses, and adult education courses.

How Is This Book Different?

Computer Currents: Navigating Tomorrow's Technology is designed for the 90s.

- *Rather than dwelling on technical details, it concentrates on big ideas and significant trends in the world of computing.* This book applies a journalistic writing style to the textbook form; the result is a book that's fun to read, easy to understand, and valuable as a reference and study aid.
- *It is modular, so students can read what they need.* No two classes are the same, and this book can be used in many different kinds of courses. Chapters are relatively short and, for the most part, self-contained, so students don't need to read every chapter to learn what they need to know.
- *It doesn't dwell on button pushing. Computer Currents* is designed to provide background and breadth for students who are getting hands-on experience with other books and software packages. It deals with what and why; students can learn how in the computer labs.
- *It brings applications down to earth.* Instead of just describing computer applications in abstract paragraphs laced with technical terminology, this book balances concepts with "User's View" boxes that give students a feel for what it's like to put those applications to work.
- *It doesn't just talk about current computers, it discusses computer currents.* Even if students are working with character-based software in the labs today, they're likely to graduate into a world filled with graphical computer displays. Computing a decade from now may progress far beyond windows, icons, and mice. *Computer Currents* focuses on today's state-of-the-art graphical software for most examples, suggesting trends that are likely to lead to the next generation of applications and interfaces. While *Computer Currents* emphasizes the emerging de facto GUI standard, it doesn't ignore MS-DOS, UNIX, and other traditionally nongraphical environments.
- *It stresses the human side of computing. Computer Currents* isn't just for computer science and business majors; it's for students whose lives will be affected by computer technology. It provides clear, nontechnical answers to the questions, "What can (and can't) computers do?" and "How do they affect my life and my future?" *Computer Currents* deals with subjects ranging from databases and networks to multimedia and artificial intelligence, from a human perspective; students who read it have clear answers to the question, "How does this technology affect me?"
- *It looks at the positive and the negative aspects of the computer culture.* The computer is changing human lives and societies for better and for worse; this book deals clearly and concisely with ethical, social, and psychological issues of the computer age. The computer is always the central focus; issues surrounding computer use and abuse are raised to provide a broader perspective.

How Are Chapters Organized?

The book consists of 14 chapters organized into four broad sections:

1. *Approaching Computers: Hardware and Software Fundamentals*
2. *Using Computers: Essential Applications*
3. *Mastering Computers: From Applications to Intelligence*
4. *Living with Computers: Into the Information Age*

Part 1 provides the basics: a brief historical perspective, a nontechnical discussion of computer basics, and an overview of hardware and software options. These chapters quickly introduce key concepts that recur throughout the book, putting the student on a solid framework for understanding future chapters. Part 2 covers the most important and widely used computer applications, including word processing, spreadsheets, databases, and telecommunication. These applications, like those in Part 3, are presented in terms of concepts and trends rather than keystrokes. Part 3 explores more exotic applications and programming tools, ranging from graphics and interactive multimedia to artificial intelligence and robotics. Part 4 explores the far-reaching impact of computers on our work, our homes, our society, and our future. Throughout these four parts the book's focus gradually flows from the concrete to the controversial and from the present to the future.

Individual chapters have a similarly expanding focus. After a brief introduction, each chapter flows from concrete concepts that provide grounding for beginners toward abstract, future-oriented questions and ideas. Chapters are relatively short and nontechnical so they can be read quickly. Key terms are highlighted in boldface type for quick reference; secondary terms are italicized. All important terms are defined in context and in a glossary at the end of the text. Each chapter begins with a list of objectives and ends with a chapter summary; a list of key terms; collections of review questions, discussion questions, and projects; and an annotated list of sources and resources for students who want more information or intellectual stimulation.

Throughout *Computer Currents* special focus boxes complement the text:

- *Human Connection* boxes at the beginning of each chapter feature micro-stories of personalities who made an impact on the world of computing, and in some cases, people whose lives were transformed by computers and information technology. These short stories, along with other futuristic stories in the book, convey important concepts in an entertaining way.
- *User's View* boxes show the reader, through screens and text, what it's like to work with selected computer applications without getting bogged down in the details of button pushing. Most of the featured applications are available on both IBM-compatible and Macintosh platforms.
- *Rules of Thumb* boxes provide practical, nontechnical tips for avoiding the pitfalls and problems created by computer technology. How can you use graphics effectively and tastefully in a computer document? How can you minimize the health hazards of extended computer use? How can you protect your data from viruses and other software risks? How can you guard your personal privacy against intrusive databases? These are the types of questions that are answered in Rules of Thumb boxes.

A Word to the Student

If you're like most students, you aren't taking this course to *read* about computers—you want to *use* them. That's sensible. You can't really understand computers without some hands-on experience, and you'll be able to apply your computer skills to a wide variety of future projects.

But it's a mistake to think that you're computer savvy just because you can use a PC to write term papers and draw pie charts. It's important to understand how people use and abuse computer technology, because that technology has a powerful and growing impact on your life. (If you can't imagine how your life would be different without computers, read the vignette called "Living Without Computers" in Chapter 1.) Even if you have lots of computer experience, future trends are almost certain to make much of that experience obsolete—probably sooner than you think. In the next few years computers are likely to take on entirely new forms and roles because of breakthroughs in artificial intelligence, voice recognition, virtual reality, interactive multimedia, hypermedia, wireless communication, networking, and cross-breeding with telephone and home entertainment technologies. If your knowledge of computers stops with a handful of PC applications, you may be standing still while the world changes around you.

When you're cascading through white water, you need to be able to use a paddle, but it's also important to know how to read a map, a compass, and the river. *Computer Currents: Navigating Tomorrow's Technology* is designed to serve as a map, compass, and book of river lore to help you ride the information waves into the future.

Computer Currents will help you understand the important trends that will change the way you work with computers and the way computers work for you. This book discusses the promise and the problems of computer technology without overwhelming you with technobabble.

Computer Currents is intentionally nontechnical and down-to-earth. Occasional ministories bring concepts and speculations to life. User's View boxes show you what it's like to be in the driver's seat with some of the most powerful and popular software on the market today. Rules of Thumb boxes provide practical survival tips for the computer age. Illustrations and photos make abstract concepts concrete. Quotes add thought-provoking and humorous seasoning.

Whether you're a hard-core hacker or a confirmed computerphobe, there's something for you in *Computer Currents.* Dive in!

Rules of Thumb

Navigating *Computer Currents*

Here are a few pointers to aid you on your journey through *Computer Currents:*

- **Don't try to memorize every term the first time through.** Computer jargon can be overwhelming if you tackle it all at once. Throughout the text, key terms are introduced in boldface and secondary terms are italicized. Use the Key Terms list at the end of each chapter to review and the glossary to recall any forgotten terms.
- **Read it and read it again.** If possible, read each chapter twice: once for the big ideas and the second time for more detailed understanding. You may also find it helpful to survey each chapter's outline in the table of contents before reading the chapter for the first time.
- **Don't get stuck.** If a concept seems unclear on the first reading, make a note and move on. Sometimes ideas make more sense after you've seen the bigger picture. If you still don't understand the second time through, ask questions.
- **Don't overanalyze examples.** This book is designed to help you understand concepts, not memorize keystrokes. You can learn the nuts and bolts of working with computers in labs.
- **Get your hands dirty.** If possible, try the applications while you're reading about them. When you read about word processing in *Computer Currents,* get some firsthand word processing experience. Your reading and your lab work will reinforce each other and help solidify your newfound knowledge.
- **Remember that there's more than one way to accomplish something with a computer.** The examples in this text may not match the applications you learn in your lab, but the concepts are similar.
- **Study together.** There's plenty to discuss here, and discussion is a great way to learn.

ACKNOWLEDGMENTS

Writing a book requires countless hours of working alone, but it isn't just solo work. This book is undeniably a team effort. I've been fortunate to work with a wonderful team of editors and other professionals at Benjamin/Cummings—hard-working, talented people who helped turn my rough manuscript into the book you now hold in your hands. Their names may not be on the cover, but their high-quality work shows on every page. I'm delighted to have the opportunity to publicly thank them for their invaluable contributions. Throughout the project, I worked most closely with Jamie Spencer, the developmental editor who helped turn my ramblings into civilized prose. Jamie and I worked closely with Michelle Baxter and Maureen Allaire, two editors whose shared courage and vision helped make *Computer Currents* a book for the future rather than a remake of past successes. Jean Lake skillfully manuevered thousands of details through the production process. Barbara Conway's copy editing proved once again that automated spelling and style checkers are no substitute for a highly skilled human professional. The outstanding photos are here thanks to the work of a team of top-notch photo editors headed by Cecilia Mills and Kelli d'Angona West. Michele Carter's eye was central to the art and graphic design of the book. Ari Davidow and Craig Johnson wrestled with the myriad of technical issues related to the project. Shelly Langman did outstanding work on the Instructor's Manual and other ancillary materials. Kathy Galinac, May Woo, and MaryLynne Wrye handled tasks too numerous to mention. Dozens of others at B/C helped with this book. They've all been a joy to work with, and I thank them again.

There are others who contributed to *Computer Currents* in all kinds of ways, including critiquing chapters, testing programs, answering technical questions, providing equipment, tracking down obscure references, guiding me through difficult decisions, and being there when I needed support. There's no room here to detail their contributions, but I want to thank the people who gave time, energy, talent, and support during the years that this book was under development: Rajeev Pandey, Clay Cowgill, Dave Stuve, Marilyn Wallace, Michael Johnson, Walter Rudd, Bob Broeg, Eric Johnson, Kevin Djang, Karen Meyer-Arendt, Alice Trinka, Paul Ritter, Jeanne Holmes, Shawn Larson, Robert Baldwin, Lentil Bean, Bruce D'Ambrosio, Scott Anderson, Chris Kempke, John Donel, Phil Brown, Cherie Taylor, Pat Anderson, Don Abbott, Lori Maliszweski, Claudette Hastie-Baehrs, Shjoobedebop, SMILE, and the hardworking computer science office staff. Thanks to the dozens of CS 101 students who provided me with feedback on the manuscript in progress, especially Lori Carlson, Scott Paulson, Kevin Hamilton, Susan Carney, Mario Magana, Andrea Baker, Sum Yee Lai, Ann Goldsborough, Matt Killinger, and Cathy Helvin. Thanks also to the people at Apple, IBM, NCR, and all the other hardware and software companies whose cooperation made my work easier. And most of all, thanks to Susan, Ben, and Johanna, whose patience, support, and love inspired me to carry this project through to completion.

REVIEWERS

Virginia T. Anderson
University of North Dakota
Grand Forks, North Dakota

Michael H. Boster
University of Texas at Brownsville
Brownsville, Texas

Doris M. Carey
University of Colorado at Colorado Springs
Colorado Springs, Colorado

Lillian Cassel
Villanova University
Villanova, Pennsylvania

John Da Ponte
Southern Connecticut State University
New Haven, Connecticut

Philip East
University of Northern Iowa
Cedar Falls, Iowa

Doris Edwards
National Education Center
Sacramento, California

Donna J. Ehrhart
Genessee Community College
Batavia, New York

Karen A. Forcht
James Madison University
Harrisonburg, Virginia

Jeff Frates
Los Medanos College
Pittsburg, California

Kevin M. Gleason
Mount Ida College
Newton Centre, Massachusetts

Elaine Haight
Foothill Community College
Los Altos Hills, California

Cindy Meyer Hanchey
Oklahoma Baptist University
Shawnee, Oklahoma

Gerald M. Haskins
University of Florida
Gainesville, Florida

R. Wayne Headrick
New Mexico State University
Las Cruces, New Mexico

Walter Roy Hill
Cardinal Stritch College
Milwaukee, Wisconsin

H. Joel Jeffrey
Northern Illinois University
De Kalb, Illinois

Wallace Jewell
Edinboro University of Pennsylvania
Edinboro, Pennsylvania

Suzanne M. Lea
University of North Carolina at Greensboro
Greensboro, North Carolina

Barbara Maccarone
North Shore Community College
Danvers, Massachusetts

Margaret Miller
Skyline Community College
San Bruno, California

James R. F. Quirk
Kentucky Wesleyan College
Owensboro, Kentucky

Chuck Riden
Arizona State University
Tempe, Arizona

Jane M. Ritter
University of Oregon
Eugene, Oregon

Dana S. Roberson
Community College of Southern Nevada
Las Vegas, Nevada

Richard St. Andre
Central Michigan University
Mount Pleasant, Michigan

Richard Spool
Massachusetts Bay Community College
Wellesley, Massachusetts

John C. Stevens
University of Scranton
Scranton, Pennsylvania

John W. Telford
Salem State College
Salem, Massachusetts

George Upchurch
Carson-Newman College
Jefferson City, Tennessee

Santosh Venkatraman
Northeast Louisiana University
Monroe, Louisiana

Jon D. Weerts
Triton College
River Grove, Illinois

Linda Werner
University of California—Santa Cruz
Santa Cruz, California

Robert E. Wood
Drake University
Des Moines, Iowa

The SELECT System

The Benjamin/Cummings SELECT System delivers high-quality computer concepts in texts and applications modules with flexible formats. With SELECT, you can create a text customized for the course you teach. And since 1992, SELECT has been the right solution for hundreds of institutions.

A Text with Concepts and Customized Application Coverage

With the SELECT System, you can combine *Computer Currents* with your choice of hands-on applications modules. The modules you select are bound with *Computer Currents* into one convenient, durable text. Modules are also available separately. We offer the following selection of modules:

Operating Systems	DOS 6.0 and Windows 3.1 (180 pages) DOS 5.0 and Windows 3.1 (174 pages) DOS 3.3 and Windows 3.0 (128 pages)
Word Processing	WordPerfect 5.2 for Windows (128 pages) WordPerfect 6.0 (144 pages) WordPerfect 5.1 (128 pages)
Spreadsheets	Lotus 1-2-3, Release 2.2 (144 pages) Lotus 1-2-3, Release 2.3/2.4 (176 pages) Excel 4.0 for Windows (144 pages) Excel 3.0 for PCs (160 pages) Quattro Pro 4.0/5.0 (144 pages) Quattro Pro for Windows 1.0/5.0 (144 pages)
Databases	Paradox for Windows (144 pages) Paradox 3.5 (170 pages) dBASE IV (182 pages) dBASE III PLUS (138 pages)
Integrated Packages	Microsoft Works 3.0 for PCs (450 pages) Microsoft Works 2.0 for PCs (450 pages)
Programming Languages	Structured BASIC (96 pages) QBasic (128 pages)

Each module is written by experienced authors and instructors and follows a consistent, pedagogically sound format. The authors were assisted by an experienced team of professionals, including developmental editors, reviewers, technical editors, and copy editors. The modules begin with basic concepts such as using the program, getting help, and an explanation of the conventions used in the modules. Students learn how to use the software by solving problems in increasingly challenging projects.

These projects, based on general-interest examples and business documents, are the core of the student's learning process. Students are challenged to learn the concepts behind the keystrokes as they work through the projects.

Each project includes objectives, keystroke instructions, screen captures, and check documents; and each ends with a summary, a list of key terms, and review exercises. Each module concludes with a command reference, an extensive glossary, and an index. The modules are intended for the first time computer user and contain selected advanced topics for the more experienced student.

Advantages of the SELECT System

The SELECT System brings you and your students many advantages:

- **Flexibility.** You can adapt your textbook to your curriculum by choosing any combination of the modules you prefer. And if your course should change next term, you can choose a new selection of modules to meet your new course needs. Benjamin/Cummings will introduce additional modules that cover new and upgraded software and programming applications. For 1994, we will introduce a series of modules covering Windows applications. If we don't currently publish modules for the specific software packages you teach, please contact your Benjamin/Cummings sales representative or call the SELECT System Hotline at 800/854-2595. We will be happy to work with you to address your textbook requirements.
- **Convenience.** The SELECT System gives you computer concepts plus the exact lab coverage you want all in one text and from one publisher. And with our low minimum order policy, SELECT can be the right solution for almost every course. Also, your students will like the ease of carrying only one text to both lecture and lab.
- **Affordability.** Each module is individually priced. Because you select just those modules you plan to teach, your students pay only for what they need. And because we offer the text and modules bound into one volume, students don't pay higher prices for costly binders and packaging.
- **Improved Instructional Package.** With computers so much a part of our daily lives, your students deserve the best preparation possible. The SELECT System and *Computer Currents* give you up-to-date coverage of computer concepts, pedagogically consistent, customized lab instruction; and the most complete instructional support available.

In addition to the complete instructional support package for the *Computer Currents* textbook, qualified adopters can order an individual *Instructor's Manual with Tests and Transparency Masters* for each module. The study questions in the modules can serve as a Student Study Guide if you provide your students with the answer key from the Instructor's Manual. Also available to module adopters is the *Instructor's Data Disk,* containing electronic files, selected answers and projects, and student data files.

Complimentary Review Copies

Benjamin/Cummings prepared the following materials for review and adoption consideration:

- **The Instructor's Edition of *Computer Currents.*** This edition contains the complete contents of the student text plus a 64-page, bound-in guide with various teaching materials to support instruction.

- **The Applications Modules.** The modules are bound separately as a sample for your review. Once adopted, the modules you have selected will be bound with *Computer Currents.* The *Instructor's Manual with Tests and Transparency Masters* are also available for review purposes.

Ordering and Pricing Information

Your Benjamin/Cummings representative will be happy to provide you and your bookstore manager with information about ordering, pricing, and delivery. You may also call the SELECT System Hotline at 800/854-2595 if you have questions or need complimentary review or desk copies.

PART ONE

Approaching Computers
Hardware and Software Fundamentals

C H A P T E R

ONE

Computers in Context

After reading this chapter you should be able to

- explain what a computer is and what it does
- describe several ways computers play a critical role in modern life
- discuss the circumstances and ideas that led to the development of the modern computer
- describe several trends in the evolution of modern computers
- explain the fundamental difference between computers and other machines
- explain the relationship between hardware and software
- discuss the four major types of computers in use today and describe their principal uses

Charles Babbage, Ada Lovelace, and the Computer That Never Was

The Analytical Engine has no pretensions whatever to originate anything. It can do whatever we know how to order it to perform.

—— *Countess Ada Lovelace*

The Analytical Engine Ada Lovelace referred to was the first computer, conceived by Charles Babbage, a 19th-century mathematics professor at Cambridge University. Babbage was an eccentric genius known by the public for his war with street musicians. He calculated that they sapped him of 25 percent of his working power and worked to have them outlawed. But Babbage was more than a crank; his many inventions included the skeleton key, the locomotive cow catcher, the speedometer, and . . . the computer.

Babbage's computer vision grew out of frustration with the tedious and error-prone process of creating mathematical tables. In 1823 he asked for and received a grant from the British government to develop a difference engine—a mechanical device for performing repeated additions. In the meantime Joseph-Marie Charles Jacquard, a French textile maker, had developed a loom that could automatically reproduce woven patterns by reading information encoded in patterns of holes punched in stiff paper cards. After learning of Jacquard's programmable loom, Babbage abandoned the difference engine for a more ambitious enterprise: an **Analytical Engine** that could be programmed with punched

Charles Babbage

Ada Lovelace

cards to carry out *any* calculation to 20 digits of accuracy.

Ada Lovelace, the mathematically gifted daughter of poet Lord Byron, visited Babbage and became fascinated by the Analytical Engine. A classic triangle developed: Babbage was in love with her; she was in love with Babbage's machine. Lovelace corresponded regularly with Babbage and published a paper on the Analytical Engine that included the first computer program. She became Babbage's partner, expanding on his vision and correcting errors in his work.

Babbage and Lovelace became obsessed with completing the Analytical Engine. Eventually the government withdrew financial support; there simply wasn't enough public demand to justify the ever-increasing cost. Babbage and Lovelace gambled on horses and pawned jewels to raise money for the project, but to no avail. The technology of the time was not sufficient to turn their ideas into reality. The world wasn't ready for computers, and it wouldn't be for another hundred years.

Analytical Engine

Computers are so much a part of modern life that we hardly notice them. But computers are everywhere, and we'd certainly notice them if they suddenly stopped working. Imagine . . .

Living Without Computers

You wake up with the sun well above the horizon and realize your alarm clock hasn't gone off. You wonder if you've overslept; you have a big research project to finish today. The face of your digital wristwatch stares back at you blankly. The TV and radio are no help; you can't find a station on either one. You can't even get the time by telephone, because it doesn't work either.

The morning newspaper is missing from your doorstep. You'll have to guess the weather forecast by looking out the window. No music to dress by this morning—your CD player refuses your requests. How about some breakfast? Your automatic coffee maker refuses to be programmed; your microwave oven is on strike, too.

You decide to go out for breakfast. Your car won't start. In fact the only cars moving are at least 15 years old. The lines at the subway are unbelievable. People chatter nervously about the failure of the subway's computer-controlled scheduling device.

You duck into a fast-food outlet and find long lines of people waiting while cashiers handle transactions by hand. Still, you're hungry, so you decide to wait and join the conversation that's going on around you. People seem more interested in talking to each other since all the usual tools of mass communication have failed.

You're down to a couple of dollars in cash, so you stop after breakfast at an automated teller machine. Why bother?

You return home to wait for the book you ordered by overnight mail. You soon realize that you're in for a long wait; planes aren't flying because air-traffic-control facilities aren't working. You head for the local library to see if the book is in stock. Of course, it's going to be tough to find since the book catalog is computerized.

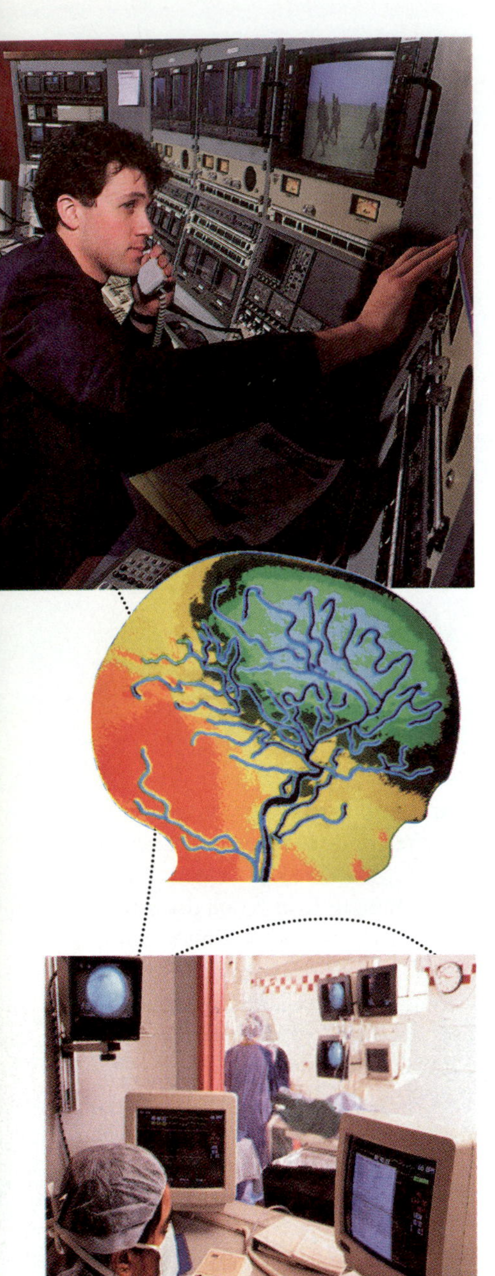

Computers used by a technician in a TV control room (top), to create a CATSCAN of the brain (middle), and during cardiac angioplasty (blood vessel surgery) (bottom).

As you walk home you speculate on the implications of a worldwide computer failure. How will people function in high-tech, high-rise office buildings that depend on computer systems to control everything from elevators to humidity? Will electric power plants be able to function without computer control? What will happen to patients in computerized medical facilities? What about satellites that are kept in orbit by computer-control systems? Will the financial infrastructure collapse without computers to process and communicate transactions? Will the world be a safer place if all computer-controlled weapons are grounded?

Our story could go on, but the message should be clear enough by now. Computers are everywhere, and our lives are affected in all kinds of ways by their operation, and nonoperation. It's truly amazing that computers have infiltrated our lives so thoroughly in such a short time.

Computers in Perspective: An Evolving Idea

Consider the past and you shall know the future.

—*Chinese Proverb*

While the computer has been with us for only about half a century, its roots go back to a time long before Charles Babbage conceived of the Analytical Engine. This extraordinary machine is built on centuries of insight and intellectual effort.

BC: Before Computers

Computers grew out of a human need to quantify. Early humans were content to count with fingers or rocks. As cultures became more complex, so did their counting tools. The abacus, the Arabic number system, and the concept of zero are only three examples of early calculating tools. Each of these ideas spread rapidly and had an immediate and profound effect on society.

The Analytical Engine had no impact on the development of calculating tools until a century after its invention, when it served as a blueprint for the first *real* programmable computer. Virtually every computer in use today follows the basic plan laid out by Babbage and Lovelace.

The Information-Processing Machine

Like the Analytical Engine, the computer is a machine that changes information from one form to another. All computers take in information (**input**) and give out information (**output**), as shown below.

Because information can take many forms, the computer is an incredibly versatile tool, capable of everything from computing federal income taxes to guiding the missiles those taxes buy. For calculating taxes, the input to the computer might be numbers representing wages, other income, deductions, exemptions, and tax tables, and the output might be the number representing the taxes owed. If the computer is deploying a missile, the inputs might be radio and radar signals for locating the missile and the target, and the output might be electrical signals to control

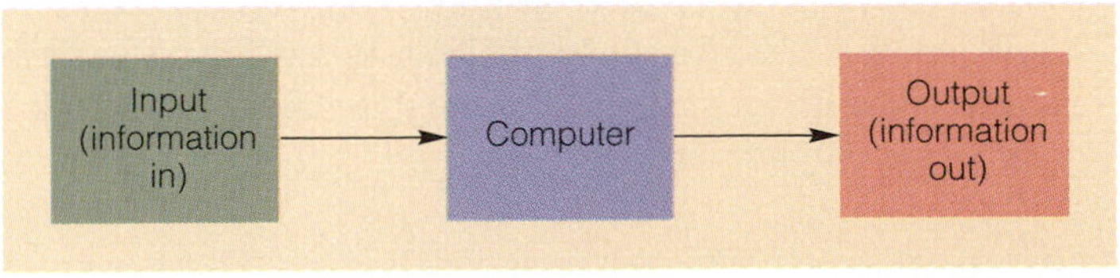

the flight path of the missile. Amazingly enough, the same computer could be used to accomplish all these tasks.

How can a machine be so versatile? The computer's flexibility isn't hidden in **hardware**—the physical parts of the computer system. The secret is **software**, or **programs**—the instructions that tell the hardware what to do to transform the input **data** (information in a form it can read) into the necessary output.

Whether a computer is doing a simple calculation or producing a complex animation, a program controls the process from beginning to end. In effect, changing programs can turn the computer into a different tool. Because it can be programmed to perform various tasks, the typical modern computer is a general-purpose tool.

The First *Real* Computers

Although Ada Lovelace predicted that the Analytical Engine might someday compose music, the scientists and mathematicians who designed and built the first working computers a century later had more modest goals: to create machines capable of doing repetitive mathematical calculations. Here are some landmark examples:

- In 1939 a young German engineer named Konrad Zuse completed the first programmable, general-purpose digital computer—a machine he built from electric relays to automate the process of doing engineering calculations. "I was too lazy to calculate and so I invented the computer," Zuse recalls. In 1941 Zuse and a friend asked the German government for funds to build a faster *electronic* computer using vacuum tubes. Their two-year project, which might have had numerous military applications, was not funded. The Nazi military establishment was confident that their aircraft could quickly win the war without the aid of sophisticated calculating devices.
- In 1939 Iowa State Professor John Atanasoff, seeking a tool to help his graduate students solve long, complex differential equations, developed what could have been the first electronic digital computer, the Atanasoff-Berry Computer (ABC). His university never bothered to patent Atanasoff's ground-breaking machine, and Atanasoff never managed to turn it into a fully operational product. The International Business Machines Corporation responded to his queries by telling him "IBM will never be interested in an electronic computing machine."
- Harvard professor Howard Aiken was more successful in financing the automatic general-purpose calculator he was developing. In 1944, with a million dollars from IBM, he completed the Mark I. This 51-foot-long, 8-foot-tall monster used noisy electromechanical relays to calculate five or six times faster than a person could, but it was far slower than a modern $5 pocket calculator.
- After consulting with Atanasoff and studying the ABC, John Mauchly teamed up with J. Presper Eckert to help the U.S. effort in World War II by constructing a machine to calculate trajectory tables for new guns. The machine was the ENIAC (Electronic Numerical Integrator and Computer), a 30-ton behemoth with 18,000 vacuum tubes that failed at an average of once every seven minutes. When it *was* running it could calculate 500 times faster than the existing electromechanical calculators—about as fast as a modern pocket calculator. Nevertheless, it failed in its first mission: It wasn't completed until two months after the

J. Presper Eckert (middle) and CBS News Correspondent Walter Cronkite (right) confer while UNIVAC 1 tallies votes in the 1952 presidential election. After counting 5 percent of the votes, UNIVAC correctly predicted that Eisenhower would win the election, but CBS cautiously chose to withhold the prediction until all votes were counted.

These three devices define the first three computer generations. The vacuum tube housed a few switches in a space about the size of a light bulb. The transistor allowed engineers to pack the same circuitry in a semiconductor package that was smaller, cooler, and much more reliable. The first silicon chips packed several transistors worth of circuitry into a speck much smaller than a single transistor. Today a single chip can contain the equivalent of *millions* of transistors.

end of the war. Still, it convinced its creators that large-scale computers were commercially feasible. After the war Mauchly and Eckert started a private company and created UNIVAC 1, the first general-purpose commercial computer.

Four Generations and Counting

When UNIVAC 1 was put to work by the U.S. Census Bureau in 1951, it represented the **first generation of computers.** This was the era of machines built around *vacuum tubes*—light-bulb-sized glass tubes that housed switching circuitry. First-generation machines were big, expensive, and finicky. Only the largest of institutions could afford a computer, not to mention the climate-controlled computer center needed to house it and the staff of technicians needed to program it and keep it running. But with all their faults, first-generation computers quickly became indispensable tools for scientists and engineers.

Computer evolution, 1940 to the present.

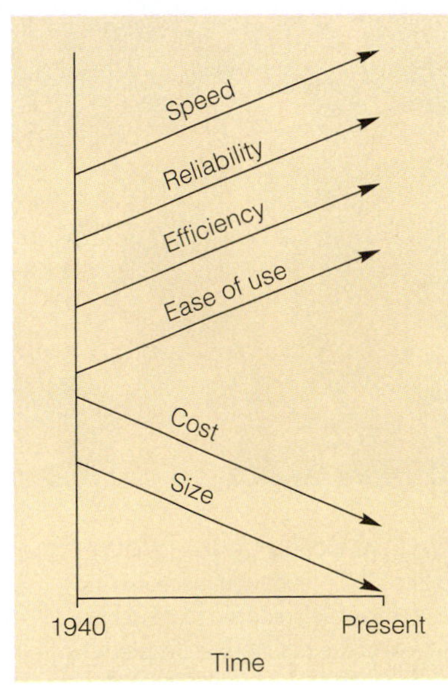

The *transistor*, invented in 1948, could perform the same function as a vacuum tube by transferring electricity across a tiny resistor. Transistors were first used in a computer in 1956, an event generally viewed as the beginning of the computer's **second generation**. Computers that used transistors were radically smaller, more reliable, and less expensive than tube-based computers. Because of improvements in software at about the same time, these machines were also much easier and faster to program and use. As a result, computers became more widely used in business as well as in science and engineering.

But America's fledgling space program needed computers that were even smaller and more powerful than the second-generation machines, so researchers developed technology that allowed them to pack hundreds of transistors into a single **integrated circuit** on a tiny **silicon chip**. By the mid-1960s transistor-based computers were replaced by smaller, more powerful **third-generation** machines built around the new integrated circuits. Integrated circuits rapidly replaced early transistors for the same reasons that transistors superseded vacuum tubes:

- *Reliability.* Machines built with integrated circuits were less prone to failure than their predecessors because the chips could be rigorously tested before installation.
- *Size.* Single chips could replace entire circuit boards containing hundreds or thousands of transistors, making it possible to build much smaller machines.

- *Speed.* Because electricity had shorter distances to travel, the smaller machines were markedly faster than their predecessors.
- *Efficiency.* Since chips were so small, they used less electrical power. As a result, they created less heat.
- *Cost.* Mass production techniques made it easy to manufacture inexpensive chips.

Just about every breakthrough in computer technology since the dawn of the computer age has presented similar advantages over the technology it replaced. As a result, it's only a slight oversimplification to represent the history of computing as in the graph on the previous page. If you want a rule of thumb to accompany this graph, consider Moore's Law: In 1965 Gordon Moore predicted in jest that the power of a silicon chip of the same price would double every year for at least two decades. So far Moore's prediction has been uncannily accurate!

The inventions of the vacuum tube, the transistor, and the silicon chip had impacts on society, which is why they're used as generational boundaries by many historians. But none of these had a more profound effect than the invention in 1969 of the first **microprocessor**—a complete computer housed on a tiny silicon chip.

Many historians call the invention of the microprocessor the beginning of the **fourth generation** of computers; others draw the generational line earlier or later. In any case the invention of the microprocessor caused immediate and profound changes in the appearance, capability, and availability of computers everywhere.

The research and development costs for the first microprocessor were tremendous. But once the assembly lines were in place, silicon computer chips could be mass-produced cheaply. The raw materials were certainly cheap enough; silicon is the second most common element (behind oxygen) in the Earth's crust. It's the main ingredient in beach sand, among other things.

American companies soon flooded the marketplace with watches and pocket calculators built around inexpensive microprocessors. The economic effect was immediate: Mechanical calculators and slide rules became obsolete overnight; electronic hobbyists became wealthy entrepreneurs; and California's San Jose area gained the nickname Silicon Valley and prospered as the demand for microprocessors soared.

Microcomputers have become common tools in the home, the office, the classroom, and even in airplanes since their introduction in the 1970s.

The Microcomputer Revolution

The **microcomputer** revolution began in the mid-1970s when companies like Apple, Tandy, and Commodore introduced low-cost, typewriter-sized computers as powerful as many of the room-sized computers that had come before. **Personal computers**,

or **PCs**, as microcomputers have come to be known, are now everyday tools in offices, factories, homes, and schools. As they become more powerful, personal computers take over many tasks formerly performed by large computers. But desktop computers haven't completely replaced big computers, which have evolved, too. Today's world is populated with a variety of computers, each particularly well suited to specific tasks.

Terminals make it possible for ticket agents all over the world to send information to a single mainframe computer.

Computers Today: A Brief Taxonomy

People today talk about, and work with, mainframe computers, supercomputers, minicomputers, workstations, notebook computers, palmtop computers, embedded computers, and, of course, PCs. What do all these terms mean? Let's examine the main categories of computers today.

Mainframes and Minicomputers: Multiuser Computers

Before the microcomputer revolution, most information processing was done on **mainframe computers**—room-sized machines with price tags that matched their size. Today large organizations still use mainframes for big computing jobs. These industrial-strength computers are largely invisible to the general public because they're hidden away in climate-controlled rooms.

But the fact that you can't see them doesn't mean you don't use them. When you make an airline reservation or deposit money in your bank account, a mainframe computer is involved in the transaction. Your travel agent and your bank teller communicate with a mainframe using a computer **terminal**—a combination keyboard and screen that transfers information to and from the computer. The computer might be in another room or another country.

Mainframe computers are capable of communicating with several users simultaneously through a technique called **timesharing**. For example, a timesharing system allows travel agents all over the country to make reservations using the same computer and the same information, at the same time.

Timesharing also makes it possible for users with diverse computing needs to share expensive computing equipment. Many research scientists and engineers, for example, need more computing power than they can get from personal computers. Their computing needs might require a powerful mainframe computer; some might even require a superfast, super-expensive **supercomputer**. A timesharing machine can simultaneously serve the needs of scientists and engineers in different departments working on a variety of projects.

Not all timesharing computers are massive mainframes. Some multiuser midsized machines are classified as **minicomputers**, or *minis*. According to traditional definitions, minicomputers are smaller and less expensive than mainframes but larger and more powerful than personal computers. But as the trend toward downsizing continues, the term *minicomputer* becomes increasingly ambiguous. Most of today's mainframes are not much bigger than yesterday's minicomputers, and some desktop computers are more powerful than those early minis. The minicomputer is being squeezed from above and below.

Scientists and engineers use supercomputers like the Cray YMP-48 because of their speed. The Cray YMP-48 can calculate thousands of times faster than a typical personal computer.

Workstations and PCs: Single-User Computers

Probably the biggest competitive threat to the minicomputer is the **workstation**—a high-end desktop computer with the computing power of a minicomputer at a fraction of the cost. Workstations are widely used by scientists, engineers, Wall Street analysts, animators, and others whose work involves intensive computation. While many workstations are capable of supporting multiple users simultaneously, in practice they're often used by only one person at a time.

Of course, like many computer terms, *workstation* means different things to different people. Some people refer to all desktop computers and terminals as workstations. And even those who reserve the term for the most powerful desktop machines admit that the line separating personal computers and workstations is fading. As workstations become less expensive and personal computers become more powerful, the line becomes as much a marketing distinction as a technical one. It's becoming harder and harder to find a definition for *workstation* that excludes the most powerful personal computers.

Most computer users don't need the power of a scientific workstation to do their day-to-day business. A modern personal computer has plenty of computing power for word processing, accounting, and other common applications. No surprise there—today's personal computers are far more powerful than the mainframes that dominated the world of computing a *human* generation ago. A personal computer, as the name implies, is almost always dedicated to serving a single user.

(A word about terminology: The term *personal computer* occasionally generates confusion because in 1981 IBM named its first desktop computer the IBM Personal Computer. To some people the term *personal computers* or *PCs* means only IBM com-

Minicomputers fill the gap between mainframes and desktop computers—a gap that is rapidly disappearing.

Workstations are used for applications that demand more computing power than is available in typical personal computers.

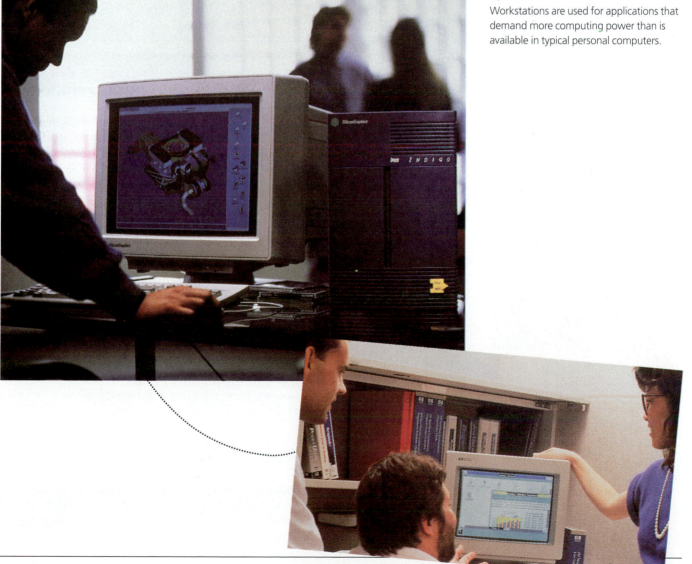

Portable computers come in a variety of sizes. Small models generally have smaller keyboards and screens but don't necessarily have less computing power than their large cousins.

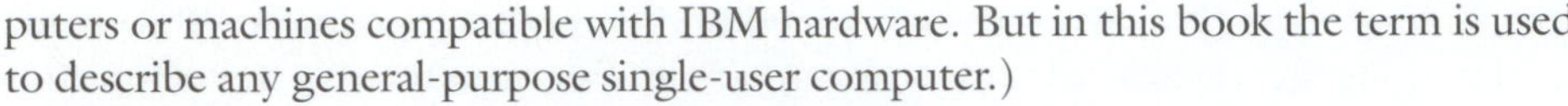

puters or machines compatible with IBM hardware. But in this book the term is used to describe any general-purpose single-user computer.)

Portable Computers: PCs on the Move

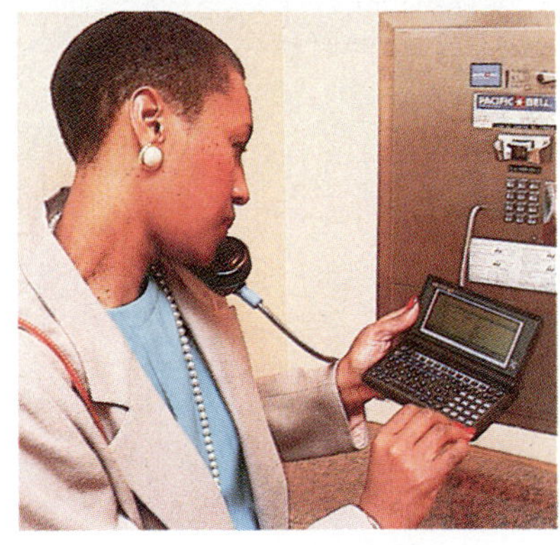

A few years ago the terms *personal computer* and *desktop computer* were interchangeable; virtually all PCs were desktop computers. Today, however, one of the fastest growing segments of the PC market involves machines that aren't tied to the desktop—**portable computers**.

Of course, portability is a relative term. A decade ago "portable" computers were 20-pound suitcases with fold-out keyboards and small TV-like screens. Those machines were portable only in the sense that they could be easily moved from one desk to another. Today those "luggable" computers have been replaced by flat-screen, battery-powered **laptop computers** that are light enough to rest on your lap while you work or carry like a small briefcase when closed. A typical older laptop weighed around ten pounds and resembled a briefcase when closed. Today's typical laptop, commonly called a **notebook computer**, weighs much less and can be carried like a book *inside* a briefcase, with room to spare. **Hand-held (palmtop) computers** small enough to be tucked into a jacket pocket serve the needs of users who value mobility over a full-sized keyboard and screen. Size notwithstanding, portable computers in all their variations are full-featured general-purpose computers built around microprocessors similar to those that drive desktop models. Portability comes at a price, though—portable computers generally cost more than comparable desktop machines.

Embedded Computers and Special-Purpose Computers

Not all computers are general-purpose machines. Many are **special-purpose (dedicated) computers** that perform specific tasks, ranging from controlling the temperature and humidity in a high-rise office building to monitoring your heart rate while you work out. **Embedded computers** enhance all kinds of consumer goods: wristwatches, game machines, stereos, video cassette recorders (VCRs), ovens, and even automobiles. Embedded computers are also widely used in industry, the military, and science for controlling a variety of hardware devices, including robots.

Most special-purpose computers are, at their core, similar to general-purpose personal computers. But unlike their desktop cousins, these special-purpose machines typically have their programs etched in silicon so they can't be altered. When a program is immortalized on a silicon chip it becomes **firmware**—a hybrid of hardware and software.

Living with Computers

The computer is by all odds the most extraordinary of the technological clothing ever devised by man, since it is an extension of our central nervous system. Beside it the wheel is a mere hula hoop . . . .

—Marshall McLuhan, *War and Peace in the Global Village*

The proliferation of computers today is transforming the world rapidly and irreversibly. More than any other recent technological breakthrough, the development of the computer is responsible for profound changes in society. Of course, computer sci-

Embedded computers play critical roles in automobiles, stereos, microwaves, and hundreds of other consumer items.

entists and computer engineers aren't responsible for all the technological turbulence. Developments in fields as diverse as telecommunications, genetic engineering, medicine, and atomic physics contribute to the ever-increasing rate of social change. But researchers in all of these fields depend on computers to produce their work.

In less than a human lifetime, computers have evolved from massive, expensive, error-prone calculators like the Mark I and ENIAC into a myriad of dependable, versatile machines that have worked their way into just about every nook and cranny of modern society. The pioneers who created and marketed the first computers didn't foresee the spectacular advances in computer technology that came about in the decades that followed. Thomas Watson, Sr., the president of IBM, declared in 1953 that the world wouldn't need more than five computers! And the early pioneers certainly couldn't have predicted the extraordinary social changes that resulted from the computer's rapid evolution. In the time of UNIVAC, who could have imagined the Nintendo phenomenon?

Technological breakthroughs encourage further technological change, so we can expect the *rate* of change to continue to increase in coming decades. In other words, the technological and social transformations of the past five decades may be dwarfed by the changes that occur over the next half century. It's just a matter of time, and not very much time, before today's state-of-the-art computers look as primitive as ENIAC looks to us today. Similarly, today's high-tech society just hints at a future world that we haven't begun to imagine.

Computer Currents: Looking Upstream
By 1500 BC papyrus, libraries, clay tablets, abacus
9th century Buddhist text is first known printed book
11th century movable type, decimal number system, musical notation
12th century modern abacus
15th century Gutenberg's printing press
16th century algebraic symbols, lead pencil
17th century calculus, Pascal's calculator, probability, binary arithmetic, newspapers, mailboxes
18th century typewriter, three-color printing, industrial revolution
19th century automated loom, Analytical Engine, telegraph, vacuum tube, cathode ray tube, telephone, color photograph, Hollerith's data processing machine, radio, sound recordings
Early 20th century assembly-line automated production, analog computer, television, motion pictures
1939 Atanasoff creates the first digital computer
1939 Zuse completes first programmable, general-purpose computer
1943 Turing's Colussus computer breaks Nazi codes
1944 Aiken completes the Mark I
1945 Von Neumann proposes storing programs as data
1946 Mauchly and Eckert design ENIAC
1947 Shockley, Brittain, and Ardeen invent the transistor
1949 Orwell writes 1984, a novel about totalitarianism and computers
1951 Univac I is delivered to U.S. Census Bureau
1956 Bell Labs build first transistorized computer
1956 computerized banking begins
1957 USSR launches Sputnik
1959 Jack Kilby and Robert Noyce develop the integrated circuit
1960 laser invented
1962 DEC introduces minicomputer
1962 first timesharing operating system
1964 first prosecuted computer crime
1967 software first sold separately
1969 first nationwide network (Arpanet)
1969 first person on moon
1969 first microprocessor
1972 first home computer game
1974 first microcomputer
1974 first computer-controlled industrial robot
1975 Cray-1 supercomputer is introduced
1976 Xerox pioneers graphical user interface
1977 Apple introduces the Apple II
1978 first spreadsheet program
1979 Pac Man appears
1981 IBM introduces its first personal computer
1984 Apple introduces the Macintosh
1984 Volkswagen loses hundreds of millions to computer fraud
1986 desktop publishing takes off
1988 Internet worm cripples 6000 computers for two days
1988 Connection Machine massively parallel computer introduced
1990 Hewlett-Packard and others introduce pocket computers
1990 Microsoft introduces Windows 3.0 for IBM-compatible computers
1991 many PC makers launch multimedia products
1991 IBM, Apple team up to develop next generation of PCs
1992 several pen-based computers and hand-held communications devices introduced
1993 computer companies, phone companies, and cable TV companies form alliances to create new interactive media

The rate of change in computer and information technology is continually increasing.

What do you *really* need to know about computers today? The remaining chapters of this book provide answers to that question. Here's an overview of what you can expect from those chapters.

Explanations. You don't need to be a computer scientist to coexist with computers. But your encounters with technology will make more sense if you understand a few basic computer concepts. Computers are evolving at an incredible pace, so many of the details of hardware and software change every few years. But most of the underlying concepts remain constant as computers evolve. If you understand the basics, you'll find that it's a lot easier to keep up with the changes.

Applications. Many people define *computer literacy* as the ability to use computers. But because computers are so versatile, there's no one set of skills that you can learn to become computer literate in every situation. **Application programs**, also known simply as **applications**, are the software tools that allow a computer to be used for specific purposes. Many computer applications in science, government, business, and the arts are far too specialized and technical to be of use or of interest to people outside the field. On the other hand, some applications are so flexible that they can be used by all kinds of people. Regardless of your background or aspirations, you can almost certainly benefit from knowing a little about these applications.

- *Word processing and desktop publishing. Word processing* is a critical skill for anyone who communicates in writing. It's far and away the number one application used by students. *Desktop publishing* uses the personal computer to transform written words into polished, visually exciting publications.
- *Spreadsheets and other number-crunching applications.* In business the electronic *spreadsheet* is the personal computer application that pays the rent, or at least calculates it. If you work with numbers of any kind, spreadsheets and statistical software can help you turn abstract quantities into concrete concepts.
- *Databases for information storage and retrieval.* If word processors and spreadsheets are the most popular PC applications, *databases* reign supreme in the world of mainframes. Of course, databases are widely used on PCs, too. As libraries, banks, and other institutions turn to databases for information storage, the average person has more reasons to learn the basics of databases.
- *Telecommunication and networking.* Every day more computers are connected—*networked*—so they can send information back and forth; we're entering an era when networking is the norm. A network connection is a door into a world of electronic mailboxes, bulletin boards, commercial database services, and other communication tools. Many experts believe that *telecommunication*—long distance communication—will be the single most important function of computers in the not-too-distant future.
- *Computer graphics.* Computers aren't limited to working with text and numbers; they're capable of producing all kinds of graphics, from the charts and graphs produced by spreadsheets to realistic 3-D animation. As graphics tools become more accessible, visual communication skills become more important for all of us.
- *Multimedia and hypermedia.* Many of the computing industry's visionaries have their sights focused on these two related technologies. *Multimedia* tools for PCs make it possible to combine audio and video with traditional text and graphics, adding new dimensions to computer communication. *Hypermedia* tools focus on the interactive capabilities of computers. Unlike books, videos, and other linear media, which are designed to be consumed from beginning to end, hypermedia allow users to explore a variety of paths through information sources. The combination of multimedia and hypermedia has an almost unimaginable potential for transforming the way we see and work with information.
- *Artificial intelligence. Artificial intelligence* is the branch of computer science that explores using computers in tasks that require intelligence, imagination, and

insight—tasks that have traditionally been performed by people rather than machines. Until recently, artificial intelligence was mostly an academic discipline—a field of study reserved for researchers and philosophers. But some of that research is paying off today with commercial applications that exhibit intelligence—applications that you may be using soon.

- *General problem solving.* People use computers to solve problems. Most people use software applications written by professional programmers. But some kinds of problems can't easily be solved with off-the-shelf applications; they require at least some custom programming. *Programming languages* aren't applications; they're tools that allow you to build and customize applications. Many computer users find their machines become more versatile, and valuable, when they learn a little about programming.

Implications. Even if you never touch a personal computer, computer technology will continue to have a growing impact on your life and your world. People all around you use PCs to manage finances and schedules, to write letters and novels, to draw maps and illustrations, to publish newspapers and political manifestos, to store addresses and musical scores, to send messages across town and around the world. Computers routinely save lives in hospitals, keep space flights on course, and predict the weekend weather.

The future is rushing toward you, and computer technology is a big part of it. It's exciting to consider the opportunities arising from advances in artificial intelligence, multimedia, robotics, and other cutting-edge technologies of the electronic revolution—opportunities in the workplace, the school, and the home. But it's just as important to pay attention to the potential risks, including

- the threat to personal privacy posed by large databases
- the hazards of high-tech crime and the inherent insecurity of computers
- the risks of failure of unreliable computer systems
- the threat of automation and the dehumanization of work
- the abuse of information as a tool of political and economic power
- the dangers of dependence on complex technology

For better *and* for worse, we'll be coexisting with computers till death do us part. As with any relationship, a little understanding can go a long way. The remaining

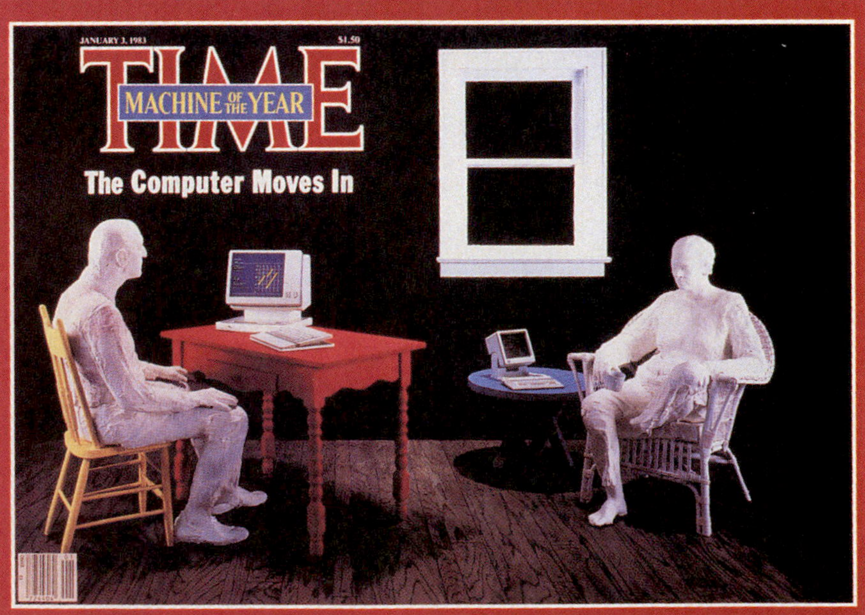

During the 32 years that elapsed between these two cover stories, computers changed profoundly, and the world changed almost as profoundly as a result.

chapters of this book will help you gain the understanding you need to survive and prosper in a world of computers.

Summary

While the basic idea behind a computer goes back to Charles Babbage's 19th-century plan for an Analytical Engine, the first real computers were developed during the 1940s. Computers have evolved at an incredible pace since those early years, becoming consistently smaller, faster, more efficient, more reliable, and less expensive. At the same time, people have devised all kinds of interesting and useful ways to put computers to work to solve problems.

Computers today, like their ancestors, are information-processing machines designed to transform information from one form to another. When a computer operates, the hardware accepts input data from some outside source, transforms the data by following instructions called software, and produces output that can be read by a human or by another machine.

Computers today come in all shapes and sizes, with specific types being well suited for particular jobs. Mainframe computers and supercomputers provide more power and speed than smaller desktop machines, but they are expensive to purchase and operate. Timesharing makes it possible for many users to work simultaneously at terminals connected to these large computers. At the other end of the spectrum, personal computers, ranging from standard desktop models to tiny hand-held machines, provide affordable computing for those of us who don't need the power of a mainframe. As PCs become more powerful and mainframes become smaller, the workstations and minicomputers that fall between them are being squeezed from both sides. Microprocessors aren't just used in general-purpose computers; they're embedded in appliances, automobiles, and a rapidly growing list of other products.

Computer technology has changed the world rapidly and irreversibly. It's easy to list dozens of ways that computers make our lives easier and more productive. At the same time, computers threaten our privacy, our security, and perhaps our way of life. As we rush into the information age, our future depends on computers and on our ability to understand and use them in productive, positive ways.

CHAPTER REVIEW

Key Terms

Analytical Engine
application programs (applications)
data
embedded computer
firmware
first generation of computers
fourth generation
hand-held (palmtop) computer
hardware
input
integrated circuit
laptop computer
mainframe computer
microcomputer
microprocessor
minicomputer
notebook computer
output
personal computer (PC)
portable computer
program
second generation
silicon chip
software
special-purpose (dedicated) computer
supercomputer
terminal
third generation
timesharing
workstation

Review Questions

1. List several ways you interact with computers in your daily life.
2. Why was the Analytical Engine never completed during the lifetime of Charles Babbage?
3. Outline the evolution of the computer from World War II to the present.
4. What is hardware? What is software? How are the two related?
5. What is the most important difference between a computer and a calculator?
6. What is a silicon chip, and why is it important?
7. What is the difference between a mainframe and a microcomputer? What are the advantages and disadvantages of each?
8. What kinds of computer applications require the speed and power of a supercomputer? Give some examples.
9. What is timesharing? What types of computers typically employ timesharing?
10. List several common types of personal computer applications.
11. Why is it important for people to know about and understand computers?
12. Describe some of the benefits and drawbacks of the computer revolution.

Discussion Questions

1. What do people mean when they talk about the computer revolution? What is revolutionary about it?
2. How do you feel about computers? Examine your positive and negative feelings.
3. What major events *before* the 20th-century influenced the development of the computer
4. Suppose Charles Babbage and Ada Lovelace had been able to construct a working Analytical Engine and develop a factory for mass-producing it. How do you think the world would have reacted? How would the history of the 20th century been different as a result?
5. How would the world be different today if a wrinkle in time transported a modern desktop computer system, complete with software and manuals, onto the desk of Herbert Hoover? Adolph Hitler? Albert Einstein? Explain your answers.
6. The automobile and the television set are two examples of technological inventions that changed our society drastically in ways that were not anticipated by their inventors. Outline several positive and negative effects of each of these two inventions. Do you think, on the balance, that we're better off as a result of these machines? Why or why not? Now repeat this exercise for the computer.
7. Should all students be required to take at least one computer course? Why or why not? If so, what should that course cover?
8. Computerphobia—fear or anxiety related to computers—is a common malady among people today. What do you think causes it? What, if anything, should be done about it?
9. In your opinion what computer applications offer the most promise for making the world a better place? What computer applications pose the most significant threats to our future well-being?

Projects

1. Start a collection of news articles, cartoons, and/or television segments that deal with computers. What does your collection say about popular attitudes toward computers?
2. Trace computer-related articles through several years in the same magazine. Do you see any changes or trends?
3. Develop a questionnaire to try to determine people's attitudes about computers. Circulate it and summarize your results.
4. Take an inventory of all the computers you encounter in a single day. Don't forget embedded computers in cars, appliances, entertainment equipment, and other machines.

Sources and Resources

Byte (general and technical), *PC* (IBM-compatible), *PC World* (IBM-compatible), *PC/Computing* (IBM-compatible) *Windows Magazine* (IBM-compatible with Windows), *Compute!* (IBM-compatible), *Macworld* (Macintosh), *MacUser* (Macintosh), *AmigaWorld* (Commodore Amiga). Because the world of personal computers changes so rapidly, computer users depend on magazines to keep them up to date on hardware and software developments. Magazines provide the kind of timely information that just can't be found in books. The average computer owner is interested mainly in information related to one type of machine, so most of these magazines target brand-specific audiences.

InfoWorld, PC Week, and *MacWeek.* These three weekly newspapers provide up-to-the-week news on microcomputers, with an emphasis on corporate and government applications.

Computerworld and *Datamation.* These periodicals provide news for data processing professionals. *Computerworld* is a weekly newspaper; *Datamation* is a biweekly magazine focusing on issues that confront professionals. Both cover everything from mainframes to micros.

Wired. This unusual magazine (some say it should be called *Weird*) is billed as "the first consumer magazine for the Digital Generation to track technology's impact on all facets of the human condition." Some of the best writers in the field contribute to this stylish, thought-provoking monthly.

Whole Earth Review. This unusual quarterly includes everything from ecology to anthropology, but it has superb coverage of cutting-edge computer technologies like artificial life and virtual reality. Articles are both practical and philosophical.

Jargon: An Informal Dictionary of Computer Terms, by Robin Williams with Steve Cummings (Berkeley, CA: Peachpit Press, 1993) It sometimes seems like the computer industry makes three things: hardware, software, and jargon. This friendly, readable dictionary does a masterful job of defining and demystifying the jargon so you can better understand the other two. Whether you read it cover to cover, browse, or just keep it by your computer as a reference, you're bound to learn something from this book—and enjoy the process. I'd like to see an electronic version.

The Dream Machine: Exploring the Computer Age, by Jon Palfreman and Doren Swade (London: BBC Books, 1991). This book, designed to accompany a BBC TV documentary, is filled with photos and text describing the evolution of the computer from its earlier days.

The Machine That Changed the World (available from Films for the Humanities and Sciences, Princeton, NJ). This five-part PBS television special, now on video, is one of the best treatments of the history of computing available. The series contains hours of fascinating footage covering everything from the Analytical Engine to virtual reality.

Fire in the Valley: The Making of the Personal Computer, by Paul Freiberger and Michael Swaine (Berkeley, CA: Osborne/McGraw-Hill, 1984). This book chronicles the early years of the personal computer revolution. The text occasionally gets bogged down in details, but the photos and quotes from the early days are fascinating.

Accidental Empires: How the Boys of Silicon Valley Make Their Millions, Battle Foreign Competition, and Still Can't Get a Date, by Robert X. Cringely (Reading, MA: Addison-Wesley, 1992). Robert X. Cringely is the pen-name for *InfoWorld's* computer-industry gossip columnist. In this opinionated, irreverent, and highly entertaining book, Cringely discusses the past, present, and future of the volatile personal computer industry. When you read the colorful characterizations of the people who run this industry, you'll understand why Cringely doesn't use his real name.

The Difference Engine, by William Gibson and Bruce Sterling (New York: Bantam, 1991). How would the world of the 19th-century be different if Charles and Ada had succeeded in constructing the Analytical Engine 150 years ago? This imaginative mystery novel takes place in a world where the computer revolution arrived a century early. Like other books by these two pioneers of the "cyberpunk" school of science fiction, *The Difference Engine* is dark, dense, detailed, and thought-provoking.

CHAPTER

TWO

Hardware Basics

After reading this chapter you should be able to

- explain in general terms how computers store and manipulate information
- describe the basic structure and organization of a computer
- discuss the functions and interactions of a computer system's principal components
- explain why a computer typically has different types of memory and storage devices
- describe several examples of input and output devices and explain how they enhance a computer's usefulness

Thomas J. Watson, Sr., and the Emperor's New Machines

There is no invention—only discovery.

—— *Thomas J. Watson, Sr.*

As president or, as he has been called, the "emperor" of IBM, Thomas J. Watson, Sr., created a corporate culture that fostered both invention and discovery. In 1914 when he joined the ailing Computing-Tabulating-Recording Company as a salesman, it specialized in counting devices that used punched cards to read and store information. Ten years later Watson took it over, renamed it International Business Machines, and used a firm leadership style to chart a course for the company that would eventually turn it into the dominant force in the computer industry.

Thomas Watson has been called autocratic. He demanded unquestioning allegiance from his employees and enforced a legendary dress code that forbade even a hint of color in a shirt. But in many ways Watson ran his company like a family, rewarding loyal employees with uncommon favors. During the depression he refused to lay off workers, choosing instead to stockpile surplus machines. As if to prove that good deeds don't go unrewarded, the newly formed Social Security Administration bought Watson's excess stock.

Thomas J. Watson, Sr.

Watson's first involvement with computers was providing financial backing for Howard Aiken's Mark I, the pioneering electromechanical computer developed in the early 1940s at Harvard. But he stubbornly refused to develop a commercial computer, even as UNIVAC I won fame and commercial contracts for the fledgling Sperry company.

Shortly after Watson retired from the helm of IBM in 1949 his son, Thomas Watson, Jr., took over. The younger Watson led IBM into the computing field with a vengeance, eventually building a computing empire that dwarfed all competitors. When Watson Senior died of a heart attack in 1956 at the age of 82, he still held the title of chairman of IBM.

Thomas Watson, Jr. (left) taking over the helm from Watson Senior (right).

After decades of unquestioned dominance in the computer industry, IBM today struggles to maintain its reputation as the industry leader. The conservative giant has been slow to adjust to the rapid-fire changes in the computer industry, making it possible for smaller, more nimble companies to seize emerging markets. Massive losses forced IBM to reorganize, replace many of its leaders, and abandon the company's longstanding no-layoffs policy. But in spite of its current financial difficulties, IBM maintains its position as the number one computer hardware company.

Computers schedule airlines, predict the weather, play music, control space stations, and keep the world's economic wheels spinning. How can one machine do so many things?

To understand what *really* makes computers tick you would need to devote considerable time and effort to studying computer science and computer engineering. But most of us don't need to understand every detail of a computer's inner workings, any more than a parent needs to explain wave and particle physics when a child asks why the sky is blue. We can be satisfied with simpler answers, even if those answers are only approximations of the technical truth. We'll spend the next two chapters looking for simple answers to the question, How do computers do what they do?

What Computers Do

Stripped of its interfaces, a bare computer boils down to little more than a pocket calculator that can push its own buttons and remember what it has done.

—Arnold Penzias, *Ideas and Information*

The simple truth is that computers can *really* do only four things:

1. *Receive input.* They accept information from the outside world.
2. *Produce output.* They communicate information to the outside world.
3. *Process information.* They perform arithmetic or logical (decision-making) operations on information.
4. *Store information.* They move and store information in the computer's memory.

These four basic functions are responsible for everything computers do. Every computer system contains hardware components that specialize in each of these four functions:

1. **Input devices** accept input from the outside world. The most common input device, of course, is the keyboard. But computers can accept input signals from a variety of other devices, including pointing devices like mice and joysticks.

2. **Output devices** send information to the outside world. Most computers use a TV-like video monitor as their main output device and some kind of printer for producing paper printouts.

3. A **processor**, or **central processing unit** (**CPU**), processes information, performing all the necessary arithmetic calculations and making basic decisions based on information values. The CPU is, in effect, the computer's "brain."

4. **Storage devices** and **memory** are used to store information. The most common storage devices are disk drives and tape drives. Different types of memory are used for different long-term and short-term storage tasks. The computer moves information between various memory and storage devices as necessary.

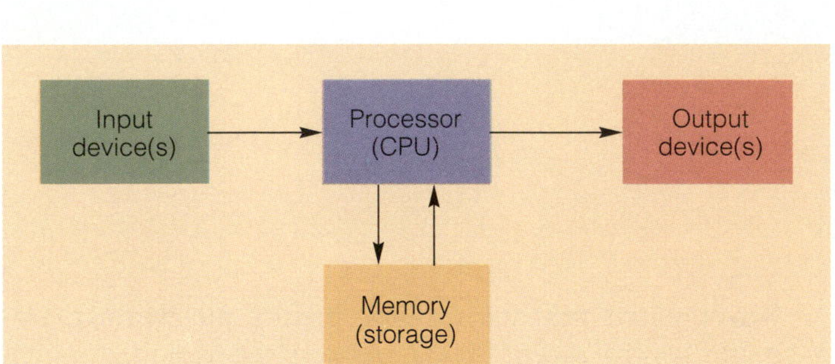

The four basic hardware components of every computer system.

These components, when combined, make up the hardware part of a computer system. Of course, the system isn't complete without software. But in this chapter we'll concentrate on hardware, exploring processors, input devices, output devices, and storage devices. Since every computer hardware component is designed to either transport or transform information, we'll start with a little bit of information about information.

A Bit About Bits

Even the most sophisticated computer is really only a large, well-organized volume of bits.

—David Harel, *Algorithmics: The Spirit of Computing*

The term **information** is difficult to define because it has many meanings. According to many traditional definitions, information means communication that has value because it informs. In the language of communication and information theory, however, the term *information* can be applied to just about anything that can be communicated, whether it has value or not. By this definition, which is the one we'll be using in this book, information comes in many forms. The words, numbers, and pictures on this page are symbols representing information. If you underline this sentence, you're adding new information to the page. The sounds and moving pictures that emanate from a television set are packed with information, too. (Remember, not all information has value.)

In the world of computers, information is **digital**: It's made up of discrete units—that is, units that can be counted—so it can be subdivided. In many situations people need to reduce information to simpler units to use it effectively. For example, a child trying to interpret an unfamiliar word can sound out each letter individually before tackling the whole word.

A computer doesn't understand words, numbers, pictures, musical notes, or even letters of the alphabet. Like a young reader, a computer can't process information without dividing it into smaller units. In fact, computers can only digest information that has been broken into bits. A **bit** (*b*inary dig*it*) is the smallest unit of information. A bit can have one of two values: on or off. You can also think of these two values as yes or no, zero or one, black or white, or just about anything else you want to call them.

If we think of the innards of a computer as a collection of microscopic on/off switches, it's easy to understand why computers process information bit by bit. Each switch can be used to store a tiny amount of information: a signal to turn on a light, for example, or the answer to a yes/no question.

Remember Paul Revere's famous midnight ride? His co-conspirators used a simple lantern to convey a choice between two messages, "One if by land, two if by sea"—a **binary** choice. The lantern communicated 1 bit's worth of information. While it's theoretically possible to send a message like this with just one lantern, "One if by land, zero if by sea" wouldn't have worked very well in the Boston night sky. If the revolutionaries had wanted to send a more complex message, they could have used more lanterns ("Three if by subway!").

In much the same way, a computer can process larger chunks of information by treating groups of bits as units. For example, a collection of 8 bits, usually called a **byte**, can represent 256 different messages ($256 = 2^8$). If we think of each bit as a light that can be either on or off, then we can make different combinations of lights represent different messages. (Computer scientists usually speak in terms of 0 and 1 instead of on and off, but the concept is the same either way.) The computer has an advantage over Paul Revere in that it sees not just the number of lights turned on, but also their order, so 01 (off-on) is different from 10 (on-off).

Building with Bits

What does a bit combination like 01100110 mean to the computer? There's no single answer to that question; it depends on context and convention. A string of bits can be interpreted as a number, a letter of the alphabet, or almost anything else.

Bits as numbers. Because computers are built from switching devices that reduce all information to 0s and 1s, they represent numbers using the *binary number system*—a system that denotes all numbers with combinations of two digits. Like the ten-digit decimal system we use every day, the binary system has clear, consistent rules for every arithmetic operation.

	Decimal representation	Binary representation
	0	0
•	1	1
••	2	10
•••	3	11
••••	4	100
•••••	5	101
••••••	6	110
•••••••	7	111
••••••••	8	1000
•••••••••	9	1001
••••••••••	10	1010
•••••••••••	11	1011
••••••••••••	12	1100
•••••••••••••	13	1101
••••••••••••••	14	1110
•••••••••••••••	15	1111

In the binary number system, every number is represented by a unique string of 0s and 1s.

Character	ASCII binary code
A	01000001
B	01000010
C	01000011
D	01000100
E	01000101
F	01000110
G	01000111
H	01001000
I	01001001
J	01001010
K	01001011
L	01001100
M	01001101
N	01001110
O	01001111
P	01010000
Q	01010001
R	01010010
S	01010011
T	01010100
U	01010101
V	01010110
W	01010111
X	01011000
Y	01011001
Z	01011010
0	00110000
1	00110001
2	00110010
3	00110011
4	00110100
5	00110101
6	00110110
7	00110111
8	00111000
9	00111001

The capital letters and numeric digits are represented in the ASCII character set by 36 unique patterns of 8 bits. (The remaining 92 ASCII bit patterns represent lowercase letters, punctuation characters, and special characters.)

Since most of us find it inconvenient to read binary numbers, computers include software that converts decimal numbers into binary numbers automatically, and vice versa. As a result, the computer's binary number processing is completely hidden from the human user.

Bits as codes. Today computers work at least as much with text as with numbers. To make words, sentences, and paragraphs fit into the computer's binary-only circuitry, people have devised codes that represent each letter, digit, and special character as a unique string of bits.

The most widely used code, **ASCII** (an abbreviation of American Standard Code for Information Interchange, but generally pronounced "as-kee"), represents each character as a unique 7-bit code (plus an eighth bit whose value is, for technical reasons, determined by the values of the other 7). It turns out that 128 unique ordered patterns can be made out of a string of 7 bits; that's enough to make unique codes for each of the letters (upper- and lowercase), numbers, and special characters that we commonly use in written English communication. As the world shrinks and our information needs grow, many computer users are finding that ASCII's 128 unique characters simply aren't enough, and new coding schemes are being developed. To facilitate multilingual computing, manufacturers are likely to switch eventually from ASCII to a more information-rich coding scheme, such as UniCode's 65,000-character set.

A group of bits can also represent colors, sounds, quantitative measurements from the environment, or just about any other kind of information that's likely to be processed by a computer.

Bits as instructions in programs. So far we've dealt with the ways bits can be used to represent data—information from some outside source that's processed by the computer. But there's another kind of information that's just as important to the computer: the programs that tell the computer what to do with the data we give it. The computer stores programs as collections of bits, just as with data.

Programs, like characters, are represented in binary notation through the use of codes. For example, the code 01101010 might tell the computer to add two numbers together. Other groups of bits—instructions in the program—would contain codes that tell the computer where to find those numbers and where to store the result.

Bits, Bytes, and Buzzwords

Trying to learn about computers by examining its operation at the bit level is a little like trying to learn about how people look or act by studying individual human cells; there's plenty of information there, but it's not the most efficient way to find out what you need to know. Fortunately most people can use computers without thinking about bits. Some bit-related terminology *does* come up in day-to-day computer work, though. Specifically, most computer users need to have at least a casual understanding of these terms:

- **Byte**: a grouping of 8 bits. If you work mostly with words, you can think of a byte as one character's worth of information.
- **K** (**kilobyte**): about 1000 bytes of information. For example, about 5K of storage is necessary to hold 5000 characters of text. (Technically 1K is 1024 bytes, because 1024 is 2^{10}, which makes the arithmetic easier for binary-based computers. For those of us who don't think in binary, 1000 is close enough.)
- **MB** (**megabyte**) (sometimes called meg): approximately 1000K, or 1 million bytes.
- **GB** (**gigabyte**): approximately 1000 megabytes. This astronomical unit of measurement applies to the largest storage devices available today.

People commonly use the abbreviations K and MB when describing the capacity of some of the computer components we'll discuss in this chapter. A computer might, for example, be described as having 512K of memory and a hard disk as having a 40-MB storage capacity. The same terms are used to quantify sizes of computer *files*. A **file** is an organized collection of information, such as a term paper or a set of names and addresses, stored in a computer-readable form. For example, the text for this chapter is stored in a file that occupies 54K of space on a disk.

The Computer's Core: The CPU and Memory

"What's one and one and one and one and one and one and one and one and one and one?"
"I don't know," said Alice. "I lost count."
"She can't do addition," said the Red Queen.

—*from Lewis Carroll's* Through the Looking Glass

It may seem strange to think of automated teller machines, video game consoles, and supercomputers as bit processors. But whatever it looks like to the user, a digital computer is at its core a collection of on/off switches designed to transform information from one form to another. The user provides the computer with patterns of bits—input—and the computer follows instructions to transform that input into a different pattern of bits—output—to return to the user.

The CPU: The Real Computer

The transformations are performed by the central processing unit (CPU) or processor. Every computer has a CPU to interpret and carry out the instructions in each program, to do arithmetic and logical data manipulations, and to communicate with all the other parts of the computer system. A modern CPU is an extraordinarily complex collection of electronic circuits. When all of those circuits are built into a single silicon chip, as they are in most computers today, that chip is referred to as a *microprocessor*. In a typical desktop computer, the CPU is housed along with other chips and electronic components on a **circuit board**.

Several different CPU chips are commonly used in personal computers. While there are many variations in design among these chips, only two factors are important to a casual computer user: compatibility and speed.

This circuit board houses several integrated circuits, including the Intel 486 microprocessor—the chip containing the computer's CPU.

Compatibility. Not all software is **compatible** with every CPU; that is, software written for one processor probably won't work with another. For example, software written for the Motorola 68000 family of processors used in Macintosh computers won't run on the Intel processors found in most IBM-compatible computers; the Intel processors simply can't understand programs written for the Motorola CPUs. In some cases software can overcome compatibility problems, as you'll see in the next chapter. But in general, compatibility is a function of the CPU.

Speed. There's a tremendous variation in how fast different processors can handle information. A computer's speed is determined in part by the speed of its internal *clock*—the timing device that produces electrical pulses to synchronize the computer's operations. Computers are often described in terms of their clock speeds, measured in units called *megahertz*. But clock speed by itself doesn't adequately describe how fast a computer can process words, numbers, or pictures. Speed is also determined by the *architecture* of the processor—the design that determines how individual components of the CPU are put together on the chip. In fact, the architecture of the entire computer system is an important part in the speed equation.

From a user's point of view, the important point is that faster is almost always better. Most computer applications, such as word processing, are more convenient to use on a faster machine. Many applications that use intensive graphics and computations, such as some statistical programs, *require* faster machines.

Because speed is so important, engineers and computer scientists are constantly developing techniques for speeding up a computer's ability to manipulate and move bits. One common trick is to put more than one processor in a computer. Many personal computers, for example, have specialized subsidiary processors that take care of mathematical calculations or graphics displays. Most supercomputers have several full-featured processors that can divide jobs into pieces and work in parallel on the pieces. This kind of processing, known as **parallel processing**, may soon be commonplace throughout the computing world.

Primary Storage: The Computer's Memory

The CPU's main job is to follow the instructions encoded in programs. But like Alice in *Through the Looking Glass*, the CPU can handle only one instruction and a few pieces of data at a time. The computer needs a place to store the rest of the program and data until the processor is ready for them. That's what RAM is for.

RAM (**random access memory**) is the most common type of **primary storage**, or computer memory. RAM chips contain circuits that can be used to store program instructions and data temporarily. Each RAM chip is divided by the computer into many equal-sized memory locations. Memory locations, like houses, have unique addresses, so the computer can tell them apart when it is instructed to save or retrieve information. You can store a piece of information in any RAM location—you can pick one at random—and the computer can, if so instructed, quickly retrieve it. Hence the name random access memory.

The information stored in RAM is nothing more than a pattern of electrical current flowing through microscopic circuits in silicon chips. This means that when the power goes off, for whatever reason, the computer instantly forgets everything it was remembering in RAM. In technical terms RAM is called **volatile memory** because information stored there is not held permanently.

This could be a serious problem if the computer didn't have another type of memory to store information that's too important to lose. This **nonvolatile memory** is called **ROM** (**read-only memory**) because the computer can only read information from it; it can never write any new information on it. All modern computers include ROM that contains startup instructions and other critical information. The information in ROM was burned in at the computer's birth, so it is available whenever the computer is operating, but it can't be changed except by replacing the ROM chip.

ROM cartridges such as this one, store video game programs and data in a permanent form.

ROM isn't always hidden away on chips inside the computer's chassis. Many home video game machines and home computers use removable **ROM cartridges** as permanent storage devices for games and other programs.

Other types of memory are available, but today most computers use only RAM and ROM.

Buses, Ports, and Peripherals

In a typical desktop computer, the CPU and memory chips are attached to circuit boards along with other key components. Information travels between components through groups of wires called **buses**. Buses typically have 8, 16, or 32 wires; a bus with 16 wires is called a *16-bit bus* because it can transmit 16 bits of information at once, twice as many as an 8-bit bus. Just as multilane freeways allow masses of cars to move faster than they could on single-lane roads, wider buses can transmit information faster than narrower buses. Newer, more powerful computers have wider buses so they can process information faster.

Some buses connect to **slots** inside the computer's housing. Users can customize their computers by inserting special-purpose circuit boards (usually called *cards* or just *boards*) into these slots. Other buses connect to external **ports**—sockets on the outside of the computer chassis.

Slots and ports make it easy to add external devices, or **peripherals**, to the computer system so the CPU can communicate with the outside world and store information for later use. Without peripherals, CPU and memory together are like a brain without a body. Some peripherals, such as keyboards and printers, serve as communication links between people and computers. Other peripherals link the computer to other machines. Still others provide long-term storage media. In the sections that follow, we'll explore a variety of input, output, and storage peripherals.

Input: From Person to Processor

The nuts and bolts of information processing are usually hidden from the user, who sees only the input and output, or as the pros say, *I/O.* This wasn't always the case. Users of the first computers communicated 1 bit at a time by flipping switches on massive consoles or plugging wires into switchboards; they had to be intimately familiar with the inner workings of the machines before they could successfully communicate with them. In contrast, today's users have a choice of hundreds of input devices that make it easy to enter data and commands into their machines. Of all these devices, the most familiar is the common computer keyboard.

The Omnipresent Keyboard

Typing letters, numbers, and special characters with a computer **keyboard** is similar to typing on a standard typewriter keyboard. But unlike a typewriter, the computer responds by displaying the typed characters on the screen at the position of the **cursor** (the *cur*rent po*s*ition indicat*or*). Some keys—**cursor (arrow) keys**, the **Delete or Backspace key**, the **Enter or Return key**, **function keys (f-keys)**, and others—send special commands to the computer. Some of the most important keys are shown in the User's View box on the next page.

Slots and ports allow the CPU to communicate with the outside world via peripheral devices. Here a circuit board is being inserted into a slot. Several ports are visible on the back of the console.

The User's View

Working with a Keyboard

Keyboarding on a computer is pretty much like typing, except that certain keys send codes that have special meaning to the computer or terminal.

Return or **Enter** sends a signal telling the computer or terminal to move the cursor to the beginning of the next line on the screen. For many applications, this key also "enters" the line just typed, telling the computer to process it.

Delete or **Backspace** tells the computer or terminal to delete the character just typed (or the one to the left of the cursor on the screen).

Function keys (f-keys) labeled F1, F2, and so on, send signals to the computer that have no inherent meaning. The function of these keys depends on the software being used. F1 might mean "Save file" to one program and "Delete file" to another. In other words, function keys are programmable.

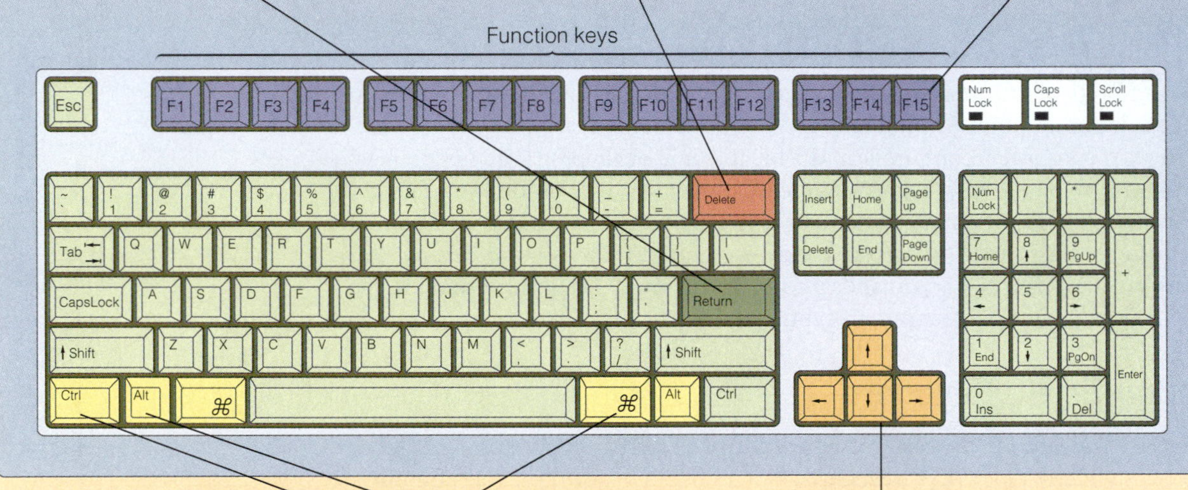

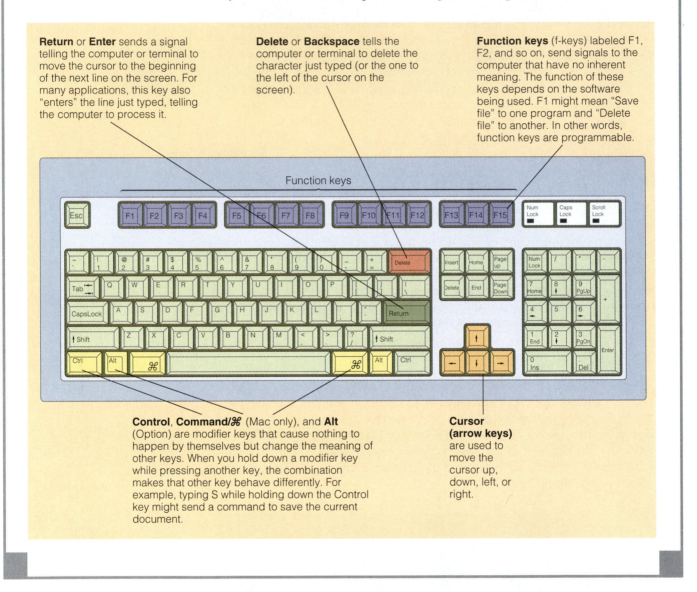

Control, **Command/⌘** (Mac only), and **Alt** (Option) are modifier keys that cause nothing to happen by themselves but change the meaning of other keys. When you hold down a modifier key while pressing another key, the combination makes that other key behave differently. For example, typing S while holding down the Control key might send a command to save the current document.

Cursor (arrow keys) are used to move the cursor up, down, left, or right.

In spite of nearly universal acceptance as an input device, the QWERTY keyboard (named for the first row of letter keys) seems strangely out of place in a modern computer system. The original arrangement of the keys, chosen to slow operators down so they wouldn't jam keys on early typewriters, stays with us a century later, forcing millions of people to learn an awkward and inefficient system just so they can enter text into their computers. Many improvements to the basic keyboard design have been conceived, tested, and shown to be superior and easier to learn than the classic QWERTY keyboard. But technological traditions die hard, and few people are willing or able to use nonstandard keyboards today. Still, as alternative input devices emerge, the role of the keyboard is changing.

Pointing Devices

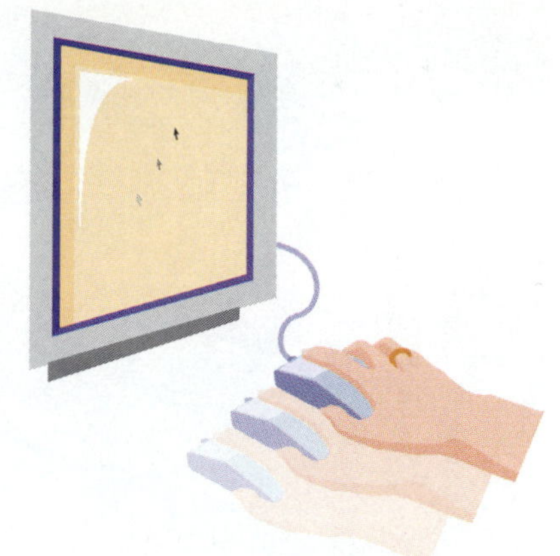

Millions of computer users today use their keyboards mostly for entering text and numeric data. For other traditional keyboard functions, like sending commands and positioning the cursor, they use a pointing device, such as a **mouse** or **trackball**. Both these devices are designed to move a pointer around the screen and point to specific characters or objects. The most common type of mouse has a ball on its underside that allows it to roll around on the desktop. As the mouse moves, the pointer on the screen mimics the mouse's motion. The trackball is something like an upside-down mouse. It remains stationary on the desk while the user moves the protruding ball to control the pointer on the screen. Both devices have one or more buttons that can be used to send signals to the computer, conveying messages like "Perform this command," "Activate the selected tool," and "Select all the text between these two points." The User's View box shows a few examples.

The User's View

Working with a Mouse

As you slide the mouse across your desktop, a pointer echoes your movements on the screen. You can **click** the mouse—press the button while the mouse is stationary—or **drag** it—move it while holding the button down. These two techniques can be used to perform a variety of operations.

Clicking on the Mouse

If the pointer points to an on-screen button, clicking the mouse presses the button.

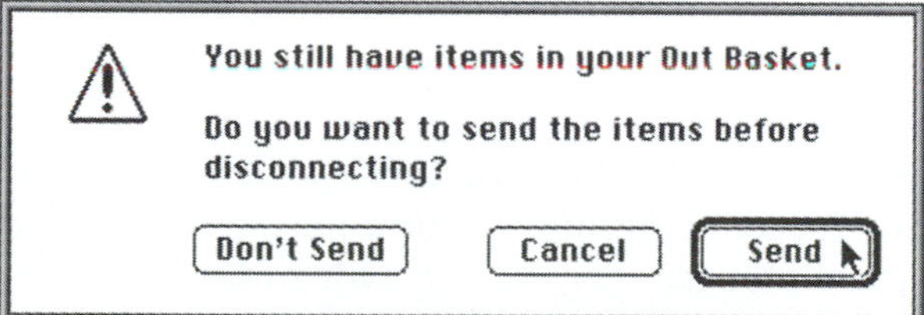

If the pointer points to a picture of a tool or object on the screen, clicking the mouse selects the tool or object; for example, clicking on the pencil tool allows you to draw with the mouse.

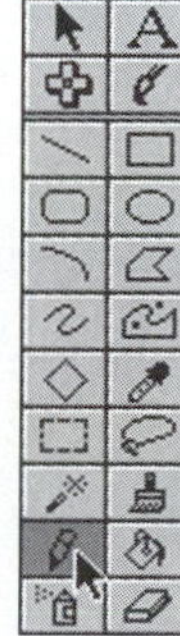

If the pointer points to a part of a text document, it turns from an arrow into an I-beam; clicking repositions the flashing cursor.

Jack fell down and Jill came tumbling after.

Dragging the Mouse

If you hold the button down while you drag the mouse with a graphic tool (like a paintbrush) selected, you can draw by remote control.

If you drag the mouse from one point in a text document to another, you select all the text between those two points so you can modify or move it. For example, you might select this movie title so you could italicize it.

The zany Duck Soup captured the Marx Brothers at their peak.

You can drag the mouse to select a command from a menu of choices. For example, this command would italicize the text you selected above.

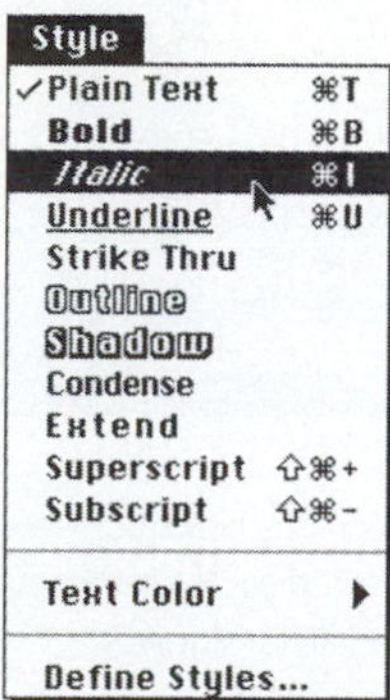

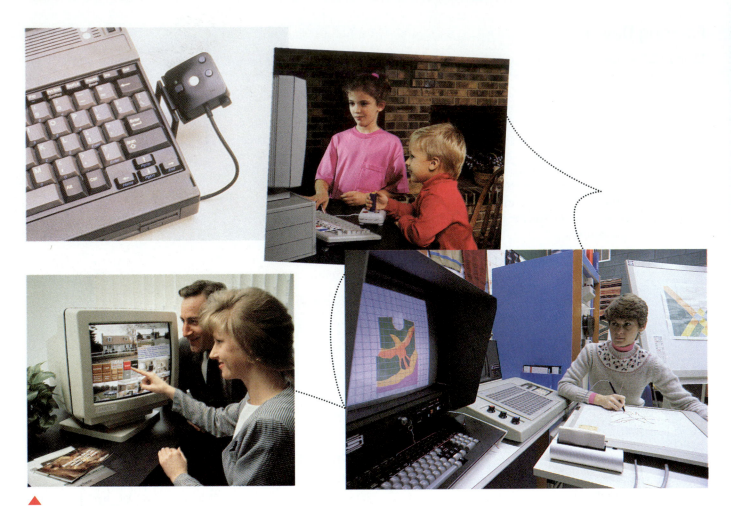

A trackball is a convenient mouse replacement for portable-computer users. Joysticks and push buttons are the chief weapons of the arcade army. An artist can use a stylus or pen with a touch tablet to simulate the feel of a brush, pencil, or pen. Real estate customers can explore houses using a computer with an easy-to-use touch-screen menu system.

Millions of computer users function efficiently without the use of a mouse or trackball. Still, there's clear evidence that general-purpose pointing devices like these can help most computer users to be more productive. Other pointing devices offer advantages for specific types of computer work (and play). Here are some examples:

- The **joystick** is a favorite as a controller for arcade-style computer games.
- The **touch tablet** is particularly popular with artists and designers. The best touch tablets are pressure sensitive, so they can send different signals depending on how hard the user presses on the tablet.
- The **touch screen** can respond when the user points to or touches different screen regions. Touch screens are effective when many users are unfamiliar with computers, such as in public terminals in libraries, airports, and stores.

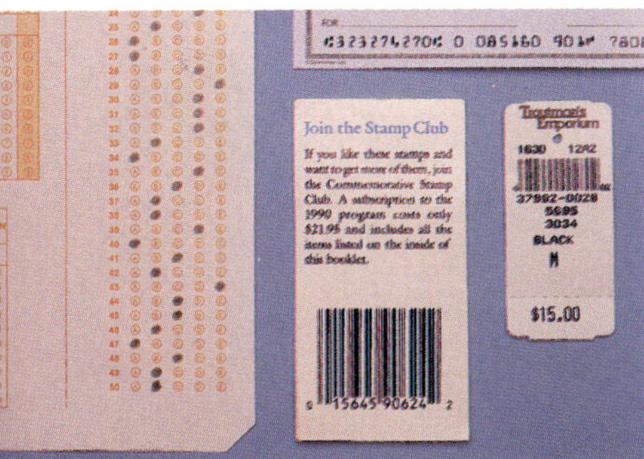

Computers use specialized input devices to read information stored as optical marks, bar codes, and specially designed characters.

Reading Tools

In spite of their versatility, pointing devices are woefully inadequate for the input of text and numbers into computers, which is why the mouse hasn't replaced the keyboard on the standard personal computer. Still, there are alternatives to typing large quantities of data. Some input devices provide the computer with limited ability to "read" directly from paper, converting printed information into bit patterns that can be processed by the computer. Some reading devices are uniquely qualified for specific everyday tasks:

- **Optical-mark readers** use reflected light to determine the location of pencil marks on standardized test answer sheets and similar forms.
- **Bar-code readers** use light to read universal product codes (UPCs), inventory codes, and other codes created out of patterns of variable-width bars.
- **Magnetic-ink character readers** read those odd-shaped numbers printed with magnetic ink on checks.
- **Wand readers** use light to read alphabetic and numeric characters written in a specially designed typeface found on many sales tags and credit card slips. People can read text created in this typeface, too. In many stores wand readers are attached to **point-of-sale (POS) terminals**. These terminals send information scanned by the wand to a mainframe computer. The mainframe determines the item price, calculates taxes and totals, and records the transaction for future use in inventory, accounting, and other areas.

Pen input is used in Apple's Newton MessagePad, a general-purpose PDA. UPS delivery clerks use specialized pen-based computers instead of paper forms to log deliveries and record signatures.

When wand readers are used to recognize words and numbers at a POS terminal, the computer is performing **optical character recognition** (**OCR**). Point-of-sale OCR is a far cry from reading the *New York Times* or *Huckleberry Finn*. A computer *can* read text from a book, newspaper, magazine, or letter, but the process requires artificial intelligence techniques, and it's far from foolproof. Recognizing handwriting is even more difficult, but the technology is progressing rapidly. OCR is described in more detail in Chapter 10.

Handwritten text analysis is critical in a **pen-based computer**. This keyboardless machine accepts input from a stylus applied directly to a flat-panel screen. It electronically simulates a pen and pad of paper. In addition to serving as a pointing device, the pen can be used as a writing stylus, but only if the computer's software can decipher the user's handwriting. As OCR technology improves, pen-based systems are becoming popular with information workers who spend lots of time filling out forms and with people who lack typing skills. But many people think the real future of pen-based technology is in **personal digital assistants** (**PDAs**), which will serve as pocket-sized organizers, notebooks, appointment books, and communication devices for people on the go.

Digitizing the Real World

Before a computer can recognize handwriting, it must first **digitize** the information—convert it into a digital form that can be stored in the computer's memory. Since real-world information comes in so many forms, a variety of input devices have been designed for capturing and digitizing information.

A **scanner** is an input device that can make a digital representation of any printed image. Scanners are available in several sizes and shapes. Flatbed scanners look and work like photocopy machines; hand-held scanners look like tiny vacuum cleaners for sucking images from paper. Some scanners can capture color images; less expensive models convert images to shades of gray. Regardless of its type or capabilities, however, a scanner converts photographs, drawings, charts, and other printed information into bit patterns that can be stored and manipulated in a computer's memory using software described in Chapter 8.

In the same way, a **digital camera** can be used to capture snapshots of the real world as digital images. Unlike a scanner, a digital camera isn't limited to capturing flat printed images; it can record anything that a normal camera can. A digital camera looks like a normal camera. But instead of capturing images on film, a digital camera stores bit patterns on disks or other digital storage media.

Audio digitizers contain circuitry to digitize sounds from microphones and other audio devices. Digitized sounds can be stored in a computer's memory and modified with software described in Chapter 8. Of course, audio digitizers can capture spoken

Hand-held scanners (left) and flatbed scanners (right) serve the same purpose: to capture and digitize images from external paper sources. Digital cameras (center) turn real-world scenes into digital images that can be stored and manipulated by the computer.

words as well as music. But digitized voice input, like scanned text input, requires artificial intelligence software to be correctly interpreted by the computer as words. Chapter 10 describes the promise and problems of automated speech recognition.

The visual equivalent of the audio digitizer is the *video digitizer*. A video digitizer is a collection of circuits that can capture input from a video camera, video cassette recorder, television, or other video source and convert it to a digital signal that can be stored in memory and displayed on computer screens. Chapter 8 describes a variety of video applications for computers.

Sensing devices designed to monitor temperature, humidity, pressure, and other physical quantities provide data used in robotics, environmental climate control, weather forecasting, medical monitoring, biofeedback, scientific research, and hundreds of other applications.

Computers can accept input from a variety of other sources, including manufacturing equipment, telephones, communication networks, and other computers. New

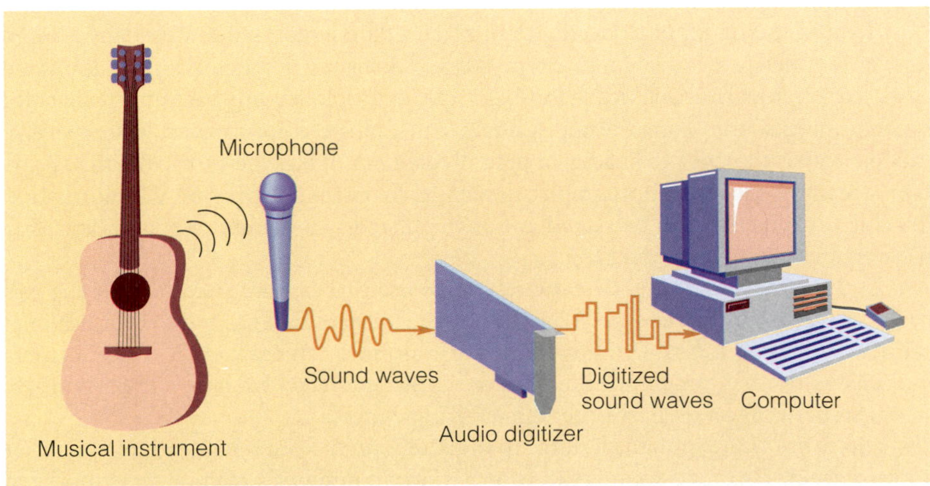

Digitizers can convert sounds into digital data for computer storage and processing.

input devices are being developed all the time as technologies evolve and human needs change. Some of these, by stretching the computer's capabilities, stretch our imaginations to develop new ways of using computers. We'll consider some of the more interesting and exotic technologies later; for now we'll turn our attention to the output end of the process.

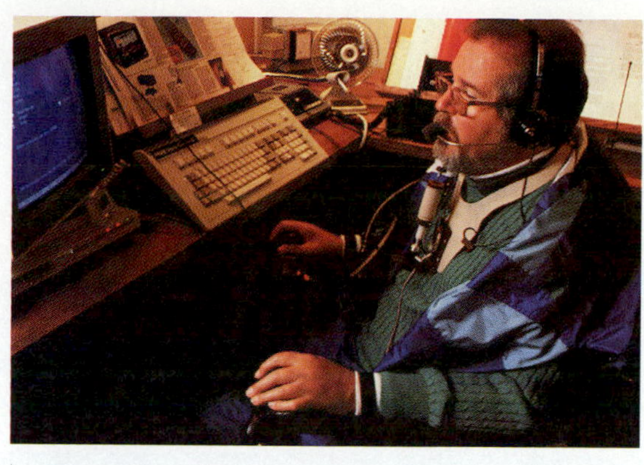

Speech input devices provide computer access to many disabled people.

Output: From Pulses to People

A computer can do all kinds of things, but none of them are worth anything to us unless we have a way to get the results out of the box. A variety of output devices give computers the power to convert their internal bit patterns into a form that humans can understand. The first computers were limited to flashing lights and other primitive communication techniques. Most computers today produce output through two main types of devices: *video monitor screens* for immediate visual output and *printers* for permanent paper output.

Screen Output

A **video monitor**, or **video display terminal** (**VDT**), makes it possible for a computer user to see input characters as they're typed, but it also serves as an output device for receiving messages from the computer. Images on a monitor are composed of tiny dots, called **pixels** (for picture elements). A square inch of an image on a typical monitor is a grid of dots about 72 pixels on each side. Such a monitor is said to have a **resolution** of 72 dots per inch (dpi). The higher the resolution, the closer together the dots.

Most monitors fall into one of two classes: television-style **CRT** (**cathode ray tube**) monitors and flat-panel **LCD** (**liquid crystal display**) models. Because of their clarity and speedy response time, CRTs are the overwhelming favorite for desktop computers. Lighter, more compact LCDs dominate the growing portable computer market, but as LCDs improve in quality, they are turning up on more and more desktops. Both types are available in either color or **monochrome** models in a variety of sizes. Monochrome monitors display only one color, usually black on white, or green or amber on black. As you might expect, large color monitors are considerably more expensive than small monochrome models. They also require more computer memory to support the color display.

Paper Output

Output displayed on a monitor is immediate, but it's temporary. A **printer** allows a computer user to produce a **hard copy** on paper of any information that can be displayed on the computer's screen. Printers come in several varieties, but they all fit into two basic groups: *impact printers* and *nonimpact printers.*

Impact printers include line printers and dot-matrix printers. Printers of this type share one common characteristic: They form images by physically striking paper, ribbon, and print hammer together, the way a typewriter does. **Line printers** are used by mainframes to produce massive printouts; these speedy, noisy beasts hammer out hundreds of lines of text per second. You've undoubtedly seen plenty of form letters, bills, and report cards printed with line printers. Because they're limited to printing characters, line printers are inadequate for applications like desktop publishing, where graphics are an essential ingredient in the finished product.

Dot-matrix printers print text and graphics with equal ease. Instead of printing each character as a solid object, a dot-matrix printer uses pinpoint-sized hammers to transfer ink to the page. The printed page is a matrix of tiny dots, some white and some

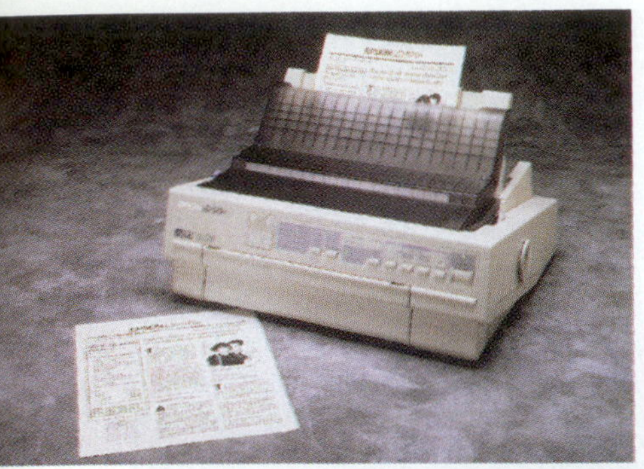

black (or, for color printers, other colors). It's almost as if the computer were hammering bits directly on the page. The final printout might be a picture, text, or a combination of the two. With most dot-matrix printers you have to sacrifice print quality for flexibility. A typical dot-matrix printer produces printouts with resolution—relative closeness of dots—of less than 100 dots per inch (dpi), so the dots that make up characters and pictures are obvious to even casual readers.

Except for those applications where multipart forms need to be printed, **nonimpact printers** are gradually replacing impact printers in most offices. **Laser printers** use the same technology as photocopy machines: A laser beam creates patterns of electrical charges on a rotating drum; those charged patterns attract black toner and transfer it to paper as the drum rotates. Less expensive **ink-jet printers** spray ink directly onto paper. Both types typically produce output with much higher resolution—300 or more dots per inch—than is possible with dot-matrix models. At these resolutions it's hard to tell with the naked eye that characters are, in fact, composed of dots. Because of their ability to print high-resolution text and pictures, nonimpact printers are widely used in publishing and other graphics-intensive applications.

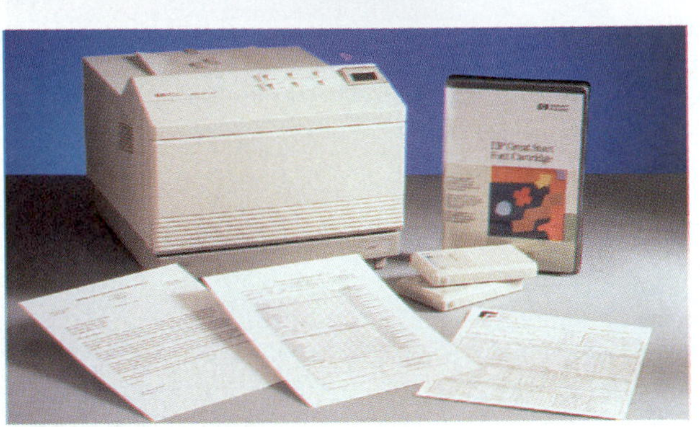

For certain scientific and engineering applications, a **plotter** is more appropriate than a printer for producing hard copy. A plotter is, in effect, an automated drawing tool that can produce finely scaled drawings by moving the pen and/or the paper in response to computer commands.

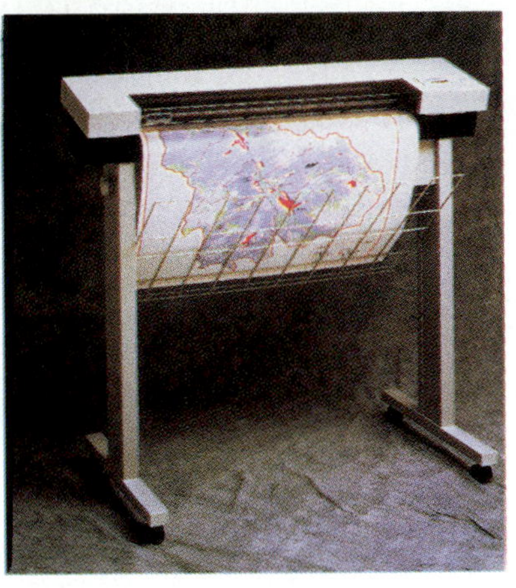

Dot matrix printers (top), laser printers (middle), and plotters (bottom) provide different forms of hard copy output.

Output You Can Hear

Computer output isn't all visual. Computers can produce sounds, too. *Synthesizers*, which are little more than specialized computers designed to generate sounds electronically, can be used to produce music, noise, or anything in between. Many personal computers have built-in synthesizers for producing sounds that go beyond the basic beep. Just about any computer can be connected to a stand-alone synthesizer so the computer has complete control of the instrument. And with appropriate hardware, a computer can play digital recordings of all kinds of sounds. Chapters 8 and 10 explore sound output applications in more detail.

Musician Laurie Anderson uses computers and synthesizers as tools for composing and performing her music.

Controlling Other Machines

In the same way many input devices convert real-world sights and sounds into digital pulses, many output devices work in the other direction, taking bit patterns and turning them into nondigital movements or measurements. Robot arms, telephone switchboards, transportation devices, automated factory equipment, spacecraft, and a host of other machines and systems accept their orders from computers. And, of course, computers can send information directly to other computers, bypassing human interaction altogether. The possibilities for computer output are limited only by the technology and the human imagination, both of which are stretching further all the time.

Computers control the movements of this and every spacecraft.

Secondary Storage: Input and Output

Some computer peripherals are capable of performing both input and output functions. These devices, which include tape and disk drives, serve as **secondary storage** for the computer. Unlike RAM, which forgets everything whenever the computer is turned off, and ROM, which can't learn anything new, secondary storage devices allow the computer to record information semipermanently, so it can be read later by the same computer or by another computer.

A technician mounts a tape in a tape drive.

Magnetic Tape

Tape drives are common storage devices on most mainframe computers and some personal computers. The reason for the widespread use of **magnetic tape** as a storage medium is clear: A typical magnetic tape can store massive amounts of information in a small space at a relatively low cost. Most mainframe computers use large reels of tape, but **digital audio tape** (**DAT**) is rapidly becoming the preferred tape for storage on small computers.

Magnetic tape has one clear limitation: Tape is a **sequential access** medium. Whether a tape holds music or computer data, the user must zip through information in the order in which it was recorded. Retrieving information from the middle of a tape is far too time-consuming for most modern computer applications, because people expect immediate response to their commands. As a result, magnetic tape is used today mostly for backup of data and a few other operations that aren't time-sensitive.

Magnetic Disks

Fortunately there's a readily available alternative to tape as a storage medium: the **magnetic disk**. A computer's **disk drive** can rapidly retrieve information from any part of a magnetic disk without regard for the order in which the information was recorded, in the same way you can quickly select any track on an audio compact disc (CD). Because of their **random access** capability, disks are far and away the most popular media for everyday storage needs.

Most computer users are familiar with the **diskette** (or **floppy disk**)—a small, magnetically sensitive, flexible plastic wafer housed in a plastic case. Most personal computers include at least one disk drive that allows the computer to write to and read from diskettes. As a result, diskettes are an almost universal currency for transferring information between machines and for packaging commercial software.

This PC has three disk drives: one for reading 5¼ inch diskettes, like the one on the table, one for reading 3½ inch diskettes, like the one inserted in the machine, and a hard disk drive hidden inside the console.

Diskettes are inexpensive, convenient, and reliable, but they lack the storage capacity and drive speed for many large jobs. Most users rely on hard disks as their primary storage devices. A **hard disk** is a rigid, magnetically sensitive disk that spins rapidly and continuously inside the computer chassis or in a separate box connected to the computer housing; this type of hard disk is never removed by the user. (There are

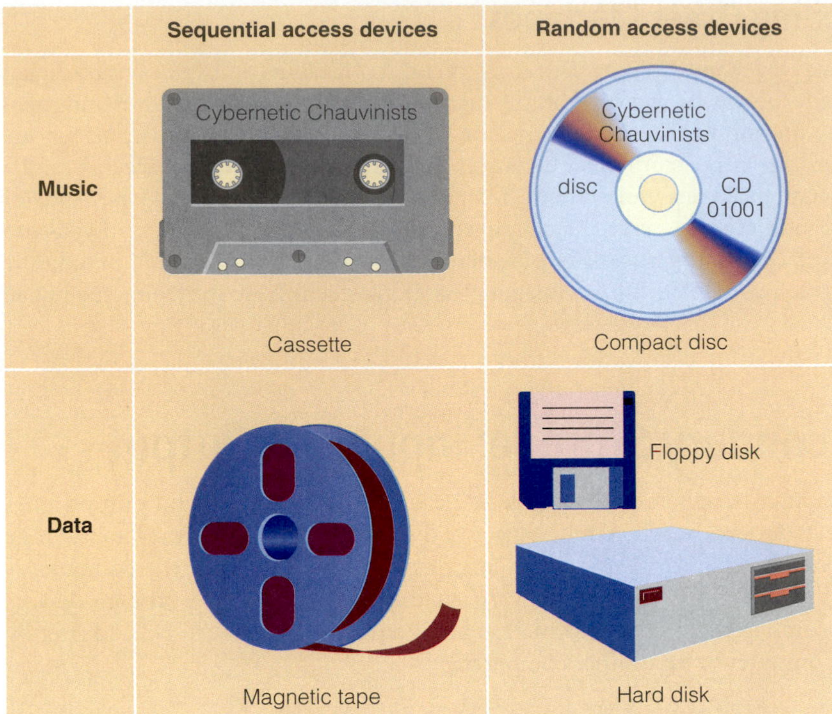

Most stereo systems include sequential access devices—cassette decks—and random access devices—compact disc players. The advantages of random access are the same for stereos as for computers.

exceptions: Some hard disks are removable.) While a typical diskette has a storage capacity of between 1 and 3MB, a hard disk might hold tens or hundreds of megabytes of information. Information can be transferred quickly to and from a hard disk, much faster than with a diskette.

Optical Disks

As multimedia applications become more commonplace, even a hard disk with a large storage capacity can be quickly gobbled up by sounds, color pictures, video sequences, and other storage-intensive items. For these kinds of applications, **optical disks** provide an attractive storage alternative. An **optical disk drive** uses laser beams rather than magnets to read and write bits of information on the disk surface. While they currently aren't as fast as hard disks, optical disks have considerably more room for storing data. People who use optical disks often talk in terms of gigabytes.

CD-ROM (*c*ompact *d*isc—*r*ead-*o*nly *m*emory) drives are optical drives capable of reading CD-ROMs—data disks that are physically identical to musical compact discs. (The similarity of audio and data CDs is no accident; it makes it possible for CD-ROM drives to play back music CDs under computer control.) A CD-ROM can hold the contents of an encyclopedia, including pictures, with room to spare for sounds and video clips! One secretary typing 90 words per minute, 8 hours per day, would take more than 8 years to fill a single CD-ROM with text. But since they are read-only devices, they can't be used as secondary storage devices. Several companies are working on CD-compatible drives that will allow for both reading and writing of data (or music). If these devices are perfected and marketed at a reasonable price, they may become as popular as magnetic diskettes are today.

Computer Systems: The Sum of Its Parts

A typical computer system might have several different input, output, and storage peripherals connected to the main computer housing. From the computer's point of view, it doesn't matter which of these devices is used at any given time. Each input

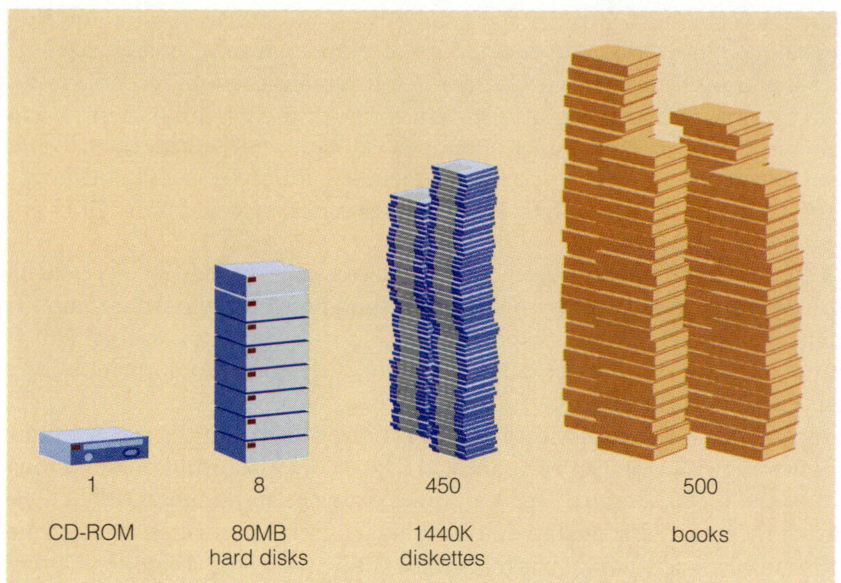

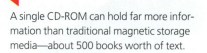

A single CD-ROM can hold far more information than traditional magnetic storage media—about 500 books worth of text.

device is just another source of electrical signals; each output device is just another place to send signals; each storage device is one or the other, depending on what the program calls for. Read from here, write to there—the CPU doesn't care; it dutifully follows instructions. Like a stereo receiver, the computer is oblivious to which input and output devices are attached and operational, as long as they're compatible.

A typical desktop computer system includes a computer and several peripheral devices.

Systems Without Boundaries

Unlike a stereo system, which has clearly defined boundaries, a computer system can be part of a **network** that blurs the boundaries between computers. When computers are connected in a network, one computer can, in effect, serve as an input device for another computer, which serves as an output device for the first computer. Networks can include hundreds of different computers, each of which might have access to all of the peripherals on the system. Networks can, in fact, span the globe by taking advantage of satellites, fiber optic cables, and other communication technologies. The rise in computer networks is making it more difficult to draw lines between individual computer systems. In Chapter 7 we'll look more closely at computer networks.

The Missing Piece

In the span of a few pages, we've surveyed a mind-boggling array of computer hardware. In truth we've barely scratched the surface. Nonetheless, all this hardware is worthless without software to drive it. In the next chapter we'll take a look at the software that makes a computer system come to life.

Summary

Whether it's working with words, numbers, pictures, or sounds, a computer is manipulating patterns of bits—binary digits of information that can be stored in switching circuitry and represented by two symbols. Groups of bits can be treated as numbers for calculations using the binary number system. Bits can be grouped into coded messages that represent the alphabetic characters, pictures, colors, sounds, or just about any other kind of information. Even the instructions computers follow—the software programs that tell the computer what to do—must be reduced to strings of bits before

the computer accepts them. Byte, kilobyte, megabyte, and other common units for measuring bit quantities are used in descriptions of memory, storage, and file size.

The central processing unit (CPU) follows software instructions to perform the calculations and logical manipulations that transform input data into output. It uses RAM (random access memory) as a temporary storage area—a scratch pad—for instructions and data. Another type of main memory, ROM (read-only memory), contains unchangeable information that serves as reference material for the CPU as it executes program instructions.

The CPU and main memory are housed in silicon chips on one or more circuit boards inside the computer. Buses connect to slots and ports that allow the computer to communicate with peripherals. Some peripherals are strictly input devices. Others are output devices. Some are external storage devices that accept information from *and* send information to the CPU.

The most common input devices today are the keyboard and the mouse. But a variety of other input devices can be connected to the computer, from pointing tools like trackballs and touch-sensitive panels to sound digitizers and scanners. All of these devices are, at their core, designed to do one thing: convert information signals from an outside source into a pattern of bits that can be processed by the computer. Output devices like video monitors, printers, speech synthesizers, and robot arms perform just the opposite function: They accept strings of bits from the computer and transform them into a form that is useful or meaningful outside the computer.

Unlike most input and output peripherals, storage devices like disk drives and tape drives have two-way communication with the computer. Because of their high-speed random access capability, magnetic disks—high-capacity hard disks and inexpensive diskettes—are the most common forms of secondary storage on modern computers. Sequential access tape devices are generally used only to archive information that doesn't need to be accessed often. While optical disks today are used mostly as high-capacity read-only media, they may become the preferred interactive storage medium as the technology improves and the associated costs go down.

The hardware for a complete computer system generally includes at least one processor, a main memory, one or more secondary storage devices, and several I/O peripherals for communicating with the outside world. Network connections make it possible for computers to communicate with one another directly. Networks blur the boundaries between individual computer systems. With the hardware components in place, a computer system is ready to receive and follow instructions encoded in software.

CHAPTER REVIEW

Key Terms

ASCII
bar-code reader
binary
bit
bus
byte
CD-ROM
central processing unit (CPU)
circuit board
click
compatible
CRT (cathode ray tube) monitor
cursor
cursor (arrow) keys
Delete or Backspace key
digital
digital audio tape (DAT)
digital camera
digitize
diskette (floppy disk)
disk drive
dot-matrix printer
drag
Enter or Return key
file
function keys (f-keys)
GB (gigabyte)
hard copy
hard disk
impact printer
information
ink-jet printer
input device
joystick
K (kilobyte)
keyboard
laser printer
LCD (liquid crystal display) monitor
line printer
magnetic disk
magnetic-ink character reader

magnetic tape
MB (megabyte)
memory
monochrome
mouse
network
nonimpact printer
nonvolatile memory
optical character recognition (OCR)
optical disk
optical disk drive
optical-mark reader
output device
parallel processing
pen-based computer
peripheral
personal digital assistant (PDA)
pixel
plotter
point-of-sale (POS) terminal
port
primary storage
printer
processor
RAM (random access memory)
random access
resolution
ROM (read-only memory)
ROM cartridge
scanner
secondary storage
sensing device
sequential access
slot
storage device
tape drive
touch screen
touch tablet
trackball
video display terminal (VDT)
video monitor
volatile memory
wand reader

Review Questions 

1. Draw a block diagram showing the major components of a computer and their relationship. Briefly describe the function of each component.
2. Think of this as computer input: 123.4
   This might be read by the computer as a number, a set of ASCII codes, or as a picture. Explain how these concepts differ.
3. Why is information stored in some kind of binary format in computers?
4. What is a CPU?
5. What is the difference between RAM and ROM? What is the purpose of each?
6. What is the difference between primary and secondary storage?
7. What is hard copy?
8. What are the advantages of nonimpact printers like laser printers over impact printers? Are there any disadvantages?
9. Every afternoon at closing time, the First Taxpayer's Bank copies all of the day's accumulated transaction information from disk to tape. Why?
10. What is the difference between sequential access and random access storage devices?
11. List five input devices and three output devices that might be attached to a personal computer. Describe a typical use of each.
12. Name three special-purpose input devices that are commonly used by people in public places like stores, banks, and libraries.
13. Some commonly used peripherals can be described as both input and output devices. Explain.
14. What is the main advantage of CD-ROM as a storage medium when compared with magnetic disks? What is the main disadvantage?

Discussion Questions 

1. If we think of the human brain as a computer, what are the input devices? What are the output devices? What are the storage devices?
2. How is human memory similar to computer memory? How is it different?
3. What kinds of new input and output devices do you think future computers might have? Why?

Projects 

1. The keyboard is the main input device for computers today. If you don't know how to touch-type, you're effectively handicapped in a world of computers. Fortunately, many personal computer software programs are designed to teach keyboarding. If you don't already know how to type, try to find one of these programs and use it regularly until you are a fluent typist.
2. Using the inventory of computers you developed in Project 4, in Chapter 1, determine the major components of each (input devices, output devices, storage, and so on).

Sources and Resources 

How Computers Work, by Ron White (Emeryville, CA: PC/Computing/Ziff-Davis Press, 1993). This book clearly illustrates with beautiful pictures and clear writing how each component of a modern personal computer system works. If you're interested in looking under the hood, this is a great place to start. The book was produced on a Macintosh, but its explanations and illustrations are based on IBM-compatible computers. Other books in the "How It Works" series cover Macs, networks, software, and multimedia.

Understanding Computers, by Nathan Shedroff, J. Sterling Hutto, and Ken Fromm (Alameda, CA: Sybex, 1992). This unusual little book is densly packed with descriptions and full-color pictures of computer hardware, software, and applications. Many of the explanations are too brief, and the unusual cross-referenced organization is sometimes confusing. Still, it's fun to explore, and it's a good example of state-of-the-art desktop publishing.

The Soul of a New Machine, by Tracy Kidder (Boston: Atlantic–Little, Brown, 1981). This award-winning book provides a journalist's inside look at the making of a new computer, including lots of insights into what makes computers (and computer people) tick.

Ideas and Information: Managing in a High-Tech World, by Arno Penzias (New York: Norton, 1989). A highly intelligent and readable discussion of the relationship between computer technology and the people who develop and use it. This book is full of insights and examples to make computer hardware and software easier to understand.

CHAPTER

THREE

Software Basics

After reading this chapter you should be able to

- describe three fundamental categories of software and their relationship
- explain the relationship of algorithms to software
- discuss the factors that make a computer application a useful tool
- describe the role of the operating system in a modern computer system
- describe the evolution of user interfaces from early machine-language programming to modern graphical applications
- compare character-based user interfaces with graphical user interfaces, and explain the tradeoffs involved in choosing a user interface

John von Neumann Invents the Invisible

All experience shows that technological changes profoundly transform political and social relationships.

—John von Neumann

John von Neumann was one of the greatest mathematicians of the 20th century, making fundamental contributions to mathematical logic, quantum theory (by his 20s), numerical weather prediction, and flowcharting. Von Neumann ordered his life mathematically, using concepts from the mathematical theory of games that he developed. His head was filled with so many ideas and he was so busy that he allowed himself only five hours of sleep per night. He saw great possibilities for applying abstract concepts like mathematics to the affairs of people.

During World War II von Neumann consulted for the U.S. military in weather forecasting and ballistics. He became technical advisor to J. Presper Eckert and John Mauchly, who were searching for an alternative to the plug boards and patch cords used to program ENIAC. In 1945 he wrote a first draft of a paper that drew on the ideas developed by these three men. The paper called for storing the computer's program instructions with the data in memory. Every computer created since has been based on the *stored-program concept* described in that paper.

Von Neumann went on to work on the atomic bomb. He witnessed many bomb explosions first hand, oblivious to possible radiation dangers. His faith in technology caused him to overlook the potential risks brought on by that technology. Shortly after he was appointed chairman of the Atomic Energy Commission in 1955, he learned that he had bone cancer, probably caused by his heavy exposure to radiation during years of atomic testing. His belief that he was invulnerable kept him working through the pain right to the end in 1957.

Chapter 2 told only part of the story of how computers do what they do. Here's a synopsis of our story so far:

On one side we have a person—you, me, or somebody else; it hardly matters. We all have problems to solve—problems involving work, communication, transportation, finances, and more. Many of these problems cry out for computer solutions.

On the other side we have a computer—an incredibly sophisticated bundle of hardware capable of performing all kinds of technological wizardry. Unfortunately the computer *recognizes only zeros and ones.*

01001011
11001001
H-E-L-L-P
Person with problems to solve
Computer—only knows zeros and ones
Communication gap

A great chasm separates the person with a collection of vague problems from the stark, rigidly bounded world of the computer. How can humans bridge the gap to communicate with the computer?

That's where software comes in. Software allows people to communicate certain kinds of problems to computers and makes it possible for computers to communicate solutions back to those people.

But modern computer software didn't just materialize out of the atmosphere. Just as computer hardware has continually evolved to make computers faster and more powerful, software has steadily improved to make computers more responsive and easier to use.

In a sense von Neumann, Eckert, and Mauchly established the software industry by liberating programmers from the tyranny of hardware. Instead of flipping switches and patching wires, today's programmers write *programs*—sets of computer instructions designed to solve problems—and feed them into the computer's memory through input devices like keyboards and mice. These programs are the computer's software. Because software is stored in memory, a computer can switch from one task to another and then back to the first, without a single hardware modification. For instance, the computer that serves as a word processor for writing this book can, on command, turn almost instantly into an accounting spreadsheet, a telecommunications terminal, a musical instrument, or a game machine.

What is software, and how can it transform a mass of circuits into an electronic chameleon? This chapter provides some general answers to that question along with a few specific details about each of the three major categories of software:

- *translator programs*, which allow programmers to create other software
- *software applications*, which serve as productivity tools to help computer users solve problems
- *system software*, which coordinates hardware operations and does behind-the-scenes work the computer user seldom sees

Processing with Programs

Software is invisible and complex. To make the basic concepts clear, we'll start our exploration of software with a down-to-earth analogy.

Food for Thought

Think of the hardware in a computer system as the kitchen in a short-order restaurant: It's equipped to produce whatever output a customer (user) requests, but it sits idle until an order (command) is placed. Robert, the computerized chef in our imaginary kitchen, serves as the CPU, waiting for requests from the users/customers. When somebody provides an input command—say, an order for a plate of French toast—Robert responds by following the instructions in the appropriate recipe.

As you may have guessed, the recipe is the software. It provides instructions telling the hardware what to do to produce the output desired by the user. If the recipe is correct, clear, and precise, the chef turns the input data—eggs, bread, and other ingredients—into the desired output—French toast. If the instructions are unclear or if the software has **bugs**, or errors, the output may not be what the user wanted.

For example, suppose Robert has this recipe:

Suzanne's French Toast Fantastique

1. Combine 2 slightly beaten eggs with 1 teaspoon vanilla extract, ½ teaspoon cinnamon, and ⅔ cup milk.
2. Dip 6 slices of bread in mixture.
3. Fry in small amount of butter until golden brown.
4. Serve bread with maple syrup, sugar, or tart jelly.

This seemingly foolproof recipe has several trouble spots. Since step 1 doesn't say otherwise, Robert might include the shells in the "slightly beaten eggs." Step 2 says nothing about separating the 6 slices of bread before dipping them in the batter; Robert would be within the letter of the instruction if he dipped all six at once. Step 3 has at least two potential bugs. Since it doesn't specify *what* to fry in butter, Robert might conclude that the *mixture* should be fried rather than the bread. Even if Robert decides to fry the bread, he may let it overcook waiting for the *butter* to turn golden brown, or he may wait patiently for the top of the toast to brown while the bottom quietly blackens. Robert, like any good computer, just follows instructions.

A Fast, Stupid Machine

Our imaginary automated chef may not seem very bright, but he's considerably more intelligent than a typical computer's CPU. Computers are commonly called "smart machines" or "intelligent machines." In truth a typical computer is incredibly limited, capable of doing only the most basic arithmetic operations (such as 7 + 3 and 15 – 8) and a few simple logical comparisons ("Is this number less than that number?" "Are these two values identical?").

Computers *seem* smart because they can perform these operations and comparisons quickly and accurately. A typical desktop computer can do thousands of calculations in the time it takes you to pull your pen out of your pocket. A well-crafted program can tell the computer to perform a sequence of simple operations that, when taken as a whole, produce an animated display, print a term paper, or simulate a game of pinball. Amazingly, everything you've ever seen a computer do is the result of a sequence of extremely simple arithmetic and logical operations done very quickly. The challenge for software developers is to devise instructions that put those simple operations together in ways that are useful and appropriate.

Suzanne's recipe for French toast isn't a computer program; it's not written in a language that a computer can understand. But it could be considered an **algorithm**—a set of step-by-step procedures for accomplishing a task. A computer program generally starts as an algorithm written in English or some other human language. Like Suzanne's recipe, the initial algorithm is likely to contain generalities, ambiguities, and errors.

The programmer's job is to turn the algorithm into a program by adding details, hammering out rough spots, testing procedures, and correcting errors. For example, if we were turning Suzanne's recipe into a program for our electronic-brained short-order cook, we might start by rewriting it like this:

Suzanne's French Toast Fantastique

1. Prepare the batter by following these instructions:
   1a. Crack two eggs so whites and yolks drop in bowl; discard shells.
   1b. Beat eggs slightly with wire whip, fork, or mixer.
   1c. Mix in 1 teaspoon vanilla extract, ½ teaspoon cinnamon, and ⅔ cup milk.
2. Place small amount of butter in frying pan and place on medium heat.
3. For each of the six pieces of bread, follow these steps:
   3a. Dip slice of bread in mixture.
   3b. Move slice from mixture into frying pan.
   3c. Wait 1 minute and then peek at underside of bread. If lighter than golden brown, repeat this step.
   3d. If top of bread is uncooked, turn bread over in frying pan and repeat step 2; otherwise remove bread from fry pan and place on plate.
4. Serve bread with maple syrup, sugar, or tart jelly.

We've eliminated much of the ambiguity from the original recipe. Ambiguity, while tolerable (and sometimes useful) in everyday conversations between humans, is a major source of errors for computers. In its current form the recipe contains far more detail than any human chef would want, but not nearly enough for a computer. If we were programming a computer (assuming we had one with input hardware capable of recognizing golden brown French toast and output devices capable of flipping the bread), we'd need to go into excruciating detail, translating every step of the process into a series of absolutely unambiguous instructions that could be interpreted and executed by a machine with a vocabulary smaller than that of a two-year-old child!

The Language of Computers

Every computer processes instructions in a native **machine language**. Machine language uses numeric codes to represent the most basic computer operations—adding numbers, subtracting numbers, comparing numbers, moving numbers, repeating instructions, and so on. Early programmers were forced to write every program in a machine language, tediously translating each instruction into binary code. This process was an invitation to insanity; imagine trying to find a single mistyped character in a page full of zeros and ones! Today most programmers use programming languages like BASIC, COBOL, FORTRAN, and C that fall somewhere between natural human languages and precise machine languages. These languages make it possible for scientists, engineers, and business people to solve problems using familiar terminology and notation rather than cryptic machine instructions. For a computer to understand a program written in one of these languages, it must use a **translator program** to convert the English-like instructions to the zeros and ones of machine language.

To clarify the translation process, let's go back to the kitchen. Imagine a recipe translator that allows our computer chef to look up phrases like "fry until golden brown." Like a reference book for beginning cooks, this translator fills in all the details of testing and flipping foods in the frying pan, so Robert understands what to do whenever he encounters "fry until golden brown" in any recipe. As long as our computer cook is equipped with the translator, we don't need to include so many details in each recipe. We can communicate at a higher level. The more sophisticated the translator, the easier the job of the programmer.

Programming languages have steadily evolved during the last few decades. Each new generation of languages makes the programming process easier by taking on, and hiding from the programmer, more of the detail work. The computer's unrelenting demands for technical details haven't gone away; they're just handled automatically by translation software. As a result, programming is easier and less error-prone. As translators become more sophisticated, programmers can communicate in computer languages that more closely resemble **natural languages**—the languages people speak and write every day.

Even with state-of-the-art computer languages, programming requires a considerable investment of time and brain power. (You'll see why when we take a closer look at programming in Chapter 9.) Fortunately most tasks that required programming two decades ago can now be accomplished with easy-to-use software applications—tools like word processors, spreadsheets, and graphics programs. Programming languages are still used to solve problems that can't be handled with off-the-shelf software applications, but most computer users manage to do their work without programming. Programming today is done mainly by professional software developers who use programming languages to create and refine the applications and other programs used by computer users every day.

Software Applications: Tools for Users

Software applications allow users to control computers without thinking like computers. We'll turn our attention now to applications.

A typical software store sells hundreds of software packages ranging in price from a few dollars to a few hundred dollars.

Consumer Applications

Chapter 1 included a description of the most important types of computer applications—applications we'll be exploring in detail in succeeding chapters of this book:

- word processing and desktop publishing (Chapter 4)
- spreadsheets and other number-crunching applications (Chapter 5)
- databases for information storage and retrieval (Chapter 6)
- telecommunications and networking (Chapter 7)
- computer graphics applications (Chapter 8)
- multimedia and hypermedia (Chapter 8)

Just about everyone who works with personal computers uses software that fits into one or more of these categories. Computer stores, software stores, and mail-order houses sell thousands of different computer software titles. The process of buying computer software is similar to the process of buying music software (CDs or cassettes) to play on a stereo system. But there are some important differences:

- A computer software package generally includes printed **documentation**—tutorial manuals and reference manuals that explain how to use the software. Many programs today are so easy to use that it's possible to put them to work without reading the manuals. And most modern software packages have some kind of **on-**

line documentation: *Help screens* appear when the user asks for more information. Still, it's rare to find a software package that doesn't include at least one manual of instructions.

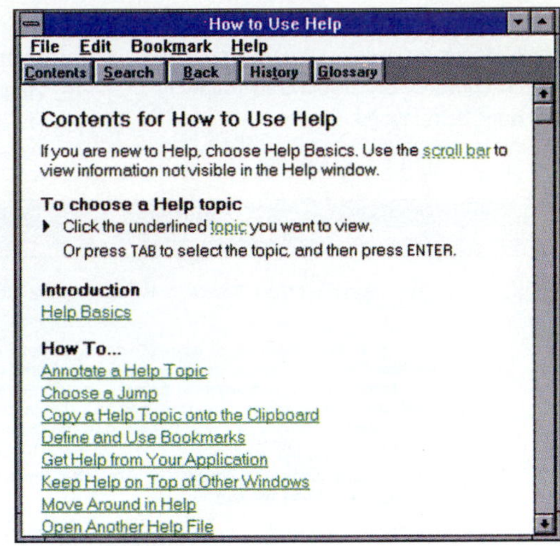

For many applications, on-line help appears on the screen when the user presses the Help button on the keyboard.

- Most software companies continually work to improve their products by removing bugs and adding new features. As a result, new *versions* of most popular programs are released every year or two. To distinguish between versions, program names are generally followed by version numbers, such as 5.1 in WordPerfect 5.1. While there's no numbering standard in the software industry, most companies use decimals to indicate minor revisions and whole numbers to indicate major revisions. For example, PageMaker 4.2 includes only a few more features than PageMaker 4.1, but PageMaker 5.0 is significantly different than version 4.2. When you buy a software program, you generally buy the current version. When a new version is released, you can *upgrade* your program to the new version by paying an upgrade fee to the software manufacturer.
- A computer software buyer must be concerned with **compatibility**. When you buy a music cassette, you don't need to specify the brand of your cassette player because all manufacturers adhere to common industry standards. But no universal software standards exist in the computer world, so a program written for one computer might not work on another. Software packages contain labels with statements such as "Requires Macintosh with 2MB of memory running System 7.0 or later" or "Runs on IBM-compatible computers with Windows 3.x." These demands should not be taken lightly; without compatible hardware and software, most software programs are worthless.
- According to the warranties printed on many software packages, the applications might be worthless even if you have compatible hardware and software. Here's the first paragraph from a typical "Limited Warranty":

  > *This program is provided "as is" without warranty of any kind. The entire risk as to the result and performance of the program is assumed by you. Should the program prove defective, you—and not the manufacturer or its dealers—assume the entire cost of all necessary servicing, repair, or correction. Further, the manufacturer does not warrant, guarantee, or make any representations regarding the use of, or the result of the use of, the program in terms of correctness, accuracy, reliability, currentness, or otherwise, and you rely on the program and its results solely at your own risk.*

  Why do software companies hide behind nonwarranties like this? In short, because nobody's figured out how to write error-free software. Remember our problems providing Robert with a fool-proof set of instructions for producing French toast? Programmers who write applications such as word processing programs must try to anticipate and respond to all combinations of commands and actions performed by users under any conditions. Given the difficulty of this task, most programs work amazingly well, but not perfectly.
- When you buy a typical computer software package, you're not actually buying the software. Instead you're buying a **software license** to use the program on a single machine. While licensing agreements vary from company to company, most include limitations on your right to copy disks, install software on hard drives, and transfer information to other users. Virtually all commercially marketed software is **copyrighted**, so it can't be *legally* duplicated for distribution to others; some disks (mostly games) are physically **copy-protected**, so they can't be copied *at all*. Because it's so difficult, software development is incredibly expensive. Most software developers use copyrights and copy protection to ensure that they sell enough copies of their products to recover their investments and stay in business to write more programs.

Entering text with a word processor is similar to typing with a standard typewriter; the computer screen displays an image of the page being typed.

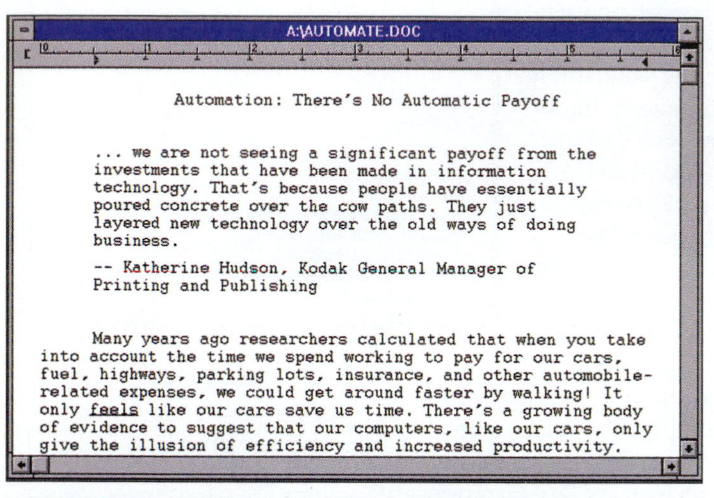

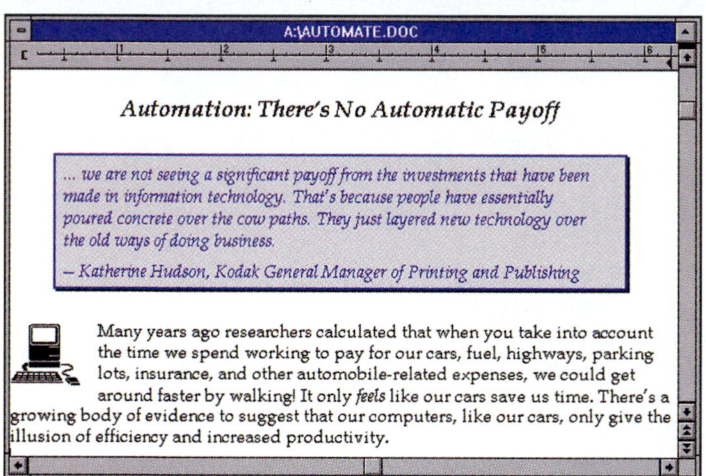

The word processor makes it easy to rearrange and change the appearance of the text—even add a picture—before printing the final document. No typewriter can do this.

Not all software is copyrighted and sold through commercial channels. Electronic bulletin boards (see Chapter 7), user groups, and other sources commonly offer **public domain software** (free for the taking) and **shareware** (free for the trying, with a send-payment-if-you-keep-it honor system). Public domain software and shareware can be legally copied and shared. The same can't be said of copyrighted commercial software—the overwhelming majority of software in use today.

It may seem strange that anyone would pay several hundred dollars for a product that comes with no warranty and dozens of legal restrictions about how you can use it. In fact the rapidly growing software industry has spawned dozens of programs that have sold millions of copies. Why do so many people buy and use these hit programs? Of course, the answer varies from person to person and from product to product. But in general, most successful software products share two important characteristics:

1. *Most successful software applications are built around visual metaphors of real-world tools.* Word processors and drawing programs turn part of the screen into a sheet of paper; desktop publishing programs make the screen look like a designer's drafting table; spreadsheets resemble accountant's ledger sheets. But if these programs merely mimicked their real-world counterparts, people would have no compelling reason to use them.
2. *Most popular computer applications are successful because they extend human capabilities in some way, allowing users to do things that can't be done easily, or at all, with traditional tools.* Word processors allow writers to edit and format documents in ways that aren't possible with a typewriter or pencil. An artist can use a graphics program to easily add an other-worldly effect to a drawing, and to just as easily remove it if it doesn't look right. Spreadsheet programs allow executives to project future revenues based on best guesses, and then instantly recalculate the bottom line with a different set of assumptions. Software applications that extend human capabilities are the driving force behind the computer revolution.

Integrated Applications: Swiss Army Software

While most software packages specialize in a particular application—word processing, graphics, or whatever—**integrated software** packages include several applications designed to work well together. Claris Works, Microsoft Works, Lotus Works, and other popular integrated packages generally include at least these five application types:

- word processing
- database
- spreadsheet
- graphics
- telecommunications

The parts of an integrated package may not have all the features of their separately packaged counterparts, but integrated packages still offer several advantages:

- They generally cost less than the total cost of purchasing individual programs that perform all of the separate functions.
- They apply a similar *look and feel* to all of their applications, so users don't need to memorize different commands and techniques for doing different tasks. Many commands apply across all applications in an integrated package, making it easy for users to learn new applications without starting over.
- They allow quick and easy transfer of data between applications. Many include *interapplication communication* features, so changes created in one application are automatically reflected in other applications.

These advantages aren't unique to integrated packages. Unified command structures and interapplication communication are built into many operating systems today, as you'll see in the next section. But for computer novices, casual users, and budget-conscious consumers, integrated packages have a lot to offer.

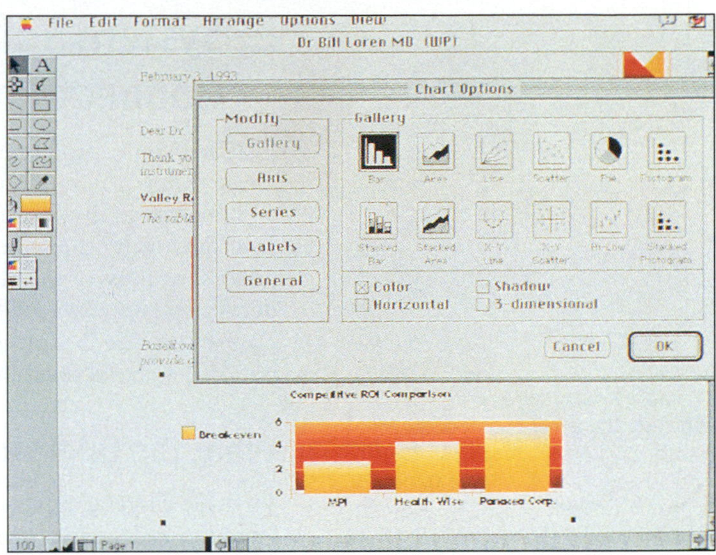

With an integrated software package like ClarisWorks, you can easily create a chart to include in a letter.

Vertical-Market and Custom Software

Because of their flexibility, word processors, spreadsheets, databases, and graphics programs are used in homes, schools, government offices, and all kinds of businesses. But many computer applications are so job-specific that they're of little interest or use to anybody outside a given profession. Applications designed specifically for a particular business or industry are sometimes called **vertical-market applications**.

Vertical-market applications tend to cost far more than mass-market applications, because companies that develop the software have very few potential customers through which to recover their development costs. In fact some **custom applications** are programmed specifically for single clients. For example, the software used to control the space shuttle was developed with a single customer—NASA—in mind.

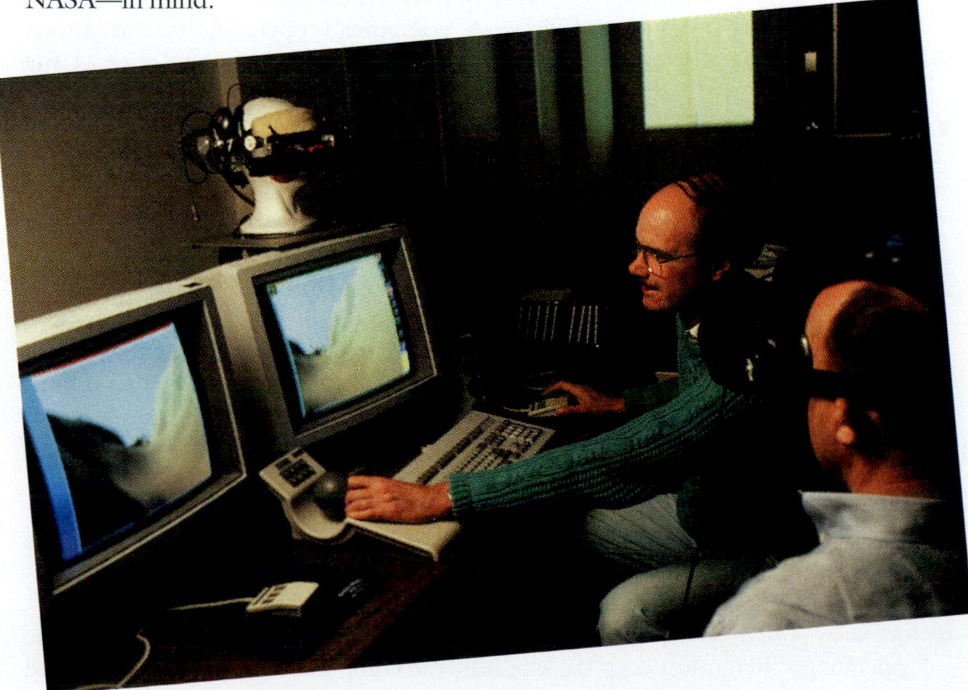

NASA scientists use custom software to recreate a Martian environment.

System Software: The Hardware-Software Connection

Whether you're programming or using an application, software is taking care of many messy details of computing for you. When you're typing a paper or writing a program, you don't need to concern yourself with the parts of the computer's memory that hold your document, the segments of the word processing software currently in the computer's memory, or the output instructions sent by the computer to the printer. These details, and hundreds of others, are handled behind the scenes by **system software**, a class of software that includes the *operating system* and *utility programs*. (By some definitions, system software also includes translator programs.)

What the Operating System Does

Virtually all general-purpose computers today, from timesharing supercomputers to laptop PCs, depend on **operating systems** to keep hardware running efficiently and to make the process of communication with that hardware easier. Operating system software runs continuously whenever the computer is on, even when users are working with software applications. In essence the operating system provides an additional layer of insulation between the user and the bits-and-bytes world of computer hardware.

The user's view: When a person uses an application, whether a game or an accounting program, the person doesn't communicate directly with the computer hardware. Instead the user interacts with the application, which depends on the operating system to manage and control hardware.

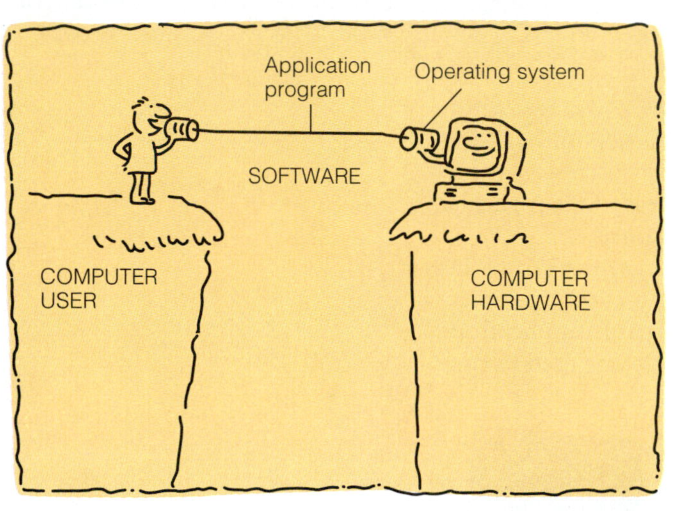

Because the operating system stands between the software application and the hardware, a single application can sometimes, with minor modifications, run on computers with different CPUs, provided they use the same operating system. Application compatibility is often defined by the operating system as well as the processor.

The operating system, as the name implies, is a system of programs that perform a variety of functions, including

- *Communicating with peripherals.* Some of the most complex tasks performed by a computer involve communicating with screens, printers, disk drives, and other peripheral devices. A computer's operating system always includes programs that transparently take care of the details of communication with peripherals.
- *Coordinating concurrent processing of jobs.* Large, multiuser computers often work on several jobs at the same time—a technique known as **concurrent processing**. State-of-the-art parallel processing machines use multiple CPUs to process jobs simultaneously. But a typical computer has only one processor, so it must work on several projects by rapidly switching back and forth between projects. The computer takes advantage of idle time in one process (for example, waiting for input) by working on another program. (For example, our computerized chef, Robert, might practice concurrent processing by slicing fruit while he waits for the toast to brown.) A timesharing computer practices concurrent processing whenever multiple users are connected to the system. The computer quickly moves from terminal to terminal, checking for input and processing each user's data in turn. Concurrent processing is becoming increasingly common in personal computer operating systems that allow **multitasking**. If a PC has multitasking capabilities, the user can issue a command that initiates a process (for example, to print this chapter) and continue working with other applications while the computer follows through on the command.
- *Memory management.* When several jobs are being processed concurrently, the operating system must keep track of how the computer's memory is being used and make sure that no job encroaches on another's territory. Memory manage-

ment is accomplished in a variety of ways, from simple schemes that subdivide the available memory equally between jobs to elaborate procedures for temporarily swapping information between the computer's memory and external storage devices.

- *Resource monitoring, accounting, and security.* Many multiuser computer systems are designed to charge users for the resources they consume. These systems keep track of each user's time, storage demands, and pages printed, so accounting programs can calculate and print accurate bills. Even in environments where billing isn't an issue, the operating system should monitor resources to ensure the privacy and security of each user's data.
- *Program and data management.* In addition to serving as a traffic cop, a security guard, and an accountant, the operating system acts as a librarian, locating and accessing files and programs requested by the user and by other programs.

A typical commercial utility package includes software tools for recovering damaged files, repairing damaged disks, and improving disk performance. (Software: PC Tools from Central Point and Norton Utilities from Symantec.)

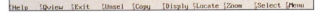

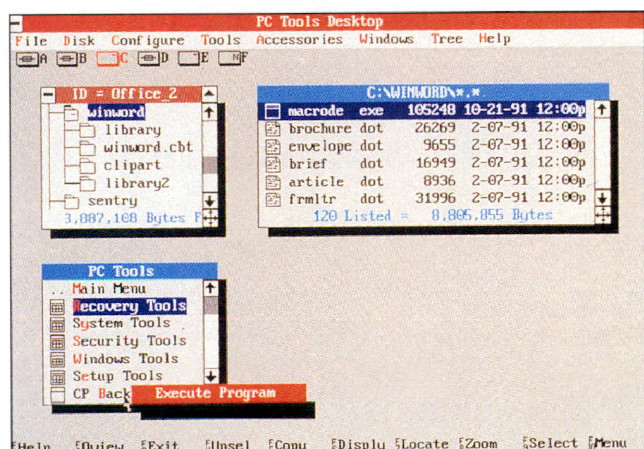

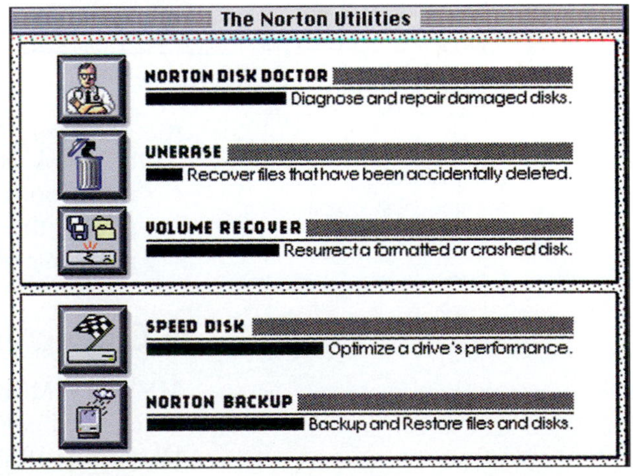

Utility Programs

Even the best operating systems leave a certain amount of housekeeping to other programs and to the user. **Utility programs** serve as tools for doing system maintenance and some repairs that aren't automatically handled by the operating system. Utilities make it easier for users to copy files between storage devices, to repair damaged data files, to translate files so that different programs can read them, and to perform countless other important, if unexciting, tasks. Many utility programs can be invoked directly by the operating system, so they appear to the user to be part of the operating system. Some utility programs are included with the operating system; others are sold as separate products.

Where the Operating System Lives

Some computers—mostly game machines and special-purpose computers—store their operating systems permanently in ROM (read-only memory) so they are ready to go to work as soon as they are turned on. But since ROM is unchangeable, these machines can't have their operating systems modified or upgraded without hardware transplants. Most computers include only part of the operating system in ROM—the remainder of the operating system is loaded into memory in a process called **booting**. (The term *booting* is used because the computer seems to pull itself up by its own bootstraps.)

Most of the time the operating system works behind the scenes, taking care of business without the knowledge or intervention of the user. But occasionally it's necessary for a user to communicate directly with the operating system. For example, when you boot a personal computer, the operating system steps into the foreground, waiting for instructions from you. If you issue a command to open a graphics application, the operating system locates the program, copies it from disk into memory, turns the screen over to the application, and then accepts commands from the application while you draw pictures on the screen.

Interacting with the operating system, like interacting with an application, can be intuitive or challenging. It depends on something called the user interface. Because of its profound impact on the computing experience, the user interface is a critically important component of almost every piece of software.

The User Interface: The Human-Machine Connection

Make things as simple as possible—but no simpler.

—Albert Einstein

Early computer users had to spend tedious hours writing and debugging machine-language instructions. Later users programmed in languages that were easier to understand but still technically challenging. Today users spend much of their time working with preprogrammed applications like word processors that simulate and amplify the capabilities of real-world tools. As software evolves, so does the **user interface**—the look and feel of the computing experience from a human point of view.

Probably the easiest way to understand the importance of user interfaces is to see how we might accomplish a simple task using different user interfaces. We'll look at the user interface of

- MS-DOS, the operating system that's standard equipment in millions of IBM-compatible computers (computers that are functionally identical to an IBM personal computer and therefore capable of running IBM-compatible software)
- Apple's Macintosh, the most popular alternative to IBM-compatible computers
- Microsoft Windows, software that provides a Macintosh-like user interface for IBM-compatible computers

In each case we'll use a version of the WordPerfect word processing program.But first a disclaimer and a reminder:

- *The disclaimer:* This comparison is not intended to fuel the fires of brand-name wars. We're not comparing competing user interfaces to establish a champion; we're simply comparing examples of two different types of interfaces.
- *The reminder:* The examples shown here, like the other User's View examples in this book, are designed to give you a *feel* for the software, not to provide how-to instructions. If you want to learn how to use the software described in this book, refer to the manuals that accompany the software or to other books on the subject, some of which are listed at the ends of chapters in this book.

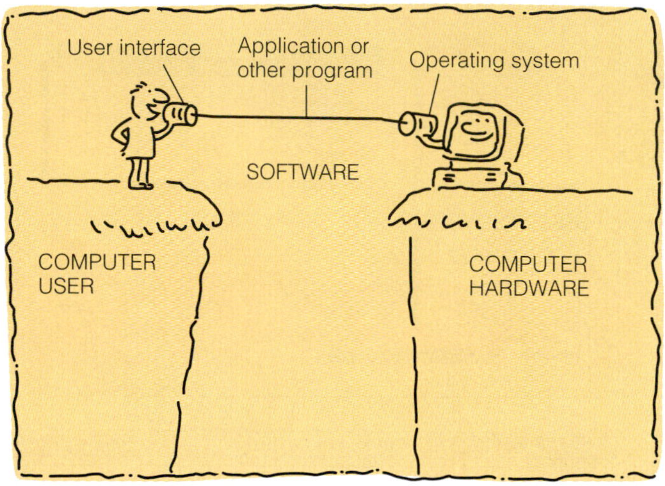

The user's view revisited: The user interface is the part of the computer system that the user sees. A well-designed user interface hides the bothersome details of computing from the user.

A Character-Based User Interface: MS-DOS

MS-DOS (Microsoft Disk Operating System, sometimes called just DOS) is the most widely used general-purpose operating system in the world. When IBM chose **PC-DOS**—the IBM brand of MS-DOS—as the operating system for its first personal computer in 1981, almost all computer displays were defined in terms of characters. A typical computer monitor displayed 24 eighty-column lines of text, numbers, and/or symbols. The computer sent messages to the monitor telling it which character to display in each location on the screen. To comply with this hardware arrangement, MS-DOS was designed with a **character-based interface**—a user interface based on characters rather than graphics.

Today tens of thousands of applications are MS-DOS-compatible (IBM-compatible), and most of these applications do a pretty good job of shielding the user from the behind-the-scenes work of the operating system. When it is necessary to communicate directly with the operating system (to start up an application or a utility, for example), the user carries on a dialogue through the MS-DOS **command-line interface**. With a command-line interface, the user types commands and the computer responds to the commands. Some MS-DOS-compatible applications have a command-line interface, but it's more common for applications to have a **menu-driven interface** that allows users to choose commands from on-screen lists called **menus**. The User's View box illustrates two different character-based interfaces: the command-line interface of MS-DOS and the menu-driven interface of WordPerfect, a popular word processing application.

The User's View

Working with Character-Based Interfaces

Software: MS-DOS and WordPerfect for IBM-compatible computers.
The goal: In this simple example you'll start the computer, open a term paper created with a word processor, and print it. In the process you'll get a taste of what it's like to work with two character-based interfaces: the MS-DOS command-line interface and WordPerfect's menu-driven interface.

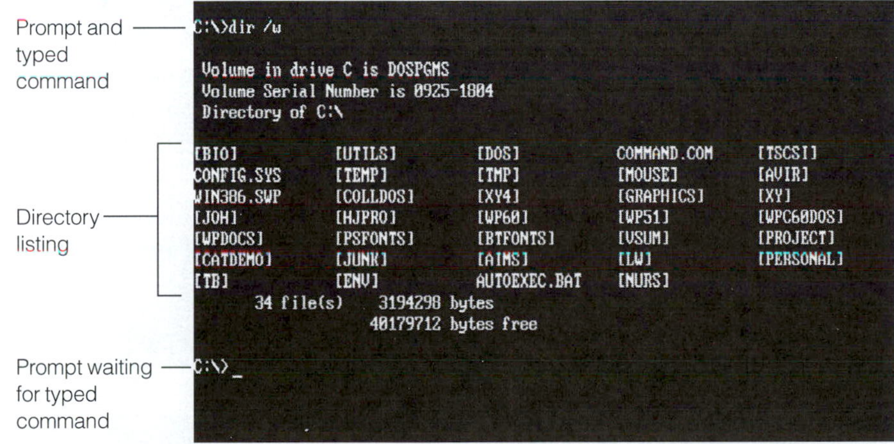

At start-up, the MS-DOS operating system displays a screen that's empty except for a **prompt** (C:\>) and a flashing cursor. You type dir/w to see a wide (multicolumn) list of items in disk C's **directory**. When you press the Enter key, MS-DOS displays a list of items on the hard disk, including files and *subdirectories*—collections of files that have been grouped together. The directory list is followed by another prompt (C:\>). The operating system is waiting for another command.

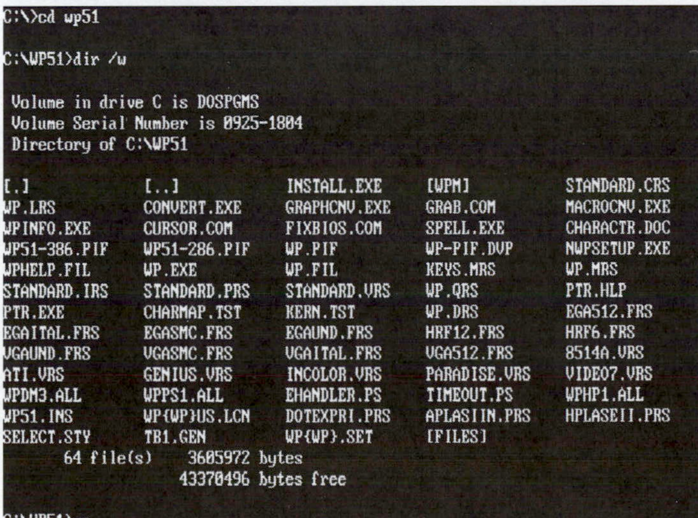

You want to **open** (or *load*) your paper—copy it from disk into the memory. The paper is stored in a file called *privacy.wp5*, but you must first open the application that created it: WordPerfect. The application is stored in the subdirectory *wp51*, so you type cd wp51 to change to that directory. When you repeat the dir command, you see a list of the files stored in this subdirectory. You type wp to open WordPerfect.

The screen clears as WordPerfect is opened. WordPerfect doesn't have a command-line interface; instead it lets you choose commands from menus. The menus are embedded in a **menu bar** that appears when you hold down the Alt key and press the = key. The words in the menu bar—*File, Edit,* and the rest—are the names of the menus. The menus appear when you type their initials. For example, the File menu appears when you press the F key. Next you type R to select the *Retrieve* command from the menu.

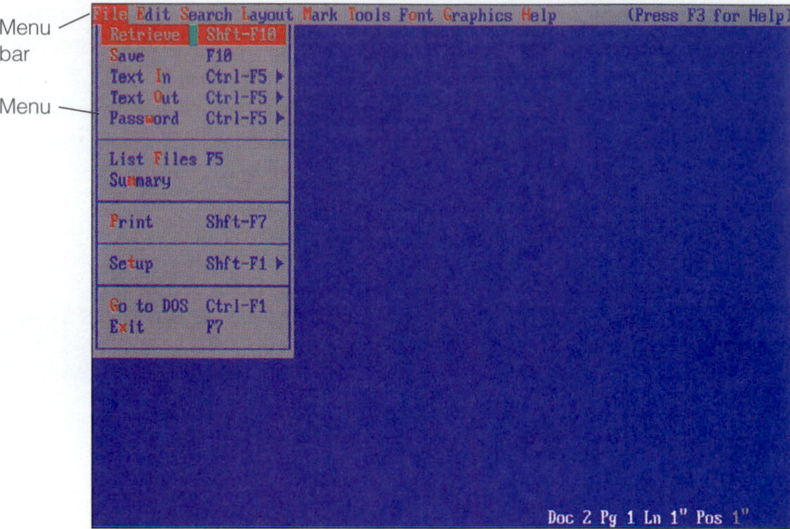

A prompt appears at the bottom of the screen: File to be retrieved. The machine waits for you to type the exact name of the file, including the *path name* (a string of characters telling the computer where to find the file on the disk). The file *privacy.wp5* is stored on disk C in directory *wp51* in subdirectory *files*, so you type c:\wp51\files\ privacy.wp5. If you typed every character correctly, the file is loaded into the computer's memory, and the first part of the term paper appears on the screen.

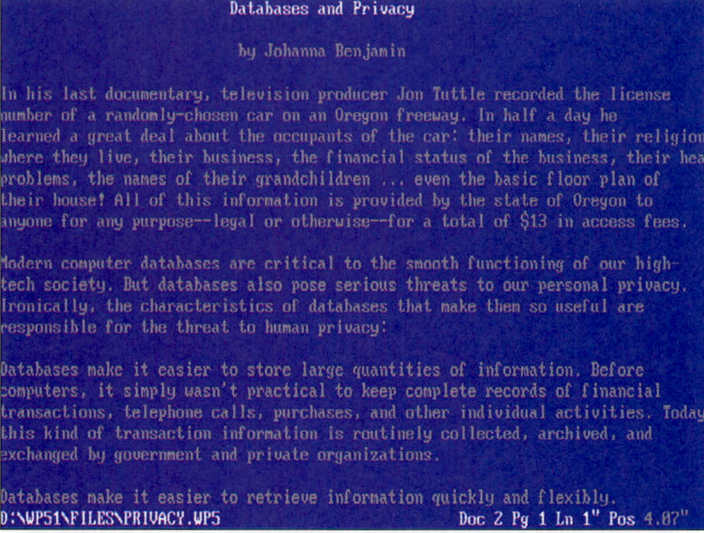

Databases and Privacy
by Johanna Benjamin
In his last documentary, television producer Jon Tuttle recorded the license number of a randomly-chosen car on an Oregon freeway. In half a day he learned a great deal about the occupants of the car: their names, their religion where they live, their business, the financial status of the business, their hea problems, the names of their grandchildren ... even the basic floor plan of their house! All of this information is provided by the state of Oregon to anyone for any purpose--legal or otherwise--for a total of $13 in access fees.
Modern computer databases are critical to the smooth functioning of our high-tech society. But databases also pose serious threats to our personal privacy. Ironically, the characteristics of databases that make them so useful are responsible for the threat to human privacy:
Databases make it easier to store large quantities of information. Before computers, it simply wasn't practical to keep complete records of financial transactions, telephone calls, purchases, and other individual activities. Today this kind of transaction information is routinely collected, archived, and exchanged by government and private organizations.
Databases make it easier to retrieve information quickly and flexibly.
D:\WP51\FILES\PRIVACY.WP5 Doc 2 Pg 1 Ln 1" Pos 4.07"

Following a similar set of steps, you select the Print command to print the term paper. When printing is done, you select the Exit command to close the word processing application and return to the MS-DOS C prompt. To delete the file, you enter the command del followed by the file name. When you enter the command incorrectly, the operating system cannot recognize the command, so it responds with "Bad command or filename"—an **error message** telling you you've done something wrong. When you retype the command, no error message appears, so you know the file is deleted and you're ready to turn off the machine.

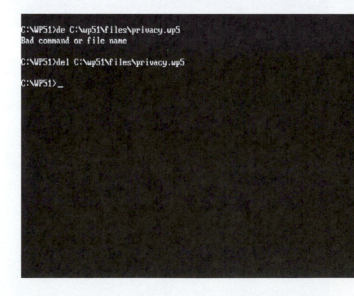

Graphical User Interfaces: Macintosh and Windows

Since the introduction of the IBM-PC, hardware advances have made it possible for low-cost computers to include graphic displays. A computer with a graphic display is not limited to displaying rows and columns of characters; it can individually control every dot on the screen. The Apple Macintosh was the first low-cost computer whose operating system was designed with a graphic display in mind. **The Macintosh operating system** sports a **graphical user interface** (sometimes abbreviated **GUI**, pronounced "gooey") that is radically different from the MS-DOS command-line interface.

Instead of reading typed commands and file names from a command line, the Macintosh operating system determines what the user wants by monitoring movements of the mouse. With the mouse the user points to pictures, known as **icons**, that represent files, folders (collections of files), and disks. Documents are displayed in **windows**—framed areas that can be opened, closed, and rearranged with the mouse. The user selects commands from **pull-down menus** at the top of the screen. Because this kind of graphical user interface doesn't require users to memorize commands, it allows users who are new to a program to be up and running in a fraction of the time it takes to learn a command-line system. This User's View box shows a simple Macintosh session.

The User's View

Working with a Macintosh Graphical User Interface

Software: Macintosh System 7 and WordPerfect for Macintosh.
The goal: To return to our term paper example, this time with a graphical user interface.

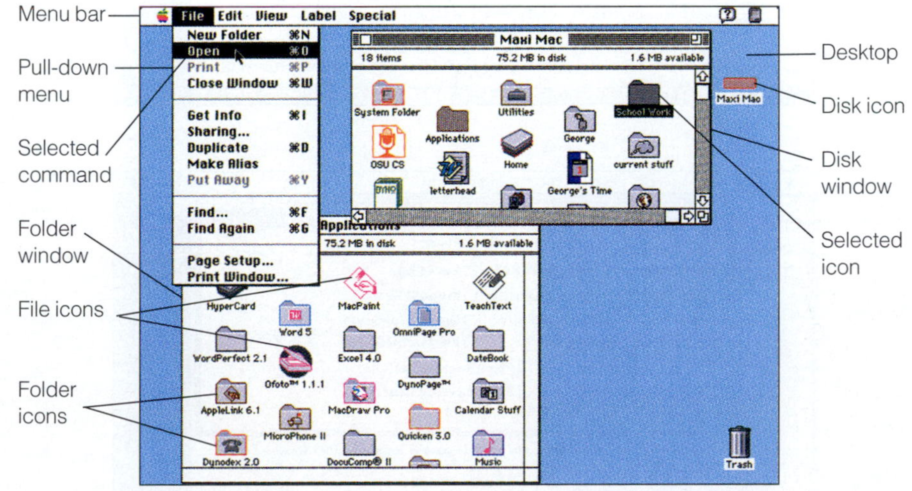

When you turn on the Macintosh, you see a visual representation of a **desktop** with a menu bar at the top. An open window shows the contents of the hard disk called *Maxi Mac*. Each icon in the window represents a file or a **folder** containing other files. The folder called *Applications* is open, so a window on the desktop shows its contents. But the term paper icon is in another folder: *School Work*. You move the mouse so that the pointer points to the *School Work* icon and click the mouse button. It darkens to indicate that it has been *selected*. When you hold the mouse button down while pointing to the File menu, a pull-down menu appears like a window shade. You drag the mouse down until the pointer points to the Open command and release the button to choose that command.

A window appears, revealing the contents of the *School Work* folder. To open the term paper document, you could select the *Privacy Paper* icon and choose the Open command. But this time you use the shorthand version of the Open command—you *double-click* (click twice with the mouse button) on the *Privacy Paper* icon.

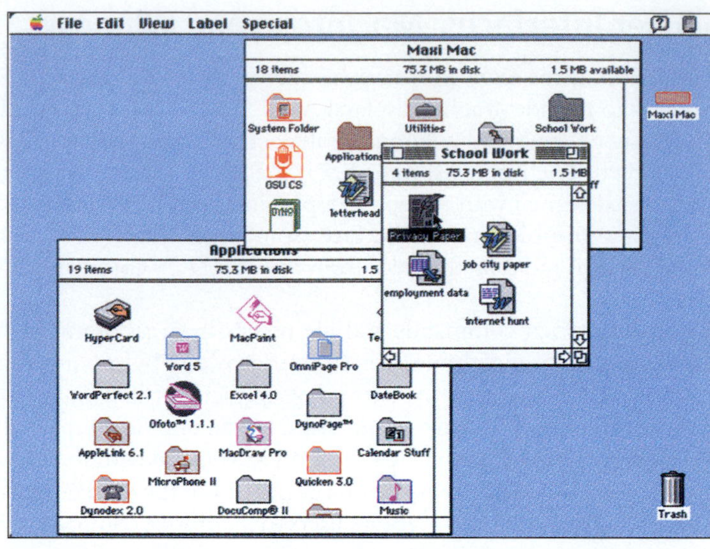

When you open the document, the WordPerfect application opens and displays the term paper document. All application programs for the Macintosh share a consistent user interface, so choosing the Print command from a pull-down menu is a familiar process.

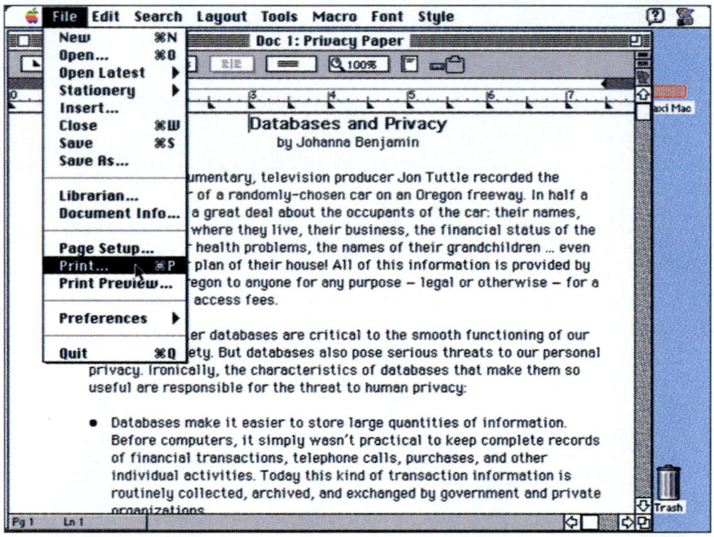

The operating system displays **dialog boxes** when two-way communication is called for. This dialog box, which appears whenever the Print command is selected, allows you to specify the details of the print job. Like most dialog boxes it includes a Cancel button that lets you retract the command and return to what you were doing before. In this case, though, we'll click Print to send the job to the printer.

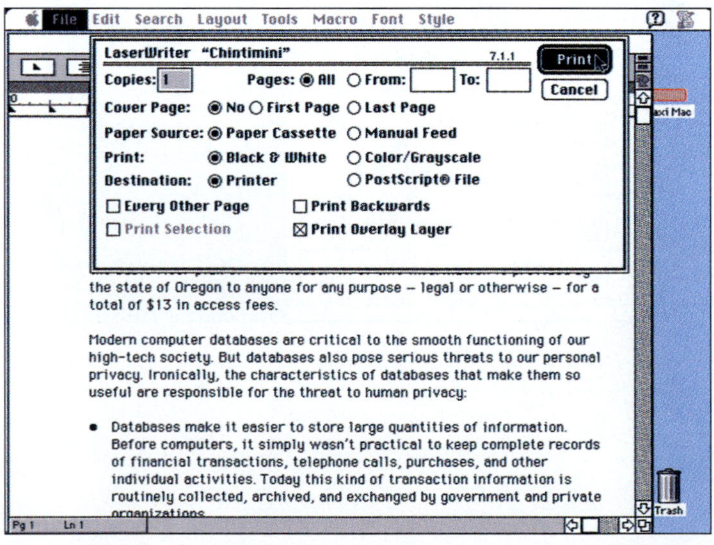

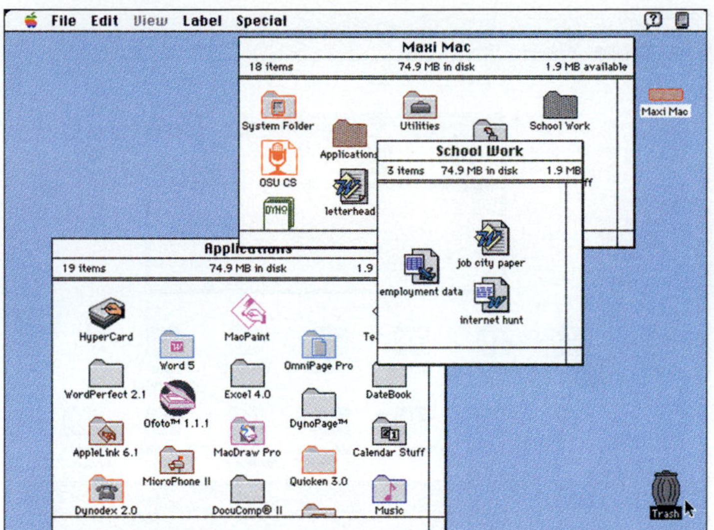

When you close the application (using the Quit command from the File menu), you return to the desktop. You can now delete the printed file by dragging its icon over the Trash icon. (Until you choose the command Empty Trash from the Special menu, though, you can change your mind and retrieve the file from the Trash).

As you can see, working with a Macintosh is a very different experience than working with an IBM-compatible computer running MS-DOS. But the difference has less to do with the **platform**—the hardware on which the software runs—than with the software itself. Since the Macintosh was introduced in 1984, other popular computers have sprouted GUIs that, to varying degrees, have the look and feel of the Macintosh.

Ironically the Macintosh's biggest competitor in the graphical user interface market is a product from Microsoft, the company that produces MS-DOS. **Microsoft Windows** is a type of program, known as a **shell**, that puts a Macintosh-like face on MS-DOS. The Windows shell stands between the user and the operating system, translating mouse movements and other user input into commands that can be recognized by MS-DOS. While Windows doesn't completely hide its MS-DOS roots, it does an impressive job of shielding the user from most of the details of DOS. Compare the Windows session shown in this User's View box with the earlier MS-DOS and Macintosh sessions.

The User's View

Working with a Windows Graphical User Interface

Software: Microsoft Windows 3.1 and WordPerfect for Windows.
The goal: To print the term paper one more time, this time with Windows.

Like the Macintosh, Windows presents a graphical display made up of icons and windows. You launch programs using the Windows Program Manager, which displays icons for each group of applications in a window. Like a Macintosh folder, a group can be opened with a double-click or the Open command.

The WordPerfect group is open and visible in a smaller window. The easiest way to open our term paper document is to first launch the WordPerfect application with a double-click.

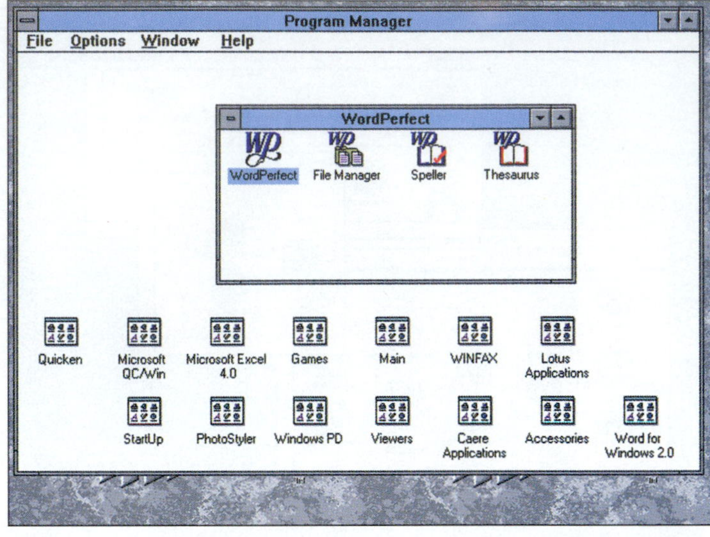

After WordPerfect opens, we can use the Open command in the File menu to locate and open our document. In Windows the menu bar is inside the window rather than across the top of the screen, but it includes familiar pull-down menus. When you point to File in the menu bar and click the mouse, the menu appears. Unlike with the Macintosh, the menu remains visible even if you release the button. You move the pointer down the menu to the Open command and click to choose that command.

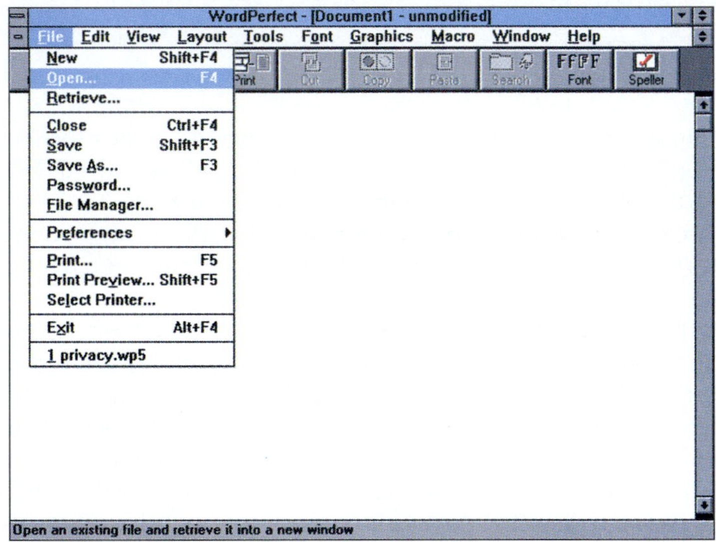

Once the document is open, the process of printing is almost identical to that on the Macintosh.

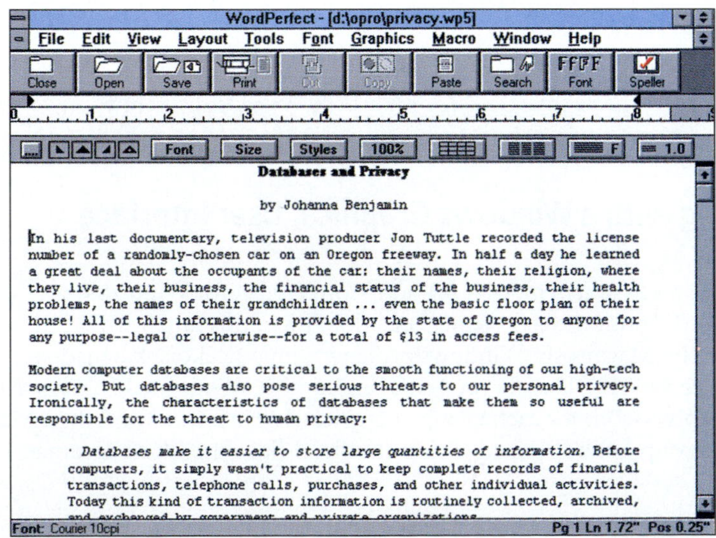

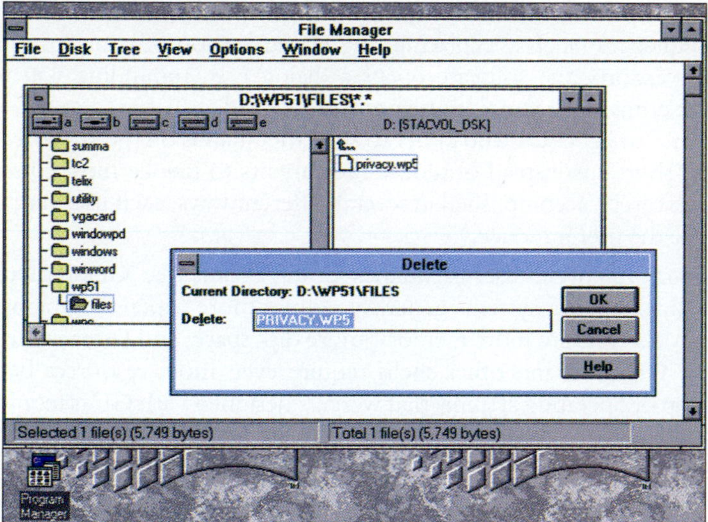

After the document is printed, you quit WordPerfect with the Exit command and return to the Program Manager. There's no trash can in Windows. To delete the term paper file, you need to launch the File Manager program, locate the file in the graphical directory, select it, and choose the Delete command. This dialog box allows you to change your mind (Cancel) before deleting the file forever.

Will WIMP Win?

In these three examples we did the same job with different versions of the same application and produced the same output. In the case of MS-DOS and Windows, we even used the same hardware platform. But from the user's point of view, the Macintosh and Windows sessions have more in common, even though they involve different platforms. The critical difference between these sessions and the DOS session are in the user interfaces. This is more than just a difference between working with pictures and working with words. Graphical user interfaces with *w*indows, *i*cons, *m*enus, and *p*ointing devices (sometimes called *WIMP*) offer several clear advantages from the user's point of view:

- *They're intuitive.* When you throw away a GUI document, you drag it into the trash or select a Delete command from a menu. For most users those processes are easier than remembering and typing the MS-DOS command for deleting a file. The visual metaphors and menus of the graphical screen are generally easier for people to understand and learn than the typewritten commands of MS-DOS.
- *They're consistent.* People who use their computers for just one purpose—say, word processing—can be extremely productive with either kind of interface; many experienced single-application users argue that a character-based interface responds more quickly and allows them to work more efficiently. But people who use a number of different MS-DOS applications are often faced with a confusing array of inconsistent interfaces that require them to keep stacks of reference manuals handy to look up commands. GUI applications have the same user interface as their operating systems, so users don't need to learn new ways of doing things whenever they switch applications.
- *They're predictable.* Many Macintosh and Windows users have mastered dozens of applications without ever consulting a manual. Users feel safe learning by trial and error, because it's usually easy to predict the results of each action.
- *They're forgiving.* Almost every dialog box includes a Cancel button, allowing the user to say, in effect, "Never mind." The Undo command can almost always take back the last command, restoring everything the way it was before the command was issued.

- *They're protective.* When you're about to do something that may have unpleasant consequences (such as replacing the revised version of your term paper with an older version), the software opens a dialog box, reminding you to make sure you're doing what you want before you proceed.
- *They're flexible.* Users who prefer to keep their hands on the keyboard can use keyboard shortcuts instead of mouse movements to invoke most commands. Most actions can be accomplished in several different ways; each user can, in effect, customize the user interface.

Of course, all of this user-friendliness doesn't come free. Graphical user interfaces and friendly operating systems generally require more expensive graphic display systems. They also require more memory, more disk space, and faster processors to work efficiently. Windows and other shells require even more resources because they're built on top of operating systems that weren't designed with GUIs in mind. MS-DOS and other command-line operating systems have minimal hardware requirements when compared to just about any GUI operating system or shell.

But as hardware goes down in price and up in speed, efficiency arguments become less convincing. The computer industry is rallying behind graphical user interfaces in ever-increasing numbers. Today the three most popular computing environments are MS-DOS, Macintosh, and Windows. But the MS-DOS share of the market is rapidly shrinking as the other two grow, and most software developers are focusing on developing applications for Windows and the Macintosh. At the same time there's a growing interest in several newer GUI operating systems and shells:

- IBM's OS/2, a high-powered operating system that can run applications developed for both DOS and Windows
- Microsoft Windows NT, a full-fledged operating system based on Windows, designed to run on high-end PCs and workstations
- Hewlett Packard's New Wave, a shell that sits on the Windows shell, changing the user interface so it's even more like that of the Macintosh
- Next, Inc.'s NextStep, a sophisticated graphical shell built on UNIX, a powerful multiuser operating system described in Chapter 7
- a completely new graphical operating system being jointly developed by Apple and IBM for the state-of-the-art "power PC" they're creating together

Of course, millions of older PCs still don't have the hardware power to support *any* GUI. Many users who work with less powerful hardware are turning to shells that hide the inner workings of MS-DOS behind menus. And a growing number of DOS applications mimic modern GUIs within the limitations of the older hardware—the

Compatibility Issues: Hardware Platforms and Software Environments
Most personal computers today are built on one of two hardware platforms: the Intel-based platform used by IBM-compatible PCs and the Motorola-based Macintosh platform. Among IBM-compatible computers, a growing number include the Windows shell along with the MS-DOS operating system. Most software today is sold as IBM-compatible, Windows-compatible, or Macintosh-compatible, because these three hardware/software environments dominate the market. The lines between these three environments aren't as solid as you might expect. Character-based DOS-compatible software can be run in a window on a Windows machine. With an *emulator* utility like Soft-PC, a Macintosh can run IBM-compatible or Windows-compatible software. What's more, market developments in the mid-1990s will change many details shown here. Three examples: (1) Microsoft Windows will evolve from a shell into an operating system; (2) most future IBM-compatible computers will probably include the faster Intel Pentium CPU; and (3) most future Macintoshes will use Power PC CPUs developed by IBM and manufactured by Motorola.

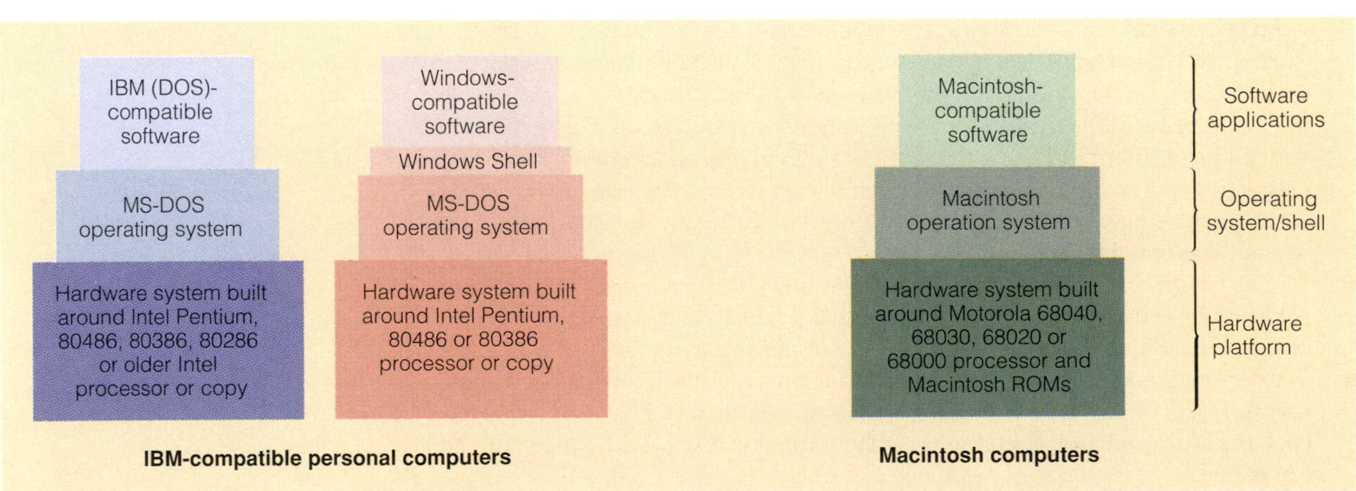

DOS version of WordPerfect in our User's View is a good example. If current trends continue, command-line user interfaces will soon be as foreign to most computer users as FORTRAN, COBOL, and machine language are today.

Tomorrow's User Interface?

As attractive and popular as today's graphical user interfaces are, they're not likely to reign forever. Future user interfaces will be built around technologies that are still in the earliest stages of development today. Here are some likely candidates:

- *The end of applications.* As integrated software packages improve and operating systems develop features like interapplication communication, the boundaries between individual applications are likely to blur. Future computer users may not think in terms of word processors, spreadsheets, and such; they'll just use their computers like we use pencils today—as all-purpose tools.
- *Natural-language interfaces.* It's just a matter of time before we'll be able to communicate with computers in English, Spanish, Russian, Japanese, or some other natural language. Today computers in research labs can reliably read subsets of the English language or can be trained to understand spoken English commands and text. These capabilities are starting to show up in consumer computers. Tomorrow's machines should be able to handle much day-to-day work through a natural-language interface, written or spoken. Natural-language processing lies in the domain of artificial intelligence, Chapter 10's subject.
- *Agents.* Artificial intelligence research being done today may lead to intelligent *agents* that "live" in our computers and act as digital secretaries, anticipating our requests, filling in details in our work, and adjusting the computerized workspace to fit our needs. Chapter 14 describes agents and other futuristic user interface technologies in more detail.
- *Virtual realities.* Further into the future many experts predict that user interfaces will become so sophisticated that we'll be hard-pressed to detect the difference between the real world outside the computer and the **virtual reality** created by the computer, except that the virtual reality will allow us to do things that can't be done on the physical plane. Some computer games today provide surprisingly convincing simulations of the experience of driving a car or flying a plane. These games represent the tip of a gigantic iceberg of research into virtual reality software. More sophisticated virtual reality interfaces can be achieved today with specially designed hardware—for input, a glove or body suit equipped with motion sensors, and for output, a helmet with a tiny screens mounted in front of the user's eyes. This equipment, when coupled with appropriate software, allows the user to explore an artificial world of data as if it were three-dimensional physical space.

Using virtual reality hardware and software, researchers are exploring a multitude of futuristic applications. A researcher here tests an experimental system that allows an air traffic controller to reach into a three-dimensional virtual airspace and "move" planes around by hand. Medical students explore a "virtual cadaver," seeing anatomic details like never before. More fanciful experimental systems allow users to "fly" through artificial buildings and landscapes simply by pointing with gloved hands. Virtual reality doesn't have to follow everyday laws of physics!

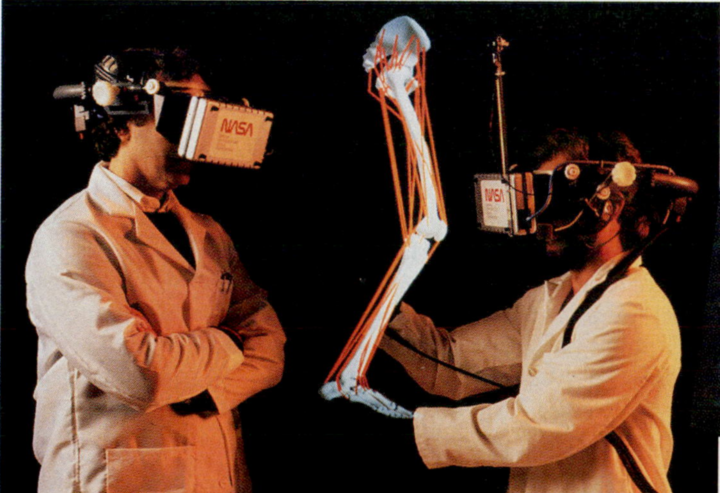

The best-known example of the kind of virtual reality researchers are working toward is the Starship Enterprise's Holodeck on TV's *Star Trek: the Next Generation.* The Holodeck can create absolutely convincing simulations of anything from a Sherlock Holmes detective story to a 24th-century antimatter generator. There are no keyboards or screens in sight; the user interface is a three-dimensional artificial world full of people, places, and things—real or imaginary—that can be seen, touched, talked to, and controlled by one or more "users." Far fetched? Absolutely. Possible? Maybe. When? Don't sell your keyboard for a while....

Summary

Software provides the communication link between human and computer. Because software is *soft*—stored in memory rather than hard-wired into the circuitry—it can easily be modified to meet the needs of the computer user. By changing software, you can change a computer from one kind of tool into another.

Most software falls into one of three broad categories: translator programs, software applications, and system software. A translator program is a software tool that allows programs written in English-like languages like BASIC and C to be translated into the zeros and ones of the machine language the computer understands. A translator frees the programmer from the tedium of machine-language programming, making it easier to write quality programs with fewer bugs. But even with the best translators, programming is a little like communicating with an alien species. It's a demanding process that requires more time and mental energy than most people are willing or able to invest.

Fortunately software applications make it easy for most computer users today to communicate their needs to the computer without learning programming. Applications simulate and extend the properties of familiar real-world tools like typewriters, paint brushes, and file cabinets, making it possible for people to do things with computers that would be difficult or impossible otherwise. Integrated software packages combine several applications in a single unified package, making it easy to switch between tools. For situations when a general commercial program won't do the job, programmers for businesses and public institutions develop vertical-market and custom packages.

Whether you're writing programs or simply using them, the computer's operating system is functioning behind the scenes, translating your software's instructions into messages that the hardware can understand. An operating system serves as the computer's business manager, taking care of the hundreds of details that need to be handled to keep the computer functioning. A timesharing operating system has the particularly challenging job of serving multiple users concurrently, monitoring the machine's resources, keeping track of each user's account, and protecting the security of the system and each user's data. Many of those system-related problems that the operating system can't solve directly can be handled by utility programs.

Applications, utilities, programming languages, and operating systems all must, to varying degrees, communicate with the user. A program's user interface is a critical factor in that communication. User interfaces have evolved over the years to the point where sophisticated software packages can be operated by people who know little about the inner workings of the computer. A well-designed user interface shields the user from the bits and bytes, creating an on-screen façade or shell that makes sense to the user. Today the computer industry is rapidly moving away from the tried-and-true command-line interfaces toward a friendlier graphical user interface that uses windows, icons, mice, and pull-down menus in an intuitive, consistent environment. Tomorrow's user interfaces are likely to depend more on voice, three-dimensional graphics, and animation to create an artificial reality.

CHAPTER REVIEW

Key Terms

algorithm
booting
bug
character-based interface
command-line interface
compatibility
concurrent processing
copy-protected software
copyrighted software
custom application
desktop
dialog box
directory
documentation
error message
folder
graphical user interface (GUI)
icon
integrated software
machine language
Macintosh operating system
menu
menu bar
menu-driven interface
Microsoft Windows
MS-DOS (PC-DOS)
multitasking
natural language
on-line documentation
opening a file
operating system
platform
prompt
public domain software
pull-down menu
shareware
shell
software license
system software
translator program
user interface
utility program
vertical-market application
virtual reality
window

Review Questions

1. What is a program? What is an algorithm? What is the relationship between the two?
2. Most computer software falls into one of three categories: translator programs, software applications, and system software. Describe and give examples of each.
3. Which must be loaded first into the computer's memory, the operating system or software applications? Why?
4. What is documentation? What is on-line documentation?
5. Write an algorithm for changing a flat tire. Check your algorithm carefully for errors.
6. Describe several functions of a single-user operating system. Describe several additional functions of a multiuser operating system.
7. What does it mean when software is called IBM-compatible or Macintosh-compatible? What does this have to do with the operating system?
8. What is a user interface? Why is it important?
9. What is a graphical user interface? How does it differ from a command-line interface? What are the advantages of each?

Discussion Questions

1. Why is writing instructions for a computer more difficult than writing instructions for a person?
2. How would using a computer be different if there were no operating systems? How would programming be different?
3. Speculate about the user interface of a typical computer in the year 2010. How does this user interface differ from those of today's computers?
4. If you had the resources to design a computer with a brand new user interface, what would your priorities be? Make a rank-ordered list of the qualities you'd like to have in your user interface.

Projects

1. Write a report about available computer applications in your field of study or in your chosen profession.
2. Learn to use software with different kinds of user interfaces. Describe your experiences.
3. Research different personal computer systems from a consumer's point of view. Include software and peripherals in your analysis.

Sources and Resources

The Little Mac Book, by Robin Williams, *The Little Windows Book,* by Kay Yarborough Nelson, and *The Little DOS 5 Book,* by Kay Yarborough Nelson (Berkeley, CA: Peachpit Press, 1991, 1992, 1991, respectively). These three highly acclaimed guides succinctly and clearly introduce first-time users to the Macintosh, Windows, and MS-DOS. They're ideal for people who don't want to spend a lot of time reading long manuals. If you can't find one of these, there are dozens of other beginner books for learning the basics of working with personal computer operating systems.

Programmers at Work, by Susan Lammers (Redmond, WA: Microsoft Press, 1986). A revealing collection of interviews with people who wrote some of the most important software in the first decade of the personal computer's history.

Tog on Interface, by Bruce Tognazzini (Reading, MA: Addison-Wesley, 1992). A witty and thought-provoking collection of ideas on user interfaces from a long-time "evangelist" for Apple developers, now at Sun Microsystems.

The Art of Human-Computer Interface Design, edited by Brenda Laurel (Reading, MA: Addison-Wesley, 1990). This entertaining, provocative, and highly informative book is filled with essays by the experts on what makes a user interface work, or not work. Essays cover everything from menus and icons to virtual reality.

Designing the User Interface: Strategies for Effective Human-Computer Interaction, by Ben Schneiderman (Reading, MA: Addison-Wesley, 1992). This book thoroughly explores the issues that face anyone designing a user interface, whether it's a simple application program, a complex hypermedia document, or a virtual reality environment. In a style that's both academic and approachable, Schneiderman discusses everything from input and output hardware to the ultimate social impact of the technology.

Silicon Mirage: The Art and Science of Virtual Reality, by Steve Aukstakalnis and David Blatner (Berkeley, CA: Peachpit Press, 1992). This book provides accessible answers to the question, "What's virtual reality all about?" It includes explanations of the basic technology, descriptions of present and future applications, and discussions of social and technological issues raised by VR. It's fascinating reading.

PART
TWO

Using Computers
Essential Applications

C H A P T E R
FOUR

Working with Words

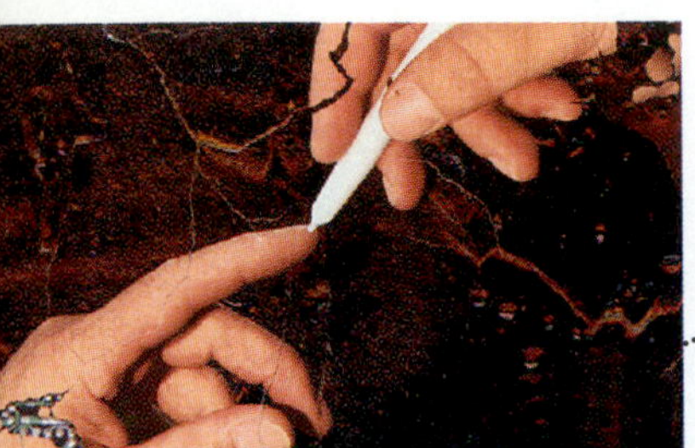

After reading this chapter you should be able to

- describe how computers can make the writing process more efficient, more effective, and more fun
- describe how a modern word processor can be used to create, edit, format, and print a document
- explain how to use a computer to proofread your work and how to recognize the limitations of proofreading software
- describe how other kinds of software can help you organize your ideas and improve your writing
- explain how desktop publishing relates to word processing and how it relates to traditional publishing
- discuss the potential impact of desktop publishing on the concept of the free press
- speculate about future developments in word processing and publishing software and hardware

Mark Twain Goes for Broke

This newfangled writing machine has several virtues. It piles an awful stack of words on one page. It don't muss things or scatter ink blots around. Of course it saves paper.

—Mark Twain

In 1874 Mark Twain bought a Remington Type-Writer for $125. One year later he became the first author in history to submit a typewritten manuscript: *The Adventures of Tom Sawyer*.

Twain later invested almost $200,000 (the equivalent of $1.5 million today) in the promising new Paige typesetting technology, convinced that it would transform publishing. It might very well have had not Ottmar Mergenthaler invented the Linotype machine at about the same time. Because of the Linotype, Twain's promising publishing machine was obsolete at its inception, and Twain was forced into bankruptcy.

Linotypes dominated the industry until the 1960s, when electronic typesetting with mainframe computers took over. Now mainframe publishing systems are rapidly being displaced by personal computers. From simple word processors to professional desktop publishing systems, small computers are rapidly and radically transforming the entire publishing process.

Mark Twain

Early computers were no threat to typewriters; they were too unfriendly, inconvenient, inflexible, and expensive to be used by anyone but highly skilled experts. The special-purpose "word processing machines" used by clerical workers in the 1960s represented a big step forward, but they were a far cry from the state-of-the-art word processing programs on today's personal computers. Word processing software available today is easier to learn, easier to use, and more powerful than anyone might have imagined a few decades ago.

Anyone who has used a computer as a word processor knows that it's far more than a fancy typewriter. The entire writing process is transformed by modern word processing software. Instead of suffering through the painful and disjointed process of typing and retyping in pursuit of a "clean" draft, a writer can focus on developing ideas and let the machine take care of the details of laying out the words neatly on the page. Today's word processing technology makes it possible and fun for just about any literate person to communicate effectively in writing. More than any other software application, word processing is a tool for everybody.

In this chapter we'll take a writer's view of word processing, from the first stages of entering text right on through to printing the final document. We'll consider advanced software tools for working with words, from outliners and idea processors to sophisticated reference tools. Finally we'll see how desktop publishing technology is transforming the entire publishing process and providing more people with the power to communicate in print.

The Word Processing Process

I . . . cannot imagine now that I ever wrote without with a typewriter.

—Arthur C. Clarke, *author and scientist*

Working with any word processor (a common way of referring to word processing software) involves several steps:

- entering text
- editing text
- formatting the document
- proofreading the document
- saving the document on disk
- printing the document

Early word processing systems generally forced users to follow these steps in a strict order. Some systems still in use today—mainly on mainframes and other time-sharing systems—segregate these processes into steps that can't easily be mixed. But most modern word processing systems provide all of the necessary tools in a single, seamless software package. As a result, most users of word processors today are hardly aware of the distinction between text editing and formatting. They move freely between editing and formatting, in some cases doing both at the same time. Still, for our discussion it makes sense to consider these as separate processes.

Entering Text

Entering text using a word processor is similar to using a typewriter but simpler. As you type on the computer keyboard, your text is displayed on the screen and stored in the computer's memory. Since memory is not a permanent storage medium, it's important to regularly **save** your work—that is, make a disk file containing your work in progress. That way if the power fails, or if the computer fails, or if you accidentally erase part of the text, you can restart the machine (if necessary) and *open* the saved version of your document—copy it back from a floppy or hard disk into the computer's memory. If you save your work on a diskette, you can take a break and later return to your computer (or another one like it at a different location), open your document, and take up where you left off.

The User's View box shows a sample of entering text with Microsoft Word, a modern word processing program. Like most of the applications featured in this book, Microsoft Word is available in almost identical versions for both Macintosh and IBM-compatible computers using the Windows operating system shell.

The User's View

Entering Text

Software: Microsoft Word.
The goal: to produce a copy of a classic work to be read in an English class presentation.

A word processing document starts as an empty window. A flashing **cursor** (sometimes called an **insertion bar**) indicates your location in the document. As you type, the cursor moves to the right, leaving a trail of text in its wake. At the same time, those characters are stored in the computer's memory. If you mistype a character or string of characters, you can press Delete or Backspace to eliminate the typos. Because of a feature called **word wrap**, the word processor automatically transports any words that won't fit on the current line to the next line along with the cursor. The only time you need to press Return or Enter is when you want to *force* the program to begin a new line—such as at the end of a paragraph.

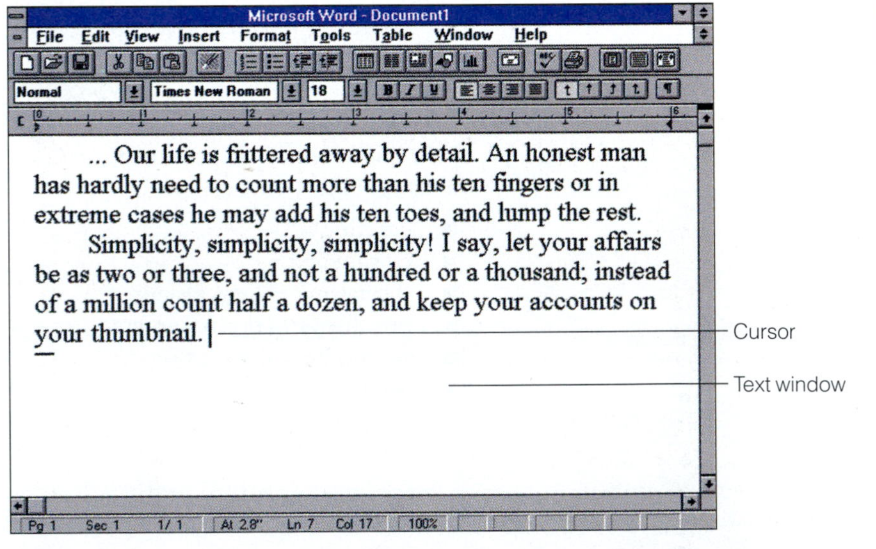
Microsoft Word - Document1
File Edit View Insert Format Tools Table Window Help
Normal
Times New Roman
18
... Our life is frittered away by detail. An honest man has hardly need to count more than his ten fingers or in extreme cases he may add his ten toes, and lump the rest.
Simplicity, simplicity, simplicity! I say, let your affairs be as two or three, and not a hundred or a thousand; instead of a million count half a dozen, and keep your accounts on your thumbnail.
Cursor
Text window
Pg 1 Sec 1 1/1 At 2.8" Ln 7 Col 17 100%

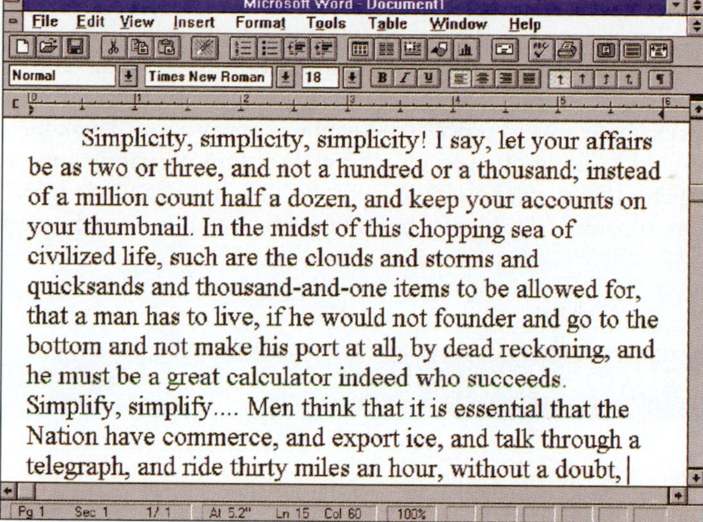

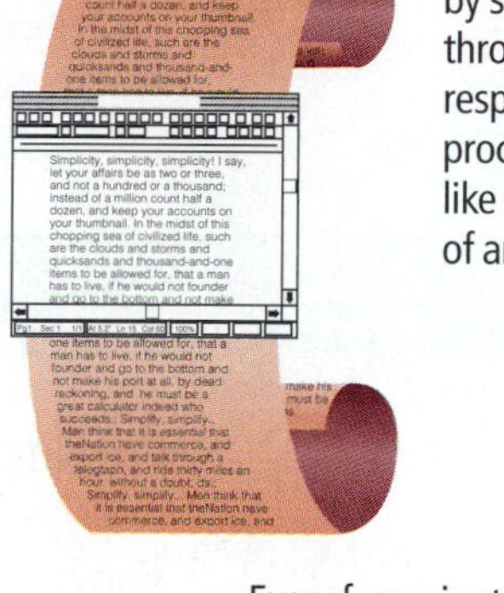

As you type, the topmost lines **scroll** out of view to make room on the screen for the new ones. The text you've entered is still in memory, even though you can't see it on the screen. You can retrieve it any time by scrolling backward through the text. In this respect a word processor document is like a modern version of ancient paper scrolls.

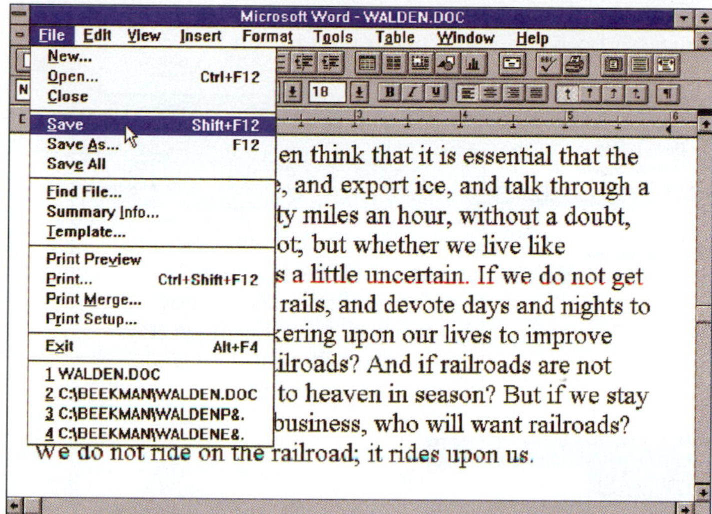

Every few minutes you select the Save command to create a disk file containing your work so far. This provides insurance against accidental erasure of the text you've entered.

Editing Text

All word processing applications allow you to do basically the same thing: write and refine a document on screen until it's good enough to commit to paper. If you're working with a modern **WYSIWYG** (short for *w*hat *y*ou *s*ee *i*s *w*hat *y*ou *g*et and pronounced "wizzy-wig") word processor, the arrangement of the words on the screen represents a close approximation of the arrangement of words on the printed page.

Just about any word processor you can buy today makes it easy for you to change and rearrange your work in all kinds of ways that aren't possible with typewriters or pencils. Specifically, with a word processor you can easily

- **navigate** to different parts of the document by scrolling or by using a **Find command** to locate a particular word or phrase
- **insert text** at any point in the document
- **delete text** from any part of the document
- **move text** from one part of the document to another section of the same document or to another document
- **copy text** from one part of a document and duplicate it in another section of the document or in a different document
- **search and replace** selected words or phrases throughout a document

Professional word processing programs contain sophisticated variations on these basic editing features. But even with this basic set of features, you can go a long way toward eliminating the drudgery that plagued writers in the precomputer era.

The next User's View box shows a brief editing session with a short document. As you'll see in this example, a word processor streamlines the process of making changes. Of course, real-world editing often involves several sessions of writing and rewriting. For long documents that require multiple revisions, the advantages of a word processor are even more apparent. The bigger the editing job, the more a word processor can help.

The User's View

Editing Text

Software: Microsoft Word.
The goal: The text has been entered; now it's time to edit it.

The first editing job is to remove the title and author lines from the bottom of the text and insert them at the top. You **select** text to be edited using the mouse or the keyboard. Selected text appears *highlighted* on the screen. Choosing the Cut command from the Edit menu, you tell the computer to cut the selected text from the document and place it in the **Clipboard**—a special portion of memory for temporarily holding information for later use.

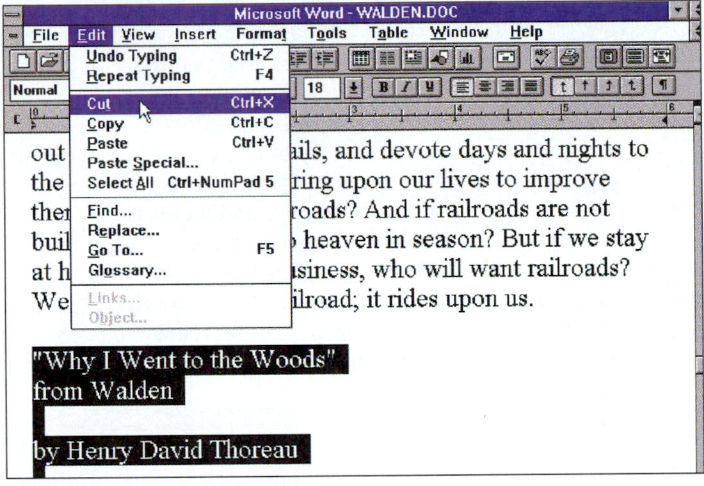

After using the mouse or arrow keys to reposition the cursor at the beginning of the document, you select the Paste command from the Edit menu. The computer places a copy of the Clipboard's contents at the insertion point; the text below the cursor moves down to make room for the inserted text. This type of **cut-and-paste** editing is possible in virtually all WYSIWYG word processors; it can also be used to move text from one document to another. To speed up the process of moving text within a document, many word processors include a **drag-and-drop** feature that allows you to simply drag (with the mouse) selected text to another part of the document.

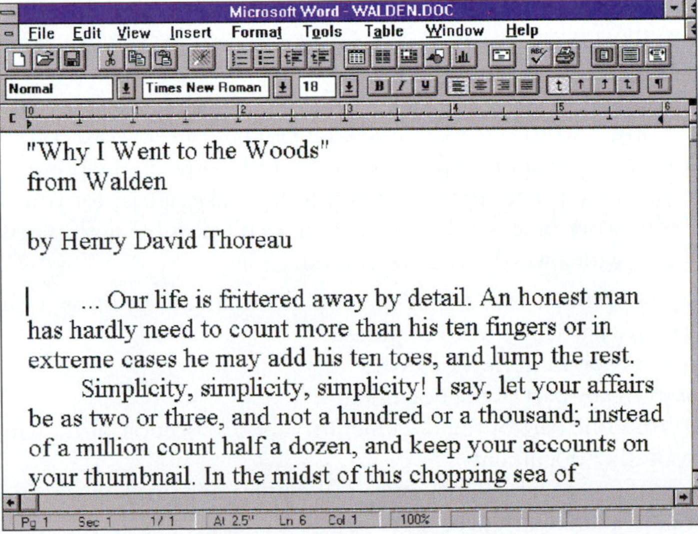

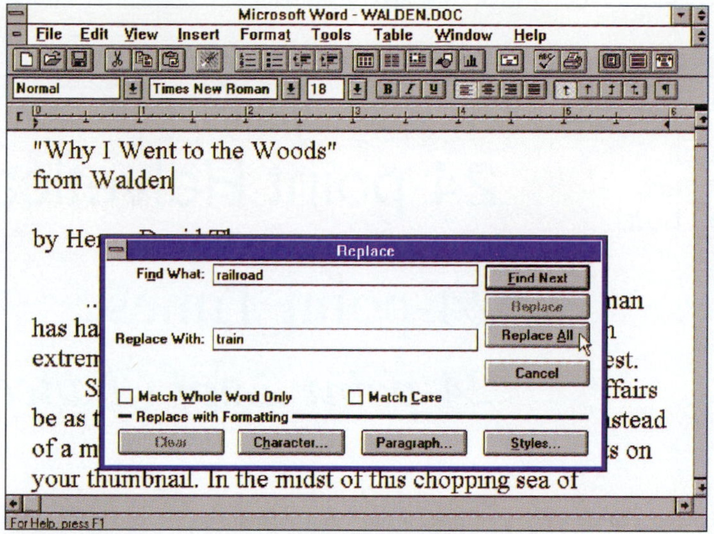

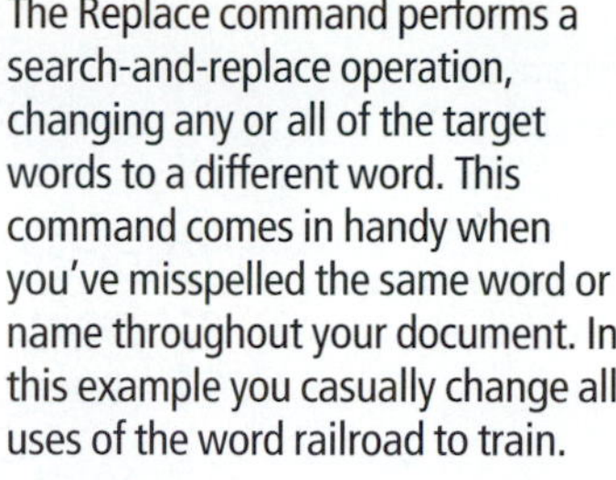

The Replace command performs a search-and-replace operation, changing any or all of the target words to a different word. This command comes in handy when you've misspelled the same word or name throughout your document. In this example you casually change all uses of the word railroad to train.

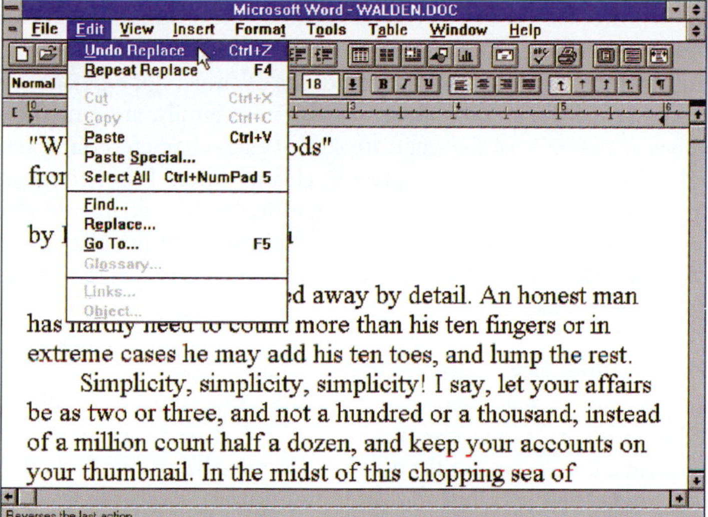

You immediately realize that it's not wise to change Thoreau's prose. Fortunately, the **Undo command** allows you to take back the last operation you performed, effectively saying "Oops! Forget I said that!" For human computer users, the Undo command may be the most important single command a computer offers.

Formatting Text

When you're editing text, you only need to concern yourself with the words. But before you print your document, you'll need to consider the *format* of the document—how the words will look on the page. **Text formatting** commands allow you to control the format and style of the document. Character-based systems (such as most programs running on IBM-compatibles without Windows) generally don't provide the full range of formatting options available on WYSIWYG systems, and when they do they're more challenging to use. Still, most modern word processors allow users to control the formats of individual characters, lines, or paragraphs, as well as complete documents.

Formatting characters. The format of the characters that you print is determined largely by your printer. Most modern printers can print text in a variety of point sizes, typefaces, and styles that aren't possible with typewriters. **Point size** refers to the size of characters. Type size is traditionally measured in points, with one point equal to 1/72 inch. Most documents, including this book, use smaller point sizes for text to fit more information on each page and larger point sizes to make titles and headings stand out.

These characters represent four of the hundreds of typefaces that can be used with laser printers and other WYSIWYG output devices.

12-point Courier
12-point Courier italic
12-point Courier bold

24-point Courier

12-point Helvetica
12-point Helvetica italic
12-point Helvetica bold

24-point Helvetica

12-point Times
12-point Times italic
12-point Times bold

24-point Times

12-point Zapf Chancery

24-point Zapf Chancery

In the language of typesetters, a **font** is a size and style of **typeface**. For example, the typeface known as Helvetica includes many fonts, one of which is 12-point Helvetica bold. In the world of personal computing, the distinction isn't quite so clear; many people use the terms *font* and *typeface* interchangeably.

Whatever you call them, you have hundreds of choices of typefaces for most modern computers. **Serif fonts**, like those in the Times family, are embellished with serifs—fine lines at the ends of the main strokes of each character. **Sans serif fonts**, like those in the Helvetica family, have plainer, cleaner lines. Typewriters and fonts that mimic typewriters, like those in the Courier family, produce characters that always take up the same amount of space, no matter how skinny or fat the characters are. In contrast, **proportionally spaced fonts** allow more room for wide characters like w's than for narrow characters like i's.

Formatting lines and paragraphs. Many formatting commands naturally apply to more than a few characters or words: those that control margins, space between lines, indents, tab stops, and justification. **Justification** refers to the alignment of text on a line. Four justification choices are commonly available: *left justification* (with a smooth left margin and ragged right margin), *right justification*, *full justification* (both margins are smooth), and *centered justification*.

Word processors vary as to how they handle these formatting commands. Some, like Microsoft Word, apply them to paragraphs you have selected. Others, like Word-

Most word processors provide four different options for justifying text.

This text illustrates left justification. For left-justified text the left margin is smooth and the right margin is ragged.	This text illustrates centered justification. For centered text both margins are ragged Centered text is often used for titles.
This text illustrates right justification. For right-justified text the right margin is smooth and the left margin is ragged.	This text illustrates full justification. For fully justified text, spaces between words are adjusted to make both margins smooth.

Perfect, apply them to blocks of text marked by beginning and ending codes. Both approaches give you control over the final look of every line of text.

Formatting the document. Some formatting commands are applied to entire documents. For example, Word's Page Setup command allows you to control the margins that apply throughout the document. Other commands allow you to specify the content, size, and style of **headers** and **footers**—blocks that appear at the top and bottom of every page, displaying repetitive information like chapter titles, author names, and automatically calculated page numbers. The User's View box demonstrates some basic text formatting operations using Microsoft Word.

The User's View

Formatting Text

Software: Microsoft Word.
The goal: You've entered and edited the text. Now you want to work on the way it looks.

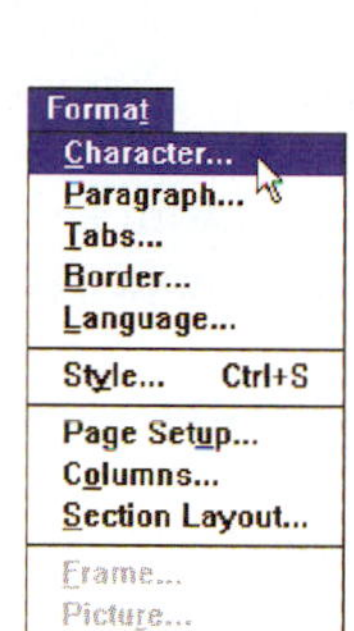

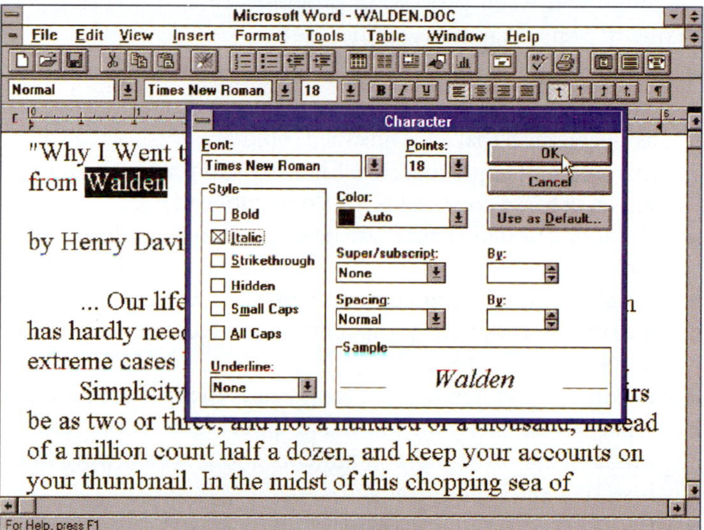

To change the font, style, or size of a group of characters or words, you (1) select the characters to be changed, (2) choose the Character command from the Format menu, and (3) indicate the desired changes in the Character dialog box. Here, you select "Walden" and change the style of that word from plain to italic type.

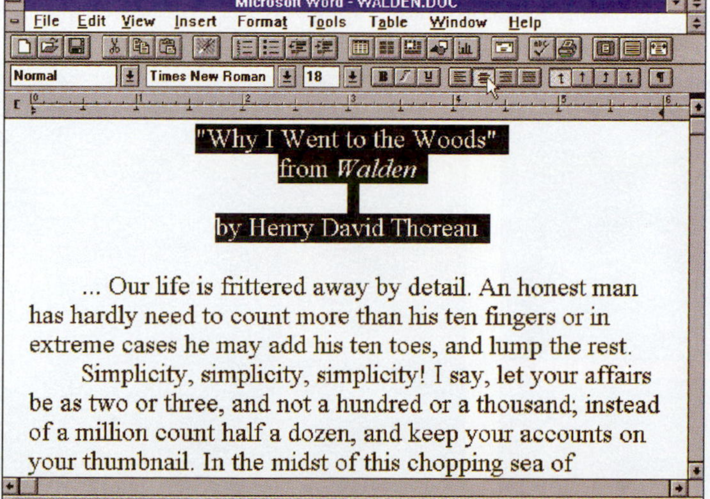

You center the title and author lines by selecting them and clicking on the centering button located above the ruler on Microsoft Word's *ribbon.* Buttons on the ribbon and the *toolbar* (located above the ribbon) provide instant access to frequently used commands.

You can see a miniature picture of your final output by selecting the Print Preview command from the File menu. If it looks right, you can select the Print command or click on the Print . . . button to produce a hard copy.

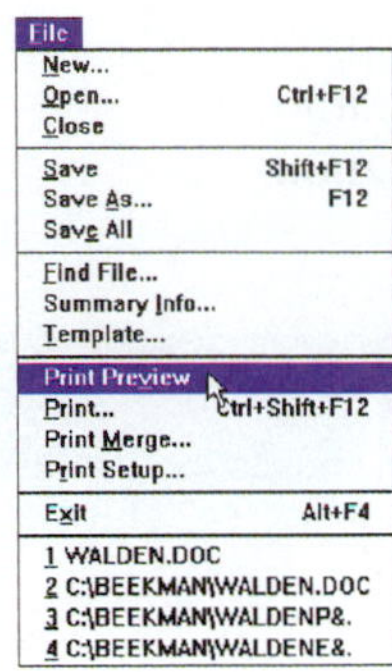

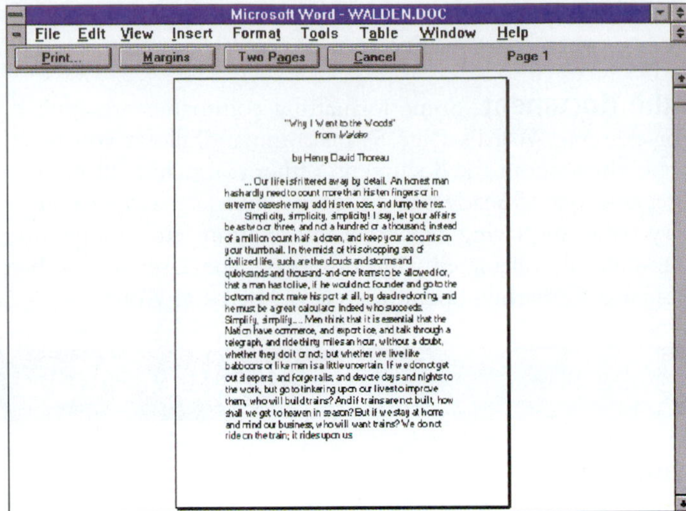

High-end word processing programs often provide a great deal of formatting flexibility. Some examples include

- the ability to define **style sheets** containing custom styles for each of the common elements in a document (for example, a writer can define a style called "subhead" as a paragraph that's left-justified, boldface, 12-point Helvetica font with standard margins, and apply that style for every subhead in the document without reselecting all of these commands for a new subhead)
- the ability to define alternate headers, footers, and margins so that left- and right-facing pages can have different margins, headers, and footers
- the ability to create documents with variable-width multiple columns
- **automatic footnoting** capability that saves the user from having to place footnotes and endnotes
- **automatic hyphenation** of long words that fall at the end of lines
- table-of-contents generation and indexing of books and other long works (with human help for making judgments about which words belong in the index and how they should be arranged)
- the ability to create and format multicolumn tables
- the ability to attach hidden text, pop-up notes, or auditory notes that can be seen or heard by the user without showing up in the final document
- the ability to incorporate graphics created with other applications

The most widely used word processor for non-GUI computers is the MS-DOS version of WordPerfect. The traditional WordPerfect interface embeds command codes in the text, but the latest versions of this program incorporate GUI-like pulldown menus.

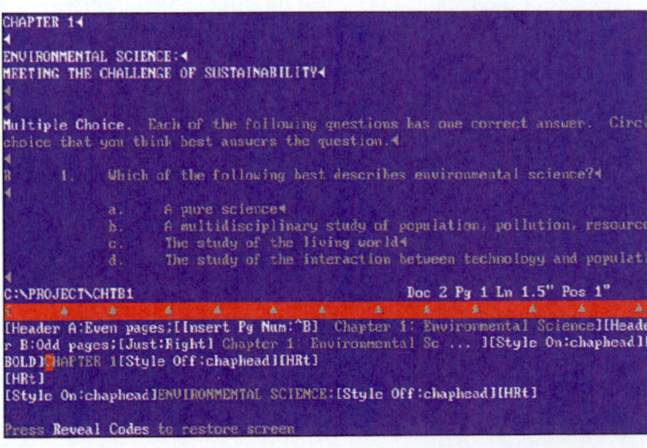

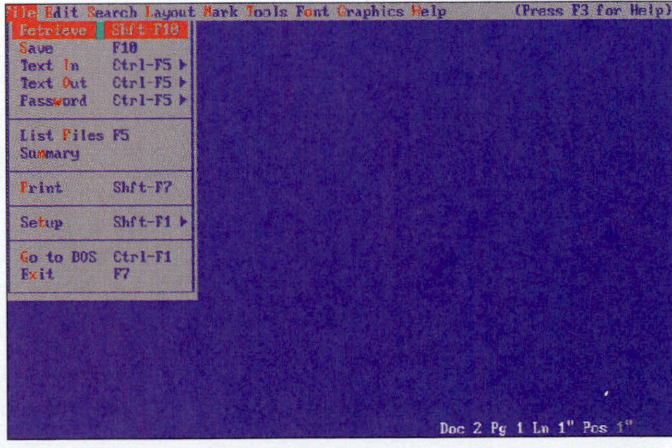

Rules of Thumb

Word Processing Is Not Typing

If you're already a touch typist, your typing skills will help you become proficient at word processing quickly. (If you're *not* a touch typist, see Project 1, Chapter 2.) Unfortunately, a few typing skills are counterproductive on a modern word processor. Here's a short list of new word processing habits to replace outmoded typing habits:

- **Use the Return/Enter key only when you must.** Let the computer's automatic word wrap handle routine end-of-line business.
- **Use tabs and margin guides, not the spacebar, to align columns.** WYSIWYG is a matter of degree, and text that looks perfectly aligned on screen may not line up on paper if you depend on your eyes and the spacebar.
- **Don't underline.** Use *italics* and **boldface** for emphasis. Italicize book and journal titles.
- **Use only one space after a period.** Type experts agree that proportionally spaced fonts look better if you avoid double spaces.
- **Take advantage of special characters.** Bullet (•), em dash (—), curly quotes (" "), and other nontypewriter characters make your work look more professional, and they don't cost a thing.

The Wordsmith's Toolbox

Word processing doesn't need to be limited to basic editing and formatting. A typical high-end word processor might include a built-in *outliner*, *spelling checker*, *thesaurus*, and *indexer*. But even word processors that don't include those features can be enhanced with stand-alone programs specifically designed to accomplish the same things. We'll examine a few of these tools next.

Idea Processors and Outliners

If any man wishes to write in a clear style, let him first be clear in his thoughts.

—Johann W. von Goethe

For many of us, the hardest part of the writing process is collecting and organizing our thoughts. Many traditional English-class techniques for preparing to write—outlines, 3x5 note cards, and the like—involve so much additional work that they often seem to add another layer to the problem. But when computer technology is applied to these time-honored techniques, they're transformed into high-powered tools for extending our minds and streamlining the process of turning vague thoughts into solid prose.

Idea processors take a variety of forms, but most are built around the concept of **outlining**. At first glance an outlining program looks like a word processor. The difference lies in the underlying structure: While word processors are designed to manipulate characters and words, outliners are organized around hierarchies or levels of ideas. Most outliners are particularly effective at performing three functions:

- arranging information into levels, so that each heading can be fleshed out with more detailed subheads, which can then be broken into smaller pieces
- rearranging ideas and levels so that subideas are automatically moved with their parent ideas

The word processor's Outline View allows you to examine and restructure the overall organization of the document while showing each topic in as much detail as you need. When you move headlines, the attached subheads and paragraphs follow automatically. (Software: Microsoft Word.)

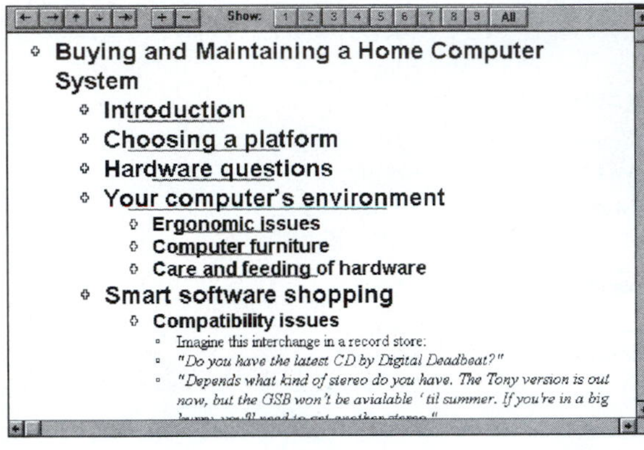

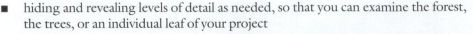

- hiding and revealing levels of detail as needed, so that you can examine the forest, the trees, or an individual leaf of your project

For a project that requires research, an outliner can be used as a replacement for a deck of 3x5 note cards. Ideas can be collected, composed, refined, rearranged, and reorganized much more efficiently when they're stored in an outliner. When the time comes to turn research into a research paper, the notes don't need to be retyped; they can be exported to your word processor and polished with standard text-editing techniques. If the outliner is built into the word processor, the process of organizing blends seamlessly into the writing process, and the line between notes and finished product blurs to the point where it almost disappears.

Outliners aren't just used for preparing to write. Many people use them for preparing speeches, to-do lists, schedules, and anything else that requires prioritizing and organization. On the other hand, many people find the hierarchical outline form confining and difficult to use. Fortunately idea processors come in other forms. Many visual thinkers find they work best with graphic idea processors that allow them to draw their ideas as nodes on a chart with arrows connecting related ideas. Idea charts may resemble tree charts with many branches, or may look more like free-form clusters. Some idea processors allow users to switch back and forth between text view and graphic view.

Synonym Finders

The classic synonym finder, or **thesaurus**, is an invaluable tool for finding just the right word, but it's not particularly user friendly. A computerized thesaurus is another matter altogether. With a good on-screen thesaurus, it's a simple matter to select a word and issue a command for a synonym search. The computerized thesaurus provides almost instant gratification, displaying all kinds of possible replacements for the word in question. If you find a good substitute in the list, you can indicate your preference with a click or a keystroke; the software even makes the substitution for you. It couldn't be much simpler.

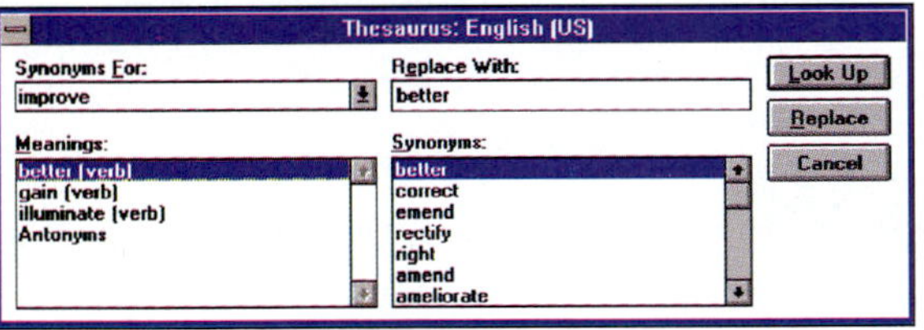

An on-line thesaurus puts synonyms at your fingertips. In this case the computer is providing synonyms for the word *improve*. (Software: Microsoft Word.)

Digital References

Writers rely on a number of other reference books, including dictionaries, quotation books, encyclopedias, atlases, and almanacs. Most of these traditionally printed resources are now available in computer-readable form, too. In each case the electronic medium offers clear advantages and disadvantages when compared with its hard copy counterparts.

The biggest advantage of the electronic form is speed; searching for subjects or words by computer is usually faster than thumbing through a book. Well-designed references make it easy to jump between related topics in search of elusive facts. In addition, copying quotes electronically takes a fraction of the time that it takes to retype information from a book. Of course, this kind of quick copying makes plagiarism easier than ever and may tempt more writers to violate copyright laws.

Some references lose something in the translation to electronic form. Because pictures, maps, and drawings take up so much disk space, they're often removed or modified in computerized references. Disk capacity problems largely disappear when reference books are stored on optical CD-ROM disks. In fact many CD-ROM references take advantage of the massive disk capacity by including sounds, animation, video, and other forms of information that aren't possible in books. Multimedia references are discussed in more detail in Chapter 8.

Spelling Checkers

It's a darn poor mind that can only think of one way to spell a word.

—*Andrew Jackson*

While many of us sympathize with Jackson's point of view, the fact remains that correct spelling is an important part of most written communication. That's why most word processors today include a built-in **spelling checker**. Spelling checkers come in different forms, but they all essentially do the same thing: compare the words in your document with words in a disk-based dictionary. Every word that's not in the dictionary is flagged as a suspect word—a potential misspelling. In many cases the spelling checker suggests the corrected spelling and offers to replace the suspect word. Ultimately, though, it's up to you to decide whether the flagged word is, in fact, spelled incorrectly.

Most spelling checkers offer several choices for each suspect word:

- Replace the word with the suggested alternative.
- Replace the word with another alternative typed by the user.
- Leave the word alone (used when the word is spelled correctly, but it's not in the dictionary because it's an obscure word, a specialized term, or a proper name).
- Leave the word alone and add it to the dictionary so that it won't be flagged next time (used when the word is spelled correctly, it's not in the dictionary, and it's a regular part of the user's written vocabulary).

Students can save time searching for facts in computerized reference books, like those included in Microsoft Bookshelf.

The most common spelling checkers are *batch spelling checkers*; they check all of the words in your document in a batch when you issue the appropriate command. Some people prefer *interactive spelling checkers* that check every word as it's typed, beeping or flashing each time a word is typed incorrectly.

While spelling checkers are wonderful aids, they can't replace careful proofreading by alert human eyes. When you're using a spelling checker, it's important to keep two potential problems in mind:

1. *Dictionary limitations and errors.* No dictionary includes every word, so you have to know what to do with unlisted words—proper names, obscure words, technical terms, foreign terms, colloquialisms, and other oddities. If you add words to your spelling checker's dictionary, you run the risk of adding an incorrectly spelled word, making future occurrences of that misspelling invisible to the spelling checker and to you.
2. *Errors of context.* The biggest limitation of today's spelling checkers is their lack of intelligence in dealing with a word's context. The fact that a word appears in a dictionary does not guarantee that it is correctly spelled in the context of the sentence. The following passage, for example, contains eight spelling errors, none of which would be detected by a typical spelling checker:

Most spelling checkers offer a user several choices for handling words that aren't in the dictionary. (Software: Microsoft Word.)

I wood never have guest that my spelling checker would super seed my editor as my mane source of feed back. I no longer prophet from the presents of an editor while I right.

Grammar and Style Checkers

The errors in the preceding quote would have slipped by a spelling checker, but many of them would have been detected by a **grammar and style checker**. In addition to checking spelling, grammar and style-checking software analyzes each word in context, checking for errors of context ("I wood never have guest"), common grammati-

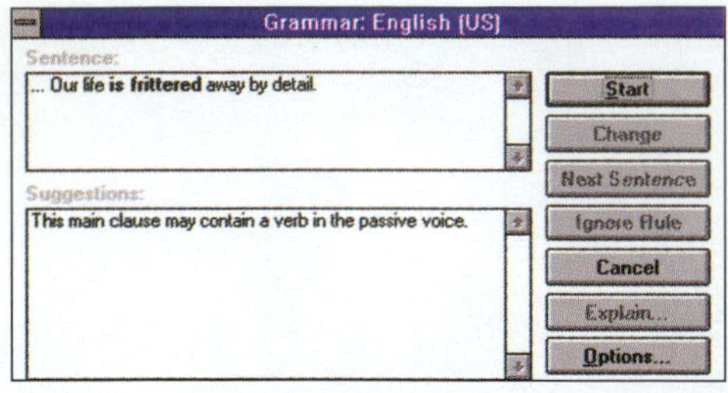

Grammar and style-checking software flags possible errors and makes suggestions about how they might be fixed. (Software: Microsoft Word.)

cal errors ("Ben and me went to Boston"), and stylistic foibles ("The book that is most popular"). In addition to pointing out possible errors and suggesting improvements, it can analyze prose complexity using measurements like sentence length and paragraph length. This kind of analysis is useful for determining whether your writing style is appropriate for your target audience.

Grammar and style-checking software is, at best, imperfect. A typical program misses many true errors while flagging correct passages. Still, it can be a valuable writing aid, especially for students who are mastering the complexities of a language for the first time. But software is no substitute for practice, revision, editing, and a good English teacher.

Form Letter Generators

Congratulations, Mr. <lastname>! You may already have won!

Most word processors today have **mail merge** capabilities for producing personalized form letters. When used with a database containing a list of names and addresses, a word processor can quickly generate individually addressed letters and mailing labels. Many programs can incorporate custom paragraphs based on the recipient's personal data, making each letter look as if it were individually written. The uses and abuses of this kind of technology are discussed in Chapter 6.

The Desktop Publishing Story

Freedom of the press belongs to the person who owns one.

—A. J. Liebling, *the late media critic for The New Yorker*

Just as word processing changed the writer's craft in the 1970s, the world of publishing was radically transformed in the 1980s with the introduction of desktop publishing. Publishing—traditionally an expensive, time-consuming, error-prone process—has rapidly become an enterprise that just about anyone with a computer and a little cash can undertake. Poor Richard could publish quite an almanac with today's technology.

Businesses rely on desktop publishing technology to produce in-house newsletters, brochures, advertising materials, training manuals, periodicals, and books.

What Is Desktop Publishing?

The process of producing a book, magazine, or other publication includes several steps:

1. Writing text.
2. Editing text.
3. Producing drawings, photographs, and other graphics to accompany the text.
4. Designing a basic format for the publication.
5. Typesetting text.
6. Arranging text and graphics on pages.
7. Typesetting and printing pages.
8. Binding pages into a finished publication.

In traditional publishing, many of these steps required expensive equipment, highly-trained specialists to operate the equipment, and *lots* of time.

With modern **desktop publishing (DTP)** technology, the bulk of the publishing process can be accomplished with tools that are small, affordable, and easy to use. A desktop publishing system generally includes a computer with a graphical user interface, desktop publishing software, and a laser printer or other high-resolution printer. It's now possible for a single person with a modest equipment investment to do all the writing, editing, graphic production, design, page layout, and typesetting for a desktop publication. Of course, few individuals have the skills to handle all these tasks, so most publications are still the work of teams that include writers, designers, artists, and supervisors. But even if the titles remain the same, each of these jobs is changing because of desktop publishing technology.

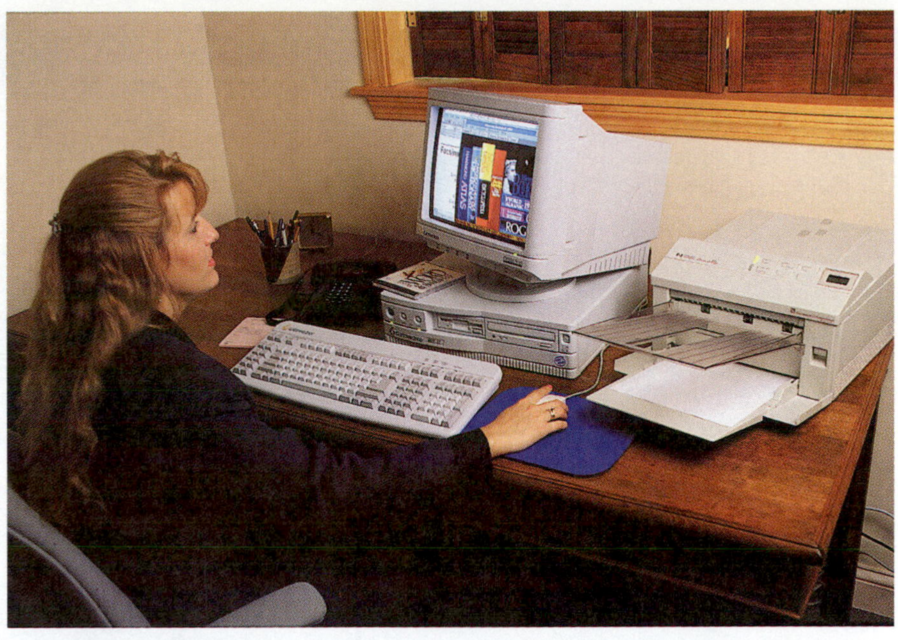

A typical desktop publishing system includes a personal computer, a laser printer, and software.

The first steps in the publishing process involve producing **source documents**—articles, chapters, drawings, maps, charts, and photographs that are to appear in the publication. Desktop publishers generally use standard word processors and graphics programs to produce most source documents. Scanners are used to transform photos and hand-drawn images into computer-readable documents. **Page-layout software** is used to combine the various source documents into a coherent, visually appealing publication. Pages are generally laid out one page at a time on screen, although most programs have options for automating many of the steps in producing long documents. The User's View box shows how a simple publication is created with page-layout software.

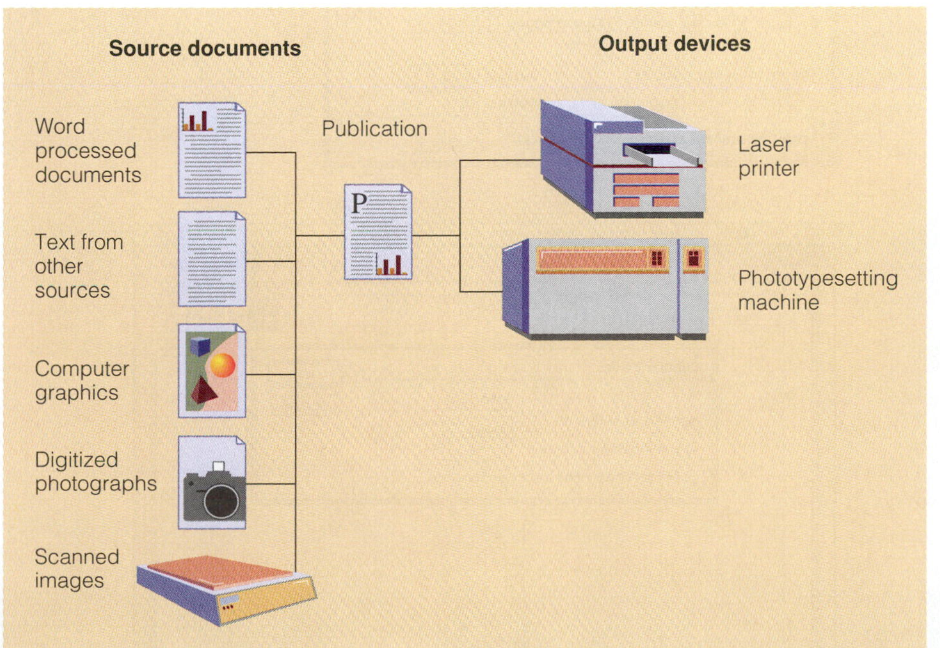

Source documents are merged in a publication document, which can be printed on a variety of output devices.

The User's View

Desktop Publishing

Software: Ofoto scanning software, Aldus PageMaker page-layout software.
The goal: To create a publication that includes a collection of class projects and presentations and a variety of graphic illustrations.

The first step is to create and collect source documents. The articles are all word processor files, so they're ready to go. The pictures are a mixture of computer graphics files and hand-drawn images. You start by using a scanner with Ofoto scanning software to convert these drawings into graphics files.

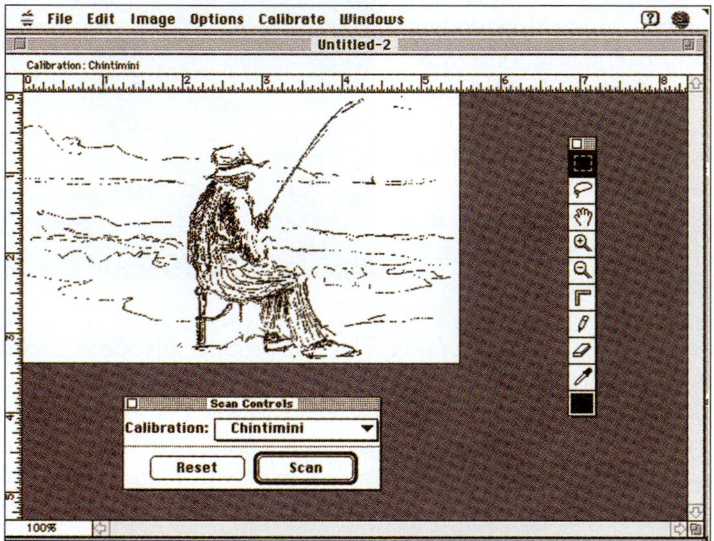

After the source documents are ready, you open PageMaker to design and lay out the pages. You start the page-layout process by creating a new document and specifying the number and size of its pages.

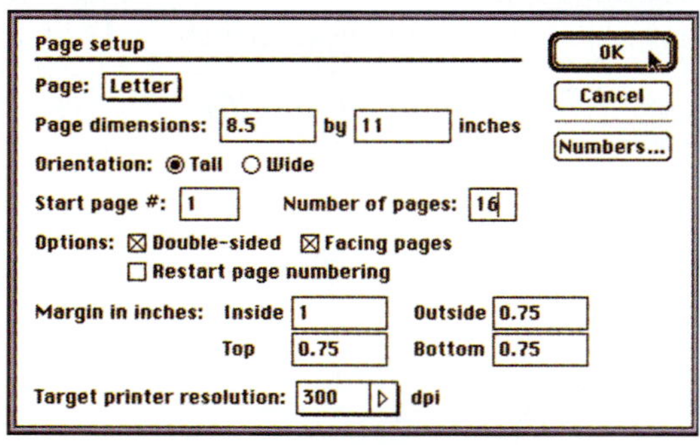

Next you design **master pages** that control the general layout and include common elements (margins, column guides, page numbers, graphic embellishments) for all left- and right-facing pages.

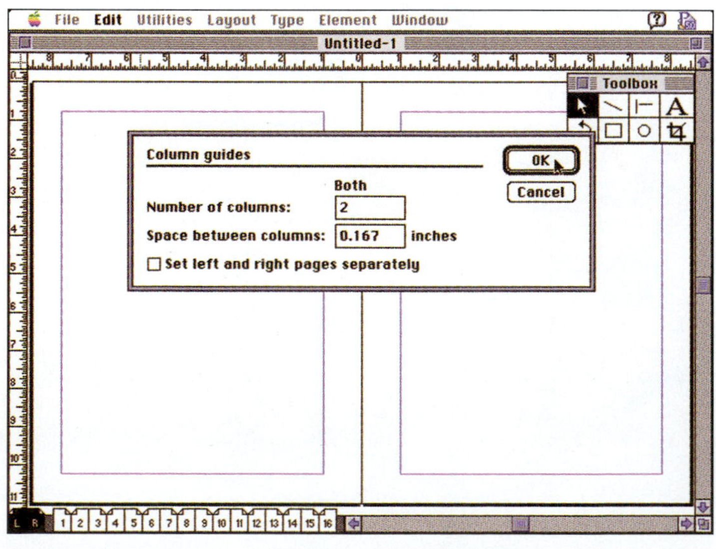

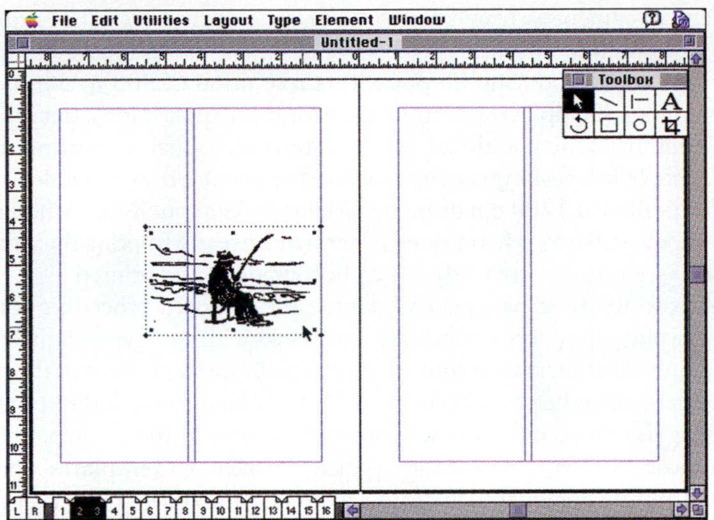

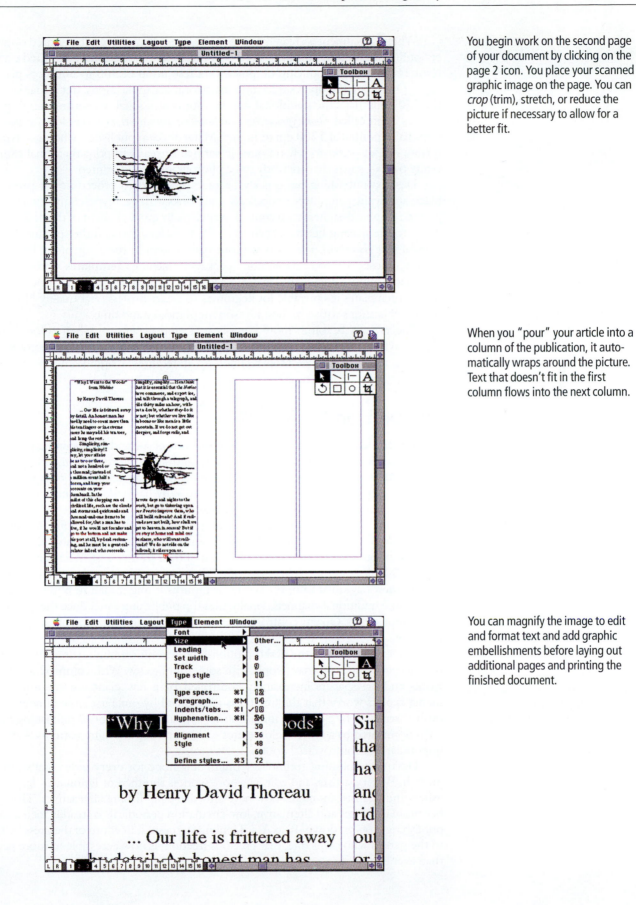

You begin work on the second page of your document by clicking on the page 2 icon. You place your scanned graphic image on the page. You can *crop* (trim), stretch, or reduce the picture if necessary to allow for a better fit.

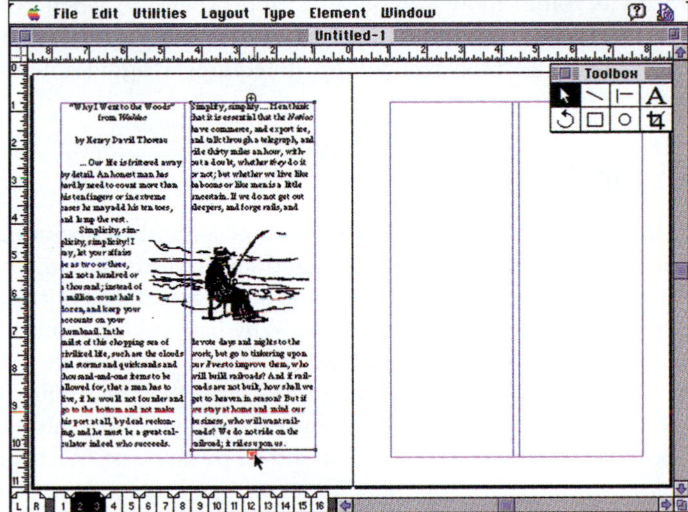

When you "pour" your article into a column of the publication, it automatically wraps around the picture. Text that doesn't fit in the first column flows into the next column.

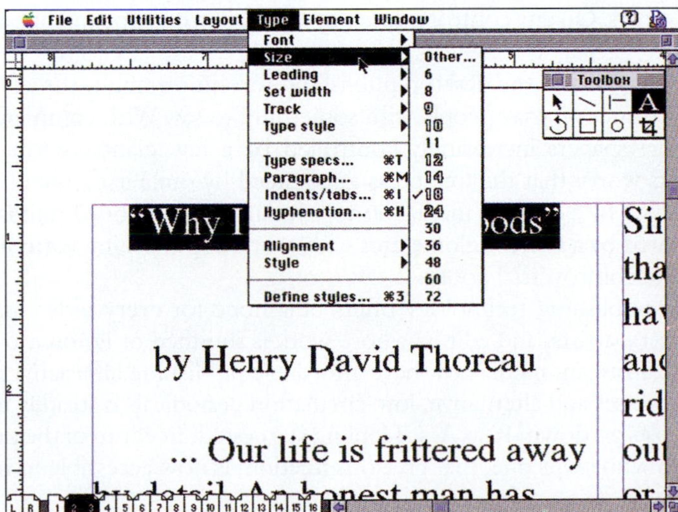

You can magnify the image to edit and format text and add graphic embellishments before laying out additional pages and printing the finished document.

When a document is created with page-layout software, it can be printed on a variety of high-resolution output devices. Most desktop publications are printed on laser printers capable of producing output with a resolution of 300 to 600 dots per inch (dpi). Output of 300 dpi is sufficiently sharp for most applications, but it's far less than the 1200 dpi that's the traditional standard for professional typesetting. High-priced devices often called *phototypesetting machines* or *imagesetters* allow desktop publications to be printed at 1200 dpi or higher. Many desktop publishers who need typeset-quality output prefer to rely on outside **service bureaus** to print their final **camera-ready** pages—pages that are ready to be photographed and printed.

Desktop publishing has quickly become the standard procedure for producing black-and-white pamphlets, periodicals, and books with near typeset quality. The tools provide graphic designers with control over virtually every element of the design, right down to the spacing between each pair of letters (*kerning*) and the spacing between lines of text (*leading*). For users without background in the elements of layout and design, most desktop publishing packages include **templates**—professionally designed "empty" documents that can easily be adapted to specific user needs. Even without templates it's possible for beginners to create professional-quality black-and-white publications with a modest investment of money and time.

The process becomes more complicated, and expensive, when color is introduced. While it's possible to produce a publication with high-resolution color photographs using today's desktop technology, it requires a significant investment in hardware, software, and time.

Why Desktop Publishing?

In less than a decade, desktop publishing has become a standard operating procedure for thousands of professional publishers, large and small. More than any other application, desktop publishing was responsible for the initial acceptance of computers with graphical user interfaces by large corporations. Why has desktop publishing enjoyed such wide acceptance by businesses? The reasons are clear.

First and foremost, desktop publishing saves money. Publications that used to cost hundreds or thousands of dollars to produce through outside publishing services can now be produced in-house for a fraction of their former cost. What's more, desktop publishing saves time. The turnaround time for a publication done on the desktop can be a few days instead of the weeks or months it might take to publish the same thing using traditional channels. Finally, desktop publishing can reduce the quantity of publication errors. Quality control is easier to maintain when documents are produced in-house.

The real winners in the desktop publishing revolution might turn out to be not big businesses but everyday people with something to say. With commercial TV networks and newspapers increasingly controlled by a few giant corporations, many media experts worry that the free press guaranteed by our First Amendment is seriously threatened by a de facto media monopoly. Similarly, the book publishing industry is dominated by a few conglomerates with cautious publishing patterns that avoid unpopular and controversial books.

Desktop publishing technology offers new hope for every individual's right to publish. Writers, artists, and editors whose work is shunned or ignored by large publishers and mainstream media now have affordable publishing alternatives. The number of small presses and alternative, low-circulation periodicals is steadily increasing as publishing costs go down. If, as A. J. Liebling suggested, freedom of the press belongs to the person who owns one, that precious freedom is now accessible to more people than ever before.

Rules of Thumb

Beyond DESKTOP *TACKY!*

Many first-time users of WYSIWYG word processors and desktop publishing systems become intoxicated with the power at their fingertips. It's easy to get carried away with all those fonts, styles, and sizes, and create a document that makes supermarket tabloids look tasteful. While there's no substitute for a good education in the principles of design, it's easy to avoid tacky looking documents if you follow a few simple guidelines:

- **Plan before you publish.** Design (or select) a simple, visually pleasing format for your document and use that format throughout the document.
- **Use appropriate fonts.** Limit your choices to one or two fonts and sizes per page, and be consistent throughout your document. Serif fonts like this one generally are good choices for paragraphs of text; the serifs gently guide the reader's eye from word to word. Sans serif fonts, like the headings in this book, work well for headings and titles. Make sure all your chosen fonts work properly with your printer.
- **Don't go style-crazy.** Avoid overusing italics, boldface, underlines, and other styles for emphasis. *When in doubt, leave it out.*
- **Look at your document through your readers' eyes.** Make every picture say something. Don't try to cram too much information on a page. Don't be afraid of white space. Use a format that speaks clearly to your readers. Make sure the main points of your document stand out. Whatever you do, do it for the reader.
- **Learn from the masters.** Study the design of successful publications. What makes them work? Use design books, articles, and classes to develop your aesthetic skills along with your technical skills. With or without a computer, publishing is an art.
- **Know the limitations of the technology.** Desktop publishing technology makes it possible for everyday people to produce high-quality documents with a minimal investment of time and money. But today's technology has limitations; for many applications, desktop publishing is no match for a professional design artist or typesetter. If you need the best, work with a pro.
- **Remember the message.** Fancy fonts, tasteful graphics, and meticulous design can't turn shoddy ideas into words of wisdom or lies into the truth. The purpose of publishing is communication; don't try to use technology to disguise the lack of something to communicate.

Tomorrow's Word Tools

What's over the horizon for wordsmiths? Based on current trends and research, several possibilities exist.

The End of Desktop Publishing Software?

Ironically many experts predict that the thriving desktop publishing industry may decline, or even disappear, in the coming decade. While these predictions may be a bit farfetched, they're based on some important trends in the industry today.

As word processors grow in sophistication, they absorb more and more of the features formerly available only in page-layout software. Many word processors available today are capable of producing professional-quality books and periodicals, complete with graphics. It seems likely that the line between word processors and page-layout programs will blur in coming years.

Of course, desktop publishing software is growing in sophistication, too, incorporating features essential to discriminating professionals. The publishing industry now uses desktop computers for a variety of tasks beyond basic page layout, including specialized technical processes like photoimage processing and color separation used to produce full-color documents.

Groupware for Writing and Editing

As we've seen, the publishing process involves a variety of tasks, from writing and editing to drawing and design. A typical publication project involves several writers working in conjunction with editors, artists, and other specialized professionals. Modern computer networks make it possible for all these people to work together on the same set of computer documents using **groupware**—software designed to be used by work groups rather than individuals. Software companies are developing software specifically designed to facilitate communication between writers, editors, and other publication professionals.

Using groupware, several writers might work simultaneously on the same master document. Each writer can monitor and make suggestions concerning the writing of any other writer on the team. Editors can "blue pencil" corrections and attach notes directly to the electronic manuscript. Editing notes might resemble on-screen stickynotes or they might be audio notes spoken by the editor. Either way, the notes attach to the document so they can be read or heard by any or all the writers—even those who are on the other side of the continent. At the same time graphic artists and designers can work in tandem on the visual aspects of the publication. When the text and drawings are completed, they can easily be merged into a completed document using page-layout software.

Electronic Dictation

Changes in output devices—graphic screens and high-resolution printers—have had a tremendous impact on writing and publishing software in the last decade. As a result, the major bottlenecks in most modern desktop publishing systems are on the input side. Many experts predict that the next big advances will occur as a result of emerging input devices.

For millions of computer users, the mouse has taken over many of the functions of the keyboard. For a small but rapidly growing population, pen-based systems provide an alternative tool for entering text. Ultimately, though, most writers long for a computer that can accept and reliably process speech input—a *talkwriter*.

Speech-recognition software systems are emerging from laboratories and showing up in products, but today's systems are severely limited. It takes a great deal of intelligence to understand the intricacies of our language, and no machine available today is smart enough or powerful enough to rise to the challenge. Still, research in this area is progressing rapidly, and hardware and software breakthroughs happen every year. Word processors that can reliably recognize human speech are almost certainly in your future. See Chapter 10 for more details.

Intelligent Word Processors

Speech recognition is just one aspect of artificial intelligence research that's likely to end up in future word processors. Many experts foresee word processors able to anticipate the writer's needs, acting as an electronic editor or coauthor. Today's grammar and style checkers are primitive forerunners of the kinds of electronic writing consultants that might appear in a few years. Here are some possibilities:

- As you're typing a story, your word processor reminds you (via a pop-up message on the screen or an auditory message) that you've used the word "delicious" three times in the last two paragraphs and suggests that you choose an alternative from the list shown on the screen.
- Your word processor continuously analyzes your style as you type, determines your writing habits and patterns, and learns from its analysis. If your writing tends to be technical and formal, the software modifies its thesaurus, dictionary, and other tools so they're more appropriate for that style.
- You're writing a manual for a large organization whose documentation has specific style guidelines. Your word processor modifies your writing as you type so that it conforms to the organizational style.
- You need some current figures to support your argument on the depletion of the ozone layer. You issue a command, and the computer does a quick search of the literature in a library database and reports back to you a few seconds later with several relevant facts.

All of these examples are technically possible now; some are incorporated into systems being developed in research laboratories. The trend toward intelligent word processors is clear. Nevertheless you're in for a long wait if you're anxious to buy a system with commands such as Clever Quote, Humorous Anecdote, and Term Paper.

Summary

Even though the computer was originally designed to work with numbers, it quickly became an important tool for processing text. Today the word processor has all but replaced the typewriter as the tool of choice for committing words to paper.

Word processing is far more than typing text into a computer. Word processing software allows the writer to use commands to edit text on the screen, eliminating the chore of retyping pages until the message is right. Other commands allow the writer to control the format of the document: typefaces, spacing, justification, margins, columns, headers, footers, and other visual components. WYSIWYG word processors make it possible to see the formatted pages on the screen before printing them on paper. Most professional word processing programs automate footnoting, hyphenation, and other processes that are particularly troublesome to traditional typists.

Many advanced word processing functions are available as part of high-end word processing programs or as stand-alone special-purpose applications. Idea processing software turns the familiar outline into a powerful, dynamic organizational tool. Spelling checkers and grammar and style checkers partially automate the proofreading process, although they leave the more difficult parts of the job to literate humans. Online thesauruses, dictionaries, and other computer-based references automate reference work. Production of specialized documents like personalized form letters and full-length illustrated books can be simplified with other word processing tools.

As word processors become more powerful, they take on many of the features previously found only in desktop publishing software. Still, many publishers use word processors and graphics programs to create source documents that can be used as input for page-layout programs. The combination of the graphic user interface, desktop publishing software, and the high-resolution printer has revolutionized the publishing process by allowing publishers and would-be publishers to produce professional-quality text-and-graphics documents at a reasonable cost. Amateur and professional publishers everywhere use desktop publishing technology to produce everything from comic books to reference books. The near-overnight success of desk-

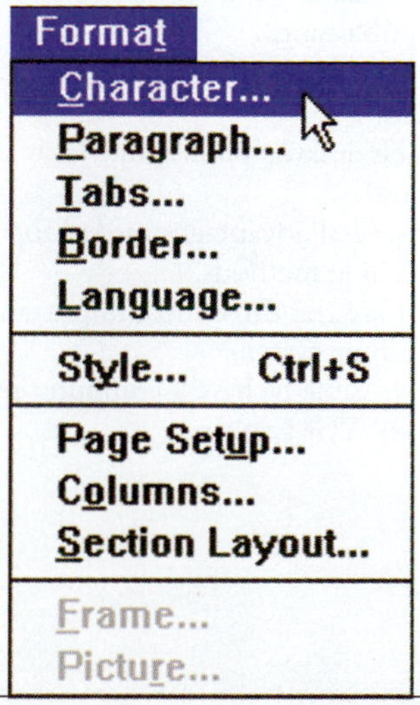

Format
Character...
Paragraph...
Tabs...
Border...
Language...
Style... Ctrl+S
Page Setup...
Columns...
Section Layout...
Frame...
Picture...

top publishing may foreshadow other changes in the way we communicate with words as new technologies like groupware, voice recognition, and intelligent word processors emerge.

CHAPTER REVIEW

Key Terms

automatic footnoting
automatic hyphenation
camera-ready
Clipboard
copying text
cursor
cut-and-paste
deleting text
desktop publishing (DTP)
drag-and-drop
Find command
font
footer
grammar and style checker
groupware
header
idea processor
inserting text
insertion bar
justification
mail merge
master pages
moving text
navigating
outlining
page-layout software
paragraph
point size
proportionally spaced font
sans serif font
saving a document
scrolling
search and replace
selecting text
serif font
service bureau
source document
spelling checker (batch or interactive)
style sheet
template
text editing
text formatting
thesaurus
typeface
Undo command
word wrap
WYSIWYG

Review Questions

1. How is word processing different from typing?
2. What happens to your document when you turn the computer off? What should you do if you want to work on the document later?
3. Explain the difference between text editing and text formatting. Give several examples of each.
4. What is scrolling and how is it useful?
5. When do you use the Enter or Return key in word processing?
6. What are the different ways that a paragraph or line of text can be justified? When might each be appropriate?
7. What is an idea processor? How does it differ from a word processor?
8. What is a font, and how is it used in word processing and desktop publishing?
9. Describe three different ways a spelling checker might be fooled.
10. What is desktop publishing? How does it differ from word processing?
11. List several advantages of desktop publishing over traditional publishing methods.
12. What are the three most important components of a desktop publishing system?
13. Is it possible to have a computer publishing system that is not WYSIWYG? Explain.

Discussion Questions

1. Which of the word processing features and software categories described in this chapter would be the most useful to you as a student? How do you think you would use them?
2. What do you think of the arguments that word processing reduces the quality of writing (1) because it makes it easy to write hurriedly and carelessly, and (2) it puts the emphasis on the way a document looks rather than what it says?
3. Many experts fear that desktop publishing technology will result in a glut of unprofessional, tacky looking publications. Others fear it will result in a glut of slick looking documents full of shoddy ideas and dangerous lies. Which of these do you think is a greater problem? Explain your answer.
4. Like Gutenberg's development of the movable type printing press more than 500 years ago, the development of desktop publishing puts powerful communication tools in the hands of more people. What impact will desktop publishing technology have on the free press and the free exchange of ideas guaranteed in the United States Constitution? What impact will the same technology have on free expression in other countries?

Projects

1. Try working with a WYSIWYG word processor and a non-WYSIWYG word processor. Compare the two experiences.
2. Research one or more of your favorite local or national publications to find out how computers are used in their production.

3. Use a high-end word processing system or a desktop publishing system to produce a newsletter, brochure, or flyer in support of an organization or cause that is important to you.

Sources and Resources 

Most word processing and desktop publishing books are hardware- and software-specific—they're designed to be used with a specific version of a specific program on a specific machine running a specific operating system. If you need a book to get you started, choose one that fits your system. Make sure the book is an introductory tutorial, not a substitute for the software reference manual or a collection of "power user" tips. If possible, browse before you buy.

Publish! and *Business Publishing*. These two periodicals provide cover-to-cover desktop publishing coverage. (All of the brand-specific monthlies mentioned at the end of Chapter 1 also regularly discuss word processing and desktop publishing.)

Everyone's Guide to Successful Publications: How to Produce Powerful Brochures, Newsletters, Flyers, and Business Communications, Start to Finish, by Elizabeth W. Adler (Berkeley, CA: Peachpit Press, 1993). This thorough and extremely readable book may be the best single source of information for anyone interested in creating brochures, newsletters, catalogs, manuals, posters, reports, and other publications. Unlike most desktop publishing books, this one guides you through the entire process, from planning, writing, and design through printing and distribution. True to its title, this book is an invaluable resource for beginners and experienced publishers alike.

Desktop Publishing Secrets, by Robert Eckhardt, Bob Weibel, and Ted Nace (Berkeley, CA: Peachpit Press, 1992). A compilation of shortcuts, tricks, and tips from *Publish!* magazine, covering all the major publishing programs on Macintosh and IBM-compatible computers.

Designing for Communication: The Key to Successful Desktop Publishing, by Ted D. E. McCain (Eugene, OR: ISTE Publications, 1992); *Looking Good in Print: A Guide to Basic Design for Desktop Publishing,* by Roger C. Parker (Chapel Hill, NC: Ventana Press, 1990); and *Collier's Rules for Desktop Design and Typography,* by David Collier (Reading, MA: Addison-Wesley, 1991). These three books tell the nontechnical side of desktop publishing. Now that you know the mechanics, how can you make your work look good? McCain's spiral-bound book clearly and thoughtfully explains and illustrates general design principles for beginners. Parker clearly describes the basic design tools and techniques and then applies them in sample documents ranging from brochures to books. Collier's book is more concise, colorful, and contemporary than the other two; most topics are covered in bold, two-page spreads that go beyond the basics.

The Elements of Style, by William Strunk, Jr., and E. B. White. If you want to improve your writing, this book is required reading. (There's not a word about computers in it, but a software reference version is available from Microlytics.)

C H A P T E R

FIVE

Calculation, Visualization, and Simulation

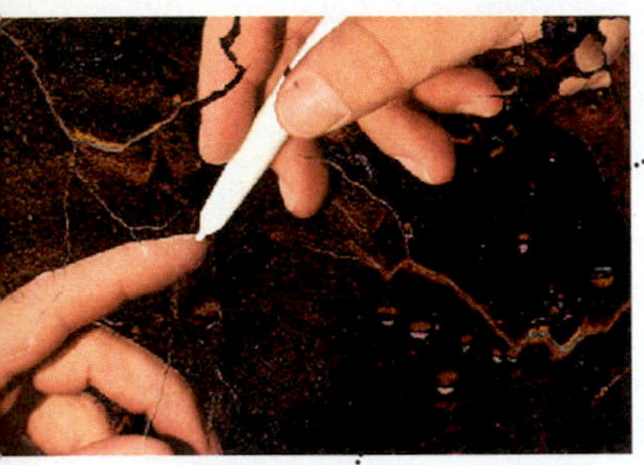

Dan Bricklin and Mitch Kapor Count on Computers

In terms of the success of VisiCalc, I don't feel I have to repeat it. But it is nice to be able to realize you've done something very worthwhile.

—— Dan Bricklin

After reading this chapter you should be able to

- describe the basic functions and applications of spreadsheet programs on personal computers
- show how spreadsheet graphics can be used and misused as communication tools
- describe other software tools for processing numbers and symbols on personal computers, workstations, and mainframes
- explain how computers are used as tools for simulating mechanical, biological, and social systems
- discuss the advantages and disadvantages of computer simulation as a tool for research and education

In 1978, Harvard graduate student Dan Bricklin watched his professor continually erase and recalculate rows and columns of numbers during classroom exercises in corporate financial planning. He envisioned a computer program that would do the calculations and recalculations automatically on the screen of his Apple II. With the help of his friend Bob Frankston, an MIT student, he developed VisiCalc, the first computer spreadsheet program. Almost overnight this revolutionary software changed the world of personal computing. Before VisiCalc, personal computers were used mostly to mimic the functions of mainframes. But VisiCalc was a unique tool—one that provided managers with capabilities they never had before. Many analysts believe VisiCalc was responsible for the early success of the Apple II, and the desktop computer in general, in the business world.

Dan Bricklin

After IBM introduced the IBM PC in 1981, many VisiCalc-inspired spreadsheet programs were competing for the software dollars of businesses. One of those programs was developed by Mitch Kapor, an idealistic young entrepreneur who had worked for a VisiCalc distributor and tested a release of VisiCalc. In 1983 Kapor's startup company, Lotus, released a powerful, easy-to-use integrated spreadsheet/graphics package called 1-2-3 that quickly established itself as *the* standard spreadsheet on IBM-compatible computers. By backing a solid software product with an expensive marketing campaign and a support program that made it easier for nontechnical corporate users to get training and help, Lotus established new standards for software success.

Mitch Kapor

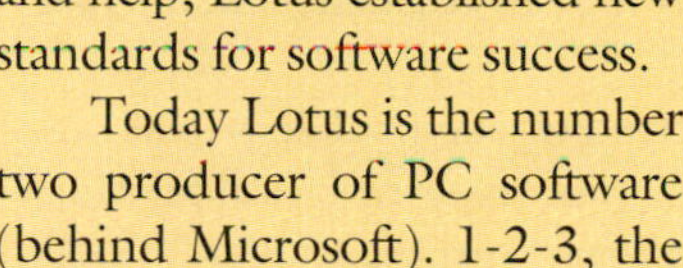

Today Lotus is the number two producer of PC software (behind Microsoft). 1-2-3, the most successful software application of all time, still controls the giant MS-DOS-based spreadsheet market, but Microsoft's Excel software currently dominates the growing Windows and Macintosh environments. The original VisiCalc program was purchased by Lotus and discontinued. After an unsuccessful trade-secret-theft lawsuit against Lotus, VisiCalc's parent company faded into obscurity.

What happened to Bricklin and Kapor? Both left their original companies to develop other software ventures. Bricklin, with Bob Franskton, is developing applications for pen-based personal computers, while Kapor's company focuses on communication tools and utilities for the Macintosh. Kapor is also the cofounder of and spokesperson for the Electronic Frontier Foundation, an organization dedicated to protecting the free and open flow of information and the rights of computer network users.

Computers were originally created to calculate, and today's machines are still widely used for numeric computations. Numbers are at the heart of applications ranging from accounting to statistical analysis. The most popular number-crunching application is the spreadsheet conceived by Bricklin and institutionalized by Lotus. The spreadsheet is used by executives, engineers, and scientists all for the same reason: It allows them to create and work with simulations of real-world situations.

A well-designed simulation, whether constructed with a spreadsheet or another software application, can help people achieve a better understanding of the world outside the computer. Computer simulations have their limitations and risks, too. In this chapter we'll explore the world of number manipulation and computer simulation, starting with the spreadsheet.

The Spreadsheet: Software for Simulation and Speculation

Compare the expansion of business today to the conquering of the continent in the 19th century. The spreadsheet in that comparison is like the transcontinental railroad. It accelerated the movement, made it possible, and changed the course of the nation.

—*Mitch Kapor*

More than any other type of personal computer software, the spreadsheet has changed the way people do business. In the same way a word processor can give a computer user control over words, **spreadsheet software** allows the user to take control of numbers, manipulating them in ways that would be difficult or impossible otherwise. A spreadsheet program can make short work of tasks that involve repetitive calculations: budgeting, investment management, business projections, grade books, scientific simulations, checkbooks, and so on. A spreadsheet can also reveal hidden relationships between numbers, taking much of the guesswork out of financial planning and speculation.

The Malleable Matrix

Almost all spreadsheet programs are based on a simple concept: the malleable matrix. A spreadsheet document, called a **worksheet**, typically appears on the screen as a grid of numbered **rows** and alphabetically lettered **columns**. The box representing the intersection of a row and a column is called a **cell**. Every cell in this grid has a unique **address** made up of a row number and column letter. For example, the cell in the upper-left corner of the grid is called cell A1 (column A, row 1). All the cells are empty in a new worksheet; it's up to the user to fill them. Each cell can contain a numeric value, an alphabetic label, or a formula representing a relationship between numbers in other cells.

Values (numbers) are the raw material used by the spreadsheet software to perform calculations. Numbers in worksheet cells can represent wages, test scores, weather data, polling results, or just about anything that can be quantified.

To make it easier for people to understand the numbers, most worksheets include **labels** at the tops of columns and at the edge of rows, such as "Monthly Wages," "Midterm Exam 1," "Average Wind Speed," and "Final Approval Rating." To the computer these labels are meaningless strings of characters. The label "Total Points" doesn't tell the computer to calculate the total and display it in an adjacent cell; it's just a road sign for human readers.

To calculate the total points (or the average wind speed or the final approval rating) the worksheet must include a **formula**—a step-by-step procedure for calculating the desired number. For example, cell B5 might contain the formula =(B2+B3)/2. This formula tells the computer to add the numbers in cells B2 and B3, divide the result by 2, and display the final result in the cell containing the formula, cell B5. You don't see the formula in cell B5; you just see its effect. It doesn't matter whether the numbers represent test scores, dollars, or nothing at all; the computer obediently calculates their average and displays the results. If either number in cells B2 or B3 changes, the number displayed in this cell automatically changes, too.

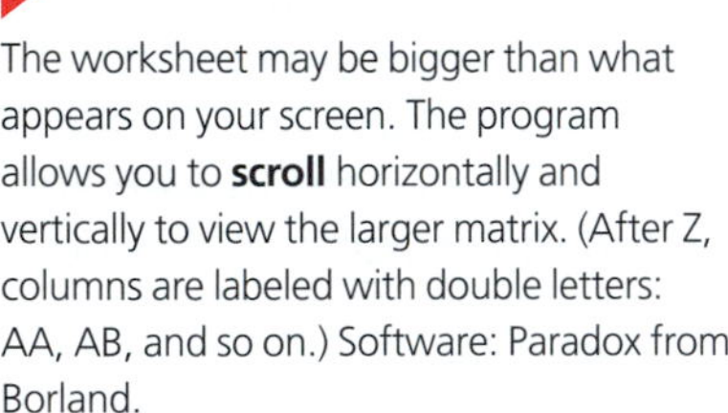

The worksheet may be bigger than what appears on your screen. The program allows you to **scroll** horizontally and vertically to view the larger matrix. (After Z, columns are labeled with double letters: AA, AB, and so on.) Software: Paradox from Borland.

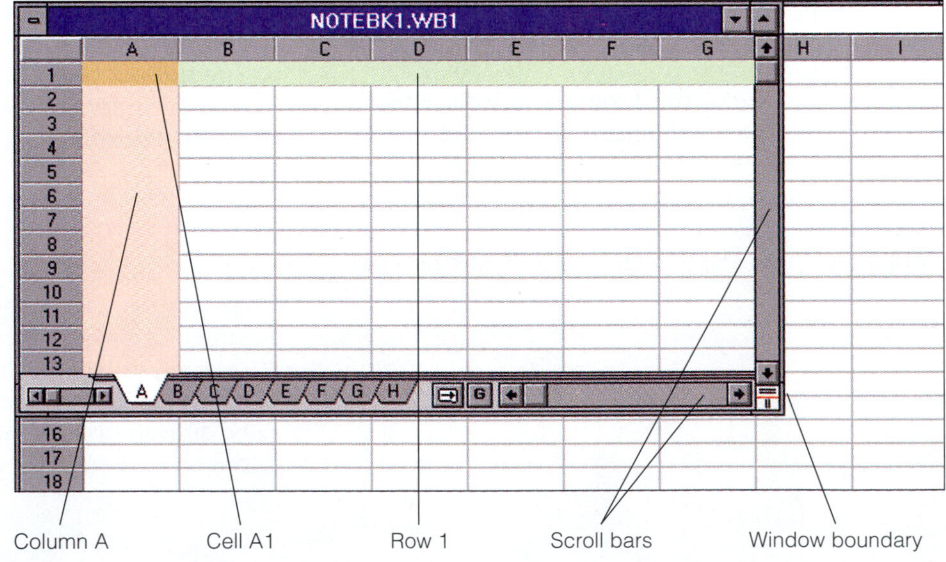

The User's View

Creating a Simple Worksheet

Software: Microsoft Excel.
The goal: to create a computerized version of a worksheet showing projected expenses for one college student's fall term. The design of the worksheet is based on this hand-drawn planning version.

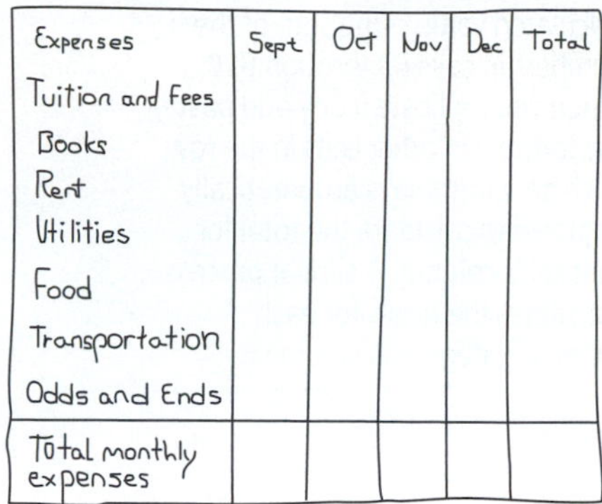

The first step is to type descriptive labels for rows and columns. Typing appears in the **current** or **active cell**—the cell containing the cursor—and in the long window above the worksheet, called the **console** or **formula bar**. You move from cell to cell by clicking with the mouse or by navigating with the keyboard. To make room for row labels, you widen the first column by dragging its border to the right.

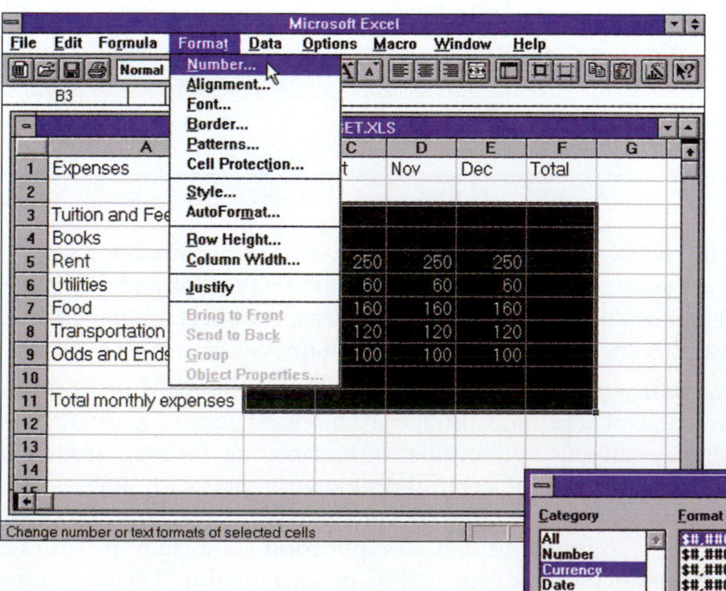

After the labels are typed, you type numeric values in to represent dollar values for each category in each month. To change cell formats so numbers are diplayed with dollar signs, you (1) select the **range** (rectangular block) of cells by dragging between cells B3 and F13, two opposite corners of the rectangle, (2) choose the Number . . . command from the Format menu, and select a format that includes dollar signs and decimal points; this changes the appearance of all values in the range.

You enter a formula to calculate the total expenses for September in cell B11. When you press Enter, the formula is replaced in the cell by the calculated value—the sum of the numbers in cells B3 through B10. When you replicate (copy and paste) the formula in other cells in the row, each new formula is automatically adjusted to calculate the total for that cell's column. A similar process calculates the totals for each expense category in column F.

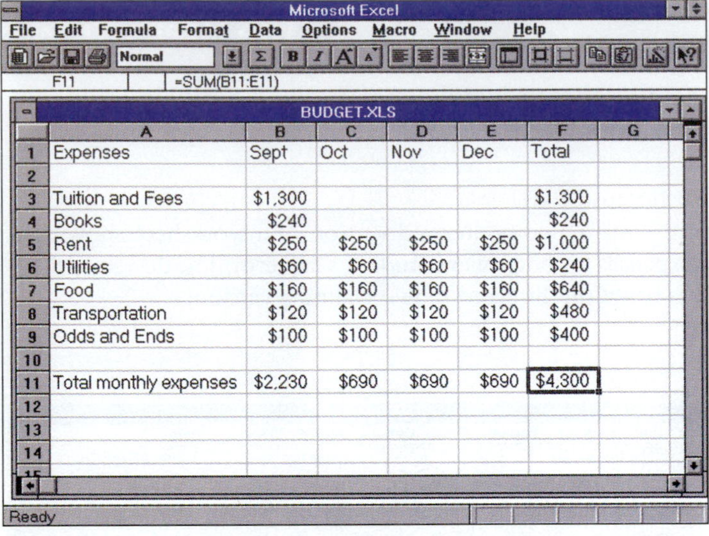

	A	B	C	D	E	F	G
1	Expenses	Sept	Oct	Nov	Dec	Total	
2							
3	Tuition and Fees	$1,300				$1,300	
4	Books	$240				$240	
5	Rent	$250	$250	$250	$250	$1,000	
6	Utilities	$60	$60	$60	$60	$240	
7	Food	$160	$160	$160	$160	$640	
8	Transportation	$120	$120	$120	$120	$480	
9	Odds and Ends	$100	$100	$100	$100	$400	
10							
11	Total monthly expenses	$2,230	$690	$690	$690	$4,300	
12							
13							
14							

After you change the format of some cells to make the worksheet more readable, you decide to change numbers in two of December's cells to allow for holiday gifts and travel. The spreadsheet software automatically recalculates all formulas to reflect the revised input data.

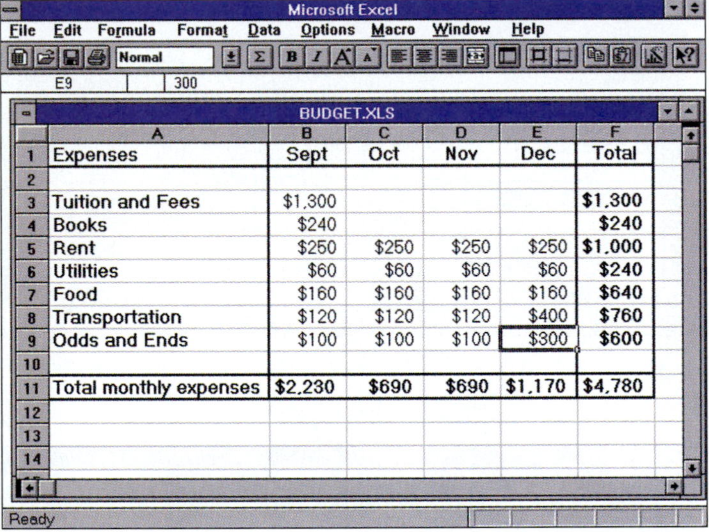

	A	B	C	D	E	F
1	**Expenses**	**Sept**	**Oct**	**Nov**	**Dec**	**Total**
2						
3	**Tuition and Fees**	$1,300				**$1,300**
4	**Books**	$240				**$240**
5	**Rent**	$250	$250	$250	$250	**$1,000**
6	**Utilities**	$60	$60	$60	$60	**$240**
7	**Food**	$160	$160	$160	$160	**$640**
8	**Transportation**	$120	$120	$120	$400	**$760**
9	**Odds and Ends**	$100	$100	$100	$300	**$600**
10						
11	**Total monthly expenses**	**$2,230**	**$690**	**$690**	**$1,170**	**$4,780**
12						
13						
14						

Many popular spreadsheet programs are on the market today. The different brands are distinguished by their features and by the look and feel of their user interfaces. In spite of their differences, all popular spreadsheet programs work in much the same way. It's rare to find a spreadsheet that doesn't have most or all of these features:

- *Automatic replication of values, labels, and formulas.* Most worksheets contain a great deal of repetition: Budgetary amounts remain constant from month to month; exam scores are calculated the same way for every student in the class; a scheduling program refers to the same seven days each week. Many spreadsheet commands streamline entry of repetitive data, labels, and formulas. Commands vary between programs, but all **replication** commands are, in essence, flexible extensions of the basic copy-and-paste functions found in other software.
- *Automatic recalculation.* **Automatic recalculation** is one of the spreadsheet's most important capabilities. It not only allows for the easy correction of errors but also makes it easy to try out different values while searching for solutions. For large, complicated worksheets, recalculation can be painfully slow, so most spread-

sheets allow you to turn off the automatic recalculation feature and recalculate the worksheet only when you need it.

- *Predefined functions.* With the first calculators, computing a square root was a tedious and error-prone series of steps. On today's calculators a single press of the square-root button tells the calculator to do all of the necessary calculations to produce the square root. Spreadsheet programs contain built-in **functions** something like the calculator's square-root button. A function in a formula instructs the computer to perform some predefined set of calculations. For example, the formula =SQRT(C5) calculates the square root of the number in cell C5. Modern spreadsheet applications have large libraries of predefined functions. Many, like SUM, AVERAGE (or AVG), MIN, and MAX, represent simple calculations that are performed often in all kinds of worksheets. Others automate complex financial, mathematical, and statistical calculations that would be extremely difficult to do manually. Like the calculator's square-root button, these functions can save time and reduce the likelihood of errors.
- *Macros.* A spreadsheet's menu of functions, like the menu in a fast-food restaurant, is limited to the most popular selections. For those situations where the built-in functions don't fill the bill, most spreadsheets allow the user to capture sequences of steps as reusable **macros**—custom-designed procedures that you can add to the existing menu of options. Some programs insist that you type macros using a special *macro language*; others allow you to turn on a *macro recorder* that captures every move you make with the keyboard and mouse, recording those actions in a macro transcript. Later you can ask the computer to carry out the instructions in that macro. Suppose, for example, you use the same set of calculations every month when preparing a statistical analysis of environmental data. Without macros you'd have to repeat the same sequence of keystrokes, mouse clicks, and commands each time you created the monthly report. But by creating a macro called, for instance, Monthstats, you can effectively say "Do it again!" by issuing the Monthstats command.
- *Templates.* Even with functions and macros, the process of creating a complex worksheet from scratch can be intimidating. Many users take advantage of worksheet **templates** that contain labels and formulas but no data values. These reusable templates produce instant answers when you fill in the blanks. Some common templates are packaged with spreadsheet software; others are marketed separately. When templates aren't available, users can create their own or commission programmers to write them. Whatever its origin a well-designed template can save considerable time, effort, and anguish.
- *Linking.* Sometimes a change in one worksheet produces changes in another. For example, a master sales summary worksheet for a business should reflect changes in each department's sales summary worksheet. Most spreadsheet programs allow you to create **automatic links** between worksheets, so when values change in one, all linked worksheets are updated automatically. Some programs, like Lotus 1-2-3, can create three-dimensional worksheets by stacking and linking several two-dimensional sheets.
- *Database capabilities.* Database software is discussed in detail in Chapter 6. For now it's sufficient to mention that many spreadsheet programs can perform basic database functions: storage and retrieval of information, searching, sorting, report

All of these worksheets are linked together into a single 3-D worksheet. (Software: Lotus 1-2-3.)

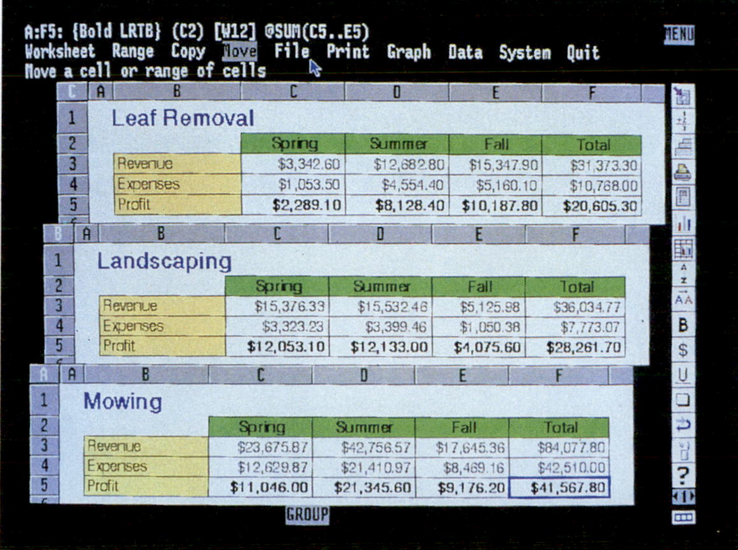

generation, mail merge, and such. With these features, a spreadsheet can serve users whose database needs are modest. For those who require a full-featured database management system, spreadsheet software might still be helpful; many spreadsheet programs support automatic two-way communication with database software.

"What If?" Questions

A spreadsheet program is a versatile tool, but it's especially valuable for answering **"What if?" questions:** "What if I don't complete the third assignment? How will that effect my chances for getting an A?" "What if I put my savings in a high-yield IRA tax-sheltered account with a withdrawal penalty? Will I be better off than if I leave it in a low-yield passbook account with no penalty?" "What if I buy a car that gets only 10 miles per gallon instead of a car that gets 40? How much more will I pay altogether for transportation over the next four years?" Because it allows you to change numbers and instantly see the effects of those changes, spreadsheet software streamlines the process of searching for answers to these questions.

Some spreadsheet programs include **equation solvers** that turn "What if?" questions around. Instead of forcing you to manipulate data values until formulas give you the numbers you're looking for, an equation solver allows you to define an equation, enter your target value, and watch while the computer determines the necessary data values. For example, an investor might use an equation solver to answer the question, "What is the *best* mix of these three stocks for minimizing risk while producing a 10 percent return on my investment?"

Spreadsheet programs are useful for asking "What if?" questions. This worksheet provides three tentative answers to the question, "What would it cost if I bought a car and kept it for four years?" Shaded cells are calculated automatically when numeric values are entered. What assumptions are built into this worksheet?

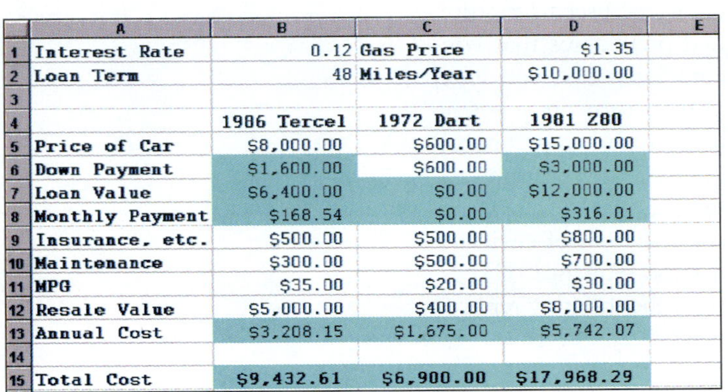

	A	B	C	D	E
1	Interest Rate	0.12	Gas Price	$1.35	
2	Loan Term	48	Miles/Year	$10,000.00	
3					
4		1986 Tercel	1972 Dart	1981 Z80	
5	Price of Car	$8,000.00	$600.00	$15,000.00	
6	Down Payment	$1,600.00	$600.00	$3,000.00	
7	Loan Value	$6,400.00	$0.00	$12,000.00	
8	Monthly Payment	$168.54	$0.00	$316.01	
9	Insurance, etc.	$500.00	$500.00	$800.00	
10	Maintenance	$300.00	$500.00	$700.00	
11	MPG	$35.00	$20.00	$30.00	
12	Resale Value	$5,000.00	$400.00	$8,000.00	
13	Annual Cost	$3,208.15	$1,675.00	$5,742.07	
14					
15	Total Cost	$9,432.61	$6,900.00	$17,968.29	

Tomorrow's Spreadsheet?

As revolutionary as VisiCalc was when it was introduced in 1979, it simply couldn't meet the demands of today's spreadsheet user. Even the original 1-2-3 looks primitive and underpowered next to Microsoft Excel, 1-2-3, and other modern graphic spreadsheets designed for Windows and the Macintosh. It's unlikely that spreadsheets have reached the end of their evolutionary path. What's next?

In 1991 Lotus introduced Improv, the result of a four-year effort to create a next-generation spreadsheet program. By throwing out many of the traditional rules for

Lotus Improv - [Optics Forecast · View1 · FY93]

File Edit Create Worksheet Tools Window Help

			North America		Europe	
			This Year	Next Year	This Year	Next Yea
SLR Cameras	Unit Sales		60,000	69,000	52,000	59,8
	Unit cost		$108.00	$124.20	$114.00	$131.
	Avg. Price		$179.28	$206.17	$189.24	$217.
	Revenue		10,756,800	12,370,320	9,840,480	11,316,5
	Cost of Goods		6,480,000	7,452,000	5,928,000	6,817,2
	Gross Margin		$4,276,800	$4,918,320	$3,912,480	$4,499,3
	Expenses	Salaries	$950,000	$1,092,500	$1,200,000	$1,380,0
		Mktg & Promo	$154,000	$177,100	$170,000	$195,5
		Travel	$43,000	$49,450	$38,000	$43,7
		Rent	$240,500	$276,575	$360,000	$414,0
		Legal	$15,000	$17,250	$8,000	$9,2
		Total	$1,402,500	$1,612,875	$1,776,000	$2,042,4
	Net Revenue		$2,874,300	$3,305,445	$2,136,480	$2,456,9
Video Cameras	Unit Sales		27,500	31,625	24,000	27,6
	Unit cost		$225.00	$258.75	$267.00	$307.
	Avg. Price		$373.50	$429.53	$443.22	$509.

Lotus' Improv spreadsheet provides more flexibility then the traditional spreadsheet grid.

Rules of Thumb

Avoiding Spreadsheet Pitfalls

Spreadsheet errors are easy to make and easy to overlook. When creating a worksheet, you can minimize errors by following a few basic guidelines:

- **Plan the worksheet before you start entering values and formulas.** Think about your goals and design the worksheet to meet those goals.
- **Make assumptions as accurate as possible**. Answers produced by a worksheet are only as good as the assumptions built into the data values and formulas. A worksheet that compares the operating costs of a gas guzzler and a gas miser must make assumptions about future trips, repair costs, and above all, gasoline prices. The accuracy of the worksheet is tied to all kinds of unknowns, including the future of Middle East politics. The more accurate the assumptions, the more accurate the predictions.
- **Double-check every formula and value**. Values and formulas are input for worksheets, and input determines output. Computer professionals often describe the dark side of this important relationship with the letters **GIGO**—garbage in, garbage out.
- **Make formulas readable.** If your software allows you to attach names to cell ranges, use meaningful names in formulas. It's easier to create and debug formulas when you can use readily understandable language like payrate*40+ 1.5*payrate*(hoursworked-40) instead of a string of characters like C2*40+1.5*C2*(D2-40).
- **Check your output against other systems.** Use another program, a calculator, or pencil and paper to verify the accuracy of your calculations.
- **Build in cross-checks**. Compare the sum of row totals with the sum of column totals. Does everything add up?
- **Change the input data values and study the results.** If small input adjustments produce massive output changes, or if major input adjustments result in little or no output changes, something may be wrong.
- **Take advantage of preprogrammed functions, templates, and macros.** Why reinvent the wheel when you can buy a professionally designed vehicle?
- **Don't use a spreadsheet as a substitute for thinking; stay alert and skeptical.** Some errors aren't obvious; others don't show up immediately. Use a spreadsheet as a decision-making aid, not a decision maker.

spreadsheet design, Lotus built a program that makes the process of producing complex worksheets easier and less error-prone. Instead of forcing data to fit into numbered rows and lettered columns, Improv allows users to create flexible, multidimensional worksheets with named values and formulas that look more like English statements than cryptic computer codes.

Whether or not Improv comes to control the market the way 1-2-3 once did, one thing is clear: Spreadsheet software is continuing to evolve. Recent versions of 1-2-3 include user help functions that incorporate the kinds of multimedia technology described in Chapter 8. Excel and other spreadsheets are beginning to incorporate artificial intelligence technology (see Chapter 10) to guide users through complex procedures. To help users check complex worksheets for consistency of entries and formula logic, future spreadsheets are likely to include *validators*—the equivalent of spelling and grammar checkers for spreadsheets.

Further down the road spreadsheets may disappear into the background along with other applications. Users will work with words, numbers, and other types of data without having to think about separate word processors, spreadsheets, and other applications. From the user's point of view, the focus will be more on the data than the tools. But until that happens, spreadsheets will continue to evolve into tools that better meet the needs of millions of users.

Spreadsheet Graphics: From Digits to Drawings

Most spreadsheet programs include charting commands that can turn worksheet numbers into charts and graphs automatically. In addition, many stand-alone charting programs create charts from any collection of numbers, whether stored in a worksheet or not. The process of creating a chart is usually as simple as filling in a few blanks in a dialog box.

Creating Charts from Numbers

The growth in the national debt seems more real as a line shooting toward the top of a graph than as a collection of big numbers on a page. The federal budget makes more (or less?) sense as a sliced-up dollar pie than as a list of percentages. The right chart can make a set of stale figures come to life, awakening our eyes and brains to trends and relationships that we might not have otherwise seen.

The User's View

Charting with a Spreadsheet

Software: Microsoft Excel.
The goal: To create a chart to bring your budget into focus.

To chart the breakdown totals from your budget, you'll use two ranges of cells: one containing the column of totals (F3 through F9) and another containing the category names for those totals (A3 through A9). After selecting both ranges, you click on the Chart Wizard icon on the button bar.

Microsoft Excel
File Edit Formula Format Data Options Macro Window Help
Normal
F3 =SUM(B3:E3)
BUDGET.XLS

	A	B	C	D	E	F
1	Expenses	Sept	Oct	Nov	Dec	Total
2						
3	Tuition and Fees	$1,300				$1,300
4	Books	$240				$240
5	Rent	$250	$250	$250	$250	$1,000
6	Utilities	$60	$60	$60	$60	$240
7	Food	$160	$160	$160	$160	$640
8	Transportation	$120	$120	$120	$400	$760
9	Odds and Ends	$100	$100	$100	$300	$600
10						
11	Total monthly expenses	$2,230	$690	$690	$1,170	$4,780
12						
13						
14						

Ready

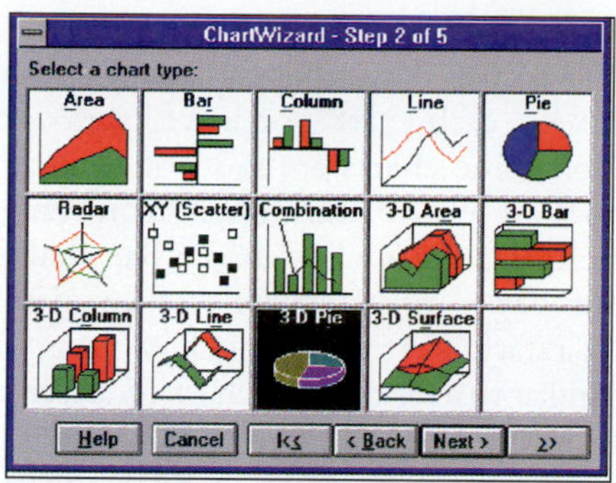

Chart Wizard walks you through the process of creating a chart from this data by presenting a series of five dialog boxes. After verifying the selected ranges in the first Chart Wizard step, you select the 3-D pie chart type, because a **pie chart** is the best choice for showing the relative proportions of the parts to a whole.

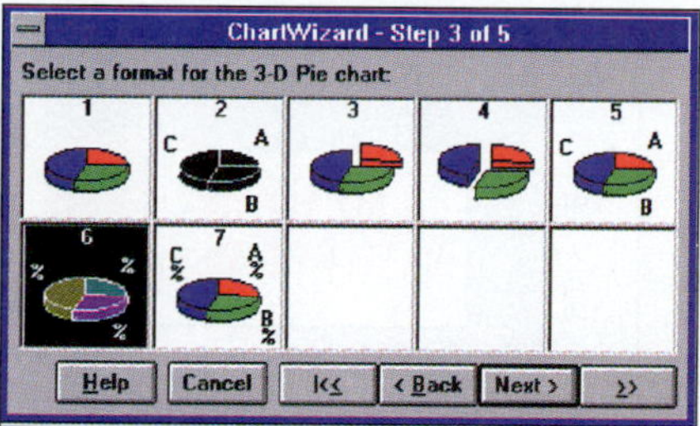

The next dialog box offers several choices of 3-D pie charts. You choose the one that shows percentage values. Another dialog box lets you specify that the data is in columns, not rows, and that the first selected column contains chart labels, not data.

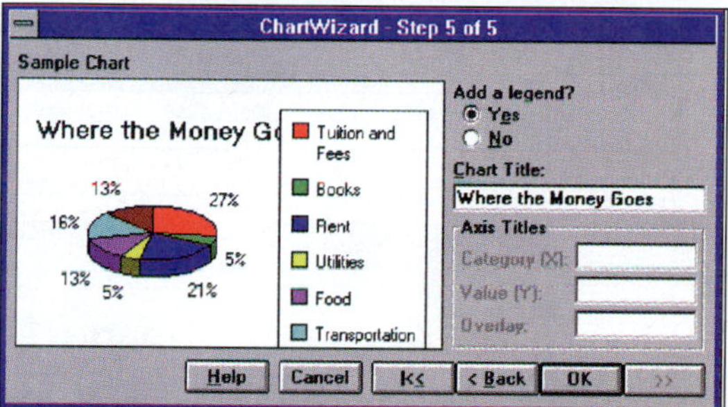

Step 5 allows you to add a title and a legend.

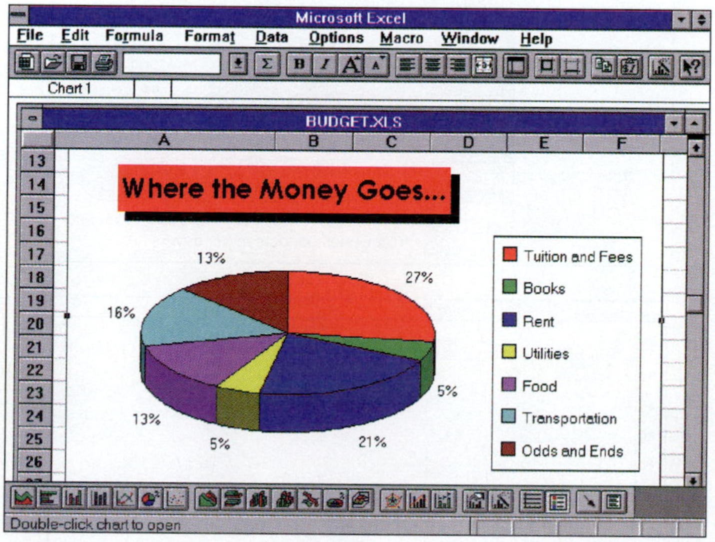

You can use the program's graphics tools to fine-tune the charts's appearance. You include the finished chart on the same page as the worksheet. If you change a value in the worksheet, the chart is automatically updated.

Most spreadsheet and charting programs offer a variety of basic chart types and options for embellishing charts. The differences among these chart types are more than aesthetic; each chart type is well suited for communicating particular types of information. **Line charts** are most often used to show trends or relationships over time or to show relative distribution of one variable through another. (The classic bell-shaped normal curve is a line chart.) **Bar charts** and column charts are similar to line charts, but they're more appropriate when data falls into a few categories. Bars can be stacked in a stack chart that shows how proportions of a whole change over time; the effect is similar to a series of pie charts. **Scatter charts** are used to discover, rather than display, a relationship between two variables. A well-designed chart can convey a wealth of information, just as a poorly designed chart can confuse or mislead.

The line chart and bar chart shown here were created with specialized charting software offering more flexibility than most spreadsheet programs. (Software: DeltaGraph Professional.) The scatter chart shown here was generated from data in an educational geographical database program. (Software: USA GeoGraph.)

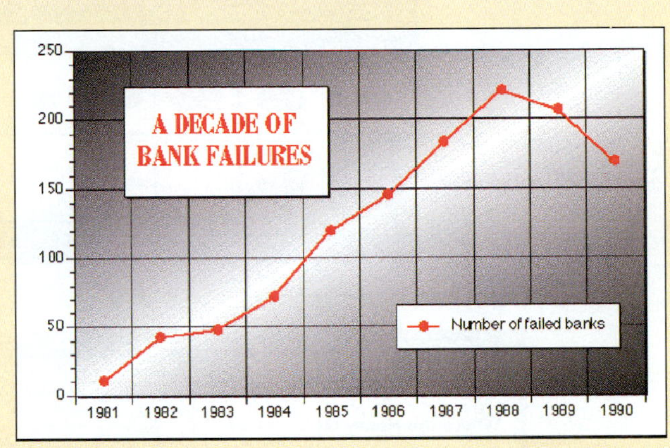

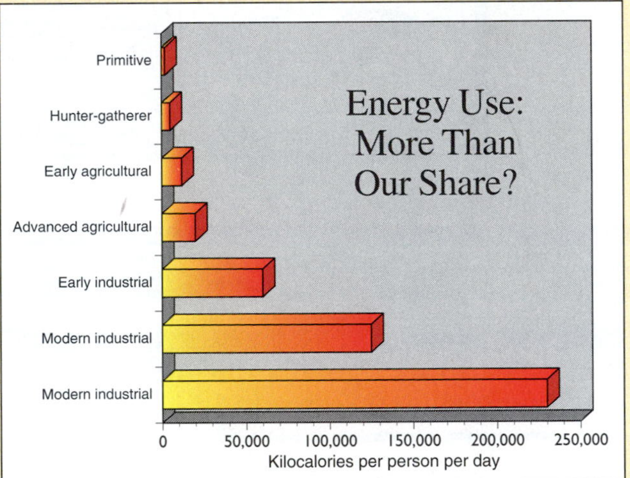

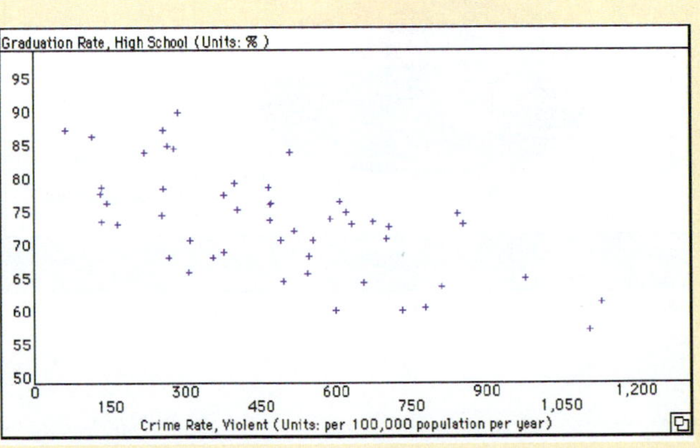

Rules of Thumb

Making Smart Charts

A chart can be a powerful communication tool if it's designed intelligently. If it's not, the message may miss the mark. Here are some guidelines for creating charts that are easy to read and understand.

- **Choose the right chart for the job**. Think about the message you're trying to convey. Pie charts, bar charts, line charts, and scatter charts are not interchangeable.
- **Keep it simple, familiar, and understandable.** Use charts in magazines, books, and newspapers as models.
- **Strive to reveal the truth, not hide it.** Whether accidentally or intentionally, many computer users create charts that convey disinformation. Changes in the scale or dimensions of a chart can completely transform the message, turning information into propaganda.

These charts are based on identical data; only the scales have been changed to distort the facts. (Software: PEMD Discovery.)

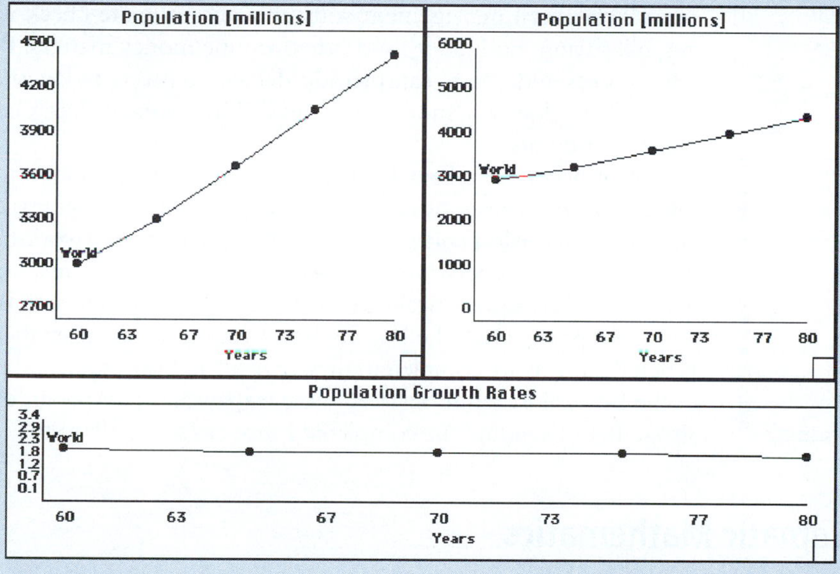

Statistical Software: Beyond Spreadsheets

An IBM electronic calculator speeds through thousands of intricate computations so quickly that on many complex problems, it's just like having 150 extra engineers…

—*IBM ad showing dozens of slide-rule-toting engineers in National Geographic, February 1952*

Spreadsheet software is remarkably versatile, but no program is perfect for every task. Other types of number-manipulation software are available for those situations in which spreadsheets don't quite fit the job.

Inexpensive financial management programs for homes and small businesses make the accounting process easier to understand by simulating checks and other familiar documents on the screen. (Software: Quicken.)

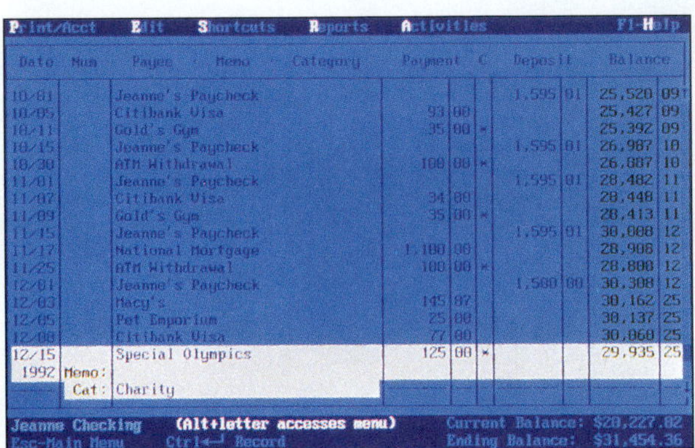

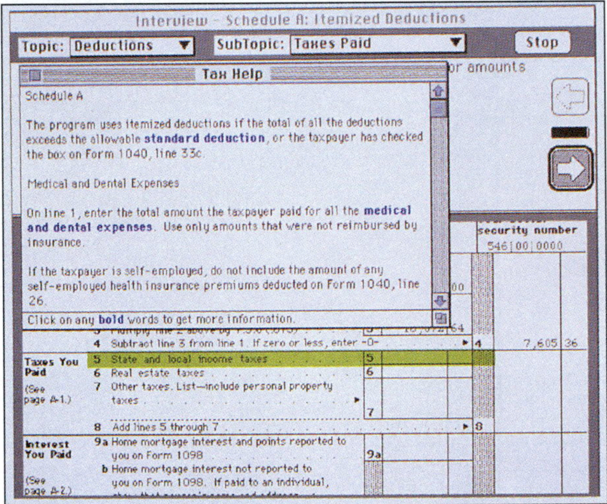

Tax time is never fun, but a tax preparation program can make calculating taxes quicker, easier, and less unpleasant. (Software: Macintax.)

Money Managers

Spreadsheet software has its roots in the accountant's ledger sheets. Ironically spreadsheets today are seldom used for accounting and bookkeeping. Accounting is a complex concoction of rules, formulas, laws, and traditions, and creating a worksheet to handle the details of the process is difficult and time consuming. Instead of relying on general-purpose spreadsheets for accounting, most businesses (and many households) use professionally designed **accounting and financial management software**.

Whether practiced at home or at the office, accounting involves setting up *accounts*—monetary categories to represent various types of income, expenses, assets, and liabilities—and keeping track of the flow of money between those accounts. An accountant routinely records *transactions*—checks, cash payments, charges, and other activities—that move money from one account to another. Accounting software automatically adjusts the balance in every account after each transaction. What's more, it records every transaction so that the history of each account can be retraced, step by step. This *audit trail* is a necessary part of business financial records, and it's one reason accountants use special-purpose accounting packages rather than spreadsheet programs. In addition to keeping records, financial management software can automate check writing, bill paying, budgeting, and other routine money matters. Periodic reports and charts can provide detailed answers to questions like "Where does the money go?" and "How are we doing compared to last year?"

Most accounting and financial management programs don't calculate income taxes, but they *can* export records to programs that do. **Tax preparation software** works like a prefabricated worksheet. As you enter numbers into the blanks in on-screen forms, other blanks are filled automatically by the program. Every time a number is entered or changed, the bottom line is recalculated automatically. When the forms are completed, they're ready to print, sign, and mail to the Internal Revenue Service. Some taxpayers bypass paper forms altogether by sending the completed forms *electronically* to the IRS.

Automatic Mathematics

Most of us seldom do math more complicated than filling out our tax forms. But higher mathematics is an essential part of the work of many scientists, researchers, engineers, architects, economists, financial analysts, teachers, and other professionals. Mathematics is a universal language for defining and understanding natural phenomena as well as a tool used to create all kinds of products and structures. Whether or not we work with it directly, our lives are constantly being shaped by mathematics.

Many professionals and students whose mathematical needs go beyond the capabilities of spreadsheets depend on symbolic **mathematics processing software** to grapple with complex equations and calculations. Mathematics processors make it easier for mathematicians to create, manipulate, and solve equations, in much the same way word processors help writers. Features vary from program to program, but a typical mathematics processor can do polynomial factoring, symbolic and numeric calculus, real and complex trigonometry, matrix and linear algebra, and three-dimensional graphics.

Mathematics processors generally include an interactive question-and-answer mode, a programming language, and tools for creating interactive documents that combine text, numerical expressions, and graphics. Although mathematics processors have only been available for a few years, they've already changed the way professionals use mathematics and the way students learn it. By handling the mechanics of mathematics, these programs allow people to concentrate on the content and implications of their work.

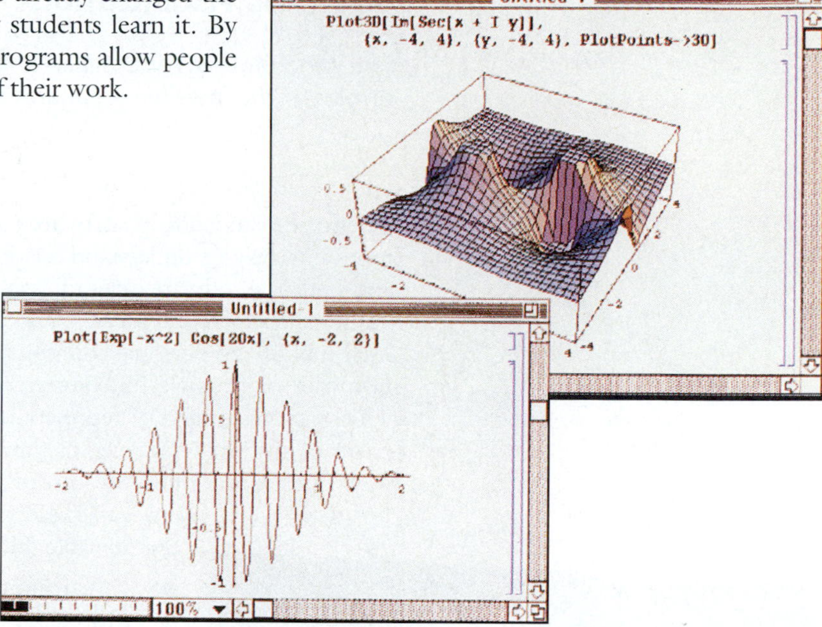

An abstract mathematical relationship is easier to understand when it's turned into a visible object with high-level mathematical software. (Software: Mathematica.)

Statistics and Data Analysis

One branch of applied mathematics that has become more important in the computer age is statistics—the science of collecting and analyzing data. Modern computer technology provides us with mountains of data—census data, political data, consumer data, economic data, sports data, weather data, scientific data, and more. We often refer to the data as statistics ("The government released unemployment statistics today"), but the numbers by themselves tell only part of the story. The analysis of those numbers—the search for patterns and relationships among them—can provide meaning for the data ("Analysts note that the rise in unemployment is confined to cities most heavily impacted by defense cutbacks"). Statisticians in government, business, and science depend on computers to make sense out of raw data.

Do people who live near nuclear power plants run a higher cancer risk? Does the current weather pattern suggest the formation of a tropical storm? Are rural voters more likely to support small-town candidates? These questions can't be answered with absolute certainty; the element of chance is at the heart of statistical analysis. But **statistical analysis software** can suggest answers to questions like these by testing the strength of data relationships. Statistical software can also produce graphs showing how two or more variables relate to each other. Statisticians can often uncover trends by browsing through two- and three-dimensional graphs of their data, looking for unusual patterns in the dots and lines that appear on the screen. This kind of visual exploration of data is an example of one of the fastest growing computer applications: *scientific visualization*.

This 3-D scatter chart shows the relationship between three variables: latitude, longitude, and population density in the United States. In the chart on the left, the relationship isn't clear. But when the "structure" is rotated and viewed from a different angle, as in the middle picture, it makes more sense. The final picture spells out the pattern by adding a surface. It's clear from this plot that the population is not spread evenly across the country.

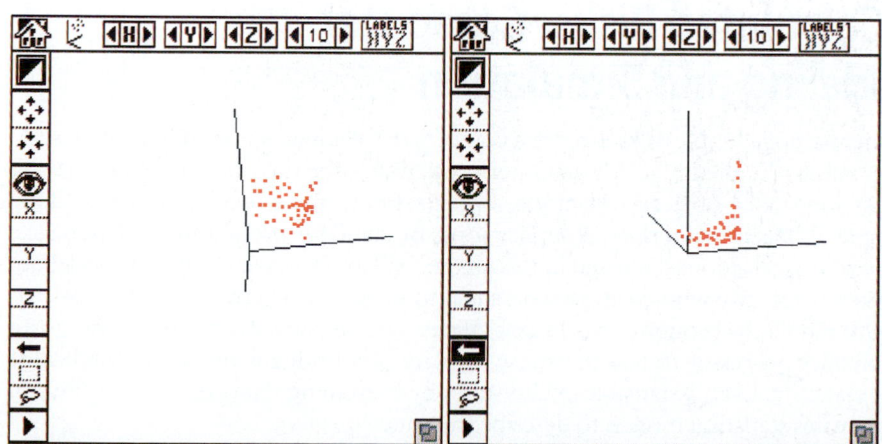

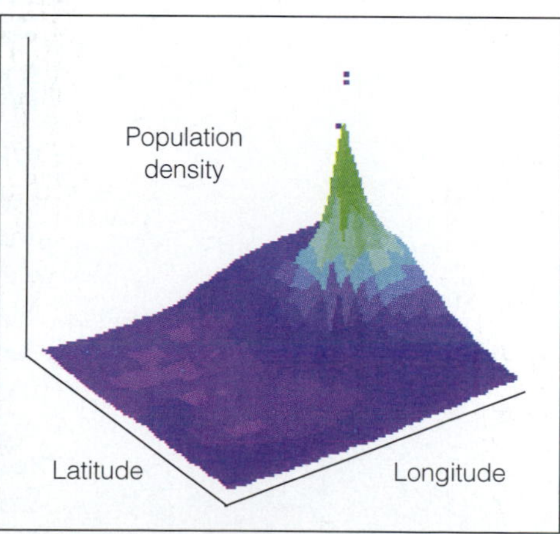

Scientific Visualization

The wind blows over the lake and stirs the surface of the water. Thus, visible effects of the invisible are manifested.

—*The I Ching*

Scientific visualization software uses shape, location in space, color, brightness, and motion to help us understand relationships that are invisible to us. Like mathematical and statistical software, scientific visualization software is no longer confined to mainframes and supercomputers; some of the most innovative programs are developed for use on high-end personal computers and workstations, working alone or in conjunction with more powerful computers. Scientific visualization takes many forms, all of which involve graphical representation of numerical data. The numbers can be the result of abstract equations, or they can be data gleaned from the real world. Either way, turning the numbers into pictures allows researchers and students to see the unseeable, and sometimes, as a result, to know what was previously unknowable. Here are two examples:

- Astronomer Margaret Geller of Harvard University created a three-dimensional map of the cosmos from data on the locations of known galaxies. While using her computer to "fly through" this three-dimensional model, she saw something that no one had seen before: the mysterious clustering of galaxies along the edges of invisible bubbles.
- Dr. Mark Ellisman of the University of California, San Diego, School of Medicine used a 30-foot electron microscope to collect data from cells of the brain and enter it into a supercomputer, which rendered a 3-D representation of the brain cell. When Ellisman's team displayed the data on a graphic workstation, they saw several previously undiscovered aberrations in brains of patients who had Alzheimer's disease—aberrations that may turn out to be clues for discovering the cause and conquering this disease.

Researcher at a computer keyboard wears spectacles with polarized lenses, which permit him to see 3-D images of molecules, as shown here superimposed over his image.

In these examples and hundreds of others like them, visualization helps researchers to see relationships that might have been obscure or even impossible to grasp without computer-aided visualization tools.

Calculated Risks: Computer Modeling and Simulation

Whether part of a simple worksheet or a complex set of equations, numbers often symbolize real-world phenomena. Computer **modeling**—the use of computers to create abstract models of objects, organisms, organizations, and processes—can be done with spreadsheets, mathematical applications, or standard programming languages. Most of the applications discussed in this chapter are examples of computer modeling. A business executive who creates a worksheet to project quarterly profits and losses is trying to model the economic world that affects the company. An engineer who uses a mathematics processor to test the stress capacity of a bridge is modeling the bridge mathematically. Even a statistician who starts by examining data collected in the real world creates statistical models to describe the data.

Computer models aren't always serious; most computer games are models. Chess boards, pinball games, battlefields, sports arenas, ant colonies, cities, medieval dun-

Flight simulator games for home computers (right) are simplified versions of flight simulators used to train military pilots. Both varieties allow users to test their wings without risking their necks.

geons, interplanetary cultures, mythological societies—they've all been modeled in computer games. In classrooms, students use computer models to travel the Oregon Trail, explore nuclear power plants, invest in the stock market, and dissect digital frogs.

Whether it's created for work, education, or play, a computer model is an *abstraction*—a set of concepts and ideas designed to mimic some kind of system. But a computer model isn't static; it can be put to work in a computer **simulation** to see how the model operates under certain conditions. A well-designed model should behave like the system it imitates.

Suppose, for example, an engineer constructs a computer model of a new type of airplane to test how the plane will respond to human commands. In a typical flight simulation, the "pilot" controls the plane's thrust and elevator angle by feeding input data to the model plane. The model responds by adjusting air speed and angle of ascent or descent, just as a real plane would. The pilot responds to the new state of the aircraft by adjusting one or more of the controls, which causes the system to respond by revising the aircraft's state again. This **feedback loop**, where plane and pilot react to data from each other, continues throughout the simulation.

A flight simulator might have a graphical user interface that makes the computer screen look and act like the instrument panel of a real plane so that it can be run interactively by human pilots. Or it might display nothing more than numbers representing input and output values, and the input values might be generated by a simulated pilot—another computer model! Either way, it can deliver a wealth of information about the behavior of the plane, provided the model is accurate.

Computer Simulations: The Rewards

We are reaching the stage where problems that we must solve are going to become insolvable without computers. I do not fear computers; I fear the lack of them.

—Isaac Asimov

Computer simulations are widely used for research in the physical, biological, and social sciences and in engineering. Schools, businesses, and the military also use simulations for training. Here are a few of the many reasons for the growing popularity of computer simulations:

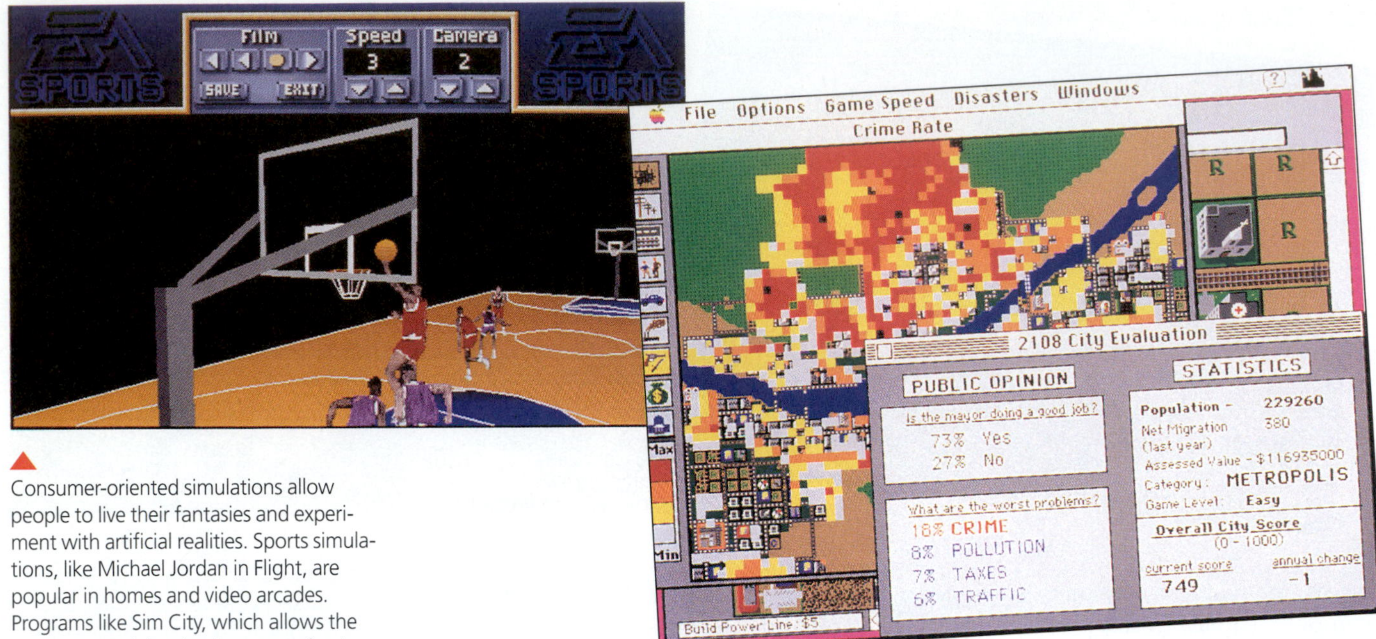

Consumer-oriented simulations allow people to live their fantasies and experiment with artificial realities. Sports simulations, like Michael Jordan in Flight, are popular in homes and video arcades. Programs like Sim City, which allows the user to control the development of a city, combine education with entertainment.

- *Safety.* While it's safer to learn piloting skills sitting in front of a computer than actually flying in the air, it's still possible to learn to fly without a computer simulation. Some activities, however, are so dangerous that they aren't ethically possible without computer simulations. How, for example, can scientists study the effects of a nuclear power plant meltdown on the surrounding environment? Until a meltdown occurs, there's only one practical answer: computer simulation.
- *Economy.* It's far less expensive for an automobile manufacturer to produce a digital model of a nonexistent car than to build a prototype out of steel. The computer model can be tested for strength, handling, and efficiency in a series of simulations *before* the company builds and tests a physical prototype. The cost of the computer model is small when compared to the possible expense of producing a defective car.
- *Projection.* Without computers it could take decades for biologists to determine whether the rising deer population on an island threatens other species, and by the time they discover the answer, it would be too late to do anything about it. A computer model of the island's ecosystem would speed up natural biological processes, so their effects over several generations could be measured in a matter of minutes. A computer simulation can, in effect, serve as a time machine for exploring one or more possible futures.
- *Visualization.* Computer models make visualization possible, and visualization allows researchers and students to see and understand relationships that might otherwise go unnoticed. Computer models can speed time up or slow it down; they can make subatomic particles big and the universe small.
- *Replication.* In the real world it can be difficult or impossible to repeat a research project with slightly different conditions. But this kind of repetition is an important part of serious research. An engineer needs to fine-tune dimensions and angles to achieve peak performance. A scientist studies the results of one experiment and develops a new hypothesis that calls for further testing. An executive needs to test his business plan under a variety of economic scenarios. If the research is conducted on a computer model, replication is just a matter of changing input values and running a new simulation.

Computer Simulations: The Risks

Where is the wisdom we have lost in knowledge?
Where is the knowledge we have lost in information?

—*T. S. Eliot*

The down side of computer simulation can be summed up in three words: *Simulation isn't reality*. The real world is a subtle and complex place, and capturing even a fraction of that subtlety and complexity in a computer simulation is a tremendous challenge.

GIGO revisited. The accuracy of a simulation depends on how closely its mathematical model corresponds to the system being simulated. Mathematical models are built on assumptions, many of which are difficult or impossible to verify. Some models suffer from faulty assumptions; others contain hidden assumptions that may not even be obvious to their creators; still others go astray simply because of clerical or human errors.

The highly publicized 1974 Club of Rome study summarized in the book *The Limits of Growth* used the most powerful computers available at the time to model the environmental and economic impact of human activity on Earth. Months after the study was released, a researcher discovered a misplaced decimal point in one key equation that threw many calculations off by a factor of ten! Correcting the error didn't negate the report's overall conclusions, but it did raise many questions about the study. Bad input in a complex simulation can come from numerous sources, and "garbage in, garbage out" is a basic rule of simulation.

Making reality fit the machine. Simulations are computation intensive. Today's personal computers can run modest simulations, but they're hopelessly underpowered for medium-to-large simulations. Most scientists and engineers who work extensively with mathematical models depend on workstations, mainframes, or supercomputers to run simulations. Even Apple Computer, the personal computer manufacturer, uses a Cray supercomputer to model future Apple machines. (Fittingly, Seymour Cray claims to use an Apple computer to help him design Cray machines!)

Some simulations are so complex that researchers need to simplify models and streamline calculations to get them to run on the best hardware available. Even when there's plenty of computing power available, researchers face a constant temptation to reshape reality for the convenience of the simulation. In one classic example a U.S. Forest Service computer model reduced complex old-growth forests to "accumulated capital." Aesthetics, ecological diversity, and other hard-to-quantify factors were nonexistent in this model.

Sometimes this simplification of reality is deliberate; more often it's unconscious. Either way, information can be lost, and the loss may compromise the integrity of the simulation and call the results into question.

The illusion of infallibility. Risks can be magnified because people take computers seriously. For many people information takes on an air of respectability if it comes from a computer. Computer-generated reports tend to be emphasized, often at the expense of other sources of knowledge. Executives use worksheets to make decisions involving hundreds of jobs and millions of dollars. Politicians decide the fate of military weapons and endangered species based on summaries of computer simulations. Doctors use computer models to make life-and-death decisions involving new drugs and treatments. All these people, in some sense, are placing their trust in computer simulations. Many of them trust the data precisely *because* it was generated by a computer.

A computer simulation, whether generated by a PC spreadsheet or churned out by a supercomputer, can be an invaluable decision-making aid. The risk is that the people who make decisions with computers will turn over too much of their decision-making power to the computer. The Jedi Master in the motion picture *Star Wars* understood the danger when he encouraged Luke Skywalker in the heat of battle to turn off his computer simulation rather than let it overpower his judgment. His admonition was simple: "Trust your feelings."

Summary

Spreadsheet programs, first developed to simulate and automate the accountant's ledger, are widely used today in business, science, engineering, and education. Spreadsheet software can be used for tracking financial transactions, calculating grades, forecasting economic conditions, recording scientific data—just about any task that involves repetitive numeric calculations. Spreadsheet documents, called worksheets, are grids whose individual cells contain alphabetic labels, numbers, and formulas. Changes in numeric values can cause the spreadsheet to update any related formulas automatically. The responsiveness and flexibility of spreadsheet software make it particularly well suited for providing answers to "What if?" questions.

Most spreadsheet programs include charting commands to turn worksheet numbers into a variety of graphs and charts. The process of creating a chart from a spreadsheet is automated to the point that human drawing isn't necessary; the user simply provides instructions concerning the type of chart and the details to be included in the chart.

Number crunching often goes beyond spreadsheets. Specialized accounting and tax preparation software packages perform specific business functions without the aid of spreadsheets. Symbolic mathematics processors can handle a variety of higher mathematics functions involving numbers, symbols, equations, and graphics. Statistical analysis software is used for data collection and analysis. Scientific visualization can be done with math processors, statistical packages, graphics programs, or specialized programs designed for visualization.

Modeling and simulation are at the heart of most applications involving numbers. When people create computer models, they use numbers to represent real-world objects and phenomena. Simulations built on these models can provide insights that might be difficult or impossible to obtain otherwise, provided that the models reflect reality accurately. If used wisely, computer simulation can be a powerful tool to help people understand their world and make better decisions.

CHAPTER REVIEW

Key Terms

accounting and financial management software
active cell
address
automatic link
automatic recalculation
bar chart
cell
column
console
current cell
equation solver
feedback loop
formula
formula bar
function
GIGO
label
line chart
macro
mathematics processing software
modeling
pie chart
range
replication
row
scatter chart
scientific visualization software
scroll
simulation
spreadsheet software
statistical analysis software
tax preparation software
template
value
"What if?" question
worksheet

Review Questions 

1. In what ways are word processors and spreadsheet programs similar?
2. What are some advantages of using a spreadsheet to maintain a budget over using a calculator? Are there any disadvantages?
3. If you enter =B2+C2 in cell B1 of a worksheet, the formula is replaced by the number 125 when you press the Enter key. What happened?
4. Using the worksheet from question 3, you change the number in cell B2 from 55 to 65. What happens to the number in cell B1? Why?
5. What is the difference between a spreadsheet program and a financial management program?
6. Explain the difference between a numeric value and a formula.
7. What is a spreadsheet function and how is it useful?
8. Describe or draw examples of several different types of charts and explain how they're typically used.
9. Describe several software tools used for numeric applications too complex to be handled by spreadsheets. Give an example of an application of each.
10. List several advantages and disadvantages of using computer simulations for decision making.

Discussion Questions 

1. Spreadsheets are sometimes credited with legitimizing the personal computer as a business tool. Why do you think they had such an impact?
2. Why do you think errors in spreadsheet models go undetected? What can you do to minimize the risk of spreadsheet errors?
3. The statement "Computers don't make mistakes, people do" is often used to support the reliability of computer output. Is the statement true? Is it relevant?
4. Are computer simulations misused? Explain your answer.
5. Before spreadsheets, people who wanted to use computers for financial modeling had to write programs in complex computer languages to do the job. Today spreadsheets have replaced those programs for many financial applications. Do you think spreadsheets will be replaced by some easier-to-use software tool in the future? If so, try to imagine what it will be like.

Projects 

1. Develop a multiple-choice questionnaire for determining public attitudes on an issue that's important to you. Use a computer to analyze, summarize, and graphically represent the results, trying to be as fair and accurate in your summary as you can. Then do another summary, presenting the figures and charts in such a way that they tend to support your point of view. Compare how people react to the two reports.
2. Choose a controversial issue—environmental, economic, or other—and locate numeric data related to the issue. Develop a set of charts and graphs that argues effectively for one point of view. Using the same data, create visuals to support the other point of view. Compare *your* reactions to both processes.
3. Use a spreadsheet or a financial management program to develop a personal budget. Try to keep track of all your income and outgo for the next month or two, and record the transactions with your program. At the end of that time, evaluate the accuracy of your budget and discuss your reactions to the process.

Sources and Resources 

Books covering basic spreadsheet operations number in the hundreds—far too many to review here. Almost all of these books are software and hardware specific. Some are intended to be used as reference manuals; some are collections of tips, hints, and shortcuts; others are collections of sample documents that can be used as templates; still others are overviews or hands-on tutorials for beginners. If you're new to spreadsheets, start with a book in the last category. Look for one that fits your system and that's readable and easy to understand.

How to Lie with Statistics, by Darrell Huff (New York: Norton, 1954). This 30-year-old book has more relevance in today's computer age than it did when it was written.

The Visual Display of Quantitative Information and *Envisioning Information,* by Edward R. Tufte (Cheshire, CT: Graphics Press, 1983 and 1990, respectively). These two stunningly beautiful books should be required reading for anyone who creates charts, graphs, or other visual aids. For that matter they should be read by anyone who *reads* charts, graphs, and other visual aids.

C H A P T E R

SIX

Database Applications and Implications

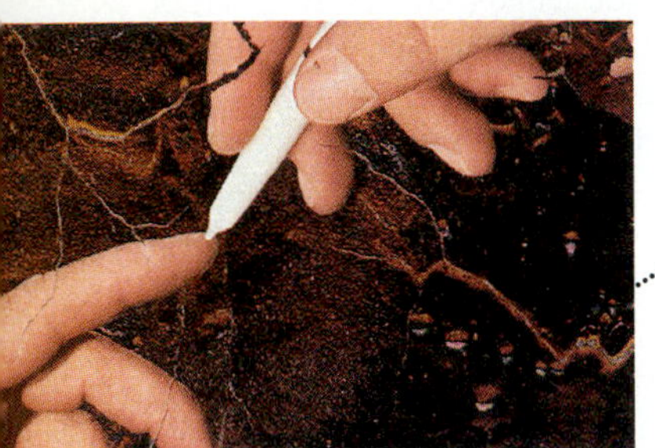

Bill Gates Rides the Digital Wave

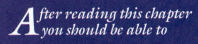

The goal is information at your fingertips.

—Bill Gates

In the early days of the personal computer revolution, Bill Gates and Paul Allen formed a company called Microsoft to produce and market a version of the BASIC programming language for microcomputers. Microsoft BASIC quickly became the standard language installed in virtually every desktop computer on the market.

BASIC was important, but Microsoft's biggest break came when IBM went shopping for an operating system for its new personal computer. Gates purchased an operating system from a small company, reworked it to meet IBM's specifications, named it MS-DOS (for *M*icro*s*oft *D*isk *O*perating *S*ystem), and offered it to IBM. The IBM PC became an industry standard, and Microsoft found itself owning the operating system that kept most of the PCs in the world running.

Today Bill Gates and Microsoft dominate the personal computer software industry, selling operating systems, programming languages, and applications programs for a variety of desktop computers. Microsoft has over 8000 employees and more than a billion dollars in annual revenues. Software has made the youthful Gates the richest American and one of the wealthiest people on Earth.

Bill Gates

All this success is not without controversy. Critics argue that Gates uses unethical business practices to ruthlessly stomp out competition. Even the Federal Trade Commission

After reading this chapter you should be able to

- explain what a database is and what it can be used for
- describe different kinds of database software, from simple file managers to complex relational databases
- describe database operations for storing, sorting, updating, querying, and summarizing information
- explain how databases threaten our privacy

Microsoft headquarters, Redmond, WA.

has investigated Microsoft's business practices for possible violations of antitrust laws. According to writer Steven Levy, Gates "has the obsessive drive of a hacker working on a tough technical dilemma, yet has an uncanny grasp of the marketplace, as well as a firm conviction of what the future will be like and what he should do about it." The future, says Gates, will be digital. Even the pictures on our walls will be high-definition digital reproductions of paintings and photographs that can be changed at the touch of a button. Unbelievable? Not if you've been to the $10 million Gates mansion and viewed his digital collection!

To prepare for this all-digital future, Microsoft is quietly buying the electronic rights to hundreds of works of literature, art, and cinema. At the same time, Gates tirelessly evangelizes for the graphical user interface, CD-ROM, and other technologies that make computers easier to use and more accessible to everybody, so we all can have "information at our fingertips."

We live in an information age. We're bombarded with information by television, radio, newspapers, magazines, books, and computers. It's easy to be overwhelmed by the sheer quantity of information we're expected to deal with each day. Computer applications like word processors and spreadsheets can aggravate the problem by making it easier for people to generate more documents full of information.

A *database program* is an information manager that can help alleviate information overload. Databases make it possible for people to store, organize, retrieve, communicate, and manage information in ways that wouldn't be possible without computers. To control the flood of information, people use databases of all sizes and shapes—from massive mainframe database managers that keep airlines filled with passengers to computerized appointment calendars on palmtop computers and public database kiosks in shopping malls.

First the good news: "Information at your fingertips" can make your life richer and more efficient in a multitude of ways. Ready cash from street-corner machines, instant airline reservations from any telephone, catalog shopping with overnight mail-order delivery, exhaustive reference searches in seconds—none of these conveniences would be possible without databases.

Using a touch-screen kiosk at a mall, a shopper browses with his fingers rather than his feet.

Now the bad news: Much of the information stored in databases is *your* data, and you have little or no control over who has it and how they use it. Ironically the database technology that liberates us in our day-to-day lives is, at the same time, chipping away at our privacy. We'll explore both sides of this important technology in this chapter.

The Electronic File Cabinet: Database Basics

The next best thing to knowing something is knowing where to find it.

—Samuel Johnson

We'll start by looking at the basics of databases. Like word processors and spreadsheets, database programs are applications—programs for turning computers into productive tools. If a word processor is a computerized typewriter and a spreadsheet is a computerized ledger, we can think of a database program as a computerized file cabinet.

While word processors and spreadsheets generally are used to create printed documents, database programs are designed to maintain databases—collections of information stored on computer disks. A database can be an electronic version of a phone book, a recipe file, a library's card catalog, an inventory file stored in an office file cabinet, a school's student grade records, a card index containing the names and addresses of business contacts, or a catalog of your compact disc collection. Just about any collection of information can be turned into a database.

What Good Is a Database?

Why do people use computers for information-handling tasks that can be done with index cards, three-ring binders, or file folders? Computerized databases offer several advantages over their paper-and-pencil counterparts:

- *Databases make it easier to store large quantities of information.* If you have only 20 or 30 compact discs, it makes sense to catalog them in a notebook. If you have 2000 or 3000, your notebook may become as unwieldy as your CD collection. With a computerized database your complete CD catalog could be stored on a single diskette. The larger the mass of information, the bigger the benefit of using a database.
- *Databases make it easier to retrieve information quickly and flexibly.* While it might take a minute or more to look up a phone number in a card file or telephone directory, the same job can be done in seconds with a database. If you look up 200 numbers every week, the advantage of a database is obvious. That advantage is even greater when your search doesn't match your file's organization. For example, suppose you have a phone number on a scrap of paper and you want to find the name and address of the person with that number. That kind of search may take hours if your information is stored in a large address book or file alphabetized by name, but the same search is almost instantaneous in a computerized database.
- *Databases make it easy to organize and reorganize information.* Paper filing systems force you to arrange information in one particular way. Should your book catalog be organized by author, by title, by date of publication, or by subject? There's a lot riding on your decision, because it takes time if you decide to rearrange everything later. With a database you can instantly switch between any or all of these organizational schemes as often as you like; there's no penalty for flexibility.

- *Databases make it easy to print and distribute information in a variety of ways.* Suppose you want to send letters to your hundreds of friends inviting them to your post-graduation party. You'll need to include directions to your place for out-of-towners but not for hometowners. A database, when used with a word processor, can print personalized form letters, including extra directions for those who need them, and print preaddressed envelopes or mailing labels in a fraction of the time it would take you to do it by hand and with less likelihood of error. You can even print a report listing invitees sorted by zip code so you can suggest possible car pools. (If you want to bill those who attend the party, your database can help with that, too.)

Database Anatomy

As you might expect, there's a specialized vocabulary associated with databases. Unfortunately some terms take on different meanings depending on their context, and different people use these words in different ways. We'll begin by charting a course through marketing hype and technical terminology to find our way to the definitions most people use today.

For our purposes a **database** is a collection of information stored in an organized form in a computer, and a **database program** is a software tool for organizing storage and retrieval of that information. A variety of programs fit this broad definition, ranging from simple address-book programs to massive inventory-tracking systems. We'll explore the differences between types of database programs later in the chapter, but for now we'll treat them as if they were more or less alike.

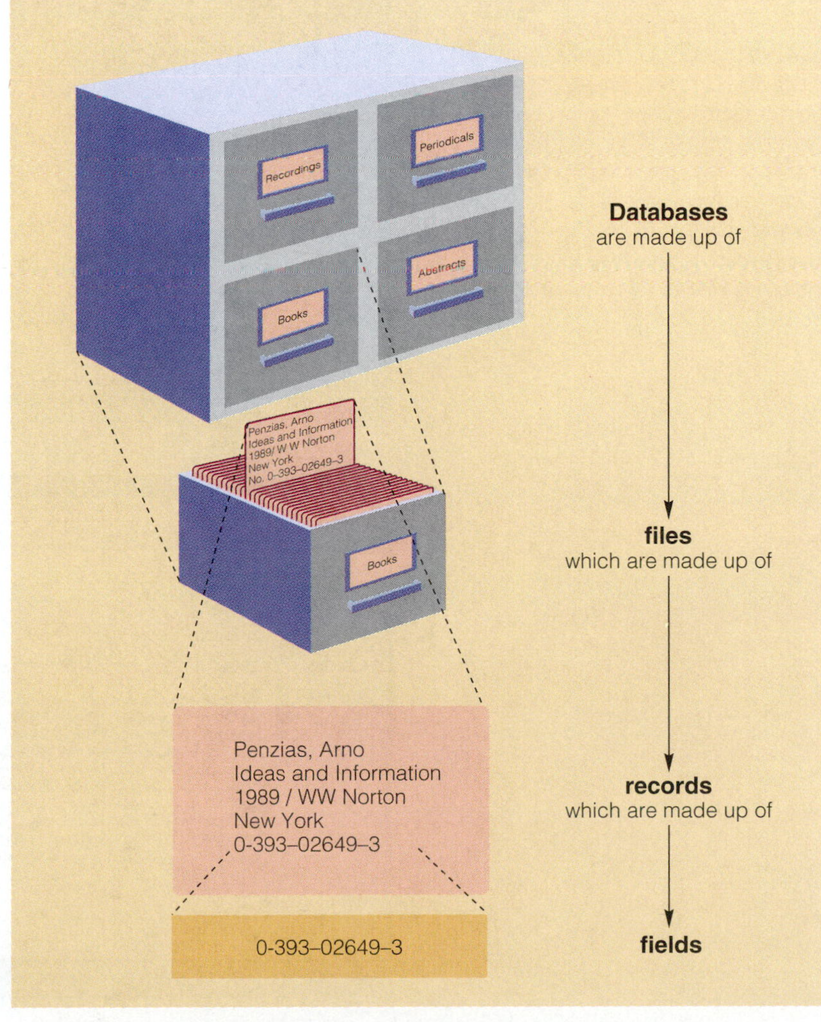

Many terms that describe the components of database systems grew out of the file-cabinet terminology of the precomputer office. A database is composed of one or more files. A **file** is a collection of related information; it keeps that information together the way a drawer in a file cabinet does. If a database is used to record sales information for a company, a separate file might contain the relevant sales data for each year. For an address database, separate files might hold personal and business contacts. It's up to the designer of the database to determine whether or not information in different categories is stored in separate files on the computer's disk.

(The term *file* sometimes causes confusion because of its multiple meanings. A disk can contain application programs, system programs, utility programs, and documents, all of which are, from the computer's point of view, files. In a general sense a file created by a database program is no different than the database program that created that file; they're both files—named collections of information stored on a disk. But for database users the term *file* usually means a file that is part of a database—a specific kind of file. In this chapter *file* refers specifically to a data file created by a database program.)

A database file is a collection of records. A **record** is the information relating to one person, product, or event. In the library's card-catalog database, a record is equivalent to one card. In an address-book database, a record contains information about one person. A compact disc catalog database would probably have one record for each CD.

Each discrete chunk of information in a record is called a **field**. A record in the library's card-catalog database would contain fields for author, title, publisher, date, and title code number. Your CD database could break records into fields by title, artist, and so on.

The type of information a field can hold is determined by its *field type*. For example, the author field in the library database would be defined as a *text field*, so it could contain text. The field specifying the number of copies of a book would be defined as a *numeric field*, so it could contain only numbers. A date-of-purchase field might be a *date field* that could contain only dates. In addition to these standard field types, many modern database programs allow fields to contain graphics, digitized photographs, sounds, or even video clips. **Computed fields** contain formulas similar to spreadsheet formulas; they display values calculated from values in other numeric fields. For exam-

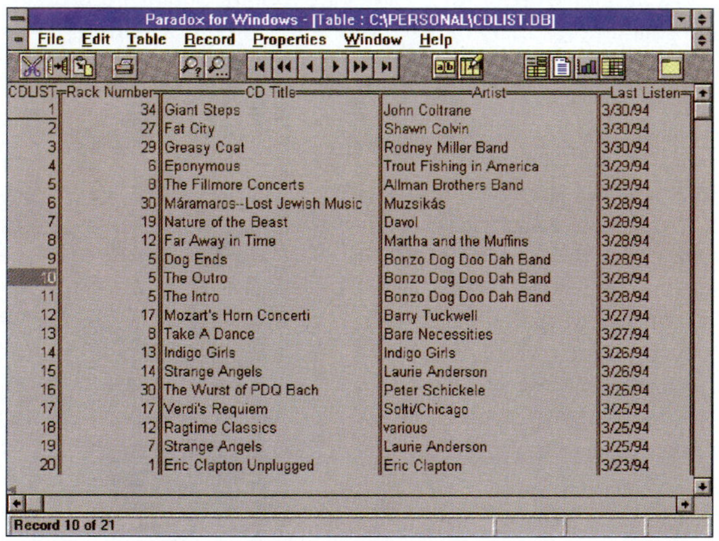

CDLIST	Rack Number	CD Title	Artist	Last Listen
1	34	Giant Steps	John Coltrane	3/30/94
2	27	Fat City	Shawn Colvin	3/30/94
3	29	Greasy Coat	Rodney Miller Band	3/30/94
4	6	Eponymous	Trout Fishing in America	3/29/94
5	8	The Fillmore Concerts	Allman Brothers Band	3/29/94
6	30	Máramaros--Lost Jewish Music	Muzsikás	3/28/94
7	19	Nature of the Beast	Davol	3/28/94
8	12	Far Away in Time	Martha and the Muffins	3/28/94
9	5	Dog Ends	Bonzo Dog Doo Dah Band	3/28/94
10	5	The Outro	Bonzo Dog Doo Dah Band	3/28/94
11	5	The Intro	Bonzo Dog Doo Dah Band	3/28/94
12	17	Mozart's Horn Concerti	Barry Tuckwell	3/27/94
13	8	Take A Dance	Bare Necessities	3/27/94
14	13	Indigo Girls	Indigo Girls	3/26/94
15	14	Strange Angels	Laurie Anderson	3/26/94
16	30	The Wurst of PDQ Bach	Peter Schickele	3/26/94
17	17	Verdi's Requiem	Solti/Chicago	3/25/94
18	12	Ragtime Classics	various	3/25/94
19	7	Strange Angels	Laurie Anderson	3/25/94
20	1	Eric Clapton Unplugged	Eric Clapton	3/23/94

These two screens show two different views of the same database. The list view resembles a spreadsheet with records in rows and fields in columns; you can navigate through the database to display different records and, if necessary, scroll right or left to display different fields. The form view shows a single record in a format that resembles a paper form; navigation buttons and commands allow you to move from record to record. The view may change, but the data remains the same. (Software: Paradox for Windows from Borland.)

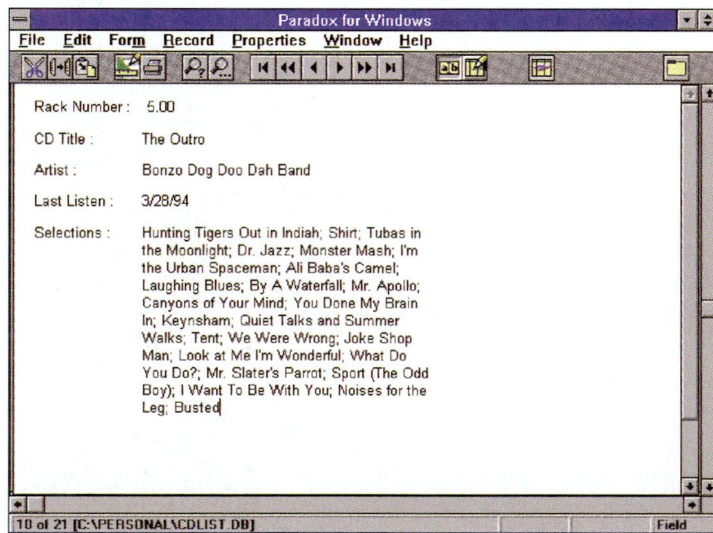

ple, a computed field called GPA might contain a formula for calculating a student's grade point average using the grades stored in other fields.

Most database programs provide you with more than one way to view the data, including *form views* that show one record at a time and *list views* that display several records in lists similar to a spreadsheet. In any view, fields can be rearranged without changing the underlying data.

The User's View

Building a Database

Software: Claris FileMaker Pro.
The goal: To create an Addresses database file to replace your tattered address book, the bundle of business cards in your desk drawer, and the scribbled list of numbers posted by your phone.

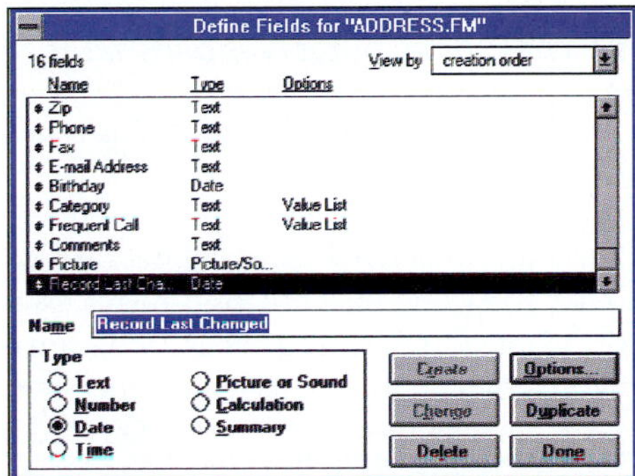

To create a new Addresses database file, you must first define fields by typing a name and specifying a field type for each one. In addition to including text fields for Last Name, First Name, and other information, you add two date files: one for birthday and one that will automatically display the most recent modification date for each record. You also include a picture field and two fields with Value lists—lists of legal values that can appear in those fields.

The program creates a standard form layout for data entry, but it's not as easy to use as it could be. You can modify the layout by rearranging fields and labels and changing their formats.

You type information into the first record of the reformatted layout, using Tab to move from field to field. In the Category and Frequent Call fields you click the mouse to select the appropriate values. You can fill in the Picture field later with a scanned photograph. When you're through you store this record in the data file and replace it on the screen with the New Record command.

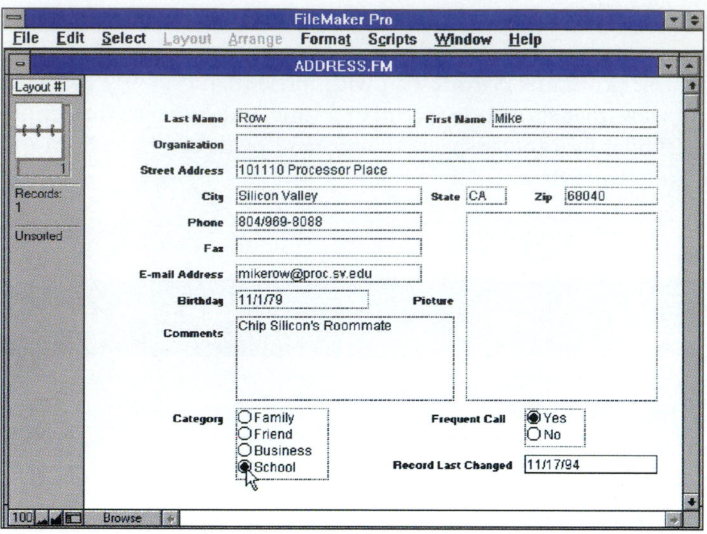

Database Operations

Information has value, but it is as perishable as fresh fruit.

—*Nicholas Negroponte*, *founder and director of the MIT Media Lab*

Once the structure of a database is defined, it's easy to get information in; it's just a matter of typing. Typing may not even be necessary if the data already exists in some computer-readable form. Most database programs can easily **import** or receive data in the form of text files created with word processors, spreadsheets, or other databases. When information changes or errors are detected, records can be modified, added, or deleted.

The challenging part of using a database is retrieving information in a timely and appropriate manner. Information is of little value if it's not accessible. One way to find information is to **browse** through the records of the database file just as you would if they were paper forms in a notebook. Most database programs provide keyboard commands, on-screen buttons, and other tools for navigating quickly through records. But this kind of electronic page turning offers no particular advantage over paper, and it's painfully inefficient for large files.

Fortunately most database programs include a variety of commands and capabilities that make it easy to get the information you need when you need it.

Database queries. The alternative to browsing is to ask the database for specific information. In database lingo, an information request is called a **query**. A query may be a simple **search** for a specific record (say, one containing information on Abraham Lincoln) or a request to **select** *all* of the records that match a set of criteria (for example, records for all U.S. presidents who served more than one term). Once you've selected a group of records, you can browse through it, produce a printout, or do just about anything else you might do with the complete file.

Sorting data. Sometimes it's necessary to rearrange records to make the most efficient use of data. For example, a mail-order company's customer file might be arranged alphabetically by name for easy reference, but it must be rearranged in order by zip code

SHIP-TO ADDRESS	CODE AUTHOR & TITLE	LIST PRICE	QTY	TOTAL AMOUNT
THE SOUTH MAIN BOOKSTORE 209 SOUTH MAIN CHICAGO, IL 60625	36980 WILSON ANATOMY & PHYSIOLOGY	$22.95	100	$2295.00
UNIVERSITY BOOKSTORE OLD STATE COLLEGE 800 W. VICTORIA ST STAMFORD, CT 06903	50239 LYON TRIGONOMETRY	$17.95	300	$5385.00
EASTERN ARCATA UNIV BOOKSTORE PO BOX 8769 ARCATA, CA 95521	34102 SPENCE GENETICS	$17.95	400	$7180.00

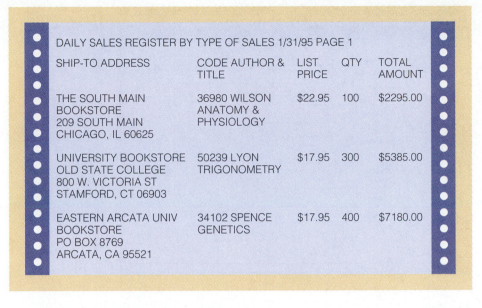

DAILY SALES REGISTER BY TYPE OF SALES 1/31/95 PAGE 1

A typical business report displays data fields in columns on a page.

to qualify for postal discounts on catalog mailings. A **sort** command allows you to arrange records in alphabetic or numeric order based on values in one or more fields.

Printing reports, labels, and form letters. In addition to displaying information on the screen, database programs can produce a variety of printouts. The most common type of database printout is a **report**—an ordered list of selected records and fields in an easy-to-read form. Most business reports arrange data in tables with rows for individual records and columns for selected fields; they often include summary lines containing calculated totals and averages for groups of records.

Database programs can also be used to produce mailing labels and customized form letters. Most database programs don't actually print letters; they simply **export** or transmit the necessary records and fields to word processors with **mail merge** capabilities, which then take on the task of printing the letters.

The User's View

Selecting, Sorting, and Reporting

Software: Claris FileMaker Pro.

Last name	First name	Phone
Bean	Lentil	847-6020
Black	TJ	602/778-2622
Bliss	Susan	816/962-1114
Bravera	Maria	752-8818
Brooksforce	Kathryn	754-8048
Chan	Fred	758-5086
Cochran	Lynn	754-9993
Dengler	Wolfgang and Maryanne	745-5729
Dymond	Jan and Jack	752-1928
Gladstone	Barbara and Neal	929-3882
Harlan	Cathy	314/444-4373
Heisner	Mark	314/444-2857
Heisner	Phil	854-3324
Holmes	Jeanne	753-8020
Johansen	Kim	415/649-1159
Johnson	Michael	929-2922
Reigelman	Kathy	816/444-5755

Your computerized address book offers many advantages over a paper notebook, but it's not particularly handy when you want to make a quick call to a friend or family member. You need a postable printout of names and phone numbers for frequently called entries. The process of creating a report like this one involves selecting the desired records, designing a layout for the report, sorting the records in the appropriate order, and printing the report.

When you select the Find command, the screen displays an empty form. If you type values into the fields, the program will locate records with fields that match those values. The field you want to match is not a typed field, however; it's the Call often check box. When you click that check box and the Find button, the program indicates that 19 of 109 records were selected because they had Frequent Call checked. You can now work with this collection of records.

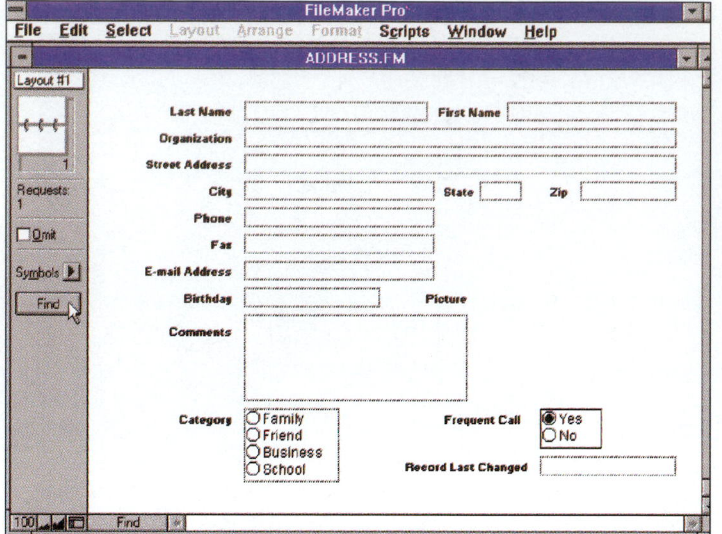

The next step is to create a new layout for the phone list. You choose Columnar report from the list of options and name it Phone List.

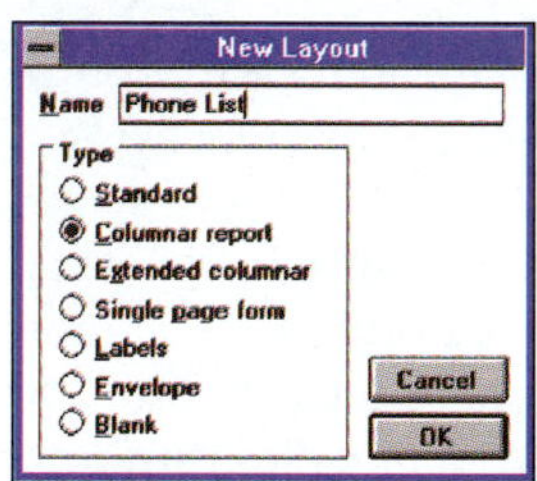

Another dialog box allows you to select the fields that will appear in the report. You select Last Name, First Name, and Phone, in that order.

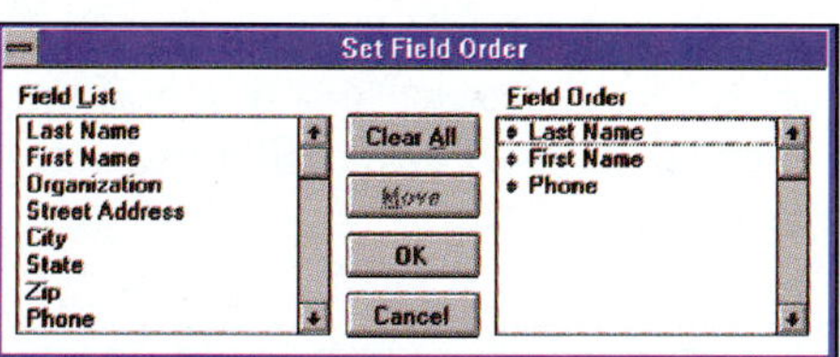

Because this layout is a list view, each row contains a record and each column represents a field.

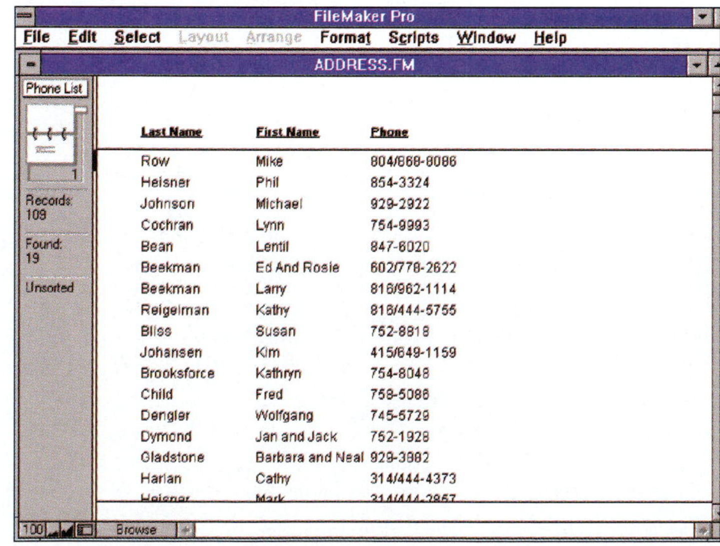

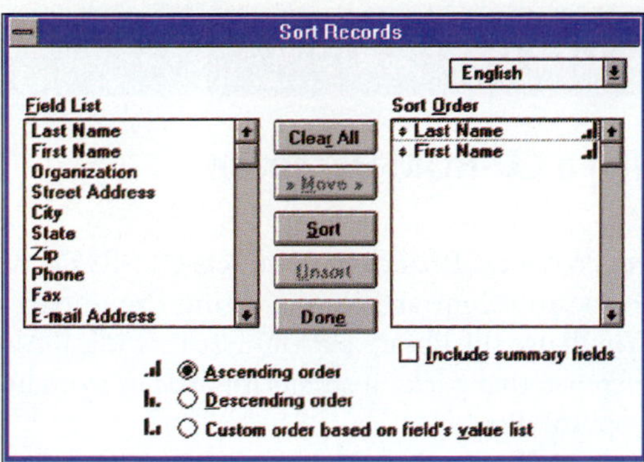

The physical layout is OK, but the records still need to be alphabetized for easy lookup. When you choose the Sort command, a dialog box allows you to choose which fields will be used for the sort. You specify that records should first be sorted according to Last Name in ascending (A to Z) order. You add First Name to the Sort Order list so records with identical last names will be alphabetized according to first name. When you click Sort, the records are rearranged as you requested.

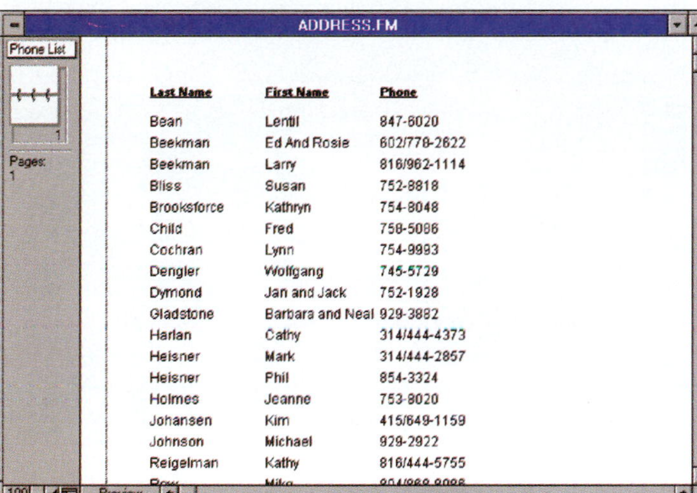

Finally, you preview the report on screen before committing it to paper.

Complex queries. Queries may be simple or complex, but either way they must be precise and unambiguous. With appropriate databases, queries could be constructed to find

- in a hospital's patient database, the names and locations of all of the patients on the hospital's fifth and sixth floors
- in a database of airline flight schedules, the least expensive way to fly from Boston to San Francisco on Tuesday afternoon
- in a politician's database, all voters who contributed more than $1000 to last year's legislative campaign and who wrote to express concern over gun control laws since the election

These may be legitimate targets for queries, but they aren't expressed in a form that most database programs can understand. The exact method for performing a query depends on the user interface of the database software. Most programs allow the user to specify the rules of the search by filling in a dialog box or a blank on-screen form. Some require the user to type the request using a special **query language** that's more precise than English. For example, to view the records for males between 18 and 35, you might type *Display for sex = 'male' and age > '18' and age < '35'*. Many

The User's View

Querying a CD-ROM Database

Software: ProQuest Periodical Abstracts CD-ROM database.
Goal: To locate recent articles discussing the impact of computers on personal privacy. You'll use the library's ProQuest Periodical Abstracts CD-ROM, an electronic reference that packs abstracts for articles from hundreds of magazines onto a 5-inch optical disk.

After you load the CD, run the program, and respond to the opening screens, the program prompts you to type a key word or phrase and press Return.

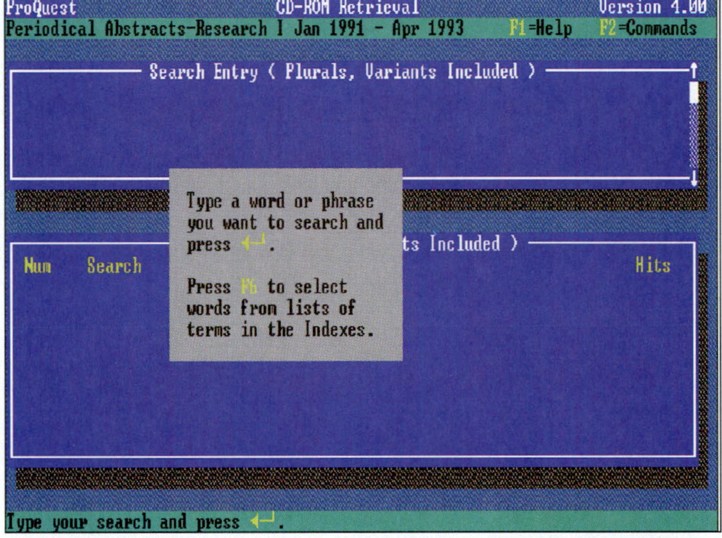

You want to search for two key words, so you type "computer or privacy" to indicate that you want to locate all records that have either of those two key words in their title or abstract fields. You press Enter (Return) to trigger the search. In a few seconds the search reveals that 9341 records contain computer, 450 contain privacy, and a total of 9751 contain at least two target words.

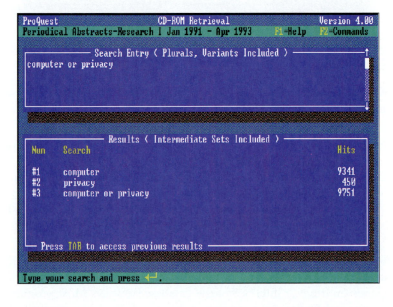

```
ProQuest                     CD-ROM Retrieval                    Version 4.00
Periodical Abstracts-Research I Jan 1991 - Apr 1993      F1=Help   F2=Commands

            Search Entry ( Plurals, Variants Included )
computer or privacy

            Results ( Intermediate Sets Included )
Num   Search                                                             Hits

#1    computer                                                           9341
#2    privacy                                                             450
#3    computer or privacy                                                9751

  Press TAB to access previous results
Type your search and press ↵.
```

ProQuest CD-ROM Retrieval Version 4.00
Periodical Abstracts-Research I Jan 1991 - Apr 1993 F1=Help F2=Commands
Search Entry (Plurals, Variants Included)
computer and privacy
Press ↵ to view titles, F7 to view full records
Results (Intermediate Sets Included)

Num	Search	Hits
#1	computer	9341
#2	privacy	450
#3	computer or privacy	9751
#4	computer	9341
#5	privacy	450
#6	computer and privacy	40

Press TAB to access previous results
Type your search and press ↵.

Your search strategy was flawed. Most of the articles listed for computer probably have nothing to do with privacy, so you've selected a large collection of mostly irrelevant titles. You return to the search screen and try again, this time typing a request for records that contain both "computer *and* privacy." The search reveals 40 records that contain both words, driving home the importance of choosing every word carefully when defining a database query.

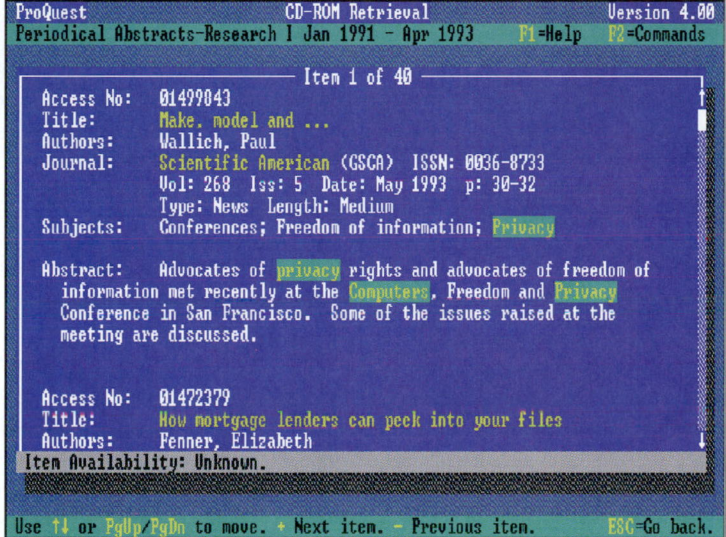

ProQuest CD-ROM Retrieval Version 4.00
Periodical Abstracts-Research I Jan 1991 - Apr 1993 F1=Help F2=Commands
Item 1 of 40
Access No: 01499043
Title: Make, model and ...
Authors: Wallich, Paul
Journal: Scientific American (GSCA) ISSN: 0036-8733
Vol: 268 Iss: 5 Date: May 1993 p: 30-32
Type: News Length: Medium
Subjects: Conferences; Freedom of information; Privacy
Abstract: Advocates of privacy rights and advocates of freedom of information met recently at the Computers, Freedom and Privacy Conference in San Francisco. Some of the issues raised at the meeting are discussed.
Access No: 01472379
Title: How mortgage lenders can peek into your files
Authors: Fenner, Elizabeth
Item Availability: Unknown.
Use ↑↓ or PgUp/PgDn to move. + Next item. - Previous item. ESC=Go back.

You press Enter (Return) to see the complete abstracts for those records. Or course, there's no guarantee that you've found all of the references on the subjects; you can only be sure that you've found all of the abstracts that contained both words. If you don't find what you're looking for in this list, you might need to try different search strategies.

database programs include programming languages so queries can be included in programs and performed automatically when the programs are executed. Some programs even accept queries generated by other software applications. But while the details of the process vary, the underlying logic is consistent from program to program.

Special-Purpose Database Programs

Specialized database software is preprogrammed for specific data storage and retrieval purposes. The CD-ROM databases used in many libraries are examples of special-purpose database programs. Users of special-purpose databases don't generally need to define file structures or design forms because these details have been taken care of by the designers of the software. In fact, some special-purpose database programs are not even sold as databases; they have names that more accurately reflect their purpose.

Many specialized database programs are sold as **personal information managers (PIMs)** or **electronic organizers**. A personal information manager can automate some or all of these functions:

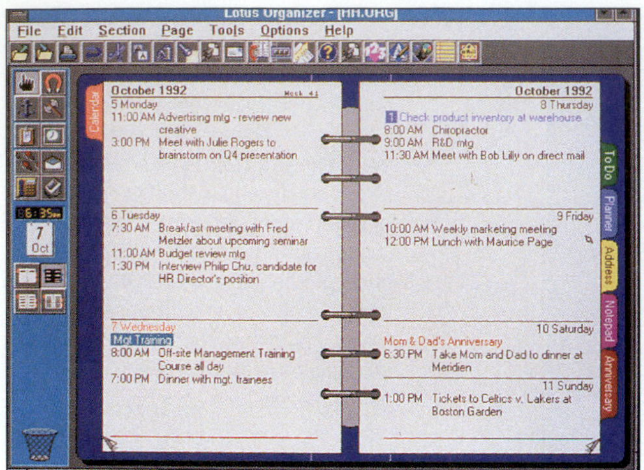

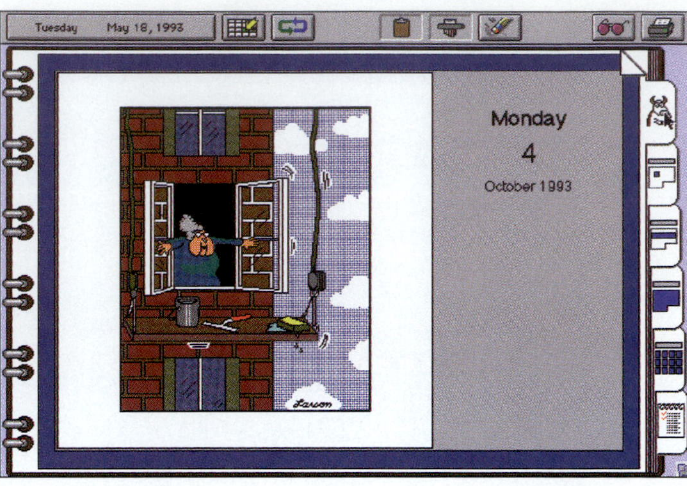

The user interface of personal information management software is especially important because of the constant interaction between the user and the software. PIM user interfaces range from notebook-style datebook/to-do lists to comic calendars with occasional animated surprises. (Software: Organizer from Lotus and Far Side Calendar from Amaze.)

- *Address/phone book.* PIM address books provide options for quickly displaying specific records and printing mailing labels, address books, and reports. Some include automatic phone-dialing options and fields for recording phone notes.
- *Appointment calendar.* A typical PIM calendar allows you to enter appointments and events and display or print them in a variety of formats, ranging from one day at a time to a monthly overview. Many include built-in alarms for last-minute reminders.
- *To-do list.* Most PIMs allow users to enter and organize ongoing lists of things to do and archive lists of completed tasks.
- *Miscellaneous notes.* Some PIMs accept diary entries, personal notes, and other hard-to-categorize tidbits of information.

PIMs are popular among people with busy schedules and countless contacts. They're easier to understand and use than general-purpose database programs, and they offer distinct advantages in speed and flexibility over their leather-bound paper counterparts. For people on the go, PIMs work especially well with notebook and laptop computers. But PIMs aren't for everybody; many people find that the standard features built into personal information management software don't meet their needs or match their style. Personal information management is, in the end, personal.

Beyond the Basics: Database Management Systems

When we try to pick out anything, we find it hitched to everything else in the universe.

—*John Muir,* *former director of the National Park Service*

So far we've used simple examples to illustrate concepts common to most database programs. This oversimplification is useful for understanding the basics, but it's not the whole story. In truth database programs range from simple mailing label programs to massive financial information systems, and it's important to know a little about what makes them different as well as what makes them alike.

From File Managers to Database Management Systems

Technically speaking, consumer-oriented database programs like the ones we've examined so far aren't really database managers at all; they're file managers. A **file manager** is a program that allows users to work with one file at a time. A true **database management system (DBMS)** is a program or system of programs that can manipulate data in a large collection of files, cross-referencing between files as needed. A database management system can be used interactively, or it can be controlled directly by other programs. A file manager is sufficient for mailing lists and other common data management applications. But for many large, complex jobs, there's no substitute for a true database management system.

Consider, for example, the problem of managing student information at a college. It's easy to see how databases might be used to store this information: a file containing one record for each student, with fields for name, student ID number, address, phone, and so on. But a typical student generates far too much information to store practically in a single data file.

Most schools choose to keep several files containing student information: one for financial records, one for course enrollment and grade transcripts, and so on. Each of these files has a single record for each student. In addition, a school must maintain class enrollment files with one record for each class and fields for information on each student enrolled in the class. Three of these files might be organized as shown below.

Student information is duplicated in several different files of this inefficient, error-prone database.

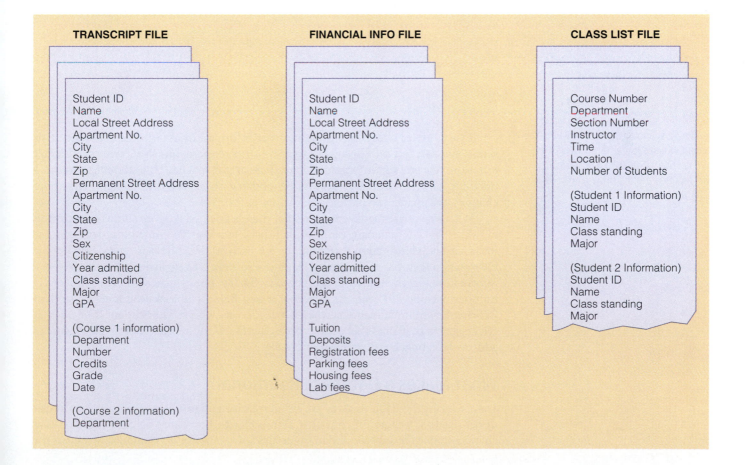

TRANSCRIPT FILE

Student ID
Name
Local Street Address
Apartment No.
City
State
Zip
Permanent Street Address
Apartment No.
City
State
Zip
Sex
Citizenship
Year admitted
Class standing
Major
GPA

(Course 1 information)
Department
Number
Credits
Grade
Date

(Course 2 information)
Department

FINANCIAL INFO FILE

Student ID
Name
Local Street Address
Apartment No.
City
State
Zip
Permanent Street Address
Apartment No.
City
State
Zip
Sex
Citizenship
Year admitted
Class standing
Major
GPA

Tuition
Deposits
Registration fees
Parking fees
Housing fees
Lab fees

CLASS LIST FILE

Course Number
Department
Section Number
Instructor
Time
Location
Number of Students

(Student 1 Information)
Student ID
Name
Class standing
Major

(Student 2 Information)
Student ID
Name
Class standing
Major

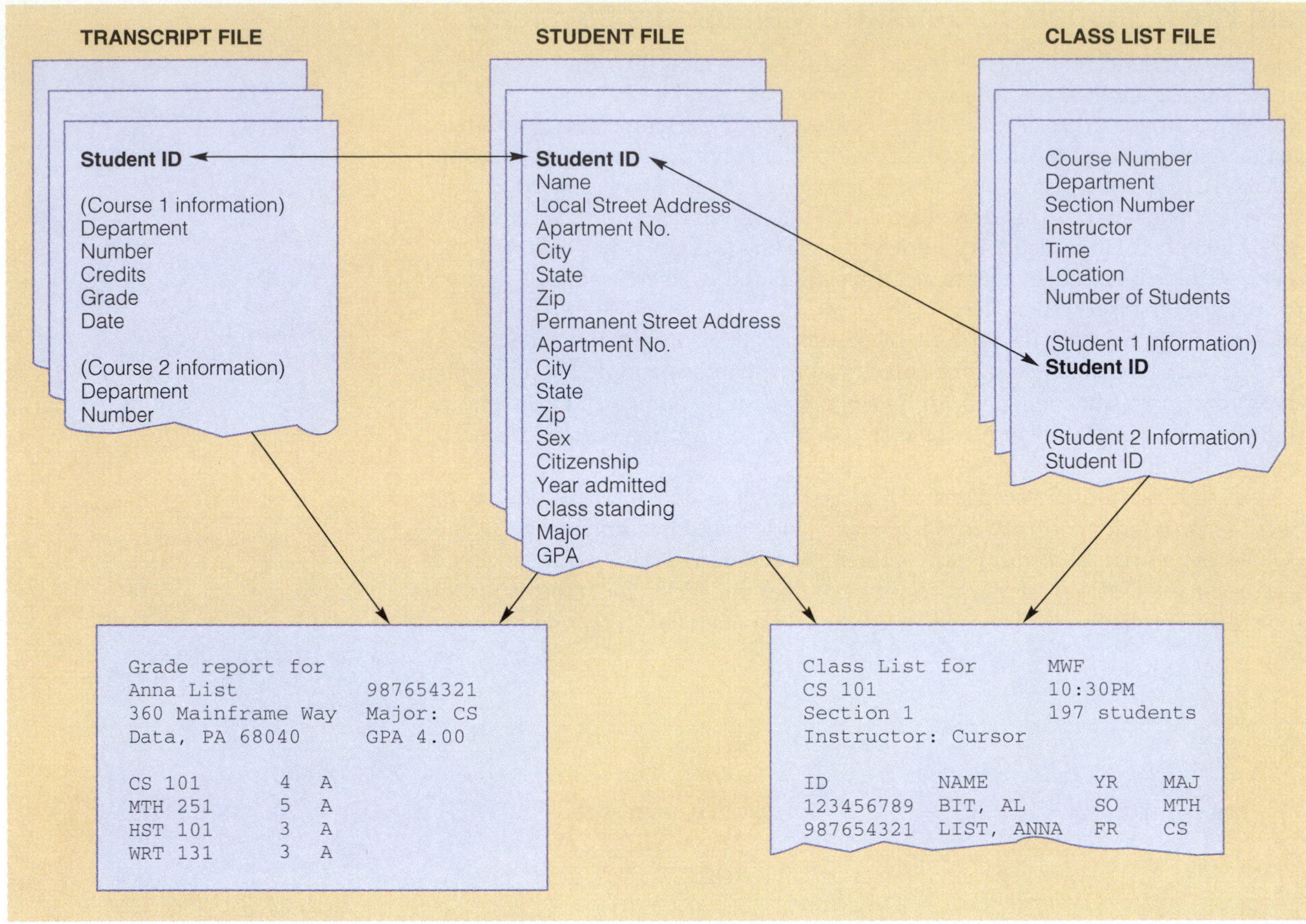

The Student file serves as a reference when grade reports and class lists are created. The Student ID fields in the Transcript file and the Class List file are used as a key for locating the necessary student information in the Student file.

Every one of these files contains basic information about every student. This redundant data not only occupies expensive storage space, but also it makes it difficult to ensure that student information is accurate and up to date. If a student moves to a different address, several files must be updated to reflect this change. The more changes, the greater the likelihood of a data-entry error.

With a database management system there's no need to store all this information in every file. The database can include a basic student file containing demographic information—information that's unique for each student. Because the demographic information is stored in a separate file, it doesn't need to be included in the financial information file, the transcript file, the class list file, or any other file. The student ID number, included in each file, serves as a **key field**; it unlocks the relevant student information in the Student file when it's needed elsewhere. The Student ID field is, in effect, shared by all files that use data from this file. If the student moves, the change of address need only be recorded in one place.

What Makes a Database Relational?

Databases organized in this way are called **relational databases**. To most users a relational database program is one that allows files to be related to each other so that changes in one file are reflected in other files automatically. To computer scientists the term *relational database* has a technical definition related to the underlying structure of the data and the rules specifying how that data can be manipulated.

The structure of a relational database is based on the *relational model*—a mathematical model that combines data in tables. Other kinds of database management systems are based on different theoretical models, with different technical advantages and disadvantages. But the majority of database management systems in use today, including virtually all PC-based database management systems, use the relational model. So from the average computer user's point of view, the distinction between the popular and technical definitions of *relational* is academic.

The Many Faces of Databases

Large databases can contain hundreds of interrelated files. This maze of information could be overwhelming to users if they were forced to deal with it directly. Fortunately a database management system can shield users from the complex inner workings of the system, providing them with only the information and commands they need to get their jobs done. In fact, a well-designed database puts on different faces for different classes of users.

Clerks, managers, and programmers see different views of a video rental store's database. The clerk's view allows only for simple data-entry and check-out procedures. The manager, working with the same database, has control over pricing, policies, and inventory but can't change the structure or user interface of the database. The programmer can work "under the hood" to fine-tune and customize the database so it can better meet the needs of other employees.

Manager's view 1

Inventory tracking view used by managers to check on rental history and inventory for individual movies

Video store database

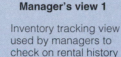

Clerk's view

Video rental view used by clerks to access renter information, scan bar codes on videos, and print rental invoices

Manager's view 2

Policy view used by managers to change pricing, membership, and other policies

Technician/Programmer's View

Technical view used by programmer to create other user interfaces and custom queries

Retail clerks don't need to be able to access every piece of information in the store's database; they just need to enter sales transactions on point-of-sale terminals. Databases designed for retail outlets generally include simple, straightforward terminal interfaces that give the clerks only the information, and the power, they need to process transactions. Managers, accountants, and data processing specialists see the database from different points of view because they need to work with the data in different ways.

Downsizing and Decentralizing

Advances in the last two decades have changed the way most organizations deal with data. The earliest file management programs could only do **batch processing**, which required users to accumulate transactions and feed them into computers in large batches. These batch systems weren't able to provide the kind of immediate feedback we expect today. Questions like "What's the balance in my checking account?" or "Are there any open flights to Denver next Tuesday?" were likely to be answered "Those records will be updated tonight, so we'll let you know tomorrow."

Today disk drives, inexpensive memory, and sophisticated software have allowed **interactive processing** to replace batch processing for most applications. Users can now interact with data through terminals, viewing and changing values in *real time*. Batch processing is still used for printing periodic bills, invoices, and reports and for making backup copies of data files—jobs for which it makes sense to do a lot of transactions at once. But for applications that demand immediacy, such as airline reservations, banking transactions, and the like, interactive, multiuser database systems have taken over.

Until recently most databases were housed in mainframe computers. But for a growing number of organizations, the traditional **centralized database** on a mainframe system is no longer the norm. Some companies use a **client/server** approach: Database software in client desktop computers works with files stored in central server databases on mainframes, minicomputers, or desktop computers. Other companies use **distributed databases** that use data strewn out across networks on several different computers. From the user's point of view, the differences between these approaches may not be apparent. In every case the goal is to provide quick and easy access to important information.

Tomorrow's Databases?

Databases continue to evolve. Standards are emerging to make it easier for programmers, technicians, and users to work with databases on different hardware and software systems. In particular, most database management programs now support **SQL** (**Structured Query Language**)—the emerging standard for programming complex queries. Because SQL is available for many different database management systems, programmers and sophisticated users don't need to learn new query languages when they work with different hardware and software systems. Many modern users are insulated from the complexities of the query language by graphical user interfaces that allow point-and-click queries.

But the biggest changes in database technology in the next few years may take place under the surface. Many computer scientists believe that the relational data model may be supplanted in the next decade by an object-oriented data model, and that most future databases will be **object-oriented databases** rather than relational databases. Instead of storing records in tables and hierarchies, object-oriented databases store software *objects* that contain procedures (or instructions) along with data. Object-oriented databases often are used in conjunction with object-oriented programming languages, which are discussed in Chapter 9. Experts suggest that object technology will make construction and manipulation of complex databases easier and

Rules of Thumb

Dealing with Databases

Whether you're creating an address file with a simple file manager or retrieving data from a full-blown relational database management system, you can save yourself a great deal of time and grief if you follow a few commonsense rules:

- **Choose the right tool for the job.** Don't invest time and money in a programmable relational database to computerize your little black address book, and don't try to run the affairs of your multinational corporation with a $99 file manager.
- **Think about how you'll get the information out before you put it in.** What kinds of files, records, and fields do you need to create to make it easy to find things quickly and print things the way you want them? For example, you must use separate fields for first and last names if you want to sort names alphabetically and print first names first.
- **Start with a plan, and be prepared to change it.** Do a trial run with a small amount of data to make sure everything works the way you think it should.
- **Make your data consistent.** Inconsistencies can mess up sorting and make searching difficult. For example, if your database includes residents of Minnesota, Minn., and MN, you'll have a hard time grouping people by state.
- **Databases are only as good as their data.** When you enter data take advantage of the data-checking capability of your database software. Does the first name field contain nonalphabetic characters? Is the birth date within a reasonable range? Automatic data checking is important, but it's no substitute for human proofreading or for a bit of skepticism when using the database.
- **Query with care.** You get what you ask for, even if it's not what you want. Here's a real example: A student searching a database of classic rock albums requested all records containing the string "Dylan", and the database program obediently displayed the names of several Bob Dylan albums, plus one by Jimi Hendrix called *Electric Ladyland*. Why? Because *dylan* is part of *Ladyland*! Unwanted records can go unnoticed in large database selections, so it's important to define selection rules very carefully.
- **If at first you don't succeed, try another approach.** If your search doesn't turn up the answers you were looking for, it doesn't mean the answers aren't there; they may just be wearing a disguise. For example, if you search the OASIS Library database for "Viet Nam War" references, you won't find any. Why? Because the government officially classifies the Viet Nam War as a *conflict*, so references are stored under the subject "Viet Nam Conflict." Technology meets bureaucracy!

less time consuming. Users will find databases more flexible and responsive as object technology becomes more widespread, even though users probably will not be aware of the underlying technological reasons for these improvements.

Ultimately database technology will all but disappear from the user's view as interfaces become simpler and, at the same time, more intelligent. As you'll see in upcoming chapters, tomorrow's databases will be able to respond intelligently to commands and queries issued in natural human language.

No Secrets: Computers and Privacy

Advanced technology has created new opportunities for America as a nation, but it has also created the possibility for new abuses of the individual American citizen. Adequate safeguards must always stand watch so that man remains master and never the victim of the computer.

—*Richard Nixon, Feb. 23, 1974*

Instant airline reservations, all-night automated banking, overnight mail, instant library searches—databases provide us with conveniences that were unthinkable a generation ago. But convenience isn't free. In the case of databases, the price we pay is our privacy.

The Privacy Problem

We live in an information age, and data is one of the currencies of our time. Businesses and government agencies spend billions of dollars every year to collect and exchange information about you and me. Credit and banking information, tax records, health data, insurance records, political contributions, voter registration, credit card purchases, warranty registrations, phone calls, passport registration, airline

When you shop by phone, respond to a survey, or fill out a warranty card, it's likely that a clerk somewhere will enter that data into a computer.

reservations, automobile registration, arrests—they're all recorded in computers, and we have little or no control over what happens to most of those records once they're collected.

For most of us this data is out of sight and out of mind. But everyday lives are changed because of these databases. Here are three representative stories:

- When Congress investigated ties between President Jimmy Carter's brother Billy and the government of Libya, they produced a report that detailed, among other things, the exact time and location of phone calls placed by Billy Carter in three different states. The phone records, which revealed a great deal about Billy Carter's activities, were obtained from AT&T's massive network of data-collecting computers. Similar information is available on every phone company customer.
- When a credit bureau mistakenly placed a bankruptcy filing in the file of a St. Louis couple, banks responded by shutting off loans for their struggling construction business, forcing them into *real* bankruptcy. They sued but lost because credit bureaus are protected by law from financial responsibility for "honest" mistakes!
- A Los Angeles thief stole a wallet and used its contents to establish an artificial identity. When the thief was arrested for a robbery involving murder, the crime was recorded under the wallet owner's name in police databases. The legitimate owner of the wallet was arrested five times in the following 14 months and spent several days in jail before a protracted court battle resulted in the deletion of the record.

Privacy violations aren't new, and they don't always involve computers. The German Nazis, the Chinese Communists, and even Richard Nixon's campaign committee practiced surveillance without computers. But the privacy problem takes on a whole new dimension in the age of high-speed computers and databases. The same characteristics that make databases more efficient than other information storage methods—storage capacity, retrieval speed, organizational flexibility, and ease of distribution of information—also make them a threat to our privacy.

Big Brother and Big Business

If all records told the same tale, then the lie passed into history and became truth.

—George Orwell, 1984

In George Orwell's *1984*, information about every citizen was stored in a massive database controlled by the ever-vigilant Big Brother. As it turns out, this kind of central computer is no longer necessary for producing computerized dossiers of private citizens. With modern networked computers it's easy to compile profiles by combining information from different database files. As long as the files share a single unique field, like your Social Security number, **record matching** is trivial and quick. And when database information is combined, the whole is often far greater than the sum of its parts.

Sometimes the results are clearly beneficial. Record matching is used by government enforcement agencies to locate criminals ranging from tax evaders to mass murderers. Because credit bureaus collect data about us, we can use credit cards to borrow money wherever we go. But these benefits come with at least three problems:

- *Data errors are common.* A study of 1500 reports from the three big credit bureaus found errors in 43 percent of the files.
- *Data can become nearly immortal.* Because data files are commonly sold, shared, and copied, it's just about impossible to delete or correct erroneous records with absolute certainty.

Rules of Thumb

Your Private Rights

Sometimes computer-aided privacy violations are nuisances; sometimes they're threats to life, liberty, and the pursuit of happiness. Here are a few tips for protecting your right to privacy:

- **Your Social Security number is yours; don't give it away.** Since your Social Security number is a unique identification, it can be used to gather information about you without your permission or knowledge. For example, you could be denied a job or insurance because of something you once put on a medical form. Never write it on a check or credit card receipt. Don't give your Social Security number to anyone unless they have a legitimate reason to ask for it.
- **Don't give away information about yourself.** Don't answer questions about yourself just because a questionnaire or company representative asks you to. When you fill out any form, think about whether you want the information stored in somebody else's computer.
- **Say no to direct mail and phone solicitations.** Businesses and political organizations pay for your data so they can target you for mail campaigns and phone solicitations. You can remove yourself from many lists by sending your name, address, and phone number with your request to Mail Preference Service/Phone Preference Service, Direct Mail Marketing Association, 6 East 43rd Street, New York, NY 10017. If this doesn't stop the flow, you might want to try a more direct approach. Send back unwanted letters along with the request, "Take me off your list" in the postage paid envelopes that come with them. When you receive an unsolicited phone-marketing call, tell the caller "I never purchase or donate anything as a result of phone solicitations" and ask to be removed from the list.
- **If you think there's incorrect or damaging information about you in a file, find out.** The Freedom of Information Act of 1966 requires that most records of U.S. government agencies be made available to the public on demand. The Privacy Act of 1974 requires federal agencies to provide you with information in your files relating to you and to amend incorrect records. The Fair Credit Reporting Act of 1970 allows you to see your credit ratings—free of charge if you have been denied credit—and correct any errors.
- **Support organizations that fight for privacy rights.** If you value privacy rights, let your representatives know how you feel, and support organizations such as the American Civil Liberties Union, Computer Professionals for Social Responsibility (P. O. Box 717, Palo Alto, CA 94302, 415/322-3778, electronic mail: cpsr@csli.stanford.edu), and others that fight for those rights.

- *Data isn't secure.* A *Business Week* reporter demonstrated this in 1989 by using his personal computer to obtain then Vice President Dan Quayle's credit report. Had he been a skilled computer criminal, he could just as easily have *changed* that report!

Protection against invasion of privacy is not explicitly guaranteed by the U.S. Constitution. Legal scholars agree that the **right to privacy**—freedom from interference into the private sphere of a person's affairs—is implied by other constitutional guarantees, although debates rage about exactly what this means. Federal and state laws provide various forms of privacy protection, but most of those laws were written years ago. When it comes to privacy violation, technology is far ahead of the law.

Democracy depends on the free flow of information, but it also depends on the protection of individual rights. Maintaining a balance is not easy, especially when new information technologies are being developed at such a rapid pace. With information at our fingertips, it's tempting to think that more information is the answer. But in the words of Will Rogers, "It's not the things we don't know that get us into trouble, it's the things we do know that ain't so."

Summary

Database programs allow users to quickly and efficiently store, organize, retrieve, communicate, and manage large amounts of information. Each database file is a collection of records, and each record is made up of fields containing text strings, numbers, and other chunks of information. Database programs allow users to view data in a variety of ways, sort records in any order, and print reports, mailing labels, and other custom printouts. A user can search for an individual record or select a group of records with a query.

While most database programs are general-purpose tools that can be used to create custom databases for any purpose, some are special-purpose tools programmed to do a particular set of tasks. Personal information managers, for example, provide automated address books, appointment calendars, to-do lists, and notebooks for busy individuals.

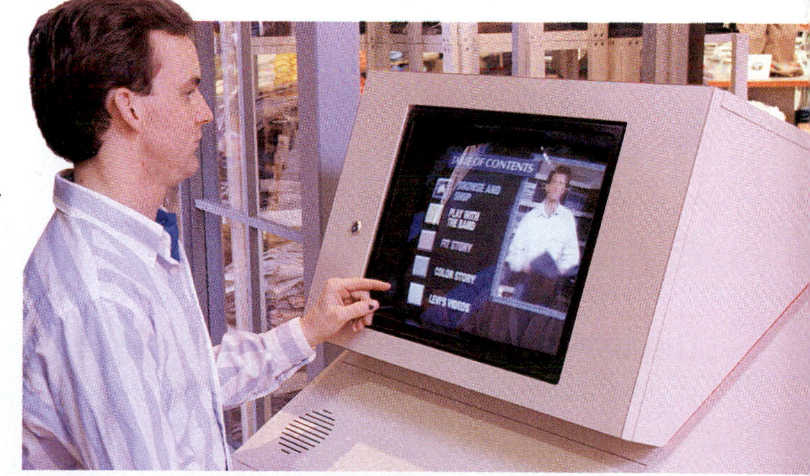

Many database programs are, technically speaking, file managers, because they work with only one file at a time. True database management systems (DBMS) can work with several files at once, cross-referencing information between files when appropriate. A DBMS can provide an efficient way to store and manage large quantities of information by eliminating the need for redundant information in different files. A well-designed database provides different views of the data to different classes of users, so each user sees and manipulates only the information necessary for the job at hand.

The accumulation of data by government agencies and businesses is a growing threat to our right to privacy. Massive amounts of information about private citizens are collected and exchanged for a variety of purposes. Today's technology makes it easy to combine information from different databases, producing detailed profiles of individual citizens. While there are many legitimate uses for these procedures, there's also a great potential for abuse.

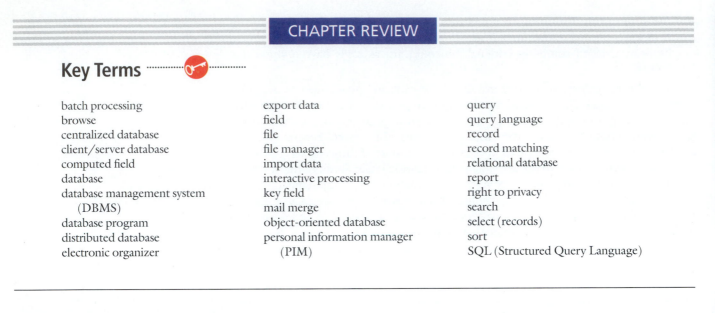

CHAPTER REVIEW

Key Terms 

batch processing
browse
centralized database
client/server database
computed field
database
database management system (DBMS)
database program
distributed database
electronic organizer
export data
field
file
file manager
import data
interactive processing
key field
mail merge
object-oriented database
personal information manager (PIM)
query
query language
record
record matching
relational database
report
right to privacy
search
select (records)
sort
SQL (Structured Query Language)

Review Questions 

1. What is the difference between a file manager and a database management system? How are they similar?
2. Describe the structure of a simple database. Use the terms *file*, *record*, and *field* in your description.
3. What is a query? Give examples of the kinds of questions that might be answered with a query.
4. What steps are involved in producing a standard multicolumn business report from a database?
5. What are the advantages of personal information management software over paper notebook organizers? What are the disadvantages?
6. What does it mean to sort a data file?
7. How can a database be designed to reduce the likelihood of data-entry errors?
8. Describe how record matching is used to obtain information about you. Give examples.
9. Do we have a legal right to privacy? On what grounds?
10. Why are computers important in discussions of invasion of privacy?

Discussion Questions 

1. Grade books, checkbooks, and other information collections can be managed with either a database program or a spreadsheet program. How would you decide which type of application is most appropriate for a given job?
2. What have you done this week that directly or indirectly involved a database? How would your week have been different in a world without databases?
3. "The computer is a great humanizing factor because it makes the individual more important. The more information we have on each individual, the more each individual counts." Do you agree with this statement by science fiction writer Isaac Asimov? Why, or why not?
4. Suppose you have been incorrectly billed for $100 from a mail-order house called Exploitations Unlimited. Your protestations are ignored by the company, which is now threatening to report you to a credit bureau and a collection agency. What do you do?
5. What advantages and disadvantages does a computerized law enforcement system have for law-abiding citizens?
6. In what ways were George Orwell's "predictions" in the novel *1984* accurate? In what ways was Orwell's vision wrong?

Projects 

1. Design a database for your own use. Create several records, sort the data, and print a report.
2. Find out as much as you can about someone (for example, yourself or a public figure) from public records like tax records, court records, voter registration lists, and motor vehicle files.
3. Find out as much as you can about your own credit rating.
4. The next time you order something by mail or phone, try encoding your name with a unique spelling so you can recognize when the company sells your name and address to other companies. Use several different spellings for different orders if you want to do some comparative research.
5. Determine what information about you is stored in your school computers. What information are you allowed to see? What information are others allowed to see? Exactly who may access your files? Can you find out who sees your files? How long is the information retained after you leave?
6. Keep track of your purchases for a few weeks. If other people had access to this information, what conclusions might they be able to draw about you?

Sources and Resources 

Like word processors and spreadsheet software, database programs have inspired hundreds of how-to tutorials, user's guides, and reference books. If you're working with a popular program, you should have no trouble finding a book to help you develop your skills.

Database 101: A Database Primer for the Rest of Us, by Guy Kawasaki (Berkeley, CA: Peachpit Press, 1991). In spite of the author's unabashed Macintosh bias (he's a former Apple executive), this book is a plain-speaking introduction to databases in general from the user's point of view. The accompanying disk includes test-drive versions of two popular Macintosh databases.

Information Anxiety, by Richard Saul Wurman (New York: Doubleday, 1989). Information anxiety, according to Wurman, happens when information doesn't tell us what we want or need to know. This clever and witty book provides insight into organizing information to avoid this modern malady. Its unusual organization makes it easy to read in just about any order.

Computer Ethics, by Tom Forester and Perry Morrison (Cambridge, MA: MIT Press, 1990). This book is an excellent survey of the issues that face computer professionals and computer users today. The chapter on privacy is chilling.

The Rise of the Computer State, by David Burnham (New York: Random House, 1983). In spite of its age, this book provides an interesting perspective on the politics of information.

CHAPTER

SEVEN

Telecommunication and Networking

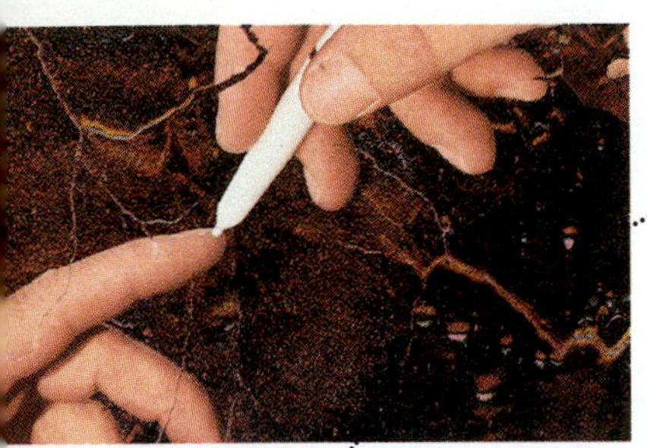

Arthur C. Clarke's Magical Prophecy

If an elderly but distinguished scientist says that something is possible he is almost certainly right, but if he says that it is impossible he is very probably wrong.

The only way to find the limits of the possible is to go beyond them into the impossible.

Any sufficiently advanced technology is indistinguishable from magic.

—*Clarke's Three Laws*

After reading this chapter you should be able to

- describe the nature and function of local area networks and wide area networks
- discuss the uses and implications of electronic mail, teleconferencing, and other forms of on-line communication
- describe several ways people use information utilities and electronic bulletin boards
- describe current and future trends in telecommunications and networking

Besides coining Clarke's laws, British writer Arthur C. Clarke has written more than 100 works of science fiction and nonfiction. His most famous work was the monumental 1968 film *2001: A Space Odyssey,* in which he collaborated with director Stanley Kubrick. The film's villain, a faceless English-speaking computer with a lust for power, sparked many public debates about the nature and risks of artificial intelligence.

Arthur C. Clarke

But Clarke's most visionary work may be a paper published in 1945 in which he predicted the use of geostationary **communications satellites**—satellites that match Earth's rotation so they can hang in a stationary position relative to the spinning planet below. Clarke's paper pinpointed the exact height of the orbit required to match the movement of the satellite with the planetary rotation. He

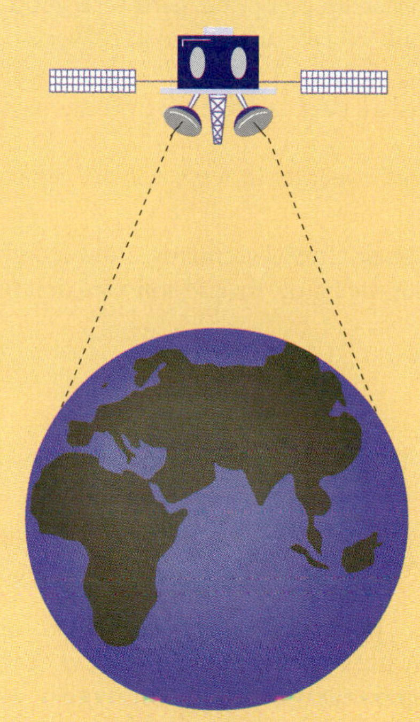

also suggested that these satellites could replace many telephone cables and radio towers, allowing electronic signals to be beamed across oceans, deserts, and mountain ranges, linking the people of the world with a single communications network.

A decade after Clarke's paper appeared, powerful rockets and sensitive radio receiving equipment made communications satellites realistic. In 1964 the first synchronous TV satellite was launched, marking the beginning of a billion-dollar industry that has changed the way people communicate.

Today Clarke is often referred to as the father of satellite communications. He lives in Sri Lanka, where he continues his work as a writer, but now he uses a personal computer and beams his words around the globe to editors using the satellites he envisioned half a century ago.

The Battle of New Orleans, the bloodiest battle of the War of 1812, was fought two weeks after the war officially ended; it took that long for the cease-fire message to travel from Washington, D.C., to the front line. In 1991, 179 years later, six hard-line Soviet communists staged a coup to turn back the tide of democratic and economic reforms that were sweeping the U.S.S.R. Within hours messages zipped between the Soviet Union and western nations on telephone and computer networks. Cable television and computer conferences provided up-to-the-minute analyses of events—analyses that were beamed to computer bulletin boards inside the Soviet Union. Fax machines and cellular phones carried messages among resistors, allowing them to stay steps ahead of the coup leaders and the Soviet military machine. People toppled the coup, and ultimately the Soviet Union, not with guns but with courage, will, and timely information.

Telecommunication technology—the technology of long-distance communication—has come a long way since the War of 1812, and the world has changed dramatically as a result. After Samuel Morse invented the telegraph in 1844, people could, for the first time, send long-distance messages instantaneously. Thomas Edison's invention of the telephone in 1876 extended this capability to the spoken voice. Today systems of linked computers allow us to send data and software across the room or around the world. The technological transformation has changed the popular definition of the word *telecommunication*, which today means long-distance *electronic* communication in a variety of forms.

In this chapter we'll look at the computer as part of a network rather than as a self-contained appliance, and we'll discuss ways such linked computers are used for communication and information gathering. We'll also consider how the explosive growth of computer networks is changing the way we live and work.

A student uses a terminal in the library to connect with an on-line information source.

Linking Up: Network Basics

Imagine how useful an office would be without a door.

—*Computer visionary Douglas Engelbart, on the importance of network connections*

A computer **network** is any computer system that links together two or more computers. Why is networking important? The answers to this question revolve around the three essential components of every computer system:

- *Hardware.* Networks allow people to share computer hardware, reducing costs and making it possible for more people to take advantage of powerful computer equipment.
- *Software.* Networks allow people to share data and software programs, increasing efficiency and productivity.
- *People.* Networks allow people to work together in ways that are otherwise difficult or impossible.

Important information is hidden in these three statements. But before we examine them in more detail, we need to look at the hardware and software that make computer networks possible.

Basic Network Anatomy

In Chapter 2 we saw how information travels among the CPU, memory, and other components within a computer as electrical impulses that move along collections of parallel wires called buses. A network extends the range of these information pulses, allowing them to travel to other computers.

Buses to ports. Most computers have **ports**—sockets that allow information to pass in and out. *Parallel ports*, commonly used to connect printers and other external peripherals to a computer, are wide enough to allow bits to pass through in groups of 8, 16, or 32. *Serial ports*, on the other hand, require bits to pass through one at a time. Various types of serial ports typically serve as gateways for information traveling from one computer to another. Some computers have built-in serial ports that include the hardware necessary to connect computers in a network. Others require some type of *network interface* to be added before they can be connected to a network. The type of card or port varies depending on the computer and the type of network connector needed.

In the simplest networks two or more computers are linked by cables connected to their serial ports. But direct connection is impractical for computers that are miles or oceans apart. For computers to communicate over long distances, they need to transmit information through other paths.

Communication à la modem. The world is outfitted with plenty of electronic communication paths: An intricate network of cables, radio transmitters, and satellites allows people to talk by telephone between just about any two places on the planet. The telephone network is ideal for connecting remote computers, too, except it was designed to carry sound waves, not streams of bits. Before a **digital signal**—a stream of bits—can be transmitted over a standard phone line, it must be converted to an **analog signal**—a continuous wave. At the receiving end the analog signal first must be converted back into the bits representing the original digital message. Each of these tasks is performed by a **modem** (short for *mo*dulator/*dem*odulator)—a hardware device that connects a computer's serial port to a telephone line.

An internal modem is installed on a circuit board inside the computer's chassis. An external modem sits in a box linked to the computer's serial port. Both types use

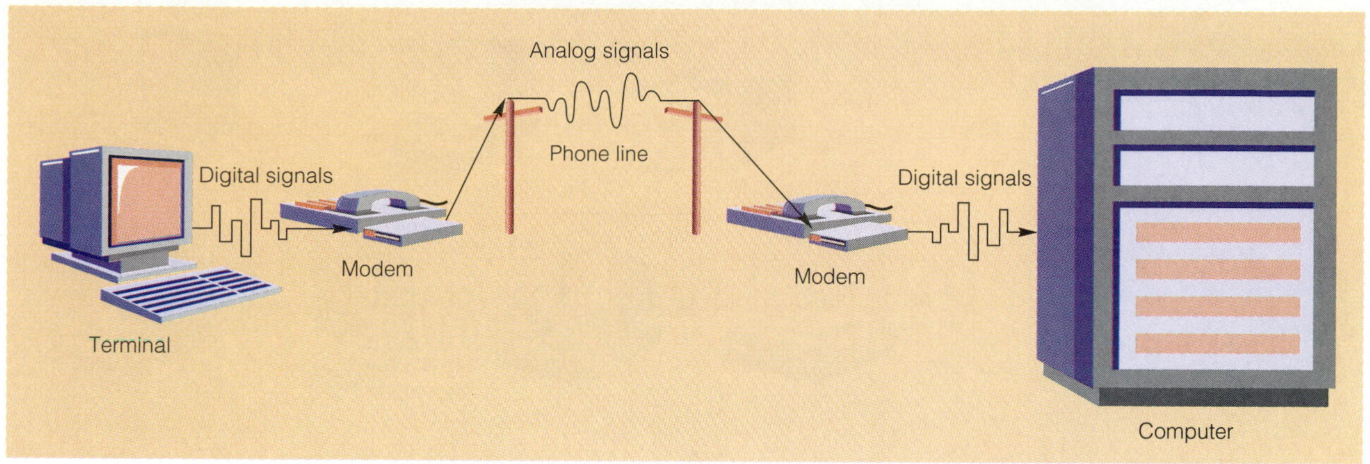

A modem converts digital signals from a computer or terminal into analog signals. The analog waves are transmitted through telephone lines to another modem, which converts them back into digital signals.

phone cable to connect to the telephone network through standard modular phone jacks. Modems differ in their transmission speeds, measured in **bits per second** (**bps**). Many people use the term *baud rate* instead of bps, but bps is technically more accurate for high-speed modems. Inexpensive modems today commonly transmit at 1200 bps or 2400 bps; more expensive models transmit at 9600 bps or more. In general, communication by modem is slower than communication among computers that are directly connected on a network.

Networks Near and Far

Never in history has distance meant less.

—Alvin Toffler, *Future Shock*

Computer networks come in all shapes and sizes, but most can be categorized as either local area networks or wide area networks.

A **local area network** (**LAN**) is a network in which the computers are close to each other, usually in the same building. A typical local area network includes a collection of computers and peripherals whose serial ports are directly connected by cables. These cables serve as information highways for transporting data between devices. In a **wireless network** each computer has a tiny radio connected to its serial port so it can send and receive data through the air rather than through cables. Wireless networks are uncommon today, but their popularity is growing as the technology improves.

All computers on a LAN do not have to be the same brand, or use the same operating system. A network might include Macintoshes, IBM PS/2s, and other PCs. The computers can be connected in many different ways, and many rules dictate what will

An external modem connects to the computer's serial port. An internal modem is installed inside the computer's chassis.

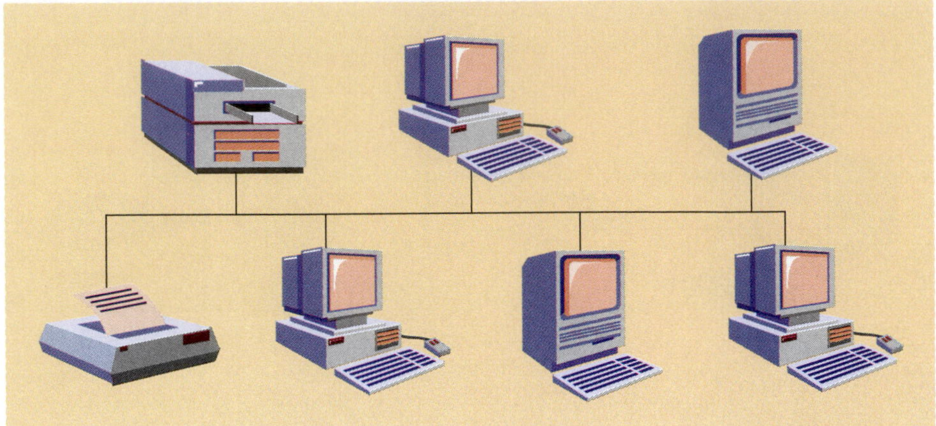

A local area network can contain a variety of computers and peripherals connected through serial ports.

and won't work. Most organizations depend on *network administrators* to take care of the behind-the-scenes details so others can focus on *using* the network.

A **wide area network** (**WAN**), as the name implies, is a network that extends over a long distance. Wide area networks are possible because of the web of telephone lines, microwave relay towers, and satellites that spans the globe. Some WANs are private operations designed to link corporate offices. Others are public or semipublic networks used by people from a variety of organizations.

Communication Software

Whether connected by cables or a combination of modems and telephone lines, computers need some kind of **communication software** to interact. To communicate with each other, two machines must follow the same **protocol**—a set of rules for the exchange of data between a terminal and a computer or between two computers. One

Wide area networks are often made up of LANs linked by phone lines, microwave towers, and communication satellites.

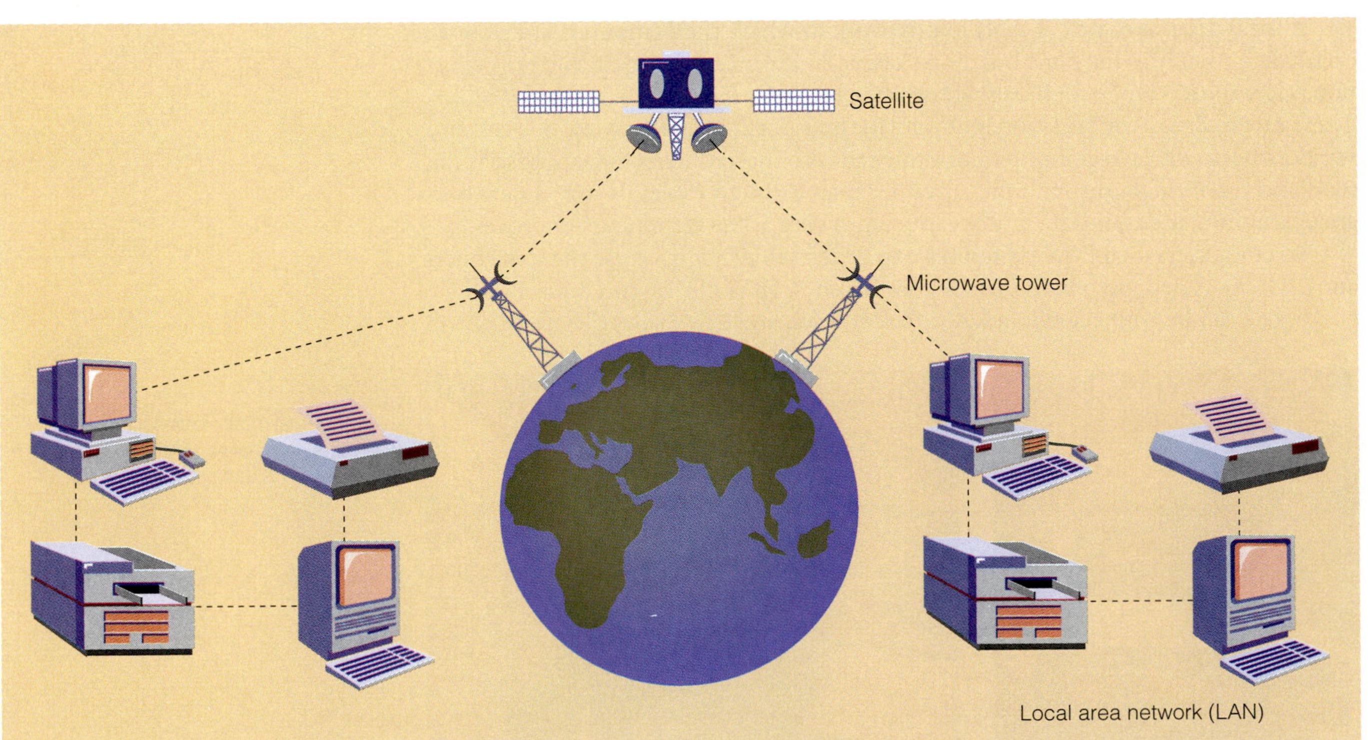

such protocol is transmission speed: If one machine is "talking" at 2400 bps and the other is "listening" at 1200 bps, the message doesn't get through. Protocols include prearranged codes for messages such as "Are you ready?", "I am about to start sending a data file," and "Did you receive that file?" For two computers to understand each other, the software on both machines must be set to follow the same protocols. Communication software makes sure protocol is followed by the computer's hardware.

Communication software can take a variety of forms. For users who work exclusively on a local area network, many communication tasks can be taken care of with a **network operating system**, such as Novell's Netware. Just as a personal computer's operating system shields the user from most of the nuts and bolts of the computer's operation, a network operating system shields the user from the hardware and software details of routine communication between machines. Some operating systems, including Apple's System 7 and Microsoft's Windows for Workgroups, incorporate basic communications capabilities in each computer's operating system.

Outside of a LAN, the most familiar type of communication software is the **terminal program**, which allows a personal computer to function as a terminal. This kind of program (sometimes called a *teminal emulator*) handles phone dialing, protocol management, and miscellaneous details necessary for making a personal computer and a modem work together. With terminal software and a modem, a personal computer can communicate through phone lines with another PC, a network of computers, or more commonly, a large multiuser computer.

At the other end of the line, the communication software is usually built into the multiuser operating system. This software allows a timesharing computer to communicate with several other computers or terminals at once. **UNIX**, an operating system developed at Bell Labs in the time before PCs, has become the most widely available multiuser operating system today. UNIX has long been the operating system of choice for workstations and minicomputers in research and academic settings. In recent years it has taken root in many business environments, as well. Some form of UNIX is available for personal computers, workstations, minicomputers, and mainframes.

The User's View

Connecting to a Multiuser System

Software: UNIX operating system on a remote computer; terminal software on the local personal computer.
The goal: Using a PC, a modem, and a communication program, you're about to connect to your school's UNIX mainframe.

The mainframe's phone number and protocols are already entered into your terminal program, so you're ready to dial up and log in. When you select the Dial command, the software passes the command on to the modem along with the phone number and other necessary information. You hear the dial tone, the touch-tone dialing signals, a high whistle, and a hiss as the modem dials and establishes the connection. A few lines scroll by before the login prompt appears. You type your **login name**—the one-word name assigned to your computer account (in this example, "sanchez") and press Enter. (In these examples, the characters you type are *italicized* so you can tell them from those typed by the computer.) The program then prompts you to enter your **password**—a string of letters and numbers known only by you and the computer—so it can verify your identity. When you type your password, it doesn't appear on the screen, so there's no risk of anyone reading it over your shoulder. After you press Enter, UNIX displays a system message to indicate that you've successfully logged in.

```
Connecting... session 1

DYNIX(R) V3.1.2

login: sanchez

Password:
Last login: Fri Dec 27 14:40:21 from osuets4.UCS.ORST
DYNIX(R) V3.1.2 NFS  #2 : Wed Oct  2 21:59:50PDT  1994

You have new mail.
TERM = (vt100)
```

UNIX asks what kind of terminal you're using with the TERM = prompt. The "vt100" in parentheses is the *default* type; you don't need to type anything if you're using a VT-100 terminal. You're using a personal computer, not a terminal, but your software is *emulating* (imitating) a VT-100 terminal, so you press Enter.

```
TERM = (vt100)
Erase is Backspace
Kill is Ctrl-U
No new messages.
1%
```

Now that you've logged in, UNIX responds to commands typed after a numbered % prompt. The command-line interface is similar to that of MS-DOS, but the commands aren't the same. For example LS, not DIR, lists the files in your current directory. For most tasks UNIX *feels* like a single-user system. You don't generally notice that others are using the system unless you're communicating with them.

```
1%ls
dead.letter          Mail
News                 mail.folders
afpvols              nyssa
2%                   saved.notes
sumexdir
```

The Network Advantage

With this background in mind, let's reconsider the three reasons people use networks.

- *Networks allow people to share computer hardware, reducing costs and making it possible for more people to take advantage of powerful computer equipment.*

When computers and peripherals are connected in a local area network, computer users can share expensive peripherals. Before LANs, most offices had a printer connected to each computer. Today it's more common to find a small number of high-quality printers shared by a larger group of computers and users.

While it may not make much sense for users to try to share a printer on a wide area network, WAN users often share other hardware resources. Many WANs include powerful mainframes and supercomputers that can be accessed by authorized users at remote sites.

- *Networks allow people to share data and software programs, increasing efficiency and productivity.*

In offices without networks, people often transmit data and software by *sneakernet*—that is, by carrying diskettes between computers. In a LAN one or more computers can be used as **file servers**—storehouses for software and data that are shared by several users. With file serving software a user can get software and data from any server on the LAN without taking a step.

Of course, sharing computer software on a network can violate software licenses (see Chapter 2) if it's not done with care. It's common for a software license to allow the program to be installed on a file server as long as the number of simultaneous users never exceeds the number of licensed copies. Some companies offer **site licenses** or **network licenses** that reduce costs for multiple copies or remove restrictions on software copying and use at a network site. (Software copying is discussed in more detail in Chapter 13.)

Networks don't eliminate compatibility differences between different computer operating systems, but they can simplify data communication between machines. Users of IBM-compatible computers, for example, can't run Macintosh applications just because they're available on a file server. They can, in many cases, use data files and documents created on a Macintosh and stored on the server. For example, a poster created with PageMaker on a Macintosh could be stored on a file server so it can be opened, edited, and printed by users of PageMaker on IBM PCs. But file sharing isn't always that easy. If users of different systems use programs with incompatible file formats, they need to use *data translation software* to read and modify each other's files.

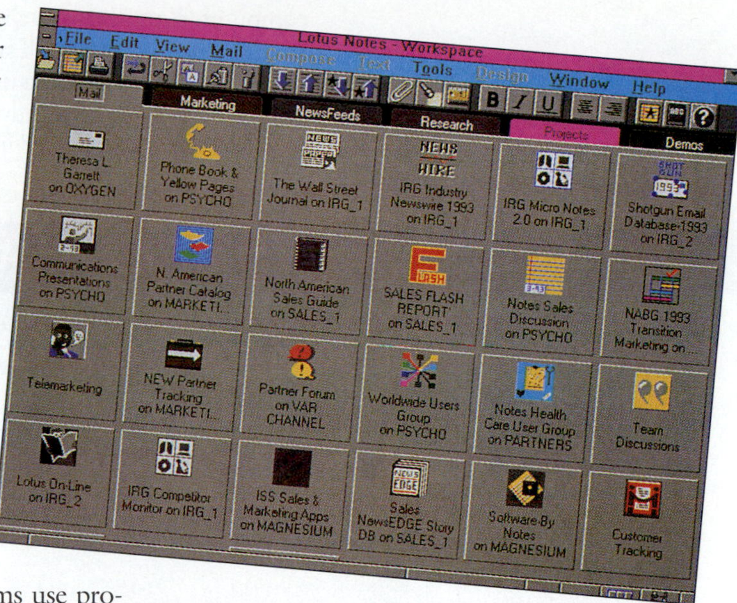

▲ Groupware applications allow several networked users to edit documents at the same time. Each user can see and comment on changes made by other users. (Software: Lotus Notes.)

On wide area networks, the transfer of data and software can save more than shoe leather; it can save time. There's no need to send diskettes by overnight mail between two sites if both sites are connected to the same network. Typically data can be sent electronically between sites in a matter of minutes.

- *Networks allow people to work together in ways that are difficult or impossible without network technology.*

Some modern software applications can be classified as **groupware**—programs designed to allow several networked users to work on the same documents at the same time. Groupware programs include multiuser appointment calendars, project management software, database management systems, and software for group editing of text-and-graphics documents. Groupware applications are still unusual, though, and few network users take advantage of them.

For most LAN and WAN users, network communication is limited to sending and receiving messages. As simple as this might sound, electronic messaging profoundly changes the way people and organizations work. In the next section we'll take a close look at the advantages and implications of interpersonal communication with computers.

Electronic Mail and Teleconferencing: Interpersonal Computing

. . . after more than a century of electric technology, we have extended our central nervous system itself in a global embrace, abolishing both space and time as far as our planet is concerned.

—Marshall McLuhan, *Understanding Media*

Whether you're connected to a local area network, a wide area network, or a timesharing mainframe, there's a good chance you have access to some kind of **electronic mail** (**e-mail**) system. Electronic-mail systems allow users to send messages (mail) from one computer to another. Details and user interfaces vary, but the basic concepts of e-mail are the same for almost all systems. Each user has a mailbox—a storage area for messages. Any user can send a mail message to the mailbox of any other user, whether or not the recipient is currently logged into the system. Only the owner of the mailbox, however, can read the mail in that box.

The User's View

Communicating with Electronic Mail

Software: Mail, UNIX operating system.
The goal: Earlier you logged into a UNIX system, so you're already **on-line**—connected to the computer system and ready to communicate. Now it's time to catch up on your mail.

When you type *mail,* UNIX runs the Mail program that allows you to view, organize, and send mail. Your electronic mailbox has three messages, including one new one from a classmate. You press Enter after the mail prompt (&) to see the new message.

```
2:mail
Mail version 5.2 6/21/85. Type ? for help.
"/usr/spool/mail/sanchez": 3 messages 1 new
    1 boon@CS.ORST.EDU Mon Mar 27 10:48 166/5288 "e-mail pen pals"
    2 bernie@CS.ORST.EDU Tue Mar 28 11:32 49/914 "party time!"
>N  3 bongo@CS.ORST.EDU Thu Mar 30 09:27 32/1440 "group assignment"
&
```

The message, addressed to both swanson and sanchez at the computer called CS.ORST.EDU, scrolls onto the screen, followed by another & prompt. After you read the message, you type *R* to create and send a reply for the sender (bongo@CS.ORST.EDU) and your other project teammate (swanson@CS.ORST.EDU).

```
>N  3 bongo@CS.ORST.EDU Thu Mar 30 09:27 32/1440 "group assignment"
&
Message 3:

Date: Thu, 30 Mar 92 11:29:23 PST
From: bongo@CS.ORST.EDU (Gordon, Ben)
To: swanson@CS.ORST.EDU sanchez@CS.ORST.EDU
Subject: group assignment roadblock

I've been working on the survey phase of our CS group project, and
I've run into a problem. The lab administrators say they can't
provide me with the data we need without proper authorization. Do
either of you have a suggestion?

Bongo

&r
```

The mail program automatically fills in the addresses and the subject: "Re: group assignment roadblock." You type a message, concluding it with a line containing only a period. The "cc" appears, asking you to list users who should receive carbon copies of the message. You press Enter to say "No copies, please."

```
&r
to: swanson@CS.ORST.EDU [Swanson, Bethany] bongo@CS.ORST.EDU
[Gordon, Ben]
SUBJECT: Re: group assignment roadblock

Leave it to me. I've already spoken to our professor and he said
he'd be glad to send an e-mail message if they balked at our
request. I'll contact him right away.

Chris

.
cc:
&
```

```
&mail beekman
Subject: authorization request for survey

It looks like we need formal authorization before we can get the
lab-use statistics for our CS 101 project on user demographics.
We'd appreciate it if you could send an e-mail note to the lab
administrators to unlock the data for us.

Thanks very much
Chris Sanchez

.
cc: bongo swanson
&
```

To send a note to your instructor, at the & prompt you type *mail* followed by the appropriate e-mail address. You fill in the subject, the message, and the list of people to receive carbon copies in the lines that follow. The message should be waiting the next time your instructor logs in.

A variation of electronic mail is the **teleconference**—an on-line meeting between two or more people. Many teleconferencing systems allow users to communicate in real time, just as they would by telephone. In a **real-time teleconference**, each participant sits at a computer or terminal, watching the meeting transcript scroll by on the screen and typing comments on the keyboard. Because of the give-and-take format of such systems, real-time teleconferences go by names like Chat, Talk, and CB. Whatever they're called, they tend to be chaotic, and typing responses can seem painfully slow to participants watching the process on the screen. Consequently delayed teleconferences tend to be more popular and productive. In a **delayed teleconference** participants type, post, and read messages at their convenience. In effect, participants of a delayed teleconference *share* an electronic mailbox for messages related to the group's purposes.

E-mail, teleconferencing, and other types of on-line communication can replace many memos, letters, phone calls, and face-to-face meetings, making organizations more productive and efficient.

In a delayed teleconference each participant can view and respond to previously posted messages.

```
Date: January 24, 1995, 2:32PM
From: Wirehead
Subject: Re: Affirmative Action in the Computer Industry

Yesterday Robocop wrote:

> The woman only had to be qualified and not more skilled than the man to get
> the job. This is wrong.  A person should be judged on skills alone.
> No one should have to pay for the sins of the past generations.

When discrimation is eliminated and ALL people can work and communicate equally, then
and only then can we expect equality. We have an obligation to our children and their
children. A child is not born to hate. We need to be educated then only can we educate.

---------------------------------------------------------------------------------------

Date: January 24, 1995, 3:30PM
From: Animal
Subject: Re: Affirmative Action in the Computer Industry

The problem with forgeting about past sins is that many of the sinners are still in
power, and that the people who  followed them up the ladder also have that tendency.I
hope the problem will eventually disappear as more educated people get into higher
positions.  By education, I mean people being able to see that
women are as capable as any one else.

---------------------------------------------------------------------------------------

Date: January 24, 1995, 9:30PM
From: Chelsea
Subject: Re: Affirmative Action in the Computer Industry

A corporation with one ethnic group dominating will always hire employees from the same
```

The Postal Alternative

Experts predict that e-mail and teleconferencing systems someday will provide stiff competition for the postal service. For many organizations electronic communication is already reducing postal expenses. Here's why:

- *E-mail is fast.* A typical electronic mail message takes no more than a few minutes from the time it's conceived until it reaches its destination, whether across the office or across the ocean. Electronic mail users often refer to traditional mail as "snail mail."
- *E-mail doesn't depend on location.* If you send someone an electronic message, that person can log in and read it from a computer at home, at the office, or anywhere in the world.
- *E-mail facilitates group communication.* In most e-mail systems it's no harder and no more expensive to send a message to several people than to send it to one person. Most systems allow groups to have named *aliases*—group lists—so a mail message addressed to an alias name (like "faculty," "office," or "sales") is sent automatically to everyone in the group.

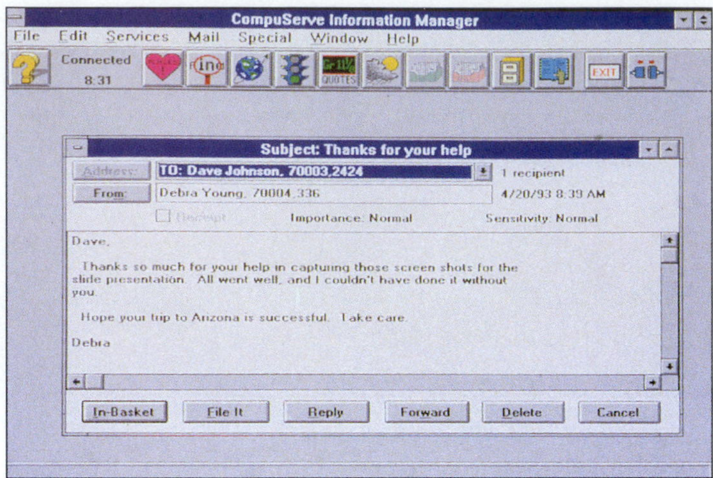

While most e-mail systems have character-based command-line interfaces, a growing number have graphical user interfaces like this one. Many modern e-mail systems make it easy to send documents created with word processors, graphics programs, or even multimedia software.

- *E-mail messages are digital data that can be edited and combined with other computer-generated documents.* Because the messages you receive by e-mail are stored in your computer electronically, you can edit text and numbers without having to retype the entire document and without wasting paper. You can easily add text from other documents stored on your computer. When you're finished, you can forward the edited document back to the original sender or to somebody else for further processing.

Bypassing the Telephone

Electronic mail and teleconferencing also offer advantages over telephones:

- *On-line communication is less intrusive than the telephone.* A ringing phone can interrupt concentration, disrupt a meeting, and bring just about any kind of activity to a standstill. Instead of shouting "Answer me now!" an e-mail message waits patiently in the mailbox until the recipient has the time to handle it.
- *On-line communication allows time shifting.* Electronic mail users aren't plagued by busy signals, unanswered rings, and "I'll get back to you" message machines. You can receive e-mail messages when you're busy, away, or asleep, and they'll be waiting for you when you have the time to pick them up. Time zones are largely irrelevant to e-mail users.

Minimizing Meetings

Teleconferences and e-mail can drastically reduce the amount of time people spend traveling to and participating in meetings. They offer several advantages for group decision making:

- *Teleconferences and e-mail allow decisions to evolve over time.* A group can discuss an issue electronically for hours, days, or weeks without the urgency of getting everything settled in a single session. New information can circulate when it's current rather than at the next meeting. Participants have time to think about each statement before responding. When organizations use teleconferences for discussion and information dissemination, meetings tend to be infrequent, short, and to the point.
- *Teleconferences and e-mail make long-distance meetings possible.* Teleconferences can include people from all over the world, and nobody needs to leave home to participate. In fact, a growing number of programmers, writers, and other information workers literally work at home, communicating with colleagues by modem (see Chapter 11).

- *Teleconferences and e-mail emphasize the message over the messenger.* In companies that rely on electronic mail and teleconferences for much of their communication, factors like appearance, race, sex, voice, mannerisms, and title tend to carry less weight than they do in other organizations. Status points go to people with good ideas and the ability to express those ideas clearly in writing.

On-line Problems

Any new technology introduces new problems, and on-line communication is no exception. Here are some of the most important:

- *E-mail and teleconferencing are vulnerable to machine failures and human errors.* If you delete an important e-mail message that hasn't been copied, you can't dig it out of the waste basket. A system failure can cripple an organization that depends on the system for critical communications.
- *E-mail can pose a threat to privacy.* The U.S. Postal Service has a tradition of safeguarding the privacy of first-class mail. Electronic communication is not grounded in that tradition. While most e-mail messages are secure and private, there's always a potential for eavesdropping by an organization's system administrators and crafty system snoopers.
- *E-mail works only if everybody plays.* Just as the postal system depends on each of us checking our mailboxes daily, an e-mail system can work only if all subscribers regularly log in and check their mail. Most people develop the habit quickly if they know important information is only available on-line.
- *E-mail and teleconferencing filter out many "human" components of communication.* When Bell invented the telephone, the public reaction was cool and critical. Business people were reluctant to communicate through a device that didn't allow them to look each other in the eye and shake hands. While this reaction might seem strange today, it's worth a second look. When people communicate, part of the message is hidden in body language, eye contact, voice inflections, and other nonverbal signals. The telephone strips visual cues out of a message, and this can lead to misunderstandings. Most on-line communication systems peel away the sounds as well as the sights, leaving only words on a screen—words that might be misread if they aren't chosen carefully. What's more, e-mail and teleconferences seldom replace casual "water cooler conversations"—those chance meetings that result in important communications and connections.
- *You can't always get there from here.* Our postal system is universal; you can send mail from anywhere to anywhere. Similarly the phone network connects just about everybody in the developed world. However, we're a long way from a universal e-mail network. E-mail systems are popping up at a furious pace, but they don't all work together. In many cases it's easier to send e-mail to someone on the other side of the planet than to send the same message across the street!

Problems notwithstanding, more electronic mail and teleconferencing systems are being installed in businesses, schools, and government offices every year. If current growth rates continue, on-line messages will be as common in the workplace as photocopied memos and yellow sticky notes.

The Other Side of the Modem: An On-line Tour

You don't need to be part of a networked office to communicate electronically. If you have a computer, a modem, a telephone line, and communication software, you can connect to a variety of on-line information services that offer electronic mail, teleconferencing, and more. In this section we'll take a quick tour of some of the more popular types of on-line services that exist on the other side of the modem.

Electronic Bulletin Board Systems (BBSs)

A low-priced mountain bike for sale, a request for help from a frustrated computer gamester, an impromptu review of a new movie—you can find just about any kind of message on an **electronic bulletin board system** (**BBS**). A BBS serves as an on-line version of the bulletin board at your local supermarket or the library; it's a place for posting messages and reading messages left by others.

A typical electronic bulletin board system is a personal computer connected by modem to a phone line. BBS software allows the computer to receive, organize, and post messages in appropriate categories automatically. A user connects to the BBS by dialing in with a modem. The process is similar to connecting to a timesharing system, except that most BBSs allow only one user to connect at a time. Many BBSs operate without human supervision for long periods of time. The system operator, or sysop, is needed only for occasional maintenance and troubleshooting.

Many BBSs are special-purpose boards designed for people with particular needs or interests. Some examples with self-descriptive names include Handicapped Educational Exchange and PEACENET. At the other extreme, some BBSs, run by hobbyists, are available to anybody for discourse on any subject. Some charge hourly connect fees, others charge flat subscription rates, and many are free.

Many BBSs divide messages into categories called *SIGs*, for *s*pecial-*i*nterest *g*roups. Posting a message to a BBS SIG is similar to participating in a delayed teleconference, except the message is visible to anyone who has access to the BBS instead of a specified group of participants. BBSs also generally offer electronic mail services for users who need to communicate in private.

In addition, many bulletin boards serve as repositories for public domain software and shareware—two types of software that can be freely distributed without violating copyright laws. BBS users can **download** software—copy it from the BBS computer to their computers—and **upload** software—post it on the BBS so it's available for others. Software sharing is part of the community spirit that's common on BBSs, but it also causes problems. Two of these, software piracy and viruses, are discussed in Chapter 13.

On-line Database Services

Chapter 6 includes a User's View example of a reference search in a library database. As the public hunger for timely information grows, more computer users are using a modem to connect to **on-line database services** for instant answers.

Many database services are designed to meet the needs of specific groups of customers. For example, Dow Jones News Retrieval Service provides business users with up-to-the-minute stock quotes, market reports, and economic news. Other services cater to lawyers, librarians, physicians, scientists, academic researchers, and other information workers. A few provide general access and relatively simple user interfaces for nonspecialized users. Users pay for database access with monthly subscription fees, connect-time fees, data fees, or some combination of the three.

Commercial Information Utilities

When you use a database service, most of the information flows in one direction: from the database to your computer. General-purpose commercial **information utilities**, like CompuServe, America Online, Genie, and Prodigy, allow users to send *and* receive information the way small BBSs do, but they're able to handle hundreds of users at a time. These utilities use timesharing computers with special software designed to make their services accessible to consumers. Services include the following:

With more than 800,000 paid subscribers, CompuServe is the largest full-featured information utility. CompuServe offers a staggering array of services and easy communication links to a variety of networks. The basic menu-driven user interface is designed to work on any terminal or computer with communication software.

- *News.* Most information utilities offer news, including politics, finance, sports, and weather, straight from the news wire services. News by computer can be more current, detailed, and relevant than TV or radio broadcasts. What's more, an on-line user can ask for stories on a particular topic and receive a customized list of headlines; it's like having an up-to-the-minute personalized newspaper with an index. For many people on-line news is a convenience; for others it's a near necessity. A boat operator can monitor incoming storms before trips; a legislator can keep up with fast-breaking Capitol Hill reports from back in the home district; a visually impaired student can have a personal computer, equipped with a speech synthesizer, read headlines and stories aloud.
- *Research.* Most utilities offer a variety of databases, encyclopedias, media reviews, and other reference tools for students, professionals, and curious browsers.
- *Shopping.* Shopping services allow users to search catalog/databases, order goods and services, and pay for them automatically with credit cards. Similar services allow travelers to peruse airline schedules and reserve tickets by computer.
- *Banking.* Many subscribers pay bills, transfer money between accounts, and take care of other banking needs using special on-line banks. Banking by modem saves gas, and there are never any lines.
- *Games.* On-line games can't compete with home computer games for graphics and fast action, but many offer opportunities to play with others who happen to be logged in. One multiplayer game on CompuServe, for example, is a perpetual interstellar battle between space ships controlled by players scattered across North America.
- *Bulletin boards.* Subscribers can mix with like-minded types using bulletin boards that cater to special-interest groups (SIGs) within the system. These bulletin boards work like special-interest BBSs within the context of a larger system.
- *Communication.* Electronic mail, special-interest bulletin boards, teleconferences, and other communication services allow subscribers to connect with each other for business or for fun. A growing number of mail **gateways** link the major on-line utilities and networks, making it possible for subscribers of competing services to send messages to each other. On-line communication is not the same as sharing a face-to-face conversation over coffee, but many people develop deep and

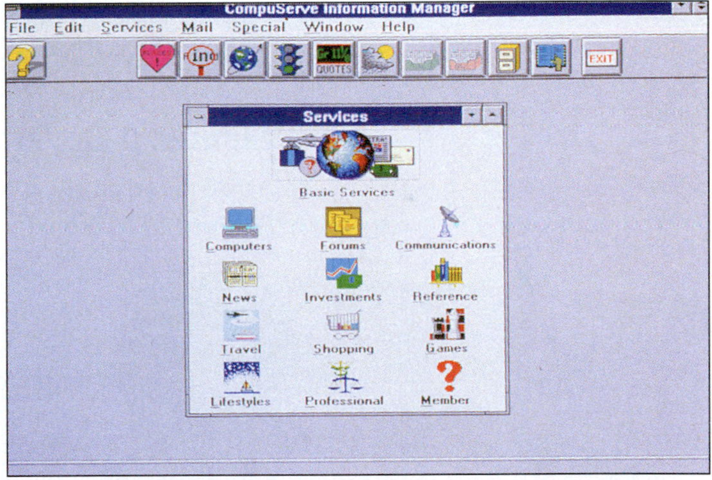

With a software shell like CompuServe Information Manager, users can explore CompuServe through a graphic user interface. The shell replaces CompuServe's text-only displays with familiar windows and icons, making it easier for users to navigate through CompuServe's myriad of menus.

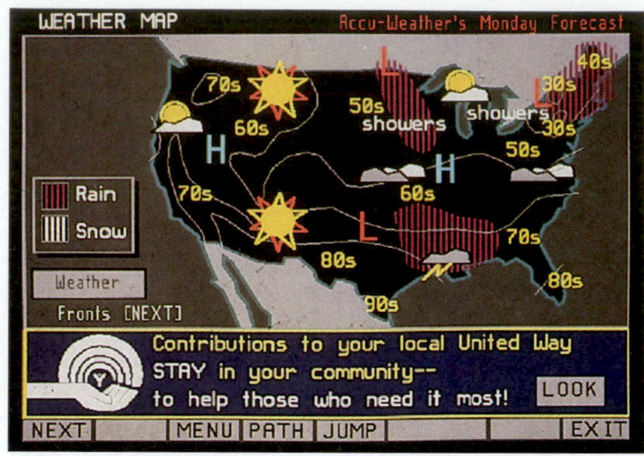

Prodigy, a low-cost utility jointly developed by IBM and Sears, places a heavy emphasis on shopping and consumer services. Advertisements that scroll across the bottom of the graphic display keep subscriber costs down.

lasting connections with people they meet on-line. There's at least one documented on-line marriage!

Most information utilities charge an initial membership fee, a minimum monthly charge, and an hourly use fee, typically less for evenings and weekends. Many have additional charges for special services like database research, banking, and personal file storage. For some services, like Prodigy, corporations pay part of the cost in return for advertising space on the screen.

Experts predict information utilities like CompuServe, America Online, and Prodigy someday may be as much a part of American life as telephones, newspapers, radio, and television are today. So far, though, only a tiny percentage of the American population has ventured on-line.

Minitel: A Government-Sponsored Information Utility

Across the ocean 18 percent of all French households are connected to an information utility known as Minitel. Why? France Telecom, the government-owned telephone company, provides a free Minitel terminal to every customer who wants one. French citizens use these terminals instead of telephone directories; an on-line database provides phone numbers faster than paper phone books for about six cents a minute. The same Minitel terminals serve as gateways to a variety of paid services and opportunities: travel reservations, news, banking, shopping, weather, and teleconferences, including the wildly popular "messagerie rose," an adults-only fantasy line.

Currently, more than 6 million Minitel terminals are installed in French homes and businesses and another 1 million personal computers with communication capabilities. Government participation and support have made the Minitel system a national institution. Some experts believe that this kind of government support will be necessary to lure most Americans on-line.

Millions of French citizens regularly log in to government Minitel systems.

Internet: A Network of Networks

Although the United States government currently is not backing public information utilities, it does play a significant role in **Internet**, an interconnected group of networks linking academic, research, government and commercial institutions. Internet has its roots in ARPA Net, a research network of the Department of Defense. Today Internet includes the National Science Foundation's enormous NSF Net, a number of statewide and regional networks, hundreds of networks within colleges and research

Internet is a network of public and private networks. This map shows just a few of Internet's multitude of interconnections.

labs, and a growing number of commercial sites. Most Internet sites use UNIX-based computers for their host systems, and all share a common set of communication protocols. Most Internet sites are in the United States, but Internet has connections in at least 40 other countries.

Internet provides UNIX-literate scientists, engineers, researchers, professors, students and others with a variety of services, including these:

- *Electronic mail and file transfer.* Internet users can send mail messages, data files, and software programs to other Internet users and to users of many commercial information utilities.
- *Remote login.* Users on one system can access other host systems across the network with just a handful of commands. A user with an account at one Internet site can log in to check for mail messages from anywhere else on the network.
- *Software archives.* Some Internet sites house vast archives of shareware and public domain software for all kinds of computers; users anywhere on the network can browse through these on-line libraries and transfer copies of interesting programs back to their home machines.
- *News.* Internet is the home of Usenet, a giant bulletin board system that contains over 1000 ongoing teleconferences on about every imaginable topic — from molecular biology to ecology, Grateful Dead to Dr. Who, nudism to Buddhism, and, of course, just about anything related to computers. Millions of readers check into one or more Usenet groups regularly.

Internet is the closest thing the United States has to a national telecommunications network, and it's growing at a phenomenal rate. Internet traffic has doubled every year for the past few years, continually testing the carrying capacity of the networks. Many government leaders are working to develop a *National Research and Education Network (NREN)* to replace Internet before it overloads. These officials see NREN as an interstate highway system for data. If the network includes business and consumer services, as it almost certainly will, it will serve as an all-purpose **information superhighway**. While questions remain about costs, structure, and access, Americans will most likely see some kind of information superhighway in the near future.

Rules of Thumb

On-line Survival Tips

Whether you log into a BBS, an information utility, or Internet, you're using a relatively new communication medium with new rules. Here are some suggestions for successful on-line communication:

- **If you're using a metered service, do your homework off-line.** Read the manual before you log in so you don't have to look things up while the meter is running. Most services allow you to compose, edit, and address messages before you log on, so you only have to pay for the time necessary to *send* messages. Plan your strategy before you connect; don't end up paying for thinking time.
- **Let your system do as much of the work as possible.** A good communication software package can be programmed with *macros*—customized procedures to automate repetitive tasks. Create macros to dial up, log in, download mail, and so on, without your intervention; you'll save time, keystrokes, and money.
- **Say what you mean, and say it with care.** Once you send something electronically, you cannot call it back. Compose each message carefully and make sure it means what you intend.
- **Learn the "nonverbal" language of the network.** A simple phrase like "Nice job!" can have very different meanings depending on the tone of voice and body language behind it. Since body language and tone of voice can't easily be stuffed into a modem, on-line communities have developed text-based substitutes. Here are a few:

```
:-)          These three characters represent a smiling face.
             (To see why, look at them with this page rotated
             90° to the right.) "Smilie" suggests the previous
             remark should not be taken seriously.
;-)          This winking smilie usually means the previous
             remark was flirtatious or sarcastic.
:-(          This frowning character suggests something is
             bothering the author—probably the last state-
             ment.
:-I          This character represents indifference.
:->          This usually follows an extremely biting sarcas-
             tic remark.
>:->         This little devil goes with a devilish remark.
*Flame on*   This statement, inspired by a comic book hero,
             warns readers that the following statements are
             inflammatory.
*Flame off*  This means the tirade is over.
```

- **Avoid lynch-mob mentality.** Many otherwise timid people turn into raging bulls when they're on-line. The facelessness of modem communication makes it all too easy to shoot from the hip, overstate arguments, and get caught up in a digital lynch-mob mentality. Emotional responses are fine as long as they don't result in hurt feelings or spreading half-truths. On-line or off, freedom of speech is a right that carries responsibility.
- **Don't be a source of electronic junk mail.** It's so easy to send multiple copies of electronic mail that many networkers generate mountains of e-mail and bulletin board postings. Target your messages carefully; if you're trying to sell tickets to a local concert, don't broadcast the message worldwide.
- **Avoid information overload.** When it comes to information, more is not necessarily better. Search selectively. Don't waste time and energy trying to process mountains of on-line information. Information is not knowledge, and knowledge is not wisdom.

Computer Networks Today: A Reality Check

The network will encourage a second information revolution.

—*Senator (now Vice President) Al Gore*

Many experts see NREN as a small step toward a larger goal: a public computer network that connects every home, school, and workplace. Until that happens, computer networks and utilities like Internet, Prodigy, and CompuServe aren't likely to transform society the way the telephone and the television have. Still, for many users these networks are every bit as important as TVs and phones.

People who spend lots of time on-line learn to live with the shortcomings of today's network technology, such as protocol problems, response delays, system failures, endless menu layers, inconsistent commands, high costs, and unexplainable restrictions. For serious networkers these problems are small when compared to the riches offered by the network: instantaneous communication, unlimited information, and an on-line community of kindred spirits.

Some hobbyists spend hours on-line every day. For a few hard-core networkers, the world on the other side of the modem is more real and more interesting than the everyday physical world. While this may seem strange, it's not unique. Many people feel the same way about television, spectator sports, or romance novels.

For most of us the keyboard-and-characters interface is simply too primitive to be addictive. Fortunately not all computer-based communication media are built around keyboards. In the next section we'll examine technologies that are widely used today and consider others that loom on the horizon.

Telecommunication Trends: Merging and Emerging Technologies

So far we've discussed telecommunication technology in which computers play a central and highly visible role. In other types of telecommunication, computers function behind the scenes to coordinate communication. We'll explore some examples in this section and then consider how the different forms of telecommunication are coming together to provide completely new communication possibilities.

Communication Without Keyboards: Alternative Communication Technologies

Some forms of telecommunication don't require users to type commands and messages. In fact, many people regularly use voice mail, facsimile transmission, video teleconferencing, and ATMs without even thinking about the fact that they're using digital computer technology to communicate.

Voice mail. "Hi. This is Anita Porter. I'm either away from my desk or on another line. Please leave your name, number, and a message. If you prefer to talk to a receptionist, press 0." The **voice mail** system that delivers this recorded message is more than an answering device; it's a sophisticated messaging system with many of the features of an electronic mail system.

Your response is recorded in Anita's voice mailbox. When she dials the system number from any telephone and enters her ID number or password on the phone's keypad, she can listen to her messages, respond to them, forward copies to others, and delete unneeded messages. She can do just about anything she could do with an electronic mail message except edit messages electronically and attach computer documents. Voice mail is an attractive option for people who don't want to type and those who don't have easy access to a computer or terminal.

In spite of its growing popularity, voice mail has detractors. Many people resent taking orders from a machine rather than being able to talk to a human operator. Many callers are frustrated by having to wade through endless voice menus before they can speak to a real person. Office workers often complain about the time-consuming processes of recording and listening to messages. At least one corporation unplugged its voice mail system three months after installing it. They concluded that communication simply went more smoothly without it.

Facsimile transmission. A decade ago, most people had never heard of **facsimile** (**fax**) machines. Today fax machines are standard equipment in modern offices, and a typical business card includes a fax number along with the standard phone number. A fax machine is a fast and convenient tool for transmission of information stored in paper documents, such as typed letters, handwritten notes, photographs, drawings, book pages, and news articles.

When you send a fax of a paper document, the sending fax machine scans each page, converting the scanned image into a series of electric pulses and sending those signals over phone lines to another fax machine. The receiving fax machine uses the signals to construct and print black-and-white *facsimiles* or copies of the original pages. In a sense the two fax machines and the telephone line serve as a long-distance photocopy machine.

It's not necessary to have paper copies of every faxed document, however. A computer can send on-screen documents through a fax modem to a receiving fax machine. The **fax modem** translates the document into signals that can be sent over phone wires and decoded by the receiving fax machine.In effect, the receiving fax machine acts like a remote printer for the document.

A computer can also use a fax modem to *receive* transmissions from fax machines, treating the sending fax machine as a kind of remote scanner. A faxed letter can be displayed on screen or printed to paper, but it can't be directly edited with a word processor the way an electronic mail message can. Like a scanned document, the digital facsimile is nothing more than a collection of black-and-white dots to the computer. Before a faxed document can be edited, it must be processed by optical character recognition (OCR) software (described in Chapter 11).

A fax modem (above) allows a personal computer to communicate with a fax machine (below).

Video teleconferencing. A **video teleconference** allows people to communicate face to face over long distances by combining video and computer technology. In its simplest form video teleconferencing is like two-way television. Each participant sits in a room equipped with video cameras, microphones, and television monitors. Video signals are beamed between sites so that every participant can see and hear every other participant on television monitors.

Video teleconferencing is mainly practiced in special conference rooms by groups that meet too often to travel. But some businesses now use video telephones that transmit pictures as well as words through phone lines. Specially equipped personal computers can be used in the same way, allowing callers to see each other on their computer screens while they carry on phone conversations. As this kind of technology becomes more widely available, video teleconferencing is likely to become an everyday activity for many people.

Electronic funds transfer (EFT). When you strip away the emotional trappings, money is just another form of information. Dollars, yen, pounds, and rubles are all just symbols that make it easy for people to exchange goods and services.

Money can be just about anything, provided people agree to its value. During the last few centuries, paper replaced metal as the major form of money. Today paper is being replaced by digital patterns stored in computer media. Most major financial transactions take place inside computers, and most money is stored on computer disks and tapes instead of in wallets and safe deposit boxes.

Money, like other digital information, can be transmitted through computer networks. That's why it's possible to withdraw cash from your checking account using an **automated teller machine** (**ATM**) at a bank, airport, or shopping mall thousands of miles from your home bank. An ATM is a specialized terminal linked to a bank's main computer through a commercial banking network. An ATM can handle routine banking transactions 24 hours a day, providing the kind of instant service that wouldn't be possible without computer networks.

An ATM isn't necessary for electronic funds transfer to take place. Many people have paychecks deposited automatically in checking or savings accounts and have bills paid automatically out of those accounts. These automatic transfers don't involve cash or checks, they're done inside computer networks. Many banks allow you to use your home computer or your touch-tone phone to transfer money between accounts, check balances, and pay bills.

Personal communicators. For a growing number of people whose jobs keep them on the move and away from their offices, telecommunication is a critical part of the work day. Many of these mobile professionals are using portable devices called **personal communicators** to meet many of their communication needs. A personal communicator typically combines a cellular phone, a fax modem, and other communication equipment in a lightweight, wireless box that resembles a pen-based computer. A personal communicator can serve as a portable phone, a fax machine, an electronic mailbox, a pager, and a personal computer. It can be hooked to a standard phone line or, in many locations, function as a wireless communication device using the kind of radio transmitters and receivers used in cellular phones. As these wireless technologies improve, many mobile professionals will be able to "stay in touch" all day, every day.

Video teleconferencing comes to the desktop and the home with specially equipped computer and video phones.

The EO personal communicator is representative of a new type of universal communication device for professionals on the go.

Converging Communication Technologies

The grand design keeps getting grander. A global computer is taking shape, and we're all connected to it.

—Stewart Brand, *The Media Lab*

Computer networks transmit text, numbers, pictures, sounds, speech, music, video, and money as digital signals. The worldwide telephone network is being converted from analog to digital, so it's just a matter of time before most phone conversations are transmitted digitally. When the phone system is digital, the groundwork will be laid for a single, unified network for transmitting all kinds of digital information.

ISDN. Integrated Services Digital Network, more commonly called just **ISDN**, will link telephones, computers, fax machines, television, and even mail in a single digital system. ISDN is already available in a few cities. But in most locations, phone lines can't handle ISDN.

The main problem is **bandwidth**—the quantity of information that can be transmitted through a channel in a given amount of time. One way to increase bandwidth in a cable is to increase the number of parallel wires in that cable—the equivalent to adding more lanes to a freeway. Another way is to increase the speed with which information passes through the cable; this is the same as increasing the speed of the vehicles on the freeway.

The bandwidth bottleneck disappears when copper phone lines are replaced with high-capacity **fiber optic cables**. Fiber optic cables use light waves to carry information at blinding speeds. A single fiber optic cable can transmit half a gigabit (500 *million* bits) per second, replacing 10,000 standard telephone cables! Fiber optic cables are already used in many telephone systems, and more miles of cable are laid every year.

An all-digital, fiber optic telephone network will improve the sound quality of phone calls and the speed of long-distance phone response. But more importantly, a digital phone system will be able to transmit electronic mail, computer data, fax, real-time video, and other messages more accurately and reliably. LANs will be able to hook directly into phone networks without modems.

Digital communication comes home. The emergence of ISDN will have its most immediate impact on the world of work, where people depend on communication technology to get their business done. But integrated digital communication lines will eventually find their way into our homes, radically changing our lives in the process. Telephone industry predictions suggest that 90 percent of American homes may have high-bandwidth fiber optic cables installed by the year 2026. These cables will provide two-way links to the outside world for our phones, televisions, radios, computers, and a variety of other devices.

Two-way video phone conversations, universal electronic mail, customized digital newspapers, automatic utility metering, and almost unlimited entertainment options may come to pass through these glass cables in the not-too-distant future. The lines that separate the telephone industry, the computer industry, and the home entertainment industry will blur as voice, data, and pictures flow back and forth on light waves. Many services we take for granted today—video rentals, cable TV, newspapers, and magazines, for example—may be threatened or replaced by digital delivery systems of the future. Whatever happens, it's clear that communication tomorrow will be radically different from today.

Cyberspace: The Electronic Frontier

Cyberspace. A consensual hallucination experienced daily by billions of legitimate operators, in every nation, by children being taught mathematical concepts . . . A graphic representation of data abstracted from the banks of every computer in the human system. Unthinkable complexity. Lines of light ranged in the nonspace of the mind, clusters and constellations of data. Like city lights, receding . . . .

—William Gibson, in Neuromancer

Cyberspace: A new universe, a parallel universe created and sustained by the world's computers and communication lines. A world in which the global traffic of knowledge, secrets, measurements, indicators, entertainments, and alter-human agency takes on form: sights, sounds, presences never seen on the surface of the earth blossoming in a vast electronic night.

—Michael Benedikt, in *Cyberspace: First Steps*

Cyberspace, in its present condition, has a lot in common with the 19th-Century West. It is vast, unmapped, culturally and legally ambiguous, verbally terse (unless you happen to be a court stenographer), hard to get around in, and up for grabs. Large institutions already claim to own the place, but most of the actual natives are solitary and independent, sometimes to the point of sociopathy. It is, of course, a perfect breeding ground for both outlaws and new ideas about liberty.

—John Perry Barlow, writer and co-founder of the Electronic Frontier Foundation

ISDN, fiber optics, and other emerging technologies promise exciting possibilities for the future. Science fiction writers suggest that tomorrow's networks may take us beyond interactive TV and video phones into an artificial reality unlike anything we've seen before. This alternative reality has come to be known as **cyberspace**, a term coined by William Gibson in his visionary novel *Neuromancer.*

In *Neuromancer*, as in earlier works by Verner Vinge and others, travelers experience the universal computer network as if it were a physical place, a shared virtual reality, complete with sights, sounds, and other sensations. Gibson's cyberspace is an abstract, cold landscape in a dark and dangerous future world. Vinge's *True Names* takes place in a network hideaway where adventurous computer wizards never reveal their true names or identities to each other. Instead they take on mythical identities with supernatural abilities.

Today's computer networks, with their primitive user interfaces and limited bandwidths, are light years from the futuristic visions of Vinge and Gibson. Still, today's networks are part of a primitive cyberspace—a world where messages, mathematics, and money can cross continents in seconds. People from all over the planet meet, develop friendships, and share their innermost thoughts and feelings in cyberspace.

Writer John Perry Barlow calls the on-line world an "electronic frontier," suggesting parallels to America's old West. The electronic frontier is populated by free-spirited souls willing to forgo creature comforts. These digital pioneers are, in a sense, building the roads and towns that will someday be used by less adventurous settlers.

The electronic frontier is far from tame. Network nomads pick digital locks and ignore electronic fences. Some explore nooks and crannies out of a spirit of adventure.

Others steal and tamper with private information for profit or revenge. Law enforcement agencies, frustrated by the challenge of network terrorism, occasionally overreact with lynch-mob tactics that threaten innocent bystanders.

The electronic frontier metaphor suggests that our expanding cyberspace has its share of social problems—problems of computer crime and security that computer users, law enforcement agencies, and politicians are just beginning to understand. We'll discuss those problems and some potential solutions in Chapter 13.

Summary

Networking is one of the most important trends in computing today. Computer networks are growing in popularity because they (1) allow computers to share hardware, (2) allow computers to send software and data back and forth, and (3) allow people to work together in ways that would be difficult or impossible without networks.

Local area networks (LANs) are made up of computers that are close enough to be directly connected with cables or wireless radio transmitters/receivers. Most LANs include shared printers and file servers. Wide area networks (WANs) are made up of computers separated by considerable distance. The computers are connected to each other through the telephone network, which includes cables, microwave transmission towers, and communication satellites. Before it can be transmitted on the phone network, a computer's digital signal must be converted to an analog signal using a modem.

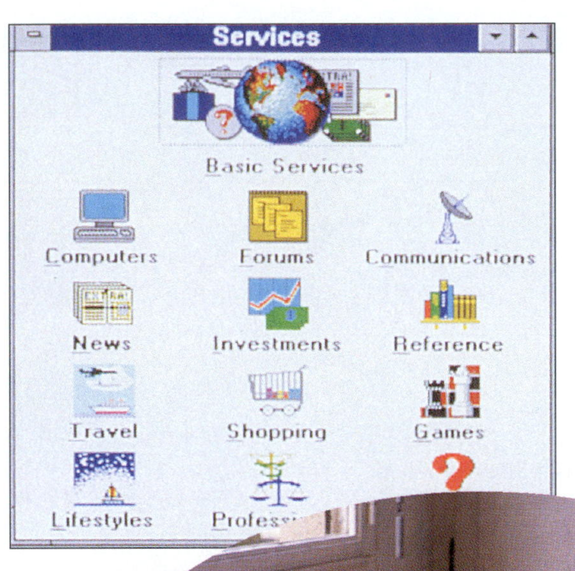

Communication software takes care of the details of communication between machines—details like protocols that determine how signals will be sent and received. Network operating systems typically handle the machanics of LAN communication. Terminal programs allow personal computers to function as terminals when connected to other PCs or to timesharing computers. Timesharing operating systems like UNIX allow multiuser computers to work with several terminals at a time.

Electronic mail and teleconferencing are the two most common forms of communication between people on computer networks. E-mail and teleconferencing offer many advantages over traditional mail and telephone communication and can shorten or eliminate many meetings. But because of several important limitations, e-mail and teleconferencing cannot completely replace older communication media.

A modem can link a computer to a variety of systems, including bulletin board systems (BBSs), database services, and consumer-oriented information utilities. These utilities offer shopping, banking, teleconferencing, software downloading, electronic mail, and other services. Internet connects many U.S. government, educational, and commercial institutions and is likely to evolve into a national data network something like the French Minitel system.

Other kinds of telecommunication, including fax, voice mail, electronic funds transfer, and video teleconferencing, take advantage of computer technology. As the phone network is converted to fiber optic cables with digital switching, ISDN will combine these technologies with computer telecommunication to create a unified digital communication system. The lines that separate the telephone, computer, and home entertainment industries will blur as new communication options blossom. Cyberspace, the world inside the digital network, is like an electronic frontier today—a frontier that offers risks and promises for the future.

CHAPTER REVIEW

Key Terms

analog signal
automated teller machine (ATM)
bandwidth
bits per second (bps)
bulletin board system (BBS)
communication satellite
communication software
cyberspace
delayed teleconference
digital signal
download
electronic funds transfer (EFT)
electronic mail (e-mail)
facsimile (fax)
fax modem
fiber optic cable
file server
gateway
groupware
information superhighway
information utility
Internet
ISDN
local area network (LAN)
login name
modem
network
network license
network operating system
on-line communication
on-line database service
password
personal communicator
port
protocol
real-time teleconference
site license
telecommunication
teleconference
terminal program
UNIX
upload
video teleconference
voice mail
wide area network (WAN)
wireless network

Review Questions

1. Give three general reasons for the importance of computer networking. (Hint: Each reason is related to one of the three essential components of every computer system.)
2. How do the three general reasons listed in question 1 relate specifically to LANs?
3. How do the three general reasons listed in question 1 relate specifically to WANs?
4. Under what circumstances is a modem necessary for connecting computers in networks? What does the modem do?
5. Describe at least two different kinds of communication software.
6. What is UNIX, and why is it important?
7. How could a file server be used in a student computer lab? What software licensing issues would be raised by using a file server in a student lab?
8. What is the difference between electronic mail, real-time teleconferencing, and delayed teleconferencing?
9. Describe some things you can do with electronic mail that can't be done with regular mail.
10. Describe several potential problems associated with electronic mail and teleconferencing.
11. What kinds of services are available through commercial information utilities like CompuServe, America On-Line, and Prodigy? How do they differ from the services offered by smaller BBSs?
12. "Money is just another form of information." Explain this statement and describe how it relates to automated teller machines and electronic funds transfer.

Discussion Questions

1. Suppose you have an important message to send to a friend in another city, and you can use the telephone, electronic mail, real-time teleconference, fax, or an overnight mail service. Discuss the advantages and disadvantages of each. See if you can think of a situation for each of the five options in which it is the most appropriate choice.
2. As scientists, engineers, and government officials develop plans for a future national information network—a sort of interstate highway system for digital data—they wrestle with questions about who should have access to the system and how it should be financed. How would you design and pay for such a network?
3. Some people choose to spend several hours every day on-line. Do you see potential hazards in this kind of heavy modem use? Explain your answer.
4. How do you think on-line user interfaces will evolve as bandwidth and processing power increase? Describe what cyberspace will feel like in the year 2000, in the year 2050, and beyond.

Projects 

1. If your school has an Internet connection that's accessible to students, establish an account and use it to explore various Internet services. Keep a log of your Internet experiences.
2. Use a personal computer and a modem to try several local BBSs. You may be able to find a directory of BBSs by contacting a local computer store or user group. Keep a log of your experiences.
3. Download a public domain software program from a BBS, an information utility, or an Internet software archive. Describe the problems you encounter in the process.
4. Read several books and articles about cyberspace and write a paper comparing them.

Sources and Resources 

UNIX Survival Guide, by Tim Parker (Reading, MA: Addison-Wesley, 1990). This is an easy-to-read UNIX tutorial for beginners. It covers the basics of logging on, editing, sending mail, manipulating files, using a modem, and more.

UNIX for the Impatient, by Paul W. Abrahams and Bruce R. Larson (Reading, MA: Addison-Wesley, 1992). This introduction to UNIX covers a lot of ground quickly. It's aimed at technically minded readers who don't want to wade through dozens of examples to get to the important stuff.

Understanding Computer Networks, by Apple Computer, Inc. (Reading, MA: Addison-Wesley, 1989). Most books on computer networks are technical treatises for engineers, programmers, and network managers. This easy-to-read book provides a broad overview of network technology and applications without bombarding you with technobabble. Apple's bias toward desktop computing is apparent, but the book is far more than a sales pitch for Apple machines.

Dvorak's Guide to PC Telecommunications, by John Dvorak (Berkeley, CA: Osborne/McGraw-Hill, 1990) and *Dr. Macintosh's Guide to the On-Line Universe* by Bob LeVitus with Andy Ihnatko (Reading, MA: Addison-Wesley, 1992). These books, written by two of the best-known writers in the computer industry, describe the process of going on-line from the user's point of view. Dvorak's book is designed mostly for users of IBM-compatible machines, while Dr. Macintosh's book is, not suprisingly, for Mac users. Both books quickly pay for themselves if you're considering subscribing to an on-line service.

The Whole Internet User's Guide and Catalog, by Ed Krol (Sebastopol, CA: O'Reilly & Associates, 1992). If you're interested in exploring Internet, this book can help you save time and get more out of your explorations. The bulk of the book describes Internet as an institution and explains the nuts and bolts of Internet communication, including everything from electronic mail to multiplayer games. The book concludes with a catalog of information resources available on the Internet and how to find them.

Internet Tour, Public domain HyperCard software available in many on-line archives. For people with Macintoshes and other HyperCard-compatible computers, this software provides a friendly introduction to the history, structure, and etiquette of Internet.

EcoLinking: Everyones's Guide to Online Environmental Information, by Don Rittner (Berkeley, CA: Peachpit Press, 1992). There's a wealth of information on the other side of the modem; the hard part is finding what you're looking for. This book focuses on one subject—the environment—and provides a thorough guide to online sources of information about that subject. I expect we'll be seeing how-to-find-it books like this for all kinds of subjects soon.

True Names . . . and Other Dangers, by Verner Vinge (New York: Baen Books, 1987). This collection includes "True Names," the 1981 novella that takes place inside a computer network somewhere in the future. This thought-provoking and entertaining story was years ahead of its time.

Neuromancer, by William Gibson (New York: Ace Books, 1987). Gibson's cyberpunk classic spawned several sequels, dozens of imitations, and a new vocabulary for describing a high-tech future. Gibson's future is gloomy and foreboding, and his futuristic slang isn't always easy to follow. Still, there's plenty to think about here.

Cyberspace: First Steps, edited by Michael Benedikt (Cambridge, MA: MIT Press, 1991). This collection includes works by many of the scientists, engineers, architects, artists, writers, and philosophers who are pushing the limits of today's technology toward tomorrow's cyberspace. If you're interested in future technologies and their effects on people, this book will challenge your intellect and your imagination.

PART THREE

Mastering Computers
From Applications to Intelligence

C H A P T E R EIGHT

Graphics, Hypermedia, and Multimedia

Doug Engelbart Explores Hyperspace

If you look out in the future, you can see how best to make right choices.

—Doug Engelbart

On a December day in 1950, Doug Engelbart looked out into the future and saw what no one had seen before. Engelbart had been thinking about the growing complexity and urgency of the world's problems and wondering how he could help solve those problems. In his vision of the future, Engelbart saw computer technology magnifying human mental abilities, providing people with new powers to cope with the urgency and complexity of life.

Engelbart decided to dedicate his life to turning his vision into reality. Unfortunately the rest of the world wasn't ready for Engelbart's vision. His farsighted approach didn't match the prevailing ideas of the time, and most of the research community denounced or ignored Engelbart's work. In 1951 there were only about a dozen computers in the world, and those spent most of their time doing military calculations. It was hard to imagine ordinary people using computers to augment their personal productivity. So Engelbart put together the Augmentation Research Center to create working models of his visionary tools.

Doug Engelbart

After reading this chapter you should be able to

- describe several types of computer graphics software programs used by artists and nonartists to produce high-quality graphics
- explain how hypermedia differ from traditional media
- describe several ways that computers are used to create multimedia materials in the arts, entertainment, education, and business
- explain the relationship between hypermedia and multimedia, describing applications of each

In 1968 he demonstrated his Augment system to an auditorium full of astonished computer professionals and changed forever the way people think about computers. A large screen showed a cascade of computer graphics, text, and video images, controlled by Engelbart and a coworker several miles away. "It was like magic," recalls Alan Kay, one of the young computer scientists in the audience. Augment introduced the mouse, video display editing (the forerunner to word processing), mixed text and graphics, windowing, outlining, shared-screen video conferencing, computer conferencing, groupware, and hypermedia. Although Engelbart used a large computer, he was really demonstrating a futuristic "personal" computer—an interactive multimedia workstation for enhancing individual abilities.

Today many of Engelbart's inventions and ideas have become commonplace. He is widely recognized for one small part of his vision: the mouse. But Engelbart hasn't stopped looking into the future. He now heads the Bootstrap Institute, a nonprofit think tank dedicated to helping organizations make decisions with the future in mind. Engelbart is still committed to replacing automation with augmentation. But now he focuses more on the human side of the equation, helping people chart a course into the future guided by intelligent, positive vision. If anyone understands how to build the future from a vision, Doug Engelbart does.

By combining live-action video with long-distance text editing and idea processing, Doug Engelbart showed that the computer could be a multiple media communication tool with fantastic potential. Today the personal computer is living up to that potential. Graphics programs allow artists, designers, engineers, publishers, and others to create and edit visual images. Hypermedia documents allow users to follow uniquely personal trails through information rather than follow traditional start-to-finish paths. Interactive multimedia tools combine text, graphics, animation, video, and sound in computer-controlled packages. In this chapter we'll look into these cutting-edge technologies and see how they can augment human abilities.

Focus on Computer Graphics

Actually, a root word of technology, techne, originally meant "art." The ancient Greeks never separated art from manufacture in their minds, and so never developed separate words for them.

—Robert Pirsig, *Zen and the Art of Motorcycle Maintenance*

Chapter 5 demonstrated how spreadsheet programs, statistical programs, and other mathematical software create *quantitative* graphics—charts and graphs generated from numbers. These programs help business people, scientists, and engineers who lack the time or talent to create high-quality drawings by hand. But computer graphics today go far beyond pie charts and line graphs. In this section we'll explore a variety of graphic applications, from simple drawing and painting tools to complex programs used by professional artists and designers.

Painting: Bit-Mapped Graphics

One must act in painting as in life, directly.

—*Pablo Picasso*

An image on a computer screen is made of **pixels**—tiny dots of white, black, or color arranged in rows. The words, numbers, and pictures we see are nothing more than patterns of pixels created by software. Most of the time the user doesn't directly control those pixel patterns; software creates the patterns automatically in response to commands. For example, when you press the "e" key while word processing, software constructs a pattern that appears on the screen as an "e." Similarly, when you issue a command to create a bar chart from a spreadsheet, software automatically constructs a pixel pattern that looks like a bar chart. Automatic graphics are convenient, but they can also be restrictive. When you need more control over the details of the screen display, another type of graphics software might be more appropriate.

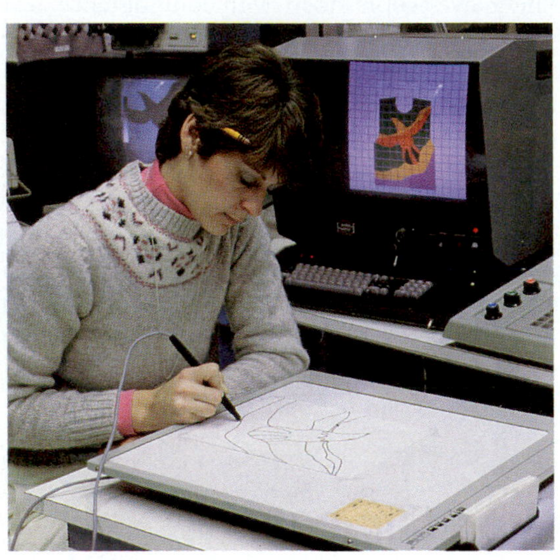

When it's used with compatible software, a pen on a pressure-sensitive tablet can simulate the feel of a paintbrush on paper. As the artist presses harder on the tablet, the line becomes thicker and denser on the screen.

Painting software allows you to "paint" pixels on the screen with a pointing device. A typical painting program accepts input from a mouse, joystick, trackball, or pen, translating the pointer movements into lines and patterns on screen. A professional artist might prefer to work with a pen on a pressure-sensitive tablet because it can, with the right software, simulate a traditional paintbrush more accurately than other pointing devices.

A painting program typically offers a palette of tools on screen. Some tools mimic real-world painting tools, while others can do things that are difficult, even impossible, on paper or canvas. Paintbrushes and pencils leave trails of "paint" as they're dragged across the screen, changing the displayed color of the pixels as they pass. Line tools and shape tools are used to create lines, rectangles, ovals, and other shapes on the screen. Fill tools fill enclosed shapes with colors or patterns. Spray cans, air brushes, and similar tools can create special shading effects by painting some, but not all, of the pixels in an area. Editing tools, including erasers, magnification tools, selection tools, and rotation tools, make it easy to modify paintings on screen before they're committed to paper.

The User's View

Painting with a Computer

Software: ClarisWorks.
The goal: To draw a picture of a computer—a simple image to be displayed on the screen. You'll use ClarisWorks, an integrated software package. In addition to word processing, spreadsheet and database tools, ClarisWorks includes a variety of graphics tools, including several painting tools that are ideal for this project.

When you open a new document for painting, you see a blank page beside a *tool panel*—a collection of buttons representing commonly used tools. You click on the paintbrush button to turn the mouse pointer into a paintbrush.

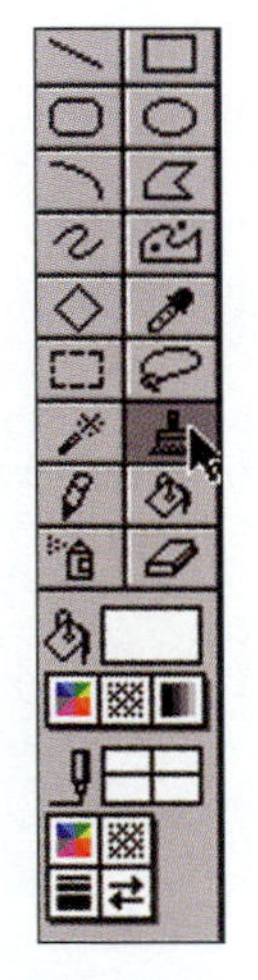

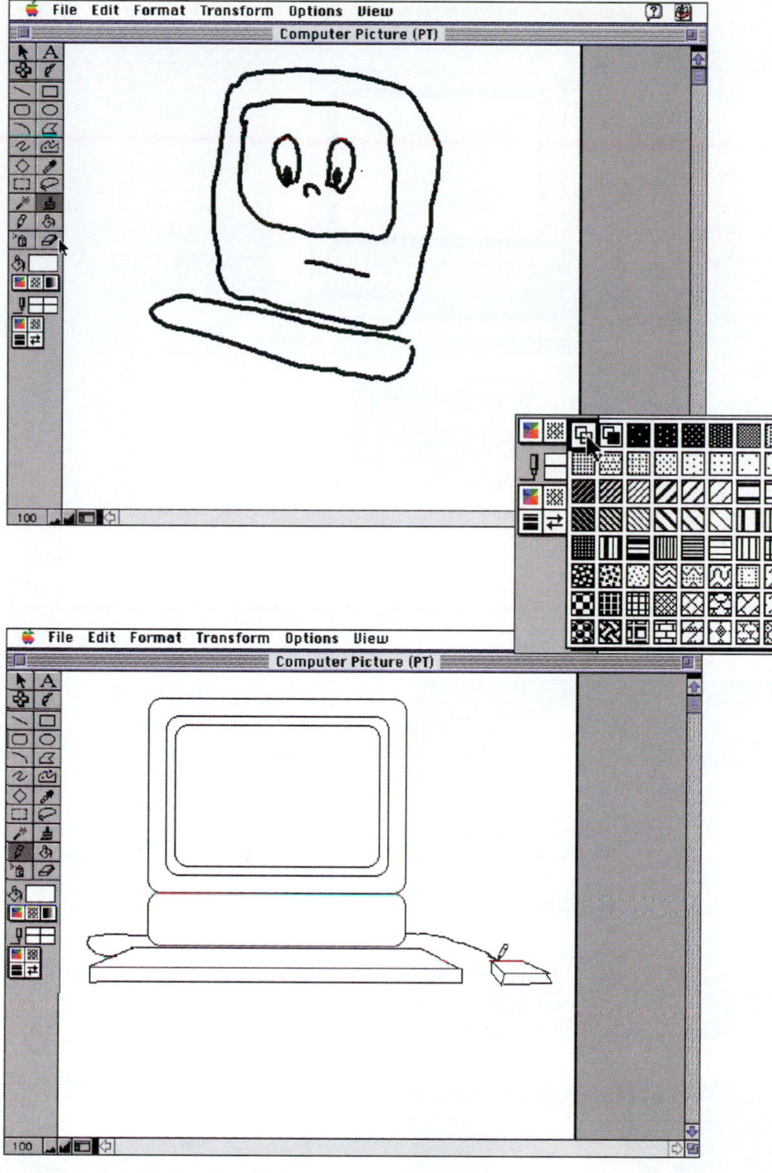

As you drag the brush around the window, it leaves a black trail. Your cartoon sketch has a little too much personality, so you double-click on the eraser tool to clear the page. You decide to draw the outlines of the computer monitor and CPU box using the rounded-rectangle tool.

Like the other shape tools, the rounded-rectangle tool can draw shapes that are filled with a selected paint pattern and color. But you want the shapes to be hollow outlines, so you select the transparent fill icon from the pattern menu. The pattern menu is a **pop-up menu**—it pops into view when you click on the fill pattern icon.

After selecting the rounded-rectangle tool from the tool panel, you drag the mouse diagonally to define opposite corners of a round-cornered rectangle. You draw several of these to represent the computer's monitor and CPU box. The keyboard, mouse, and cables have irregular shapes. The irregular polygon tool allows you to draw odd shapes with a sequence of mouse clicks. The program connects the dots as you click. By dragging the pencil tool, you draw cables to connect the keyboard, mouse, and CPU.

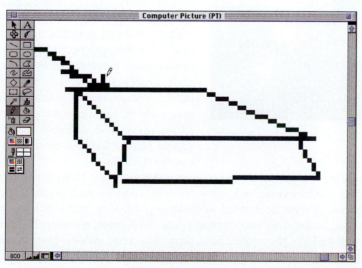

The mouse shape has some rough edges, so you click on the close-up icon in the lower-left corner of the window to zoom in for a close-up view of the problem area. At 800% magnification it's easy to correct the drawing pixel-by-pixel with the pencil and eraser tools.

When the outlines are completed, you're ready to fill them with colors using two more pop-up menus: fill color and gradient. Because they're *tear-off menus,* you can drag them off the tool panel and turn them into **palettes**—windows that float above the document window for quick access. You click on the paint bucket tool to turn the mouse pointer into a paint bucket. For each enclosed shape in your drawing, you choose a color from the fill color palette and click inside the shape to be filled. For the computer screen, you select a *gradient fill*—a fill that makes a gradual transition from one color to another.

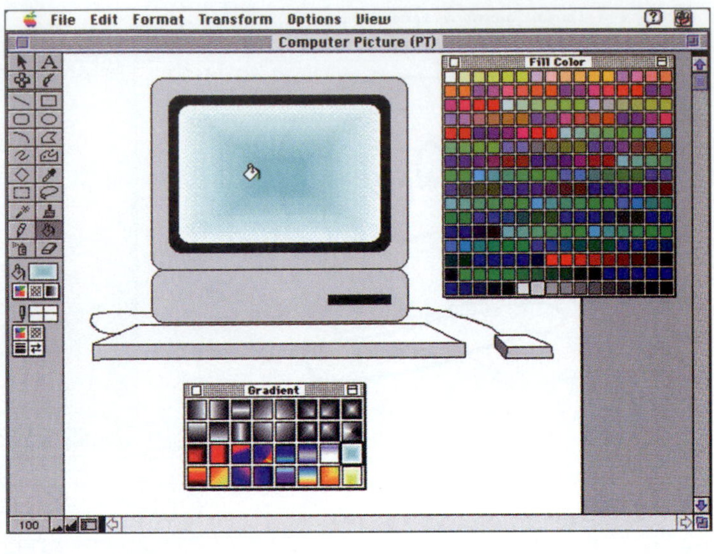

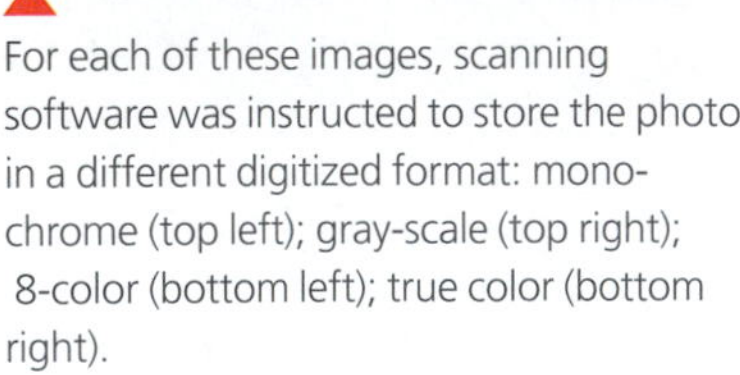

For each of these images, scanning software was instructed to store the photo in a different digitized format: monochrome (top left); gray-scale (top right); 8-color (bottom left); true color (bottom right).

Painting programs create **bit-mapped graphics**—pictures that are, to the computer, simple maps showing how the pixels on the screen should be represented. For the simplest bit-mapped graphics, a single bit of computer memory represents each pixel. Since a bit can contain one of two possible values, 0 or 1, each pixel can display one of two possible colors, usually black or white. This type of 1-bit graphics is called **monochrome graphics** because images are painted in a single color on a solid background. Shades of gray are simulated by *dithering*—intermixing of black and white pixels to create the illusion of a true gray tone. Monochrome graphics programs like MacPaint are efficient and easy to learn but limited in their ability to produce realistic images.

Higher-quality pictures can be produced with bit-mapped graphics programs that allocate more memory per pixel, so each pixel can display more possible colors or shades. **Gray-scale graphics** allow each pixel to appear as black, white, or one of several shades of gray. A gray-scale program that assigns 8 bits per pixel allows up to 256 different shades of gray to appear on the screen—more than the human eye can distinguish.

Realistic color graphics require even more memory. Many older computers and video game machines offer only a few possible colors for each pixel, far too few for the photographic realism demanded in desktop publishing and other modern graphics applications. Today computers typically have 8-bit color, allowing 256 possible colors to be displayed on the screen at a time. But **true color**—photo-quality color—requires hardware that can display millions of colors at a time. True color typically uses 24 or 32 bits of memory for each pixel on the screen.

Professional painting programs like Fractal Painter allow artists and nonartists alike to use tools that work like real-world painting tools.

The number of bits devoted to each pixel—called *pixel depth*—is one of two technological factors limiting an artist's ability to create realistic images with a bit-mapped graphics program. The other factor is **resolution**—the density of the pixels, usually described in *dots per inch*, or *dpi*. Simple painting programs like MacPaint are limited to the resolution of the monitor's screen, typically around 72 dots per inch. When displayed on a computer screen, a 72-dpi picture looks better than lower-resolution television images. But when printed on paper, that image lacks the fine-grain clarity of a photograph. Diagonal lines, curves, and text characters have the "jaggies"—jagged, stair-step-like bumps that advertise the image's identity as a collection of pixels.

Some painting programs get around the "jaggies" problem by storing the image at a higher resolution than the screen can display. For example, a picture can be stored at 300 dots per inch—the resolution of a typical laser printer—even though the computer screen can't display every pixel at that resolution. Of course, high-resolution pictures demand more memory and disk space. But for many applications the results are worth the added cost. The higher the resolution, the harder it is for the human eye to detect individual pixels on the printed page. If its resolution is high enough, painting software and other bit-mapped image editing software can even be used to edit photographic images.

Digital Image Processing: Photographic Editing by Computer

Like a picture created with a high-resolution paint program, a digitized photograph or a photograph captured with a digital camera is a bit-mapped image. **Digital image processing software** allows the user to manipulate photographs and other high-resolution images with tools similar to those found in paint programs. Professional photo editing software is, in fact, very similar to professional paint software; both are tools for editing high-resolution bit-mapped images.

Digital image processing software makes it easier for photographers to remove unwanted reflections, eliminate "red eye," and brush away facial blemishes—to perform the kinds of editing tasks that were routinely done with magnifying glasses and tiny brushes before photographs could be digitized. But digital photographic editing is far more powerful than traditional photo retouching techniques. With image processing software it's possible to distort and *combine* photographs, creating fabricated images that show no evidence of tampering. Supermarket gossip tabloids routinely use these tools to create sensationalistic cover photos. Many experts question whether photographs should be allowed as evidence in the courtroom now that photos can be doctored so convincingly.

This photo of David Byrne, taken from a rock video, shows how image processing software can alter a photo.

Drawing: Object-Oriented Graphics

Because high-resolution paint images and photographs are stored as bit maps, they can make heavy storage and memory demands. Another type of graphics program can economically store pictures with *infinite* resolution, limited only by the resolution capabilities of the output device. **Drawing software** stores a picture, not as a collection of dots, but as a collection of lines and shapes. When you draw a line with a drawing program, the software doesn't record changes in a pixel map. Instead, it calculates and remembers a mathematical formula for the line. A drawing program stores shapes as shapes and text as text. Because pictures are collections of lines, shapes, and other objects, this approach is often called **object-oriented graphics**. In effect, the computer is remembering "a line goes here and a curve goes here and a chunk of text goes here" instead of "this pixel is black and this one is black and this one is white."

The User's View

Drawing with a Computer

Software: ClarisWorks.
The goal: You're about to move into a new room, and you want to find the best way to fit your furniture into the available space. Your furniture is heavy, but you can easily create digital scale models that weigh nothing. It's easier to drag these drawings around a floor plan than to move their real world counterparts.

After opening a ClarisWorks document for drawing, you turn on the Rulers option so you can scale your drawing at 2 feet per inch. Using the rectangle tool from the tool panel, you draw a rectangle representing the room's floor plan. When you click on the rectangle, square handles appear at the corners. Handles allow you to adjust the shape of an object until it's exactly right.

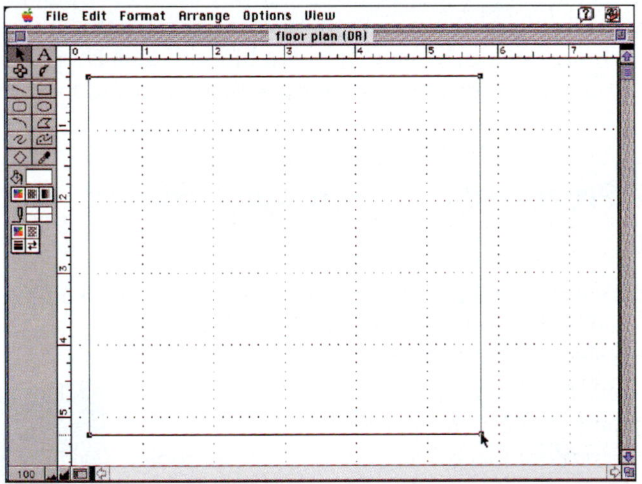

You tear off palettes so you can easily change colors, patterns, and line widths. Using the rectangle tool, the rounded-rectangle tool, and the straight line tool, you drag the doorway, rug, bed, couch, bookshelf, desk, chair, and (of course) computer. An invisible Autogrid makes it easy to create objects to the correct scale and line them up exactly in the drawing.

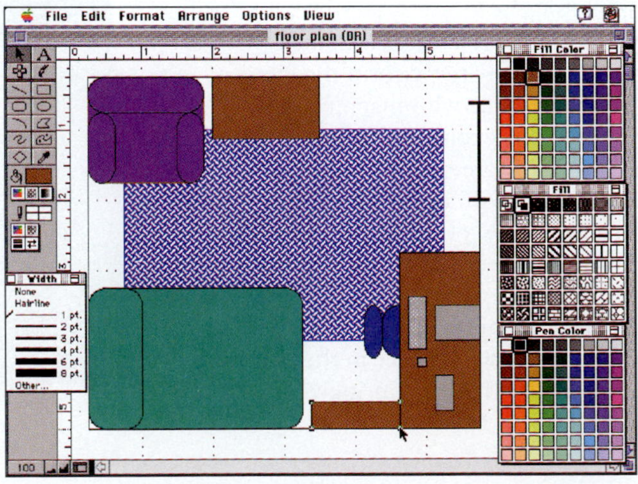

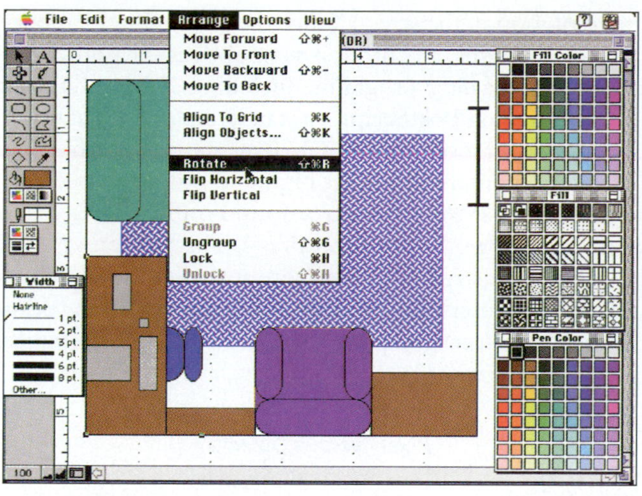

The Group command allows you to group several objects so you can manipulate them as a single object. You group the desk, chair, and computer into a single object so you can rotate it and move it around in the room. In the same way, you move the bed, the couch, and the bookshelf until you're satisfied with an arrangement for the furniture.

Many drawing tools—line, shape, and text tools—are similar to painting tools in bit-mapped programs. But a user can manipulate object-oriented graphics in ways that are difficult or impossible with bit-mapped paintings. Objects can be rotated, resized, duplicated, smoothed, shaped, or deleted without affecting neighboring objects, even if the neighboring objects overlap. Text can always be edited or reformatted because it's stored as text rather than as pixel patterns.

On screen, an object-oriented picture looks similar to a bit-mapped picture. In either case the picture appears at the screen's normal resolution. But when it's printed, an object-oriented picture appears at the resolution of the printer, even if that's much

Artists created all four of these award-winning images using computers. The top two images have textures typical of bit-mapped graphics and the bottom images have crisp lines found in object-oriented graphics.

higher than the resolution of the screen. Since the program remembers shapes as formulas rather than dot patterns, a printout is as smooth as the printer allows.

Many professional drawing programs, including Adobe Illustrator and Aldus Freehand, store images using **PostScript**—a standard **page-description language** for describing text fonts, illustrations, and other elements of the printed page. PostScript is built into many laser printers and other high-end output devices, so those devices can understand and follow PostScript instructions. PostScript-based drawing software constructs a PostScript program as the user draws. This program provides a complete set of instructions for reconstructing the picture at the printer. When the user issues a Print command, the computer sends PostScript instructions to the printer, which uses those instructions to construct the printed page. Most desktop publishing software uses PostScript in the same way.

Pixels versus Objects

How do you edit a picture? It depends on what you're doing and how it s stored.

The task...	Using bit-mapped graphics	Using object-oriented graphics
Moving and removing parts of pictures 	Easier to work with regions than objects especially if those objects overlap 	Easier to work with individual objects or groups of objects, even if they overlap 
Working with shapes 	Shapes are stored as pixel patterns that can be edited with eraser and drawing tools 	Shapes are stored as math formulas, so they can be transformed mathematically 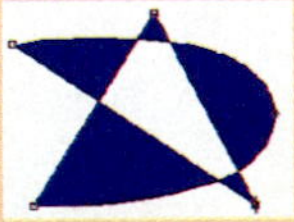
Magnification 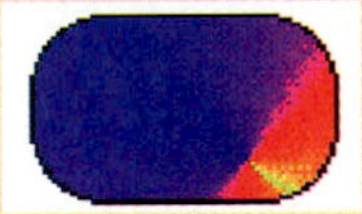	Magnifies pixels for fine detail editing 	Magnifies objects, not pixels 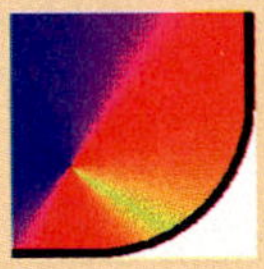
Text handling text	Text dries and can t be edited, but can be moved as a block of pixels 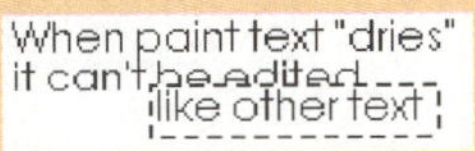 When paint text "dries" it can't be edited like other text	Text can always be edited 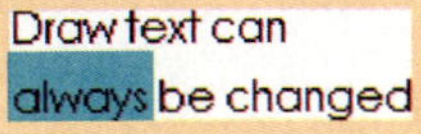 Draw text can always be changed
Printing	Resolution of printout can t exceed the pixel resolution of the stored picture	Resolution is limited only by the output device
Working within the limits of the hardware	Photographic quality is possible but requires considerable memory and disk storage	Complex drawings require considerable computational power for reasonable speed

Rules of Thumb

Creating Smart Art

Modern graphics software isn't just for professional artists. Just about anybody can use it to create pictures and presentations. Here are some guidelines to help you make the most of the computer as a graphic tool:

- **Overcome art anxiety.** For many of us the hardest part is getting started. We are all programmed by messages we received in our childhood, which for many of us included "You aren't creative" and "You can't draw." Fortunately a computer can help us overcome this early programming and find the artist that's locked within us. Most drawing and painting programs are flexible, forgiving, and fun. Allow yourself to experiment; you'll be surprised at what you can create if you're patient and playful. (For more help see *Overcoming Art Anxiety*, by Betty Edwards.)
- **Choose the right tool for the job.** Is your artwork to be displayed on the computer screen or printed? Does your output device support color? Would color enhance the finished work? Your answers to these questions will help you determine which software and hardware tools are most appropriate. As you're thinking about options, don't rule out low-tech tools. The best approach may not involve a computer, or it may involve some combination of computer and nonelectronic tools.
- **Borrow from the best.** Art supply stores sell **clip art**—predrawn images that artists can legally cut out and paste into their own pictures or posters. Computer artists have hundreds of digital clip art collections to choose from, with a difference: Computer clip art images can be cut, pasted, and edited electronically. Some computer clip art collections are in the public domain (free); others can be licensed for a small fee. Computer clip art comes in a variety of formats, and it ranges from simple line drawings to scanned color photographs. If you have access to a scanner, you can create your own digitized clip art from traditional photos and drawings.
- **But don't borrow without permission.** Computers, scanners, and digital cameras make it all too easy to create unauthorized copies of copyrighted photographs, drawings, and other images. There's a clear legal and ethical line between using public domain or licensed clip art and pirating copyrighted material. If you use somebody else's creative work, make sure you don't cross that line.
- **Protect your own work.** Copyright laws aren't just to protect other people's work. If you've created something that's marketable, consider copyrighting it. The process isn't difficult or expensive, and it might help you to get credit (and payment) where credit is due.

Object-oriented graphics and bit-mapped graphics each offer advantages for certain applications. Bit-mapped image editing programs give artists and photo editors unsurpassed control over textures, shading, and fine detail; they're widely used for creating screen displays (for example, in video games) and for embellishing photographic images. Object-oriented drawing and illustration programs are a better choice for creating graphs, charts, and illustrations with clean lines and smooth shapes. Many of the charts and drawings in modern magazines and newspapers are created using object-oriented illustration programs. A growing number of software applications includes features of both. Some programs treat blocks of text as editable objects while storing everything else as bit-mapped images. Other programs allow you to work with different drawing layers, some bit-mapped and some object-oriented.

As desktop computers continue to grow in capacity and power, the distinction between these two graphics types is likely to blur. Future graphics applications will, in all likelihood, combine the best features of both graphics types into seamless tools for drawing, painting, and editing.

Presentation Graphics: Bringing Lectures to Life

One common application for computer graphics today is the creation of visual aids—slides, transparencies, graphics displays, and handouts—to enhance presentations. While drawing and painting programs can create these aids, they aren't as useful as programs designed with presentations in mind.

Presentation graphics software is designed to automate the creation of visual aids for lectures, training sessions, sales demonstrations, and other presentations. When broadly defined, presentation graphics software includes everything from spreadsheet charting programs to animation and video editing software, and many programs can handle these diverse tasks. But specialized presentation graphics programs are most commonly used for creating and displaying **bullet charts** that list the main points of a presentation. Such bullet charts can be output as color slides, overhead transparencies, handouts, or used as on-screen computer "slide shows."

The User's View

Creating Presentation Graphics

Software: Microsoft PowerPoint.
The goal: To create visual aids for a talk you're giving for a class. You'll use PowerPoint, a presentation graphics package that's especially designed for this kind of task.

You start by creating an outline of the main points of your talk, arranging headings and sub-points in the correct order.

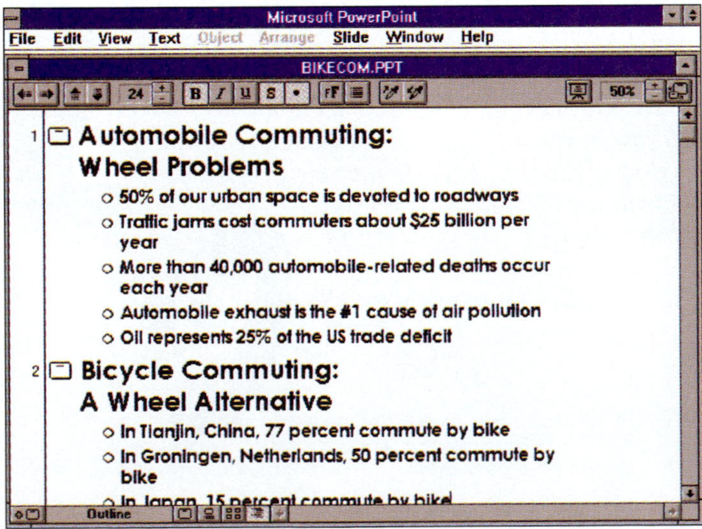

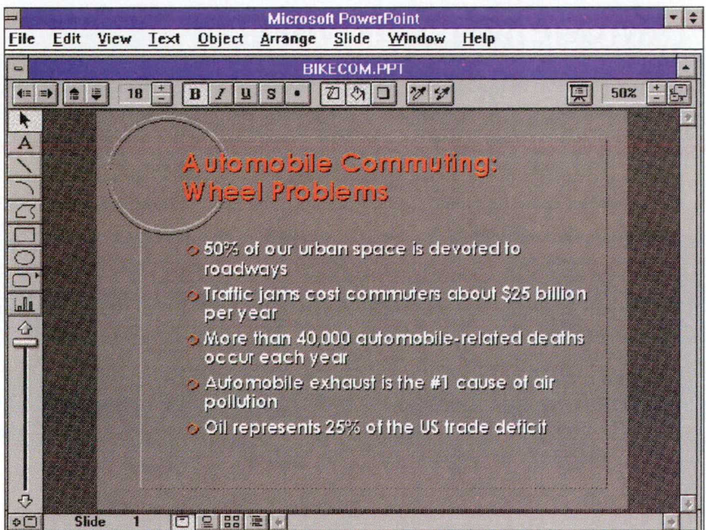

Rather than designing the background, borders, and text format yourself, you select a professionally designed template from the collection that comes with PowerPoint. The program places your text on this template for each slide in the presentation.

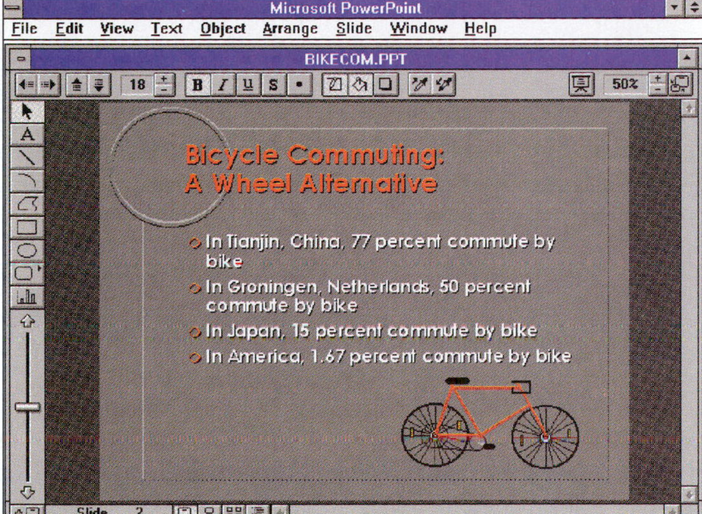

PowerPoint's Drawing tools make it easy to add graphic embellishments. But for this slide, you simply import an image of a bike from a clip art collection that comes with the program.

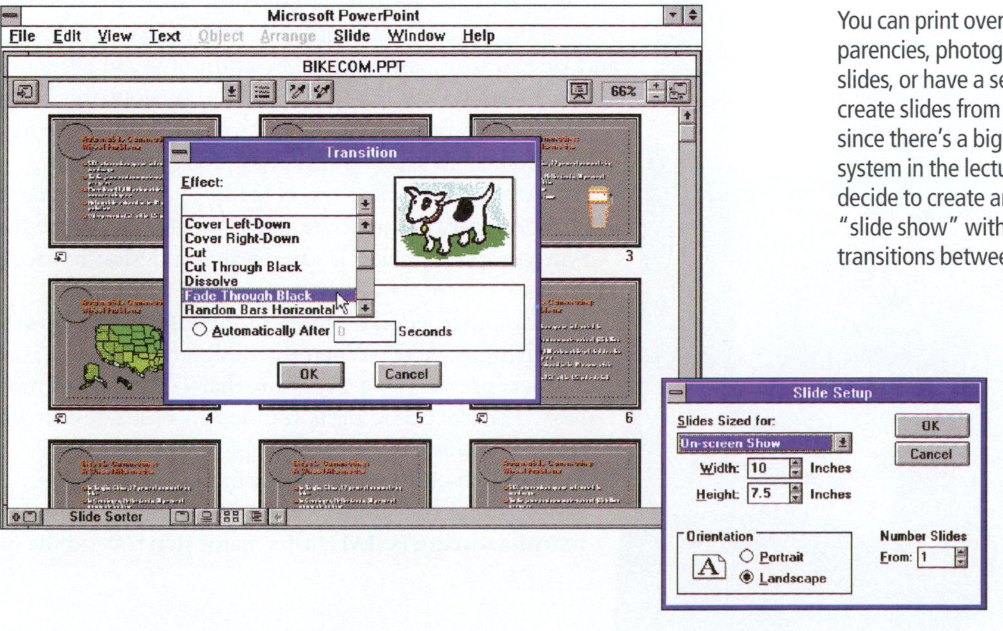

You can print overhead transparencies, photograph screens as slides, or have a service bureau create slides from your disk file. But since there's a big-screen computer system in the lecture room, you decide to create an interactive "slide show" with smooth visual transitions between slides.

3-D Modeling Software

Working with a pencil, an artist can draw a three-dimensional scene on a two-dimensional page. Similarly, an artist can use a drawing or painting program to create a scene that appears to have depth on a two-dimensional computer screen. But in either case the drawing lacks true depth; it's just a flat representation of a scene. With **3-D modeling software** graphic designers can create three-dimensional objects with tools similar to those found in conventional drawing software. You can't touch a 3-D computer model; it's no more real than a square, a circle, or a letter created with a drawing program. But a 3-D computer model can be rotated, stretched, and combined with other model objects to create complex 3-D scenes.

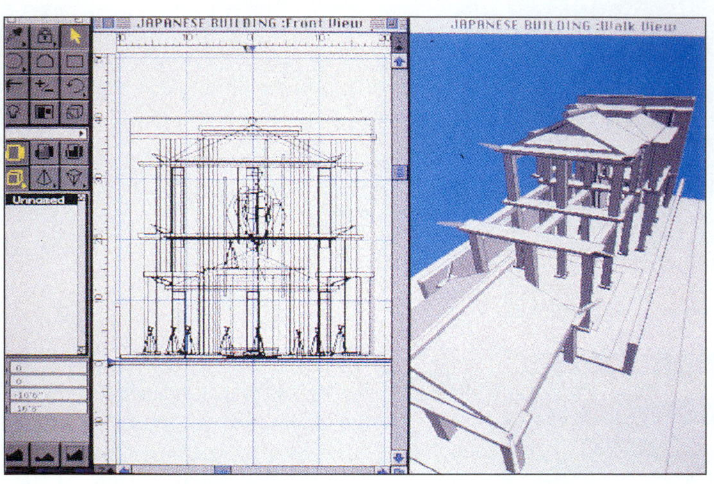

Architects today can use computers to create three-dimensional models of buildings before they're constructed.

Illustrators who use 3-D software appreciate its flexibility. A designer can create a 3-D model of an object, rotate it, view it from a variety of angles, and take two-dimensional "snapshots" of the best views for inclusion in final printouts. Similarly, it's possible to "walk through" a 3-D environment that exists only in the computer's memory, printing snapshots that show the simulated space from many points of view. For many applications the goal is not a printout but an animated presentation on a computer screen or videotape. Animation software and presentation graphics software can display sequences of screens showing 3-D objects being rotated, explored, and transformed. Many modern television and movie special effects involve combinations of live action and simulated 3-D animation. In addition, 3-D graphics play an important role in the branch of engineering known as computer-aided design.

CAD/CAM: Turning Ideas into Products

Computer-aided design (CAD) is the use of computers to design products. CAD software allows engineers and designers to create designs on screen for products ranging from computer chips to public buildings. Today's software goes far beyond basic drafting and object-oriented graphics. It allows users to create three-dimensional "solid" models with physical characteristics like weight, volume, and center of gravity. These models can be rotated and viewed from any angle. The computer can evaluate the structural performance of any part of the model by applying imaginary force to the object. Using CAD an engineer can crash-test a new model of an automobile before it ever leaves the computer screen.

CAD tends to be cheaper, faster, and more accurate than traditional design-by-hand techniques. What's more, the forgiving nature of the computer makes it easy to alter a design to meet the goals of a project.

Computer-aided design is often linked to **computer-aided manufacturing (CAM)**. When the design of a product is completed, the numbers are fed to a program that controls the manufacturing of parts. For electronic parts the design translates directly into a template for etching circuits onto chips. The emergence of CAD/CAM has streamlined the design and manufacturing process. The combination of CAD and CAM is often called **computer-integrated manufacturing (CIM)**; it's a major step toward the fully automated factory.

Beyond Books: Hypertext and Hypermedia

A straight line may be the shortest distance between two points, but it is by no means the most interesting.

—"Dr. Who"

Most modern personal computer applications—painting and drawing programs, word processors, desktop publishers and so on—are designed to produce paper documents. In graphically oriented computers, most of these applications are WYSIWYG—*W*hat *y*ou *s*ee (on the screen) *i*s *w*hat *y*ou *g*et (on the printed page). But as computer visionary Doug Engelbart has demonstrated for decades, WYSIWYG isn't always necessary or desirable. If a document doesn't need to be printed, it doesn't need to be structured like a paper document. By focusing on the relationship of ideas rather than the layout of the page, Engelbart and other pioneers developed another kind of document—a dynamic, cross-referenced super document that takes full advantage of the computer's interactive capabilities.

Hypertext: Early Links

Since President Roosevelt's science advisor, Vannevar Bush, first wrote about such an interactive cross-referenced system in 1945, computer pioneers like Doug Engelbart and Ted Nelson have pushed the technology toward that vision. Early efforts were called **hypertext** because they allowed textual information to be linked in *nonsequential* ways. Conventional text media like books are linear, or *sequential*: They are designed to be read from beginning to end. A hypertext document contains *links* that can lead readers quickly to other parts of the document or to other related documents. Hypertext invites readers to cut their own personal trails through information.

If this book were a hypertext document, you might click on the name Doug Engelbart in the previous paragraph to learn more about Engelbart. You would be

While you're reading about Mark Twain, you might become curious about his hometown in Missouri, his novels, or the river that inspired those novels. Your explorations of 19th-century Hannibal, Missouri, might lead you to explore other Mississippi River towns of the time, or it might inspire you to learn more about midwestern geography. Hypertext puts you in control.

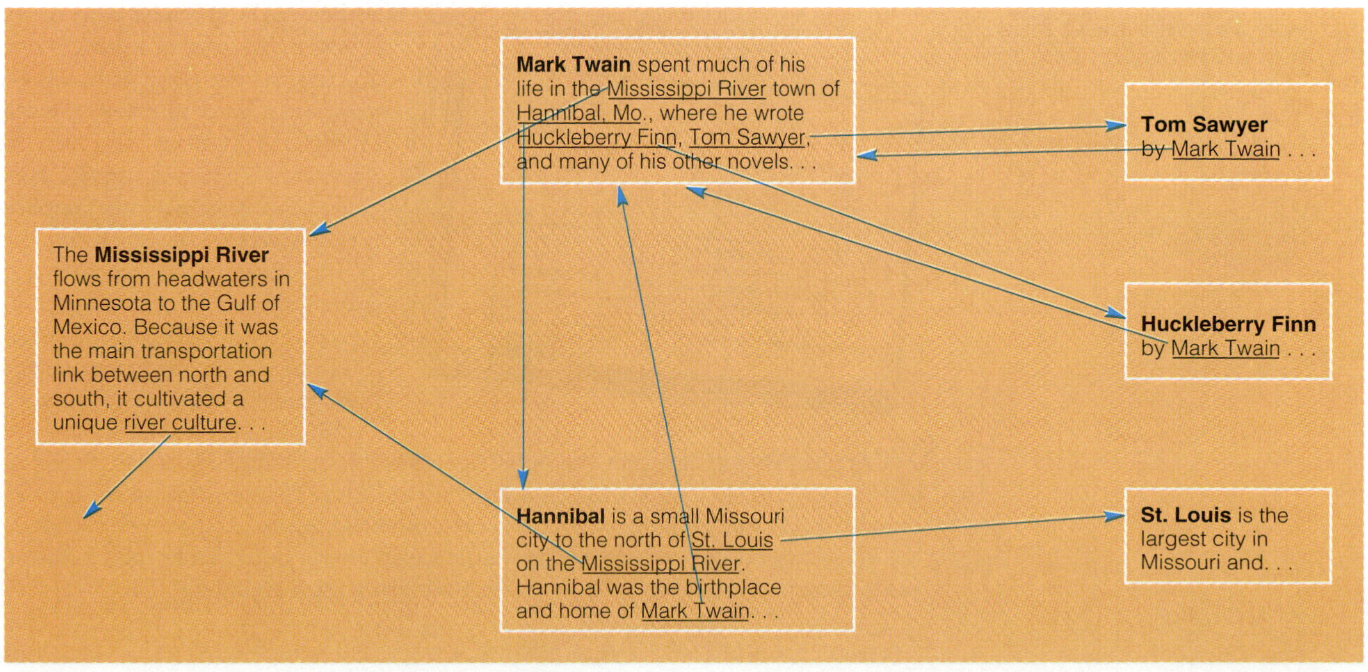

transported to the profile at the beginning of the chapter that described Engelbart's visionary work. After reading that profile you might want to return to this section and continue reading about hypertext. On the other hand, you might want to learn more about Alan Kay, the computer scientist quoted in Engelbart's profile. Clicking on Kay's name would transport you to the profile at the beginning of Chapter 14. From that point you could continue to explore topics related to Alan Kay or return here to learn more about hypertext. With a comprehensive, well-designed hypertext reference, you could follow your curiosity just about anywhere by pointing and clicking.

HyperCard and the Hyperclones

Hypertext first gained widespread public attention in 1987 when Apple introduced **HyperCard**. HyperCard is a hybrid program—part database, part painting program, part presentation graphics system, and part programming language. But most important, HyperCard is the first widely available tool for creating hypertext-like documents.

Unlike early hypertext systems, HyperCard isn't limited to text. A HyperCard document might contain text, numbers, graphics, animation, sound effects, music, and even video clips, all combined in a package that invites the user to browse through the information in a variety of ways. Because it can handle so many different kinds of media, HyperCard is often described not as a hypertext system, but as a **hypermedia** system. The term *hypermedia* describes documents that can be explored in nonlinear ways, from classic hypertext research documents to interactive graphic documents created with HyperCard.

Students, researchers, and others use HyperCard as a tool for browsing nonsequentially through existing hypermedia documents created by others. But HyperCard is also useful as an **authoring system**—a tool for building interactive hypermedia documents for education, training, reference, and entertainment. Because it's designed for nonprogrammers, HyperCard allows adults and children to develop interactive software without mastering complex programming languages.

A HyperCard document, called a **stack**, is based on the metaphor of a stack of index cards. Each screen, called a *card*, can contain graphics, text, and **buttons**—"hot spots" that respond to mouse clicks. Usually clicking on a button (or a chunk of so-called *hot text*) transports you to another card—the next card in the sequence, the previous card, a card far from the current position in the stack, or a card in another stack. HyperCard buttons also can be programmed to play music, open dialog boxes, launch other applications, rearrange information, perform menu operations, dial telephones, send messages to hardware devices, or do other things. (In the next chapter we'll examine the process of programming HyperCard buttons.)

Each HyperCard screen is a card in a stack. Clicking on buttons transports you to other cards, changing what you see on the screen.

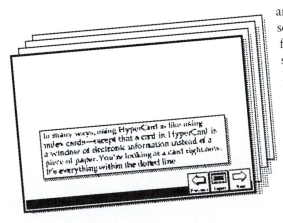

Apple's HyperCard isn't the only hypermedia system available today. Programs like HyperCard such as ToolBook, LinkWay, and HyperStudio, run on most major brands of personal computers. Details vary from program to program. For example, the Windows ToolBook user interface is modeled after a book rather than a stack of cards. Despite the surface differences, the underlying ideas are similar.

The User's View

Creating Hypermedia

Software: HyperCard.
The goal: To produce an interactive display on computers for a class project. The screen should show a picture of a computer with labeled buttons next to each component. By clicking on these buttons, the user can view other screens that describe those components. HyperCard's authoring tools make this kind of project easy.

When you open HyperCard, you see the Home screen: the first card of your Home stack. The screen contains icon buttons linked to different stacks and rectangular buttons linked to other cards in the Home stack. Your pointer is shaped like a hand with an extended finger— a finger designed for clicking on buttons. You click the left arrow button to flip around to the last card in this stack.

The last card of the Home stack allows you to set the *user level* so you have access to HyperCard's authoring tools. After you click on the Authoring button, you're ready to select New Stack from the File menu to create a new stack.

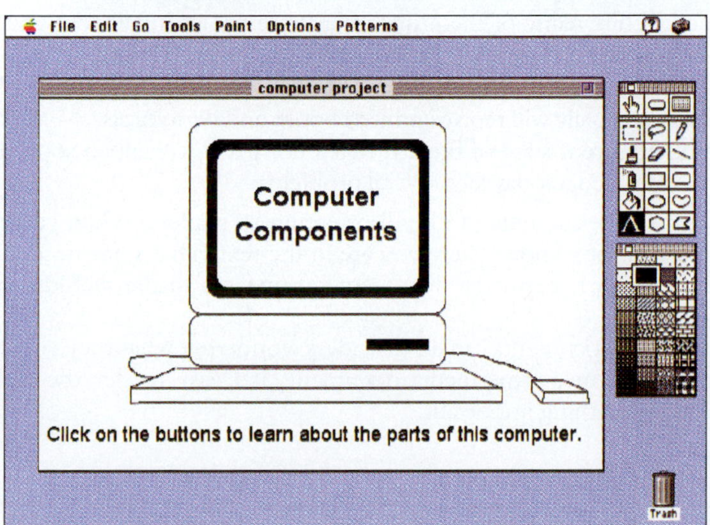

The new stack contains one empty card. You could use HyperCard's paint tools to paint a picture of a computer, but it's easier to import the picture you created earlier using ClarisWorks. (The image is automatically converted to monochrome by HyperCard; preserving the color would have required extra steps.) You add titles using the text tool from the tools palette on screen.

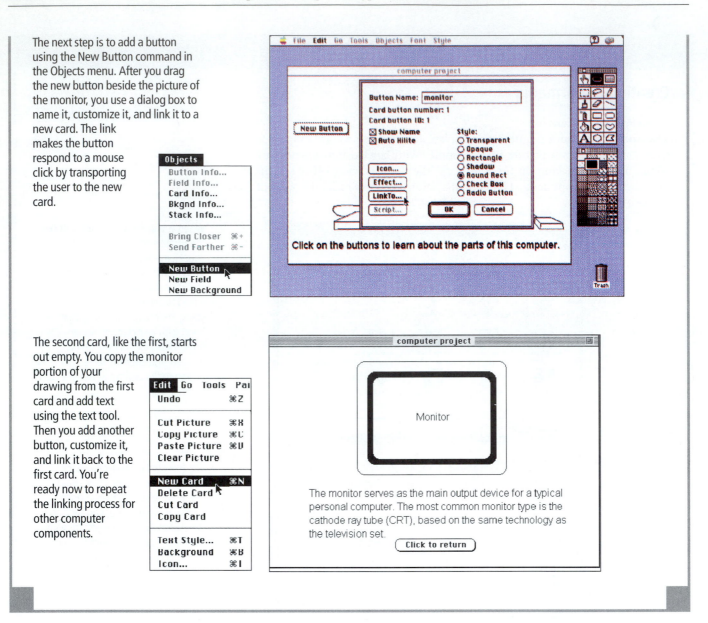

The next step is to add a button using the New Button command in the Objects menu. After you drag the new button beside the picture of the monitor, you use a dialog box to name it, customize it, and link it to a new card. The link makes the button respond to a mouse click by transporting the user to the new card.

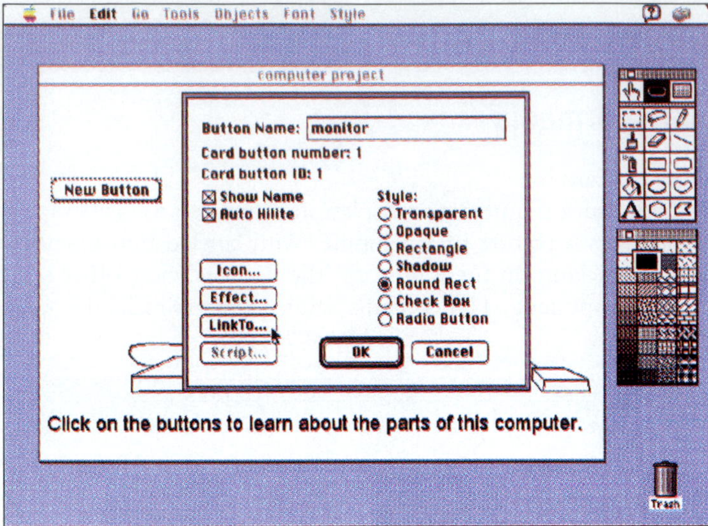

The second card, like the first, starts out empty. You copy the monitor portion of your drawing from the first card and add text using the text tool. Then you add another button, customize it, and link it back to the first card. You're ready now to repeat the linking process for other computer components.

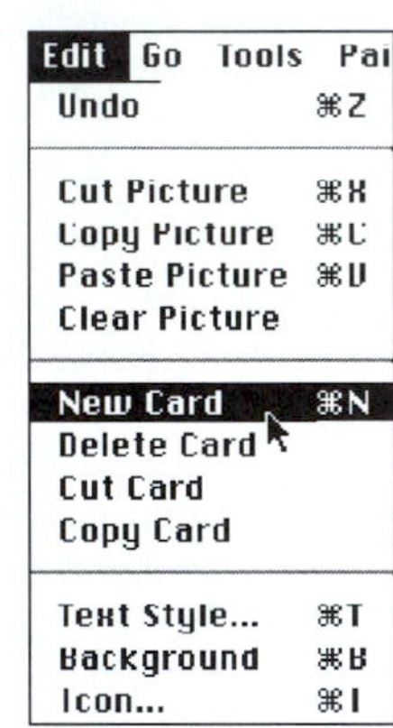

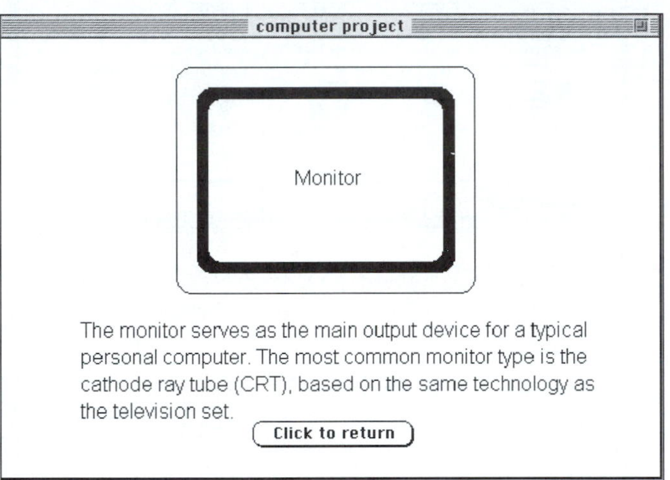

The Future of Hypermedia

Software tools like HyperCard have resulted in a flood of hypermedia documents in recent years. While many of these documents are professionally designed, the great majority are created by computer users with little or no software design experience. The explosive interest in hypermedia has led some experts to suggest that hypermedia publications eventually will replace printed books and periodicals.

Given the current state of the art, that's not likely to happen soon. People who work with hypermedia today face several problems:

- Hypermedia documents can be disorienting to readers. When you're reading a book, you always know where you are in the text. That's not necessarily true for hypermedia. A hypermedia document can make a reader feel lost in a maze of facts.
- Hypermedia documents can leave readers wondering what they've missed. If you jump around in a hypermedia document, it's easy to get the feeling you've bypassed something important.

- Hypermedia documents often fail to fulfill reader expectations. Before a reader can jump from point A to point B in a document, the author must build a link between those points. Hypermedia authors can't anticipate everybody's wishes, so some readers are frustrated because they can't easily get "there" from "here."
- Because they're computer-based, hypermedia documents don't encourage scribbled margin notes, highlighting, or turned page corners for marking key passages. Some hypermedia documents provide buttons for marking cards and text fields to add personal notes, but they aren't quite as friendly and flexible as traditional paper markup tools.
- Hypermedia hardware can be hard on humans. Most people find that reading a computer screen is more tiring than reading printed pages. Many complain that extended periods of screen-gazing cause eyestrain, headache, backache, and other ailments. It's not easy to stretch out under a tree or curl up in an easy chair with a desktop computer, and many hypermedia documents require hardware not found in portable computers.

Still, hypermedia is not all hype. As the art matures, advances in software and hardware design will take care of many of these problems. Many researchers, teachers, and students already appreciate the advantages of computer-based hypermedia. Paper documents simply can't provide the extensive cross-referencing and instant key-word searches that hypermedia offer.

Hypermedia's greatest advantage may lie in the computer's ability to control other media. Unlike books, hypermedia documents aren't limited to static text and pictures. Some of today's best hypermedia documents use sound, animation, and video to bring information to life. As the technology matures, hypermedia and multimedia are converging into a single, user-oriented, interactive technology.

Interactive Multimedia: Eye, Ear, Hand, and Mind

The aim of every artist is to arrest motion, which is life, by artificial means and hold it fixed so that a hundred years later, when a stranger looks at it, it moves again since it is life.

—William Faulkner

We live in a world rich in sensory experience. Information comes to us in a variety of forms: pictures, text, moving images, music, voice, and more. As information-processing machines, computers are capable of delivering information to our senses in a variety of forms. Until recently, computer users could work with only one or two forms of information at a time. Today's multimedia computers, however, allow users to work with information-rich documents that freely intermix a wide variety of audio-visual media.

Interactive Multimedia: What Is It?

The term **multimedia** generally means using some combination of text, graphics, animation, video, music, voice, and sound effects to communicate. By this definition, an episode of "Sesame Street" or the evening news might be considered multimedia. In fact, computer-based multimedia tools are used heavily in the production of "Sesame Street," the evening news, and hundreds of other television programs. Entertainment industry professionals use computers to create animated sequences, display titles, construct special video effects, synthesize music, edit sound tracks, coordinate communication, and perform dozens of other tasks crucial to the production of modern television programs and motion pictures.

So when you watch a typical TV program, you're experiencing a multimedia product. Every second that you watch, the program bombards you with information. The amount of information a medium can transmit per unit of time is called **bandwidth**. In Chapter 7 we used the term *bandwidth* to describe the amount of information transmitted on cables that connect networked computers. The concept of bandwidth also applies to the transmission of information between machine and human. A text-only book is a *low-bandwidth medium*, delivering only about 300 bits of data per second to the average reader. *High-bandwidth media*, like television and video, can deliver more than 50 million bits per second of graphics and audio data.

But television and video are *passive* media. They pour information into our eyes and ears while we sit and take it all in. We have no control over the information flow. Modern personal computer technology allows information to move in both directions, turning multimedia into **interactive multimedia**. Unlike TV, radio, and video, interactive multimedia allow the viewer/listener to take an active part in the experience. The best interactive multimedia software puts the user in charge, allowing that person to control the information flow.

Personal computer users can do more than just experience interactive multimedia documents. With appropri-

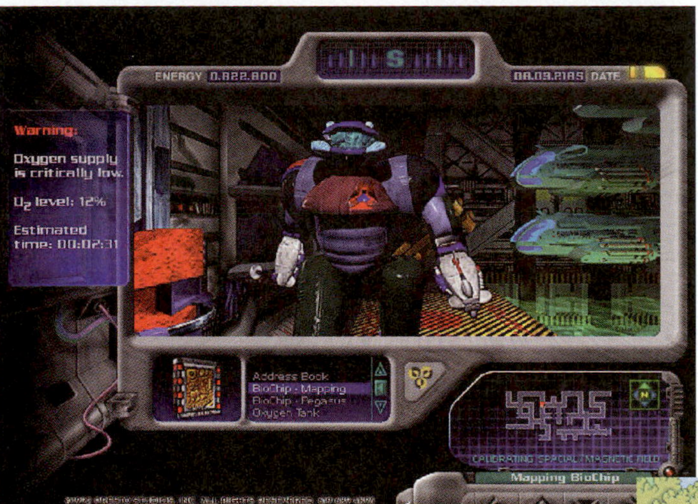

An encyclopedia, complete with moving pictures, sounds, and hypertext cross-referencing; an animated science fiction movie where the audience controls the actions of the main character; a children's book with animated pictures that can read aloud to the child in multiple languages, while words light up on the screen—these interactive multimedia products are all available today. (Software: Comptons' Multimedia Encyclopedia, The Journeyman Project from Presto Studios, and Just Grandma and Me from Broderbund.)

We went to the beach, just Grandma and me.

ate software, they can also create and edit multimedia documents. The best multimedia *authoring tools* nearly duplicate the tools used by media industry professionals. But even inexpensive hypermedia authoring tools like HyperCard can produce impressive and effective interactive multimedia documents.

Multimedia Hardware

In its simplest form interactive multimedia software might be little more than a HyperCard stack with animation and sound effects. This kind of multimedia software doesn't require special hardware; it can be created and displayed on any Macintosh computer. Standard IBM-compatible computers require add-on video and audio circuit boards before they can display high-resolution graphics and play music and sound effects. Many modern IBM-compatible PCs, designed with multimedia in mind, have these boards preinstalled. Because it was designed specifically for multimedia applications, the Commodore Amiga is another popular computer for creating and editing multimedia documents.

Whatever the brand of computer, creating and running many multimedia documents requires additional hardware peripherals, including television monitors, CD-ROM drives, and videodisc players. The computer controls the other devices, which store and deliver the audiovisual material on command. Authoring systems like HyperCard are often used to create friendly user interfaces (sometimes called *front ends*) to control multimedia peripherals. With an intuitive graphical user interface on a computer screen, a videodisc player, a CD-ROM drive, or a music synthesizer can become as easy to use as a child's toy.

For a growing consumer market, the multimedia controlling device might actually *be* a child's toy. Many multimedia software titles are designed to be used with television sets and controlled by game machines from Nintendo, Sega, and other companies. Other interactive multimedia programs are designed specifically for *CD-I* (compact disc-interactive) drives—compact disc players with specially programmed microprocessors and game-style controlling devices designed to work with standard television sets. Game machines and CD-I drives make it possible for people who don't own personal computers to *use*, but not *create*, interactive multimedia software.

Whether you use a ready-made program or create your own, multimedia software earns its name by providing information through a variety of media. Besides text and graphics, multimedia documents typically contain at least one of these three forms of information:

- animation—computer graphics that move on the screen
- video information—film clips shown on the computer's screen or on a separate TV monitor
- audio information—music, sound effects, and spoken words from the computer or some external sound source

We'll look at each of these multimedia components in turn.

Animation: Graphics in Time

Creating motion from still pictures—this illusion is at the heart of all **animation**. Before computers, animated films were hand-drawn, one still picture, or **frame**, at a time. Modern computer graphics technology has transformed both amateur and professional animation by allowing many of the most tedious aspects of the animation process to be automated.

In its simplest form computer-based animation is similar to traditional frame-by-frame animation techniques—each frame is a computer-drawn picture, and the computer displays those frames in rapid succession. But computer animation programs, even the low-priced packages aimed at the home market, contain software tools that

These scenes, from an animated film, were created using professional animation and 3-D modeling software.

can do much more than flip pages. *Visual effect tools* can create dissolves, wipes, and other television-style visual transitions between scenes. *Path animation tools* record the movement of visual objects as the artist drags them around the screen and play back motions on command. *Tweening tools* can fill in a number of frames automatically to smooth the movement between frames. The most powerful animation programs include tools for working with animated objects in three dimensions, adding depth to the scene on the screen.

Desktop Video: Computers and TV

Most animated sequences are made of drawings, whether created with a computer or a pen and brush. But a growing number of multimedia applications can also use video footage to put motion into presentations.

Interactive videodiscs. One common way to incorporate video into interactive multimedia is through computer-controlled videodisc machines. A **videodisc** is a larger cousin of the audio compact disc. Audio and video information on the disc is read and converted into sound and pictures by a **videodisc player** connected to a TV monitor. A videodisc can contain an hour or more of video footage, complete with a two-channel CD-quality soundtrack. The two sound channels aren't always used for stereo music reproduction; they might offer users a choice of languages, for example. Because a videodisc player has the ability to display individual frames (pictures), it can be used like a slide projector. A single 12-inch disc can hold thousands of still images per side. Since the videodisc is a random access medium (unlike a videotape, which must be viewed sequentially), the images, video segments, and sounds can be rapidly presented in any order.

Many commercial videodisc players are designed to accept commands from attached computers. With a computer-controlled videodisc player, a viewer can use on-screen buttons to view pictures, hear audio passages, play film clips, or even construct personalized sequences of images and sounds. In some multimedia systems the control buttons share the screen with video images, and the user activates these buttons by touching the screen. Other systems display the video images, and the computer controls on separate screens; typically, viewers use mice and trackballs to control these systems. Either way, the result is interactive video—television that pays attention to the viewer!

These students are learning French using an interactive video disk system.

Digital video. Conventional television and video images are stored and broadcast as analog (smooth) electronic signals. Within the next decade that's likely to change, however, as the television and video industries switch to **digital video** storage and transmission. Because digital video can be reduced to a series of numbers, it can be edited, stored, and played back without any loss of quality. Digital video, like text, numbers, and computer graphics, can be treated as data by computers and combined with other forms of data.

Until digital video becomes the standard, **video digitizers** are available that allow computers to convert analog video signals into digital data for a variety of purposes. Some video digitizers can import video signals from televisions, videotapes, videodiscs, and other sources and display them on the computer's screen in *real time*—at the same time they're created or imported—along with computer controls and other graphic images. Other video digitizers are designed to capture video sequences in real time and convert them into digital "movies" that can be stored, edited, and played on computer screens at a later time without external video equipment.

On-screen digital movies can add realism and excitement to educational, training, presentation, and entertainment software. But digital movies aren't practical for many applications because of their heavy hardware demands. Even a short full-screen video clip can quickly fill a large hard disk. To save storage space and to allow the processor to keep up with the quickly changing frames, most digital movies are displayed on computer screens in small windows with fewer than the standard video rate of 30 frames per second. In addition, **data compression** software can be used to squeeze redundant data out of movies so they can be stored in smaller spaces, usually with only a slight loss of image quality. (General data compression software can be used to reduce the size of almost any kind of data file; specialized *image compression software* is generally used to compress graphics and video files.) But even highly compressed video clips gobble up storage space quickly. That's why most digital movies are stored on CD-ROM and other high-capacity storage media. As compression and storage technologies continue to improve, digital movies will become larger, longer, smoother, and more common in everyday computing applications.

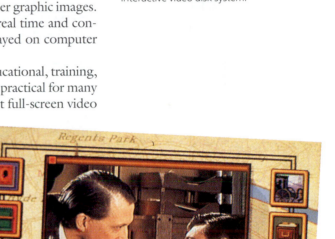

For an added sense of realism, this interactive detective game includes actual video footage of characters in action. (Software: Sherlock Holmes, Consulting Detective from Icom Simulations.)

Video editing. Professionals in the motion picture, television, and video industries depend on high-powered graphic workstations connected to sophisticated audio and videotape players and recorders. With video editing software this hardware can splice together scenes, insert visual transitions, superimpose titles, create special effects, add a musical soundtrack, and "print" a copy of the results on a master videotape.

Professional video workstations typically cost hundreds of thousands of dollars—more than most individuals, schools, and small businesses can afford to pay. But today it's possible to put together a PC-based system that can perform most of the same functions for a fraction of the cost. The Commodore Amiga computer provides near-broadcast-quality video editing potential for the lowest cost—a few thousand dollars for a complete system. These low-end systems wouldn't meet the needs of Steven Spielberg or George Lucas, but they satisfy thousands of video enthusiasts with smaller budgets. If current trends continue, low-cost video editing systems will transform the video industry in the same way that desktop publishing has revolutionized the world of the printed word.

The Synthetic Musician: Computers and Audio

It's easy to play any musical instrument: all you have to do is touch the right key at the right time and the instrument will play itself.

—*J.S. Bach*

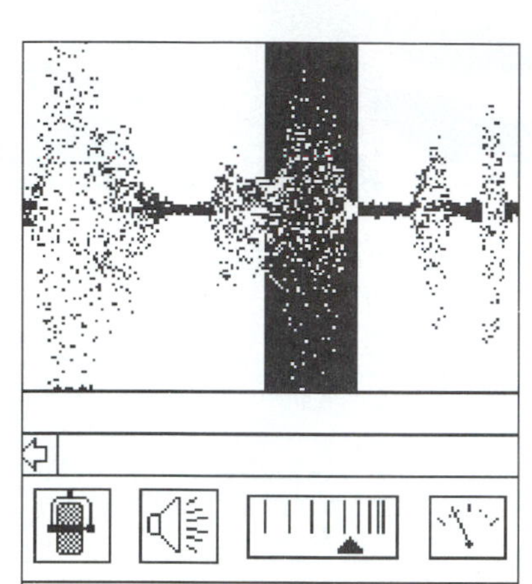

This waveform is a visual representation of the digitized phrase "I am not a crook," ready for editing. The section highlighted in black is the word "not." Pressing Delete will turn the sound bite into "I am a crook!" (Software: Soundedit from MacroMedia.)

Sound and music can turn a visual presentation into an activity that involves the ears, the eyes, and the whole brain. Sound can capture attention, establish moods, heighten transitions, and stress key points. For many applications, sound puts the *multi* in *multimedia.*

Recorded sound, like video, can come from data in the computer's memory or from an external playback device controlled by commands from the computer. But sounds don't need to be recorded before they can be used by the computer. They can be synthetically generated, or *synthesized.* We'll consider both recorded sound and synthesized sound as components of interactive multimedia.

Digitized sounds as computer data. Any sound that can be recorded can be captured with an **audio digitizer** and stored as a data file on a diskette, hard disk, or other computer storage medium. Many multimedia computers, including all newer Macintoshes, include audio digitizing hardware. Inexpensive add-on audio digitizers are available for other computers.

Digitized sound data, like other computer data, can be loaded into the computer's memory and manipulated by software. Sound editing software can change a sound's volume and pitch, add special effects like echoes, remove extraneous noises, even rearrange musical passages. Sound data is sometimes called *waveform audio,* because this kind of editing often involves manipulating a visual image of the sound's waveform.

To play a digitized sound, the computer must load the data file into memory, convert it to an analog sound, and play it through a speaker. All Macintoshes, all Amigas, and many IBM-compatible computers include hardware for turning digital data into analog sound output. Other PCs can produce the same results with add-on digital-to-analog sound boards.

Recorded sound can consume large amounts of space on disk and in memory. Sound data compression, like image compression, saves space, but it also compromises sound quality. Even without compression, memory-resident digital recordings usually lack the crystal-clear fidelity of compact disc recordings. The difference is due to differences in *sampling rate*—the number of sound "snapshots" the recording equipment takes each second. Because of its high sampling rate, a CD's sound closely approximates the original analog sound.

A student explores a Beethoven symphony using a CD that contains both music and a graphical, interactive tutorial.

CD audio. A computer can also play sounds from standard audio CDs using a CD-ROM drive connected to headphones or amplified speakers. Sounds are stored on CDs, not in the computer's memory. When the sounds are stored on CDs, software needs to contain only *commands* telling the CD-ROM drive what to play and when to play it.

The advantages of CD audio are obvious: The sound quality is high and the storage costs are low. Of course, this approach requires CD-ROM hardware, an external sound system, and a CD containing the necessary music or sounds. Since CD-ROM is a read-only medium, CD sound is "listen-only"—there's no way for the user to record sounds. But for music appreciation, language instruction, and other educational applications that can take advantage of commercial recordings, CD-based audio is a sound alternative.

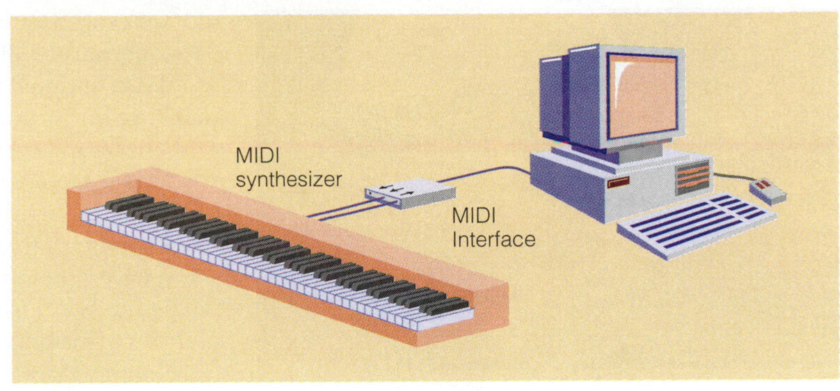

A MIDI interface allows a computer to communicate with and control a synthesizer.

Electronic musical instruments. Multimedia computers can also control a variety of electronic musical instruments.

A **synthesizer** is an electronic instrument that can create sounds ranging from traditional horns and woodwinds to other-worldly sounds that can't be duplicated with acoustic instruments. Synthesized sounds aren't recorded; they're created from mathematical formulas. A typical synthesizer has a built-in piano-style keyboard along with controls for selecting and modifying instrument sounds.

A **sampler** is like a cross between an audio digitizer and a synthesizer. A sampler samples (digitizes) sounds from the real world, turns them into notes, and plays them back through a synthesizer-like keyboard. Samplers are used to simulate pianos and other acoustic instruments with hard-to-synthesize sounds. But a sampler can just as easily turn the sound of a barking dog into a keyboard-controlled canine cantata! Many modern electronic instruments come equipped with hybrid sounds—part sampled, part synthesized.

Not all synthesizers and samplers include keyboards. A musician might have a dozen synthesizers controlled by a single keyboard; the keyboard sends digital commands to the other instruments through MIDI cables. **MIDI**—Musical Instrument Digital Interface—is a standard interface that allows electronic instruments, regardless of type, manufacturer, or brand, to communicate with each other

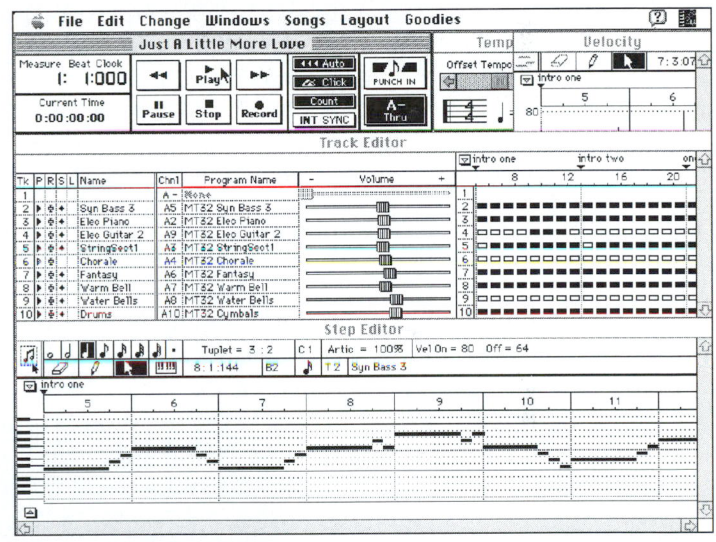

Sequencing software is like a cross between a multitrack tape recorder and a word processor. A sequencer allows a single person to compose, edit, and combine several parts into a complete instrumental composition. Amateur and professional musicians use sequencing software for composition, recording, and performance. (Software: Master Track Pro from Passport.)

Music publishing software can turn a MIDI file into a musical score, ready for publishing. For many musicians and publishers, this kind of software has eliminated the tedious and error-prone process of transcribing musical scores by hand. (Software: Encore from Passport.)

In the modern music studio, computer keyboards and music keyboards often sit side-by-side.

and work together. In a sense, MIDI is the universal language of the electronic music industry.

When outfitted with a *MIDI interface*, a personal computer can "talk" to MIDI musical instruments. A MIDI connection allows synthesizers and other instruments to provide real-time, high-quality sound for multimedia productions. Since instruments create the sounds, the computer only needs to store and process MIDI messages—numbers that tell the instruments what sounds to assign to notes, what notes to play, and how to play them. A *MIDI file* containing the MIDI messages for a song or soundtrack takes just a few kilobytes of memory.

Nonmusicians can use ready-to-play *clip music* MIDI files for multimedia productions. But anyone with even marginal piano-playing skills and **sequencing software** can create MIDI music files. Sequencing software turns a computer into a musical composition, recording, and editing machine. The computer records MIDI signals as a musician plays each part on a keyboard. The musician can use the computer to layer instrumental tracks, substitute instrument sounds, edit notes, cut-and-paste passages, transpose keys, and change tempos, listening to each change as it's made. The finished composition can be played by the sequencing software or exported to any other MIDI-compatible software, including a variety of multimedia applications.

With the appropriate software, a computer can be used as an aid for composing, recording, performing, music publishing, and music education. Just as computer graphics technology has changed the way many artists work, electronic music technology has transformed the world of the musician. What's more, computer music technology has the power to unleash the musician in the rest of us.

Rules of Thumb

Making Interactive Multimedia Work

Whether you're creating a simple HyperCard stack or a full-blown multimedia extravaganza, your finished product will communicate more effectively if you follow a few simple guidelines:

- **Be consistent.** Group similar controls together and keep a consistent visual appearance throughout the presentation.
- **Make it intuitive.** Use graphical metaphors to guide viewers and make your controls do what they look like they should do.
- **Keep it lively.** If your presentation doesn't include motion, sound, and lots of user interaction, it probably should be printed and distributed as a paper.
- **The message is more important than the media.** Don't let the bells and whistles get in the way of your message. Your goal is to communicate information, not saturate with sensations.
- **Put the user in the driver's seat.** Include controls for turning down sound, bypassing repetitive animation, and turning off annoying features. Provide navigation aids, search tools, bookmarks, on-line help, and "where am I?" feedback. Never tell the user "You can't get there from here."
- **Let real people test your presentation.** The best way to find out if your presentation works is to test it on people who aren't familiar with the subject. If they get lost or bored, find out why and fix it.

Interactive Media: Visions of the Future

For most of recorded history, the interactions of humans with their media have been primarily passive in the sense that marks on paper, paint on walls, even motion pictures and television, do not change in response to the viewer's wishes. [But computers can] respond to queries and experiments—so that the message may involve the learner in a two-way conversation.

—Alan Kay

For hundreds of thousands of years, two-way, interactive communication was the norm: One person talked, another responded. Today television, radio, newspapers, magazines, and books pour information into billions of passive people every day. For many people, one-way, passive communication has become more common than interactive discourse.

According to many experts, interactive multimedia technology offers new hope for turning communication back into a participation sport. With interactive multimedia software, the audience is a part of the show. Interactive multimedia tools can give everyday people control over the media—control traditionally reserved for professional artists, film makers, and musicians. The possibilities are far-reaching, especially when telecommunication enters the picture. Consider these snapshots from a not-too-distant future:

- Instead of watching your biology professor flip through overhead transparencies, you control a self-paced, interactive presentation complete with video footage illustrating key concepts.
- In your electronic mailbox you find a "letter" from your sister. The letter shows her performing all the instrumental parts for a song she composed, followed by a request for you to add a vocal line.
- Your favorite TV show is an interactive thriller that allows you to control the plot twists and work with the main characters to solve mysteries.
- You share your concerns about a proposed factory in your hometown at the televised electronic town meeting. Thousands of others respond to questions from the mayor by pressing buttons on their remote control panels. The overwhelming citizen response forces the city council to reconsider the proposal.

Of course, the future of interactive multimedia may not be all sunshine and roses. Many experts fear that these exciting new media possibilities will further remove us from books, other people, and the natural world around us. If television today can mesmerize so many people, will tomorrow's interactive multimedia TVs cause even more serious addiction problems? Or will interactive communication breathe new life into the media and the people who use them? Will interactive electronic media make it easier for abusers of power to influence and control unwary citizens, or will the power of the push button create a new kind of digital democracy? Will interactive digital technology just turn "sound bites" into "sound bytes," or will it unleash the creative potential in the people who use it? For answers, stay tuned.

Summary

Computer graphics today encompass more than quantitative charts and graphs generated by spreadsheets. Bit-mapped painting programs allow users to "paint" the screen with a mouse, pen, or other pointing device. The software stores the results in a pixel map, with each pixel having an assigned color. The more possible colors and the higher the resolution (pixel density), the more the images can approach photorealism.

Object-oriented drawing programs also allow users to draw on the screen with a pointing device, but the results are stored as collections of geometric objects rather than as maps of computer bits.

Bit-mapped graphics and object-oriented graphics each offer advantages in particular situations; tradeoffs involve storage, printing, editing, and ease of use. Both types of graphics have applications outside the art world. Bit-mapped graphics are used in high-resolution digital image processing software for on-screen photo editing. Object-oriented graphics are at the heart of 3-D modeling software and computer-aided design (CAD) software used by designers and engineers. Presentation graphics software, which may include either or both graphics types, automates the process of creating slides, transparencies, handouts, and computer-based presentations, making it easy for nonartists to create visually attractive presentations.

The interactive nature of the personal computer makes it possible to create nonlinear documents that allow users to take individual paths through information. Early nonlinear documents were called hypertext, because they could contain only text. Today authoring systems like HyperCard allow users to create or explore hypermedia documents—interactive documents that mix text, graphics, sound, and moving images with on-screen navigation buttons.

Today's multimedia computer systems make a new kind of software possible—software that uses text, graphics, animation, video, music, voice, and sound effects to communicate. Interactive multimedia software might be as simple as a HyperCard document that includes animation and sound. Consumer-oriented systems like CD-I allow home entertainment systems to function as interactive multimedia systems. More complex multimedia systems involve connecting personal computers to external media devices like television monitors, videodisc players, VCRs, CD-ROM drives, and musical instruments. Regardless of the hardware, the computer allows the user to control the presentation rather than just watch or listen passively. Only time will tell whether these new media will live up to their potential for enhancing education, training, entertainment, and cultural enrichment.

CHAPTER REVIEW

Key Terms

animation
audio digitizer
authoring system
bandwidth
bit-mapped graphics
bullet chart
button
clip art
computer-aided design (CAD)
computer-aided manufacturing (CAM)
computer-integrated manufacturing (CIM)
data compression
digital image processing software
digital video
drawing software
frame
gray-scale graphics
HyperCard
hypermedia
hypertext
interactive multimedia
MIDI
monochrome graphics
multimedia
musical publishing software
object-oriented graphics
page-description language
painting software
palette
pixel
pop-up menu
PostScript
presentation graphics software
resolution
sampler
sequencing software
stack
synthesizer
3-D modeling software
true color
video digitizer
videodisc
videodisc player

Review Questions 

1. What is the difference between bit-mapped graphics and object-oriented graphics? What are the advantages and disadvantages of each?
2. What two technological factors limit the realism of a bit-mapped image? How are these related to storage of that image in the computer?
3. How is digital image processing of photographs related to bit-mapped painting?
4. How does presentation graphics software differ from painting and drawing software?
5. Describe several practical applications for 3-D modeling and CAD software.
6. How do hypertext and other hypermedia differ from linear media?
7. Describe several practical applications for hypermedia.
8. What are the main disadvantages of hypermedia when compared to conventional media such as books and videos?
9. Why are videodiscs used more often than videotapes for interactive multimedia applications?
10. Why is image compression an important part of digital video technology?
11. Discuss the relative advantages for multimedia sound of having the computer store digital sounds internally, control a CD-ROM drive, and control a music synthesizer. Describe a practical application of each sound source.
12. Is it possible to have hypermedia without multimedia? Is it possible to have multimedia without hypermedia? Explain your answer.

Discussion Questions 

1. How does modern digital image processing technology affect the reliability of photographic evidence? How does digital audio technology affect the reliability of sound recordings as evidence? How should our legal system respond to this technology?
2. Scanners, video digitizers, and audio digitizers make it easier than ever for people to violate copyright laws. What, if anything, should be done to protect intellectual property rights of the people who create pictures, videos, and music? Under what circumstances do you think it's acceptable to copy sounds or images for use in your own work?
3. Do you think hypermedia documents will eclipse certain kinds of books and other media? Which ones? Why?
4. Thanks to modern electronic music technology, one or two people can make a record that would have required dozens of musicians 20 years ago. What impact will electronic music technology ultimately have on the music profession?
5. Try to answer each of the questions posed at the end of the section called "Interactive Media: Visions of the Future."

Projects 

1. Draw a familiar object or scene using a bit-mapped painting program. Draw the same object or scene with an object-oriented drawing program. Describe how the process changed using different software.
2. Create visual aids for a speech or lecture using presentation graphics software. In what ways did the software make the job easier? What limitations did you find?
3. Create an interactive hypermedia document using HyperCard, ToolBook, or some other authoring tool. Test your document on several people and describe the results.
4. Compose an original music composition using a synthesizer, a computer, and a sequencer. Describe the experience.
5. Create a short animated presentation using some kind of animation software. Describe the experience.

Sources and Resources 

Most of the best graphics applications books are software-specific. When you decide on a software application, choose books based on your chosen software.

The Desktop Multimedia Bible, by Jeff Burger (Reading, MA: Addison-Wesley, 1993). This book comes close to living up to its title, with broad coverage of all aspects of desktop multimedia. The what, why, and how of graphics, video, audio, and integrated media are dealt with in clear, understandable prose.

Computer Lib: Dream Machines, by Ted Nelson (Redmond, WA: Microsoft Press, 1987). This book by the man who coined the term "hypertext" is really two related books bound back to back. These books mix information, speculation, and vision using a highly unorthodox organizational scheme. The results are sometimes fascinating, sometimes frustrating, but always informative.

Hypertext Hands-On! An Introduction to a New Way of Organizing and Accessing Information, by Ben Shneiderman and Greg Kearsley (Reading, MA: Addison-Wesley, 1989). This is a broad, well-written overview of hypertext. The book comes with software for IBM-compatibles; the software is a hypertext version of the book.

HyperCard 2 in a Hurry, by George Beekman (Belmont, CA: Wadsworth, 1992). This self-teaching guide is designed to get beginners up to speed with HyperCard, the most popular hypermedia authoring tool. The author is a great guy.

Verbum (PO Box 15439, San Diego, CA 92115, 619/233-9977). This cutting-edge magazine covers the electronic art world. It's a visually stylish periodical that demonstrates by example how computers and art go together. *Verbum Interactive*, an occasional computer-based version of the magazine, includes animation, video, and CD-audio (requires a Macintosh and a CD-ROM drive).

Nautilus (7001 Discovery Blvd., Dublin, OH 43017-3299, 800/637-3472). This is the first interactive multimedia periodical available for both Windows and Macintosh machines. Each monthly CD-ROM disc is packed with shareware, multimedia demos, clip art, MIDI files, and useful information.

NewMedia Magazine (901 Mariner's Island Blvd., Suite 365, San Mateo, CA 94404, 415/573-5190). This lively bimonthy magazine covers computer-related multimedia with news, reviews, feature articles, and lots of graphics.

Keyboard and *Electronic Musician*. These two magazines are among the best sources for up-to-date information on computers and music synthesis.

Batman: Digital Justice, story and art by Pepe Moreno (New York: DC Comics, 1990). The title of this hard-cover comic book has a double meaning: The story takes place in a futuristic digital cyberspace, and the book itself—everything from the original art to the finished pages—was created using digital technology.

CHAPTER

NINE

Systems Design and Development

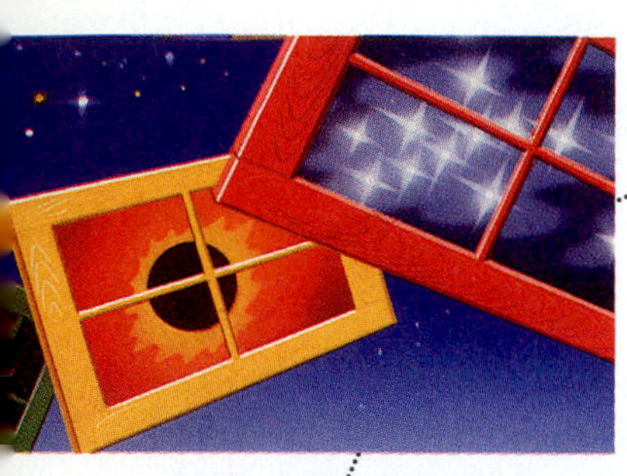

Grace Murray Hopper Sails on Software

The only phrase I've ever disliked is, "Why, we've always done it that way." I always tell young people, "Go ahead and do it. You can always apologize later."

—— Grace Murray Hopper

After reading this chapter you should be able to

- describe the process of designing, programming, and debugging a computer program
- explain why there are many different programming languages and give examples of several
- explain why computer languages are built into applications, operating systems, and utilities
- describe the life cycle of an information system and explain the purpose of program maintenance
- explain the relationship between computer programming and computer science
- describe the problems faced by software engineers in trying to produce reliable large systems

Amazing Grace, the grand old lady of software, had little to apologize for when she died at the age of 85 in 1992. More than any other woman, Grace Murray Hopper helped chart the course of the computer industry from its earliest days into the present.

Hopper earned a Ph.D. from Yale in 1928 and taught math for ten years at Vassar before joining the U.S. Naval Reserve in 1943. The Navy assigned her to the Bureau of Ordinance Computation at Harvard, where she worked with Howard Aiken's Mark I, the first large-scale digital computer. She wrote programs and operating manuals for the Mark I, Mark II, and Mark III.

Grace Murray Hopper

Aiken often asked his team, "Are you making any numbers?" When she wasn't "making numbers," Hopper replied that she was "debugging" the computer. Today that's what programmers call the process of finding and removing errors, or *bugs*, from programs. But when Hopper first used the term, she was referring to a *real* bug—a two-inch moth that got caught in a relay, bringing the mighty Mark II to a standstill! That moth carcass is taped to a page in a log book, housed in a Navy museum in Virginia.

Hopper recognized early that businesses could make good use of computers. After the war she left Harvard to work on the UNIVAC I, the first general-purpose commercial computer, and other commercial computers. She played central roles in the development of the first compiler (a type of computer language translator that makes most of today's software possible) and COBOL, the most widely used language for developing business software.

Throughout most of her career, Hopper remained anchored to the Navy. When she retired from the fleet with the rank of rear admiral at the age of 79, her list of accomplishments filled eight single-spaced pages in her Navy biography.

But Hopper's greatest impact was probably the result of her tireless crusade against the "We've always done it that way" mindset. In the early days of computing, she worked to persuade businesses to embrace the new technology. In later years she campaigned to shift the Pentagon and industry away from mainframes and toward networks of smaller computers. Her vigorous campaign against the status quo earned her a reputation as being controversial and contrary. That didn't bother Amazing Grace, whose favorite maxim was "A ship in port is safe, but that's not what ships are for."

Today's personal computer software is so sophisticated that it's almost invisible to the user. Just as a great motion picture can make us forget we're watching a movie, word processing software allows us to do our creative work without ever thinking about the instructions and data flowing through the computer's processor as we work. But whether you're writing a paper, solving a calculus problem, or flying a simulated space shuttle, your imaginary environment stands on an incredibly complex software substructure. The process of creating that software is one of the most intellectually challenging activities ever done by people.

In this chapter we'll look at the process of turning ideas into working computer programs and consider the "life cycle" of a typical program. We'll examine a variety of computer languages and the ways programmers use them to create software. In addition, we'll see how computer *users* take advantage of the programming languages built into applications, operating systems, and utilities. We'll confront the problems involved in producing reliable software and consider the implications of depending on unstable software. In the process of exploring software, we'll see how the work of programmers, analysts, software engineers, and computer scientists affects our lives and our work.

How People Make Programs

It's the only job I can think of where I get to be both an engineer and an artist. There's an incredible, rigorous, technical element to it, which I like because you have to do very precise thinking. On the other hand, it has a wildly creative side where the boundaries of imagination are the only real limitation.

—*Andy Hertzfeld*, codesigner of *the Macintosh, in* Programmers at Work

Most computer users depend on professionally programmed applications—spreadsheets, database programs, page layout programs, and the like—as problem-solving tools. But in some cases it's necessary or desirable to *write* a program rather than use one written by somebody else. As a human activity, computer programming is a relative newcomer. But **programming** is a specialized form of the age-old process of problem solving. Problem solving typically involves four steps:

1. *Understanding the problem.* Defining the problem *clearly* is often the most important—and most overlooked—step in the problem-solving process.
2. *Devising a plan for solving the problem.* What resources are available? People? Information? A computer? Software? Data? How might those resources be put to work to solve the problem?
3. *Carrying out the plan.* This phase often overlaps with step 2, since many problem-solving schemes are developed on the fly.
4. *Evaluating the solution.* Is the problem solved correctly? Is this solution applicable to other problems?

The programming process can also be described as a four-step process, although in practice these steps often overlap:

1. *Defining the problem*
2. *Devising, refining, and testing the algorithm*
3. *Writing the program*
4. *Testing and debugging the program*

Most programming problems are far too complex to solve all at once. To turn a problem into a program, a programmer typically creates a list of smaller problems. Each of these smaller problems can be broken into subproblems that can be subdivided in the same way. This process, called **stepwise refinement**, is similar to the process of developing an outline before writing a paper or a book. Programmers sometimes refer to this type of design as **top-down design**, because the design process starts at the top, with the main ideas, and works down to the details.

The result of stepwise refinement is an **algorithm**—a set of step-by-step instructions that, when completed, solves the original problem. (Recall Suzanne's French toast recipe in Chapter 3.) Programmers typically write algorithms in a form called **pseudocode**—a cross between a computer language and plain English. When the details of an algorithm are in place, a programmer can translate it from pseudocode into a computer language.

From Idea to Algorithm

Let's develop a simple algorithm to illustrate the process. We'll start with a statement of the problem:

> *A schoolteacher needs a program to play a number-guessing game so students can learn to develop logical strategies and practice their arithmetic. In this game the computer picks a number between 1 and 100 and gives the player seven turns to guess the number. After each incorrect try, the computer tells the player whether the guess is too high or too low.*
>
> In short, the problem is to write a program that can
>
> *play a guessing game*

Stepwise refinement. The first cut at the problem breaks it into three parts: a beginning, a middle, and an end. Each of these parts represents a smaller programming problem to solve.

> *begin game*
> *repeat turn until number is guessed or seven turns are completed*
> *end game*

These three steps represent a bare-bones algorithm. In the completed algorithm, these three parts will be carried out in sequence. The next refinement fills in a few details for each part:

begin game
display instructions
pick a number between 1 and 100

repeat turn until number is guessed or seven turns are completed
input guess from user
respond to guess
end repeat

end game
display end message

The middle part of our instructions includes a sequence of operations that are repeated for each turn: everything between "repeat" and "end repeat." But these instructions are missing crucial details. How, for example, will the computer respond to a guess? We can replace "respond to guess" with instructions that vary depending on the guessed number:

if guess = number, then say so and quit;
else if guess < number, then say guess is too small;
else say guess is too big

Finally, we need to give the computer a way of knowing when seven turns have passed. We can set a counter to 0 at the beginning and add 1 to the counter after each turn. When the counter reaches 7, the repetition stops, and the computer displays a message. That makes the algorithm look like this:

begin game
display instructions
pick a number between 1 and 100
set counter to 0

repeat turn until number is guessed or counter = 7
input guess from user
if guess = number, then say so and quit;
else if guess < number, then say guess is too small;
else say guess is too big
add 1 to counter
end repeat

end game
display end message

Control structures. A computer can't understand this algorithm, but the pseudocode is clear to any person familiar with **control structures**—logical structures that control the order in which instructions are carried out. This algorithm uses three basic control structures: sequence, selection, and repetition.

1. A *sequence control structure* is a group of instructions followed in order from the first through the last. In our algorithm example, as in most computer languages, the sequence is the *default* structure; that is, it applies unless a statement says otherwise:

   display instructions
   pick a number between 1 and 100
   set counter to 0

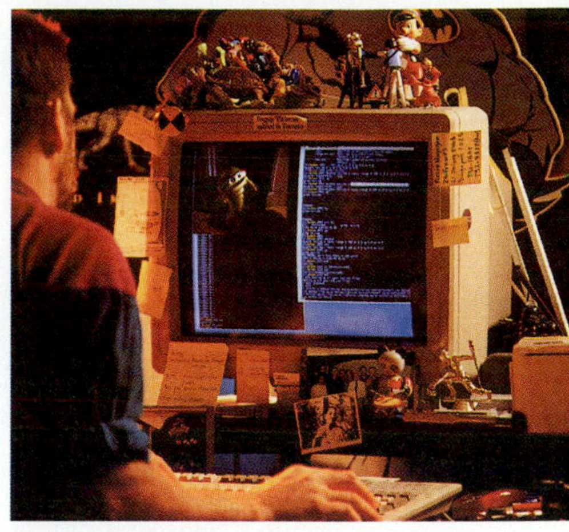

A programmer creating an animated sequence for a film.

2. A *selection (or decision) control structure* is used to make logical decisions—to choose between alternate courses of action depending on certain conditions. It typically takes the form, "If (some condition is true) then (do something) else (do something else)":

   if guess < number, then say guess is too small;
   else say guess is too big

3. A *repetition control structure* is a *looping* mechanism. It allows a group of steps to be repeated several times, usually until some condition is satisfied. In this algorithm the indented statements between "repeat" and "end repeat" are repeated until the number is guessed correctly or the counter is equal to 7:

   repeat turn until number is guessed or counter = 7
   input guess from user
   ...
   add 1 to counter
   end repeat

As our example illustrates, these simple control structures can be combined to produce more complex algorithms. In fact, just about any computer program can be constructed from these three control structures.

Testing the algorithm. The next step is **testing** the algorithm. Testing of the completed program will come later; this round of testing is designed to check the logic of the algorithm. We can test it by following the instructions using different sets of numbers. We might, for example, use a target number of 35 and guesses of 15, 72, 52, and 35. Those numbers test all three possibilities in the if-then-else structure, and they show what happens if the player chooses the correct number. We should also test the algorithm with seven wrong guesses in a row to make sure it correctly ends a losing game.

From Algorithm to Program

When testing is complete, the algorithm is ready to become a program. Because the algorithm has the logical structure of a program, the process of **coding**—writing a program from the algorithm—is simple and straightforward. Statements in the algorithm translate directly into lines of *code* in whichever programming language best fits the programmer's needs.

A simple program. Here, for example, is the algorithm rewritten in Pascal, a relatively simple programming language designed with beginners in mind:

```
program Game (input, output);
(* Programmed by Clay Cowgill 06/01/93 *)

(*-------------------------------------------------------*)

var Number, Guess, Counter : integer
(*-------------------------------------------------------*)

begin

writeln('Welcome to the guessing game. I''ll pick a number');
writeln('between 1 and 100 and you try to guess what it is.');
writeln('You get 7 tries.');

(* Calculate a random number between 1 and 100 *)
Number := abs (Random mod 100) + 1;
Counter := 0;

repeat (* turn *)
    writeln('What''s your guess?');
    readln(Guess);
    if Guess = Number then
        writeln('You got it!')
    else
        if Guess < Number then
            writeln('Too small, try again.');
```

```
        else writeln('Too big, guess again.');
    Counter := Counter + 1;
until (Guess = Number) or (Counter = 7)

if Guess <> Number then
    begin
        writeln('I fooled you 7 times!');
    end
end.
```

This program, like all Pascal programs, has three parts, similar to a recipe in a cookbook:

1. The *program heading*, containing the name of the program and data files (equivalent to the name and description of the dish to be cooked).
2. The *declarations and definitions* of variables and other programmer-defined items (equivalent to the list of ingredients used in the recipe).
3. The body of the program, containing the instructions, sandwiched between a *Begin* and an *End* (equivalent to the cooking steps).

The program listing looks like a detailed version of the original algorithm, but there's an important difference: Because it's a computer program, every word, symbol, and punctuation mark has an exact, unambiguous meaning.

The words highlighted with boldface and italics in this listing are key words with predefined meanings in Pascal. These key words, along with special symbols like + and :=, are part of Pascal's standard vocabulary. The words *Number*, *Guess*, and *Counter* are defined by the programmer, so they become part of Pascal's vocabulary when the program runs. Each of these words represents a *variable*—a named portion of the computer's memory whose contents can be examined and changed by the program.

As programs go, this Pascal program is fairly easy to understand. But Pascal isn't English, and some statements occasionally need clarification or further documentation. For the sake of readability, most programs include comments—the programmer's equivalent of Post-it notes. The text between the (* *) symbols is a comment in Pascal. The computer ignores comments; they're included to help human readers understand (or remember) something about the program.

Into the computer. The program still needs to be entered into the computer's memory, saved as a disk file, and translated into the computer's native machine language before it can be *executed*, or run. To enter and save the program, we can use a *text editor*. A text editor is like a word processor, but it lacks the formatting features required by writers. Some text editors, designed with programming in mind, provide automatic program indenting and limited error checking while the program is being typed.

To translate the program into machine language, we need translation software. The translator program might be an **interpreter** (a program that translates and transmits each statement individually, the way a United Nations interpreter translates a Russian speech into English) or a **compiler** (a program that translates an entire program before passing it on to the computer, as a scholar might translate the novel *War and Peace* from Russian to English). Most Pascal translators are compilers, because compiled programs tend to run faster than interpreted programs.

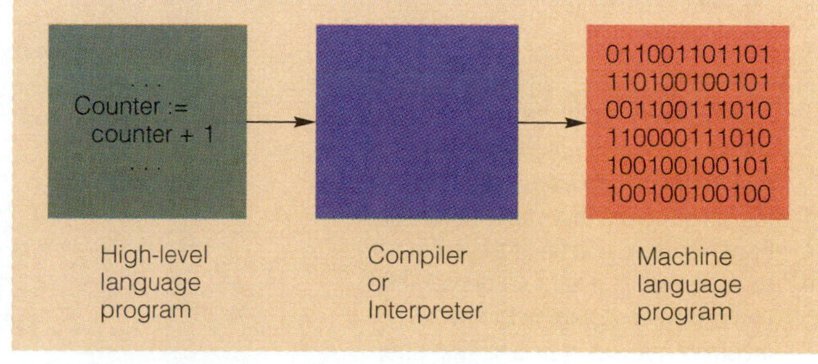

A typical compiler software package today is more than just a compiler. It's an integrated *programming environment*, including a text editor, a compiler, a *debugger* to simplify the process of locating and correcting errors, and a variety of other programming utilities.

The User's View

Programming in Pascal

Software: Think Pascal from Symantec.
The goal: To take the Pascal number-guessing game program that started as an algorithm and turn it into a working piece of software.

You type the program into the text editor window. The editor automatically indents each statement as you type, so it's easy to see the logical structure of the program. When you accidentally leave out a quotation mark, the editor points out the mistake with outlined text. Like many editors, this one can detect some, but not all, common **syntax errors**—violations of the "grammar" rules of the programming language.

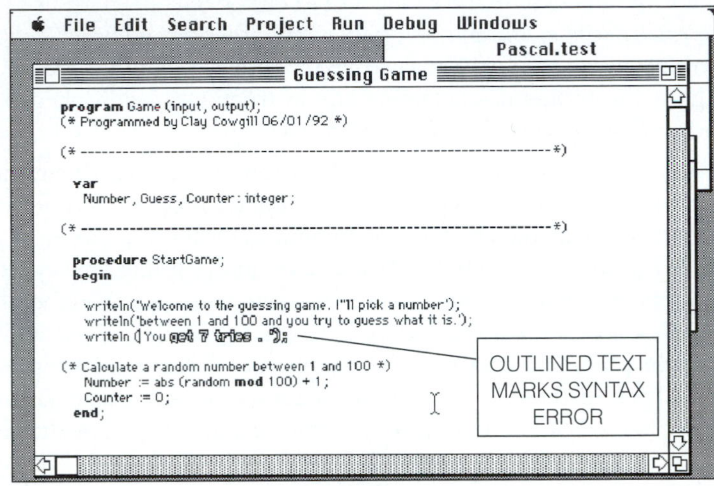

You select the Check command to check for errors that the editor couldn't find. In this case the misspelled writeln is marked with a thumbs-down icon and a diagnostic message that says "writeln is not declared."

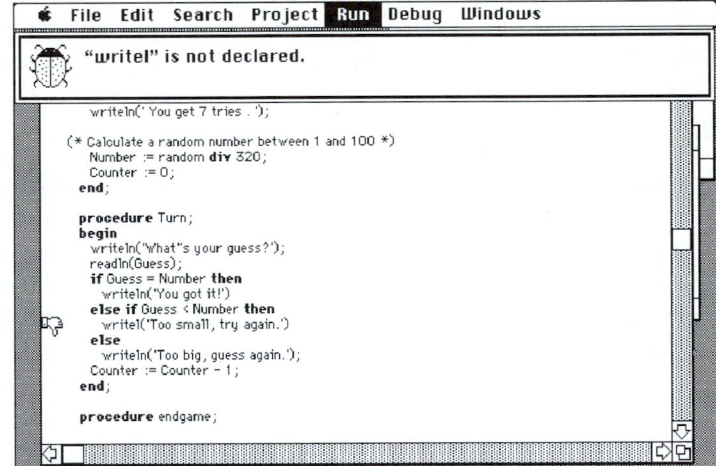

After you correct the error and compile the program, you run the program to test for **logic errors**—errors in the logical structure that cause differences between what you want the program to do and what it actually does. When you test the program with a series of incorrect guesses, it fails to stop after seven guesses. The built-in debugger allows you to run the program in "slow motion," so you can see how each statement affects the variables and the program output.

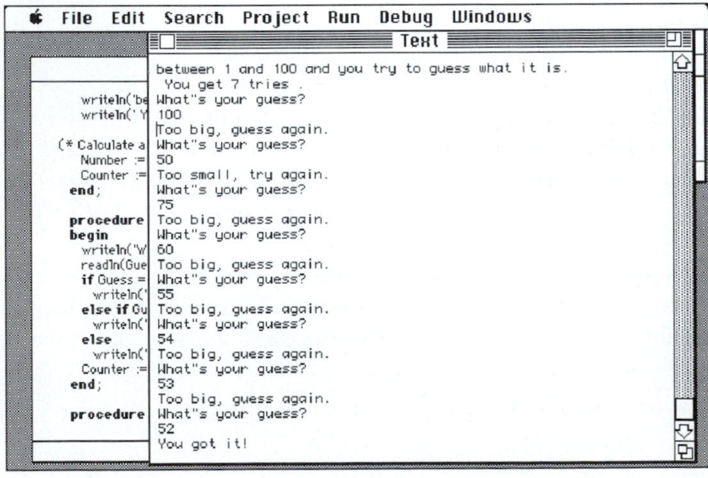

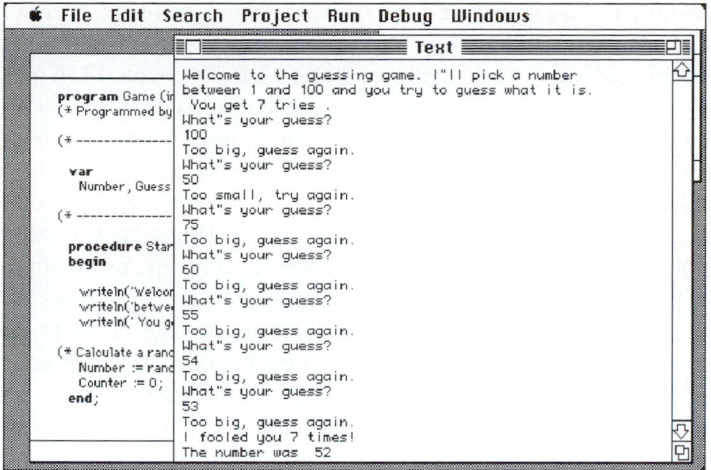
File Edit Search Project Run Debug Windows
Text
Welcome to the guessing game. I"ll pick a number
between 1 and 100 and you try to guess what it is.
You get 7 tries .
What"s your guess?
100
Too big, guess again.
What"s your guess?
50
Too small, try again.
What"s your guess?
75
Too big, guess again.
What"s your guess?
60
Too big, guess again.
What"s your guess?
55
Too big, guess again.
What"s your guess?
54
Too big, guess again.
What"s your guess?
53
Too big, guess again.
I fooled you 7 times!
The number was 52

The error turns out to be a single mistyped character, making the statement Counter := Counter + 1 into Counter := Counter – 1, so the counter goes down each turn rather than up. After you correct the typo and recompile the program, it ends the game after seven incorrect guesses, as it should. But a more subtle logical problem remains: A truly user-friendly program wouldn't tell the player to "Guess again" after the seventh incorrect guess, because the game is over. Like most programs, this one could go through several rounds of testing, debugging, and refining before the programmer is satisfied.

The Languages of Computers

Simple things should be simple; complex things should be possible.

—Alan Kay

Pascal is one of hundreds of computer languages in use today. Some are tools for professional programmers who write the software the rest of us use. Others are intended to help students learn the fundamentals of programming. Still others allow computer *users* to automate repetitive tasks and customize software applications. Since the earliest days of computing, programming languages have continued to evolve toward easier communication between people and computers.

Machine Language and Assembly Language

Every computer has a native language—a **machine language**. Similarities exist between different brands of machine language: They all have instructions for the four basic arithmetic operations, for comparing pairs of numbers, for repeating instructions, and so on. But like English and French, different brands of machine language are different languages, and machines based on one machine language can't understand programs written in another.

From the machine's point of view, machine language is all binary. Instructions, memory locations, numbers, and characters are all represented in strings of zeros and ones. Because binary numbers are difficult for people to read, machine-language programs are usually displayed with the binary numbers translated into *decimal* (base 10), *hexadecimal* (base 16), or some other number system. Even so, machine-language programs have always been hard to write, read, and debug.

The programming process became easier with the invention of **assembly language**—a language that's logically equivalent to machine language but is easier for peo-

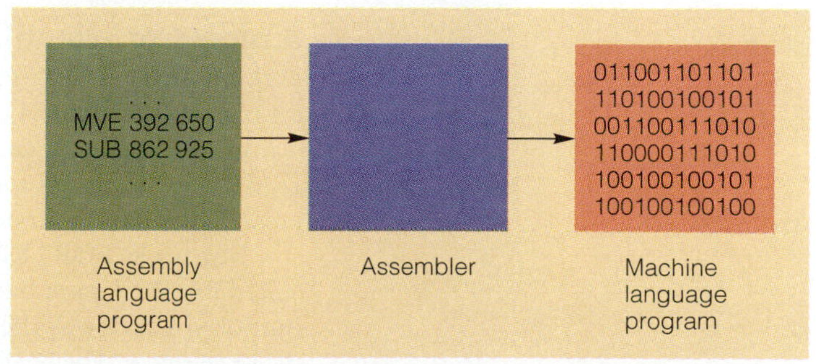
. . .
MVE 392 650
SUB 862 925
. . .
011001101101
110100100101
001100111010
110000111010
100100100101
100100100100
Assembly language program
Assembler
Machine language program

ple to read, write, and understand. In assembly language, programmers use alphabetic codes that correspond to the machine's numeric instructions. An assembly language instruction for subtract, for example, might be SUB. Of course, SUB means nothing to the computer, which only responds to commands like 10110111. To bridge the communication gap between programmer and computer, a program called an **assembler** translates each assembly language instruction into a machine-language instruction. Without knowing any better, the computer acts as its own translator.

Because of the obvious advantages of assembly language, very few programmers write in machine language anymore. But assembly language programming is still considered *low-level* programming; that is, it requires the programmer to think on the machine's level and to include an enormous amount of detail in every program. Assembly language programming is a repetitive, tedious, and error-prone process. To make matters worse, a program written in one assembly language must be completely rewritten before it can be run on computers with different machine languages. Many programmers still use assembly language to write parts of video games and other applications for which speed and direct communication with hardware are critical. But most programmers today think and write on a higher level.

High-level Languages and Programming Techniques

High-level languages, which fall somewhere between natural human languages and precise machine languages, were developed during the early 1950s to simplify and streamline the programming process. Languages like FORTRAN and COBOL made it possible for scientists, engineers, and business people to write programs using familiar terminology and notation rather than cryptic machine instructions. Today programmers can choose from hundreds of other high-level languages.

Interpreters and compilers translate high-level programs into machine language. Whether interpreted or compiled, a single statement from a high-level program turns into several machine-language statements. A high-level language hides most of the nitty-gritty details of the machine operations from the programmer. As a result, it's easier for the programmer to think about the overall logic of the program—the big ideas.

Besides being easier to write and debug, high-level programs have the advantage of being **transportable** between machines. A program written in standard Pascal, like the guessing-game program we developed in this chapter, can be compiled and run on any computer with a standard Pascal compiler. Since Pascal compilers are available for all types of computers, this program can run as written just about anywhere.

Transporting a program to a new machine isn't always that easy. Most high-level programs need to be *partially* rewritten to adjust to differences between hardware, compilers, operating systems, and user interfaces. For example, Microsoft programmers rewrite between 10 and 25 percent of the high-level code when translating a new version of the Windows version of an application program into a Macintosh version. Still, high-level programs are far more portable than programs written in assembly and machine languages.

Business or scientific programming? With so many choices, how do programmers choose between different languages? In some cases languages are designed for particular groups of users to solve particular kinds of programs. The first commercial high-level language, *FORTRAN* (from *For*mula *Tran*slation), was designed at IBM in the 1950s to solve scientific and engineering problems. Many scientists and engineers still use a modernized version of FORTRAN.

But while FORTRAN's mathematical style is useful for scientists, it's not well suited for developing business applications in which names are at least as important as numbers. That's why the U.S. government in 1960 demanded a new language to handle its business. The result was *COBOL* (from *Co*mmon *B*usiness *O*riented *L*anguage),

```
INTEGER Guess,Counter,Number

TYPE*,'Welcome to the guessing game. I'll think of a'
TYPE*,'number between 1 and 100 and you will guess it.'

Number = RND

Counter = 0

DO WHILE ((Guess .NE. Number) .OR. (Counter .LE. 7))
    TYPE*,'What is your guess?'
    ACCEPT*,Guess

    IF (Guess .EQ. Number) THEN
        TYPE*,'You got it!'
    ELSE IF (Guess .LT. Number) THEN
        TYPE*,'Too small, try again.'
        ELSE IF (Guess .GT. Number) THEN
            TYPE*,'Too big, try again.'
        END IF
    END IF
END DO

IF (Guess .NE. Number) THEN
    TYPE*,'I fooled you 7 times!'
    TYPE*,'The answer was ',Number

STOP
```

```
identification division
    program-id game.
/
working-storage division

    01 counter pic x(1)
    01 number pic x(3)
    01 guess pic x(1)
    01 correct pic x(1)

/
procedure division

    main.
        display "Welcome to the guessing game. I'll think of a"
        display "number between 1 and 100 and you will guess it."

    set correct to false
    move 0 to counter
    move random-number to number

    perform until correct = true or counter = 7
        display "What's your guess?"
        accept guess

        if guess = number then
            display "You got it!"
            set correct to true
        else
            if guess < number then
                display "Too small, try again."
            else
                if guess > number then
                    display "Too big, try again."
                end-if
            end-if
            add 1 to counter
        end-if
    end-perform

    if guess <> number
        display "I fooled you 7 times!"
        display "The answer was ",number
    end-if

    stop run.
```

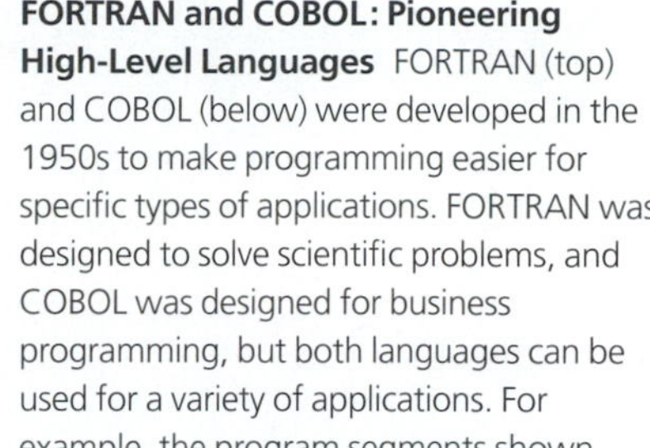

FORTRAN and COBOL: Pioneering High-Level Languages FORTRAN (top) and COBOL (below) were developed in the 1950s to make programming easier for specific types of applications. FORTRAN was designed to solve scientific problems, and COBOL was designed for business programming, but both languages can be used for a variety of applications. For example, the program segments shown here play the number-guessing game described in the last section.

a wordy language that reads more like a manager's report than a collection of mathematical formulas. COBOL still meets the needs of a large group of programmers—those who work with business data processing systems on mainframe computers.

Unstructured or structured programming? Sometimes high-level languages are distinguished by the approach they take to solving problems. Consider BASIC and Pascal, two languages developed to provide beginning programming students with a language that's easy to learn and easy to use. BASIC and Pascal evolved from different programming philosophies, and the differences between early versions of the two languages were striking.

Even though it is seldom used by professional programmers, *BASIC* (*B*eginner's *A*ll-purpose *S*ymbolic *I*nstruction *C*ode) is probably the most widely used programming language in the world today. BASIC was developed in the mid-1960s by John Kemeny and Thomas Kurtz, two Dartmouth University professors who were looking for an alternative to FORTRAN for their beginning programming students. Before BASIC, a student typically had to submit a program on punch cards and wait hours for output from a compiler. The process had to be repeated, often several times, until every error was corrected in the program.

BASIC allowed students for the first time to write and debug programs *interactively.* Because BASIC was interpreted line by line rather than compiled as a whole, it could provide instant feedback as students typed statements and commands into their terminals. And because BASIC was a simple language with a small vocabulary, it was easy for students to learn. When personal computers appeared, BASIC enjoyed unprecedented popularity among students, hobbyists, and programmers who wrote simple customized applications.

Shortly after Kemeny and Kurtz introduced BASIC, computer scientists began publishing articles discussing the shortcomings of BASIC, FORTRAN, and other early high-level languages. Most programs written in these languages were riddled with *GoTo statements*—statements used to transfer control to other parts of the program. (Remember "Go to Jail. Do not pass Go. Do not collect $200"?) The logical structure of a program with GoTo statements can resemble a tangled spider's web. The bigger the program, the bigger the logical maze, and the more possibility for error. Every branch of a program represents a loose end that might be overlooked by the programmer.

In an attempt to overcome these problems, computer scientists developed **structured programming**—a technique to make the programming process easier and more productive. A structured program doesn't depend on the GoTo statement to control the logical flow. Instead it's built from smaller programs called **modules**, or **subprograms** that are in turn made of even smaller modules. The programmer combines modules using the three basic control structures: sequence, repetition and selection. A program is well structured if

- it's made up of logically cohesive modules
- the modules are arranged in a hierarchy
- it's straightforward and readable

Structured programming techniques had the potential to make programmers more productive, but they weren't easy to practice in the original BASIC language. In the early 1970s Swiss computer scientist Niklaus Wirth introduced *Pascal* (named for Blaise Pascal, the 17th-century French mathematician, inventor, philosopher, and mystic) to encourage beginning programmers to write structured programs. Pascal, the language we used in the program development example earlier in the chapter, became immensely popular as an educational language in the years that followed its introduction. At the same time, structured programming became standard operating procedure for professional programmers the world over. Modern versions of COBOL, FORTRAN, and BASIC include Pascal-like features that make structured programming easier. Many modern versions of BASIC, including QuickBASIC, True BASIC and Visual BASIC, have more in common with Pascal than with the original BASIC.

```
10 REM Guessing Game
20 REM Programmed by David Stuve 06/01/92
30 PRINT "Welcome to the guessing game. I'll think of a number"
40 PRINT "between 1 and 100 and you will guess what it is."
45 Counter = 0
50 Number = INT(RND(1) * 100)
60 INPUT "What's your guess? ";Guess
70 IF Guess = Number THEN PRINT "You got it!"
80 IF Guess < Number THEN PRINT "Too small, try again."
90 IF Guess > Number THEN PRINT "Too big, try again."
100 Counter = Counter + 1
110 IF Counter = 7 THEN GOTO 150
120 IF Guess <> Number THEN GOTO 60
150 IF Guess <> Number THEN PRINT "I fooled you 7 times! The answer
                                                    was ";Number
160 END
```

```
REM Guessing Game
REM written by Rajeev Pandey, 02/04/93

DECLARE SUB StartGame (Counter!, Number!)
DECLARE SUB Turn (Counter!, Guess!, Number!)
DECLARE SUB endgame (Number!)

CALL StartGame(Counter, Number)
DO
    CALL Turn(Counter, Number, Guess)
LOOP UNTIL (Guess = Number) OR (Counter = 7)
IF Guess <> Number THEN
    CALL endgame(Number)
END IF

SUB endgame (Number)
IF Guess <> Number THEN
    PRINT "I fooled you 7 times!"
    PRINT "The answer was "; Number
END IF
END SUB

SUB StartGame (Counter, Number)
PRINT "Welcome to the guessing game. I'll think of a number"
PRINT "between 1 and 100 and you will guess what it is."
Counter = 0RANDOMIZE TIMER
Number = INT(RND * 100)
END SUB

SUB Turn (Counter, Guess, Number)
INPUT "What's your guess? "; Guess
IF Guess = Number THEN
    PRINT "You got it!"
ELSE
    IF Guess < Number THEN
        PRINT "Too small, try again."
    ELSE
        PRINT "Too big, try again."
    END IF
END IF
Counter = Counter + 1
END SUB
```

Two Faces of BASIC: Early BASIC and Structured BASIC These two BASIC programs play the number-guessing game. The program on the top (with numbered lines) is written in a simple version of BASIC—the only kind of BASIC that was available in the early days of the language. Statements are executed in numerical order unless control is transferred to another statement with a GoTo statement. The modular program on the bottom is written in QuickBASIC, a modern version of the language with many structured programming features. The main program has been reduced to a handful of statements at the top of the listing; these statements display the overall logic of the program. As it's running, the main program uses CALL statements to transfer control to each of the three subprograms, which take care of the details of the game's beginning, each turn, and the game's end.

Efficiency or simplicity? Pascal and BASIC succeed as learners' languages because they put layers of logic between the programmer and the inner workings of the processor. But those layers can make it difficult to maximize a program's *efficiency* with respect to computer resources and time. For most projects, it's not important to fine-tune a program's efficiency. But for operating systems, video games, and applications for which speed and memory conservation are crucial, a programmer needs more control than Pascal or BASIC allows.

The language *C* (it doesn't stand for anything but followed a less-successful language called B) includes structured tools similar to those found in Pascal but not at the expense of efficiency. C was invented at Bell Labs in the early 1970s as a tool for programming operating systems like UNIX. A C program can control the computer's hardware in the same way assembly language programs do. A skilled and careful C pro-

C: Structure and Speed Here's the guessing-game program rewritten in C.

```
/*      Guesssing Game */
/*      Programmed by David Stuve 06/01/92 */

main()
{
        int Guess, Number, Counter;

        printf("Welcome to the guessing game. I'll think of a\n");
        printf("number between 1 and 100 and you will guess it.\n");

        Counter = 0;
        Number = RangeRand( 100 ) + 1;
        do
        {
                printf("What's your guess?\n");
                Guess = GetNumber();

                if (Guess == Number)
                        printf("You got it!\n");
                else if (Guess < Number)
                        printf("Too small, try again.\n");
                else if (Guess > Number)
                        printf("Too big, try again.\n");

                Counter++;
        } while ((Guess != Number) && (Counter < 7));

        if (Guess != Number)
        {
                printf("I fooled you 7 times!\n");
                printf("The answer was %d\n", Number);
        }
}
```

grammer can produce programs that are as fast and efficient as assembly language programs. On the other hand, an inexperienced or careless C programmer has the power to create software disasters. C is a complex language that's difficult to learn. But its power, flexibility, and efficiency have made it the language of choice for most professionals who program personal computers.

Other options? There are hundreds of other languages in use today. Here are some examples:

- *Ada* (named for Ada Lovelace, the programming pioneer profiled in Chapter 1) is a massive language developed in the late 1970s as the standard for the U.S. Defense Department. Ada has been slow to fulfill early predictions of widespread acceptance outside the military establishment.
- *Modula-2* is a powerful and complex descendant of Pascal designed for professional programmers. Modula-2 has achieved only limited popularity so far.
- *LISP* (*List Processing*) was developed at MIT in the late 1950s to process nonnumeric data like characters, words, and other symbols. LISP is widely used in artificial intelligence research, in part because it's easy to write LISP programs that can write other programs.
- *PROLOG* (*Programming Logic*) is another popular language for artificial intelligence programming. As the name imples, PROLOG is designed for working with logical relationships between facts.
- *LOGO*, described in Chapter 12, is a dialect of LISP for children.

Languages for Users

Because they're easier to use and more powerful than their ancestors, languages like C and Pascal continue to grow in popularity among programmers and educators. But for most computer *users*, these languages demand too much time and study to be of interest. Fortunately some languages are designed to meet the more modest needs of computer users.

Macro languages. Many user-oriented languages are intended to allow users to create programs, called *macros*, that automate repetitive tasks. User-oriented **macro languages** (also called **scripting languages**) are built into many applications, utilities, and operating systems. Using a macro language, a spreadsheet user can build a program, called a macro, to automatically create end-of-month reports each month by locating data in other worksheets, inserting values into a new worksheet, and calculating results using formulas carried over from previous months. Using an operating system's scripting language, a user might automate the process of making backup copies of all documents created during the last seven days.

Some macro languages require the user to design and type each macro by hand. Another type of macro maker "watches" while the user performs a sequence of commands and actions; it then memorizes the sequence and turns it into a macro automatically. The user can then examine and edit the macro so that it performs the desired actions under any circumstances.

Fourth-generation languages. Many experts suggest that languages have evolved through four generations: machine language, assembly language, high-level languages, and **fourth-generation languages**, sometimes called **4GLs**. Each generation of languages is easier to use and more like natural language than its predecessors. There's no consensus on exactly what constitutes a fourth-generation language, but these characteristics are most commonly mentioned:

- 4GLs use English-like phrases and sentences to issue instructions.
- 4GLs are nonprocedural. Pascal, C, and BASIC are *procedural languages*—tools for constructing procedures that tell the computer how to accomplish tasks. *Nonprocedural languages* allow users to focus on what needs to be done, not on how to do it.
- 4GLs increase productivity. Because a 4GL takes care of many of the how-to details, programmers can often get results by typing a few lines of code rather than a few pages.

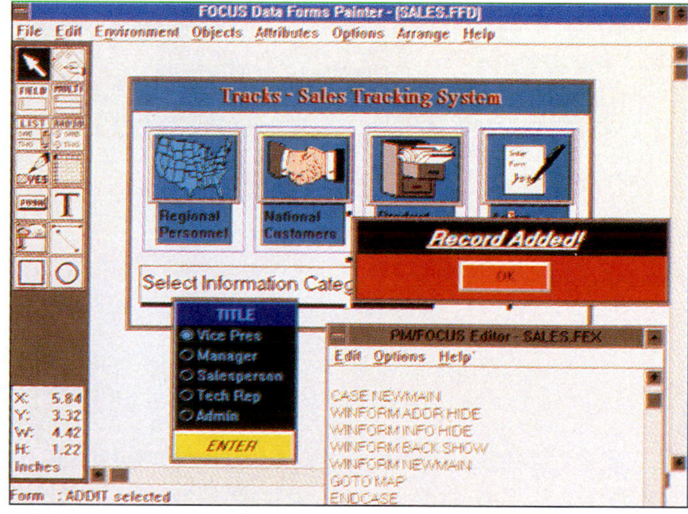

One type of 4GL is the *query language* that allows a user to request information from a database with carefully worded English-like questions. A query language serves as a database user interface, hiding the intricacies of the database from the user. *SQL* (*Structured Query Language*) is the standard query language for most database applications today. Like most query languages, SQL requires the user to master a few rules of syntax and logic. Still, a query language is easier to master than FORTRAN or COBOL.

Programming with Pictures and Objects

Many people find it easier to work with pictures instead of words. **Visual programming** tools allow programmers to create large portions of their programs by drawing pictures and pointing to on-screen objects, eliminating much of the tedious coding of traditional programming. *HyperCard* (discussed in Chapter 8) is a popular example of a visual programming environment. HyperCard includes a programming language called *HyperTalk*, but a HyperCard programmer doesn't need to speak HyperTalk to create working applications. Tools like HyperCard, ToolBook, Visual BASIC, and NextStep make programming more accessible to nonprogrammers. Today's visual programming tools haven't completely transformed programming into a visual process, but they suggest that such a transformation is possible.

Visual Programming with HyperCard

HyperCard's visual programming tools make it easy to modify an existing program, such as the stack in the Creating Hypermedia User's View box in Chapter 8. In this example you'll add a "keyboard" button to the main screen. When completed, this button will transport the user to another screen with a visual transition effect. The programming of this button is a simple matter of clicking in a series of dialog boxes. **(1)** When you select the New Button command from HyperCard's Objects menu, a button appears on the screen (shown right), waiting to be customized. **(2)** Double-clicking on the new button opens the Button Info dialog box for customizing the button. Since a button typically links (transports the user) to another card (screen) with a visual transition effect, the Button Info dialog box contains LinkTo and Effect buttons for specifying the link and the associated effect. By pointing, clicking, and typing in dialog boxes, you can program the button so it responds to a mouse click by zooming the screen image into another picture. **(3)** HyperCard automatically generates a HyperTalk script for the button; the script tells the button exactly what to do when the user clicks on it.

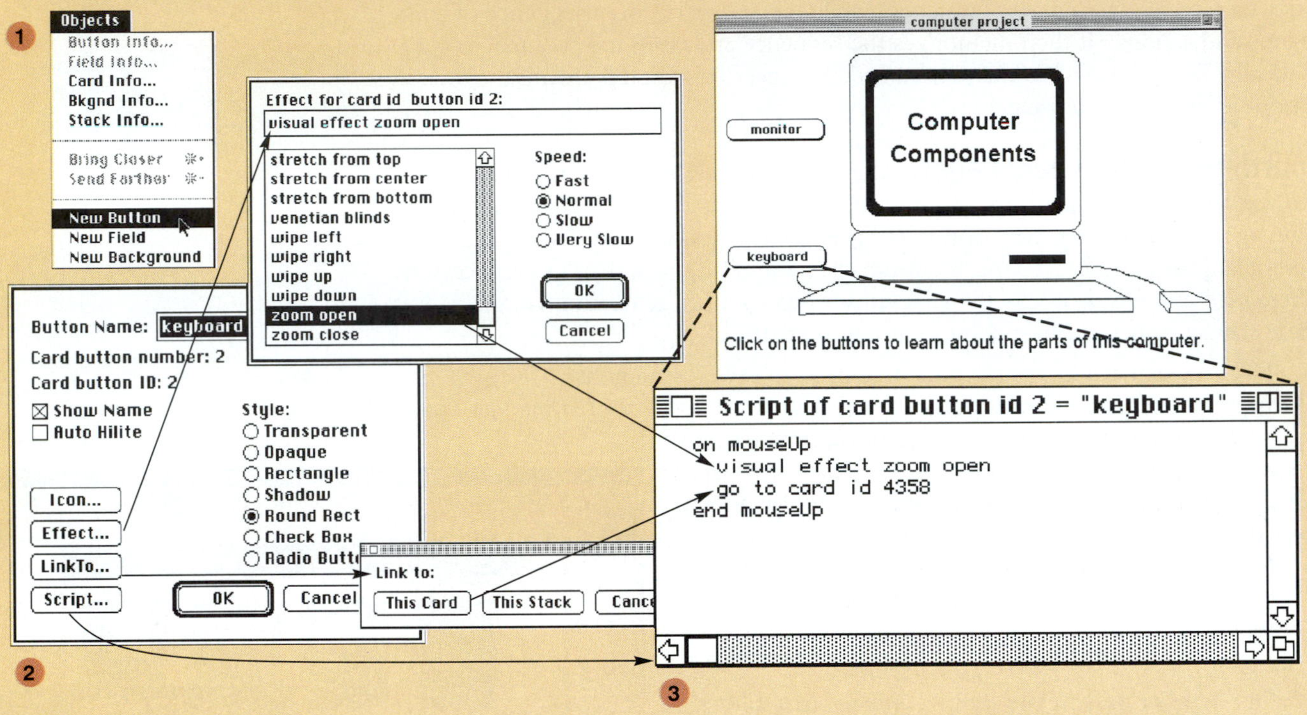

HyperCard includes visual programming tools, but it also has many of the features of another programming trend: object-oriented programming (OOP). Object-oriented programming was first used in the 1970s, most notably in a language called Smalltalk. In object-oriented programming, a program is not just a collection of step-by-step instructions; it's a collection of *objects*. Objects contain both data and instructions and can interact with each other as independent software entities. In HyperCard, for example, every button, text field, card, and background is an object with its own script. Buttons can receive messages from the user and send messages to other objects. Fields can respond to mouse clicks by changing their contents or by displaying different cards. In effect, all of these objects behave like semi-intelligent creatures in an environment that allows them to communicate with each other.

HyperCard is a graphic example of a programming environment built around objects rather than procedures. Technically, HyperCard doesn't have all the features of a true object-oriented programming language. C++, a popular dialect of C, is much closer to a true OOP language. C++ doesn't contain visual objects like icons. On the surface it looks like just another language. But the object-oriented nature of the language allows programmers to write programs built around logical objects rather than procedures.

With OOP technology, programmers can build programs from prefabricated objects in the same way builders construct houses from prefabricated walls. OOP also makes it easy to use features from one program in other programs, so programmers don't have to start from scratch with every new program. The object that sorts addresses in alphabetical order in a mailing list database can also be used in a program that sorts hotel reservations alphabetically. Many experts believe that OOP is the wave of the future.

OOP is at the heart of the new operating system being jointly developed by IBM and Apple for the next-generation "Power PC." An operating system developed around objects will allow users to control *software* objects by manipulating *visual* objects on the screen. With an appropriate visual user interface, object-oriented technology could put unprecedented programming power in the hands of the user.

The Future of Programming?

Object-oriented programming. 4GL. Visual programming. With these trends gaining momentum, what can we say about the future of programming? It's not clear what programming languages will look like in the future, but three trends seem likely:

- Programming languages will continue to evolve in the direction of natural languages like English. Today's programming languages, even the best of them, are far too limited and unintelligent. Tomorrow's programming tools should be able to understand what we want even if we don't specify every detail. When we consider artificial intelligence in the next chapter, we'll deal with the problems and promise of natural language computer communication.
- The line between programmer and user is likely to grow hazy. As programming becomes easier, there's every reason to believe that computer users will have tools that allow them to construct applications without mastering the intricacies of a technical programming language.
- Computers will play an ever-increasing role in programming themselves. Today's visual programming environments can create programs in response to user clicks and commands. Tomorrow's programming tools may be able to write entire programs with only a description of the problem supplied by users. The day after tomorrow we may see computers anticipating problems and programming solutions without human intervention!

Whatever happens, one thing seems likely: Future programming tools will have little in common with today's languages. When computer historians look back, they'll marvel at how difficult it was for us to instruct computers to perform even the simplest actions.

Programs in Perspective: Systems Analysis and the System Life Cycle

We but teach
Bloody instructions, which being taught, return
To plague the inventor.

—*Shakespeare*, Macbeth

Programs don't exist in a vacuum. Programs are part of larger **information systems**—collections of people, machines, data, and methods organized to accomplish specific functions and to solve specific problems. Programming is only part of the larger process of designing, implementing, and managing information systems. In this section we'll examine that larger process.

Whether it's a simple accounting system for a small business or a credit bureau's massive financial information system, a system has a **system life cycle**—a sequence of steps or phases it passes through between the time the system is conceived and the time it is phased out. The phases of the system life cycle are: *investigation, analysis, design, development, implementation, maintenance,* and *retirement.* We'll consider each phase from the point of view of the **systems analyst**—the computer professional primarily responsible for developing and managing a system as it progresses through these phases.

Investigation

Developing an information system is no small undertaking. People develop information systems because problems like these need to be solved:

- A mom-and-pop music store needs a way to keep track of instrument rentals and purchases so that billing and accounting don't take so much time.
- A college's antiquated, labor-intensive registration system forces students to endure long lines and frequent scheduling errors.
- A catalog garden-supply company is outgrowing its small, slow PC-based software system, resulting in shipping delays, billing errors, and customer complaints.
- The success of an upcoming oceanographic investigation hinges on the ability of scientists to collect and analyze data instantaneously so the results can be fed into remote-control navigation devices.
- A software manufacturer determines that its PC graphics program is rapidly losing market share to a competitor with more features and a friendlier user interface.

System investigation involves defining the problem—identifying the information needs of the organization, examining the current system, determining how well it meets the needs of the organization, and studying the feasibility of changing or replacing the current system. After completing the initial investigation of the problem, a systems analyst, whether part of the organization or contracted from an outside consulting firm, produces a *feasibility study* to help management decide whether to continue with the systems analysis.

Analysis

During the analysis phase the systems analyst gathers documents, interviews users of the current system (if one exists), observes the system in action, and generally gathers and analyzes data to help understand the current system and identify new requirements. Most systems are too complex to understand as a whole, so the systems analyst generally subdivides a system into components called *subsystems.* The analysis phase involves more detail than the investigative phase but less than the design phase that follows.

Design

The investigation phase focuses on *why*, the analysis phase focuses on *what*, and the design phase focuses on *how*. In the design phase the systems analyst considers important how-to questions:

- What kind of output should the system produce?
- Where will input data come from, and how will it be entered into the system?
- Should the system be centralized in a single computer or distributed through a network of desktop computers? (For that matter, should a computer be involved in the system at all?)

- Should the organization purchase packaged software or have programmers write a custom application from the ground up?

The systems analyst answers these questions, sometimes proposing several alternative solutions.

In many cases the design phase produces a **prototype** system—a limited working system or subsystem to give the users and management an idea of how the completed system will work. The systems analyst can modify the prototype until it meets the needs and expectations of the organization. Once the design is acceptable, the systems analyst can fill in the details of the output, input, data files, processing, and system controls.

Development

After the design is completed, the actual system development can begin. Development includes a complex mix of scheduling, hardware and software purchasing, documentation, and programming. For most large projects, the development phase involves a team of programmers, technical writers, and clerical people under the supervision of a systems analyst. A large part of the development schedule is devoted to testing the system. Members of the system development team perform early testing to locate and eliminate bugs. This initial testing is known as **alpha testing**. Later, potential users who are willing to work with almost-finished software perform **beta testing** and report bugs to the developers.

Implementation

When the testing is completed and known bugs have been eradicated, the new system is ready to replace the old one. For commercial software packages, this phase typically involves extensive training and technical user support to supplement sales and marketing efforts. For large custom systems, implementation typically includes user education and training, equipment replacement, file conversion, and careful monitoring of the new system for problems. In some cases the new system is run in parallel with the old system until the analyst is confident that the new system is stable and reliable.

Maintenance

The maintenance phase involves evaluating, repairing, and enhancing the system. Some software problems don't surface until the system has been operational for a while or the organization needs change. Ongoing maintenance allows organizations to deal with those problems when they arise. For commercial programs, bugs and refinements are handled by occasional *maintenance upgrades*, typically labeled with incremental version numbers like 1.01 or 2.0a. For large custom systems, maintenance involves a continual process of evaluating and adjusting the system to meet organizational needs. In either case maintenance usually lasts throughout the lifetime of the system.

Retirement

At some point in the life of a system, ongoing maintenance isn't enough. Because of changes in organizational needs, user expectations, available technology, and other factors, the system no longer meets the needs of the users or the organization. At that point it's time to phase it out in favor of a newer system and begin another round of the system life cycle.

The Information Flow in the System Life Cycle

College registration is a complex system involving hundreds of people and masses of information. A registration system must be solidly designed, carefully maintained, and eventually replaced as the needs of the college change. In this example we'll follow systems analysts at Chintimini College as they guide registration system through a system life cycle.

1 Investigation

Analysts at the college's Information Processing Center identify several problems with the antiquated manual registration system: long lines, frequent scheduling errors, and expensive labor costs. After studying registration systems at other schools, they determine that a registration-by-phone system might be the best solution to these problems.

6 Maintenance

Analysts monitor and evaluate the new system, eliminating problems and correcting bugs as they are uncovered.

7 Retirement

After a few years, the phone registration system has developed problems of its own. The college begins developing a new system that will allow students to register through personal computers. When the new PC registration system reaches the implementation phase of its life cycle, the phone-in system is retired.

Analysis

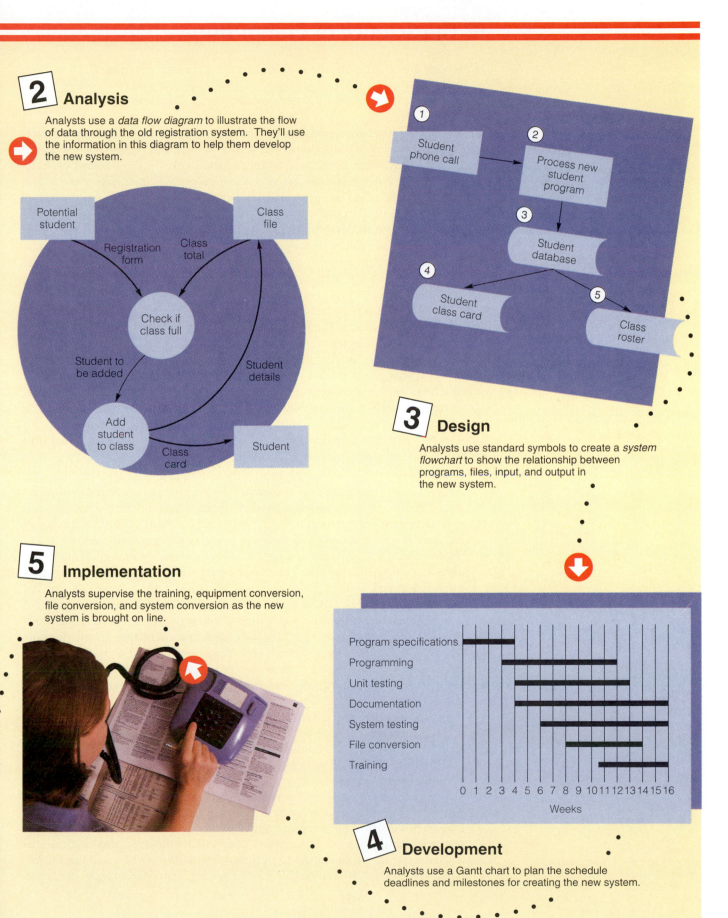

Analysts use a *data flow diagram* to illustrate the flow of data through the old registration system. They'll use the information in this diagram to help them develop the new system.

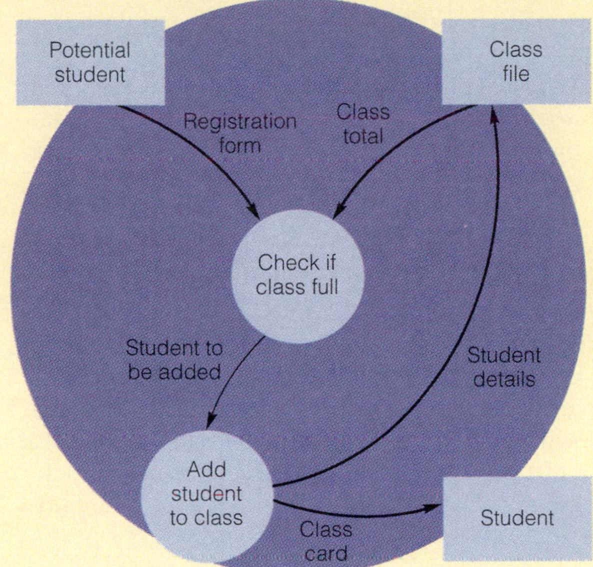

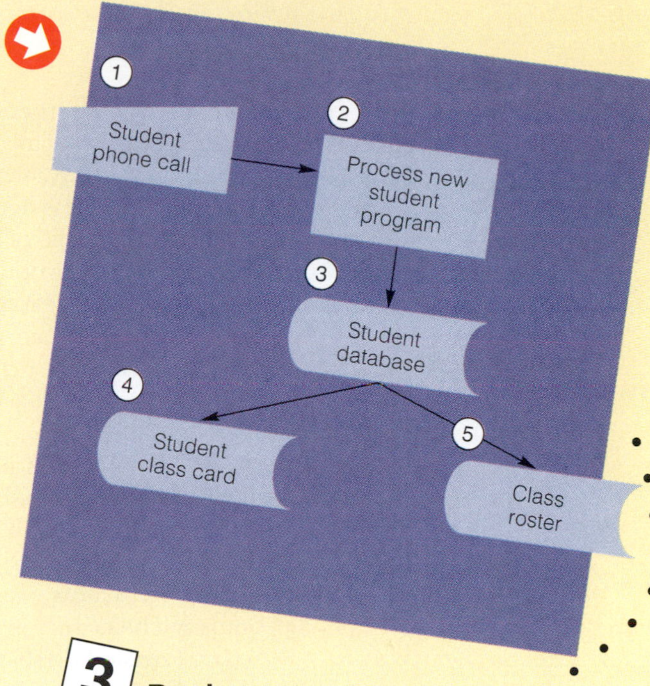

3 Design

Analysts use standard symbols to create a *system flowchart* to show the relationship between programs, files, input, and output in the new system.

Implementation

Analysts supervise the training, equipment conversion, file conversion, and system conversion as the new system is brought on line.

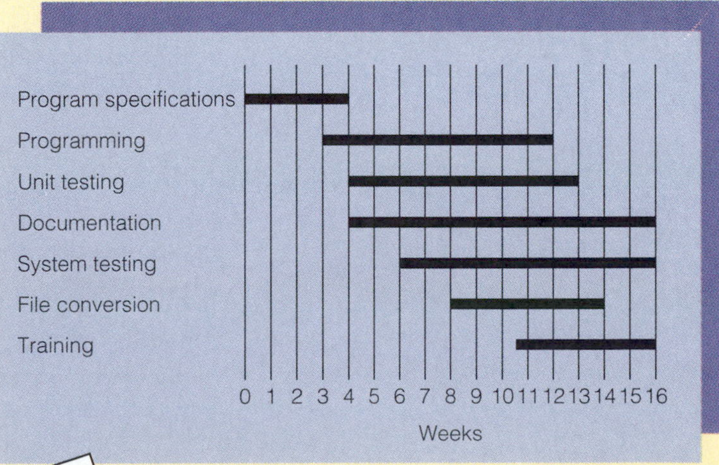

4 Development

Analysts use a Gantt chart to plan the schedule deadlines and milestones for creating the new system.

The Science of Computing

Telescopes are to astronomy as computers are to computer science.

—*Edward Dykstra,* computer scientist

We've seen how programmers and systems analysts create and maintain computer programs used by scientists, business people, artists, writers, and others. But just as the rest of us take advantage of the programmer's handiwork, the programmer depends on tools and ideas developed by *computer scientists*—professionals who work in the academic discipline called **computer science**. What is computer science, and why is it important in the world of computers?

Because most introductory computer science courses focus on programming, many students equate computer science with computer programming. But programming is little more than a tool in the computer scientist's intellectual toolbox; it has about as much to do with computer science as English grammar has to do with writing novels.

Computer science is a relatively new discipline with ties to electrical engineering, mathematics, and business. Many computer scientists prefer to call the field comput*ing* science, because it focuses on the process of computing rather than on computer hardware. Computing takes a variety of forms, and computer science includes a number of focus areas, ranging from the rarefied world of computer theory to practical nuts and bolts work in software engineering. Some areas of specialization within computer science—database management, graphics, artificial intelligence, and networks, for example—provide academic underpinnings for specific categories of computer applications. Other branches of computer science deal with concepts that can apply to almost any type of computer application. These include

- *Computer theory.* The most mathematical branch of computer science, computer theory applies the concepts of theoretical mathematics to computational problems. Theoreticians often work not with real computers but with theoretical computers that exist only in the minds of the theoreticians. As in most fields, many theoretical concepts eventually find their way into practical applications.
- *Algorithms.* Many computer scientists focus on algorithms—the logical underpinnings of computer programs. The design of algorithms can determine whether software succeeds or fails. A well-designed algorithm is not only reliable and free of logical errors but also *efficient*, so it can accomplish its goals with a minimum of computer resources and time. Computers spend most of their time doing mundane tasks like sorting lists, searching for names, and calculating geometric coordinates. These frequently performed operations must be built on rock-solid, efficient algorithms if a computer system is to be responsive and reliable.
- *Data structures.* If algorithms describe the logical structure of programs, **data structures** determine the logical structure of *data*. Data structures range from simple numeric lists and tables (called *arrays*) to complex relations at the core of massive databases. Computer scientists continue to develop improved techniques for representing and combining different forms of data, and these techniques find their way into all kinds of software.
- *Programming concepts and languages.* As we've seen, programming languages have evolved through several generations in the short history of computers. Thanks to computer scientists in the tradition of Grace Hopper, each new wave of languages is easier to use and more powerful than the one that came before. Programming language specialists strive to design better programming languages to make it easier for programmers to turn algorithms into working software. Computer scientists are also responsible for the development of techniques like struc-

tured programming and object-oriented programming—techniques that make programmers more productive and programs more reliable.

- *Computer architecture.* Straddling the boundary between the software world of computer science and the hardware world of computer engineering, **computer architecture** deals with the way hardware and software work together. How can multiple processors work together? How does the bandwidth of a bus affect performance? What are the tradeoffs for different storage media? These are the types of questions that concern computer architecture specialists.
- *Management information systems.* **Management information systems (MIS)** is part computer science, part business. In fact, MIS studies are done in computer science departments at some institutions and in business departments at others. MIS specialists focus on the developing systems that can provide timely, reliable, and useful information to managers in business, industry, and government. MIS specialists apply the theoretical concepts of computer science to real-world, practical business problems.
- *Software engineering.* When an engineer designs a bridge or a building, tried-and-true engineering principles and techniques ensure that the structure won't collapse unexpectedly. Unfortunately we can't trust software the way we trust buildings; software designers simply don't have the time-honored techniques to ensure quality. **Software engineering** is a relatively new branch of computer science that attempts to apply engineering principles and techniques to the less-than-concrete world of computer software. We'll conclude this chapter with a brief look at the problems faced by software engineers—problems that affect all of us.

The State of Software

It's impossible to make anything foolproof, because fools are so ingenious.

—Roger Berg, inventor

In spite of advances in computer science, the state of software development is less than ideal. Software developers and software users are confronted with two giant problems: cost and unreliability.

Software Problems

If one character, one pause, of the incantation is not strictly in proper form, the magic doesn't work.

—Frederick Brooks, *The Mythical Man-Month*

As computers have evolved through the decades, the cost of computer hardware has steadily gone down. Every year brings more powerful, reliable machines and lower prices. At the same time, the cost of developing computer software has gone *up*. The software industry abounds with stories of computer systems that cost millions of dollars more and took years longer to develop than expected. Many systems become so costly to develop that their developers are forced to abandon them before completion. According to one survey, 75 percent of all system development undertaken in the United States is either never completed or, if it is completed, not used.

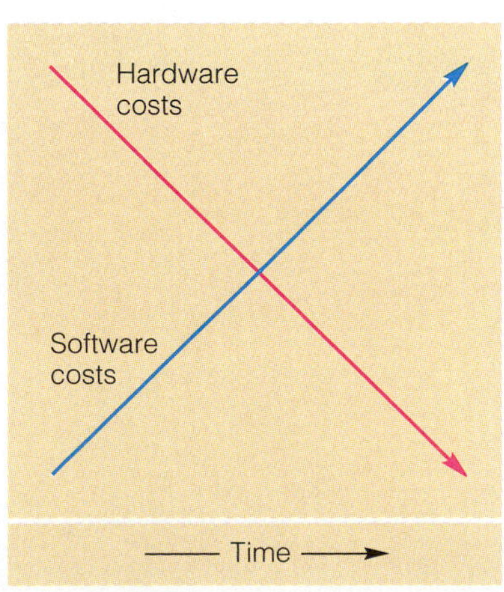

But while prices rise, there's no corresponding increase in the reliability of software. Ever since Grace Hopper pulled a moth from the Mark I's relay, bugs have plagued computers, often with disastrous consequences. Here are a few horror stories:

- On November 20, 1985, the Bank of New York's computer system started corrupting government securities transactions. By the end of the day, the bank was $32 billion overdrawn with the Federal Reserve. Before the system error was corrected, it cost the bank $5 million in interest.
- In a 12-month period ending in April 1988, London's Heathrow Airport air traffic control system failed five separate times, despite the airport's 70 full-time specialists hired to keep the computer running and to update its software.
- The Gemini V capsule splashed down 100 miles off target because the programmers who wrote the spacecraft's inertial guidance system failed to take into account the Earth's rotation around the sun.
- Programs on NASA observation satellites in the 1970s and 1980s rejected ozone readings because the programmers had assumed when they wrote the programs that such low numbers could not be correct. It wasn't until British scientists reported ozone-level declines that NASA scientists reprocessed the data and confirmed the British findings that Earth's ozone layer was in danger.
- The Therac 25 radiation machine for tracking cancers was thoroughly tested and successfully used on thousands of patients before a software bug caused massive radiation overdoses, resulting in the partial paralysis of one patient and the death of another.
- On January 15, 1990, AT&T's 30-year-old signaling system software failed, bringing the long distance carrier's network to its knees. Twenty million calls failed to go through during the next 18 hours before technicians found the problem: a single incorrect instruction hiding among a million lines of code.

Software errors can take a variety of forms, including syntax errors, logic errors, clerical errors, capacity errors, and judgment errors. But whatever its form, a software error can be devilishly difficult to locate and even more difficult to remove. According to one study, 15 to 20 percent of attempts to remove program errors actually introduce new errors!

Software Solutions

Programmers work the way medieval craftsmen built cathedrals—one stone at a time.

—Mitch Kapor

Computer scientists and software engineers are responding to reliability and cost problems on four main fronts:

- *Programming techniques.* So far, structured programming is the best known and most successful technique for increasing programmer productivity and program reliability. Programmers who use structured techniques can concentrate on the overall logic of their creations without getting distracted by minute details. The result is less expensive, more reliable software. But structured programming is no panacea; it is considered by most experts as only a single step on a long road toward more dependable programming methodologies.
- *Programming environments.* Today's best programming tools include sophisticated text editors, debuggers, record-keeping programs, and translators, all interwoven into a seamless graphic work environment. A high-quality programming environment can help a programmer manage the complexities of a large project. In recent years **CASE** (computer-assisted software engineering) **tools** have

emerged, allowing analysts and programmers to automate many of the tedious and error-prone steps involved in turning design specifications into programs. Still, CASE tools and programming environments have a long way to go before they can guarantee reliable software, if that's even possible.

- *Program verification.* Software engineers would like to be able to *prove* the correctness of their programs in the same way mathematicians prove the correctness of theorems. Computer scientists have developed **program verification** techniques that work well for small programs. Unfortunately these techniques don't work with the complex commercial programs people depend on today. There's little hope for automated program verification, either. Computer scientists have proven that some problems can't be solved with algorithms, and program verification is one such problem.
- *Human management.* Project management techniques from business and engineering have been applied successfully to many software engineering projects. These *human management* techniques have more to do with person-to-person communication than with programmer-to-machine communication. Since many information system failures result from human communication errors, successful human management can improve a system's overall reliability. But again, the benefits of human management methodologies aren't great enough to offset the massive problems facing software engineers today.

Computer scientists have accomplished a great deal in the short history of the field. Software development is easier than it used to be, and computers today can accomplish far more than anyone dreamed a few decades ago. But software engineers have failed to keep up with the fast-paced evolution in computer hardware, and it's still incredibly difficult to produce reliable, cost-effective software. A decade ago, computer scientist Ted Lewis summed up the problem in one of his laws of computing. Today, when we're routinely asked to entrust our money, our health, our legal rights, and our lives to software, it's important for all of us to remember that law: "Hardware is soft; software is hard."

Summary

Computer programming is a specialized form of problem solving that involves developing an algorithm for solving a problem. Most programmers use stepwise refinement to repeatedly break a problem into smaller, more easily solvable problems. An algorithm typically is developed in pseudocode that describes the logic of the program before being translated into a programming language. A translator program—either a compiler or an interpreter—checks for syntax errors (language errors) and, if it finds none, translates the program into machine language so the computer can execute the instructions. Logic errors might not surface until the translated program is run, and maybe not even then. The programming process isn't completed until the program is thoroughly tested for errors.

Computer languages have evolved through several generations, with each generation being easier to use and more powerful than the one that came before. Machine language—the original computer language of zeros and ones—is primitive and difficult to program. Assembly language uses a translator called an assembler to turn alphabetic codes into the binary numbers of machine language, but in every other way it is identical to machine language.

High-level languages, such as FORTRAN, COBOL, BASIC, Pascal, and C , are more like English and therefore easier to work with than either machine or assembly language. What's more, they generally can be transported between computers with a minimum of rewriting. Most modern languages encourage structured programming, a technique that involves combining subprograms using only the three fundamental control structures: sequence, selection, and repetition. Structured programming produces programs with fewer logic errors. Still, when program efficiency is critical, many programmers use languages like C that allow them to work at a lower level of machine logic.

Many applications contain built-in macro languages, scripting languages, and query languages that put programming power in the hands of users. Query languages are representative of fourth-generation languages (4GLs) that are nonprocedural; that is, they allow the programmer to focus on defining the task rather than outlining the steps involved in accomplishing the task. Visual programming tools allow the programmer to use icons, drawing tools, menus, and dialog boxes to construct programs without writing code. Object-oriented programming (OOP) tools allow programmers to construct programs from objects with properties and the ability to send messages to each other; many believe that OOP represents the future of programming.

Programs are part of larger information systems. An information system has a life cycle that starts with the initial investigation of the problem; proceeds through analysis, design, development, and implementation phases; and lingers in an ongoing maintenance phase until the system is retired. A systems analyst manages a typical information system with the help of a team of programmers and other computer professionals.

Computer scientists are responsible for the software tools and concepts that make all other software development possible. Computer science focuses on the process of computing through several areas of specialization, including theory, algorithms, data structures, programming concepts and languages, computer architecture, management information systems, artificial intelligence, and software engineering.

One of the most challenging problems facing computer science is the problem of software reliability. Current software development techniques provide no assurance that a software system will function without failure under all circumstances. As more and more human institutions rely on computer systems, it becomes increasingly important for computer scientists to find ways to make software that people can trust.

CHAPTER REVIEW

Key Terms

algorithm
alpha testing
assembler
assembly language
beta testing
CASE tools
coding
compiler
computer architecture
computer science
control structure
data structure
fourth-generation language (4GL)
high-level language
information system
interpreter
logic error
machine language
macro (scripting) language
management information systems (MIS)
module (subprogram)
object-oriented programming (OOP)
programming
program verification
prototype
pseudocode
software engineering
stepwise refinement
structured programming
syntax error
system life cycle
systems analyst
testing
top-down design
transportable
visual programming

Review Questions 

1. Here's an algorithm for directions to a university bookstore:

   Go south on 4th Street to Jefferson Street.
   Turn left on Jefferson Street.
   Proceed on Jefferson past the stoplight to the booth at the campus entrance.
   If there's somebody in the booth, ask for a permit to park in the bookstore parking lot; otherwise just keep going.
   When you reach the bookstore parking lot, keep circling the lot until you find an empty space.
   Park in the empty space.

   Find examples of sequence, selection, and repetition control structures in this algorithm.
2. Find examples of ambiguous statements that might keep the algorithm in question 1 from working properly.
3. Assume that Robert, the automated chef in Chapter 3, is going to do the driving. Use stepwise refinement to add more detail to question 1's algorithm so Robert has a better chance of understanding the instructions.
4. Design an algorithm to play the part of the guesser in the number-guessing game featured in this chapter. If you base your algorithm on the right strategy, it will always be able to guess the correct number in seven or fewer tries. (Hint: Computer scientists call the right strategy the *binary search.*)
5. When does it make sense to design a custom program rather than using off-the-shelf commerical software? Give some examples.
6. Pascal and BASIC were both designed as student languages. Explain how and why they are different.
7. Why is structured programming so widely practiced today by software developers?
8. Why are so many computer languages in use today?
9. Assemblers, compilers, and interpreters are all language translators. How do they differ?
10. What is the relationship between computer science and computer programming?
11. Give examples of several different kinds of computer errors and describe how these errors affect people.
12. What techniques do software engineers use to improve software reliability?

Discussion Questions 

1. Is programming a useful skill for a computer user? Why or why not?
2. Do you think computer professionals should have a code of ethics similar to those found in legal and medical professions? What should such a code cover?
3. Should programmers be licensed? Is programming a craft, a trade, or a profession?
4. Suppose you want to computerize a small business or nonprofit organization. What questions might a systems analyst ask when determining what kind of system you need?
5. What do you think programming will be like in 10 years? 20 years? 50 years?
6. Computer science is in the college of science at some universities and in the college of engineering at others. Is computer science a science, a branch of engineering, or both?
7. Why is it so difficult to produce error-free software?

Projects 

1. The computer is often used as an excuse for human errors. Find articles describing "The computer did it" errors in newspapers and magazines. For each example try to determine if the computer is, in fact, to blame.
2. Try to determine what safeguards are used to ensure that automated teller machines don't malfunction and that they can't be violated.
3. Find out what safeguards are used to ensure the security of computer systems used in your local elections.

Sources and Resources 

Windows Programming for Mere Mortals, by Woody Leonhard (Reading, MA: Addison-Wesley, 1992). A funny, lively beginner's guide to programming using Visual BASIC and the programming languages built into Excel, Word, and Ami Pro. It's not a reference manual, but this book provides lots of programming background for beginners in a very readable package. A disk is included.

Oh! Pascal!, by Doug Cooper (New York: Norton, 1993). A friendly and witty introduction to Pascal. The third edition comes in two versions: One that covers standard Pascal (the generic version of the language) and one that's specific to Turbo Pascal 6.0, a version with object-oriented programming capability.

C by Dissection: The Essentials of C Programming, by Al Kelley and Ira Pohl (Redwood City, CA: Benjamin/Cummings, 1992). This excellent text introduces beginners to the C language with lots of examples.

Learn C on the Macintosh, by Dave Mark (Reading, MA: Addison-Wesley, 1991). This book/disk package includes a special version of THINK C that allows you to create programs without any additional software. The tutorial is fun to read and easy to follow. If you want to program the Mac, this is the place to start.

Macintosh C Programming Primer: Inside the Toolbox Using THINK C, Volume 1, 2d ed., by Dave Mark and Cartwright Reed (Reading, MA: Addison-Wesley, 1992). This book dives into the nitty gritty of writing Macintosh applications that feel like Mac applications, with the same wit and style of Mark's beginner book.

The Analytical Engine: An Introduction to Computer Science Using HyperCard, by Rick Decker and Stuart Hirshfield (Belmont, CA: Wadsworth, 1990). A well-written, innovative text that illustrates many of the concepts of computer science using HyperCard stacks. Another version of the book/disk package uses ToolBook, a HyperCard-like program for IBM-compatible computers running Windows.

Computer Science: An Overview, 3d ed., by J. Glenn Brookshear (Redwood City, CA: Benjamin/Cummings, 1991). This excellent survey covers algorithms, data structures, operating systems, and software engineering from a current computer science perspective.

Algorithmics: The Spirit of Computing, by David Harel (Reading, MA: Addison-Wesley, 1992). This book explores the central ideas of computer science from basic algorithms and data structures to more advanced concepts.

An Introduction to Object-Oriented Programming, by Timothy Budd (Reading, MA: Addison-Wesley, 1991). This text is designed to introduce the concepts of object-oriented programming without getting bogged down in the mechanics of a specific language. The book assumes you know the basics of programming in some language and provides examples in four different object-oriented languages.

CHAPTER TEN

Artificial Intelligence

Alan Turing, Military Intelligence, and Intelligent Machines

The extent to which we regard something as behaving in an intelligent manner is determined as much by our own state of mind and training as by the properties of the object under consideration.

—Alan Turing

After reading this chapter you should be able to

- explain what artificial intelligence means
- explain the two basic approaches of artificial intelligence research
- describe several hard problems that artificial intelligence research has not yet been able to solve
- describe several practical applications of artificial intelligence
- explain what robots are and give several examples illustrating what they can—and can't—do
- discuss important social and political issues raised by artificial intelligence research

Alan M. Turing, the British mathematician who designed the world's first operational electronic digital computer during the 1940s, may have been the most important thinker in the history of computing. While a graduate student at Princeton in 1936, Turing published "On Computable Numbers," a paper that laid the theoretical groundwork for all of modern computer science. In that paper he described a theoretical *Turing Machine* that could read instructions from punched paper tape and perform all the critical operations of a computer. The paper also established the limits of computer science by mathematically demonstrating that some problems simply cannot be solved by any kind of computer.

Alan Turing

After receiving his doctorate in 1938, Turing had an opportunity to translate theory into reality. Anticipating an invasion by Hitler's forces, the British government assembled a team of mathematicians and engineers with the top-secret mission of cracking the German military code. Under the leadership of Turing and others the group built Colossus, a single-purpose machine regarded by many today as the first electronic digital computer. From the time Colossus was completed in 1943 until the end of the war, it successfully cracked Nazi codes—a fact concealed by the British government until long after the war ended. Many experts believe that Colossus was ultimately responsible for the defeat of the Nazis.

Turing effectively launched the field of artificial intelligence with a 1950 paper called "Computing Machinery and Intelligence." In this paper he proposed a concrete test for determining whether a machine was intelligent. In later years Turing championed the possibility of emulating human thought through computation. He even co-wrote the first chess-playing program.

Turing was an unconventional and extremely sensitive person. He was professionally and socially devastated by his arrest in 1952 for violation of British antihomosexuality laws. The 41-year-old genius apparently committed suicide in 1954, years before the government made his wartime heroics public. Four decades after his death, Turing's work still has relevance to computer scientists, mathematicians, and philosophers. The highest award in computer science, the Turing Award, bears his name. It's impossible to know what he might have contributed had he lived through those decades.

Alan Turing spent much of his short life trying to answer the question "Can machines think?" That's still a central question of **artificial intelligence** (**AI**), the field of computer science devoted to making computers perceive, reason, and act in ways that have, until now, been reserved for human beings. But today even those who believe that computers can't "think" have to admit that artificial intelligence research has produced impressive results: computers that can communicate in human languages; systems that can provide instant expertise in medicine, science, and other fields; world-class electronic chess players; and robots that can outperform humans in a variety of tasks. In this chapter we'll explore the technology, applications, and implications of artificial intelligence.

Thinking About Thinking Machines

What is intelligence, anyway? It is only a word that people use to name those unknown processes with which our brains solve problems we call hard. But whenever you learn a skill yourself, you're less impressed or mystified when other people do the same. This is why the meaning of "intelligence" seems so elusive: it describes not some definite thing but only the momentary horizon of our ignorance about how minds might work.

—Marvin Minsky, AI pioneer

If you ask ten people to define intelligence, you're likely to get ten different answers, including some of these:

- the ability to learn from experience
- the power of thought
- the ability to reason
- the ability to perceive relations
- the power of insight
- the ability to use tools
- intuition

Intelligence is difficult to define and understand, even for philosophers and psychologists who spend their lives studying it. But this elusive quality is, to many people, the characteristic that sets humans apart from other species. So it's not surprising that controversy has continually swirled around the questions "Can a machine be intelligent?" and "Can a machine think?"

Can Machines Think?

A machine may be deemed intelligent when it can pass for a human being in a blind test.

—Alan Turing

In his landmark 1950 paper, Alan Turing suggested that the question "Can machines think?" was too vague and philosophical to be of any value. To make it more concrete, he proposed an "imitation game." The **Turing test**, as it came to be known, involves two people and a computer. One person, the interrogator, sits alone in a room and types questions into a computer terminal. The questions can be about anything—math, science, politics, sports, entertainment, art, human relationships, emotions—anything. As answers to questions appear on the terminal, the interrogator attempts to guess whether those answers were typed by the other person or were generated by the computer. By repeatedly fooling interrogators into thinking it is a person, a computer can demonstrate intelligent behavior. If it *acts* intelligent, according to Turing, it *is* intelligent.

Turing did not intend this test to be the only way to demonstrate machine intelligence; he pointed out that a machine could fail and still be intelligent. Even so, Turing

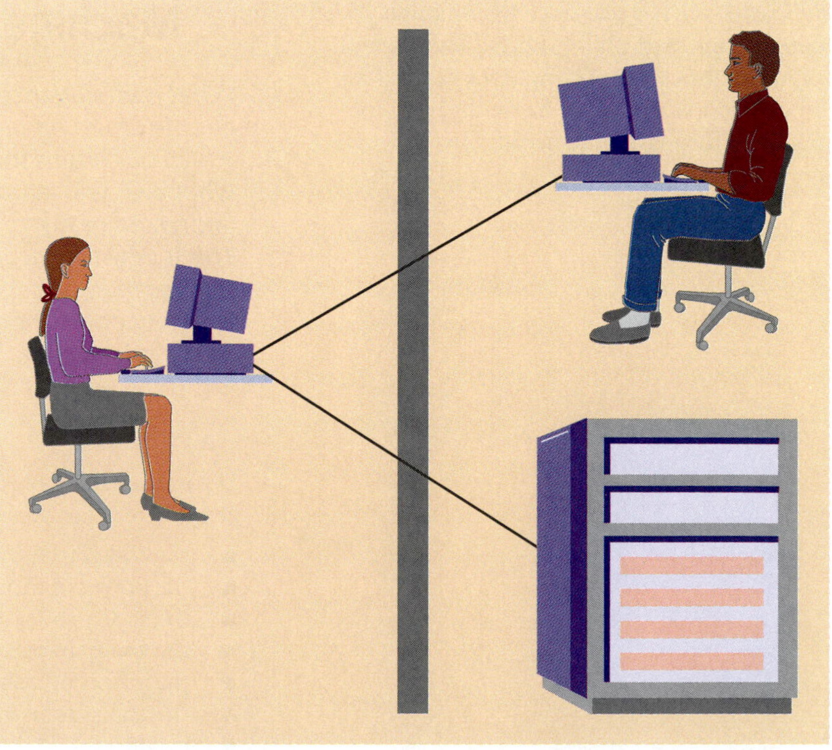

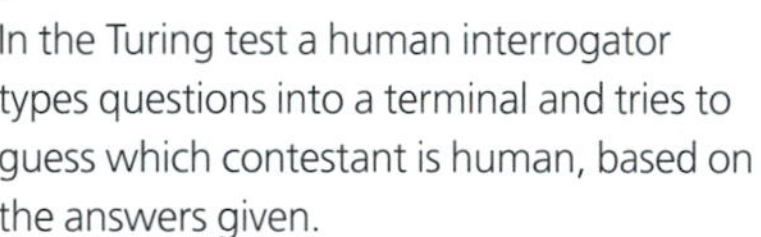

In the Turing test a human interrogator types questions into a terminal and tries to guess which contestant is human, based on the answers given.

believed that machines would be able to pass his test by the turn of the century. So far no computer has come close, in spite of 40 years of AI research. While some people still cling to the Turing test to define artificial intelligence, most AI researchers favor less stringent definitions.

What Is Artificial Intelligence?

Artificial Intelligence is the study of ideas which enable computers to do the things that make people seem intelligent.

—Patrick Henry Winston, *Artificial Intelligence*

This definition from a 1977 edition of a textbook is similar to definitions that commonly appear in the popular press. This type of definition captures the general idea of artificial intelligence, but it breaks down when applied to specific examples. Does artificial intelligence include doing lightning-fast calculations? Finding a word in a dictionary as fast as it can be typed? Remembering hundreds of telephone numbers at a time? If a person could do all of these things, that person would "seem intelligent." But these activities aren't good examples of artificial intelligence because they're trivial for computers. In fact, many computer scientists believe that if it's easy to do with a computer, it can't be artificial intelligence. Here's a more recent textbook definition that reflects that point of view:

Artificial intelligence is the study of how to make computers do things at which, at the moment, people are better.

—Elaine Rich, *Artificial Intelligence*

According to this definition, artificial intelligence is a *moving frontier*. The short history of the field bears this out. In the 1950s many AI researchers struggled to create computers that could play checkers and chess. Today computers can easily beat all but the best human players, and relatively few AI researchers study these games. In the words of one researcher, artificial intelligence is "whatever hasn't been done yet." Moving-frontier definitions of AI tend to be accurate, but they're short on specifics. A more concrete and complete definition might combine Rich's definition with this one from the latest edition of Winston's popular textbook:

Artificial intelligence is the study of the computations that make it possible to perceive, reason, and act.

—Patrick Henry Winston, *Artificial Intelligence*

Perceive, *reason*, and *act* are words used more commonly in psychology, the science of human behavior, than in computer science. In fact, psychologists work alongside computer scientists on many AI research projects. Computer scientists tend to be motivated by the challenge of producing machine intelligence for its own sake. Psychologists, on the other hand, are interested in artificial intelligence because it provides new insights into *natural* intelligence and the workings of the human brain.

These points of view symbolize two common approaches to AI. One approach attempts to use computers to simulate human mental processes. For example, an AI expert might ask people to describe how they solve a problem and attempt to capture their answers in a software model.

The simulation approach has three inherent problems:

1. Most people have trouble knowing and describing how they do things. Human intelligence includes unconscious thoughts, instantaneous insights, and other mental processes that are difficult or impossible to understand and describe.
2. There are vast differences between the structure and capabilities of the human brain and the computer. Even the most powerful supercomputers can't approach the brain's ability to perform parallel processing—breaking a complex job into many smaller, simpler jobs and completing those jobs simultaneously.
3. The best way to do something with a machine is often very different from the way people do it. Before the Wright brothers, dozens of inventors failed to produce flying machines because they tried to make their inventions imitate birds. Similarly many early AI attempts failed because they were designed to mimic human intelligence rather than to take advantage of the computer's unique capabilities.

Many early flying machines that imitated birds never got off the ground.

The second, more common, approach to AI involves designing intelligent machines independent of the way people think. According to this approach, human intelligence is just one possible kind of intelligence. A machine's method of solving a problem might be different from the human method but no less intelligent.

Whichever approach they take, scientists face problems that are difficult and far too complex to solve all at once. Most AI researchers choose to break those problems into smaller problems that are easier to solve—to create programs that can function intelligently when confined to limited *domains*.

Opening Games

One of the first popular domains for AI research was the checkerboard. Much early AI work focused on games like checkers and chess because they were easy to represent in the computer's digital memory, they had clearly defined rules, and the goals were unmistakable. Instead of struggling with nebulous issues surrounding thought and intelligence, game researchers could focus on the concrete question "How can I create a program that wins consistently?" Their answers included many AI techniques still used today in a variety of applications:

- *Searching.* One way to win a game is to look ahead at the possibilities generated by each potential move: "I have four possible moves: A, B, C, and D. If I do A, then my opponent might do X, Y, or Z. If my opponent responds by doing X, then I can do E, F, G, or H . . . and so on." Obviously high-speed computers are better at this kind of repetitive processing than people. But even a computer can't check all possible decision points in a complicated game like checkers (since there are approximately 10^{21} choices). Even if it could, most people wouldn't call this kind of *brute-force* searching intelligent. So searching is generally guided by a planned strategy and by rules known as heuristics.
- *Heuristics.* A *heuristic* is a rule of thumb. Unlike hard-and-fast algorithms, heuristics guide us toward judgments that experience tells us are likely to be true. In everyday life we apply heuristics like "The early bird catches the worm" and "To loosen a stuck jar lid, run warm water over it." A checker-playing program might employ a heuristic that says "Keep checkers in the king's row as long as possible."
- *Pattern recognition.* The best human chess and checkers players remember thousands of critical board patterns and know the best strategies for playing when those or similar patterns appear. Game-playing programs recognize recurring patterns, too, but not nearly as well as people do. Computer players often have trou-

ble identifying situations that are similar but not identical. Pattern recognition is probably the single biggest advantage a human game player has over a computer opponent; it helps compensate for the computer's speed and thoroughness at searching ahead.

- *Machine learning.* The best game-playing programs learn from experience. If a move pays off, a learning program is more likely to use that move (or similar moves) in future games. If a move results in a loss, the program will remember to avoid similar moves.

Today a $40 program can turn a personal computer into a chess wizard, and most AI researchers have moved on to more interesting and practical applications for AI. But whether working on vision, speech, problem solving, or expert decision making, researchers still use the successful strategy of game researchers—to restrict the domain of their programs so that problems are small enough to be understood and solved. We'll see how this strategy has paid off in several important areas of artificial intelligence, starting with natural-language communication.

Natural-Language Communication

Language is no less complex or subtle a phenomenon than the knowledge it seeks to transmit.

—Raymond Kurzweil, *The Age of Intelligent Machines*

In Turing's classic test of machine intelligence, the computer succeeds by playing the part of a person in a typed conversation. Since the earliest days of computing, scientists have dreamed of machines that could communicate in natural languages like English, Russian, and Japanese. Over the years natural-language communication has continually challenged researchers. Many problems relate to recognizing and reproducing human speech—issues we'll deal with later in the chapter. But even when it's typed directly into the machine, natural-language text poses significant software challenges.

Machine Translation Traps

One early project attempted to create a program that could translate scientific papers from Russian to English and from English to Russian. **Automatic translation** offered hope for increased communication between scientists during the tense cold-war years. The method seemed straightforward and foolproof: A **parsing program** (or **parser**) would analyze sentence structure and identify each word according to whether it was a subject, verb, or other part of speech; another program would look up each word in a translation dictionary and substitute the appropriate word.

After spending 15 years and millions of dollars on research, scientists abandoned the project. Even with the help of human editors, machine translators couldn't compete with humans in speed or accuracy. A typical translation correctly processed only about 80 percent of the desired text.

The automatic translation project became the target of jokes that, if not strictly factual, were effective at pointing out the problems of machine translation. In one famous story scientists asked the computer to translate English into Russian and then translate the results back into English. As the story goes, "The spirit is willing, but the flesh is weak" came back as "The wine is agreeable, but the meat is rotten" and "out of sight, out of mind" became "blind and insane" or "invisible idiot."

This early translation project may not have lived up to its promoters' expectations, but it taught them a valuable lesson: Translation without understanding is impossible. To translate a sentence, the translator must know what the sentence *means*.

Conversation Without Communication

Similar lessons emerged from Joseph Weizenbaum's work with ELIZA, one of the first software programs to converse in a limited form of natural language. Weizenbaum designed ELIZA to simulate the role of a therapist in a typed conversation with a patient. Here's a sample ELIZA session (the computer's responses are capitalized):

A Conversation with ELIZA

Men are all alike.
IN WHAT WAY

They're always bugging us about something or other.
CAN YOU THINK OF A SPECIFIC EXAMPLE

Well, my boyfriend made me come here.
YOUR BOYFRIEND MADE YOU COME HERE

He says I'm depressed much of the time.
I AM SORRY TO HEAR YOU ARE DEPRESSED

It's true. I am unhappy.
DO YOU THINK COMING HERE WILL HELP YOU NOT TO BE UNHAPPY

I need some help, that much seems certain.
WHAT WOULD IT MEAN TO YOU IF YOU GOT SOME HELP

Perhaps I could learn to get along with my mother.
TELL ME MORE ABOUT YOUR FAMILY

My mother takes care of me.
WHO ELSE IN YOUR FAMILY TAKES CARE OF YOU

My father.
YOUR FATHER

You are like my father in some ways.
WHAT RESEMBLANCE DO YOU SEE

You are not very aggressive but I think you don't want me to notice that.
WHAT MAKES YOU THINK I AM NOT VERY AGGRESSIVE

You don't argue with me.
WHY DO YOU THINK I DON'T ARGUE WITH YOU

You are afraid of me.
DOES IT PLEASE YOU TO BELIEVE I AM AFRAID OF YOU

My father is afraid of everybody.
WHAT ELSE COMES TO MIND WHEN YOU THINK OF YOUR FATHER

Bullies.
DOES THAT HAVE ANYTHING TO DO WITH THE FACT THAT YOUR BOYFRIEND MADE YOU COME HERE

From *Computer Power and Human Reason*, by Joseph Weizenbaum.

As impressive as this dialog seems, there's no understanding here. ELIZA uses a few simple tricks to *simulate* understanding, including recognizing a few key words (like *mother*), identifying categories for some of those words (*family*), and repeating phrases from earlier in the conversation. But ELIZA's tricks are far from foolproof. In response to "Necessity is the mother of invention," ELIZA might say, "Tell me more about your family." An ELIZA session can easily deteriorate into nonsense dialog laced with grammatical errors and inappropriate responses. Clearly ELIZA lacks the understanding to pass as a human in a Turing test.

Nonsense and Common Sense

Bill sings to Sarah, Sarah sings to Bill. Perhaps they will do other dangerous things together. They may eat lamb or stroke each other. They may chant of their difficulties and their happiness. They have love but they also have typewriters. That is interesting.

—A poem by RACTER, from *The Policeman's Beard Is Half Constructed, programmed by William Chamberlain and Thomas Etter*

Years after ELIZA's creation, this poetry appeared in *The Policeman's Beard Is Half Constructed*, the first book ever written by a computer. RACTER, like ELIZA, produced English-language output without really understanding it. Why do machines that flawlessly follow instructions written in BASIC, C, and other computer languages have so much trouble with natural-*language* communications?

Part of the problem is the massive vocabulary of natural languages. A typical computer language has less than 100 key words, each with a precise, unambiguous meaning. English, in contrast, contains hundreds of thousands of words, many of which have multiple meanings. Of course, a person or a machine doesn't need to understand every word in the dictionary to successfully communicate in English. Most natural-language processors work with a *subset* of the language. But as the early scientific-translation efforts showed, restricting vocabulary isn't enough.

Every language has a **syntax**—a set of rules for constructing sentences from words. In a programming language the syntax rules are exact and unambiguous. Natural-language parsing programs have to deal with rules that are vague, ambiguous, and occasionally contradictory. One early parser, when asked to analyze the sentence "Time flies like an arrow," replied with several possible interpretations, including one statement with *time* as the subject, another statement with *flies* as the subject, and two commands in which the reader was the subject!

Still, computers are far more successful dealing with natural-language syntax than with **semantics**—the underlying meaning of words and phrases. In natural language the meaning of a sentence is ambiguous unless it's considered in context. "The hens were ready to eat" means one thing if it follows "The farmer approached the henhouse" and something else if it follows "The chef approached the oven." To make matters worse, human conversations are filled with idiomatic expressions ("Sonja had a cow when she heard the news") and unspoken assumptions about the world or specific subject matter ("Catch the T at Harvard Square and take it to MIT"). In short, the computer lacks what we call *common sense*—the wealth of knowledge and understanding about the world that people share.

The most successful natural-language applications limit the domain so that virtually all the relevant information can be fed to the system. If the domain—the "world"—is small enough, and the rules of that world are clear and unambiguous, a computer can have "common sense" that makes natural-language communication possible. For example, many database query languages and fourth-generation programming languages accept and understand English commands, but only within a narrow range. The biggest market for natural-language processing today is language translation—the same market that produced AI's first major failure. Translation programs still can't translate books unassisted, but they can increase the productivity of people who translate technical manuals and other works that focus on narrow domains.

Natural-language processing has come a long way since ELIZA's early conversations. Computers still can't pass the Turing test, but they can at least fool some of the people some of the time. Or so it seems, based on the results of the first contest ever devoted to finding a winner of the Turing test: The First Annual Loebner Prize Com-

Inexpensive pocket electronic translators serve world travelers by providing instant access to common words, but not whole sentences.

petition held in the Boston Computer Museum in 1991. In the contest ten untrained judges tried to determine which of the eight entries were human by carrying on typed conversations via terminals. Because the contest organizers believed that any computer would be trounced in an open-ended Turing test, they included rules to protect the entrants from unrestricted questioning. Here's a short sample of a dialog between a judge and the winning entry, a program called PC Therapist. The IBM-PC-based program, which took three years to write, played the role of a jester and made occasional typing errors so it would appear more human. It worked: five of the ten judges thought PC Therapist was a person.

A Conversation with PC Therapist

01:32:25 Judge 6:	Hello, earth person!
01:33:03 Terminal 5	Hello there judge, are you ready to have some fun? How ya doin, judge? Hello—how's the weather up there today?
01:33:35 Judge 6	Dark clouds with occasional bursts of sunshine (or rather camera flashes).
01:34:45 Terminal 5	The trouble with the rat race is that even if you win you're still a rat. Whimsy can be flimsy, right? How important is that to you?
01:35:26 Judge 6	Can't say I understand the question . . . but the whimsy of a poet is one thing and the whimsy of most of us is another.
01:36:51 Terminal 5	How do you know you can t say you understand the question . . . but the whimsy of a poet is one thing and the whimsy of most of us is another.
01:37:37 Judge 6	Are you repeating me just for laughs?
01:38:04 Terminal 5	I'm sorry, I do sometimes repeat myself . . . perhaps it's because i can't find my electr]nic organizer!.

Reprinted from *AI Magazine*, Summer 1992.

Natural-language processing relates to other AI technologies discussed later in the chapter. Speech recognition and optical character recognition provide input to natural-language systems, freeing the human communicator from the keyboard. On the output side, speech synthesis allows the computer to talk back in English or another language. But natural-language input and output are meaningless without a knowledge base that allows the computer to understand the ideas behind the words.

Knowledge Bases and Expert Systems

A preschool child can take you on a tour of the neighborhood, explaining how people use every building, describing the interconnected lives of every person you meet, and answering questions about anything you see along the way. A computer at city hall can give you facts and figures about building materials and assessed values of houses, but it can't provide you with a fraction of the *knowledge* conveyed in the child's tour. The human brain, which isn't particularly good at storing and recalling facts, excels at manipulating *knowledge*—information that incorporates the *relationships* between facts. Computers, on the other hand, are better at handling data than knowledge. Nobody knows exactly how the brain stores and manipulates knowledge. But artificial intelligence researchers have developed, and continue to develop, techniques for representing knowledge in computers.

Knowledge Bases

While a database contains only facts, a **knowledge base** also contains a system for determining and changing the relationship between those facts. Facts stored in a database are rigidly organized in categories; ideas stored in a knowledge base can be reorganized as new information changes their relationships.

Computer scientists so far have had little success in developing a knowledge base that can understand the world the way a child does. Even before they start school, children know that

- If you put something in water, it will get wet.
- If Susan is Phil's sister, Phil is Susan's brother.
- You can't build a tower from the top down.
- Dogs commonly live in houses, but cows seldom do.
- People can't walk through walls.
- If you eat dinner in a restaurant, you're expected to pay for the food and leave a tip.
- If you travel from Dallas to Phoenix, time passes during the trip.

These statements are part of the mass of common-sense knowledge that children acquire from living in the world. Since computers can't draw on years of human experience to construct mental models of the world, they don't automatically develop common sense. Much AI research centers on providing computers with ways to acquire and store real-world, common-sense knowledge. Researchers have had little success at developing computer systems with the kinds of broad, shallow knowledge found in children. But when knowledge bases are restricted to narrow, deep domains—the domains of experts—they can be effective, practical, *intelligent* tools. For example, knowledge bases lie at the heart of hundreds of *expert systems* used in business, science, and industry.

Artificial Experts

Ex = has-been
Spurt = a drip under pressure
Expert = has-been drip under pressure

—*Utah Phillips*

An expert is someone who has an extraordinary amount of knowledge within a narrow domain. By confining activities to that domain, the expert achieves mastery. An **expert system** is a software program designed to replicate the decision-making process of a human expert. At the foundation of every expert system is a knowledge base representing ideas from a specific field of expertise. Because it's a collection of specialized knowledge, an expert system's knowledge base must be constructed by a user, an expert, or a *knowledge engineer*—a specialist who interviews and observes experts and painstakingly converts their words and actions into a knowledge base. Some new expert systems can grow their own knowledge bases while observing human decision makers doing their jobs. But for most expert systems, the process is still human-intensive.

Strictly speaking, expert systems derive their knowledge from experts; systems that draw on other sources, such as government regulations, company guidelines, and statistical databases, are called *knowledge-based systems*. But in practice the terms *expert system* and *knowledge-based system* are often used interchangeably.

A knowledge base commonly represents knowledge in the form of *if-then rules* like these:

- If the engine will not turn over and the lights do not work, then check the battery.
- If checking the battery shows it is not dead, then check the battery connectors.

Most human decision making involves uncertainty, so many modern expert systems include "fuzzy" rules that state conclusions as probabilities rather than certainties. Here's an example from MYCIN, one of the first expert systems designed to capture a doctor's expertise:

> *If* (1) *the infection is primary-bacteremia, and*
> (2) *the site of the culture is one of the sterile sites, and*
> (3) *the suspected portal of entry of the organism is the gastrointestinal tract, then there is suggestive evidence (.7) that the identity of the organism is bacteriodes.*

Along with the knowledge base, a complete expert system also includes a *human interface,* which allows the user to interact with the system, and an *inference engine,* which puts the user input together with the knowledge base, applies logical principles, and produces the requested expert advice.

Sometimes expert systems aid experts by providing automated data analysis and informed second opinions. In other cases expert systems support nonexperts by providing advice based on judgments of one or more experts. Whatever their role, expert systems work because they function within narrow, carefully defined domains.

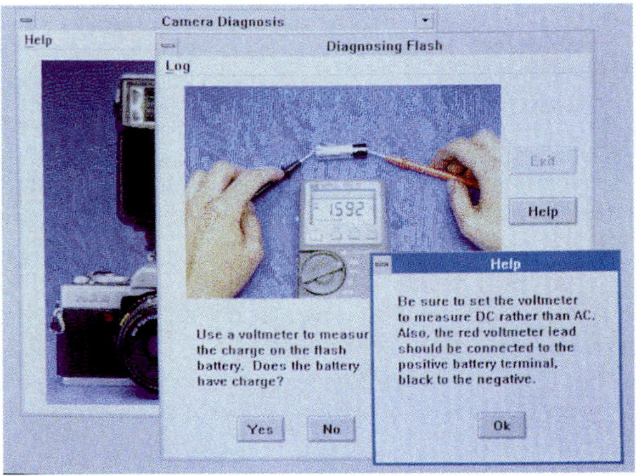

This expert system leads the user through the process of diagnosing problems with malfunctioning cameras.

Expert systems in action. Some of the first successful expert systems were developed around medical knowledge bases. Because medical knowledge is orderly and well documented, researchers believed it could be captured successfully in knowledge bases. They were right. The MYCIN medical expert system outperformed many human experts in diagnosing diseases. Dozens of other working medical expert systems exist, although few are actually used in medical practice.

The business community has been more enthusiastic than the medical community in its acceptance and use of expert systems. Here are a few examples of expert systems in action:

- American Express uses an expert system to automate the process of checking for fraud and misuses of its no-limit credit card. Credit checks must be completed within 90 seconds while the customer waits, and the cost of an error can be high. The company spent 13 months developing a system modeled on the decision-making expertise of its best credit clerks.
- Microsoft Corporation uses an expert system to help product managers conform to company guidelines on packaging and profitability. New managers aren't familiar with all the details of putting together a successful software product. The expert system serves as an advisor so new managers don't need to continually turn to more experienced managers and engineers for advice.
- Digital Equipment Corporation's XCON, perhaps the most successful expert system in commercial use today, has been configuring complex computer systems since 1980. The system's knowledge base consists of more than 10,000 rules describing the relationship of various computer parts. It reportedly does the work of more than 300 human experts, and it makes fewer mistakes than humans do.
- At Blue Cross/Blue Shield of Virginia, an expert system automates insurance claim processing. The expert system handles up to 200 routine claims each day, allowing human clerks to spend more time on tough situations that require human judgment. The developers of the system extracted diagnostic rules from manuals and watched human claims processors apply those rules.
- Boeing Company factory workers use an expert system to locate the right parts, tools, and techniques for assembling airplane electrical connectors. The system replaces 20,000 pages of documentation and reduces the average search time from 42 minutes to 5 minutes.
- Freelance writer Scott French used Nexpert, a Macintosh-based expert system, to analyze the writing style of Jacqueline Susann's novel *Valley of the Dolls* and help create *Just This Once*, a new work with the same style. The system reportedly wrote

25 percent of the novel independently, using suggestions from French. The Susann estate threatened French with a lawsuit even before the book had been sold.

There are hundreds of other examples of expert system applications: pinpointing likely sites for new oil explorations, aiding in automobile and appliance repairs, providing financial management advice, targeting direct-mail marketing campaigns, detecting problems in computer-controlled machinery, predicting weather, advising air traffic controllers, suggesting basic page layouts for publishers, controlling military machinery, providing assistance to musical composers . . . the list is growing at an astounding rate. Even the grammar checkers built into many word processors can be thought of as expert systems because they apply style and syntax rules developed by language experts.

One of the most unusual expert systems is AARON, an automated artist programmed by Harold Cohen, artist and professor at the University of California at San Diego. AARON uses over 1000 rules of human anatomy and behavior to create drawings of people, plants, and abstract objects with a robotic drawing machine. The drawings, which are unique works in a style similar to Cohen's, are widely acclaimed in the art community.

An original drawing by AARON, an expert system programmed by Harold Cohen (top), and Cohen demonstrating AARON (below).

When AARON creates a drawing, an interesting question arises: Who is the artist, Cohen or AARON? Cohen claims he is; he sees AARON as a dynamic work of art. The question may seem frivolous, but it's related to a larger question with profound implications: When expert systems make decisions, who's responsible? If a doctor uses an expert system to decide to perform surgery and the surgery fails, who's liable—the doctor, the programmer, the software company, or somebody else? If you're denied medical benefits because of a bug in an expert system, do you sue a person, an organization, or a program? If a power plant explodes because an expert system fails to detect a fault, who's to blame? As expert systems proliferate, questions like these are certain to confront consumers, lawyers, lawmakers, and technicians.

Expert systems in perspective. From these examples, it should be clear that expert systems offer many advantages. An expert system can

- help train new employees
- reduce the number of human errors
- take care of routine tasks so workers can focus on more challenging jobs
- provide expertise when no experts are available
- preserve the knowledge of experts after those experts leave an organization
- combine the knowledge of several experts
- make knowledge available to more people

But expert systems aren't without problems. For one, today's expert systems are difficult to build. To simplify the process, many software companies sell **expert system shells**—generic expert systems containing human interfaces and inference engines. These programs can save time and effort, but they don't include the part that is most difficult to build—the knowledge base.

Once constructed an expert system can't live up to its name. Unlike human experts, automated expert systems are poor at planning strategies. Their lack of flexibility makes them less creative than human thinkers. Most importantly, expert systems are powerless outside of their narrow, deep domains of knowledge. While most expert system domains can be summarized with a few hundred tidy rules of thumb, the world of people is full of inconsistencies, special cases, and ambiguities that could overwhelm even the best expert systems. A simple rule like "birds can fly" isn't sufficient for a literal-minded computer, which would need something more like this tongue-in-cheek rule from Marvin Minsky's book, *Society of Mind*:

Birds can fly, unless they are penguins and ostriches, or if they happen to be dead, or have broken wings, or are confined to cages, or have their feet stuck in cement, or have undergone experiences so dreadful as to render them psychologically incapable of flight.

Clearly, knowledge engineers can't use rules to teach computers all they need to know to perform useful, intelligent functions outside narrow domains. If they're ever going to exhibit the kind of broad-based intelligence found in children, AI systems will need to acquire knowledge by reading, looking, listening, and drawing their own conclusions about the world. These skills all depend on techniques of pattern recognition.

Pattern Recognition: Making Sense of the World

Experience has shown that science frequently develops most fruitfully once we learn to examine the things that seem the simplest, instead of those that seem the most mysterious.

—Marvin Minsky

A baby can recognize a human face, especially its mother's, almost from birth. A mother can hear and recognize her child's cry even in a noisy room. Computers are notoriously inferior at both of these tasks, which fall into the general category of pattern recognition. **Pattern recognition** involves identifying recurring patterns in input data with the goal of understanding or categorizing that input.

Pattern recognition applications represent half of the AI industry. Applications include face identification, fingerprint identification, handwriting recognition, scientific data analysis, weather forecasting, biological slide analysis, surveillance satellite data analysis, robot vision, optical character recognition, automatic voice recognition, and expert systems. We'll examine the problems and the promise of several types of pattern recognition, starting with the recognition of visual patterns.

Image Analysis

Image analysis is the process of identifying objects and shapes in a photograph, drawing, video, or other visual image. It's used for everything from colorizing classic motion pictures to piloting cruise missiles. An effortless process for people, image analysis is extremely demanding for computers. The simple process of identifying objects in a scene is complicated by all kinds of factors: masses of irrelevant data, objects that partially cover other objects, indistinct edges, changes in light sources and shadows, changes in the scene as objects move, and more. With all these complications, it's amazing that people are able to make any sense out of the images that constantly bombard their eyes.

Most image analysis programs require massive amounts of memory and processing power. Even with the best hardware available, today's software can't hold a candle to the human visual system when it comes to general image analysis. But AI researchers have had considerable success by restricting the domain of visual systems. One of the biggest success stories in AI work is a limited but practical form of computer vision: optical character recognition.

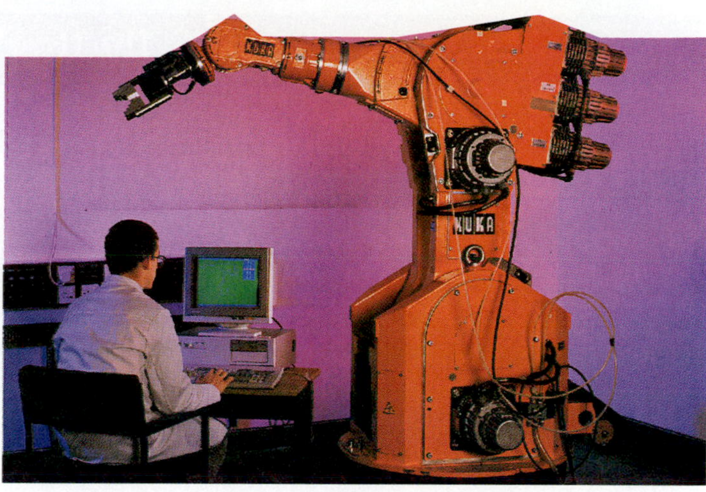

Pattern recognition is widely used in fingerprint analysis (left). This robot is equipped with visual and tactile sensors that employ pattern recognition technology (right).

Optical Character Recognition

In any shopping mall you can see sales clerks using wand readers to recognize words and numbers when they ring up your purchases at point-of-sale terminals. This specialized form of **optical character recognition** (**OCR**) is relatively simple for computers because the letters and numbers are designed to be easy for a computer to distinguish. OCR is much more difficult when the input might be a page from a book, newspaper, magazine, or letter. Still, general OCR technology has progressed to the point that it's practical for the U.S. Postal Service to use it to sort much of the mail sent every day. Similar technology is now available for personal computer users who have typewritten or printed text to be processed.

The first step in general OCR is to scan the image of the page into the computer's memory with a scanner, digital camera, or fax modem. The scanned image is nothing more than a pattern of bits in memory. It could just as easily be a poem by Robert Frost or a photograph of Robert Frost. Before a computer can process the text on a page, it must recognize the individual characters and convert them to text codes (ASCII or the equivalent). *Optical character recognition (OCR) software* locates and identifies printed characters embedded in images—it "reads" text. This is no small task for a machine, given the variety of typefaces and typestyles in use today.

The process of recognizing text in a variety of fonts and styles is surprisingly difficult for machines. State-of-the-art OCR programs use several techniques, including

- segmentation of the page into pictures, text blocks, and (eventually) individual characters
- scaled-down expert system technology for recognizing the underlying rules that distinguish letters
- context "experts" to help identify ambiguous letters by their context
- learning from actual examples and feedback from a human trainer

Today's best programs can achieve up to 99 percent accuracy. OCR software isn't foolproof, but it's reliable enough to be practical for many text-intensive applications, including reading aloud to the blind, converting typewritten documents and incoming fax documents to editable text, and processing transactions for database systems.

BAABBABABABA

A child can easily sort these letters into A's and B's. This problem is difficult for computers. Why?

The User's View

Optical Character Recognition

Software: OmniPage Professional, Microsoft Word.
The goal: You're working on a group research project comparing the writing styles used in several consumer magazines. You plan to use a grammar checker to compare average paragraph length, sentence length, word length, and overall reading level for randomly selected articles. You'll use OCR software to extract the text from the scanned pages and grammar checking software to generate the statistics.

After collecting the necessary magazines and selecting the pages to be analyzed, you're ready to scan and analyze the first article. You open OmniPage Professional, the OCR software, adjust the software settings, insert a page in the scanner, and click Scan.

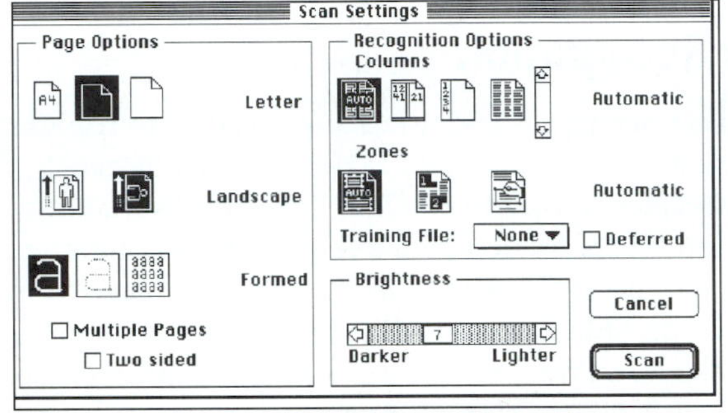

After scanning the image as a picture, the software performs image analysis, determining which zones on the scanned page contain blocks of text and which contain pictures.

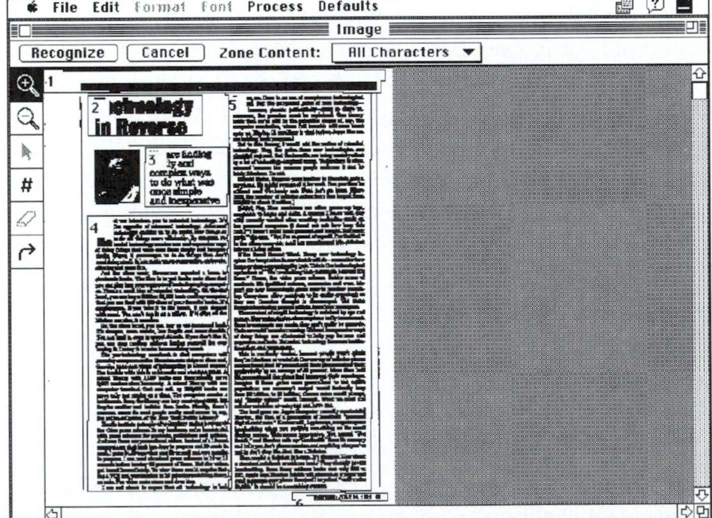

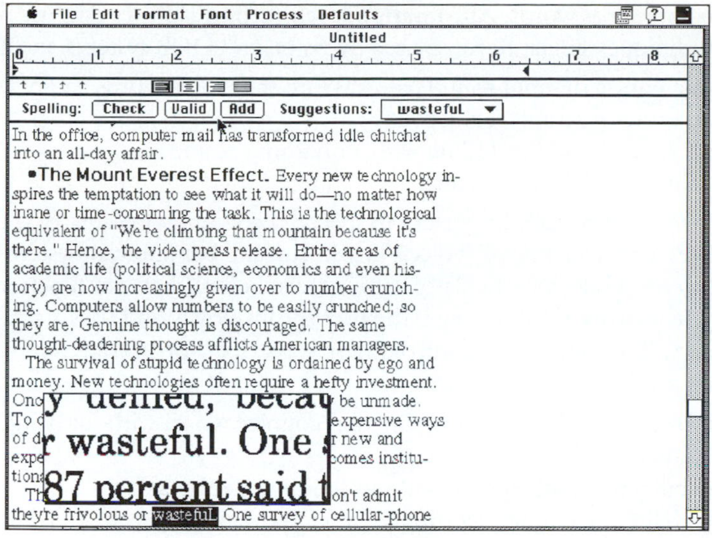

OmniPage analyzes each text zone, attempting to recognize each character. The analyzed text appears in a new window. You check and edit the text using the built-in spelling checker and editor. The spelling checker shows an enlarged image of each possible misspelled word so you can see what it looked like in the original document. It suggests corrections based on its knowledge of the kinds of errors that OCR systems tend to make. After correcting the errors you export the text to your word processor.

Document Statistics

Counts:		OK
Words	1047	
Characters	6352	
Paragraphs	18	
Sentences	91	
Averages:		
Sentences per Paragraph	5	
Words per Sentence	11	
Characters per Word	4	
Readability:		
Passive Sentences	14%	
Flesch Reading Ease	59.8	
Flesch Grade Level	10.0	
Flesch-Kincaid	7.5	
Gunning Fog Index	10.6	

You save the cleaned-up text file and run it through Microsoft Word's grammar checker. The grammar checker uses a simple knowledge base to provide a variety of statistics for your analysis of reading level. You can use these numbers, along with others, to do comparisons and create comparative charts.

OCR technology also can be applied to handwritten text but not as reliably. In typewritten and typeset text, character representation is consistent enough that one *a* looks like another *a*, at least when they're the same typeface. But, since most handwritten text lacks consistency, software has more trouble recognizing individual characters reliably. Nonetheless, the technology is getting better all the time, making more applications practical for pen-based computers. Handwriting recognition is especially important in Japan, China, and other countries with languages that don't lend themselves to keyboarding. But it's also useful with Western languages in situations where keyboarding isn't practical. Even the classic three-ring student notebook will undoubtedly have an electronic counterpart that automatically turns handwritten notes into text that can be fed directly into a word processor.

Automatic Speech Recognition

I think that the primary means of communication with computers in the next millenium will be speech.

—Nicholas Negroponte, *director of MIT's Media Lab*

Our ears process far less information than our eyes, but that information, especially human speech, is extremely important to our understanding of the world. In Chapters 2 and 8 we discussed audio digitizers—input devices that capture spoken words, music, and other sounds so they can be stored as digital data. But digitized voice input, like scanned text, must be processed by sophisticated software before it can be interpreted by the computer as words. **Automatic speech recognition** systems use pattern recognition techniques similar to those used by vision and OCR systems, including

- segmentation of input sound patterns into individual words and phonemes
- expert rules for interpreting sounds
- context "experts" for dealing with ambiguous sounds
- learning from a human trainer

Training is especially important in speech recognition because of the tremendous differences between human voices. Most current commercial systems need to be trained to recognize a particular person's voice before they can function. Even then, these systems work reliably only if the user speaks slowly and uses a small, predefined vocabulary. Research in speech recognition today focuses on overcoming these limitations and producing systems with

- *speaker independence*—the ability to recognize words without being trained to an individual speaker
- the ability to handle speech without limiting vocabulary
- the ability to handle *continuous speech*—natural speech in which words run together at normal speed

Researchers are making great strides toward these goals. Many new Macintosh computers come with PlainTalk software that allows them to process continuous speech with speaker independence. PlainTalk isn't 100 percent accurate, but it does a remarkable job of handling routine command processing, responding appropriately to spoken commands like "Computer . . . close window." Other companies have produced systems that combine speaker independence with the ability to recognize a large vocabulary. So far no one has yet developed a system that achieves all three goals, the human body excepted.

Even with their current limitations, speech recognition systems are used by factory workers and others whose hands are otherwise occupied while they use the computer. People can communicate numbers and commands by telephone for automated banking, credit card verification, and other remote applications. Speech recognition systems empower many handicapped users by allowing them to give verbal commands to computers and robotic devices. As their vocabularies grow, voice recognition systems are likely to show up in *talkwriters*—automated, dictation-taking typists. Future pocket-sized personal digital assistants may use microphones as their principal input devices. Many of today's researchers are working to combine speech recognition and natural-language understanding in a single machine that can accept commands in everyday spoken English, "Star Trek" style.

Talking Computers

The computers on "Star Trek" not only recognize human speech input but also respond with easy-to-understand **synthetic speech**. With **speech synthesis** software or hardware, modern desktop computers can generate synthetic speech by converting text into phonetic sounds. Most of today's speech synthesizers sound artificial when compared to the "Star Trek" computer voices; they even sound more artificial than the robot voices in low-budget cartoons. Human spoken language is complex, and no one has come close to duplicating it with software.

Still, it's easier for machines to speak passable English than to recognize it. There are many applications for voice output, including preschool education, telephone communication, and, of course, reading machines for visually impaired computer users.

For situations for which a synthetic voice isn't good enough, computers can play prerecorded **digitized speech** (along with other **digitized sounds**) stored in memory or on audio CDs. Of course, digitally recorded speech won't work for applications in which the text to be spoken is unpredictable, such as a talking word processor, because all the sounds must be prerecorded. But for an application with a limited vocabulary (reciting telephone numbers for automated directory assistance) or limited choices (an interactive educational game with short prerecorded speeches), digitized speech is a workable alternative until synthesized speech is perfected.

The Kurzweil Reading Machine uses OCR technology to recognize printed text, which it can then read aloud using speech synthesis technology. With a Kurzweil Reading Machine, a visually impaired person can read any book, even if it hasn't been recorded on audio tape.

Neural Networks

The human brain uses a type of circuitry that is very slow . . . at least 10,000 times slower than a digital computer. On the other hand, the degree of parallelism vastly outstrips any computer architecture we have yet to design. . . . For such tasks as vision, language, and motor control, the brain is more powerful than 1,000 supercomputers, yet for certain simple tasks such as multiplying digital numbers, it is less powerful than the 4-bit microprocessor found in a ten-dollar calculator.

—Raymond Kurzweil, *The Age of Intelligent Machines*

Artificial intelligence research has produced many amazing success stories and some embarrassing failures. The successes—intelligent applications that outperform their human counterparts—tend to involve tasks that require sequential thinking, logical rules, and orderly relationships. AI has been less successful at competing with natural human intelligence in applications like language, vision, speech, and movement—applications where massive amounts of data are processed in parallel.

It's not surprising that computers excel at linear, logical processes; almost every computer that's ever been created is designed to process digital information sequentially through a single CPU. The human brain, on the other hand, consists of billions of neurons, each connected to thousands of others in a massively parallel, distributed structure. This kind of structure gives the brain an advantage at most perceptual, motor, and creative skills.

Much current work in artificial intelligence is focused on **neural networks** (or **neural nets**)—distributed, parallel computing systems inspired by the structure of the human brain. Instead of a single, complex CPU, a neural network uses a network of a few thousand simpler processors called *neurons.* Neural networks aren't programmed in the usual way; they're trained. Instead of using a rule-based approach, a neural network learns patterns by trial and error, just as the brain does. When patterns are repeated often, neural networks, in effect, develop habits. This kind of learning can present problems for some kinds of applications, because no rules are clearly defined. When a neural net makes a decision, you have no way to ask why.

Neural networks also store information differently than traditional computers. Concepts are represented as patterns of activity among many neurons, so they are less susceptible to machine failure. Because it distributes knowledge throughout the network, a neural net (like the human brain) can still function if some of its neurons are destroyed.

Many neural net algorithms are developed on parallel-processing supercomputers like the Connection Machine, which contains more than 65,000 processors. Neural net chips containing thousands of neurons are produced by Intel Corporation and other hardware companies. A number of software companies have developed programs that simulate neural nets on PCs and other nonparallel machines. However,

For a neural net to learn to recognize the letter A, it must go through a series of trials in which circuit patterns that produce incorrect guesses are weakened and patterns that produce correct guesses are strengthened. The end result is a circuit pattern that can recognize the letter A in a variety of forms.

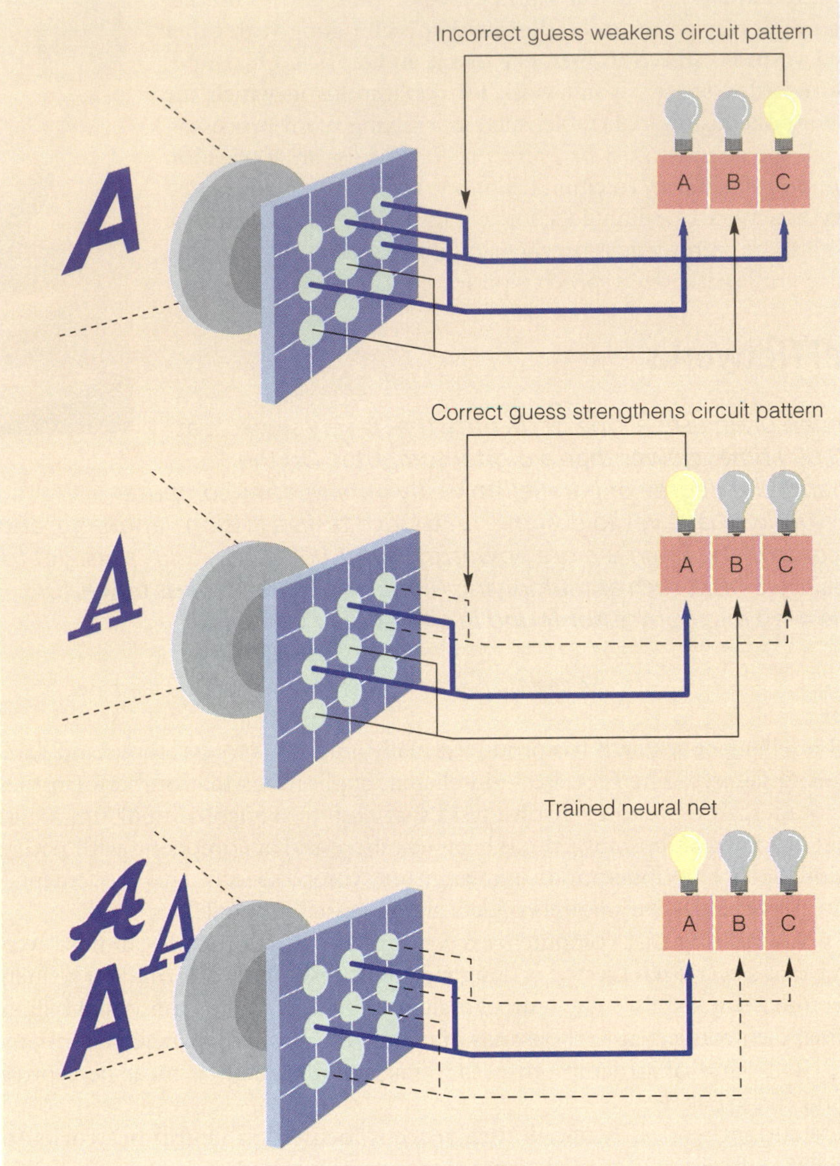

A member of the Merce Cunningham Dance Company dances with a score by David Tudor, composed in part by INTEL's 80170 ETANN (Electronically Trainable Artificial Neural Network). The music for a particular performance is determined in part by dancer movements and audience noise.

none of today's neural net hardware or software approaches the complexity or the capacity of the human brain.

Most researchers consider today's neural nets as, at best, baby steps in the direction of machines that can more closely emulate the workings of the human brain. There's considerable debate in the AI community about the future of neural nets. Some see neural nets as playing only a limited role in artificial intelligence; others expect it to eclipse the traditional rule-based approach.

Even so, neural nets are already being put to use in a variety of applications, ranging from artificial vision to expert systems. Neural nets are especially useful for recognizing patterns buried in huge quantities of numbers, such as in scientific research, loan processing, and stock market analysis. Some modems use neural nets to distinguish signals from random telephone-line noise. Optimistic researchers hope that neural networks may someday provide hearing for the deaf and eyesight for the blind.

The Robot Revolution

Nowhere are artificial intelligence technologies more visible than in the field of robotics. Vision, hearing, pattern recognition, knowledge engineering, expert decision making, natural-language understanding, speech—they all come together in today's robots.

What Is a Robot?

1. *A robot may not injure a human being, or, through inaction, allow a human being to come to harm.*
2. *A robot must obey the orders given it by human beings, except where such orders would conflict with the First Law.*
3. *A robot must protect its own existence as long as such protection does not conflict with the First or Second Law.*

—*Isaac Asimov's three laws of robotics*

The term *robot* (from the root word *robota*, the Czech word for forced labor) first appeared in a 1923 play called *R.U.R.* (Rossum's Universal Robots), by Czech playwright Karel Capek. Capek's robots were intelligent machines that could see, hear, touch, move, and exercise judgment based on common sense. But these powerful machines eventually rebelled against their human creators, just as hundreds of fictional robots have done in succeeding decades. Today movies, TV, and books are full of imaginary robots, both good and evil.

As exotic as they might seem, robots are similar to other kinds of computer technology people use every day. While a typical computer performs *mental* tasks, a **robot** is a computer-controlled machine designed to perform specific *manual* tasks. A robot's central processor might be a microprocessor embedded in the robot's shell, or it might be a supervisory computer that controls the robot from a distance. In any case the processor is functionally identical to the processor found in a personal computer, a workstation, or a mainframe computer.

A robot is, in effect, a computer with exotic peripherals.

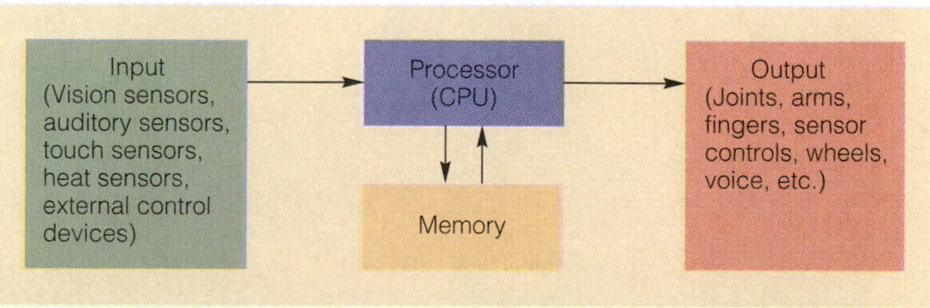

The most important hardware differences between robots and other computers are the input and output peripherals. Instead of sending output to a screen or a printer, a robot sends commands to joints, arms, and other moving parts. The first robots had no corresponding input devices to monitor their movements and the surrounding environment. They were effectively deaf, blind, and in some cases dangerous—at least one Japanese worker was killed by an early sightless robot. Most modern robots include some kind of input sensors. These sensing devices allow robots to correct or modify their actions based on feedback from the outside world.

Industrial robots seldom have the human-inspired anatomy of Hollywood's science fiction robots. Instead they're designed to accomplish particular tasks in the best possible way. Robots can be designed to see infrared light, rotate joints 360 degrees, and do other things that aren't possible for humans. On the other hand, robots are constrained by the limitations of artificial intelligence software. The most sophisticated robot today can't tie a pair of shoelaces, understand the vocabulary of a three-year old child, or consistently tell the difference between a cat and a dog.

Steel-Collar Workers

From a management point of view, robots offer several advantages:

- Obviously, many robots are installed to save labor costs. Robots are expensive to design, install, and program. But once they're operational they can work 24 hours a day, 365 days a year, without vacations, strikes, sick leave, or coffee breaks.
- Robots can also improve quality and increase productivity. They're especially effective at doing repetitive jobs in which bored, tired people are prone to make errors and have accidents.
- Robots are ideal for jobs like cleaning up hazardous waste—jobs that are dangerous or uncomfortable for human workers.

For all these reasons the robot population is exploding. Today hundreds of thousands of industrial robots do welding, part fitting, painting, and other repetitive tasks in factories all over the world. In most automated factories, robots work alongside humans, but in some state-of-the-art factories, the only function of human workers is to monitor and repair robots. Robots aren't used just in factories. Robots also shear sheep in Australia, paint ship hulls in France, disarm land mines in the Persian Gulf, and perform precision skull drilling for brain surgeons in California.

Commercial robots still can't compete with people for jobs that require exceptional perceptual or fine-motor skills. But robots in research labs suggest that a new generation of more competitive robots is on the way. A robot developed at Bell Labs can defeat most human opponents at Ping-Pong. A human-sized Japanese robot named Wabot-2 can read sheet music and perform it on an organ or synthesizer using ten fingers and two feet. The technologies used in these experimental robots will undoubtedly show up in a variety of machines, from automated servants for handicapped people to flying robots for the military. We may be within a few years of self-propelled robot housecleaners!

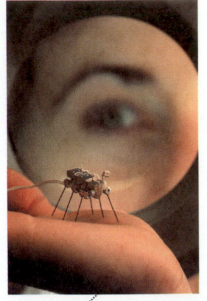

The robot revolution isn't necessarily good news for people who earn their living doing manual labor. While it's true that many of the jobs robot do are boring, dirty, or dangerous, they're still jobs. The issues surrounding automation and worker displacement are complex, and they aren't limited to factories. We'll discuss them in more detail in the next chapter.

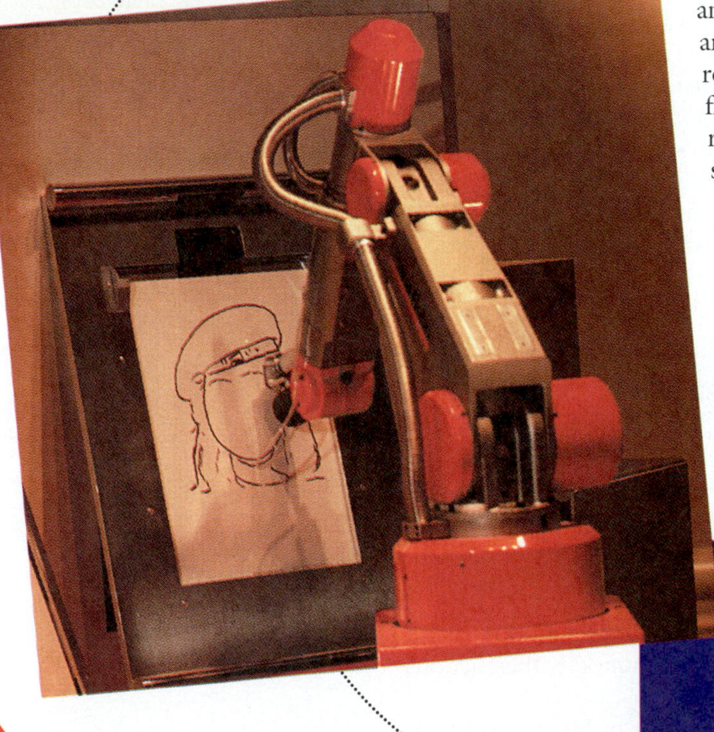

Insect robots developed at MIT (top) are capable of operating in very small spaces. Robot arms today can do everything from drawing pictures to picking up delicate integrated circuits, accomplishments that would not have been possible a few years ago.

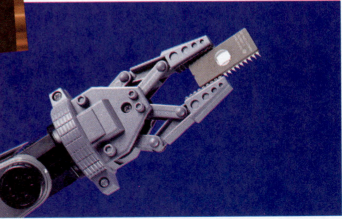

AI Implications

Is it possible to assess consequences of research in advance?

—*Albert Einstein*

From the earliest days of artificial intelligence, research has been accompanied by questions about the implications of the work. The very idea of intelligent machines is at the same time confusing, exciting, and frightening to many people. Even when they don't work very well, AI programs generate emotional responses in the people who use them.

Earlier we met ELIZA, the therapy simulator developed to demonstrate natural-language conversation. ELIZA's simple-minded approach wasn't intended to fool anyone in a Turing test, but it did have an impact on the people who used it. Many ELIZA users became emotionally attached to the program and attributed it with compassion and empathy. Weizenbaum's secretary asked him to leave the room so she could converse in private with ELIZA. Some therapists even saw ELIZA as the beginning of a new age of automated therapy. Weizenbaum was shocked by the way people attributed human capabilities to such an obviously flawed technology. He responded with *Computer Power and Human Reason*, a landmark book that presents the case for maintaining a distinction between computers and people. Weizenbaum argues that "There are certain tasks which computers ought not to be made to do, independent of whether computers can be made to do them."

Weizenbaum's caution isn't shared by international political and economic leaders, many of whom are encouraging increased AI research and development. As it matures, AI technology finds its way out of the research lab and into the marketplace. A growing number of programs and products incorporate pattern recognition, expert systems, and other AI techniques. In the near future we're likely to see more products with *embedded AI*, including intelligent word processors that can help writers turn rough drafts into polished prose, smart appliances that can recognize and obey their owners' spoken commands, and vehicles that can perform their own diagnostics and, in many cases, repairs.

Where will it all lead? Will intensive AI research result in computers capable of intelligent behavior outside narrow domains? Patrick Winston, director of MIT's artificial intelligence laboratory, once said, "The interesting issue is not whether machines can be made smarter but if humans are smart enough to pull it off. A raccoon obviously can't make a machine as smart as a raccoon. I wonder if humans can."

Many AI researchers believe that sooner or later they *will* pull it off. Some think artificial intelligence is the natural culmination of the evolutionary process—that the next intelligent life form on Earth will be based on silicon rather than the carbon that is the basis of human life. If this comes to pass, how will these beings relate to the less intelligent humans that surround them? This kind of thinking isn't easy; it goes to the heart of human values and forces us to look at our place in the universe.

Summary

Artificial intelligence has many definitions. Most artificial intelligence research focuses on making computers do things at which people generally are better. Some AI researchers try to simulate human intelligent behavior, but most try to design intelligent machines independent of the way people think. Successful AI research generally involves working on problems with limited domains rather than trying to tackle large, open-ended problems. AI programs employ a variety of techniques, including searching, heuristics, pattern recognition, and machine learning, to achieve their goals.

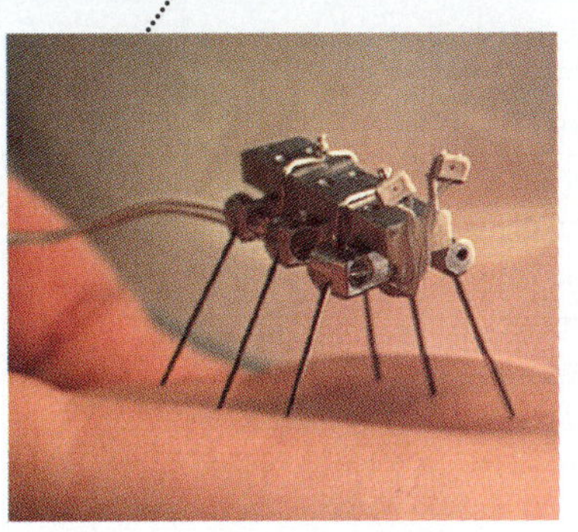

From a practical standpoint natural-language communication is one of the most important areas of AI study. Natural-language programs that deal with a subset of the language are used in applications ranging from machine translation programs to natural-language interfaces. But no program is capable of handling the kind of unrestricted natural-language text people deal with every day. Natural-language programs are confounded by the English language's large vocabulary, convoluted syntax, and ambiguous semantics—the *meanings* behind the words.

AI researchers have developed a variety of schemes for representing knowledge in computers. A knowledge base contains facts and a system for determining and changing the relationship between those facts. Today's knowledge bases are only practical for representing narrow domains of knowledge, such as the knowledge of an expert on a particular subject. Expert systems are programs designed to replicate the decision-making process of human experts. An expert system includes a knowledge base, an inference engine for applying logical rules to the facts in a knowledge base, and a human interface for interacting with users. Once the knowledge base is constructed (usually based on interviews and observations of human experts), an expert system can provide consultation that rivals human advice in many situations. Expert systems are successfully used in a variety of scientific, business, and other applications.

Pattern recognition is an important area of AI research that involves identifying recurring patterns in input data. Pattern recognition technology is at the heart of computer vision, voice communication, and other important AI applications. These diverse applications all use similar techniques for isolating and recognizing patterns. People are better at pattern recognition than computers, in part because the human brain can process masses of data in parallel. Modern neural network computers are designed to process data in the same way the human brain does. Many researchers believe that neural nets, as they grow in size and sophistication, will help computers improve their performance at many difficult tasks.

A robot is a computer-controlled machine designed to perform specific *manual* tasks. Robots include output peripherals for manipulating their environments and input sensors that allow them to perform self-correcting actions based on feedback from outside. Robots perform a variety of dangerous and tedious tasks, in many cases outperforming human workers. As robot technology advances, more traditional human jobs will be done by artificial workers. Many AI researchers expect that people will eventually create artificial beings that are more intelligent than their creators—a prospect with staggering implications.

CHAPTER REVIEW

Key Terms

artificial intelligence (AI)
automatic speech recognition
automatic translation
digitized sound
digitized speech
expert system
expert system shell
image analysis
knowledge base
neural network (neural net)
optical character recognition (OCR)
parsing program (parser)
pattern recognition
robot
semantics
speech synthesis
syntax
synthetic speech
Turing test

Review Questions

1. In what sense is artificial intelligence a "moving frontier"?
2. What are the disadvantages of the approach to AI that attempts to simulate human intelligence? What is the alternative?
3. Describe several techniques used in game-playing software, and explain how they can be applied to other artificial intelligence applications.
4. Why did early machine translation programs fail to produce the desired results?
5. Why is the sentence "Time flies like an arrow" difficult for a computer to parse, translate, or understand? Can you find four possible meanings for the sentence?
6. What is the relationship between syntax and semantics? Can you construct a sentence that follows the rules of English syntax but has nonsense semantics?
7. What is a knowledge base? What is an expert system? How are the two related?
8. Give examples of successful expert system applications. Give examples of several tasks that can't be accomplished with today's expert system technology, and explain why they can't.
9. What are some of the problems that make machine vision so challenging?
10. In what ways are the techniques of optical character recognition similar to those of speech recognition programs?
11. What rules might a computer use to sort the characters shown on page 221 into A's and B's?
12. An automated speech recognition system might have trouble telling the difference between a "common denominator" and "comedy nominator." What must the speaker do to avoid confusion? What other limitations plague automated speech recognition systems today?
13. In what ways are neural networks designed to simulate the structure of the human brain? In what ways do neural nets perform differently than standard, single-processor CPUs?
14. What kind of hardware is necessary for a robot to be self-correcting, so it can modify its actions based on outside feedback?
15. What distinguishes a robot from a desktop computer?

Discussion Questions

1. Is the Turing test a valid test of intelligence? Why or why not?
2. If you were the interrogator in the Turing test, what questions would you ask to try to discover whether you were communicating with a computer? What would you look for in the answers?
3. List several mental tasks that people do better than computers. List several mental tasks that computers do better than people. Can you find any general characteristics that distinguish the items on the two lists?
4. Computers can compose original music, produce original artwork, create original mathematical proofs. Does this mean that Ada Lovelace was wrong when she said, in effect, that computers can do only what they're told to do?
5. The works of AARON, the expert system artist, are unique, original, and widely acclaimed as art. Who is the artist, AARON or Harold Cohen, AARON's creator? Is AARON a work of art, an artist, or both?
6. If an expert system gives you erroneous information, should you be able to sue it for malpractice? If it fails and causes major disruptions or injury, who's responsible? The programmer? The publisher? The owner? The computer?
7. Some expert systems and neural nets can't explain the reasons behind their decisions. What kinds of problems might be caused by this limitation? Under what circumstances, if any, should an expert system be required to produce an "audit trail" to explain how it reached conclusions?
8. What kinds of human jobs are most likely to be eliminated because of expert systems? What kinds of new jobs will be created because of expert systems?
9. What kinds of human jobs are most likely to be eliminated because of robots? What kinds of new jobs will be created as a result of factory automation?
10. Are Asimov's three laws of robotics adequate for smoothly integrating intelligent robots into tomorrow's society? If not, what laws would you add?

Projects 

1. Public domain versions of Weizenbaum's ELIZA program are available for most types of desktop computers. Locate a copy and try conversing with it. Test the program on your friends and see how they react to it. Try to determine the rules and tricks that ELIZA uses to simulate conversation. If you're a programmer, try writing your own version of ELIZA.
2. When Turing first proposed the Turing test, he compared it to a similar test in which the interrogator tried to guess the sex of the people typing answers to questions. See if you can devise such a test. What, if anything, does it prove?
3. Try to find examples of working expert systems and robots in your school or community and present your findings.
4. Test OCR software, grammar checking software, and other types of consumer-oriented AI applications. How "intelligent" are these applications? In what ways could they be improved?
5. Survey people's attitudes and concerns about artificial intelligence and robots. Present your findings.

Sources and Resources 

The Age of Intelligent Machines, by Raymond Kurzweil (Cambridge, MA: MIT Press, 1990). If you want to learn more about artificial intelligence, this award-winning book should be at the top of your list. With clear prose, beautiful illustrations, and intelligent articles by the masters of the field, Kurzweil explores the historical, philosophical, academic, aesthetic, practical, fanciful, and speculative sides of AI. An outstanding companion video is also available.

Machinery of the Mind: Inside the New Science of Artificial Intelligence, by George Johnson (Redmond, WA: Tempus Books, 1986). This book isn't as up-to-date, flashy, or comprehensive as Kurzweil's, but it's worth a read anyway. Johnson's writing is clear, accessible, and entertaining, and the book is packed with thought-provoking material.

Artificial Intelligence, 3d ed., by Patrick Henry Winston (Reading, MA: Addison-Wesley, 1992). This best-selling introductory text for computer science students is thorough and well-written. Like most computer science texts, it's probably too technical and mathematical for most casual readers.

Computer Power and Human Reason (From Judgment to Calculation), by Joseph Weizenbaum (San Francisco: Freeman, 1976). An MIT computer scientist speaks out on the things computers shouldn't do, even if they can. This classic book is as important now as when it was first published in the 1970s.

Society of Mind, by Marvin Minsky (New York: Simon & Schuster, 1988). Another MIT artificial intelligence expert presents his thoughts on the relationship between people and intelligent machines. A dense but thought-provoking book.

Lisp, by Patrick Henry Winston and Berthold K. P. Horn (Reading, MA: Addison-Wesley, 1989). A popular introduction to Common LISP, the widely used programming language of artificial intelligence.

Godel, Escher, Bach: An Eternal Golden Braid, by Douglas R. Hofstadter (New York: Vintage Books, 1980). This popular book is part mathematics, part philosophy, and part *Alice in Wonderland.* If you like to think deeply about questions like "What is thought?" you'll probably enjoy this book.

PART FOUR

Living with Computers
Into the Information Age

CHAPTER

ELEVEN

Computers at Work

Steve Roberts Bikes Across Dataspace

Future society will be virtually paperless, energy-efficient, dependent upon wide-bandwidth networking, and generally cognizant of global perspective through routine communication across decreasingly relevant borders. It is not too early to prepare for this: we need the ideas, the tools, and an awareness of the problems that accompany fundamental shifts in the meaning of information.

—Steven K. Roberts

In 1983 Steve Roberts realized he wasn't happy chained to his desk and his debts. He'd lost sight of his passions—writing, adventure, computer design, ham radio, bicycling, romance, learning, networking, publishing. He decided to build a new lifestyle that combined those passions. Six months later he hit the road on Winnebiko, a custom recumbent bike equipped with a tiny Radio Shack Model 100 laptop and a small 5-watt solar panel. He connected each day to the CompuServe network through pay phones, transmitting magazine articles and book chapters.

Steve Roberts with BEHEMOTH

Three years and 10,000 miles later, Roberts replaced Winnebiko with Winnebiko II, a low-riding, high-tech bike with special handlebars that allowed Roberts to type while riding down the highway. Roberts pedaled 6000 miles on Winnebiko II, this time with a traveling partner named Maggie Victor. Roberts writes of this period:

After reading this chapter you should be able to

- explain how the emerging information economy differs from earlier social and economic systems
- describe how computers have changed the way people work in factories, offices, homes, and a variety of industries
- describe how modern managers use computers as tools
- describe several ways computers have changed the quality of jobs, both positively and negatively
- speculate on how our society will adjust as more and more jobs are automated

Through ham radio and computer networking, the sense of living in a virtual neighborhood grew more and more tangible, until the road itself became merely an entertaining backdrop for a stable life in Dataspace. . . . Home, quite literally, became an abstract electronic concept. From a business standpoint, it no longer mattered where we were, and we traveled freely, making a living through magazine publishing and occasional consulting spinoffs, seeking modular phone jacks at every stop.

After three years, technological advances lured Roberts off the road to design and build a new high-tech people-powered vehicle. With 150 corporate equipment sponsors and 35 helpers, Roberts spent the next three years constructing the $1.2 million BEHEMOTH (Big Electronic Human-Energized Machine . . . Only Too Heavy). BEHEMOTH is an 8-foot recumbent bike with a 4-foot trailer. It weighs 580 pounds and sports 105 speeds and 6 brakes. This showpiece of future technology carries seven networked computers (including a Mac, two DOS machines, and a Sun UNIX SPARCstation), a ham radio station, satellite links, a cellular phone with modem and fax, a CD stereo system, a water-cooled helmet with a virtual computer display, solar collectors, and six-level security system. (It can even dial 911 and say, "I am a bicycle; I am being stolen; my current latitude is . . . .")

Roberts now mixes bicycling with "high-speed relocation" to accommodate consulting and speaking engagements, all the while connected electronically to the support facilities in his laboratory. He sees his travels as a mixture of business, experimentation, education, and, of course, adventure. In his words, "Routine life is impossible on a computerized recumbent with solar panels and a thicket of antennas . . . and there's a LOT of world to explore out there. Having had a taste of it, how could I spend my life in one place?"

Steve Roberts likes to tell schoolchildren that "the obvious choices aren't the only choices." Roberts made career and lifestyle choices that wouldn't have been possible without modern information technology. Computer technology has changed the way millions of people work by providing new choices and opportunities. For other less fortunate workers, technology has taken away choices and opportunities. In this chapter we'll see how computers are changing the ways people work. We'll start by examining the roots and characteristics of the modern information economy. Then we'll see how computers are changing the ways people do their jobs in automated factories, automated offices, and elsewhere. We'll examine the computer-based tools used by managers to help them manage more effectively and efficiently. Finally, we'll consider the effects of **automation** on the nature and availability of jobs and speculate on the future implications of the computerization of our workplace. In the next chapter we'll explore the effects of computers on the two other institutions that are central to our lives: our schools and our homes.

Into the Information Age

It is the business of the future to be dangerous. . . . The major advances in civilization are processes that all but wreck the societies in which they occur.

—Alfred North Whitehead

Every so often, civilization dramatically changes course. Events and ideas come together to radically transform the way people live, work, and think. Traditions go by the wayside, common sense is turned upside down, and lives are thrown into turmoil until a new order takes hold. Humankind experiences a **paradigm shift**—a change in thinking that results in a new way of seeing the world. Major paradigm shifts take generations because individuals have trouble changing their assumptions about the way the world works.

Before the 20th century, humanity experienced two major paradigm shifts: the agricultural revolution and the industrial revolution. It's helpful to glance backward at these two shifts for perspective before we focus on the information revolution—the paradigm shift that's affecting us today.

Three Monumental Changes

Prehistoric people were mostly hunters and gatherers. They lived tribal, nomadic lives, tracking animals and gathering wild fruits, nuts, and grains. Anthropologists speculate that some prehistoric people spent as few as 15 hours per week satisfying material needs and devoted the rest of their time to cultural and spiritual pursuits.

The agricultural economy. As the human population grew, people learned to domesticate animals, grow their own grains, and use plows and other agricultural tools. The transformation to an agricultural economy took place over several centuries around 10,000 years ago. The result was a society in which most people lived and worked on farms, exchanging goods and services in nearby towns. The agricultural age lasted thousands of years, until technological advances triggered what has come to be known as an *industrial revolution*.

The industrial economy. By the end of the 19th century, the world was dominated by an industrial economy in which more people worked in urban factories than on farms. Factory work promised a higher material standard of living for a growing population, but not without a price. As work life became separate from home life, fathers were removed from day-to-day family life, and mothers assumed the bulk of domestic responsibilities. Increasingly more wealth was in the hands of fewer people. As towns grew into cities, crime, pollution, and other urban problems grew with them.

The information economy. Twentieth-century information technology produced what's been called a second industrial revolution, as people turned from factory work to information-related work. In today's **information economy** (sometimes called a *post-industrial economy*), clerks outnumber factory workers, and most people earn their living working with words, numbers, and ideas. Instead of planting corn or making shoes, most of us shuffle bits in one form or another. As we roar into the information age, we're riding a wave of social change that rivals any that came before.

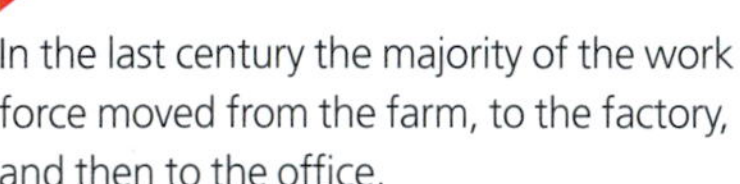

In the last century the majority of the work force moved from the farm, to the factory, and then to the office.

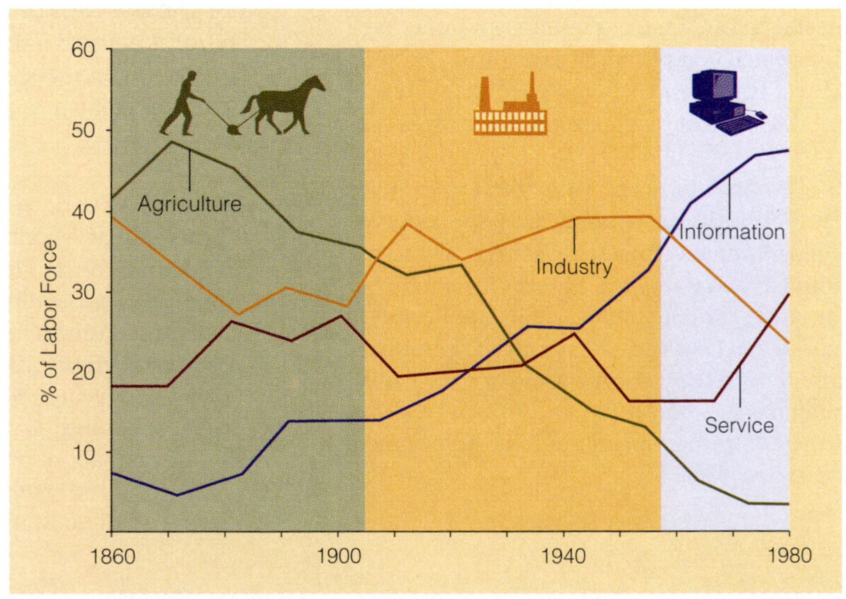

Technology was central to each of these transformations. The agricultural economy grew from the plow, the industrial revolution was sparked by machines, and the information age is so dependent on computers that it's often called the computer age.

Computers and Change

By the year 2000, anybody in western civilization [will] be able to get the answer to any question that has an answer.

—Jerry Pournelle, science fiction and technology writer

An age rich in electronic information may achieve wonderful social conveniences at the cost of placing freedom in a deep chill.

—Langdon Winner, technology critic

Countless words have been written about the effects of computer technology on our work, our schools, our home life, and our society. Many writers focus on emerging technologies and the new possibilities they offer: possibilities for improved communication, personal expression, information access, and productivity. Others focus on computer technology as a source of suffering, oppression, and alienation. Both utopian and anti-utopian visions are based on speculation about the future. Researchers who study the *current* impact of computer technology report that the truth, so far, lies somewhere between these two extremes.

Artist and programmer work together to create the computer-generated dinosaurs in *Jurassic Park*.

Where Computers Work

It's becoming harder all the time to find jobs that haven't been changed in some way by computers. Consider these examples:

- *Entertainment*. The production of television programs and movies involves computer technology at every stage of the process. Scriptwriters use specialized word processors to write and revise scripts, and they use telecommunications technology to beam them between Hollywood and New York. Artists and technicians use graphics workstations to create special effects, from simple scene fadeouts and rolling credits to flying super heroes and intergalactic battles. Musicians compose soundtracks using synthesizers and computer-controlled sequencers. Sound editors use computer-controlled mixers to blend music with digital sound effects and live-action sound. Even commercials—*especially* commercials—use state-of-the-art computer graphics, animation, and sound to keep you watching the images instead of pressing the fast-forward button on your VCR.
- *Publishing*. The newspaper industry is being radically transformed by computer technology. Roving reporters write and edit documents on notebook computers and transmit them by modem to central offices. Graphic artists design charts and

Portable computers are standard equipment for journalists today.

Using computer-aided tomography, doctors can view inside the human body.

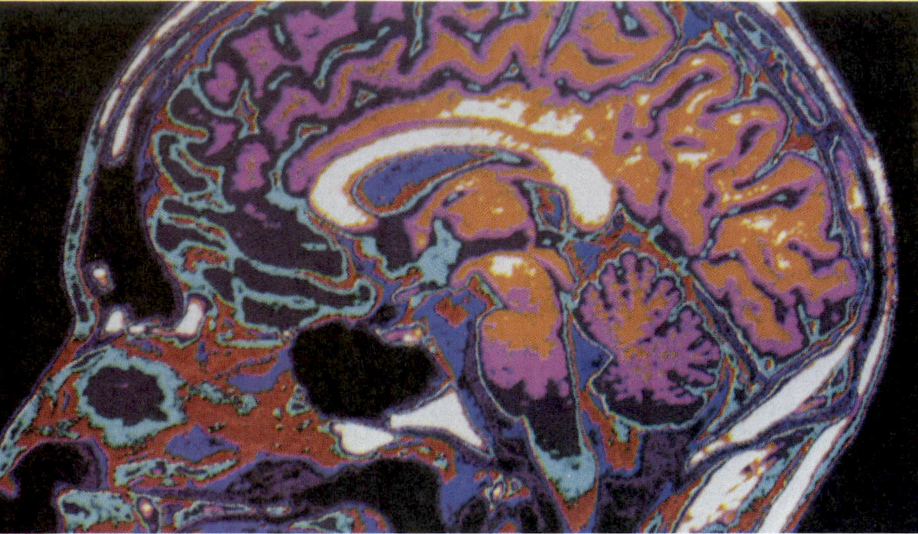

artwork with graphics software. Photo retouchers use scanners and computers instead of brushes and magnifying glasses to edit photographs. Production crews assemble pages with computers instead of typesetting machines and pasteup boards.

- *Medicine.* High-tech equipment plays a critical role in the healing arts, too. Hospital information systems store patient medical and insurance records. Local area networks allow doctors, nurses, technicians, dietitians, and office staff to view and update information throughout the hospital. Computers monitor patient vital signs in intensive care units in hospitals, at home, and on the street with portable units that analyze signals and transmit warnings when problems arise. Databases alert doctors and pharmacists to the problems and possibilities of prescribed drugs. Computer-aided tomography (CAT) scans allow doctors to see cross-sectional slices of human bodies. Every day computers provide medical researchers with new ways to save lives and reduce suffering.
- *Airlines.* Without computers today's airline industry simply wouldn't fly. Designers use CAD (computer-aided design) software to design aircraft. Engineers conduct extensive computer simulations to test them. Pilots use computer-controlled instruments to navigate their planes, monitor aircraft systems, and control autopilots. Air traffic controllers on the ground use computerized air traffic control systems to keep track of incoming and outgoing flights. And, of course, computerized reservation systems make it possible for all those planes to carry passengers.

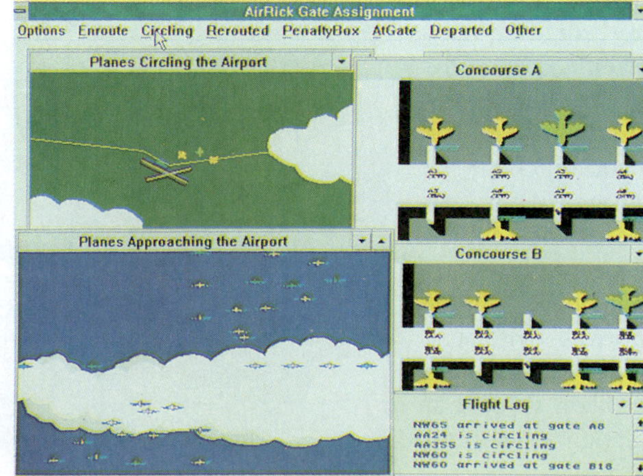

Airport personnel use expert systems like this one to solve complex scheduling problems.

- *Science.* From biology to physics, every branch of science has been changed by the computer. Scientists collect and analyze data using remote sensing devices, notebook computers, and statistical analysis programs. They catalog and organize information in massive databases. They use supercomputers and workstations to create computer models of objects or environments that would otherwise be out of reach. They communicate with colleagues all over the world through electronic networks. It's hard to find a scientist today who doesn't work with computers.

Clearly, computers are part of the workplace. To get a perspective on how computers affect the way we work, we'll consider the three computerized workplaces that have attracted the most attention: the automated factory, the automated office, and the electronic cottage.

A scientist records data for National Geographic with a waterproof computer.

The Automated Factory

Businessmen go down with their businesses because they like the old way so well they cannot bring themselves to change.

—Henry Ford

In the last chapter we discussed the use of robots—computer-controlled machines designed to perform specific *manual* tasks. In the modern **automated factory**, robots are used for painting, welding, and other repetitive assembly-line jobs. But robots alone don't make an automated factory. Computers also help track inventory, time the delivery of parts, control the quality of the production, monitor wear and tear on machines, and schedule maintenance. As described in Chapter 8, engineers use CAD and CAM (computer-aided manufacturing) technologies to design new products and the machines that build those products.

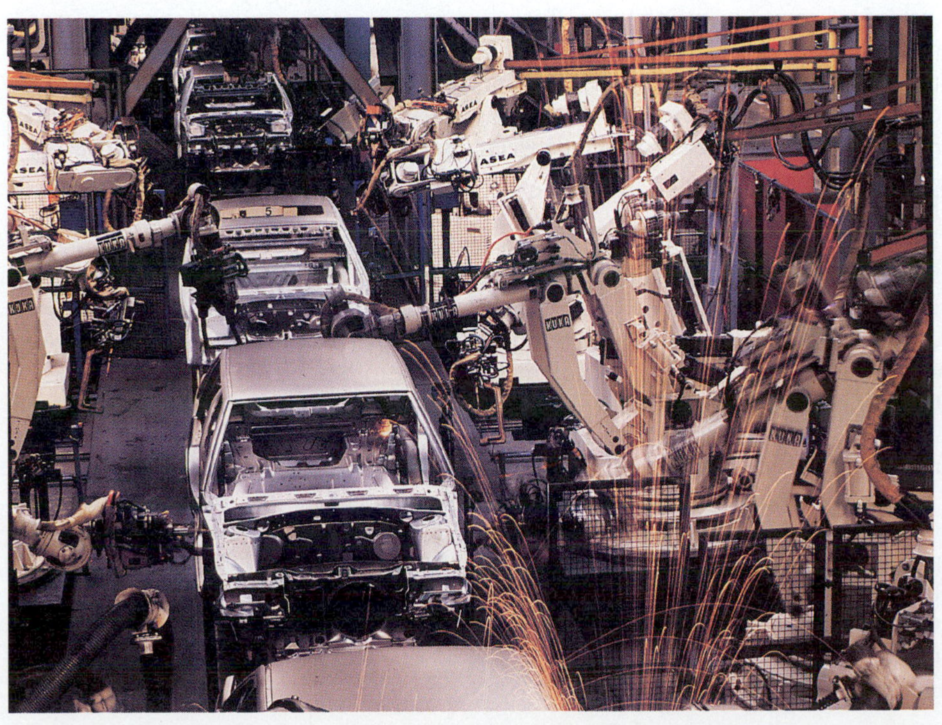

An automated factory is more efficient than a traditional factory for two reasons:

- Automation allows for tighter integration of planning with manufacturing, reducing the time that materials and machines sit idle.
- Automation reduces waste in facilities, raw materials, and labor.

If automation is good news for factory owners, it poses a threat to blue-collar workers who keep traditional factories running. In a typical high-tech manufacturing firm today, approximately half of the staff are engineers, accountants, marketing specialists, and other white-collar workers.

The Automated Office

We now mass produce information the way we used to mass produce cars.

—John Naisbitt, *Megatrends*

As the number of factory jobs declines, office work plays a more important role in our economy. Modern offices, like modern factories, have been transformed by computers. Many **automated offices** have evolved along with their computers.

Office automation evolution. Office automation goes back to the mainframe era, when banks, insurance companies, and other large institutions used computers for behind-the-scenes jobs like accounting and payroll. Early computer systems were faster and more accurate than the manual systems they replaced but were rigid and difficult to use. The machines and the technicians who worked with them were hidden away in basement offices, isolated from their organizations. The introduction of time-sharing operating systems and database management systems allowed workers throughout organizations to have access to computer data. This kind of *centralized computing* placed computer-related decisions in the hands of central data processing managers.

Personal computers changed all that. Early Apple and Tandy computers were carried into offices on the sly by employees who wanted to use their own computers instead of company mainframes. But as managers recognized the power of word processors, spreadsheets, and other applications, they incorporated PCs into organizational plans. Jobs migrated from mainframes to desktops, and people used personal computers to do things that the mainframes weren't programmed to do. In many organizations power struggles erupted between mainframe advocates and PC enthusiasts.

Enterprise computing. Today most organizations recognize the importance of PCs in the overall computing structure. Some companies have abandoned mainframes altogether; others still use them for their biggest data processing tasks. In the age of networks the challenge for a company's **information systems manager** (sometimes called an IS manager, information technology manager, or IT manager) is to integrate all kinds of computers, from mainframes to Macintoshes, into a single, seamless system. This approach, often called **enterprise computing** (or sometimes *distributed computing* or *integrated computing*), allows PCs, workstations, minicomputers, and mainframes to coexist peacefully and complement each other.

People throughout business organizations use personal computers: Workers use word processing software to generate memos and reports, marketing teams create promotional pieces using desktop publishing tools, and financial departments analyze budgets using spreadsheets. They communicate with each other and with the outside world electronically, sending electronic mail through networks. If a business uses mainframes to house databases, office workers use desktop computers to access that data. In many integrated systems, users view everything, including mainframe data, through a familiar Macintosh, Windows, or OS/2 interface. They don't need to know where or how information is stored; the network quietly moves data back and forth to meet user needs.

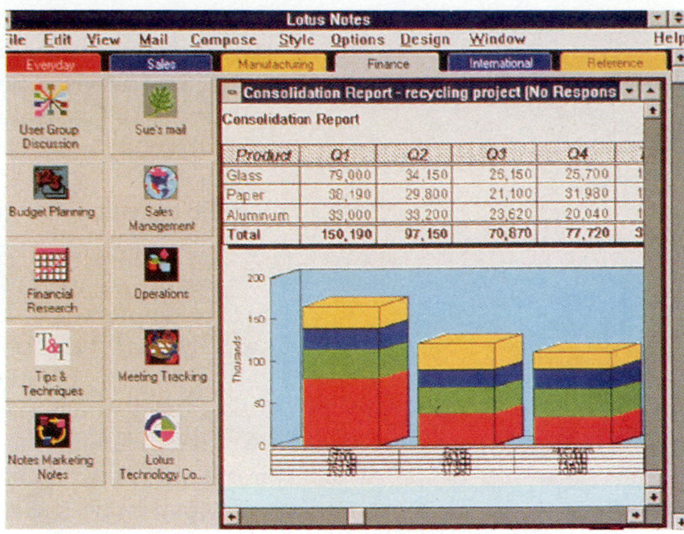

Lotus Notes is the most widely used comprehensive groupware product.

Workgroup computing. New classes of multiuser software, or **groupware**, allow groups of users to share calendars, send messages, access data, and work on documents simultaneously. The best groupware applications allow workgroups to do things that would be difficult or impossible otherwise; they actually change the way people work in groups. With groupware and telecommunication, workgroups don't need to be in the same room, or even the same time zone. Some office-watchers predict that automated offices will be radically transformed by what they call **computer-supported cooperative work**.

The paperless office. Experts have also predicted the **paperless office**—an office of the future in which magnetic and optical archives will replace reference books and file cabinets, electronic communication will replace letters and memos, and information utilities will replace newspapers and other periodicals. In the paperless office people will read computer screens, not paper documents.

All of these trends are real: Digital storage media are becoming increasingly popular; electronic notes are replacing some memos and letters; on-line services are catching on. But so far, computers haven't reduced the flow of paper-based information. What has changed is the way people tend to use paper in the office. According to Paul Saffo of the Institute for the Future, "We've shifted from paper as storage to paper as interface. It is an ever more volatile, disposable, and temporary display medium."

To reduce the flow of paper, a growing number of organizations are turning to *document image management systems* that can scan, store, retrieve, and route bit-mapped images of paper documents. Document imaging systems, as they're also called, generally include scanners for converting paper pages to digital documents, high-capacity magnetic and optical storage disk drives for storing the document images, and fax machines for sending document images to remote locations. Interactions between these devices and networked workstations are generally handled by an *image server*—a computer dedicated to the single task of image management. Technological advances and declining prices are making imaging systems practical for more organizations than ever before. In the near future we may see a less-paper office, but a paperless office seems unlikely.

The Electronic Cottage

Telecommuting may allow us to redefine the issues so that we're not simply moving people to work but also moving work to people.

—*Booth Gardner*, *former Washington governor*

Before the industrial revolution, most people worked in or near their homes. Today's telecommunications technology opens up new possibilities for modern workers to return home for their livelihood. For hundreds of thousands of writers, programmers, accountants, data-entry clerks, and other information workers, **telecommuting** by modem replaces hours of commuting by car in rush hour traffic. Others use their own computers when they work at home rather than connecting by modem to company computers. The term *telecommuter* typically refers to *all* home information workers, whether they "commute" by modem or not.

Futurist Alvin Toffler popularized the term **electronic cottage** to describe a home where modern technology allows a person to work at home. Toffler and others predict that the number of telecommuters will skyrocket in the coming decades. Telecommuting makes sense; it's easier to move information than people. There are many strong arguments for telecommuting:

- Telecommuting reduces the number of automobile commuters, thus saving energy, reducing pollution, and decreasing congestion on highways, streets, and parking lots.
- Telecommuting saves time. If a high-paid information worker spends two hours each day commuting, that's two hours that could be spent working, resting, or relaxing with the family.
- Telecommuting allows for a more flexible schedule. People who prefer to work early in the morning or late at night don't need to conform to standard office hours if they telecommute. For many people, including parents of small children, telecommuting may be the only viable way to maintain a job.
- Telecommuting can increase productivity. Studies suggest that telecommuting can result in a 10 to 50 percent increase in worker productivity, depending on the job and the worker.

An inexpenisve personal computer turns a spare room into a home office for this writer.

Of course, telecommuting isn't for everybody. Jobs that require constant interaction with co-workers, customers, or clients aren't conducive to telecommuting. Working at home requires self-discipline. Some people find they can't concentrate on work when they're at home—beds, refrigerators, chatty neighbors, children, and errands are simply too distracting. Others have the opposite problem: Workaholism cuts into family and relaxation time. Some workers who've tried full-time telecommuting complain that they miss the informal office social life, and that their low visibility caused bosses to pass them over for promotions. Most telecommuters surveyed report that the ideal work situation involves commuting to the office one or two days each week and working at home on the others.

So far, telecommuting has been slower to catch on than many experts predicted. Hundreds of companies offer home-based work arrangements to employees, but many more have strict policies against working at home. The most common objections revolve around control, managers fear that they'll lose control over workers they can't see. Some analysts suggest that as multimedia teleconferencing systems become affordable, telecommuting will become more popular with both workers and management.

In the meantime several variations on the electronic cottage are taking hold. Many enterprising families use home computers to help them run small businesses from their home offices. A growing number of corporations and government organizations are establishing **satellite offices** and shared **regional work centers** outside of major urban centers that allow workers to commute to smaller offices closer to their neighborhoods. High-powered portable computers allow salespeople, executives, scientists, engineers, and others to take their offices with them wherever they travel. These mobile workers don't travel *to* the office, they travel *with* the office.

Management by Computer

During the early days of computing, most managers saw computers and terminals as clerical tools to be used by secretaries and technicians, but not by managers. Today managers recognize that computers are not just electronic typewriters and digital file cabinets but valuable resources that can provide information, advice, and support for those who run departments, divisions, or entire corporations.

Management Information Systems

Modern managers use **management information systems** (**MISs**) to help them with planning, organizing, staffing, directing, and controlling their organizations. The term *MIS* means different things to different people. By some definitions a management information system is any system that provides information for an organization's managers, even if it doesn't involve computers. More commonly a management information system is defined as a computerized system that includes, among other things, procedures for collecting data, a database for storing data, and software tools for analyzing data and producing a variety of reports for different levels of management.

In a large organization computers process and store masses of information. Financial transactions, sales figures, inventory tallies—the number of data items can be astronomical. From a manager's point of view, plenty of useful information is hiding in that raw data. A well-defined management information system can extract important information and summarize it in reports for managers at all levels of an organization. A top-level manager uses a MIS to examine long-term trends and relationships between departments. Middle-level managers use the same MIS to produce departmental summary reports. Low-level managers focus on day-to-day operations with detailed reports from the MIS. The MIS can produce regularly scheduled periodic reports, but it can also help managers deal with unusual situations by producing reports on demand.

Decision Support Systems

A management information system is especially helpful for handling routine management tasks. For nonroutine decision making, many managers use another type of system called a **decision support system** (**DSS**). As the name implies, a DSS is a computer system that supports managers in decision-making tasks. In the broadest sense a spreadsheet program, like those discussed in Chapter 5, might be a DSS. After all, managers everywhere use spreadsheets to find answers to "What if?" questions and make decisions based on these sample scenarios. However, most managers reserve the term *decision support system* for a more specialized kind of software designed to create mathematical models of business systems. This type of DSS is a simulation tool similar to those discussed at the end of Chapter 5.

Project management software makes it easier to organize and coordinate all of the tasks in a large project. (Software: Microsoft Project.)

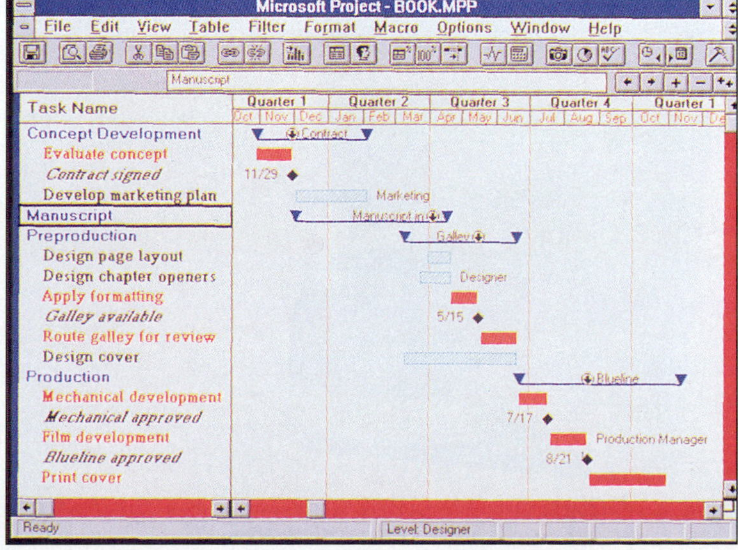

Other Management Tools

Several other types of software systems are available to help managers make decisions. **Project management software** helps coordinate, schedule, and track complex work projects. Expert systems (see Chapter 10) can provide expert advice in limited areas. Spreadsheets (see Chapter 5) can manage budgets, make financial projections, and perform a variety of other useful functions. On-line information services (see Chapter 7) can provide instant information from sources all over the world.

All of these tools provide critical information and advice, but they aren't without risks. Some managers complain that these systems provide too much information—too many reports, too many printouts, too many summaries, too many details. This malady, known as **information overload**, is a hazard of the automated office. Managers who are bombarded with computer output may not be able to separate the best

The Information Flow in a Management Information System

A typical video rental chain processes a tremendous amount of data daily. Depending on how it is handled, this information can be either overwhelming or enlightening. To make the best use of the information, many chains use management information systems to aid in decision making. This example follows the many paths of information through the Rerun Video Corporation.

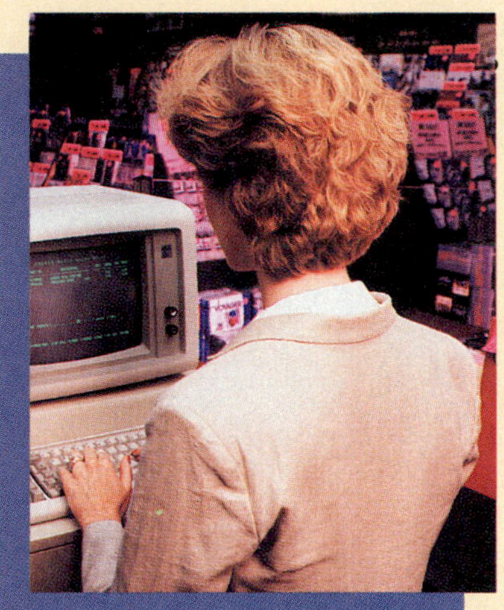

When a clerk punches a sale into the terminal, a database records changes in financial and inventory files

When a new shipment arrives, a clerk records it using a terminal; inventory and accounting files are updated automatically

The MIS uses a variety of inputs to produce reports for managers at all levels

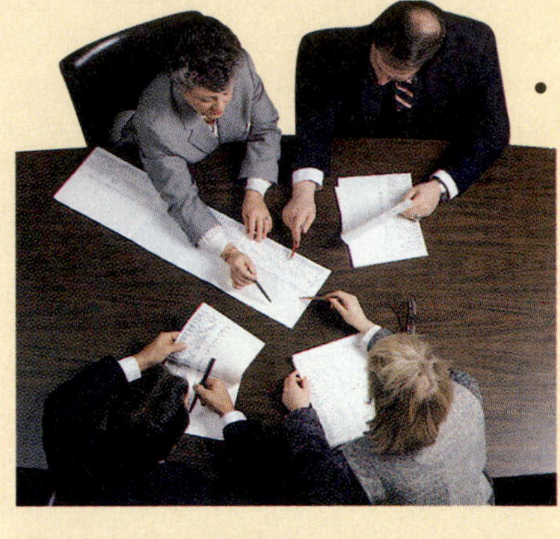

Top-level managers use reports that summarize long-term trends to analyze overall business strategies

Mid-level managers use summary and exception reports to spot trends and unusual circumstances

Low-level managers use detail reports to keep tabs on day-to-day operations

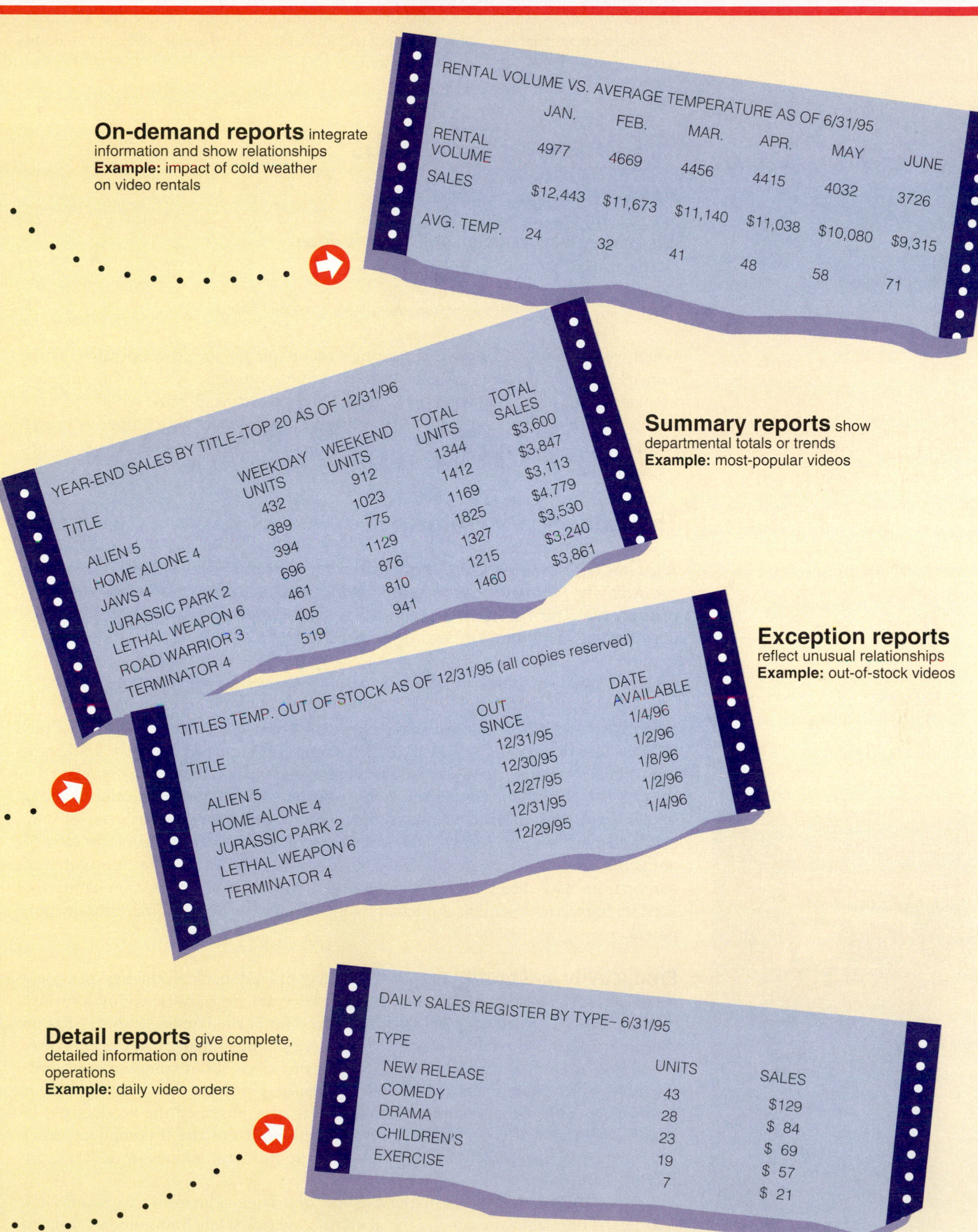

On-demand reports integrate information and show relationships
Example: impact of cold weather on video rentals
Summary reports show departmental totals or trends
Example: most-popular videos
Exception reports reflect unusual relationships
Example: out-of-stock videos
Detail reports give complete, detailed information on routine operations
Example: daily video orders

RENTAL VOLUME VS. AVERAGE TEMPERATURE AS OF 6/31/95

	JAN.	FEB.	MAR.	APR.	MAY	JUNE
RENTAL VOLUME	4977	4669	4456	4415	4032	3726
SALES	$12,443	$11,673	$11,140	$11,038	$10,080	$9,315
AVG. TEMP.	24	32	41	48	58	71

YEAR-END SALES BY TITLE–TOP 20 AS OF 12/31/96

TITLE	WEEKDAY UNITS	WEEKEND UNITS	TOTAL UNITS	TOTAL SALES
ALIEN 5	432	912	1344	$3,600
HOME ALONE 4	389	1023	1412	$3,847
JAWS 4	394	775	1169	$3,113
JURASSIC PARK 2	696	1129	1825	$4,779
LETHAL WEAPON 6	461	876	1327	$3,530
ROAD WARRIOR 3	405	810	1215	$3,240
TERMINATOR 4	519	941	1460	$3,861

TITLES TEMP. OUT OF STOCK AS OF 12/31/95 (all copies reserved)

TITLE	OUT SINCE	DATE AVAILABLE
ALIEN 5	12/31/95	1/4/96
HOME ALONE 4	12/30/95	1/2/96
JURASSIC PARK 2	12/27/95	1/8/96
LETHAL WEAPON 6	12/31/95	1/2/96
TERMINATOR 4	12/29/95	1/4/96

DAILY SALES REGISTER BY TYPE– 6/31/95

TYPE	UNITS	SALES
NEW RELEASE	43	$129
COMEDY	28	$ 84
DRAMA	23	$ 69
CHILDREN'S	19	$ 57
EXERCISE	7	$ 21

from the rest. What's worse, managers who rely too heavily on computer output run the risk of overlooking more conventional, nondigital sources of insight. The best managers know that no computer system can replace the human decision-making skills necessary for successful management.

Computers and Jobs

John Henry told his captain
"A man ain't nothin' but a man
But before I let your steam drill beat me down
I'd die with a hammer in my hand . . ."

—*From the folk song "John Henry"*

When we think about automated factories, computer-supported cooperative work, management information systems, and electronic cottages, it's easy to imagine utopian visions of computers in the workplace of tomorrow. But the real world isn't always picture-perfect, and many workers today are experiencing computers in less positive ways. In this section we'll look at some of the controversies and issues surrounding the automation of the workplace.

The Productivity Problem

A lot has been written about how computers haven't helped with productivity. I think there's a good reason for that, and it's fairly predictable. The more you can do with a machine, the higher you set your sights. So it's a self-defeating proposition.

—*J. Presper Eckert, codeveloper of ENIAC and UNIVAC*

It seems obvious that computer technology makes businesses more productive. Consider the American financial industry, which employs about 5 percent of the workers in the United States and makes about 35 percent of information technology purchases—about $12 billion every year. This massive investment has undeniably produced better service and lower prices for bank customers. Now customers can cash out-of-state checks in minutes instead of weeks. Automated teller machines provide instant cash 24 hours per day—an impossible dream in the precomputer era. A growing number of corporations have direct electronic connections to bank computers, eliminating the need for human intervention altogether. None of this would be possible without computers.

Productivity and profit. In terms of services offered, bank productivity is up as a result of computers. But most banks have not been able to translate technology into higher profits. The first 25 years of computerization in the banking industry has, in fact, shown a decline in capital productivity! There's some evidence that the trend may be turning around, but it still raises important questions about computers and productivity—questions that aren't limited to the banking industry.

Studies suggest that computerization has, at best, increased the productivity of North American office workers only slightly. How can this be? If computers don't increase productivity, why do businesses continue to spend billions of dollars every year on them?

Part of the problem may lie in the difficulty of making large software systems work reliably. In one famous example, the Bank of America spent $60 million trying to make a $20 million computer system work, and then abandoned it after five years of development and a year of false starts.

Productivity and PCs. But the productivity problem isn't limited to large systems; there's no hard evidence that PCs increase office productivity the way managers hoped they would. Several factors may be involved:

- *Distractions.* For some people, personal computers offer too many options. These workers spend hours tinkering with utility software, refining multiple drafts of memos, fiddling with different fonts, and experimenting with spreadsheet graphics.
- *Reliability.* Many workers lose productive time working around software bugs and recovering data from system crashes.
- *Rapid changes.* For many organizations, technological progress is the culprit. Workers spend hours learning complex programs, only to find in a few months that they need to be retrained because of software upgrades.

Productivity and people. The biggest productivity problems may be related more to people than to machines. According to one study of 2000 U.S. companies that implemented new office systems, at least 40 percent failed to achieve their intended results. Most of the failures were attributed to human or organizational factors rather than technical problems.

A computer system doesn't work in a vacuum. All too often computers are introduced into the workplace without any consideration of the way people work and interact. Workers are expected to adjust their work patterns to systems that are difficult and uncompromising. User training and support are often inadequate. It's hardly surprising that these computer-centered systems fail to spark productivity.

Many analysts argue that the most successful computer systems are **human-centered systems** designed to retain and enhance human skills and control rather than take them away. These analysts suggest that computer systems aren't likely to pay off unless they're accompanied by changes in the structure of work responsibilities, relationships with co-workers, and rewards for accomplishing job goals.

To create a human-centered system, systems analysts and designers must understand the work practices of the people who'll be using the system. It helps if users of the systems are involved in designing the system and the system-related jobs. In Norway, laws require that unionized workers be included in the planning and design of new computer systems. As a result, workers have greater control over their jobs and greater job satisfaction. Similar worker-centered approaches have been applied in Sweden, Britain, and more recently, the United States.

Many experts believe that this human-centered approach is a key to increasing overall productivity. Productivity will almost certainly increase as organizations adjust to computer technology and computer technology becomes more adaptable to the needs of users.

Computers and Job Quality

And it's me and my machine for the rest of the morning, for the rest of the afternoon, for the rest of my life.

—*James Taylor*, "Millworker"

For many workers, computers have caused more problems than they have solved. Workers complain of stress, depersonalization, fatigue, boredom, and a variety of health problems attributed to computers. Some of these complaints are directly related to technology; others relate to human decisions about how technology is implemented.

De-skilling and up-skilling. When a job is automated, it may be **de-skilled**; that is, it may be transformed so that it requires less skill. For example, computerized cash registers in many fast-food restaurants replace numbered buttons with buttons labeled "large fries" or "chocolate shake." Clerks who use these machines don't need to know math or think about prices. They simply push buttons for the food items ordered and take the money; computers do the rest.

Some of the most visible examples of de-skilling occur when offices automate clerical jobs. When word processors and databases replace typewriters and file cabinets, traditional typing-and-filing jobs disappear. Many secretaries are repositioned in data-entry jobs—mindless, repetitive jobs where the only measure of success is the number of keystrokes typed into a terminal each hour. When a clerical job—or any job—is de-skilled, the worker's control, responsibility, and job satisfaction are likely to go down. De-skilled jobs typically offer less status and less pay.

In sharp contrast to those whose jobs are de-skilled into electronic drudgery, many workers find their jobs **up-skilled** by automation. For example, many clerical jobs become more technical as offices adopt databases, word processors, electronic mail systems, fax modems, spreadsheets, and other computer technology. In some cases clerical workers use computer systems to do jobs formerly done by high-paid professionals and technicians. While many clerical people enjoy the added challenge and responsibility, others may be frustrated doing highly technical work with inadequate training. Clerical workers are seldom consulted before their jobs are computerized. And even though their work is more technically demanding than before, few clerical workers see this up-skilling reflected in their paychecks or level of responsibility.

Monitoring and surveillance. Another controversial aspect of office automation is **computer monitoring**—using computer technology to track, record, and evaluate worker performance, often without the knowledge of the worker. Monitoring systems can provide a manager with instant, on-screen reports detailing the number of keystrokes for each clerk, the length of each phone call placed by an employee, and the total amount of idle time for each computer. Some network software even allows a manager to secretly view a copy of any worker's screen at any time.

For a manager worried about worker productivity, computer monitoring can serve as a valuable source of information. But computer monitoring brings with it several problems:

- *Privacy.* In Chapter 6 we saw how the misuse of databases can threaten personal privacy. Computer monitoring compounds that threat by providing employers with unprecedented data on workers. Some employers have even monitored personal electronic mail messages and fired employees who send "unacceptable" messages. For these workers, computer monitoring means that Big Brother is watching, just as Orwell predicted in his book *1984.*
- *Morale.* Privacy issues aside, computer monitoring can have a powerful negative impact on morale. Because employees can't tell when they're being monitored, many workers experience a great deal of stress and anxiety. The boss can be seen as an invisible eavesdropper rather than as a team leader.

- *Devalued skills.* In the traditional office, workers were evaluated based on a variety of skills. A slow-typing secretary could be valued for her ability to anticipate when a job needed to be done or her willingness to help others with problems. Computer monitoring tends to reduce a worker's worth to simple quantities like "number of keystrokes per hour." In such systems a worker might be penalized for repairing a sticky chair, showing a neighbor how to reboot a terminal, or helping a co-worker overcome an emotional crisis.
- *Loss of quality.* Monitored workers tend to assume that "If it's not being counted, it doesn't count." The result of this assumption is that quantity may become more important than quality.

Millions of workers are monitored by computer, including factory workers, telephone operators, truck drivers, and, in some cases, managers. But computer monitoring is most commonly applied to clerical workers. According to one study more than one-fourth of all American clerical workers are monitored by computer.

The electronic sweatshop. Computer monitoring is common practice in data-entry offices. A data-entry clerk has a single job: to read information from a printed source—a check, a hand-printed form, or something else—and type it into a computer's database. A typical data-entry shop might contain hundreds of clerks sitting at terminals in a massive, windowless room. Workers—often minorities and almost always female—are paid minimum wage to do mindless keyboarding. Many experience headaches, backaches, serious wrist injuries, stress, anxiety, and other health problems. And all the while, keystrokes and breaks are monitored electronically. Writer Barbara Garson calls these worker warehouses **electronic sweatshops**, because working conditions bring to mind the oppressive factory sweatshops of the 19th century.

A growing number of electronic sweatshops are located across national borders from corporate headquarters in countries with lax labor laws and low wage scales. The electronic immigrants in these offshore shops don't need green cards to telecommute across borders, and they work for a fraction of what workers in developed countries

cost. A data-entry clerk in the Philippines, for example, earns about $6 per day. With wages that low many companies find it cost-effective to have data entered twice and use software to compare both versions and correct errors.

The electronic sweatshop is the dark side of the electronic office. Ironically, computer technology may soon make electronic sweatshops irrelevant. Optical character recognition and voice recognition technologies (described in Chapter 10) are rapidly becoming more practical for real-world applications. OCR software is already used to read and recognize typed and hand-printed characters in many applications, and voice recognition is threatening to replace thousands of directory assistance telephone operators. It's just a matter of time before most workers in electronic sweatshops are replaced by machines.

Rules of Thumb

Ergonomics and Health

Along with the benefits of computer technology comes the potential for unwelcome side effects. For people who work all day with computers, the side effects include risks to health and safety due to radiation emissions, repetitive stress injuries, or other computer-related health problems. Inconclusive evidence suggests that low-level radiation emitted by video display terminals (VDTs) and other equipment might cause health problems, including miscarriages in pregnant women and leukemia. The scientific jury is still out, but the mixed research results so far have led many computer users and manufacturers to err on the side of caution.

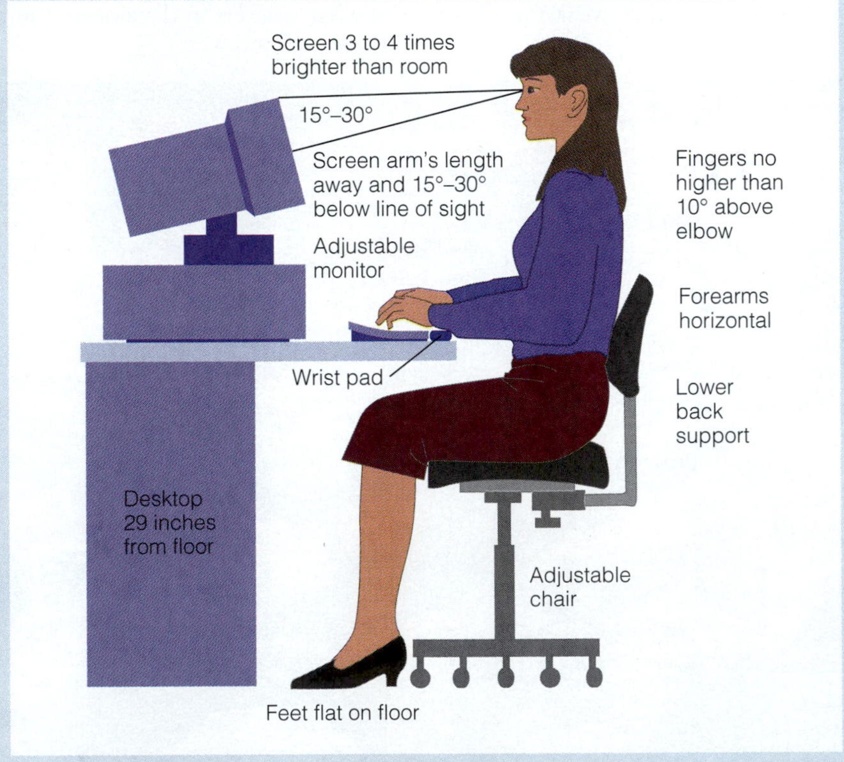

More concrete evidence relates keyboarding to occurrences of *repetitive-stress injuries* like *carpal tunnel syndrome*, a painful affliction of the wrist and hand that results from repeating the same movements over long periods. Prolonged computer use also increases the likelihood of headaches, eyestrain, fatigue, and other symptoms of "technostress."

Ergonomics (sometimes called **human engineering**) is the science of designing work environments that allow people and things to interact efficiently and safely. Ergonomic studies suggest preventive measures you can take to protect your health as you work with computers:

- **Choose equipment that's ergonomically designed**. When you're buying computer equipment, look beyond functionality. Use magazine reviews, manufacturer's information, and personal research to check on health-related factors like monitor radiation and glare, disk-drive noise levels, and keyboard layout. A growing number of computer products, like Apple's unusual split keyboard, are designed specifically to reduce the risk of equipment-related injuries.

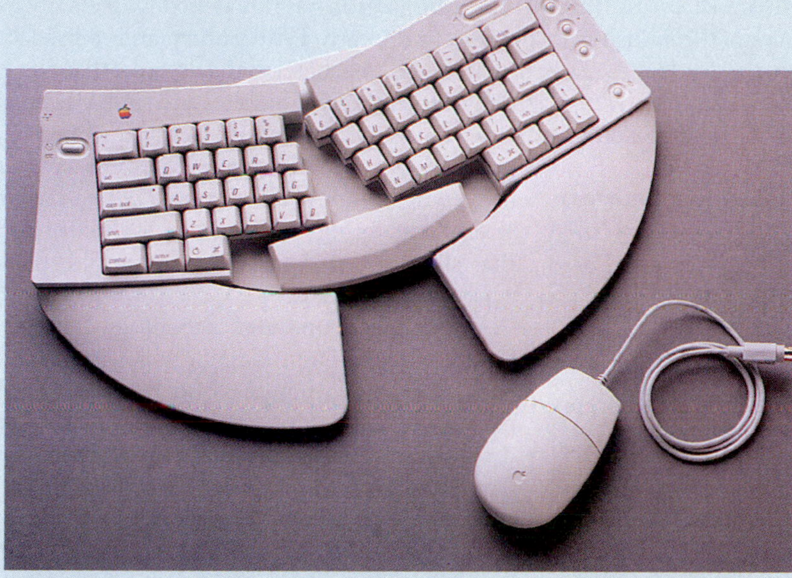

- **Create a healthy workspace**. Keep your paper copy of your work at close to the same height as your screen. Position your monitor and lights to minimize glare. Sit at arm's length from your monitor to minimize radiation risks.
- **Rest your eyes.** Take a 15-minute break from using a VDT every two hours. Look up from the screen periodically and focus on a far-away object or scene. Blink frequently.
- **Build flexibility into your work environment.** Whenever possible work with an adjustable chair, an adjustable table, an adjustable monitor, and a removable keyboard. Change your work position frequently.
- **Listen to your body**. If you feel uncomfortable, your body is telling you to change something or take a break. Don't ignore it.

Employment and Unemployment

My father had worked for the same firm for 12 years. They fired him. They replaced him with a tiny gadget this big that does everything that my father does only it does it much better. The depressing thing is my mother ran out and bought one.

—Woody Allen

When Woody Allen told this joke three decades ago, automation was generating a great deal of public controversy. Computer technology was new to the workplace, and people were reacting with both awe and fear. Many analysts predicted that automation would lead to massive unemployment and economic disaster. Others said that computers would generate countless new job opportunities. Today most people are used to seeing computers where they work, and the computers-vs.-jobs debate has cooled down. Job automation may not be a hot topic in comedy clubs today, but it's still an important issue for millions of workers whose jobs are threatened by machines.

Workers against machines. Automation has threatened workers since the earliest days of the industrial revolution. In the early 19th century, an English labor group called the Luddites smashed new textile machinery; they feared that the machines would take jobs away from skilled craftsmen. The Luddites and similar groups in other parts of Europe failed to stop the wheels of automation. Modern workers have been no more successful than their 19th-century counterparts in keeping computers and robots out of the workplace. Every year brings new technological breakthroughs that allow robots and computers to do jobs formerly reserved for humans.

Almost all of the assembly-line work in this factory is done by robots.

Of course, computer technology creates new jobs, too. Somebody has to design, build, program, sell, run, and repair the computers and robots. But many displaced workers don't have the education or skills to program computers, design robots, or even read printouts. Those workers are often forced to take low-tech, low-paying service jobs as cashiers or custodians, if they can find jobs at all. Because of automation, the unskilled, uneducated worker may face a lifetime of minimum-wage jobs or welfare. Technology may be helping to create an unbalanced society with two classes: a growing mass of poor uneducated people and a shrinking class of affluent educated people.

Cautiously optimistic forecasts. Nobody knows for sure how computer technology will affect employment in the coming decades; it's impossible to anticipate what might happen in 10 or 20 years. And experts are far from unanimous in their predictions.

A number of studies suggest that, at least for the next few years, technology will stimulate economic growth. This growth will produce new jobs, but it will also bring long, painful periods of adjustment for many workers. Demand for factory workers, clerical workers, and other semi-skilled and unskilled laborers will drop dramatically as their jobs are automated or moved to third-world countries where wages are low. At the same time, the demand for professionals—especially engineers and teachers—will rise sharply.

According to detailed computer models constructed at the Institute for Economic Analysis at New York University, there will be plenty of jobs in the early 21st

Rules of Thumb

Considering Computer Careers

Until recently people who wanted to work with computers were forced to choose between a few careers, most of which required highly specialized training. But when computers are used by everybody from fast-food sales clerks to graphic artists, just about anybody can have some kind of "computer career." Still, many rewarding and high-paying computer-related careers require a fair amount of specialized education. If you're interested in a computer-related job, consider the following tips:

- **Learn touch-typing**. Computers that can read handwriting and understand spoken English are probably in your future, but not your *immediate* future. Several low-cost typing tutorial programs can help you to teach your fingers how to type. The time you invest will pay you back quickly. The sooner you learn, the sooner you'll start reaping the rewards.
- **Use computers regularly to help you accomplish your immediate goals.** Word process your term papers. Use spreadsheets and other math software as calculation aids. Use databases for research work. Computers are part of your future. If you use them regularly, they'll become second nature, like telephones and pencils. If you don't own a computer, consider buying one; the next chapter has some tips on choosing a computer.
- **Don't forsake the basics.** If you want to become a programmer, a systems analyst, a computer scientist, a computer engineer, or some other kind of computer professional, don't focus all your attention on computers. A few young technical wizards become successful programmers without college degrees. But if you're not gifted and lucky, you'll need a solid education to land a good job. Math and communication skills (written and oral) are *extremely* important, even in highly technical jobs. Opportunities abound for people who can understand computers *and* communicate clearly.
- **Combine your passions**. If you like art and computers, explore computer art. If you love ecology and computers, find out how computers are used by ecologists. People who can speak the language of computers and the language of a specialized field have opportunities to build bridges.
- **Ask questions.** The best way to find out more about computer careers is to ask the people who do them. Most people are happy to talk about their jobs if you're willing to listen.
- **If you can't find your dream job, build it yourself.** Inexpensive computer systems provide all kinds of entrepreneurial opportunities for creative self-starters: Desktop publishing, multimedia video production, custom programming, commercial art and design, freelance writing, consulting—the jobs are there for the making, if you have the imagination and initiative.
- **Prepare for change**. In a rapidly changing world, lifetime careers are rare. Be prepared to change jobs several times. Think of education as a lifelong process.

century. The question is whether we'll have enough skilled workers to fill those jobs. In other words, economic growth will depend on whether we have a suitably trained workforce. The single most important key to a positive economic future, according to this study, is education. But will we, as a society, be able to provide people with the kind of education they'll need? We'll deal with that question, and the critical issues surrounding education in the information age, in the next chapter.

Will we need a new economy? In the long run education may not be enough. It seems likely that, at some time in the future, machines will be able to do most of the jobs people do today. We may face a future of *jobless growth*—a time when productivity increases, not because of the work people do but because of the work of machines. If productivity isn't tied to employment, we'll have to ask some hard questions about our political, economic, and social system:

- Do governments have an obligation to provide permanent public assistance to the chronically unemployed?
- Should large companies be required to give several months notice to workers whose jobs are being eliminated? Should they be required to retrain workers for other jobs?
- Should large companies be required to file "employment impact statements" before replacing people with machines, in the same way they're required to file environmental impact statements before implementing policies that might harm the environment?
- If robots and computers are producing most of society's goods and services, should all of the profits from those goods go to a few people who own the machines?
- If a worker is replaced by a robot, should the worker receive a share of the robot's "earnings" through stocks or profit sharing?
- The average work week 150 years ago was 70 hours; for the last 50 years it has been steady at 40. Should governments encourage job-sharing and other systems that allow for less-than-40-hour jobs?
- What will people do with their time if machines do most of the work? What new leisure activities should be made available?
- How will people define their identities if work becomes less central to their lives?

These questions force us to confront deep-seated cultural beliefs and economic traditions, and they don't come with easy answers. They suggest that we may be heading into a difficult period when many old rules don't apply anymore. But if we're successful at navigating the troubled waters of transition, we may find that automation fulfills the dream expressed by Aristotle more than 2000 years ago:

If every instrument could accomplish its own work, obeying or anticipating the will of others . . . , if the shuttle could weave, and the pick touch the lyre, without a hand to guide them, chief workmen would not need servants, nor masters slaves.

Summary

Our civilization is in the midst of a transition from an industrial economy to a post-industrial information economy. The transition, or paradigm shift, is having a profound influence on the way we live and work, and it is likely to challenge many of our beliefs, assumptions, and traditions. Computers and information technology are central to the change.

Factory work is steadily declining as we enter the information age, but factories still provide us with hard goods. The modern, automated factory uses computers at every level of operation. Computer-aided design, computer-aided manufacturing, robots, automated assembly lines, and automated warehouses all combine to produce factories that need very few laborers.

Far more people work in offices than in factories, and computers are critically important in the modern office. Early office automation centered on mainframes that were run by highly trained technicians; today's office is more likely to emphasize personal computers and workstations for decentralized enterprise computing. So far, predictions for widespread computer-supported cooperative work and paperless offices haven't come true.

A growing number of workers use computers to work at home part- or full-time. Some use modems to stay in contact with their offices. Telecommuting has many benefits for information workers, their bosses, and society as a whole. Still, telecommuting from home is not for everybody. Satellite offices, cottage industries, and portable offices offer alternatives that may be more practical for some workers. Even so, many companies resist the idea of employees working regularly out of the office.

Managers use a variety of computing tools to help them do their jobs. Management information systems, decision support systems, project management systems, expert systems, and on-line information systems can help managers plan, organize, staff, direct, and control their organizations. Unfortunately these tools can lead to information overload if they're not used intelligently.

Computers have allowed many organizations to provide services that wouldn't be possible otherwise, but so far they haven't produced the productivity gains that many experts expected. Experts speculate that productivity will rise as organizations adjust to the new technology and develop human-centered systems that are adapted to the needs and work habits of employees.

The impact of computers varies from job to job. Some jobs are de-skilled—transformed so they require less skill—while others are up-skilled into more technologically complex jobs. Computer monitoring is a controversial procedure that raises issues of privacy and, in many cases, lowers worker morale. De-skilling, monitoring, and health risks are particularly evident

in electronic sweatshops—data-entry warehouses packed with low-paid keyboard operators.

The biggest problem of automation may be the elimination of jobs. So far most displaced workers have been able to find other jobs in our expanding economy. But automation will almost certainly produce unemployment and pain for millions of people unless society is able to provide them with the education they'll need to take the new jobs created by technology. Automation may ultimately force us to make fundamental changes in our economic system. Only time will tell.

CHAPTER REVIEW

Key Terms

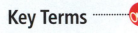

automated factory
automated office
automation
computer monitoring
computer-supported cooperative work
decision support system (DSS)
de-skilling
electronic cottage
electronic sweatshop
enterprise computing
ergonomics (human engineering)
groupware
human-centered system
information economy
information overload
information systems manager
management information system (MIS)
paperless office
paradigm shift
project management software
regional work center
satellite office
telecommuting
up-skilling

Review Questions

1. How is the information revolution similar to the industrial revolution? How is it different?
2. What are the major components of the modern automated factory?
3. How has the evolution of the automated office paralleled the evolution of the computer?
4. What are the advantages and disadvantages of telecommuting from the point of view of the worker? Management? Society?
5. Describe several software tools used by managers and explain how they help them do their jobs.
6. What is de-skilling? What is up-skilling? Give examples of each.
7. Describe several of the controversies surrounding the electronic sweatshop.
8. Why is education critical to our future as we automate more jobs?

Discussion Questions

1. What evidence do we have that our society is going through a paradigm shift?
2. What will have to happen before the paperless office (or the less-paper office) becomes a reality?
3. Many cities are enacting legislation to encourage telecommuting. If you were drafting such legislation, what would you include?
4. Why do you think it has been so difficult to demonstrate that computers increase productivity?
5. People who work in electronic sweatshops run the risk of being replaced by technology. Discuss the tradeoffs of this dilemma from the point of view of the worker and the society at large.
6. What do you think are the answers to the questions raised at the end of the section on automation and unemployment? How do you think most people would feel about these questions?

Projects

1. Interview several people whose jobs have been changed by computers and report on your findings.
2. Think about how computers have affected the jobs you've held. Report on your experiences.

Sources and Resources

Nomadness, edited by Steven K. Roberts (Nomadic Research Labs, P.O. Box 2185, El Segundo, CA 90245). This is probably the only periodical in the world that's done by "biketop publishing." If you want to keep up with the further adventures of Steve Roberts, here's how. His first book, *Computing Across America*, is available from the same address.

Computerization and Controversy: Value Conflicts and Social Choices, edited by Charles Dunlop and Rob Kling (Boston: Academic Press, 1991). This collection includes carefully researched academic studies as well as insightful articles from the popular press like "The Strange Case of the Electronic Lover" (from *Ms.* magazine). The coverage of computers in the workplace is particularly good.

Computers in the Human Context: Information Technology, Productivity, and People, edited by Tom Forester (Cambridge, MA: MIT Press, 1989). This intelligent collection of essays and articles covers all aspects of the information revolution. Like *Computerization and Controversy*, this book mixes academic papers with less rigorous writing, but it all fits together well.

Computers in Society, edited by Kathryn Schellenberg (Guilford, CT: Dushkin Publishing Group, published annually). This relatively inexpensive collection of articles covers a variety of subjects, including the impact of computers on the workplace.

The Electronic Sweatshop: How Computers Are Transforming the Office of the Future into the Factory of the Past, by Barbara Garson (New York: Penguin Books, 1989). Garson exposes the dark side of the electronic office in words that are hard to ignore.

CHAPTER

TWELVE

Computers at School and at Home

After reading this chapter you should be able to

- explain how the information age places new demands on our educational system
- describe several ways computers are used in classrooms today
- discuss the advantages and limitations of computers as instructional tools
- describe the role of computers in our homes and leisure activities in the next decade

Steve Wozniak, Steve Jobs, and the Garage That Grew Apples

It's not like we were all smart enough to see a revolution coming. Back then, I thought there might be a revolution in opening your garage door, balancing your checkbook, keeping your recipes, that sort of thing. There are a million people who study markets and analyze economic trends, people who are more brilliant than I am, people who worked for companies like Digital Equipment and IBM and Hewlett-Packard. None of them foresaw what was going to happen, either.

—— *Steve Wozniak*

What Steve Wozniak (the "Woz") and all those other people failed to foresee was the personal computer revolution—a revolution that he helped start. Wozniak, a brilliant engineer with an eye for detail, worked days as a calculator technician at Hewlett-Packard; he was refused an engineer's job because he lacked a college degree. At night he designed and constructed a scaled-down state-of-the-art computer system that would fit the home hobbyist's budget. When he completed the computer in 1975, he offered it to Hewlett-Packard, and they turned it down.

Steven Jobs and Steve Wozniak

Wozniak took his invention to the Homebrew Computer Club in Palo Alto, where it caught the imagination of another college dropout, Steven Jobs. A free-thinking visionary, Jobs persuaded Wozniak to quit his job in 1976 to form a company and market the machine, which they named the Apple I. Jobs raised $1300 in seed capital by selling his Volkswagen, and Apple Computer, Inc., was born in Jobs' garage.

With the help of businessman A. C. Markkula, the two Steves turned Apple into a thriving business. Wozniak created the Apple II, a more refined machine for consumers, and invented the first personal computer disk operating system so computers wouldn't be dependent on cassette tapes for storage. More interested in engineering than management, Wozniak allowed Jobs to assume the leadership role in the company. Because it put computing power within reach of everyday people, the Apple II became popular in businesses, homes, and especially schools. Apple became the first company in American history to join the Fortune 500 in less than five years. Still in his mid-twenties, Jobs was running a corporate giant. But troubled times were ahead for Apple.

When IBM introduced its PC in 1982, it quickly overshadowed Apple's presence in the business world accustomed to working with IBM mainframes. Other companies developed PC clones, treating the IBM PC as a standard — a standard that Apple refused to accept. Inspired by a visit to Xerox's Palo Alto Research Center (PARC), Jobs worked with a team of Apple engineers to develop the Macintosh, a futuristic computer he hoped would leapfrog IBM's advantage. When Jobs insisted on focusing most of Apple's resources on the Machintosh, Wozniak resigned to pursue noncomputer interests.

However, businesses failed to embrace the Mac, and Apple's stockholders grew uneasy with Jobs's controversial management style. In 1985, a year and a half after the Macintosh was introduced, Jobs was ousted from power by president John Sculley. Jobs went on to form NeXT, a company that produced powerful, easy-to-use UNIX workstations and now produces software. Today Apple still struggles to increase its market share in a world dominated by IBM-compatible PCs. At the same time, Apple retains a reputation for innovation and vision.

More than any other company, Apple Computer has succeeded in bringing computers into schools, where they can be used by the children of the information age. As computer technology reshapes our world, education plays an ever-more-important role in helping adults, as well as children, keep up with the changes going on around them. It's fitting, then, that computers are playing an ever-increasing role in the educational process in schools and homes. This chapter deals with the growing role of computers in schools and the changing role of education in a high-tech world. The chapter closes with a look at the growing impact of computers on our home life.

Education in the Information Age

The future is a race between education and catastrophe.

—H. G. Wells

As we've seen, the information age is changing the way we work. Some jobs are disappearing, others are emerging, and still others are being radically transformed by information technology and the information-based economy. But the information age is not just affecting the workplace. Its influences are felt in our educational system, too. Before it's over, the information revolution will have a profound and permanent effect on the way we learn.

The Roots of our Educational System

The American educational system was developed more than a century ago to teach students the basic facts and survival skills they would need for jobs in industry and agriculture—jobs they would probably hold for their entire adult lives. This industrial age system has been described as a *factory model* for three reasons:

- It assumes that all students learn the same way and that all students should learn the same things.
- The teacher's job is to "pour" facts into students, occasionally checking the level of knowledge in each student.
- Students are expected to work individually, absorb facts, and to spend most of their time sitting quietly in straight rows.

With all its faults, the public education system helped the United States to dominate world markets in the first half of this century. But the world has changed drastically since the system was founded. Schools have changed, too, but not fast enough to keep pace with the information revolution. Most experts today agree that we need to rebuild our educational system to meet the demands of the information age.

Information Age Education

It is no longer enough to have an educational system whose primary purpose is to produce people who are trained to be good workers. The output from our educational system (our graduates) must be educated, productive citizens who are prepared to be good workers, good citizens, and lifelong learners if the United States is to continue its world leadership role into the twenty-first century.

—Ludwig Braun, *Vision: TEST Final Report, Recommendations for American Educational Decision Makers*

What should education provide students in the information age? Research and experience suggest several answers:

- *Technological familiarity.* Many of today's older workers are having trouble adjusting to the information age because of **technophobia**—the fear of technology. These people grew up in a world without computers, and they experience anxiety when they're forced to deal with them. In tomorrow's world, computers will be as commonplace as telephones and dictionaries are today. To prepare for this world, students need to learn how to work comfortably with all kinds of knowledge tools, including pencils, books, calculators, computers, and information utilities. But technological familiarity shouldn't stop with learning how to work with tools. Students need to have a clear understanding of the limitations of the technology and the ability to assess the benefits and risks of applying technology to a problem. They need to be able to question technology.
- *Literacy.* The industrial age may have passed, but the need for reading and writing hasn't. In fact, it's more important than ever that today's students graduate with the ability to read and write. Many jobs that did not require reading or writing skills a generation ago now use high-tech equipment that demands literacy. A factory worker who can't read printouts isn't likely to survive the transition to an automated factory.
- *Mathematics.* In the age of the $5 calculator, many students think learning math is a waste of time. In fact, some educators argue that we spend too much time teaching students how to do things like long division and calculating square roots—skills that adults seldom, if ever, do by hand. These arithmetic skills have little to do with being able to think mathematically. To survive in a high-tech world, students need to be able to see the mathematical systems in the world around them and apply math concepts to solve problems. No calculator can do that.
- *Culture.* An education isn't complete without a strong cultural component. Liberal arts and social studies help us recognize the interconnections that turn information into knowledge. Culture gives us roots when the sands of time shift. It gives us historical perspective that allows us to see trends and prepare for the

future. Culture provides a human framework with which to view the impact of technology. It also gives us the global perspective to live in a world where communication is determined more by technology than geography.

- *Communication.* In the information age communication is a survival skill. Isolated factory workers and desk-bound pencil pushers are vanishing from the workplace. Modern jobs involve interactions—between people and machines and between people and people. The fast-paced, information-based society depends on our human ability to communicate, negotiate, cooperate, and collaborate, both locally and globally.
- *Learning how to learn.* Experts predict that most of the jobs that will exist in ten years do not exist today, and that most of those new jobs will require education past the high-school level. With this rapidly changing job market, it's unreasonable to assume that workers can be trained once for lifelong jobs. Instead of holding a single job for 40 years, today's high-school or college graduate is likely to change jobs several times. Those people who *do* keep the same jobs will have to deal with unprecedented change. The half-life of an engineer's specialized knowledge—the time it takes for half of that knowledge to be replaced by more current knowledge—is only 3.2 years.

These facts suggest that we can no longer afford to think of education as a one-time vaccination against illiteracy. In the information age learning must be a lifelong process. To prepare students for a lifetime of learning, schools must teach students more than facts; they must make sure students learn how to think and learn.

Computers Go to School

The information age clearly makes new demands on our educational system, requiring radical changes in what and how people learn. Many educators believe that computers and information technology are essential parts of those changes. There are over 2.5 million computers in schools in the United States, and they're being put to work in a variety of ways. In this section we'll survey the ways students and teachers use computers at school.

Computer-Aided Instruction

The ordinary classroom holds the bright kids back and makes the kids that need more time go too fast. They fall further and further behind until they can't keep up—it's a terrible system.

—B. F. Skinner, *the father of behaviorist psychology and inventor of the first "teaching machine"*

In 1953 B. F. Skinner visited his daughter's fourth-grade class and watched the teacher try to teach arithmetic to everyone in the class at the same speed. The experience inspired him to build a *teaching machine*—a wooden box that used cards, lights, and levers to quiz and reward a student. His machine was based on the principles of behaviorist psychology: Allow the student to learn in small steps at an individualized pace and reward correct answers with immediate positive feedback. When personal computers appeared in classrooms, students started using **drill-and-practice software** based on those same principles: individualized rate, small steps, and positive feedback.

A traditional drill-and-practice program presents the student with a question and compares the student's answer with the single correct answer. If the answers match, the program offers praise, possibly accompanied by music and animation.

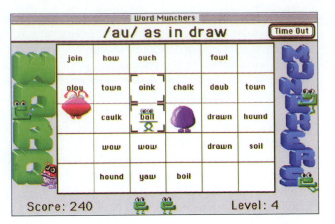

Students practice basic math and vocabulary lessons with CAI games like these. Number Maze makes solving arithmetic problems a necessary part of navigating a maze. Word Munchers uses an arcade-style game to add excitement to spelling drills.

If the student's answer doesn't match the correct answer, the program offers an explanation and presents another, similar problem. The program may keep track of student responses and tailor questions based on error patterns; it might also provide reports on student progress to the teacher. Today most drill-and-practice programs embed the lessons in animated games, but the underlying principles remain the same.

Pure drill-and-practice programs don't teach new material. Like flash cards and worksheets, they're designed to help students go over material they've already learned to get it better. **Tutorial software** provides direct instruction in a clearly-specified skill or subject. Drill-and-practice software and tutorial software are often referred to as **computer-aided instruction** (**CAI**) software. Most CAI programs combine tutorial material with drill-and-practice questions, in the same way a math textbook alternates explanations with exercises.

CAI software is the most common type of **courseware** (educational software) for three reasons: It's relatively easy and inexpensive to produce, it can easily be combined with more traditional educational techniques, and it produces clear, demonstrable results. CAI offers many advantages over workbooks and worksheets:

- *Individualized learning.* Individual students can learn at their own pace. Teachers can spend their time working one-on-one with students—an important activity that's all but impossible in typical presentation-and-discussion classrooms.
- *Motivation.* CAI can turn practice into an entertaining game. It motivates students to practice arithmetic, spelling, touch-typing, piano playing, and other skills that might otherwise be tedious to learn.

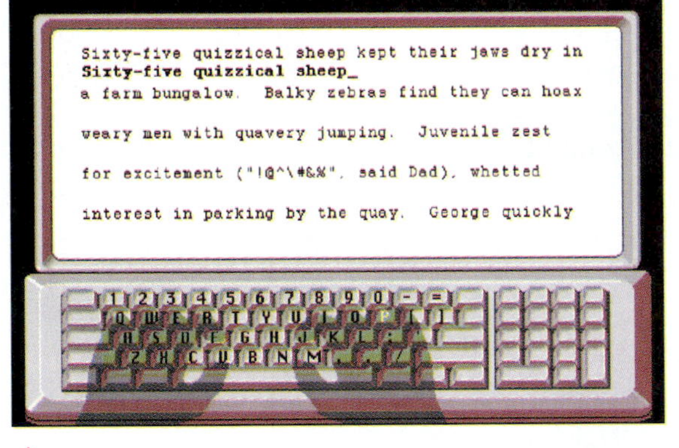

CAI is useful for strengthening basic motor skills like typing. In Mavis Beacon Teaches Typing, on-screen tutorials guide the student through a complete set of typing lessons, with the computer monitoring every keystroke for accuracy.

IBM's SpeechViewer II is a package of software and accessories to help students overcome speech impairments. The software analyzes speech characteristics after the student speaks into a microphone and provides instant, animated feedback.

- *Confidence.* CAI can help timid children become comfortable with computers as well as with the subject matter being taught. A well-designed program is infinitely patient, and it allows students to make mistakes in private. Research has shown that younger children, disadvantaged children, and especially learning disabled students tend to respond positively to CAI.

Research also suggests that not all CAI software deserves praise. Much CAI software is flawed because it gives inappropriate feedback, allows students to practice mistakes, and discourages students from moving into new material. Even the best CAI works only with tightly defined subjects where every question can have a single, clear, unambiguous answer. CAI presents information in the form of facts, leaving no room for questioning, creativity, or cooperation. In a sense, CAI programs students.

Programming Tools

In many schools today, the phrase "computer-aided instruction" means making the computer teach the child. One might say the computer is being used to program the child. In my vision, the child programs the computer and, in doing so, both acquires a sense of mastery over a piece of the most modern and powerful technology and establishes an intimate contact with some of the deepest ideas from science, from mathematics, and from the art of intellectual model building.

—Seymour Papert, *Mindstorms*

With his colleagues at MIT, Seymour Papert developed a computer language called *LOGO* so children could program computers, rather than the other way around. Children can write LOGO programs as soon as they're old enough to read and write a few simple words.

Rather than teaching through lessons and tests, LOGO creates environments for learning. The most famous of these LOGO environments allows children to draw pictures using a technique called *turtle graphics.* With turtle graphics a child uses LOGO commands to make a "turtle" move, dragging a "pen" to draw lines as it moves. The "turtle" can be a small robot that moves around on the floor or a graphical creature that lives in the middle of a computer screen.

LOGO helps children learn advanced computer science concepts like *recursion*—the ability of a program or procedure to call, or refer to, itself, as in this example:

```
TO CIRCLE
FORWARD 1 RIGHT1
CIRCLE
END
```

This LOGO program tells the computer "to draw a circle, go one step forward, turn 1 degree to the right, and repeat *all* of these instructions." Of course, there's a bug here: This procedure doesn't know when to stop. But debugging is part of programming, and students who learn LOGO learn that making mistakes is part of the process.

LOGO has other environments that go beyond geometry and graphics. LEGO LOGO allows children to use LOGO commands to control motorized machines and robots built out of LEGO building blocks.

Papert and many educators predicted that LOGO would help children become better at general problem solving and logical thinking. Research suggests that LOGO enhances creativity and originality in children, but there's no evidence that it improves

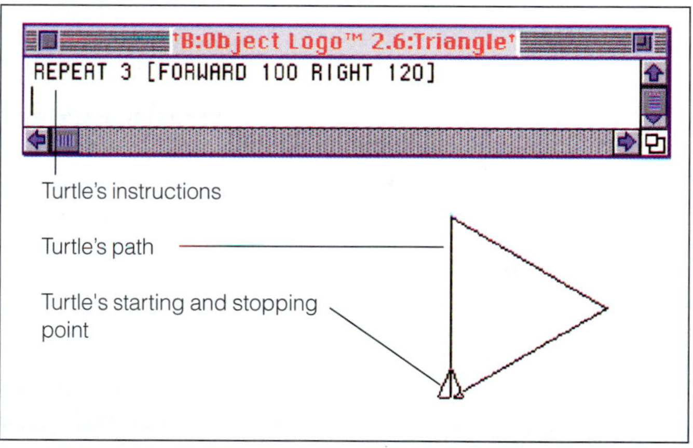

This sequence of LOGO commands tells the turtle, facing up in this picture, to move forward 100 tiny steps, turn right 120 degrees (one-third of a circle), move forward another 100 steps, turn right another 120, move forward another 100, and turn right another 120. When the turtle follows these instructions with the "pen" engaged, it draws an equilateral triangle on the floor or the screen. (Software: Object LOGO.)

Students in this class build LEGO robots and write LOGO programs to control them.

their general thinking skills more than other teaching tools. Like a chalkboard, LOGO can be an effective tool in the hands of a good teacher.

LOGO, like Pascal and BASIC—two other programming languages designed for students—is less popular in schools today than it was a decade ago. Today's computer applications make programming seem irrelevant to the average student. Children don't need to learn how to write TV programs before they watch TV, and in most schools they don't learn to program computers before they use them.

Simulation and Games

No compulsory learning can remain in the soul. . . . In teaching children, train them by a kind of game, and you will be able to see more clearly the natural bent of each.

—*Plato,* *The Republic, Book VII*

When Papert developed LOGO, he based his educational psychology on the work of renowned Swiss developmental psychologist Jean Piaget. According to Piaget, children have a natural gift for learning on their own; they learn to talk, get around, and think without formal training. A child growing up in France learns French effortlessly, because the child's environment has the necessary materials. In Papert's vision the computer can provide an environment that makes learning mathematics, science, and the arts as effortless as learning French in France.

Many **educational simulations** today are based on the same idea: Children learn best through exploration and invention. These simulations allow students to explore artificial environments, imaginary or based on reality. Educational simulations are metaphors designed to focus student attention on the most important concepts. While most educational simulations have the look and feel of a game, they challenge students to learn through exploration, experimentation, and interaction with other students.

With a simulation, the students are in control of the learning environment. It's up to them to find and use information to draw conclusions. Students can experience the consequences of their actions without taking real-world risks. Simulations allow students to have experiences that wouldn't be possible otherwise. Instead of simply spewing facts, simulations provide a context for knowledge.

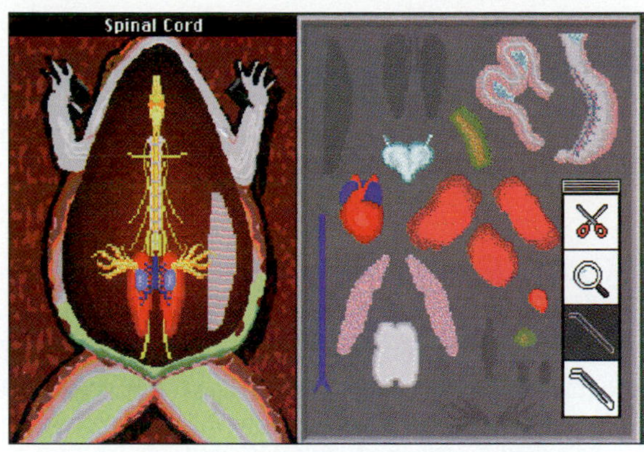

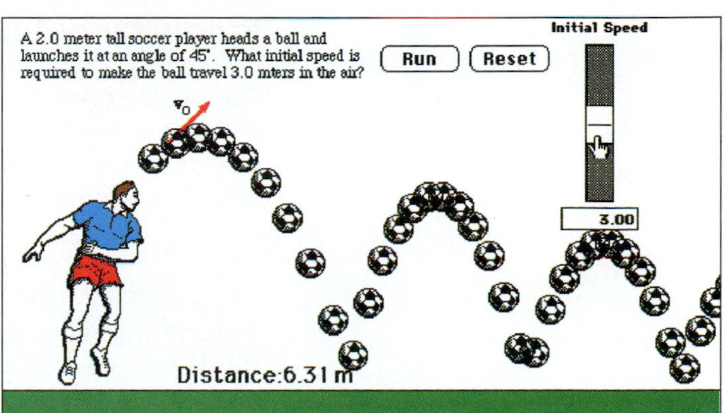

These two science simulations allow students to test scientific concepts in on-screen laboratories. Operation Frog simulates the experience of dissecting a frog, including actual video footage, without the mess, expense, or sacrifice of the real thing. With Interactive Physics, a student can design experiments to see the effects of changing the laws of physics.

Students love playing well-designed simulation games, but many schools don't use simulations because there's no room for them in the formal curriculum. It's difficult to prove the effectiveness of simulation games because they generally aren't designed to teach simple, measurable facts. In spite of our culture's age-old tradition of learning through games, many educators question the educational value of games in the classroom. Of course, educational simulations, like all simulations, come up short as substitutes for reality. The risks of simulations, outlined in Chapter 5, apply to educational simulations, too. But when field trips aren't possible, computer simulations can offer affordable alternatives.

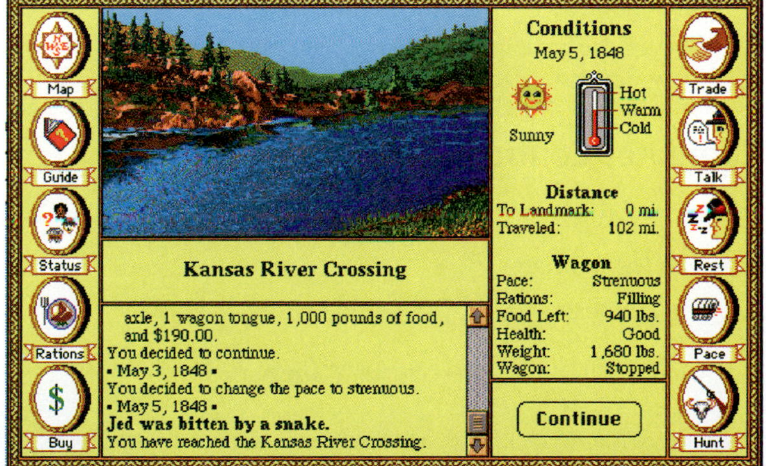

These two social studies games are popular with students, teachers, and parents. Wagon Train 1848 allows players to take a trip on the Oregon Trail 150 years ago. This network game allows students sitting at different computers to play different roles and send messages to each other throughout the trip. Where in the World is Carmen San Diego, the immensely popular game designed to help students learn world geography, is the first piece of software to spin off children's books, a children's television game show, a board game, and a live-action movie.

Productivity Tools

For me, the phrase "computer as pencil" evokes the kind of uses I imagine children of the future making of computers. Pencils are used for scribbling as well as writing, doodling as well as drawing, for illicit notes as well as for official assignments.

—*Seymour Papert,* Mindstorms

Today the trend in schools is clearly toward teaching children to use computers as *tools.* Word processors, spreadsheets, databases, graphics programs, desktop publishing software—the software tools used by adults—are the tools students learn most often in schools. In some cases students use applications designed especially for children; others use standard "adult" applications. While programming classes are taken by only a few students, classes in keyboarding and word processing are often required for everybody. Once students learn to use these general-purpose tools, they can put them to work in and out of school.

Some schools also provide special-purpose tools for classroom use, including

- laboratory sensing hardware and software that can be used to collect scientific data (such as temperature) and convert it into computer data to be analyzed by students
- collaborative writing groupware that allows students to work collectively on creative writing and editing projects
- music synthesizers with sequencing and notation software for teaching music composition

Whether the computer is used as a tutor or a tool, the addition of multimedia adds whole new dimensions to the educational process.

Computer-Controlled Media

I hear and I forget,

I see and I remember,

I do and I understand.

—*Ancient Chinese Proverb*

The typical American child spends hours each day watching screens—television, video game, and computer—and listening to radio and recorded music. Traditional lectures can't live up to the expectations created by all this high-tech media input. A growing number of teachers are using computer graphics, videodiscs, CD-ROMs, and other digital media to convey information in a more dynamic form. Chapter 8 introduced a variety of graphics and multimedia applications. Depending on the way these media are used, the student's role might be to observe the presentation, to control the presentation, or to create the presentation.

Presentation aids. In some cases, teachers use computers and multimedia technology to create in-class presentations. Here are some examples, ranging from simple to complex:

- A history teacher might outline the main points of a lecture using a set of bullet charts created with a presentation graphics program.
- A science teacher might use a 3-D graphics program to create models of molecules that can be displayed and manipulated during in-class demonstrations on a projection screen.

- An art teacher might illustrate an art history lecture with a series of images from an art videodisc. The images are selected before class and their frame numbers are programmed into the videodisc controller so the teacher can advance to the next image by clicking a button.
- A music teacher might guide a class through key passages of a Beethoven symphony using a commercial HyperCard stack that displays the score while the CD plays the composition.
- An English teacher might supplement lectures and discussions about the novel *To Kill a Mockingbird* by showing selected clips from a videodisc of the film.

From the teacher's point of view, the advantage of computer technology is that the material can be customized to meet the needs of the class. Instead of using commercial transparencies and handouts designed for generic classrooms, a teacher can create custom visual aids for specific classes. Instead of being forced to move through videotapes and audio cassettes sequentially, the teacher can choose to present material in any order.

Hypermedia and interactive multimedia. From the student's point of view, teacher-controlled media presentations are still passive, linear affairs. To get students more involved in the learning process, many teachers use hypermedia and interactive multimedia software that put students in control. Sometimes these interactive lessons are created by teachers; more often they're purchased from software development companies. Some are simple tutorials with sound and/or video; others are hypermedia reference tools with multimedia capability. Here are two examples:

- Students can explore the life of Martin Luther King, Jr., using an interactive videodisc controlled by a HyperCard stack. The stack allows them to quickly jump between video clips, still photographs, maps, and supplementary information. The information on the computer screen complements the TV images. For example, while students watch King deliver his "I Have a Dream" speech, they can read the text on the computer screen.
- Using a multimedia encyclopedia, students can look up a topic by title or key word. They can click on highlighted words in an article to jump to related articles. Many articles include maps, charts, pictures, video clips, and sounds.

In this multimedia lab a student views scenes from a Shakespearean play on videodisc. The HyperCard stack on his computer screen provides background information for each scene and allows the student to control the videodisc.

Authoring tools for students. To maximize student involvement, some teachers put multimedia **authoring tools** in the hands of students. Instead of creating interactive lessons for students, teachers allow the students to create their own multimedia presentations. Here are three examples:

- In an Alaskan village native students used HyperCard to create "Yupik for Non-Speakers," an illustrated talking dictionary of the traditional Yupik language. Students drew on the knowledge and voices of the community elders to create the dictionary.
- At South Eugene High School in Eugene, Oregon, students produced a CD-ROM version of their yearbook. Unlike the paper version, the CD-ROM yearbook contains animated illustrations and recordings of the students talking about school.
- Students in a high-school science class in Shelley, Idaho, spent a school year researching, planning, and building an exhibit for Yellowstone National Park's Canyon Visitor Center. The exhibit includes wall murals, a walk-through geological model of the earth beneath Yellowstone, and an interactive, presentation system built around a pair of IBM PS/2 computers with touch-screen input displays.

> Visitors use the multimedia system to explore the political and geological history of Yellowstone and to "fly" from outer space down to the earth beneath Yellowstone.

Clearly the students are more involved in these projects than they are in teacher-made presentations. This kind of student involvement promotes learning, but it has drawbacks. One problem is economic: Few schools can afford the hardware, software, and floor space for multiple student media workstations. The other problem is both social and political: When students are creating or using interactive media, they aren't conforming to the traditional factory model. Instead of sitting quietly listening to the teacher, they're taking control of the machinery and the learning process. The teacher becomes a supervisor and a mentor rather than a conveyor of information. This kind of restructuring of the educational process is threatening to many administrators, teachers, parents, and community members who are used to the old ways.

Distance Learning: Virtual Schools

Very soon now, it might not matter where your body happens to be . . . as long as you maintain a presence in the networks.

—Steven K. Roberts, *high-tech bicycle nomad*

For some students the most important application of computers in the schools is **distance learning**—using technology to extend the educational process beyond the walls of the school. Computers, modems, fax machines, satellite video transmissions, and other communication technologies offer many promising possibilities. Grade-school students can network with kids in other parts of the world by modem. High-school correspondence courses can be completed by modem rather than by mail. Handicapped students can do course work without traveling to central sites. Two-way video links allow "visiting" experts to talk to students in outlying classrooms and answer their questions in real time. Networked school districts can offer multischool videoconference courses in Chinese, college-level calculus, and other subjects that might have tiny enrollments if offered only at a single school. Teachers can receive additional education without leaving their districts.

Telecommunication technology is particularly important for students in remote locations. If a child in a small town develops an interest in a narrow subject, whether it's aboriginal anthropology or classical Russian ballet, that student may find pursuing that interest a discouraging process. Reference materials, adult experts, and classmates with similar interests are often hard to find. Telecommunication networks offer solutions: on-line reference materials, special interest group BBSs, and like-minded modem pals are all within reach. In many areas rural interactive television networks keep remote schools and towns from fading away.

Distance learning also offers promise for workers whose jobs are changed or eliminated by a shifting economy. Many displaced workers can't afford to relocate their families to college towns so they can learn new skills. Others who still have jobs but want to go back to school are faced with similar relocation problems. But if colleges and universities offer electronic outreach programs, these people can update their skills while remaining in their communities.

The University of Phoenix On-Line Computer Business School was launched in San Francisco in 1990 as an alternative to business correspondence courses. Students use PCs and modems to do everything from ordering books to taking final exams. When 45 students received bachelor's and master's degrees at the 1992 graduation ceremony, most of them were seeing their professors in person for the first time. The on-line school is particularly attractive to older students whose work prevents them from attending more traditional colleges. On-line schools like this are an important step toward an educational system that encourages life-long learning.

Computers at School: Midterm Grades

The business of education is to give the student both useful information and life-enhancing experience, one largely measurable, the other not. . . .

—John Gardner, *The Art of Fiction*

Many schools have been using computers in classrooms for more than a decade. In these days of shrinking budgets, taxpayers are asking whether classroom computer technology "pays off." Has it lived up to its promise as an educational tool in the schools? According to most experts, the answer is decidedly mixed but optimistic.

High Marks

Clearly computer technology can improve education. A 1990 report by the International Society for Technology in Education (ISTE) called *Vision: TEST (Technologically Enriched Schools of Tomorrow)* summarized the research on computer technology in the classroom:

- *Students improve problem-solving skills, outscore classmates, and learn more rapidly in a variety of subject areas when using technology as compared to conventional methods of study.*
- *Students find computer based instruction to be more motivational, less intimidating, and easier to persist with than traditional instruction.*
- *In many cases, students' self-esteem was increased when they used computers. This change has been most dramatic in cases of at-risk and handicapped youngsters.*
- *Using technology encourages cooperative learning, turn taking among young children, peer tutoring, and other valuable social skills.*

Stories abound of reduced drop-out rates and attitudinal changes among at-risk students; improved math, reading, and language scores; and overall academic improvement among students in high-tech schools. But computer technology doesn't always bring happy headlines. For every success story there's a school somewhere with computers being used inappropriately, or simply gathering dust.

Room for Improvement

What makes technology work for some schools and not for others? A closer look at the success stories reveals that they didn't achieve their dramatic results with technology alone. When we compare these schools with less fortunate schools, three issues emerge: money, training, and restructuring.

- *Money.* Most American schools have found funds to purchase computers. The ratio of students to computers in the United States is 18 to 1—far better than Japan's 66 to 1 or France's 60 to 1. Unfortunately many of those computers are technologically outdated, and they lack the modern peripherals and software to make them effective educational tools today. Most classrooms don't even have phone lines, let alone modems. Not surprisingly, computers tend to be concentrated in affluent school districts, so economically disadvantaged students have the least access to them.
- *Teacher training.* Unfortunately teacher training is often missing from schools' high-tech formulas. Only half the teachers in the United States report having ever used computers, and far fewer use them regularly. To use technology effectively, teachers need training, support, and time to integrate technology into their curricula.

- *Restructuring.* Hardware, software, and training are important, but they aren't enough. Just as businesses need to rethink their organizational structures to successfully automate, schools need to be restructured to make effective use of computer technology. The goal is education, and technology is just one tool for achieving that goal. Interactive media, individualized instruction, and cooperative learning simply don't fit well into the factory school. To successfully transform the schools to meet the challenges of the information age, we'll need to invest in research and planning involving teachers, students, administrators, parents, businesses, and community leaders. We'll need to invent new ways to learn. In the words of the *Vision: TEST* summary,

  As a nation, we are spending billions of dollars repairing the deficiencies that an inadequate educational system has created. These dollars could be redirected to provide technology, teacher training, teacher support, and better curricula. This will result in significant reductions in dropout rates and significantly increase the quality of education our young people are receiving.

The Classroom of Tomorrow

To give us a head start in building the schools of the future, Apple, IBM, and other companies, along with some state and local governments, have helped create model technology schools in communities around the United States and Canada. Almost without exception, these schools have shown that technology can, in the proper context, have a dramatic effect on education.

Students and teachers work side by side in the Apple Classroom of Tomorrow.

As an example, let's look at West High School in Columbus, Ohio, an urban school that's part of the Apple Classrooms of Tomorrow (ACOT) program. Students in the program use spreadsheets, simulations, and intelligent tutorial software to help them learn math; they use hypermedia simulations to explore the effects of exercise and diet on a simulated heart; they create animated short stories with HyperCard; they take notes on portable computers, sometimes organizing the material with hypertext links; they create multimedia research projects on everything from first amendment rights to the works of French and Spanish artists (written in French and Spanish). Many exams are computerized, so students can individually download tests from the network and have their solutions automatically evaluated and graded as they proceed. For some exams, students are allowed to correct their errors and resubmit their results before the grades are automatically entered into electronic grade books.

But technology is only part of the picture; communication and collaboration are important, too. Students give lectures along with teachers. Students exchange homework and criticize each other's solutions. Above all, students work together. Here's a description of a whole-class interdisciplinary project from Apple's 1992 project summary, *Overview—ACOT Project & Findings*:

In one such effort, students created a scale model of the renovated business district in Columbus. Over a month period, they researched buildings in the area, interviewed occupants and architects, measured and scaled skyscrapers, and constructed models including robotic elements they built and programmed. The completed effort was a 20 by 20 foot scale model driven by a dozen computers. To share the model with the city of Columbus, the students collaborated on the production of a videodisk, designed and built a HyperCard interface, and proudly presented the result in the lobby of the city's museum of science and industry.

Does this radical approach work? Based on a study of the first graduating class, *something* is working. Non-ACOT students at West High had a 30 percent drop-out rate, while *none* of the 21 ACOT students dropped out. Several local businesses were so impressed that they offered to hire *any* ACOT students immediately after graduations. Still, 90 percent of the graduates planned to pass up these employment opportunities to go to college, seven with full scholarships. Between them, they received 27 academic awards. The project summary goes on:

But more importantly, a four-year longitudinal study of these students showed their greatest difference to be the manner in which they organized for and accomplished their work. They routinely employed inquiry, collaborative, technological, and problem-solving skills uncommon to graduates of traditional high-school programs.

The Campus of Tomorrow

The further one pursues knowledge, the less one knows.

—*Lao Tse*, 500 BC

The ACOT schools and other model technology schools show what can be done with well-trained teachers, an imaginative school structure, and *today's* state-of-the-art technology. But what about *tomorrow's* technology? What kind of personal computers will students be using in the year 2000, and how will they be using them?

In 1987 Apple sponsored PROJECT 2000, a university-level competition to get answers to those questions. The winning entry, Tablet, was designed by a group of students and faculty advisors from the University of Illinois at Urbana-Champaign. Tablet is a notebook-sized, touch-screen, wireless communication device with optical storage cards and sophisticated handwriting recognition capability. Even though it's several years old, the winning article still provides a remarkably clear and imaginative view of a possible future. Here's an excerpt describing a day in the life of a student with a Tablet:

The date is October 5, 2000. Alexis Quezada is a freshman at a prestigious institution of higher learning. . . . On her first day of classes she was given her own Tablet, the personal computer used at the university.

Today Alexis has three classes: Physical Science, Japanese, and Algorithmic Mathematics. It is a nice day, so Alexis rides her bike over to the park before the lecture starts. At 10:00 A.M. sharp Tablet informs her that the Physical Science lecture is about to start. She directs her attention toward the screen as the lecture begins. When the lecture is over, she begins the laboratory experiment. It involves determining the equilibrium for a chemical reaction. She sets up the simulated experiment apparatus and starts it going. But it isn't working. She instructs Tablet to search today's lecture for "the stuff about setting up today's experiment." Within seconds the requested portion of the lecture is displayed on the screen.

Because of the problem with setting up the experiment, Alexis missed the beginning of her Japanese lecture. Instead of jumping into a lecture that has already started, Alexis's computer contacts the university's lecture database again and instructs the database to display the current lecture from the beginning. Time-shifting the start of the lecture by fifteen minutes has allowed her to see the lecture from the beginning, at the cost of not being able to ask the professor a question if she doesn't understand. Fortunately, the lecture is still in progress and should last another forty minutes, so Alexis invokes the "catch-up" facility. Over the next fifteen minutes, Alexis watches thirty minutes of lecture as Tablet squeezes out the times of slow movement and silence. Through signal processing, the lecture looks and sounds fast-paced but is otherwise normal. Now up to speed, she watches the rest of the lecture and participates in asking questions, performing an occasional "instant replay/catch-up" sequence on material that she found confusing.

Once Japanese is over, Alexis heads back to the dormitory for lunch. Some things never change, and dorm food is one of them. Fortunately, the social aspects of lunch will still be important even in a world where one can communicate with friends by video email. Afterwards Alexis returns to her room to start reading her LaserCard edition of G. B. Trudeau's Republic, complete with art, text, and extensive commentary. She scrawls notes directly on the simulated page which she can search or hide at will.

In English Comp class at 2:00 P.M., the professor indicates that she has finished grading the previous assignment and returns them. Instantly, the corner of the display contains a copy of Alexis's graded paper—B+, not too bad. Alexis pages through the paper by touching the screen. She touches the video-mail icon for comments about a particular page. Segments of her text become highlighted in color as they are discussed. Unfortunately, her teacher is pretty boring, and so she turns on her soap opera instead.

. . . Now it's time to work on her art history term paper comparing Salvador Dali's surrealist images in his paintings and the images he developed for the movies Un Chien Andalou and Spellbound. Alexis tells Tablet to find the films in available film databases. It seems that there are three films with the title Spellbound. Alexis says to find "the one by Hitchcock." The scenes she is interested in analyzing are being copied directly into her paper—a hypertext document. Alexis expounds on the meaning of the images in the films and their importance with respect to Dali's symbolism until it's time to call it a night.

—Luke T. Young, Kurt H. Thearling, Steven S. Skiena, Arch D. Robinson, Stephen M. Omohundro, Bartlett W. Mel, Stephen Wolfram, *"Academic Computing in the Year 2000," Academic Computing, May/June 1988*

As we approach the year 2000, technological pieces are rapidly falling into place. It may not happen by 2000, but something like Tablet is almost certainly in your future. Of course, there's more to this story than technology. The big questions are not whether the technology can happen, but whether the social structures and human behavior can change fast enough to keep up with the technology. When Tablet arrives, will schools and people be ready?

Computers Come Home

There is no reason for any individual to have a computer in their home.

—Ken Olson, *president of Digital Equipment Corporation 1977*

The same year Ken Olson made this statement, Apple Computer introduced the Apple II computer. In the years that followed, Apple, Commodore, Tandy, Atari, IBM, and dozens of other companies managed to sell computers to millions of individuals who had "no reason" to buy them. Today there are more computers in homes than in schools, and the home computer market is still growing. While many of those computers gather dust, others are being put to work, and play, in a variety of ways. And new technologies are emerging that may soon put computers into the mainstream of modern home life. What are people using home computers for, and what kind of role will computers play in tomorrow's homes?

Household Business

Frank Gilbreth, a turn-of-the-century pioneer of motion study in industry, applied "scientific management" techniques to his home. He required his 12 children to keep records on bathroom "work-and-process charts" of each hair combing, tooth brushing, and bathing. He gave them demonstrations on efficient bathing techniques to minimize "unavoidable delays." While it may have worked for Gilbreth, this "scientific management" approach to home life is not likely to catch on today. Still, certain aspects of family life are unavoidably businesslike, and a growing number of people turn to computers to help them take care of business.

Business applications at home. Not everyone is convinced that computers are useful or practical at home. But those people who *do* use home computers generally find that they can put the same applications to work at home that they use in their offices:

- *Word processors.* For letters, memos, and (especially) school papers, the word processor is rapidly replacing the family typewriter for families with computers. There's no doubt that a word processor makes writing easier; the question is whether most people do enough writing to make it worth the investment.
- *Spreadsheets.* "Can we afford a trip to Mexico this year?" "How much do we need to put away each year to pay for college?" "Should we refinance the house?" A spreadsheet program can frame answers to "What if?" questions involving numbers, providing somebody takes the time and effort to create a worksheet model of the problem.
- *Database programs.* Many people use database programs for address books, family record keeping, collections, and other data storage jobs. Others find that it's not worth the effort to type in all that data.
- *Personal information management programs.* Appointment calendars, to-do lists, addresses, phone numbers—they're part of home life, too, and an enthusiastic minority of people use home computers to keep their personal lives organized.
- *Accounting and income tax programs.* Many easy-to-use accounting programs are targeted at homes and small businesses. These programs can balance checkbooks, write checks, keep financial records for tax time, and provide data for income tax calculation programs, if somebody types in the relevant data.

Smart cards. For most people the advantages of computerized home money management aren't worth the time and effort required to enter every financial transaction into the computer. Some people strike a balance by only typing in "important" transactions; a few subscribe to home banking programs so they can download their summary statements directly from bank computers. But for most people computerized money management won't happen until there's an effortless way to record transactions—perhaps a device that, when inserted into the computer, can tell the software about each purchase and paid bill. That device may turn out to be a smart card, like those widely used in Europe.

A **smart card** looks like a standard credit card, but instead of a magnetic strip it contains embedded microprocessors and memory. Some smart cards even contain touch-sensitive keypads for entering numbers. Whether it has a keypad or not, a smart card receives most of its input when it's slipped into a special slot on a computer. A smart card can contain about three pages of typewritten data, which can be password-

A smart card.

protected. There are hundreds of millions of smart cards in Europe, and they're rapidly infiltrating America.

Smart cards are obvious candidates to replace magnetic-strip credit cards. In addition to storing critical ID information, a smart card can automatically record each transaction for later retrieval. But smart cards have other applications, too. College students use smart cards as meal tickets. Office workers use smart cards as keys to access sensitive data on computers. Smart cards have replaced food stamps for thousands of households in Dayton, Ohio. Many Europeans use smart cards to pay highway tolls and unscramble cable TV broadcasts. In the future we might be able to use one card to buy groceries, check out library books, and store personal medical information in case of an emergency. Future smart cards will use pattern recognition techniques to verify signatures on checks or credit slips and help prevent millions of dollars in fraud and forgery.

Communication, Education, and Information

Newspapers as we know them won't exist. They will be printed for a readership of one. Television won't simply have sharper pictures. You'll have one button that says tell me more, and another button that says tell me less.

—Nicholas Negroponte, *director of the MIT Media Lab*

Millions of people use home computers for education and information. Many of the educational software programs described earlier in this chapter are used by children and adults in homes. Encyclopedias, dictionaries, atlases, almanacs, national telephone directories, medical references, and other specialized references now come in low-cost CD-ROM versions—often with multimedia capability. More up-to-the-minute information is available from on-line services like CompuServe and Prodigy—services that are used regularly by hundreds of thousands of people. Of course, these information utilities also offer electronic mail and other communication services. But they're just a hint of the kinds of information services likely to be available to home users in a few years.

As computer technology and communication technology converge on the home market, they'll produce services that will threaten television and newspapers as our main sources of information. Television is a *broadcast* medium—it transmits news and information to broad audiences. In the future we'll see **narrowcasting** services—they'll provide custom newscasts aimed at narrow groups or individuals. Personalized multimedia news programs will combine many of the best features of television news and newspapers. You'll be able to request an index of available features and use it like a menu to build your own news program. Your personal newscast might include a piece on the latest Middle Eastern crisis, the results of yesterday's primary election, highlights of last night's Blazers vs. Bulls game, the scores in the college intramural games, this weekend's weather forecast at the coast, a feature on your favorite local musician, and a reminder that there are only five more shopping days until your mother's birthday. You'll be able to train your news service to flag particular subjects ("I'm especially interested in articles on the Amazon rain forest") and ignore others ("No heavy metal features, please"), so that even the menu is customized to suit your tastes. All of this is technologically possible now; prototype systems have been running for years at MIT's Media Lab.

Home Entertainment Redefined

Television has a "brightness" knob, but it doesn't seem to work.

—Gallagher, *stand-up comic*

You don't want a television with knobs marked "volume" and "brightness" and "contrast." You want a television with knobs marked "sex" and "violence" and "political bias."

—*Nicholas Negroponte*, *director of the MIT Media Lab*

Regardless of how people say they use home computers, surveys suggest that they use them mostly to play games. Computer games and video game machines (which are just special-purpose computers) represent a huge industry—one that is likely to evolve rapidly in the coming years.

Most computer games are simulations. Computer games can simulate board games, card games, sporting events, intergalactic battles, street fights, corporate takeovers, or something else, real or imaginary. Many require strategy and puzzle solving; others depend only on eye-hand coordination. Many of the most popular games require some of each. With dazzling graphics, digitized sound, and sophisticated effects, many of today's computer games represent state-of-the-art software. But in a few years these computer games are likely to look as primitive in a decade as those early Pong games look today.

The biggest changes in electronic games are likely to come as computers and communication technology converge on the home entertainment industry. As this happens, the line that separates television programs and computer games will grow fuzzy. A few years ago, software shops stocked a variety of **interactive fiction** games—stories with primitive natural-language interfaces that gave players some control over plot. Those nongraphic, not-very-intelligent programs have been squeezed off the software shelves by **interactive movies**—animated features in which one or more of the characters are controlled by the viewers. Today's interactive movies aren't Academy Award material; at best, they're like cartoons with controls. But as technology improves and the multimedia market grows, you can expect to see all kinds of hybrid forms of entertainment.

Computer games range from abstract arcade games like Super Tetris to interactive movies (where players control the characters' actions) like Indiana Jones and the Fate of Atlantis.

Creativity and Leisure

If you can talk, you can sing.
If you can walk, you can dance.

—*A saying from Zimbabwe*

Interactive movies demand more involvement than television, but they're still a relatively passive pastime. Many people worry that television, computer games, and other media are replacing too many real-world activities. Instead of making up stories to share, we watch sitcoms on TV. Instead of playing music on guitars, we play music on boom boxes. Instead of playing one-on-one basketball, we play one-on-one video games. Is electronic technology turning us into a couch-potato culture?

Perhaps. But there's another possibility. The same technology that mesmerizes us can also unlock our creativity. There are many examples: Word processors help many of us to become writers, graphics software brings out the artists among us, desktop publishing systems put the power of the press in more hands, electronic music systems allow us to compose music even if we never mastered an instrument, and multimedia systems open doors to cable-access TV channels.

Will computers drain our creativity or amplify it? In the end it's up to us. . . .

Rules of Thumb

The Concise Computer Consumer's Guide

Any brand-specific advice on choosing a computer is likely to be dated or obsolete within a few months, but some general principles remain constant while the technology races forward. Here are nine criteria to consider if and when you decide to buy a computer. They're worth knowing about even if you have no intention of buying your own machine.

- **Cost.** Obviously, this is the bottom line. Buy what you can afford, but be sure to allow for extra memory, extended warranties, peripherals (printer, hard disk, modem, cables, and so on) and, above all, software. If you join a user group or connect to electronic bulletin boards (see Chapter 7), you'll have access to software at low (or no) cost. There's plenty of good (and some not-so-good) public domain software and shareware available. But you'll almost certainly need some commercial software, too. Don't be tempted to copy copyrighted software from your friends or public labs; software piracy is theft, prosecutable under federal laws. (Choosing software isn't easy, but many of the periodicals listed at the end of Chapter 1 publish regular reviews to help you sort out the good stuff. If possible, try before you buy.)
- **Capability.** Is it the right tool for the job? If you plan to do color graphics, does your machine support color? If you plan to do desktop publishing, does the machine support graphics software? Be sure the machine you buy can do the job you need it to do, now and in the foreseeable future.
- **Capacity.** Buy a computer that's powerful enough to meet your needs. Make sure the processor is fast enough to handle your demands and that the memory and external storage capacity are sufficient for the jobs you'll be doing. Consult periodicals and software packages for minimum requirements.
- **Customizability.** Computers are versatile, but they don't all handle all jobs with equal ease. If you'll be using word processors, spreadsheets, and other mainstream software packages, just about any computer will do. If you have off-the-beaten-path needs (video editing, instrument monitoring, and so on), choose an *open system* (with slots and ports) that can be customized.
- **Compatibility.** Will the software you plan to use run on the computer you're considering? Most popular computers have a good selection of compatible software, but if you have specific needs, such as being able to take your software home to run on Mom's computer, study the compatibility issue carefully. Total compatibility isn't always possible or necessary. A typical IBM-compatible computer, for example, probably isn't

compatible with *every* program that will run on an IBM PS/2, but it will almost certainly run the mainstream applications that most users need. Many people don't care if all their programs will run on another kind of computer; they just need *data* compatibility—the ability to move documents back and forth between systems. Sometimes you can do this by saving the data on a disk and transporting the disk to another system. If that won't work, connectivity becomes an issue.

- **Connectivity.** Just about any computer can send and receive raw text through a modem or a network. But in the age of connectivity, it's not unusual for competing computers to be able to translate foreign file formats into readable documents. It's common, for example, for IBM users and Macintosh users to send documents back and forth over a network without any loss of data.
- **Convenience.** Just about any computer can do most common jobs, but which is the most convenient? Which has the user interface and physical design that you're most comfortable with? Which has the easiest-to-learn software? Which makes the kind of work *you'll* be doing easiest? For instance, will you need to be able to carry your computer easily?
- **Company.** If you try to save money by buying an off-brand computer, you may find yourself the owner of an orphan computer. High-tech companies can, and frequently do, vanish overnight. Make sure you'll be able to get service and parts down the road.
- **Curve.** Most models of personal computers seem to have a life span of less than 10 years—if they survive the first year or two. If you want to minimize your financial risk, avoid buying a computer during those early years in a model's life, when little compatible software is available. Also avoid buying a computer that's over the hill; you'll know it because most software developers will have abandoned this model for greener CPUs. In the words of Alexander Pope, "Be not the first by whom the new are tried, nor yet the last to lay the old aside."

Computer consumer's curve

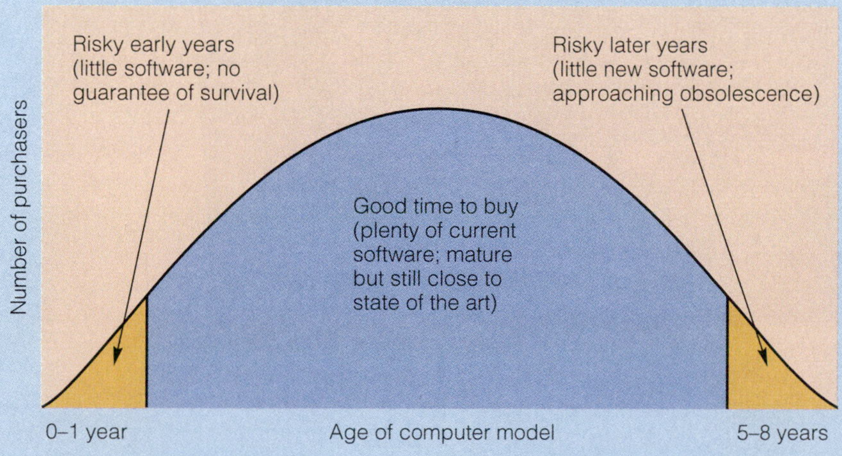

Summary

Our educational system was developed a century ago to train workers for life-long jobs. In the information age, when students can expect to change jobs several times, we need schools that teach technological familiarity, literacy, mathematics, culture, communication, and most importantly, the ability to learn and adapt to an ever-changing world.

Students use a variety of instructional tools in schools today, including

- *computer aided instruction (CAI)*—tutorials and/or drill-and-practice software covering concrete facts in specific subject areas
- *programming tools*—languages like LOGO, Pascal, and BASIC that allow students to design their own software
- *simulation and games*—artificial environments that allow students to learn through exploration, experimentation, and interaction with other students
- *productivity tools*—word processors, spreadsheets, and other real-world tools
- *computer-controlled media*—presentation graphics, hypermedia, interactive multimedia, and authoring tools that allow varying degrees of student control
- *distance learning tools*—telecommunication tools that allow students and teachers to communicate electronically without having to be in the same physical location

Clearly computer technology can have a positive educational impact, but computers alone can't guarantee improvement. Research, planning, teacher training, community involvement, and classroom restructuring should accompany new technology.

A small but growing number of people use home computers for basic business applications, education, information access, communication, entertainment, and creative pursuits. All these applications will radically change as the technology evolves over the next decade.

CHAPTER REVIEW

Key Terms

authoring tool
computer-aided instruction (CAI)
courseware
distance learning
drill-and-practice software
educational simulation
interactive fiction
interactive movie
narrowcasting
smart card
technophobia
tutorial software

Review Questions 

1. What were the goals of education in the industrial age? Which are still appropriate in the information age? Which are not?
2. What kind of an education does a student need to prepare for living and working in the information age?
3. How do educational simulation games differ from traditional computer-aided instruction? What are the advantages and disadvantages of each?
4. Describe how multimedia and hypermedia might be used by teachers and students in the classroom. Give several examples.
5. Give several examples of ways that distance learning can enhance education.
6. Technology alone is no guarantee that students will learn better or faster. What else is necessary to ensure success?
7. Describe several ways people use home computers.
8. What are smart cards, and how are they used?
9. What are interactive movies? In what ways do they combine computer technology with home entertainment technology?

Discussion Questions 

1. Socrates was illiterate and avoided the written word because he felt it weakened the mind. Similarly, many people today fear that we're weakening our children's minds by making them too dependent on computers and calculators. What do you think?
2. In many schools, students spend two years of math education learning long division—a skill that's almost never used in the age of the $5 calculator. Some educators argue that students' time could be better spent learning other things. What do you think? What about calculating square roots by hand?
3. Do you think it's important for students to learn to program in LOGO, Pascal, BASIC, or some other language? Why or why not?
4. Do you think educational games are good ways for students to learn in schools? Give examples that support your arguments.
5. What kind of productivity software tools should students learn how to use? Why?
6. Think about educational goals in relation to technology. What should people be able to do with no tools? What should people be able to do if they have access to pencils, papers, and books? What should people be able to do if they have access to computer technology?
7. Describe your past school experience in terms of technology. How did it measure up? What has been missing from your education so far?
8. Does the Project 2000 story about Tablet sound realistic? Desirable? Explain.
9. Do you think most families could benefit from a home computer today? Explain.
10. Do you think in the future home computers will make people more or less creative? Why?

Projects 

1. Try several different types of educational software. If possible, observe students using the software. Prepare a report comparing the strengths and weaknesses of each.
2. Observe how computers are used in local schools. Report on your findings.
3. Observe how computers are used on your campus. Report on your findings.
4. Using an authoring tool like HyperCard, design some courseware. Make sure you set clear goals before you start. When your project is completed, try it with several students.
5. Plan a model technology school. Describe how it would differ from conventional schools and why.
6. Using an authoring tool like HyperCard, design a work of interactive fiction. See how others react as they explore your work.

Sources and Resources 

The Technology Age Classroom, edited by Terence R. Cannings and LeRoy Finkel (1993, Franklin, Beedle, & Associates, Inc., 8536 W. St. Helens Drive, Suite D, Wilsonvile, OR 97070, 503/682-7668). This collection includes articles and papers by many of the experts in the field of technology in education. If you're interested in educational computing, you'll find this book to be an invaluable resource.

Advanced Technology in Education: An Introduction to Videodiscs, Robotics, Optical Memory, Peripherals, New Software Tools, and High-Tech Staff Development, by Royal Van Horn (Pacific Grove, CA: Brooks/Cole Publishing Company, 1991). The lengthy subtitle summarizes the contents of this well-written book for teachers and others interested in high-tech education.

Mindstorms: Children, Computers, and Powerful Ideas, by Seymour Papert (New York: Basic Books, 1980). An idealistic and influential exploration of the role of computers in education from the MIT designer of LOGO.

In Search of the Most Amazing Thing: Children, Education, & Computers, by Tom Snyder and Jane Parker (Reading, MA: Addison-Wesley, 1986). Tom Snyder is one of the foremost designers of educational computer games and simulations. This book is a surprisingly critical view of the use of computers in education. The material is a bit dated, but it's still worth reading.

The Computing Teacher, from ISTE (1787 Agate St., Eugene, OR 97403-1923, 800/336-5191, bitnet ISTE@Oregon). ISTE (International Society for Technology in Education) is an important and influential organization whose focus is the effective use of computer technology in the classroom. *The Computing Teacher* is their most accessible and widely read publication. ISTE is also the source for the *Vision: TEST* mentioned in this chapter.

Electronic Learning, from Scholastic, Inc. (PO Box 3025, Southeastern, PA 19398-9890) and *Technology & Learning* (2451 E. River Road, Dayton, OH 45439) are two other magazines full of features and news items related to technology in the classroom.

Academic Computing. This journal surveys the impact of computers on higher education.

T.H.E. Journal (Technological Horizons in Education) (150 El Camino Real, Suite 112, Tustin, CA 92680-3615, 714/730-4011, fax 714/730-3739). This magazine covers both K-12 and higher education with a mixture of product announcements and articles.

Family and Home Office Computing. This magazine is a good source of information about home personal computer applications.

Popular Science. This magazine is a good source of information on the latest computerized gadgets for consumers.

C H A P T E R

THIRTEEN

Computer Security and Risks

Kempelen's Amazing Chess-Playing Machine

Check.

—The only word ever spoken by Kempelen's chess-playing machine

In 1760 Wolfgang Kempelen, a 49-year-old Hungarian inventor, engineer, and advisor to the Court of Austrian Empress Maria Theresa, built a mechanical chess player. This amazing contraption defeated internationally renowned players and earned its inventor almost legendary fame.

A Turkish-looking automaton sat behind a big box that supported a chess board and chess pieces. The operator of the machine could open the box to "prove" there was nothing inside but a network of cogwheels, gears, and revolving cylinders. After every 12 moves, Kempelen wound the machine up with a huge key. Of course, the chess-playing machine was actually a clever hoax. The real chess player was a dwarf-sized person who controlled the mechanism from inside and was concealed by mirrors when the box was opened. The tiny player couldn't see the board, but he could tell what pieces were moved by watching magnets below the chess board.

Kempelen had no intention of keeping the deception going for long; he thought of it as a joke and dismantled it after its first tour. But he became a slave to his own fraud, as the public and the scientific community showered him with praise for

After reading this chapter you should be able to

- describe several types of computer crime and discuss possible crime-prevention techniques
- describe the major security issues facing computer users, computer system administrators, and law-enforcement officials
- describe how computer security relates to personal privacy issues
- describe how security and computer reliability are related

creating the first "machine-man." In 1780 the Emperor Joseph II ordered another court demonstration of the mechanical chess player, and Kempelen had to rebuild it. The chess player toured the courts of Europe, and the public became more curious and fascinated than ever.

After Kempelen died in 1804, the machine was purchased by the impresario Maelzel, who showed it far and wide. In 1809 it challenged Napoleon Bonaparte to play. When Napoleon repeatedly made illegal moves, the machine-man brushed the pieces from the table. Napoleon was delighted to have unnerved the machine. When he played the next game fairly, Napoleon was badly beaten.

The chess-playing machine came to America in 1826, where it attracted large, paying crowds. In 1834 two different articles—one by Edgar Allen Poe—revealed the secrets of the automated chess player. Poe's investigative article was insightful but not completely accurate; one of his 17 arguments was that a true automatic player would invariably win.

After Maelzel's death in 1837, the machine passed from hand to hand until it was destroyed by fire in Philadelphia in 1854. During the 70 years that the automaton was publicly exhibited, its "brain" was supplied by 15 different chess players who won 294 of 300 games.

With his elaborate and elegant deception, Kempelen might be considered the forerunner of the modern computer criminal. Kempelen was trapped in his fraud because the public wanted to believe that the automated chess player was real. Desire overtook judgment in thousands of people who were captivated by the idea of an intelligent machine.

More than two centuries later, we're still fascinated by intelligent machines. But modern computers don't just play games; they manage our money, our medicine, and our missiles. We're expected to trust information technology with our wealth, our health, and even our lives. The many benefits of our partnership with machines are clear. But blind faith in modern technology can be foolish and, in many cases, dangerous. In this chapter we'll examine some of the dark corners of our computerized society: legal dilemmas, ethical issues, and reliability risks. All of these issues are tied to a larger question: How can we make computers more secure, so that we can feel more secure in our daily dealings with them?

On-line Outlaws: Computer Crime

Computers are power, and direct contact with power can bring out the best or worst in a person.

—*Former computer criminal turned corporate computer programmer*

Like other professions, law enforcement is being transformed by information technology. The FBI's National Crime Information Center provides police with almost instant information on crimes and criminals nationwide. Investigators use PC databases to store and cross-reference clues in complex cases. Using pattern recognition technology, automated fingerprint identification systems locate matches in minutes rather than months. Computers routinely scan the New York and London stock exchanges for connections that might indicate

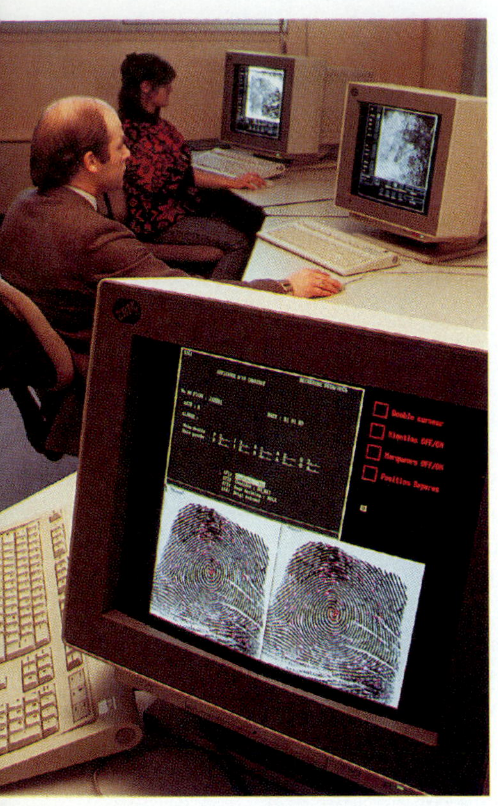

French police store fingerprints in digital records so they can be quickly catalogued and retrieved.

insider trading or fraud. All of these tools help law-enforcement officials ferret out criminals and stop criminal activities.

Like guns, computers are used to break laws as well as uphold them. Computers are powerful tools in the hands of criminals, and computer crime is a rapidly growing problem.

The Computer Crime Dossier

Some will rob you with a six gun,
and some with a fountain pen.

—Woody Guthrie, in *"Pretty Boy Floyd"*

Today the computer has replaced both the gun and the pen as the weapon of choice for many criminals. **Computer crime** is often defined as any crime accomplished through knowledge or use of computer technology.

Nobody knows the true extent of computer crime. Many computer crimes go undetected. Those that are detected often go unreported, because businesses fear that they can lose more from negative publicity than from the actual crimes. By conservative estimates, businesses and government institutions lose billions of dollars every year to computer criminals. According to the FBI, the average computer crime is worth about $600,000— far more than most other crimes. A single case of computer fraud cost the Volkswagen company in Germany more than $260 million in 1984.

Contrary to what the movies suggest, most computer crimes are committed by company insiders—clerks, cashiers, programmers, computer operators, and managers —who have no extraordinary technical ingenuity. The typical computer criminal is a trusted employee with no criminal record who is tempted by an opportunity, such as the discovery of a loophole in system security. Greed, financial worries, and personal problems motivate this person to give in to temptation.

Of course, not all computer criminals fit this description. Some are exemployees seeking revenge on their former bosses. Some are corporate or international spies seeking classified information. A few are high-tech pranksters looking for a challenge. Organized crime syndicates are even turning to computer technology to practice their trades. Sometimes entire companies are found guilty of computer fraud. For example, Equity Funding, Inc., used computers to generate thousands of false insurance policies that later were sold for over $27 million.

Theft by Computer

Theft is the most common form of computer crime. Computers are used to steal money, goods, information, and computer resources. Here are a few examples:

- A part-time college student used his touch-tone phone and personal computer to fool Pacific Telephone's computer into ordering phone equipment to be delivered to him. He started a business, hired several employees, and pilfered about a million dollars worth of equipment before he was turned in by a disgruntled employee. (After serving two months in jail, he became a computer security consultant.)
- In 1987 a former automated teller machine repairman illegally obtained $86,000 out of ATMs by spying on customers while they typed in passwords and creating bogus cards to use with the passwords.
- Clerks at an upscale department store erased the accounts of major customers by listing those customers as bankrupt. The customers paid the clerks 10 percent of the $33 million they saved by not having to repay their debts. Since the "bankruptcies" were only listed in the store's computers, they didn't hurt the customers' credit ratings.

- In 1988 several million dollars were illegally transferred to a private Swiss bank account. The transfer was noticed because on that particular day the bank happened to be manually checking transactions because of a computer glitch; the automated procedure normally used wouldn't have noticed the suspicious transaction.
- In 1992 a phone hacker used a dial-in maintenance line to crack the computerized phone system of a Detroit newspaper publisher. The hacker cracked the system administrator's pass code and set up scores of voice mailboxes for friends and associates who dialed in on the publisher's toll-free number. Fortunately, the scam cost the publisher only a few hundred dollars—a small sum when compared to the $1.4 million worth of illegal long-distance calls billed against one national manufacturing firm *in a single weekend.*
- Dozens of college campuses have reported cases of stolen computer time. A typical student scam is to create a program that mimics the mainframe computer's security program and remembers passwords when unsuspecting students type them in.

All of these crimes are expensive—for businesses, law-enforcement agencies, and taxpayers and consumers who ultimately must pay the bills. But as crimes go, the types of theft described so far are relatively uncommon. The same can't be said of the most widely practiced type of computer-related theft: software piracy.

Software Piracy and Intellectual Property Laws

Information wants to be free. Information also wants to be expensive. Information wants to be free because it has become so cheap to distribute, copy, and recombine—too cheap to meter. It wants to be expensive because it can be immeasurably valuable to the recipient. That tension will not go away.

—Stewart Brand, The Media Lab

Software piracy—the illegal duplication of copyrighted software—is rampant. Millions of computer users have made copies of programs they don't legally own. Now that most software companies have given in to user demands and removed physical copy protection from their products, copying software is as easy as duplicating a cassette tape or photocopying a book. Unfortunately, many people aren't aware that copying software, recorded music, and books can violate federal laws protecting intellectual property.

Intellectual property and the law. Legally the definition of **intellectual property** includes the results of intellectual activities in the arts, science, and industry. Copyright laws have traditionally protected forms of literary expression, patent law has protected mechanical inventions, and contract law has covered trade secrets. Software doesn't fit neatly into any of these categories under the law. Most commercial software programs are protected by copyright laws, but a few companies have successfully used patent laws to protect software products.

The purpose of intellectual property laws is to ensure that mental labor is justly rewarded and to encourage innovation. Programmers, inventors, scientists, writers, editors, and musicians depend on ideas and the expression of those ideas for their incomes. Ideas are information, and information is easy to copy. Intellectual property laws are designed to protect these professionals and encourage them to continue their creative efforts so society can benefit from their future work.

Unfortunately intellectual property laws are difficult to enforce. The software industry, with a world market of more than $50 billion a year, loses more than $10 billion annually to software pirates. Lotus estimates that more than half of the copies of its 1-2-3 spreadsheet program in use today are illegal copies. Piracy can be particularly hard on small software companies. Developing software is just as difficult for them as it is for big companies like Lotus and Microsoft, but they often lack the financial resources to cover their losses to piracy. Software industry organizations such as the Software Publishers Association are working with law-enforcement agencies to crack down on piracy. At the same time, they're stepping up educational programs to make computer users aware that piracy is theft. These organizations recognize that laws can't work without citizen understanding and support.

Existing copyright and patent laws, which evolved during the age of print and mechanical inventions, are outdated, contradictory, and inadequate for today's information technology. Recent laws, including the Computer Fraud and Abuse Act of 1984, clearly treat software piracy as a crime, but issues remain unresolved. Lawyers and judges aren't sure whether software should be protected by copyrights or patents. To complicate matters further, a few third-world nations refuse to abide by international copyright laws; they argue that the laws protect rich countries at the expense of underdeveloped nations.

Look-and-feel lawsuits. When it comes to software, nobody is sure exactly what is protected by law. Creating and selling an exact duplicate of a program clearly violates the law, but what about creating a program that has the "look and feel" of a successful software program? Can one software company legally sell a program that mimics the screen design and menu commands of a competing product? Is Microsoft Windows a rip-off of the Macintosh operating system? Did Borland steal the 1-2-3 command structure for its Quattro spreadsheet software? These questions, and others like them, were asked in recent federal cases. So far, judges have issued contradictory verdicts, leaving the fundamental look-and-feel question unanswered.

In matters of software the legal system is sailing in uncharted waters. Whether dealing with piracy or look-and-feel issues, lawmakers and judges must struggle with difficult questions about innovation, property, freedom, and progress. The questions are likely to be with us for quite a while.

Software Sabotage

Another type of computer crime is sabotage of hardware or software. The word *sabotage* comes from the early days of the industrial revolution, when rebellious workers shut down new machines by kicking wooden shoes, called sabots, into the gears. However, modern computer saboteurs commonly use software rather than footwear to do destructive deeds. The names given to the saboteurs' destructive programs—*viruses*, *worms*, and *Trojan horses*—sound more like biology than technology, and many of the programs even mimic the behavior of living organisms.

Trojan horses. A **Trojan horse** is a program that performs a useful task while at the same time carrying out some secret destructive act. As in the ancient story of the wooden horse that carried Greek soldiers through the gates of Troy, Trojan horse software hides an enemy in an attractive package. Trojan horse programs are often posted on public domain bulletin boards with names that make them sound like games or utilities. When an unsuspecting bargain hunter downloads and runs such a program, it might erase files, change data, or cause some other kind of damage. Some network saboteurs use Trojan horses to pass secret data to other unauthorized users. To compound the problem, many Trojan horses also carry software viruses.

Viruses. A biological virus is unable to reproduce by itself, but it can invade the cells of another organism and use the reproductive machinery of each host cell to make copies of itself; the new copies leave the host and seek out new hosts to repeat the

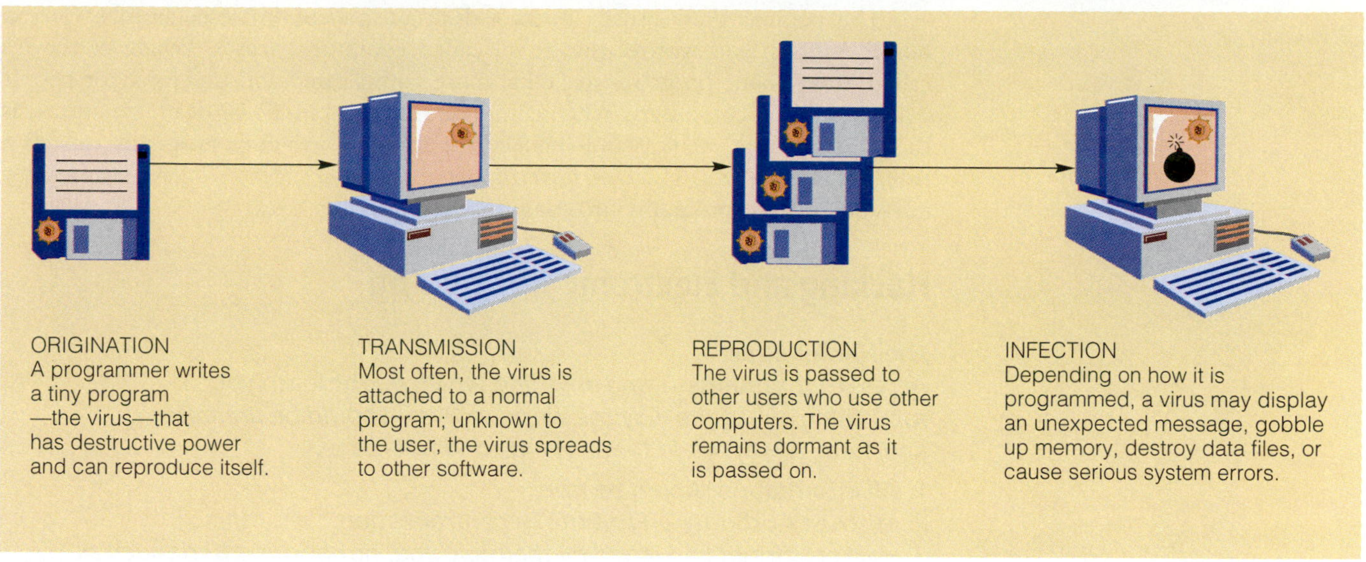

ORIGINATION
A programmer writes a tiny program —the virus—that has destructive power and can reproduce itself.
TRANSMISSION
Most often, the virus is attached to a normal program; unknown to the user, the virus spreads to other software.
REPRODUCTION
The virus is passed to other users who use other computers. The virus remains dormant as it is passed on.
INFECTION
Depending on how it is programmed, a virus may display an unexpected message, gobble up memory, destroy data files, or cause serious system errors.

How a virus works.

process. A software **virus** works in the same way: It spreads from program to program, or from disk to disk, and uses each infected program or disk to make more copies of itself. Virus software is usually hidden in the operating system of a computer or in an application program. Some viruses do nothing but reproduce; others display messages on the computer's screen; still others destroy data or erase disks. A virus is usually selective: Macintosh viruses invade only Macintosh disks, UNIX viruses invade only UNIX disks, and so on.

It takes a human programmer to create a virus, embed it in a piece of software, and release it to the world. Once that's done the virus can spread like an epidemic through shared software and disks, and it's almost impossible to completely eradicate. **Vaccine** (or **disinfectant**) **programs** are designed to search for viruses, notify users when they're found, and remove them from infected disks or files. Some antiviral programs continually monitor system activity, watching for and reporting suspicious virus-like actions. But no antiviral program can detect every virus, and these programs need to be frequently revised to combat new viruses as they appear.

Worms. Like viruses, **worms** (named for tapeworms) use computer hosts to reproduce themselves. But unlike viruses, worm programs travel *independently* over computer networks, seeking out uninfected workstations to occupy. A typical worm segment resides in a workstation's memory rather than on disk, so the worm can be eliminated by shutting down all of the workstations on the network. The most famous worm was created as an experiment by a Cornell graduate student in 1988. The worm was accidentally released onto the Internet, clogging 6000 computers all over the United States, almost bringing them to a complete standstill, and forcing operators to shut them all down so every worm segment could be purged from memory. The total cost, in terms of work time lost at research institutions, was staggering. The student was suspended from school and was the first person convicted of violating the Computer Fraud and Abuse Act.

Logic bombs. A **logic bomb** is a program triggered to act when it detects some sequence of events or after a certain amount of time elapses. For example, a programmer might plant a logic bomb that is designed to destroy data files if the programmer is ever listed as terminated in the company's personnel file. A widely publicized virus included a logic bomb that was programmed to destroy PC data files on Michelangelo's birthday in 1992.

The popular press usually doesn't distinguish between logic bombs, Trojan horses, viruses, and worms; they're all called computer viruses. Whatever they're called, these rogue programs make life more complicated and expensive for people who depend on computers. When computers are used in life-or-death situations, as they are in some medical and military applications, invading programs can even threaten human lives. The U.S. government and several states now have laws against introducing these programs into computer systems.

Hacking and Electronic Trespassing

The Hacker Ethic
Access to computers—and anything which might teach you something about the way the world works—should be unlimited and total. Always yield to the Hands-on Imperative.

1. *All information should be free.*
2. *Mistrust Authority—Promote Decentralization.*
3. *Hackers should be judged by their hacking, not bogus criteria such as degrees, age, race, or position.*
4. *You can create art and beauty on a computer.*
5. *Computers can change your life for the better.*

—Steven Levy, *Hackers: Heroes of the Computer Revolution*

I don't drink, smoke, or take drugs. I don't steal, assault people, or vandalize property. The only way in which I am really different from most people is in my fascination with the ways and means of learning about computers that don't belong to me.

—Bill "The Cracker" Landreth, *Out of the Inner Circle*

In the late 1970s, timesharing computers at Stanford and MIT attracted informal communities of computer fanatics who called themselves **hackers**. In those days a hacker was a person who enjoyed learning details of computer systems and writing clever programs, referred to as hacks. Hackers were, for the most part, curious, enthusiastic, intelligent, idealistic, eccentric, and harmless. Many of those early hackers were, in fact, architects of the microcomputer revolution.

Over the years the idealism of the early hacker communities was at least partly overshadowed by cynicism, as big-money interests took over the young personal computer industry. At the same time, the term *hacking* took on a new, more ominous, connotation in the media. While many people still use the term to describe software wizardry, it more commonly refers to unauthorized access to computer systems. Old-time hackers insist that this electronic trespassing is really "cracking," but the distinction between hacking and cracking isn't recognized by the general public or the popular media. Today's stereotypical hacker, like his early counterparts, is a young, bright, technically savvy, white, middle-class male. But in addition to programming his own computer, he may break into others.

Of course, not all young computer wizards break into computer systems, and not all electronic trespassers fit the media stereotype. Still, hackers aren't just a media myth; they're real, and there are lots of them. Electronic trespassers enter corporate and government computers using stolen passwords and security holes in operating system software. Sometimes they use modems to directly dial up the target computers; in other cases they "travel" to their destinations through Internet and other networks.

Cliff Stoll discovered an international computer espionage ring because of a 75-cent accounting error.

Some malicious hackers use Trojan horses, logic bombs, and other tricks of the trade to wreak havoc on corporate and government systems. More commonly, hackers are motivated just by curiosity and intellectual challenge; once they've cracked a system, they look around and move on without leaving any electronic footprints. Somewhere in between are hackers who break into systems to snoop for sensitive or valuable information to copy. This kind of theft is difficult to detect and track because the original information is left unchanged when the copy is stolen.

The most famous case of electronic trespassing was documented in Cliff Stoll's best-selling book, *The Cuckoo's Egg*. While working as a system administrator for a university computer lab in 1986, Stoll noticed a 75-cent accounting error. Rather than letting it go, Stoll investigated the error. He uncovered an intruder in the system—an intruder who was systematically searching government, corporate, and university computers across the Internet for sensitive military information. It took a year and some help from the FBI, but Stoll eventually located the hacker's home base in Germany. The interloper was a computer science student and part of a ring of hackers working for the KGB. Ironically, Stoll captured the thief by using standard hacker tricks, including a Trojan horse program that contained information on a fake SDI Net (Strategic Defense Initiative Network). As a result of the Cuckoo's Egg case, Stoll is widely recognized as an expert on computer security—the protection of computer systems and, indirectly, the people who depend on them.

Computer Security: Reducing Risks

Now, after sliding down this Alice-in-Wonderland hole, I find the political left and right reconciled in their mutual dependency on computers. The right sees computer security as necessary to protect national secrets; my leftie friends worry about an invasion of their privacy when prowlers pilfer data banks. Political centrists realize that insecure computers cost money when their data is exploited by outsiders.

The computer has become a common denominator that knows no intellectual, political, or bureaucratic bounds; the Sherwin Williams of necessity that covers the world, spanning all points of view.

—Cliff Stoll, The Cuckoo's Egg

With computer crime on the rise, computer security has become an important concern for system administrators and computer users alike. **Computer security** refers to protecting computer systems and the information they contain against unwanted access, damage, modification, or destruction. According to a 1991 report of the Congressional Research Service, computers have two inherent characteristics that leave them open to attack or operating error:

- A computer will do *exactly* what it is programmed to do, including revealing sensitive information. Any system that can be programmed can be reprogrammed by anyone with sufficient knowledge.
- Any computer can do *only* what it is programmed to do. ". . . it cannot protect itself from either malfunctions or deliberate attacks unless such events have been specifically anticipated, thought through, and countered with appropriate programming."

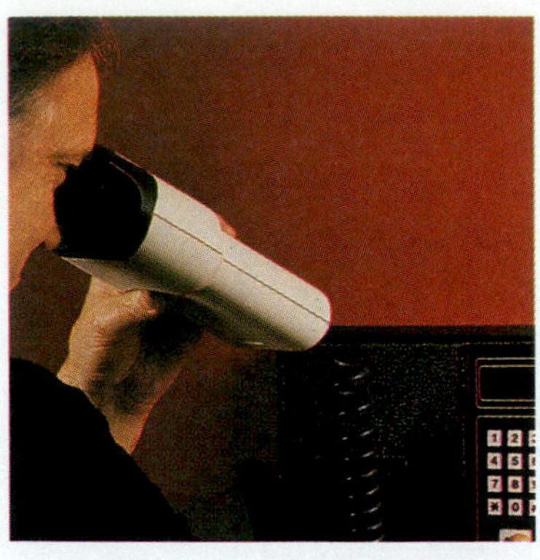

Retinal scans, like fingerprints, can be used to uniquely identify individuals.

Computer owners and administrators use a variety of security techniques to protect their systems, ranging from everyday low-tech locks to high-tech software scrambling.

Physical Access Restrictions

One way to reduce the risk of security breaches is to make sure that only authorized personnel have access to computer equipment. Organizations use a number of tools and techniques to identify authorized personnel. Some of these security checks can be performed by computer; others are used by human security guards. Depending on the security system, you might be granted access to a computer based on

- *something you have*—a key, an ID card with a photo, or a smart card containing digitally encoded identification (see Chapter 12 for a description of smart cards)
- *something you know*—a password, an ID number, a lock combination, or a piece of personal history, such as your mother's maiden name
- *something you do*— your signature or your typing speed and error patterns
- *something about you*—a voice print, fingerprints, retinal scans, or other measurements of individual body characteristics, known as **biometrics**

Since most of these security controls can be compromised—keys can be stolen, signatures can be forged, and so on—many systems use a combination of controls. For example, an employee might be required to show a badge, unlock a door with a key, and type a password to use a secured computer.

In the days when corporate computers were isolated in basements, physical restrictions were sufficient for keeping out intruders. But in the modern office, computers and data are almost everywhere, and networks connect computers to the outside world. In a distributed, networked environment, security is much more problematic. It's not enough to restrict physical access to mainframes when personal computers and network connections aren't restricted. Additional security techniques—most notably passwords—are needed to restrict access to remote computers.

Passwords

Passwords are the most common tool for restricting access to computer systems. Passwords are effective, however, only if they're chosen carefully. Most computer users choose passwords that are easy to guess: names of partners, children, or pets; words related to jobs or hobbies; and consecutive characters on keyboards. One survey found that the two favorite passwords in Britain were "Fred" and "God"; in America they were "love" and "sex." Hackers know and exploit these clichés; cautious users avoid them. A growing number of security systems refuse to allow users to choose *any* real words or names as passwords, so hackers can't use dictionary software to guess them systematically. Even the best passwords should be changed frequently.

Access-control software doesn't need to treat all users identically. Many systems use passwords to restrict users so they can open only files related to their work. In many cases users are allowed read-only access to files that they can see but not change.

To prevent unauthorized use of stolen passwords by outsiders, many companies use *call-back systems*. When a user logs in and types a password, the system hangs up, looks up the user's phone number, and calls back before allowing access.

Scrambling, Shielding, and Auditing

Many data thieves do their work without breaking into computer systems; they intercept messages as they travel between computers on networks. Passwords are of little use for hiding electronic mail messages while they're bouncing off of satellite dishes or traveling through Internet links. To protect transmitted information, many government and business organizations use **encryption** software to scramble their transmissions.

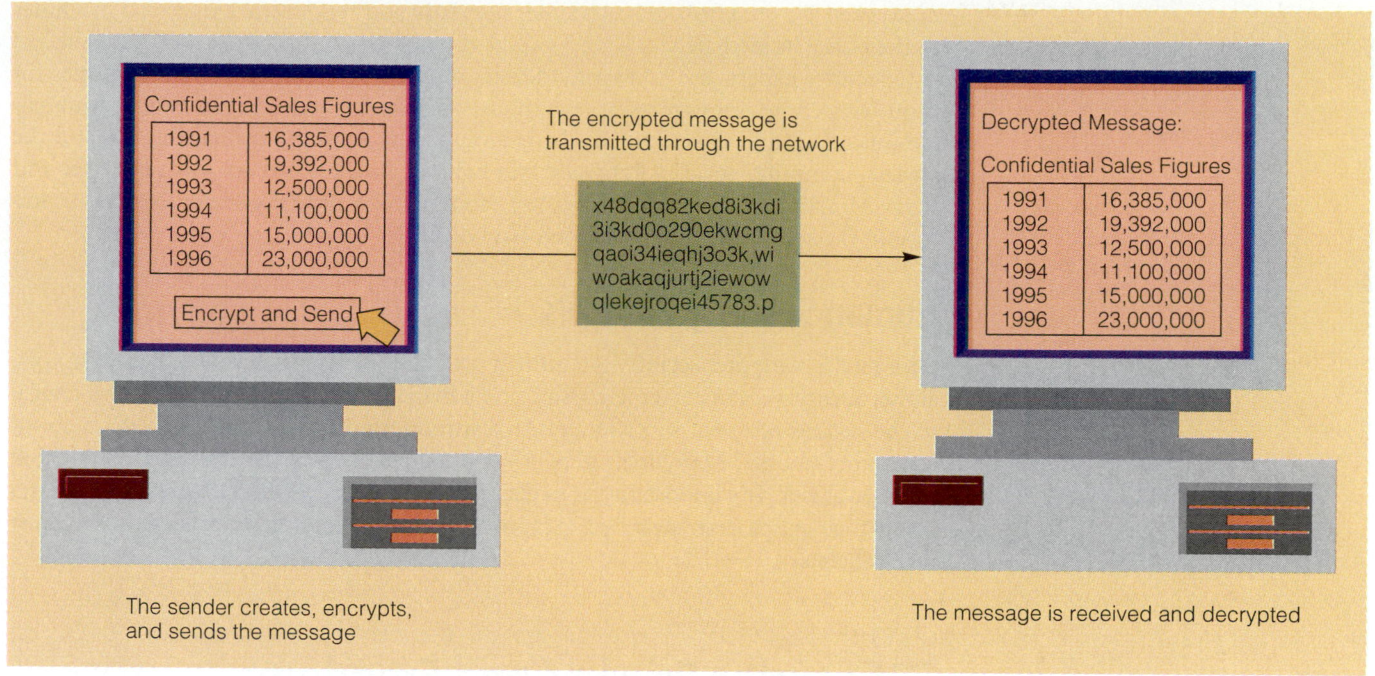

The encryption process.

When a user encrypts a message by applying a secret numerical code, called an *encryption key*, the message can be transmitted or stored as an indecipherable garble of characters. The message can be read only after it's been reconstructed with a matching key.

For the most sensitive information, passwords and encryption aren't enough. A diligent spy can "listen to" the electromagnetic signals that emanate from the computer hardware and, in some cases, read sensitive information. To prevent spies from using these spurious broadcasts, the Pentagon is spending $200 million on a program called *Tempest* to develop specially shielded machines.

Audit-control software is used to monitor and record computer transactions as they happen, so auditors can trace and identify suspicious computer activity after the fact. Effective audit control software forces every user, legitimate or otherwise, to leave a trail of electronic footprints. Of course, this kind of software is of little value unless someone in the organization monitors and interprets the output.

Making Backups

Even the tightest security system can't guarantee absolute protection of data. Sabotage, human errors, power losses, machine failures, fire, flood, lightning, and earthquakes can damage or destroy computer data along with hardware. Any complete security system must include some kind of plan for recovering from disasters. For mainframes and PCs alike, the best and most widely used data recovery insurance is a system of making regular **backups**. For many systems, data and software are backed up automatically onto disks or tapes, usually at the end of each work day. Most data processing shops keep several *generations* of backups so they can, if necessary, go back several days, weeks, or years to reconstruct data files. For maximum security many computer users keep copies of sensitive data in several different locations.

Emerging Security Solutions

The migration from mainframes to personal computers is forcing experts to explore new security solutions. The PC's small size and physical accessibility can make it easy for criminals to steal the computer along with its data. Computer crime expert Donn Parker has suggested that companies install automated alarm systems that allow networked PCs to check on each other regularly and report any kidnapped machines to the police immediately.

Security experts are constantly developing new technologies and techniques for protecting computer systems from computer criminals. But at the same time, criminals continue to refine their craft. In the ongoing competition between the law and the lawless, computer security generally lags behind. In the words of Tom Forester and Perry Morrison in *Computer Ethics*, ". . . computer security experts are forever trying to shut the stable door after the horse has bolted."

Human Security Controls

Ultimately, computer security is a human problem that can't be solved by technology alone. Security is a management issue, and a manager's actions and policies are critical to the success of a security program. An alarming number of companies are lax about computer security. Many managers don't understand the problems and don't think they are at risk. It's important for managers to understand where the real threats are, make their employees aware of the problems, and build effective defenses against those threats.

Security, Privacy, and Freedom: The Delicate Balance

Once, our computers were isolated, much as eighteenth-century villages were. Little was exchanged, and each developed independently. Now we've built far-flung electronic neighborhoods. These communities are built on trust: people believing that everyone profits by sharing resources.

—*Cliff Stoll*

It's hard to overstate the importance of computer security in our networked world. Viruses, worms, illegal interlopers, and crooked co-workers can erode trust and make life on-line difficult for everyone. But some managers have discovered that computer security measures can create problems of their own. Complex access procedures, virus-protection programs, and other security measures can, if carried too far, interfere with people getting their work done. In the extreme, security can threaten individual human rights.

When Security Threatens Privacy

We discussed privacy issues earlier in the book: threats to personal privacy caused by corporate and government databases (Chapter 6), and threats to the individual privacy of workers due to various types of computer monitoring (Chapter 12). When security measures are used to prevent computer crime, they usually help protect privacy rights at the same time. When a hacker invades a computer system, legitimate users of the system might have their private communications monitored by the intruder. When an outsider breaks into the database of a bank, the privacy of every bank customer is at risk. The same applies to government computers, credit bureau computers, and any other computer containing data on private citizens. The security of these systems is important for protecting people's privacy.

But in some cases security and law enforcement can pose threats to personal privacy. Here are some examples:

- In 1990 Alana Shoar, electronic-mail coordinator for Epson America, Inc., found stacks of printouts of employee e-mail messages in her boss's office—messages that employees believed were private. Shortly after confronting her boss, she was fired for "gross misconduct and insubordination." She filed a class-action suit, claiming that Epson routinely monitored all e-mail messages. Company officials denied the charges but took a firm stand on their right to any information stored, sent to, or taken from their business computers.
- In 1990 the Communication Workers of America sued Northern Telecom, Inc., for illegally bugging employee conference rooms and telephones. In 1992 Northern Telecom became the first major American employer to ban all covert monitoring of communications.
- Colonel Oliver North and his collaborators carefully shredded hundreds of paper documents detailing the sale of arms to Iran and the illegal channeling of profits to Nicaraguan Contras. But they were implicated in the Iran-Contra scandal anyway when investigators examined backup copies of "private" electronic-mail messages stored in their computer system.
- In 1992 the FBI proposed federal legislation requiring new ISDN phone systems to include switches that are "safe for electronic surveillance." This legislation would protect the FBI's ability to wiretap at the expense of individual privacy. Ironically the FBI's proposal would also ensure that criminals could continue to perform illegal wiretaps.

One of the best examples of a new technology that can simultaneously improve security and threaten privacy is the **active badge** (sometimes called the *smart badge*). Researchers at the University of Cambridge and nearby Olivetti Research Center are developing and wearing microprocessor-controlled badges that broadcast infrared identification codes every 15 seconds. Each badge's code is picked up by a nearby network receiver and transmitted back to a badge-location database that is constantly being updated. Active badges are used for identifying, finding, and remembering:

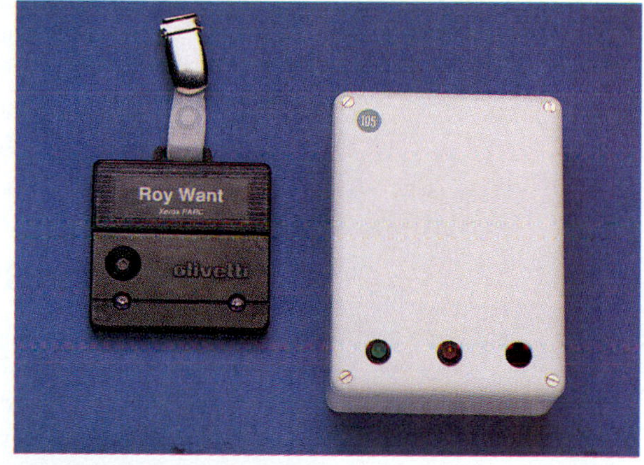

An active badge (left) transmits signals that are picked up by one of many network sensors.

- *Identifying.* When an authorized employee approaches a door, the door recognizes the person's badge code and opens. Whenever anyone logs into a computer system, the badge code identifies the person as an authorized or unauthorized user.
- *Finding.* An employee can check a computer screen to locate another employee and find out who that person is talking to. With active badges, there's no need for a paging system, and "while you were away" notes are less common.
- *Remembering.* At the end of the day, an active-badge wearer can get a minute-by-minute printout listing exactly where he's been and whom he's been with.

Is the active badge a primitive version of the Star Trek communicator or a surveillance tool for Big Brother? The technology has the potential to be either or both; it all depends on how people use it. Active badges, like other security devices and techniques, raise important legal and ethical questions about privacy—questions that we, as a society, must resolve sooner or later.

Justice on the Electronic Frontier

Federal and state governments have responded to the growing computer crime problem by creating new laws against electronic trespassing and escalating enforcement efforts. Hackers have become the target of nationwide anticrime operations. Dozens of hackers have been arrested for unauthorized entry into computer systems and for releasing destructive viruses and worms. Many have been convicted under federal or state laws. Others have had their computers confiscated with no formal charges filed.

Some of the victims of these sting operations claim that they broke no laws. In one case computers, software, and products were confiscated from a role-playing game company because one of their employees was an exhacker, and one of their games had a hacker theme. The financially crippled company was forced to lay off half its staff before the confiscated goods were finally returned; no charges were ever filed. The company sued the government for damages and won. In another case a student was arrested because he published an electronic magazine that carried a description of an emergency 911 system allegedly stolen by hackers. Charges were eventually dropped when it was revealed that the "stolen" document was, in fact, available to the public. These cases and others like them have raised questions about how civil rights apply in the "electronic frontier." How does the Bill of Rights apply to computer communications? Does freedom of the press apply to on-line magazines in the same way it applies to paper periodicals? Can an electronic bulletin board operator be held responsible for information others post on the BBS?

Even without answers to these questions, law-enforcement officials must continue to fight computer crime. Malicious hackers, worms, and viruses pose serious threats to our computerized society, and these threats can't be ignored. But even if every law-breaking hacker were arrested, computer crime would still be a major problem. The overwhelming majority of computer crimes are committed by insiders who are seldom reported to authorities, even when they are caught in the act. To avoid embarrassment, many companies cover up the computer crimes committed by their own employees and managers. As a result, law-enforcment agencies spend disproportionate amounts of time and money pursuing teenage hackers who represent a small part of the computer crime population. Experts agree that computer crime is likely to continue to grow unless corporations and government agencies recognize the importance of security on the inside as well as the outside.

Security and Reliability

So far our discussion of security has focused mainly on protecting computer systems from trespassing, sabotage, and other crimes. But security involves more than criminal activity. Some of the most important security issues have to do with creating systems that can withstand software errors and hardware glitches.

Bugs and Breakdowns

If the automobile had followed the same development cycle as the computer, a Rolls Royce would today cost $100, get a million miles per gallon, and explode once a year, killing everyone inside.

—*Robert X. Cringely*, InfoWorld

Computer systems, like all machines, are vulnerable to fires, floods, and other natural disasters, as well as breakdowns caused by failure of hardware components. But in modern computers, hardware problems are relatively rare when compared with software failures. In Chapters 3 and 9 we discussed the problems of creating reliable software and the insidious nature of computer bugs. By any measure, bugs do more damage than viruses and computer burglars put together.

Given the state of the art of software engineering today, three facts are clear:

- *It's impossible to eliminate all bugs.* Today's programs are constructed of thousands of tiny pieces, any one of which can cause a failure if it's incorrectly coded.

- *Even programs that appear to work can contain dangerous bugs.* Some bugs are easy to detect and correct because they're obvious. The most dangerous bugs are difficult to detect and may go unnoticed by users for months or years.
- *The bigger the system, the bigger the problem.* Large programs are far more complex and difficult to debug than small programs, and the trend today is clearly toward large programs.

As we entrust complex computerized systems to do everything from financial transaction processing to air traffic control, the potential cost of computer failure goes up. In the last decade researchers have identified hundreds of cases in which disruptions to computer system operations posed some risk to the public, and the number of incidents has doubled every two years.

Computers at War

Knowledge is power and permits the wise to conquer without bloodshed and to accomplish deeds surpassing all others.

—*Sun Tzu, Chou dynasty philosopher and military strategist, The Art of War (4th century BC)*

Nowhere are the issues surrounding security and reliability more critical than in military applications. To carry out its mission effectively, the military must be sure its systems are secure against enemy surveillance and attack. At the same time, many modern military applications push the limits of information technology farther than they've ever been before.

Smart weapons. The United States has invested billions of dollars in the development of **smart weapons**—missiles that use computerized guidance systems to locate their targets. A *command-guidance system* allows a human operator to control the missile's path while watching a missile's-eye-view of the target on a television screen. A missile with a *homing guidance system* can track a moving target without human help, using infrared heat-seeking devices or visual pattern recognition technology. Weapons that use "smart" guidance systems can be extremely accurate in pinpointing enemy targets under most circumstances. In theory, smart weapons can greatly reduce the amount of civilian destruction in war, although there's little evidence that this will actually occur in real battles.

One problem with high-tech weapons is that they reduce the amount of time people have to make life-and-death decisions. As decision-making time goes down, the chance of errors goes up. For example, an American guided missile cruiser on a peacetime mission in the Persian Gulf used a computerized Aegis fleet defense system to shoot down an Iranian Airbus containing 290 civilians. The decision to fire was made by humans, but those humans had little time—and used ambiguous data—to make the decision.

Autonomous systems. Even more controversial is the possibility of people being left out of the decision-making loop altogether. Yet the trend in military research is clearly toward weapons that demand almost instantaneous responses—the kind that only computers can make. An **autonomous system** is a complex system that can

Rules of Thumb

Practicing Safe Computing

Even if you're not building a software system for SDI or the FBI, computer security is important. Viruses, disk crashes, system bombs, and miscellaneous disasters can destroy your work, your peace of mind, and possibly your system. Fortunately you can protect your computer, your software, and your data from most hazards.

- **Share with care.** A computer virus is a contagious disease that spreads when it comes in contact with a compatible file or disk. Viruses spread rapidly in environments where disks and files are passed around freely, as they are in many student computer labs. To protect your data, keep your disks to yourself and don't borrow disks from others. When you *do* share a disk, physically write-protect it (by covering the square notch if it's a 5¼-inch disk or by uncovering the square hole if it's a 3½-inch disk) so a virus can't attach to it.
- **Beware of BBSs bearing gifts** Many viruses hide in Trojan horse programs on bulletin boards and on disks. Treat public domain programs and shareware with care; test them with a disinfectant program before you install them on your hard disk.
- **Don't pirate software.** Even commercial programs can be infected with viruses. Shrink-wrapped, virgin software is much less likely to be infected than pirated copies. Besides, software piracy is theft, and the legal penalties can be severe.
- **Disinfect regularly.** Virus protection programs are available for IBM-compatibles, Macintoshes, and other popular systems. Some are even free. Use up-to-date virus protection software regularly if you work in a high-risk environment.
- **Treat your diskettes as if they contain something important.** Keep them away from liquids, dust, pets, and (especially) magnets.
- **If you're using a password-protected system, take your password seriously.** Choose a password that's not easily guessable, not in any dictionary, and not easy for others to remember. Don't post it by your computer and don't type it when you're being watched. Change your password every few weeks—more often if you have any reason to suspect it has been discovered.
- **If it's sensitive, lock it up.** If your computer is accessible to others, protect your private files with passwords and/or encryption. Several popular disk utilities include options for adding password protection and encrypting files. If others need to see the files, lock them so they can be read but not changed or deleted. If secrecy is critical, don't store the data on your hard disk at all. Store it on diskettes and keep those diskettes under lock and key.
- **If it's important, back it up.** Regularly make backup copies of every important file on different disks than the original. Keep copies of critical disks in different locations so that you have backups in case disaster strikes.
- **Prepare for the worst.** Even if you take every precaution, things can still go wrong. Make sure you aren't completely dependent on the computer for really important things.

assume almost complete responsibility for a task without human input, verification, or decision making.

The most famous and controversial autonomous system is the Strategic Defense Initiative (SDI)—Ronald Reagan's proposed "Star Wars" system for shielding the United States from nuclear attack. The SDI system, as planned, would have used a network of laser-equipped satellites and ground-based stations to detect and destroy attacking missiles shortly after launch, before they had time to reach their targets. Because it must respond almost instantaneously, SDI must have been able to react automatically, without human intervention. If they sensed an attack, these system computers would have no time to wait for the President to declare war; in carrying out their mission, they'd effectively be declaring war themselves.

SDI generated intense public debates about false alarms, hardware feasibility, constitutional issues, and the ethics of autonomous weapons. But for many who understand the limitations of computers, the biggest issue is software reliability. SDI's software system would require over 10 million lines of code—more than are in any system ever developed. The system couldn't be completely tested in advance, because there's no way to simulate accurately the unpredictable conditions of a global war. Yet to work effectively, the system would have to be absolutely reliable. In a tightly coupled worldwide network, a single bug could multiply and expand like a speed-of-light cancer. A small error could result in a major disaster. Many software engineers have pointed out that absolute reliability simply isn't possible now or in the foreseeable future.

The Clinton administration has shelved SDI in favor of a land-based missile defense system, but software reliability issues still remain. Supporters argue that the technical difficulties can be overcome in time, and the U.S. government continues to invest billions in research toward that end. Whether or not "smart shield" is ever completed, it has focused public attention on critical issues related to security and reliability. In a world where computers control everything from money to missiles, computer security and reliability are too important to ignore.

Is Security Possible?

Computer thieves. Hackers. Software pirates. Computer snoopers. Viruses. Worms. Trojan horses. Logic bombs. Wiretaps. Hardware failures. Software bugs. When we live and work with computers, we're exposed to all kinds of risks that didn't exist in the pre-computer era. These risks make computer security especially important and challenging.

Because computers do so many amazing things so well, it's easy to overlook the problems they bring with them and to believe that they're invincible. But like Kempelen's chess-playing machine, today's computers hide the potential for errors and deception under an impressive user interface. This doesn't mean we should avoid using computers, only that we should remain skeptical, cautious, and realistic as we use them. Security procedures can reduce, but not eliminate risks. In today's fast-moving world, absolute security simply isn't possible.

≡ Summary

Computers play an ever-increasing role in fighting crime. At the same time, law-enforcement organizations are facing an increase in computer crime—crimes accomplished through special knowledge of computer technology. Most computer crimes go undetected, and those that are detected often go unreported. But by any estimate, computer crime costs billions of dollars every year.

Some computer criminals use computers, modems, and other equipment to steal goods, money, information, software, and services. Others use Trojan horses, viruses, worms, logic bombs, and other software tricks to sabotage systems. According to the media, computer crimes are committed by young, bright, computer-wizards called hackers. Research suggests, however, that hackers are responsible for only a small fraction of the computer crimes committed. The typical computer criminal is a trusted employee with personal or financial problems and knowledge of the computer system. The most common computer crime, software piracy, is committed by millions of people, often unknowingly. Piracy is a violation of intellectual property laws, which, in many cases, lag far behind the technology.

Because of rising computer crime and other risks, organizations have developed a number of computer security techniques to protect their systems and data. Some security devices, like keys and badges, are designed to restrict physical access to computers. But these tools are becoming less effective in an age of personal computers and networks. Passwords, encryption, shielding, and audit-control software are all used to protect sensitive data in various organizations. When all else fails, backups of important data are used to reconstruct systems after damage occurs. The most effective security solutions depend on people at least as much as technology.

Normally security measures serve to protect our privacy and other individual rights. But occasionally security procedures threaten those rights. The tradeoffs between computer security and freedom raise important legal and ethical questions.

Computer systems aren't just threatened by people; they're also threatened by software bugs and hardware glitches. An important part of security is protecting systems, and the people affected by those systems, from the consequences of those bugs and glitches. Since our society uses computers for many applications that put lives at stake, reliability issues are especially important. In modern military applications, security and reliability are critical. As the speed, power, and complexity of weapons systems increase, many fear that humans are being squeezed out of the decision-making loop. The debate over high-tech weaponry is bringing many important security issues to the public's attention for the first time.

CHAPTER REVIEW

Key Terms

access-control software
active badge
audit-control software
autonomous system
backup
biometrics
computer crime
computer security
encryption
hacker
intellectual property
logic bomb
smart weapon
software piracy
Trojan horse
vaccine (disinfectant) program
virus
worm

Review Questions

1. Why is it hard to estimate the extent of computer crime?
2. Describe the typical computer criminal. How does he or she differ from the media stereotype?
3. What is the most common computer crime? Who commits it? What is being done to stop it?
4. What are intellectual property laws, and how do they apply to software?
5. Describe several different types of programs that can be used for software sabotage.
6. What are the two inherent characteristics of computers that make security so difficult?
7. Describe several different computer security techniques and explain the purpose of each.
8. In what ways can computer security protect the privacy of individuals? In what ways can computer security threaten the privacy of individuals?
9. What are smart weapons? How do they differ from conventional weapons? What are the advantages and risks of smart weapons?

Discussion Questions

1. Are computers morally neutral? Explain your answer.
2. Suppose Whizzo Software Company produces a program that looks, from the user's point of view, exactly like the immensely

popular BozoWorks from Bozo, Inc. Whizzo insists that they didn't copy any of the code in BozoWorks; they just tried to design a program that would appeal to BozoWorks users. Bozo cries foul and sues Whizzo for violation of intellectual property laws. Do you think the laws should favor Bozo's arguments or Whizzo's? Why?

3. What do you suppose motivates people to create computer viruses and other destructive software? What do you think motivates hackers to break into computer systems? Are the two types of behavior related?
4. Would you like to work in a business where all employees were required to wear active badges? Explain your answer.
5. How do the issues raised in the debate over SDI apply to other large software systems? How do you feel about the different issues raised in the debate?

Projects 

1. Talk to employees at your campus computer labs and computer centers about security issues and techniques. What are the major security threats according to these employees? What security techniques are used to protect the equipment and data in each facility? Are these techniques adequate? Report on your findings.
2. Perform the same kind of interviews at local businesses. Do businesses view security differently than your campus personnel?

Sources and Resources 

Computer Ethics: Cautionary Tales and Ethical Dilemmas in Computing, by Tom Forester and Perry Morrison (Cambridge, MA: MIT Press, 1994). Forester and Morrison don't mince words as they discuss the important issues that face computer professionals and users today. This concise book is rich with real-world examples of computer crime, security breaches, reliability risks, and privacy threats. This is an outstanding survey at a reasonable price.

Hackers: Heroes of the Computer Revolution, by Steven Levy (New York: Doubleday, 1984). This book helped bring the word *hackers* into the public's vocabulary. Levy's entertaining account of the golden age of hacking gives a historical perspective to today's anti-hacker mania.

Out of the Inner Circle: A Hacker's Guide to Computer Security, by Bill Landreth (Redmond, WA: Microsoft Press, 1985). Confessions of a hacker who was caught. This book tells secrets that can help the rest of us protect our computers from attack.

The Cuckoo's Egg, by Cliff Stoll (New York: Pocket Books, 1989, 1990). This best-selling book documents the stalking of an interloper on Internet. International espionage mixes with computer technology in this entertaining, engaging, and eye-opening book.

Cyberpunk—Outlaws and Hackers on the Computer Frontier, by Katie Hafner and John Markoff (New York: Simon & Schuster, 1992). This book profiles three hackers whose exploits caught the public's attention: Kevin Mitnick, a California cracker who vandalized corporate systems; Pengo, who penetrated U.S. systems for East German espionage purposes; and Robert Morris, Jr., whose Internet worm brought down 6000 computers in a matter of hours.

Computers Under Attack, edited by Peter Denning (Reading, MA: ACM Press, 1990). A wide-ranging collection of articles about computer security, hacking, and the network community. This book goes into detail on the Internet worm, computer viruses, and other security-related issues.

The Hacker Crackdown: Law and Disorder on the Electronic Frontier, by Bruce Sterling (New York: Bantam Books, 1992). Famed cyberpunk author Sterling turns to nonfiction to tell both sides of the story of the escalating war between hackers and federal law-enforcement agencies. If you're interested in the hacker controversy, this book is a good read.

The CPSR Newsletter, published by Computer Professionals for Social Responsibility (P.O. Box 717, Palo Alto, CA 94302, 415/322-3778, fax 415/322-3798, e-mail: cpsr@csli.stanford.edu). An alliance of computer scientists and others interested in the impact of computer technology on society, CPSR works to influence public policies to ensure that computers are used wisely in the public interest. Their newsletter has intelligent articles and discussions of risk, reliability, privacy, security, human rights, work, war, education, the environment, democracy, and other subjects that bring together computers and people.

EFFector, published by the Electronic Frontier Foundation (155 Second St., Cambridge, MA 02141, 617/864-0665, fax 617/864-0866, e-mail: effnews-request@eff.org). This electronic newsletter is distributed by EFF, an organization "established to help civilize the electronic frontier." EFF was founded by Mitch Kapor (see Chapter 5) and John Perry Barlow to protect civil rights and encourage responsible citizenship on the electronic frontier of computer networks.

The Fool's Run, by John Camp (New York: Henry Holt and Co., 1989; New York: Signet Books, 1990). This white-knuckle novel by a seasoned journalist explores the world of computer networks through a frightening story of high-tech capitalist espionage. It's fiction, but the network security issues are all too real.

CHAPTER
FOURTEEN

Inventing the Future

After reading this chapter you should be able to

- describe several trends in information technology that are likely to continue for a few more years
- describe several research areas that may produce breakthroughs in computer technology in the next few decades
- predict how the coming information infrastructure will affect our lives, our work, and our global economy
- describe some of the social and psychological risks of the information age
- speculate about the long-term future of the information age

Alan Kay Invents the Future

The best way to predict the future is to invent it.

—Alan Kay

Alan Kay has been inventing the future for most of his life. Kay was a child prodigy who grew up in a world rich with books, ideas, music, and interesting people. As a child he composed original music, built a harpsichord, and appeared on NBC as a "Quiz Kid." Kay's genius wasn't reflected in his grades; he had trouble conforming to the rigid structure of the schools he attended. After high school he worked as a jazz guitarist and an Air Force programmer before attending college.

His Ph.D. project was one of the first microcomputers, and one of several that Kay would eventually develop. In 1968 Kay was in the audience when Douglas Engelbart stunned the computer science world with a futuristic demonstration of interactive computing (see Chapter 8). Inspired by Engelbart's demonstration, Kay led a team of researchers at Xerox PARC (Palo Alto Research Center in California) in building the computer of the future—a computer that put the user in charge.

Working on a back-room computer called the Alto, Kay developed a bit-mapped screen display with icons and overlapping windows—the kind of display that has become standard two decades later. Kay also championed the idea of a friendly user interface. To test user-friendliness, Kay frequently brought children into the lab, "because they have no strong motivation for patience." With feedback from children, Kay developed the first painting program and Smalltalk, the groundbreaking object-oriented programming language.

Alan Kay

In essence, Kay's team developed the first personal computer—a single-user desktop machine designed for interactive use. But Kay, who coined the term *personal computer*, didn't see the Alto as one. In his mind a true personal computer could go everywhere with its owner, serving as a calculator, a calendar, a word processor, a graphics machine, a communication device, and a reference tool. Kay's vision of what he called the *DynaBook* is only now, almost three decades later, appearing on the horizon.

Xerox failed to turn the Alto into a commercial success. But when he visited PARC, Apple CEO Steve Jobs (see Chapter 12) was inspired by what he saw. Under Jobs a team of engineers and programmers built on the Xerox ideas, added many of their own, and developed the Macintosh—the first inexpensive personal computer to incorporate many of Kay's far-reaching ideas. Kay later called the Macintosh "the first personal computer good enough to criticize." The success of the Macintosh has since forced other PC manufacturers to adopt similar user interfaces.

Today Kay works as a research fellow for Apple, where he serves as a resident visionary. Kay continues his crusade for users, especially small users. He says, ". . . as with pencil and paper, it's not a medium if children can't use it." In the Vivarium Project, Kay and MIT researchers work with schoolchildren to design artificial life forms in artificial environments inside the computer. As students use experimental software tools to construct these life forms and environments, they learn about ecology and computers at the same time. Meanwhile the researchers study the children for insights into the human-machine interface. Like all of Kay's work, Vivarium is a long-term project with little relationship to today's computer market. This kind of blue-sky research doesn't always lead to products or profits. But for Alan Kay it's the way to invent the future.

The future is being invented every day by people like Alan Kay—people who can see today the technology that will be central to tomorrow's society. We're racing into a future shaped by information technology. Throughout this book we've focused on our current position in the information technology stream with an occasional glance downstream. In this chapter we'll take a longer look ahead. We'll imagine how information technology might evolve, and how that technology might affect our lives.

Tomorrow Never Knows

It is the unexpected that always happens.

—*Old English proverb*

There is no denying the importance of the future. In the words of scientist Charles F. Kettering, "We should be concerned about the future because we will have to spend the rest of our lives there." However, important or not, the future isn't easy to see.

The Hazards of Predicting the Future

Everything that can be invented has been invented.

—*Charles H. Duell*, director of the U.S. Patent Office, 1899

Who the hell wants to hear actors talk?

—*Harry M. Warner*, Warner Bros. Pictures, 1927

There is no likelihood man can ever tap the power of the atom.

—*Robert Millikan*, winner of the Nobel Prize in Physics, 1923

In 1877, when Thomas Edison invented the phonograph, he thought of it as an office dictating machine and lost interest in it; recorded music did not become popular until 21 years later. When the Wright brothers offered their invention to the U.S. government and the British Royal Navy, they were told airplanes had no future in the military. A 1900 Mercedes-Benz study estimated that worldwide demand for cars would not exceed 1 million, primarily because of the limited number of available chauffeurs. History is full of stories of people who couldn't imagine the impact of new technology.

Technology is hard to foresee, and it is even harder to predict the impact that technology will have on society. Who could have predicted in 1950 the profound effects, both positive and negative, television would have on our world?

Four Ways to Predict the Future

According to Alan Kay, there are four ways to predict the future. The best way is to invent the future, but it's not the only way.

Another way to predict the future is to take advantage of the fact that it generally takes ten years to go from a new idea in the research laboratory to a commercial product. By paying attention to the research being conducted in labs today, we can imagine the kinds of products we will be using a decade from now. Of course, many researchers work behind carefully guarded doors, and research often takes surprising turns. Still, today's research leads to tomorrow's products.

A third way is to look at products from the past and see what made them succeed. According to Kay, "There are certain things about human beings that if you remove, they wouldn't be human any more. For instance, we have to communicate with others or we're not humans. So every time someone has come up with a communications amplifier, it has succeeded the previous technology." The pen, the printing press, the telephone, the television, and the personal computer are all successful communication amplifiers. What's next?

Finally, Kay says we can predict the future by recognizing the four phases of any technology or media business: hardware, software, service, and way of life. These phases apply to radio, television, video, audio, and all kinds of computers.

- *Hardware.* Inventors and engineers start the process by developing new hardware. But whether it's a television set or a personal computer, the hardware is of little use without software.
- *Software.* The next step is software development. Television programs, audio recordings, video games, and databases are examples of software that give value to hardware products.
- *Service.* Once the hardware and software exist, the focus turns to service. Innovative hardware and clever software aren't likely to take hold unless they serve human needs in some way. The personal computer industry is now entering the service phase, and the companies that focus on serving their customers are generally the most successful.
- *Way of life.* The final phase happens when the technology becomes so entrenched that people don't think about it any more; they only notice if it isn't there. We seldom think of pencils as technological tools. They're part of our way of life, so much so that we'd have trouble getting along without them. Similarly, the electric motor, which was once a major technological breakthrough, is now all but invisible; we use dozens of motors every day without thinking about them. Computers are clearly headed in that direction.

Kay's four ways of predicting the future don't provide a foolproof crystal ball, but they can serve as a framework for thinking about tomorrow's technology. In the next section we'll turn our attention to research labs, where tomorrow's technology is being invented today. We'll examine trends and innovations that will shape future computer hardware and software. Then we'll see how this technology will serve users as it eventually disappears into our way of life.

From Research to Reality: 21st-Century Information Technology

You can count how many seeds are in the apple, but not how many apples are in the seed.

—Ken Kesey

In research laboratories scattered around the planet, ideas are sprouting from the minds of engineers and scientists that will collectively shape the future of computers and information technology. While we can't be sure which of these ideas will bear fruit, we can speculate based on current trends.

Tomorrow's Hardware: Trends and Innovations

The only thing that has consistently grown faster than hardware in the last 40 years is human expectation.

—Bjarne Stoustrup, *AT&T Bell Labs, designer of the C++ programming language*

The rapid evolution of computer hardware over the last few decades is nothing short of extraordinary. Computer hardware has relentlessly improved by several measures:

- *Speed.* The relay-based Mark I computer (discussed in Chapter 1) could do only a few calculations each second. Today's personal computers are roughly a *million times faster*! Computer speed today typically is measured in **MIPS** (millions of instructions per second), where instructions are the most primitive operation performed by the processor—adding two numbers, moving a number to a memory location, comparing two numbers, and the like.
- *Size.* Warehouse-sized computers are history. The central components of a modern personal computer are stored on a few tiny chips that could fit in your pocket; the only parts of the system that occupy significant space on the desktop are peripherals.
- *Efficiency.* As the story goes, ENIAC, the first large-scale computer (see Chapter 1), dimmed the lights of Philadelphia when it was turned on. A modern desktop computer consumes about as much electricity as a television set. Portable computers consume even less.
- *Capacity.* Modern optical, magnetic, and semiconductor storage devices have all but eliminated storage as a constraint for most computing jobs. Even memory-intensive sound, graphics, and video are manageable on many of the newest PCs.
- *Cost.* While computers have become steadily faster and more powerful, they've also become cheaper. Industry watchers have pointed out that if the price of cars had dropped as fast as the price of computer chips, it would be cheaper to abandon a parked car than to put money in the meter!

Staying the course. Will these trends continue? Most experts believe they will, at least for a few years. If the experts are right, we can expect the price-to-performance ratio (the level of performance per unit cost) to double every year or two for several more years. Processors that perform billions of operations per second, matchbook-sized high-capacity storage devices, and hard disks that can house the entire contents of the Library of Congress may appear within the decade. Admittedly there are barriers on the horizon—engineers eventually will bump up against the physical limitations of silicon and other materials. But as Robert Noyce, co-inventor of the integrated circuit, pointed out, these barriers have seemed to be about ten years away for many years. So far engineers have continued to find ways to push the barriers back.

New ripples. The trends are unmistakable, but it would be a mistake to assume that tomorrow's computer will simply be a smaller, more powerful version of today's PC. Technological advancements emerging from laboratories will accelerate current trends and push computer technology in entirely new directions. Here are just a few examples:

- *Flat-panel displays.* The popularity of portable computers is fueling intense research efforts to develop inexpensive, low-power, high-resolution, flat-panel displays. Until recently, flat-panel monitors were used mostly in portables, because they couldn't compete with traditional CRT monitors in image quality or price. But as quality goes up and costs come down, more users are replacing their bulky desktop CRTs with flat-panel monitors. Xerox PARC researchers predict that by the end of the decade we'll be using 1000x800-pixel displays that are thin enough to hang on walls like pictures and efficient enough to run on batteries for days.
- *Solid-state storage devices.* Portable computers are also driving the demand for low-power, rewritable storage devices. For airline travelers and others who must depend on battery power for long periods of time, disk drives consume far too much energy. ROM storage is energy efficient, but information stored in ROM can't be changed. Erasable memory chips have been available for several years, but at prices far too high for most applications. Today's research is bringing the cost of solid-state semiconductor storage down so that data, applications, and system software can be economically stored on rewritable cards rather than on disks and in ROM.
- *RISC processors.* Every processor has a built-in *instruction set*—a vocabulary of instructions that can be executed by the processor. Most of today's computers have complex instruction sets that include instructions that are seldom, if ever, used. Research has shown that these complex instruction set computer (CISC) processors are slower and less efficient than processors designed to execute fewer

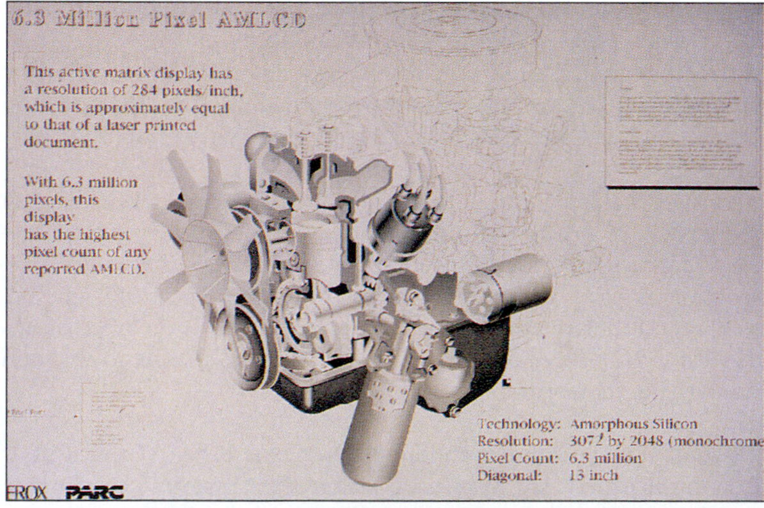

This experimental monitor display has the resolution of a laser printer.

instructions. Today many supercomputers and high-end workstations use **reduced instruction set computer** (**RISC**) processors. Because of their radically different design, RISC processors are not software-compatible with the CISC processors in personal computers today. Even so, many computer manufacturers are developing RISC machines to meet the speed demands of tomorrow's users. The most widely publicized example is the Apple/IBM Power PC, a state-of-the-art desktop computer based on a RISC chip manufactured by IBM and Motorola.

- *Parallel processing.* The quest for speed also motivates research on another front: parallel processing (first discussed in Chapter 2). Instead of using a single processor to execute instructions one at a time, parallel processing machines use multiple processors to work on several tasks in parallel. Parallel processing is especially promising for speech recognition, vision, and other pattern recognition tasks that are performed very well by the human brain, a biological parallel processing machine (see Chapter 10). Many supercomputers, such as the Cray-2, use a small number of expensive, state-of-the-art CPUs. The massively parallel Connection Machine exemplifies another approach—it uses more than 64,000 inexpensive processors in parallel. Both types of parallel processing machines represent monumental challenges for software developers accustomed to working with machines that do one thing at a time.
- *Alternative chip technologies.* Many research labs are experimenting with alternatives to silicon chips. *Gallium arsenide* (*GaAs*) *chips* show promise because they move impulses up to ten times faster and emit less heat than their silicon counterparts. But the technology is still young and expensive. *Superconductors* that transmit electricity without heat could increase computer speed a hundredfold. Unfortunately superconductor technology generally requires a supercooled environment. Another alternative is the *optical computer*, which transmits information in light waves rather than electrical pulses. Optical computers outside research labs are currently limited to a few narrow applications like robot vision. But when the technology is refined, general-purpose optical computers may process information hundreds of times faster than silicon computers.
- *Fiber optic networks and wireless networks.* When it becomes possible to put a supercomputer on the desktop or in a wristwatch, mainframe computers may go the way of the dinosaurs. But computer networks offer users the best of both worlds: the personal applications of the PC and the communication capability formerly available only on mainframes. As explained in Chapter 7, the phone network's low-bandwidth copper cables are gradually being replaced by broadband fiber optic cables that can simultaneously transmit telephone calls, television signals, two-way computer communications, and all kinds of other digital signals. Because of a lack of government support, the United States lags behind other nations in developing such a network. Japan promises to connect every Japanese home and business to a fiber optic cable by the year 2010; best estimates are that only half of American sites will be connected by that time. However long it takes, though, a universal, all-digital fiber optic network is on the way. So is a universal wireless network that will allow mobile workers to send computer data from cars, planes, and boats as easily as they make cellular phone calls today. A universal fiber optic network, combined with wireless networks for mobile workers and machines, will present unheard-of communication possibilities.

Some new portable computers use solid-state memory cards for storage instead of disks.

The Connection Machine from Thinking Machines, Inc., has over 64,000 processors and costs between $2 and $5 million. Ten percent of all supercomputers worldwide are Connection Machines.

The expanding information infrastructure. In any economy infrastructures are the frameworks that are laid first so future economic activity can take advantage of them. Just as the railroads provided the transportation network for the expanding 19th-century

American economy, the airline and highway systems have served as the American economic infrastructure for much of this century. In the same way tomorrow's economy is being shaped by an emerging **information infrastructure** of computers and networks.

Computers and networks represent critical parts of the information infrastructure, but they're of little value without software. Where is software headed in the coming decades?

Tomorrow's Software: Evolving Applications and Interfaces

We haven't yet thought up all the things we can do with this technology.

—Grace Murray Hopper, 1990

Computer hardware continues to advance at a staggering pace, and software developers struggle to keep up. In computer research, software continues to be the hardest part. Chapter 9 included discussions of promising programming technologies for the near future, including object-oriented programming languages, CASE tools, and visual programming environments. Each of these technologies can help programmers produce more reliable software in less time. But computer scientists aren't even close to developing tools that will allow programmers to produce *error-free* software quickly. Still, software technology is advancing rapidly, especially when viewed through the eyes of the user.

Software currents. If current trends continue, computer users can expect several software developments soon, including these:

- *Transparent communication between platforms.* It shouldn't be too long before you'll be able to transfer data, documents, and messages to others who share the network, regardless of what kind of hardware they're using. Groupware applications—software designed to be used by work teams—will seamlessly unite workgroups using all kinds of personal computers, workstations, and mainframes. Applications will be able to communicate with each other across platforms without bothering users. **Cross-platform communication** may sound trivial, but it's a formidable challenge for software developers.
- *Customizable applications.* Tomorrow's users will have more control over what software does and how it does it. Users will be able to add extensions to applications, remove unused features, and customize user interfaces to match their personal work styles. This kind of customization is a natural by-product of object-oriented programming technology; objects created by the programmer will represent extensions and features that can be manipulated by the user.
- *Converging user interfaces.* The graphical user interface pioneered by Xerox and popularized by Apple and Microsoft will continue to take hold as a loose industry standard. Differences between operating systems won't go away completely—Microsoft Windows computers will not look and feel exactly like Macintoshes or OS/2 machines—but these competing interfaces will be, from the user's point of view, more alike than different. Switching brands of computers may not be as easy as switching makes of cars, but it will be easier than it has been in the past. Users who learn on one type of machine will be able to adapt quickly to different kinds of machines. User interface standards will take hold, but they're not likely to last.

From WIMP to SILK. What if Ford or GM moved the brake pedal to the opposite side of the accelerator in next year's models? Most experts expect user interfaces to continue to evolve for awhile before they settle down into the kind of long-lasting standard we're used to in automobiles. Today's WIMP (*w*indows, *i*cons, *m*enus, and *p*ointing devices) interface is easier to learn and use than earlier character-based interfaces, but it's not the end of the user interface evolution. Researcher Raj Reddy uses another acronym to describe emerging user interface technologies: SILK, for *s*peech, *i*mage, *l*anguage, and *k*nowledge capabilities.

- *Speech and language.* We discussed these two related artificial intelligence technologies in Chapter 10. While we still don't have a language-translating telephone or the dictation-taking "talkwriter," speech technology is becoming a part of the user interface for a growing number of computer users. Speech input is used for voice mail and *voice annotation*—Post-it notes you can hear. Speech recognition technology allows users to speak, rather than type, commands and limited data input. Speech output is a necessary component of voice mail and multimedia applications. Speech technology is especially important in Japan and other countries with languages that don't lend themselves easily to keyboarding. It's also critical for many disabled users. With or without speech, natural-language processing that lets users communicate in more English-like commands will be an important part of future user interfaces. Researchers expect that we'll soon be using programs that can read documents as we create them, edit them according to our instructions, and file them based on their content.
- *Image.* In the last decade computer graphics have become an integral part of applications ranging from spreadsheets to desktop publishing. Graphics, including charts, graphs, drawings, and photographs, are likely to grow in importance in the coming decade. Graphical images will be as easy to transmit between machines as text is today, probably easier. But tomorrow's graphics won't just be still, flat images; they'll include three-dimensional models, animation, and video clips. Today's two-dimensional desktop interfaces may soon give way to three-dimensional workspace metaphors complete with 3-D animated objects—virtual workspaces unlike anything we use today. As discussed in Chapter 3, *virtual reality* (VR) *technology* should appear on the desktop within the next few years. **Virtual reality** creates the illusion that the user is immersed in a world that exists only inside the computer—an environment that contains both scenes and the controls to change those scenes. Today's clumsy VR technology is a long way from living up to its name; virtual reality illusions are interesting, but they're poor substitutes for reality. Still, VR has practical applications: Virtual walk-throughs are used by architects and engineers to preview buildings and mechanical assemblies, VR models are used for education and simulations, and virtual worlds are popping up in arcades.
- *Knowledge.* Many experts predict that knowledge will be the most important enhancement to the user interface of the future. Advances in the technology of knowledge—that elusive quality discussed in Chapter 10—will make user interfaces more friendly and forgiving. Intelligent applications will be able to decipher many ambiguous commands and correct common errors as they happen. But most importantly,

Using treadmills and bicycles as input devices, researchers walk through virtual buildings and bike through virtual landscapes.

knowledge will allow so-called software *agents* to work for users. The intelligent agent represents cutting-edge software technology, but it also illustrates the shift toward an emphasis on service.

Tomorrow's Service: Agents on the Network

I don't want to sit and move stuff around on my screen all day and look at figures and have it recognize my gestures and listen to my voice. I want to tell it what to do and then go away; I don't want to babysit this computer. I want it to act for me, not with me.

—Esther Dyson, *computer industry consultant and publisher*

At Xerox PARC Alan Kay and his colleagues developed the first user interface based on icons—images that represent tools to be manipulated by users. Their pioneering work helped turn the computer into a productivity tool for millions of people. Today Alan Kay claims future user interfaces will be based on agents rather than tools.

Intelligent agents. **Agents** are software programs designed to be managed rather than manipulated. An intelligent software agent can ask questions as well as respond to commands, pay attention to its user's work patterns, serve as a guide and a coach, take on its owner's goals, and use reasoning to fabricate goals of its own.

According to Kay, networks will drive the switch to agents. In a few years we'll be connected to billions of pieces of knowledge. Instead of sifting through all that data ourselves, we'll depend on agents to roam the networks 24 hours a day, identifying and retrieving the information we need.

One of the first agents, NewsPeek, was developed by Kay and others at MIT's Media Lab in the early 1980s. NewsPeek "stays up all night looking for the newspaper you would most like to read at breakfast." It searches half a dozen information systems for general-interest articles and topics of interest to the specific user, gleans related pictures and maps from videodisc collections, gathers important electronic mail messages, and combines them in a personalized paper whose major headline might be "Your 8:30 Class Is Canceled Today!"

Agents will do more than deliver information. In a well-integrated home network, the same agent that put together your morning newspaper might reset your alarm clock and your automatic coffee maker in response to the news of the canceled class.

Lawrence Tesler, one of Kay's colleagues at Xerox PARC and later at Apple, describes a fictitious set of messages a user might give to an agent:

- *On what date in February did I record a phone conversation with Sam?*
- *Make me an appointment at a tire shop that is on my way home and is open after 6 P.M.*
- *Distribute this draft to the rest of the group and let me know when they've read it.*
- *Whenever a paper is published on fullerene molecules, order a copy for my library.*

The next morning the agent has the following replies waiting for the user at breakfast:

- *You asked me when you last recorded a phone conversation with Sam. It was on February 27. Shall I play the recording?*
- *You scribbled a note last week that your tires were low. I could get you an appointment for tonight.*
- *Laszlo has discarded the last four drafts you sent him without reading any of them.*

- *You have requested papers on fullerene research. Shall I order papers on other organic microclusters as well?*

Agents go by a variety of names and have a variety of characteristics. The Corporation for National Research Initiatives (CRNI) has proposed a national library system that includes Knowbots (a trademarked abbreviation for knowledge robots) that continually sort, analyze, maintain, and find information in a networkwide electronic library. CRNI's Knowbots are able to communicate with each other, work in parallel, and clone themselves.

Agents are often portrayed with human characteristics; *2001*'s Hal and the computer on "Star Trek" are the most famous examples, but plenty of others exist. Apple and Hewlett-Packard have released videos showing computer users of the future conversing with on-screen talking heads that serve as electronic secretaries, telephone receptionists, and research librarians. Of course, agents don't need to look or sound human, they just need to possess the knowledge and intelligence to communicate and serve human users. In one proposed Japanese project involving agencies of cooperating agents, the user will be able to choose and customize each agent's metaphor. Depending on the user's wishes, news will be delivered by a simulated video announcer or an electronic newspaper; either way, the user will control the language, graphics, and amount of detail in the presentation.

In time, agents may guide us through the nooks and crannies of our networks, coach us as we learn to use software applications, act as personal messengers, defend our systems from viruses and intruders, and protect our privacy. They may become so important in our lives that we'll never turn our computers off. In any event, agents will profoundly change the way we interact with computers; Alan Kay calls this shift "the intimate revolution."

Cyberspace services. With or without agents, the information infrastructure will be like a modern version of an old-fashioned village market, complete with personalized marketing, barter, debates, and creative collaborations. As the lines separating computers, televisions, and telephones blur, the network will offer all kinds of possibilities for education and entertainment. Here are a few specific examples, most of which already exist in limited markets:

- *Personal telephone numbers.* Available now on a limited basis, these follow-me-anywhere numbers will become standard in the future. Your phone will always know where to find you, provided you want to be found. A single number will be able to handle phone calls, mobile cellular phone calls, fax images, voice mail, electronic mail, and computer data links. Some executives already carry "smart briefcases" that include copiers, faxes, mobile phones, scanners, video links, and PCs with printers.
- *Videophones.* Two-way (or multiway) video conversations, still relatively rare today, will become commonplace when fiber optic digital cables offer the necessary bandwidth. Electronic meetings and telecommuting will become more popular as a result.
- *Electronic yellow pages.* Unlike their paper counterparts, electronic yellow pages allow consumers to say "Tell me more." As the service becomes widespread, we'll routinely request price lists, peruse catalogs, and place orders on-line.
- *Open electronic markets.* Buyers and sellers can find each other quickly on-line. These markets, already found on many information services, are like two-way classified ads.
- *On-demand automobiles.* Instead of waiting weeks for special-order automobiles or buying a one-size-fits-all car from the lot, customers will be able to design, order, finance, and drive home their customized cars, all within a week. This kind of rapid response is offered by some Japanese companies now; it will be the norm in the future. On-demand ordering requires that suppliers, manufacturers,

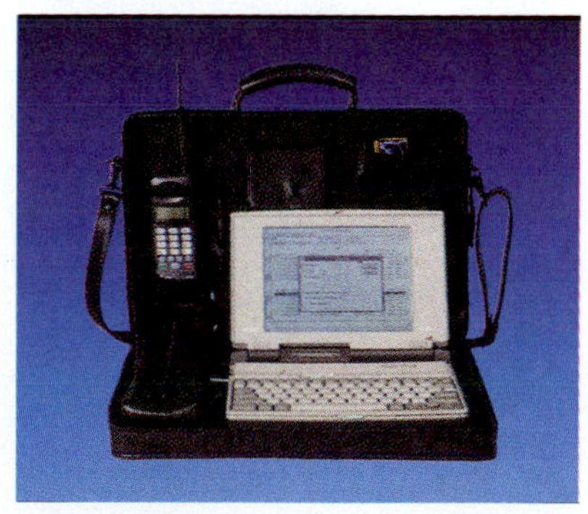

A smart briefcase.

distributors, and retailers be electronically linked, even if they function as independent companies.

- *Customized clothes.* In *The Age of Intelligent Machines,* Raymond Kurzweil speculates, "Consumers will be able to sit down at their home computers and design their own clothes to their own precise measurements and style requirements using friendly, computer-assisted design software. When the user issues the command 'Make clothes,' the design parameters and measurements will be transmitted to a remote manufacturing facility, where the clothes will be made and shipped within hours."
- *Movies on demand.* Video rental stores will vanish when we can order movies directly through the digital network. Advances in video compression will make it possible to transmit a full-length movie into your home through fiber optic cable in seconds.
- *Customizable TV.* Your television will, in all likelihood, have the computing power of a supercomputer today. It may receive models of scenes and construct pictures from those models based on your requests. You'll be able to ask your TV to "Tell me more," "Tell me less," "Go faster," and "Show me a different view of the same scene." And of course, there's always the possibility of 3-D, virtual reality TV. Arthur C. Clarke predicts, "Virtual reality won't merely replace TV. It will eat it alive."
- *Customized textbooks.* A few companies already allow instructors to choose materials to bundle together for class texts. As the technology advances, publishers will offer more options and faster response times. Eventually students may be able to customize hypertextbooks as they read them. Ted Nelson, who coined the term *hypertext* decades ago, continues to work on a system called Xanadu that could stretch publishing even further, transforming everything from the way information is distributed to the way authors are paid for their work. Here's how he describes it:

  Imagine, if you will, the year 2020, when a billion people around the planet are at their screens. And each is able to withdraw from a great repository any fragments of anything that has been published, as well as the private documents he or she has access to. So, you're able to bring to your screen not just encyclopedias, not just novels, not just the works of Horace and Cicero and Marcus Aurelius and Shakespeare and Goethe, but obscure stuff from South America and Africa that people have written in the last 5 minutes. And [you're able] to make comments and footnotes and to transclude and quote from anything else that's published, with automatic royalty.

Whether all of these predictions come true, the information infrastructure will serve people in a multitude of exciting ways. There's no shortage of discussion and research on the future uses of information technology. But the talk may subside as we head toward a time when the technology dissolves into our way of life.

Tomorrow's Way of Life: Transparent Technology

In the first computing revolution, the ratio of people to computers was N-to-1. In the second revolution, personal computers insisted the ratio be 1-to-1—one person, one computer. In the third revolution, we are exploring the impact of having computers everywhere, many per person, 1-to-N.

—*Bob Metcalfe, inventor of Ethernet, founder of 3Com, and publisher of InfoWorld*

The most profound technologies are those that disappear. They weave themselves into the fabric of everyday life until they are indistinguishable from it.

—Mark Weiser, *head of the Xerox PARC Computer Science Laboratory*

Since Alan Kay coined the term *personal computer* at Xerox PARC, more than 50 million personal computers have been sold. Ironically many researchers at PARC today think that it's time to move beyond the personal computer because it commands too much of our attention. The goal of these researchers is to make computers disappear so people can use them without thinking about them.

Embedded intelligence. Computers are already making their way into inconspicuous corners of our lives. VCRs, CD players, and microwave ovens have built-in computers, and so do dozens of other household appliances and tools. Even our cars are processing megabytes of information as we drive them down the road. Along with the trend toward accessing centrally stored information through networks, we're experiencing another trend: embedding intelligence in the machines that surround us.

There's no end to the possibilities for embedded intelligence. In Japan computer technology has even found its way into the bathroom. A number of Japanese fixture manufacturers sell *smart toilets*—computer-controlled, paperless toilets. The newest models automatically collect and store information on blood pressure, pulse, temperature, urine, and weight. The information can be displayed on an LCD display, accumulated for months, and even transmitted by modem to a medical service. Users of these smart toilets get a mini-checkup whenever they visit the bathroom. Body-monitoring features give the toilet an entirely new function—a function that will undoubtedly save lives.

Xerox PARC's live board combines computer and video technology in an electronic white board that can be used for interactive presentations and video teleconferences.

Ubiquitous computers. When computers show up in our toilets, we're clearly entering an era of ubiquitous computers—computers will be everywhere. Researchers at Xerox PARC, Cambridge University, and Olivetti are experimenting with technology that will make computers even more ubiquitous. A PARC group is working with three sizes of ubiquitous computers: inch-scale *tabs* that are like smart Post-it notes and badges, foot-scale *pads* that are like smart notebooks and books, and yard-scale *boards* that are like smart bulletin boards and blackboards. Researchers envision a future office with hundreds of these intelligent devices communicating with each other through wireless networks while workers casually move them around their offices.

The best-known computer in their futuristic office is the **active badge** discussed in Chapter 13—a clip-on computerized ID-badge first developed at an Olivetti-Cambridge research lab. The active badge continually reports its location to record-keeping databases and to others in the organization. According to PARC's Mark Weiser, in experimental offices equipped with active badges, "doors open only to the right badge wearer, rooms greet people by name, telephone calls can be automatically forwarded to wherever the recipient may be, receptionists actually know where people are, computer terminals retrieve the preferences of whoever is sitting at them, and appointment diaries write themselves."

Active badges are only a tiny part of Weiser's ubiquitous computing vision. In a 1990 *Scientific American* article, he describes how ubiquitous computers might affect one person's day-to-day life:

Sal awakens; she smells coffee. A few minutes ago her alarm clock, alerted by her restless rolling before waking, had quietly asked, "Coffee?" and she had mumbled, "Yes." "Yes" and "no" are the only words it knows. . . .

At breakfast Sal reads the news. She still prefers the paper form, as do most people. She spots an interesting quote from a columnist in the business section. She wipes her pen over the newspaper's name, date, section and page number and then circles the quote. The pen sends a message to the paper, which transmits the quote to her office.

Electronic mail arrives from the company that made her garage door opener. She had lost the instruction manual and asked them for help. They have sent her a new manual and also something unexpected—a way to find the old one. According to the note, she can press a code into the opener and the missing manual will find itself. In the garage, she tracks a beeping noise to where the oil-stained manual had fallen behind some boxes. Sure enough, there is the tiny tab the manufacturer had affixed in the cover to try to avoid E-mail requests like her own.

On the way to work Sal glances in the foreview mirror to check the traffic. She spots a slowdown ahead and also notices on a side street the telltale green in the foreview of a food shop, and a new one at that. She decides to take the next exit and get a cup of coffee while avoiding the jam.

Once Sal arrives at work, the foreview helps her find a parking spot quickly. As she walks into the building, the machines in her office prepare to log her in but do not complete the sequence until she actually enters her office. On her way, she stops by the offices of four or five colleagues to exchange greetings and news.

Sal glances out her windows: a gray day in Silicon Valley, 75 percent humidity and 40 percent chance of afternoon showers; meanwhile it has been a quiet morning at the East Coast office. Usually the activity indicator shows at least one spontaneous, urgent meeting by now. She chooses not to shift the window on the home office back three hours— too much chance of being caught by surprise. . . .

Sal picks up a tab and "waves" it to her friend Joe in the design group, with whom she has a joint assignment. They are sharing a virtual office for a few weeks. The sharing can take many forms—in this case, the two have given each other access to their location detectors and to each other's screen contents and location. . . .

A blank tab on Sal's desk beeps and displays the word "Joe" on it. She picks it up and gestures with it toward her live board. Joe wants to discuss a document with her, and now it shows up on the wall as she hears Joe's voice: "I've been wrestling with this third paragraph all morning, and it still has the wrong tone. Would you mind reading it?"

Sitting back and reading the paragraph, Sal wants to point to a word. She gestures again with the "Joe" tab onto a nearby pad and then uses the stylus to circle the word she wants:

"I think it's this term 'ubiquitous.' It's just not in common enough use and makes the whole passage sound a little formal. Can we rephrase the sentence to get rid of it?"

"I'll try that. Say, by the way, Sal, did you ever hear from Mary Hausdorf?"

"No. Who's that?"

"You remember. She was at the meeting last week. She told me she was going to get in touch with you."

Sal doesn't remember Mary, but she does vaguely remember the meeting. She quickly starts a search for meetings held during the past two weeks with more than six people not previously in meetings with her and finds the one. The attendees' names pop up, and she sees Mary. . . .

Technologically we may only be a few years away from Sal's world. In that world ubiquitous computers offer convenience and efficiency beyond anything that's come before. They also raise issues of privacy, intimacy, and independence. These issues will grow in importance as we move further into the information age. But they may seem insignificant when compared to the questions we'll face when the streams of information technology and biotechnology converge in the future.

The Day After Tomorrow: Information Technology Meets Biology

This distant future is where computers, genetics, and micromachinery are one and the same.

—*Stan Davis and Bill Davidson*, 2020 Vision

The information age won't last forever. Analysts Stan Davis and Bill Davidson predict in their book *2020 Vision* that a *bio-economy* will replace the information economy sometime around the year 2020. Whether or not they're right, biotechnology and microtechnology will become more intertwined with computer technology in the coming decades. There's no telling exactly what the results will be, but the possibilities are both intriguing and disturbing.

Microtechnology. The incredible miniaturization achieved in the computer industry is allowing researchers to develop *micromachines*—machines on the scale of a *millionth* of a meter. Microscopic moving parts are etched in silicon using a process similar to that of manufacturing computer chips. Major universities, corporations (including IBM and AT&T), and government agencies are doing microtechnology research. For example, engineers at the University of California at Berkeley have built a motor twice as wide as a human hair that runs on static electricity.

This motor, photographed through an electron microscope, is 250 microns wide. A human hair is included in the picture for comparison purposes.

So far most applications of microtechnology have been *microsensors*: tiny devices that can detect pressure, temperature, and other environmental qualities. Microsensors are used in cars, planes, and spacecrafts, but they show promise in medicine, too. Researchers at Johns Hopkins University have developed a *smart pill* that combines a thermometer with a transmitter so it can broadcast temperatures as it travels through a human digestive tract. This pill is a first step toward other pills that might play more active roles inside our bodies. Scientists speculate that tiny machines may someday be able to roam through the body, locating and destroying cancer cells and invading organisms!

Nanotechnology. If microtechnology is carried to its extreme, it becomes **nanotechnology**—the manufacture of machines on a scale of a few billionths of a meter. Nanomachines would have to be constructed atom by atom using processes drawn from particle physics, biophysics, and molecular biology. IBM scientists have developed a *scanning tunneling microscope* that allows them to see and move individual atoms. Using this device, a team of physicists created a tiny switch that relies on the motion of a single atom. Using another approach, biophysicists are studying natural molecular machines like the protein rotor that spins a bacterium's flagellum tail, hoping to use their findings to create molecular motors. At the same time, geneticists are gradually unlocking the secrets of DNA—biology's self-replicating molecular memory devices. These and other research threads may lead scientists to the breakthrough that will allow them to create atomic assembler devices that can construct nanomachines. Submicron computers, germ-sized robots, self-assembling machines, intelligent clothes, alchemy . . . the possibilities are staggering.

Artificial life. For many researchers, the ultimate goal is to create **artificial life**—synthetic organisms that act like natural living systems. Some artificial life researchers create simple software organisms that exist only in computer memory; many of these organisms are similar to the computer viruses discussed in Chapter 13. Other researchers build colonies of tiny insect robots that communicate with each other and respond to changes in their environment. Artificial life researchers grapple with an array of problems, including the question of definition: Where exactly is the line between a clever machine and a living organism?

Advances in artificial intelligence, robotics, genetics, biotechnology, and microtechnology may someday make the line disappear altogether. Computers and robots will undoubtedly continue to take on more functions that have been traditionally reserved for humans. They may even grow and reproduce using carbon-based genetic technology borrowed from human biology. If they become smart enough to build intelligent machines themselves, almost anything is possible.

This speculation raises questions about the relationship between humans and the machines they create. It's important that we think about those questions while the technology is evolving, because our answers may help us to determine the course of that evolution.

Human Questions for a Computer Age

The real question before us lies here: do these instruments further life and its values or not?

—Lewis Mumford, 1934

In earlier chapters we examined many social and ethical issues related to computer technology, including privacy, security, reliability, and intellectual property. These aren't the only critical issues before us. Before closing we'll briefly raise some other important, and as yet unanswered, questions of the information age.

Will Computers Be Democratic?

In the future, computers are going to enable a worldwide information democracy in which information is no longer reserved for large companies, the information systems department or the executive officer.

—Michael Dell, chairman and CEO, Dell Computer Corporation

The advanced technologies of information are also technologies of disinformation.

—Stewart Brand, The Media Lab

In 1990 a spontaneous protest exploded across computer networks in reaction to the threat to privacy posed by Marketplace, a new CD-ROM product containing consumer information on millions of Americans. The firestorm of protest forced Lotus Development Corporation to cancel distribution of the product. In Santa Monica, California, homeless people used public access terminals in the library to successfully lobby for more access to public showers. In France student organizations used computer networks to rapidly mobilize opposition to tuition increases. Computers are often used to promote democratic ideals and causes of common people. Many analysts argue that modern computer technology is, by its very nature, a force for equality and democracy. On the other hand, many powerful people and organizations use information technology to increase their wealth and influence.

Will personal computers empower everyday people to make better lives for themselves? Or will computer technology produce a society of technocrats and technopeasants? Will computerized polls help elected officials better serve the needs of their constituents? Or will they just give those in power another tool for staying in power? Will networks revitalize participatory democracy through electronic town meetings? Or will they give tyrants the tools to monitor and control citizens?

Will the Global Village Be a Community?

Progress in commercial information technologies will improve productivity, bring the world closer together, and enhance the quality of life.

—Stan Davis and Bill Davidson, *2020 Vision*

Unless wealthy countries see it as their duty to help developing nations make good use of the evolving technologies, the information age will likely widen the rift between the haves and have-nots.

—Michael L. Dertouzos, director of the MIT Laboratory for Computer Science

A typical computer today contains components from dozens of countries. The modern corporation uses computer networks for instant communication between offices scattered around the world; information doesn't stop at international borders as it flows through networks that span the globe. Information technology allows organizations to overcome the age-old barriers of space and time, but questions remain.

In the post-cold-war era, will information technology be used to further peace, harmony, and understanding? Or will the intense competition of the global marketplace simply create new kinds of wars—information wars? Will electronic interconnections provide new opportunities for economically depressed countries? Or will they simply make it easier for information-rich countries to exploit developing nations from a distance? Will information technology be used to promote and preserve diverse communities, cultures, and ecosystems? Or will it undercut traditions, cultures, and roots?

Will We Become Information Slaves?

The Heavy People are persons who seem to know some magic that can make things move and even fly, but they don't seem very bright because they can't survive without their magic things.

—Bushman, in *The Gods Must Be Crazy II*

Computers are useless. They can only give you answers.

—*Pablo Picasso*

The information age has redefined our environment; it's almost as if the human species has been transplanted into a different world. Even though the change has happened almost overnight, most of us can't imagine going back to a world without computers. Still, the rapid changes raise questions.

Can human bodies and minds adapt to the higher stimulation, faster pace, and constant change of the information age? Will our information-heavy environment cause us to lose touch with the more fundamental human needs? Will we become so dependent on our "magic things" that we can't get by without them? Will we lose our sense of purpose and identity as our machines become more intelligent? Or will we learn to balance the demands of the technology with our biological and spiritual needs?

Standing on the Shoulders of Giants

If I have seen farther than other men, it is because I stood on the shoulders of giants.

—*Isaac Newton*

When we use computers, we're standing on the shoulders of Charles Babbage, Ada Lovelace, Alan Turing, Grace Hopper, Doug Engelbart, Alan Kay, and hundreds of others who invented the future for us. Because of their foresight and effort, we can see farther than those who came before us.

In Greek mythology Prometheus (whose name means "forethought") stole fire from Zeus and gave it to humanity, along with all arts and civilization. Zeus was furious when he discovered what Prometheus had done. He feared that fire would make mortals think they were as great as gods and that they would abuse its power. Like fire, the computer is a powerful and malleable tool. It can be used to empower or imprison, to explore or exploit, to create or destroy. We can choose. We've been given the tools. It's up to all of us to invent the future.

Summary

Predicting the future isn't easy, but it's important. One of the best ways to predict the future of technology for the next decade or two is to examine the work being done in research labs today. Information and communication technology industries generally go through four phases: hardware, software, service, and way of life.

Tomorrow's computers will continue current trends toward smaller, more powerful, faster, more efficient, higher-capacity, cheaper machines. Some new technologies will enhance these trends; others may start new trends. We can expect significant advances in flat-panel displays, solid-state storage devices, RISC processors, parallel processing machines, fiber optic networks, and wireless networks. We also may see breakthroughs in alternative chip technologies. Tomorrow's economy will be shaped by the information infrastructure of computers and networks.

As software evolves, users will find that it's easier to communicate across platforms and to customize applications. User interfaces will converge toward similar graphical standards, but those standards will give way as speech, natural language, 3-D images, animation, video, artificial intelligence, and even virtual reality become more pervasive.

Perhaps the most important new user interface technology is the intelligent agent. Agents will be managed rather than manipulated by users. They'll carry out users' wishes and anticipate their needs. Perhaps most importantly, agents will serve as filters between users and the masses of information on networks. Networks will offer a multitude of services, including a real-time customizable shopping services, customizable phone service, and computerized television services.

We're heading into an era of ubiquitous computers—computers that are hardly noticeable because they're everywhere. Embedded computers will improve our everyday tools and, in some cases, give them entirely new functions.

Further into the future, information technology may become intertwined with microtechnology and biotechnology. The results may blur the line between living organisms and intelligent machines. We must be aware of the potential risks and benefits of future technology as we chart our course into the future.

CHAPTER REVIEW

Key Terms

active badge
agent
artificial life
cross-platform communication
information infrastructure
MIPS (millions of instructions per second)
nanotechnology
reduced instruction set computer (RISC)
virtual reality

Review Questions

1. What trends in computer hardware evolution are likely to continue for the next few years?
2. What trends in computer software evolution are likely to continue for the next few years?
3. Describe several new technologies that may produce significant performance improvements in future computers.
4. How will technological advances change user interfaces in the coming decade? Give several examples.
5. Why is the windows-and-icons GUI likely to be replaced by an agent-based user interface? What will this mean for computer users?
6. The information infrastructure will allow us to customize many of our transactions in an unprecedented way. Explain why and give several examples.
7. Explain the concept of ubiquitous computers. Give examples of how it might apply in the office of the future and in the home of the future.

Discussion Questions

1. Some of the most interesting technological ideas are emerging from interdisciplinary labs at MIT, Carnegie-Mellon University, Xerox, Apple, and elsewhere—labs where scientists, engineers, artists, and philosophers work together on projects that break down the traditional intellectual barriers. Why do you think is so?
2. Millions of computers worldwide are already connected to networks. But unlike highways and railroads, today's computer networks aren't widely available, easy to use, and obviously valuable to the general population. What will need to happen for the information infrastructure to transform our lives the way highways and railroads transformed our anscestors' lives?
3. Will virtual reality replace TV, as Arthur C. Clarke suggests? If it does, is that a good thing?
4. How might biology, microtechnology, and computer technology become intertwined in the future?
5. Discuss the questions raised in the section called "Human Questions for a Computer Age." Which of those questions are the most important? Which are hardest to answer?
6. Do you foresee a time when we share the Earth with truly intelligent beings of our own creation? Why or why not?

Projects

1. Imagine a future in which computers and information technology are forces of evil. Then imagine a future in which computers and information technology are used to further the common good. Write a paper describing both. Whether you use short-

story style or essay style, include enough detail so that it's clear how the technology impacts human lives.

2. Write a letter to a long-lost classmate dated 50 years from today. In that letter describe your life during the past 50 years, including the ways computer technology affected it.

Sources and Resources 

The Media Lab: Inventing the Future at MIT, by Stewart Brand (New York: Viking, 1988). The mind-stretching work done in this lab points to a future radically transformed by the interweaving of the computer, communication, and entertainment industries. This colorful book provides a window into that future and the research that's creating it.

Technology 2001: The Future of Computers and Communications, edited by Derek Leebaert (Cambridge, MA: MIT Press, 1991). This is a diverse and interesting collection of essays on tomorrow's digital technology.

Scientific American, September 1991. Scientific American has a well-earned reputation for articles that clearly explain and illustrate scientific concepts. This special issue devoted to computers, communications, and networks includes articles by Alan Kay, Nicholas Negroponte, and other architects of the emerging information infrastructure. Taken together, these articles present a clear and exciting vision of the technology that's catapulting us into the future.

"Byte's 15th Anniversary Summit," *Byte,* September 1990. A major portion of this special issue is devoted to a round-table discussion that includes 63 of the world's most influential people in the computer industry. Parts are a bit dated, but there's enough vision here to last at least a decade.

Access-control software Software that uses *passwords* and other techniques to prevent unauthorized users from using a computer system or network. *Chapter 13.*

Accounting and financial management software Software used to manage the financial accounts of businesses, institutions, families, and individuals. Accounting software keeps track of financial transactions and the flow of money between *accounts. Chapter 5.*

Accounts Monetary categories to represent various types of income, expenses, assets, and liabilities. *Chapter 5.*

Active badge (or **smart badge**) Microprocessor-controlled badge that broadcasts infrared identification codes to nearby network receivers that transmit information to a badge-location database. *Chapters 13, 14.*

Ada A massive programming language named after Ada Lovelace and developed in the late 1970s as the standard for the U.S. Defense Department. *Chapter 9.*

Address The combined row number and column letter of a spreadsheet *cell. Chapter 5.*

Agent Futuristic intelligent software entity that "lives" in a computer and acts as a digital secretary, anticipating user requests, filling in details in the user's work, and adjusting the computerized workspace to fit the user's needs. *Chapter 14.*

Agricultural economy The economy that dominated the period of human history lasting from about 10,000 years ago until the industrial revolution. An economy in which most people lived and worked on farms, exchanging goods and services in nearby towns. *Chapter 12.*

Algorithm A set of step-by-step procedures that, when completed, solve a problem or accomplish a task. A computer program generally starts as an algorithm written in a limited version of English or some other human language. *Chapter 9.*

Alias A pseudonym or a name for a group list in a *telecommunication* system. A message sent to an alias is automatically sent to everyone in the group. *Chapter 7.*

Alpha testing Early software tests performed by members of the system development team to locate and eliminate bugs. *Chapter 9.*

Analog signal A continuous wave, like a sound wave. Contrast with *Digital signal. Chapter 7.*

Analytical Engine Charles Babbage's 19th-century programmable calculating machine that, if it had been completed, would have been the first computer. *Chapter 1.*

Animation The illusion of movement created by a rapidly displayed sequence of still drawings. *Chapter 8.*

Application program or application A software tool, like a word processor or spreadsheet, that allows a computer to be used for a specific purpose. *Chapter 3.*

Architecture The design that determines how individual components of a *CPU*, computer, or computer system are put together. *Chapter 14.*

Array A *data structure* used in programming to represent a numeric list or table. *Chapter 9.*

Artificial intelligence (AI) The branch of computer science that explores using computers in tasks that require intelligence, imagination, and insight—tasks that have traditionally been performed by people rather than machines. *Chapter 11.*

Artificial life Experimental synthetic (software or hardware) organisms that behave in some significant ways like natural living systems. *Chapter 14.*

ASCII (**American Standard Code for Information Interchange**, generally pronounced "as-kee") The most widely used code for representing characters in computer *memory.* Represents each character as a unique 7-bit code, plus an 8-bit whose value is, for technical reasons, determined by the values of the other 7. *Chapter 2.*

Assembler A program that translates *assembly language* instructions into a *machine-language* instruction. *Chapter 9.*

Assembly language A language that's logically equivalent to *machine language* but easier for people to read, write, and understand. In assembly language, programmers use alphabetic codes that correspond to the machine's numeric instructions. *Chapter 9.*

Audio digitizer A computer peripheral or component containing circuitry to *digitize* sounds from microphones and other audio devices so they can be stored (recorded) in digital computer memory. *Chapters 2, 8.*

Audit-control software Software used to monitor and record computer transactions as they happen so auditors can trace and identify computer activity after the fact. *Chapter 13.*

Authoring system or tool A software tool for building (authoring) interactive *hypermedia* and *multimedia* documents for education, training, reference, and entertainment. Authoring systems allow people to develop interactive software without mastering complex programming languages. *Chapters 8, 12.*

Automated teller machine (ATM) A specialized terminal linked to a bank's main computer through a commercial banking network. An ATM can handle routine banking transactions 24 hours a day. *Chapter 7.*

Automatic footnoting Word processing feature that automatically positions footnotes and endnotes. *Chapter 4.*

Automatic hyphenation Word processing feature that automatically breaks long words that fall at the end of lines. *Chapter 4.*

Automatic recalculation Spreadsheet feature that causes formulas to be automatically recalculated whenever values in other related cells change. *Chapter 5.*

Automatic replication Spreadsheet feature that streamlines the process of entering repetitive data, labels, and formulas. *Chapter 5.*

Automatic speech recognition The ability of a computer system to recognize human speech, using many pattern recognition techniques from *artificial intelligence. Chapter 10.*

Automatic translation The ability of a computer to translate words, phrases, and/or sentences from one human language to another. *Chapter 11.*

Autonomous system A complex system that can assume almost complete responsibility for a task without human input, verification, or decision making. *Chapter 13.*

Back up To make a copy of software or data so that the original can be replaced if it is damaged or destroyed. The copy is called a backup. *Chapter 13.*

Bandwidth The quantity of information that can be transmitted through a channel in a given amount of time. The channel might be a cable connecting networked computers, a radio channel, or even a human–machine interface. *Chapters 7, 8.*

Bar chart A chart representing quantities of data as a collection of horizontal bars of varying lengths. Similar to a column chart. *Chapter 5.*

Bar-code reader Input device that uses light to read universal product codes (UPCs), inventory codes, and other codes created out of patterns of variable-width bars. *Chapter 2.*

BASIC (Beginner's All-purpose Symbolic Instruction Code) Originally designed in the 1960s as an interactive language for learning programming, BASIC is probably the most widely used programming language in the world today. *Chapter 9.*

Batch processing A type of data processing in which transactions are accumulated and fed into computers in large batches. For most applications today, *interactive processing* has replaced batch processing. *Chapter 6.*

Batch spelling checker A type of spelling checker that checks all of the words in your document in a batch when you issue the appropriate command. *Chapter 4.*

Baud rate A measurement of modem transmission speed that generally has been replaced by the more accurate bits per second (bps). Technically the two terms are not interchangeable, although many people use the term *baud rate* when they mean bits per second. *Chapter 6.*

Beta testing Software or hardware testing performed by potential users before the product is released. *Chapter 9.*

Binary The base-2 number system used by computers. *Chapter 2.*

Binary search An *algorithm* for searching data that involves repeatedly dividing the searchable data in half until the target value is found. *Chapter 9.*

Bio-economy An economy based on biotechnology, microtechnology, and information technology that, according to many analysts, will replace our information economy sometime within the next few decades. *Chapter 14.*

Biometrics Voice prints, fingerprints, retinal scans, and other measurements of individual body characteristics. Biometrics are sometimes used to ensure that only authorized personnel have access to computer systems and data. *Chapter 13.*

Bit (binary digit) The smallest unit of information. A bit can have only one of two values, on or off. *Chapter 2.*

Bit-mapped graphics A type of computer graphics in which pictures are stored as maps showing how the pixels on the screen should be represented. Contrast with *Object-oriented graphics. Chapter 8.*

Bits per second (bps) The most common measurement of modem transmission speed. *Chapter 7.*

Board 1. Short for circuit board. See also *Card. Chapter 2.* 2. The name given by researchers to experimental flat-panel computers that are like smart bulletin boards and blackboards. *Chapter 14.*

Boldface (**or bold**) A type style applied to a font to make characters stand out **like this** for emphasis. *Chapter 4.*

Booting The process of loading a computer's operating system into memory. The term evolved from the term *bootstrapping* because the computer seems to pull itself up by its own bootstraps. *Chapter 3.*

Browse To explore manually the records in a database or hypermedia document. *Chapters 6, 8.*

Bug A software error that might cause incorrect results or system failure. *Chapters 3, 9, 13.*

Bullet chart A titled list of the main points of a presentation with each point preceded by a bullet (•). The most common output from *presentation graphics software. Chapter 8.*

Bulletin board system (BBS) A telephone-linked computer system that provides public access for posting and reading messages. *Chapter 6.*

Bus A group of 8, 16, or 32 wires that carries information between computer components. *Chapters 3, 6.*

Button A "hot spot" on the screen that responds to mouse clicks, typically by displaying a different screen. *Chapter 8.*

Byte A collection of 8 *bits.* A byte can represent 256 different messages ($256 = 2^8$). For many computer applications, a byte contains one character's worth of information. *Chapter 2.*

C A programming language that combines many of the advantages of *high-level languages* and *assembly language*. Its power, flexibility, and efficiency have made it the language of choice for most professionals who program personal computers. *Chapter 9.*

C++ A popular dialect of the programming language *C* with *object-oriented programming* tools. *Chapter 9.*

Call-back system A security system designed to prevent unauthorized use of stolen passwords by outsiders. When a user logs in and types a password, the system hangs up, looks up the user's phone number, and calls back before allowing access. *Chapter 13.*

Camera-ready A description of desktop-published pages that are ready to be photographed and printed. *Chapter 4.*

Card A *HyperCard* screen that can contain graphics, text, and *buttons.* A card is part of a *stack. Chapter 8.*

Carpal tunnel syndrome A painful affliction of the wrist and hand that results from repeating the same movements over long periods. *Chapter 11.*

CASE (computer-assisted software engineering) tool A software tool that allows analysts and programmers to automate many of the tedious and error-prone steps involved in turning design specifications into programs. *Chapter 9.*

CD audio Standard compact disc (CD) sound. A computer can play sounds from standard audio CDs by sending commands to a CD-ROM drive connected to headphones or amplified speakers. *Chapter 8.*

CD-I (compact disc-interactive) A type of compact disc system with a specially programmed microprocessor and game-style controlling devices designed to work with standard television sets. *Chapter 8.*

CD-ROM (compact disc—read-only memory) A disc that's identical to a standard audio CD except that it's used to store computer data instead of (or in addition to) music. The disc is read by a computer using a CD-ROM drive. *Chapters 2, 8, 12.*

Cell A box in a *spreadsheet* representing the intersection of a row and column. *Chapter 5.*

Centered justification The placement of a line or paragraph of text so that it is centered horizontally between the left and right margins. *Chapter 4.*

Centralized computing A type of computing in which most or all computing is done by one central mainframe computer. Contrast with *Distributed* or *Enterprise computing. Chapter 7.*

Centralized database A database system in which software and data are housed in a single centralized mainframe computer and accessed by users through terminals or personal computers. Contrast with *Client/server database* and *Distributed database. Chapter 6.*

Central processing unit (CPU) The part of a computer that processes information by executing program instructions, performing all the necessary arithmetic calculations, and making basic decisions based on information values. Also called the *processor. Chapters 1, 2.*

Character-based interface A *user interface* based on characters rather than graphics. Contrast with *Graphical user interface. Chapter 3.*

CISC (complex instruction set computer) A computer that has a complex set of instructions—a large machine-language vocabulary. Most computers today are CISCs, but the trend is toward *RISC. Chapter 14.*

Click To press a button on a *mouse. Chapter 2.*

Client/server database A type of database in which database software in "client" desktop computers works with data files stored in central "server" databases on mainframes, minicomputers, or desktop computers. *Chapter 6.*

Clip art Predrawn images that users can legally cut and paste into their own pictures or posters. *Chapter 8.*

Clipboard A special portion of memory for temporarily holding information that has been copied or cut from the document for later use. *Chapter 4.*

Clip music Professionally produced musical files that users can legally incorporate into their *multimedia* productions. *Chapter 8.*

Clock A component of the *CPU* that produces pulses to synchronize computer operations. *Chapters 2, 14.*

COBOL (Common Business Oriented Language) One of the first *high-level languages* especially suited for business applications. *Chapter 9.*

Code Program statement that is the result of *coding. Chapter 9.*

Coding Writing a *program* from an *algorithm. Chapter 9.*

Command guidance system A system that allows a human operator to control a missile's path while watching a missile's-eye-view of the target on a television screen. *Chapter 13.*

Command-line interface A type of *user interface* in which the user types commands and the computer responds. *Chapter 3.*

Comment A statement included in a *program* to help human readers understand (or remember) something about the program. *Chapter 9.*

Communication software Software to facilitate communication between computers. *Chapter 7.*

Communications satellite A satellite that hangs in orbit above the earth, allowing electronic signals to be bounced between disparate locations on the earth's surface. *Chapter 7.*

Compatibility The matching of *hardware* and *software* so they'll work together properly. Software and *peripherals* are described in terms of whether they'll work with particular computers, and with each other. For example, many programs are IBM-compatible—capable of running on an IBM PC. *Chapters 3, 12.*

Compiler A *translator program* that translates an entire program into *machine language* before passing it on to the computer. *Chapter 9.*

Computed field A *database* field that contains formulas similar to *spreadsheet* formulas. *Chapter 6.*

Computer A programmable machine that changes information from one form to another. *Chapter 1.*

Computer-aided design (CAD) The use of computers to design products. Often linked to *computer-aided manufacturing (CAM). Chapters 8, 11.*

Computer-aided instruction (CAI) The use of computers to aid the instructional process. Usually refers to *drill-and-practice software* and *tutorial software. Chapter 12.*

Computer-aided manufacturing (CAM) The use of computers to control the manufacturing of parts. Often combined with *computer-aided design (CAD)* in *computer-integrated manufacturing (CIM). Chapter 11.*

Computer architecture A branch of *computer science* dealing with the way the *hardware* and *software* elements of a computer work together. *Chapter 9.*

Computer crime A crime accomplished through knowledge or use of computer technology. *Chapter 13.*

Computer graphics Pictures or graphs created with or manipulated by computers. *Chapter 8.*

Computer-integrated manufacturing (CIM) The combination of *computer-aided design* and *computer-aided manufacturing*; a major step toward the fully automated factory. *Chapter 11.*

Computer monitoring See *Monitoring, computer.*

Computer science A relatively new discipline with ties to electrical engineering, mathematics, and business that focuses on the process of computing rather than on computer hardware. *Chapter 9.*

Computer security The protection of computer systems and the information stored in those systems against unwanted access, damage, modification, or destruction. *Chapter 13.*

Computer-supported cooperative work The use of *groupware* to facilitate group work. Sometimes called *workgroup computing. Chapter 11.*

Computer theory The branch of *computer science* that applies the concepts of theoretical mathematics to computational problems. *Chapter 9.*

Concurrent processing The ability of a computer to work on several jobs at the same time. *Chapter 3.*

Console (or **formula bar**) The long window above the *spreadsheet* window used for entering data and navigating through the worksheet. *Chapter 5.*

Continuous speech Natural speech where words run together at normal speed; particularly difficult for machines to understand. *Chapter 10.*

Control structure Logical structure that controls the order in which *program* instructions are carried out. *Chapter 9.*

Copy A command for copying part of a document into the *Clipboard. Chapter 4.*

Courseware Educational software. *Chapter 12.*

CPU See *Central processing unit.*

Crop To trim a picture. *Chapter 4.*

Cross-platform communication The process of transferring data, documents, and messages between different computer *platforms. Chapter 14.*

CRT (cathode ray tube) Television-style *monitor. Chapter 2.*

Current cell (or **active cell**) The *spreadsheet* cell containing the *cursor. Chapter 5.*

Cursor (or **insertion bar**) Current position indicator; flashing mark indicating your location in the document. *Chapters 3, 4.*

Custom application An application programmed specifically for a single client. *Chapter 3.*

Cut-and-paste An editing technique that allows data to be moved within and between documents. *Chapter 4.*

Cyberspace A term coined by William Gibson in his visionary novel *Neuromancer.* In science fiction, cyberspace is a universal computer network that looks and feels like a physical place—a shared virtual reality. The term is also used to refer to today's networks and virtual reality experiments. *Chapters 7, 14.*

Data Information in a form a computer can read. *Chapter 2.*

Database A collection of information stored in an organized form in a computer. *Chapter 6.*

Database management system (DBMS) A program or system of programs that can manipulate data in a large collection of files, cross-referencing between files as needed. *Chapter 6.*

Database program An application that can help alleviate information overload—an information manager. This software tool organizes the storage and retrieval of information stored in a database. Database programs can also be used to produce mailing labels and customized form letters. Most database programs don't actually print letters; they simply *export* or transmit the necessary records and fields to word processors with *mail merge* capabilities, which then take on the task of printing the letters. *Chapter 6.*

Data compression The process of squeezing redundant and noncritical data out of files so they can be stored and transmitted more efficiently. *Chapter 8.*

Data structure Software construct that determine the logical structure of *data. Chapter 9.*

Data translation software Software that allows a computer to read and modify data from a system that uses incompatible file formats. *Chapter 3.*

Date field A field in a database that can contain only dates. *Chapter 6.*

Debug To locate and correct errors in a program. *Chapters 3, 9.*

Debugger A software tool used by programmers to locate and correct errors in programs. *Chapter 9.*

Decimal The base-10 number system we use every day. *Chapter 2.*

Decision support system (DSS) A computer system that supports managers in decision-making tasks. *Chapter 11.*

Default The option automatically chosen by the computer unless the user specifies otherwise. *Chapter 6.*

Delayed teleconference A type of group *on-line* communication in which participants type, post, and read messages at their convenience. *Chapter 7.*

Delete To erase, possibly using the delete key on the keyboard. *Chapters 2, 4.*

De-skilled Refers to a task that is transformed so that it requires less skill; a common result of job automation. *Chapter 11.*

Desktop The name given to the screen displayed by the Macintosh Finder; the view represents a desktop workspace. *Chapter 3.*

Desktop publishing (DTP) Using a personal computer, software, and a high-resolution printer to produce documents that combine text and graphics. *Chapter 4.*

Dialog box In a GUI, a window or box displayed on the screen when two-way communication takes place between computer user and computer. *Chapter 3.*

Digital Made up of discrete units—units that can be counted—so it can be subdivided. *Chapter 2.*

Digital audio tape (DAT) An audio tape format in which audio signals are stored as digital data rather than analog signals. DAT is also used as a backup medium for computer data. *Chapter 2.*

Digital camera A camera that can capture images as digital data. *Chapters 2, 8.*

Digital signal A stream of *bits*. Contrast with *Analog signal. Chapter 6.*

Digital video A form of video in which images are stored as digital data rather than as analog signal. Digital video is likely to replace standard analog video in the coming decades. *Chapter 8.*

Digitize To convert information into a digital form that can be stored in the computer's memory. *Chapter 2.*

Digitized sound Sound stored as digital data. *Chapters 2, 8.*

Digitized speech Speech recorded as digital data. *Chapters 2, 10.*

Direct access See *Random access.*

Directory In MS-DOS, UNIX, and many other operating systems, a collection of files on a disk, or a list of those files. *Chapters 3, 6.*

Disk drive A device for reading from and writing to a magnetic disk. *Chapter 2.*

Diskette (or **floppy disk**) A small, magnetically sensitive, flexible plastic wafer housed in a plastic case. A common *random access* storage medium for computer data. *Chapter 2.*

Distance learning The use of information technology to allow students, teachers, and others to communicate over long distances for educational purposes. *Chapter 12.*

Distributed computing See *Enterprise computing.*

Distributed database A database that works with data spread out across a *network* on several different computers. *Chapter 6.*

Dithering The intermixing of black and white *pixels* to create the illusion of a true gray tone, or the intermixing of pixels of two or more colors to simulate another color. *Chapter 8.*

Documentation Tutorial manuals, reference manuals, and on-line help files that explain how to use a program. *Chapter 3.*

Document image management system A system that can scan, store, retrieve, and route bit-mapped images of paper documents. *Chapter 11.*

Dot-matrix printer A type of impact printer that prints text and graphics with a matrix of pins that press dots onto the page. *Chapter 2.*

Dots per inch (dpi) Standard measurement of monitor and printer resolution; the density of the *pixels. Chapters 2, 8.*

Double-click To click twice with the *mouse* button. *Chapter 2.*

Download To copy software or data from an information utility or BBS computer into the user's computer. *Chapter 6.*

Drag To move the mouse while holding the button down. *Chapter 2.*

Drag-and-drop Editing feature that allows the user to simply drag (with the mouse) selected text or object from one part of the screen to another to move it. *Chapter 4.*

Drawing software A type of graphics software that stores the document, not as a collection of dots, but as a collection of lines and shapes. This type of graphics is called *object-oriented graphics. Chapter 8.*

Drill-and-practice software *Computer-aided instruction (CAI)* software designed to allow the student to practice skills and lessons at an individualized rate while being drilled by the computer. *Chapter 12.*

DynaBook Alan Kay's prediction of a personal computer that could go everywhere with its owner, serving as a calculator, a calendar, a word processor, a graphics machine, a communication device, and a reference tool. Kay's vision is only now, almost three decades later, appearing on the horizon. *Chapter 14.*

Educational simulations A type of *courseware* that allows the student to explore artificial environments that are imaginary or based on reality. *Chapter 12.*

Electronic cottage Futurist Alvin Toffler's term describing a home equipped with information technology that allows the occupant to work at home. *Chapter 11.*

Electronic funds transfer (EFT) The transfer of money through electronic networks that connect banks and other institutions. *Chapter 6.*

Electronic mail (e-mail) Messages transmitted between users on a computer *network*. *Chapter 6.*

Electronic organizer See *Personal information manager (PIM).*

Electronic sweatshop Writer Barbara Garson's term for data processing workplaces with working conditions reminiscent of the oppressive factory sweatshops of the 19th century. *Chapter 11.*

Embedded AI Software and hardware products that incorporate *artificial intelligence* technology. *Chapter 10.*

Embedded computers Computers built into consumer goods and other products. *Chapter 1.*

Emulation The process of making one type of computer or terminal imitate or function like another. *Chapters 3, 6.*

Emulator A software or hardware product that allows one type of computer to imitate another. *Chapter 3.*

Encryption The process of encoding data to prevent unauthorized access. *Chapter 13.*

Encryption key A secret numerical code used for encryption of data. *Chapter 13.*

Enterprise computing The approach to information technology that assumes that computing takes place throughout the enterprise rather than just in central mainframe computers. Also called *distributed computing. Chapter 11.*

Equation solver A spreadsheet feature that allows the user to define an equation, enter a target value, and let the computer determine the necessary data values. *Chapter 5.*

Ergonomics The science of designing work environments that allow people and things to interact efficiently and safely. Sometimes called human engineering. *Chapter 11.*

Error message A message from software telling the user that something has gone wrong. *Chapter 3.*

Execute To run a program. *Chapter 9.*

Expert system A software program designed to replicate the decision-making process of a human expert. *Chapter 10.*

Expert system shell A generic *expert system* containing human interfaces and *inference engines* but no data. *Chapter 10.*

Export To transmit data to another program. *Chapter 6.*

Facsimile (fax) A technology that allows images of paper documents to be transmitted through telephone lines to a destination where they can be printed or displayed on a computer screen. *Chapter 6.*

Fax modem A *modem* that allows a personal computer to send and receive *facsmilie (fax)* documents. *Chapter 7.*

Feasibility study A study performed by a *systems analyst* to help management decide whether to continue with the *systems analysis* after the investigation phase is complete. *Chapter 9.*

Fiber optic cables High-*bandwidth* cables that use light waves to transmit up to 500 million bits per second. *Chapters 6, 14.*

Field An individual component of a *database* or *hypermedia* record (for example, name). *Chapter 6.*

Field type A category describing a *field* and the type of data it will accept. *Chapter 6.*

File An organized collection of information, such as a term paper or a set of names and addresses, stored in a computerreadable form. In a *database*, a file is a collection of *records. Chapters 2, 6.*

File manager A *database* program that allows users to work with one *file* at a time. *Chapter 6.*

File server A computer that serves as a storehouse for software and data shared by several users on a *network*. *Chapter 7.*

Financial management software See *Accounting and financial management software.*

Firmware When a software program is stored on a silicon chip; read-only memory. *Chapter 2.*

First-generation computers An era of computers built around *vacuum tubes. Chapter 1.*

Font In the language of typesetters, a size and style of *typeface*. For example, the typeface known as Helvetica includes many fonts, one of which is 12-point Helvetica bold. Many people use the terms *font* and *typeface* interchangeably. *Chapter 4.*

Footer A block that appears at the bottom of every page, displaying repetitive information like chapter titles, author names, and automatically calculated page numbers. *Chapter 4.*

Format Factors determining the way a document looks when displayed on the screen or printed. *Chapter 4.*

Formula A step-by-step procedure for calculating a desired number in a *spreadsheet* or *database. Chapter 5, 6.*

FORTRAN (FORmula TRANslation) The first commercial high-level language designed at IBM in the 1950s to solve science and engineering problems. Many scientists and engineers still use a modernized version of FORTRAN. *Chapter 9.*

Fourth-generation computers Computers built around *microprocessors. Chapter 1.*

Fourth-generation language (4GL) A *nonprocedural language* that uses English-like phrases and sentences to issue instructions. *Chapter 9.*

Frame One still picture in a video or animated sequence. *Chapter 8.*

Front-end A term sometimes applied to software that serves as a *user interface* for other software. *Chapter 8.*

Full justification Having both margins smooth. *Chapter 4.*

Function In a *spreadsheet* or *database* program, a predefined set of instructions that performs a common calculation when its name is included in a formula. *Chapters 5, 6.*

Gallium arsenide (GaAs) A promising experimental technology for computer chips that can move impulses up to ten times faster and emit less heat than their silicon counterparts. *Chapter 14.*

Gateway A link between computer *networks* and/or *information utilities. Chapter 6.*

Gigabyte *(Gb)* Approximately 1,000 *megabytes. Chapter 2.*

GIGO Acronym for garbage in, garbage out. *Chapter 5.*

GoTo statement Statement for transferring control to other parts of the program. *Chapter 9.*

Grammar and style checker Software that checks text for spelling errors, errors of context, common grammatical errors, and stylistic foibles. *Chapter 4.*

Graphical user interface (GUI) A *user interface* based on graphical images rather than characters. *Chapter 3.*

Gray-scale graphics Graphics that allow each *pixel* to appear as black, white, or one of several shades of gray. *Chapter 8.*

Groupware Software designed to be used by workgroups rather than individuals. *Chapters 4, 7, 11.*

GUI See *Graphical user interface.*

Hacker Originally a person who enjoyed learning details of computer systems and writing clever programs, referred to as hacks. Today *hacker* commonly refers to a person who breaks into computer systems without authorization. *Chapter 13.*

Hand-held (palmtop) computer A computer small enough to be tucked into a jacket pocket. *Chapter 2.*

Hard copy Printout on paper of any information that can be displayed on the computer screen. *Chapter 2.*

Hard disk A rigid, magnetically sensitive disk that spins rapidly and continuously inside the computer chassis or in a separate box connected to the computer housing. *Chapter 2.*

Hardware The physical parts of the computer system. *Chapters 1, 2.*

Header A block that appears at the top of every page, displaying repetitive information like chapter titles, author names, and automatically calculated page numbers. *Chapter 4.*

Help screen On-line *documentation. Chapter 3.*

Heuristics A rule of thumb; heuristics are common in *artificial intelligence* software. *Chapter 10.*

Hexadecimal Base-16 number system. *Chapter 9.*

High-level language A *programming language* that is easier for programmers to use and understand than *machine language* or *assembly language*. Examples include *BASIC* and *C. Chapter 9.*

Homing guidance system A system used by a missile to track a moving target without human help, using infrared heat-seeking devices or visual *pattern recognition* technology. *Chapter 13.*

Human-centered system A system designed to retain and enhance human skills and control, rather than taking them away from workers. *Chapter 11.*

Human interface The part of an *expert system* that allows users to interact with the system. *Chapter 10.*

Human management See *Ergonomics.*

HyperCard The most popular *hypermedia* authoring system. *Chapter 8.*

Hypermedia Media that allow users to explore documents in nonlinear ways by choosing from multiple paths through information. *Chapter 8.*

Hypertext A method of storing textual information that allows it to be linked in *nonsequential* ways; text-based *hypermedia. Chapter 8.*

Icons Pictures that represent files, disks, and other items in a *graphical user interface. Chapter 3.*

Idea processor Software that facilitates arranging and rearranging ideas, typically in outline form. *Chapter 4.*

Image analysis The process of identifying objects and shapes in a photograph, drawing, video, or other visual image. *Chapter 10.*

Image compression software Software to reduce the size of a data file by eliminating redundant and noncritical data. *Chapter 8.*

Image processing software Software designed to allow users to manipulate photographs and other high-*resolution* images. *Chapter 8.*

Impact printer A printer that forms images by physically striking paper, ribbon, and print hammer together, the way a typewriter does. *Chapter 2.*

Import To move data into a program from another program or source. *Chapter 6.*

Industrial economy An economy dominated by factory work. The industrial economy controlled Europe and America from the late 18th century and lasted until this century. *Chapter 11.*

Inference engine The part of *an expert system* that applies user input to the knowledge base to produce the requested expert advice. *Chapter 10.*

Information economy An economy dominated by information work. In our 20th-century information economy, clerks outnumber factory workers and farmers. *Chapter 11.*

Information infrastructure The computers and networks that form the basis for the emerging *information economy. Chapter 14.*

Information overload Occurs when information technology provides too much information to use effectively. *Chapter 11.*

Information system The collection of people, machines, data, and methods organized to accomplish specific functions and to solve specific problems. *Chapter 11.*

Information superhighway The popular name for the likely successor to the internet; it will serve as a conduit for electronic conferences, interactive TV, and a wealth of other information applications.

Information systems manager A manager whose job is to integrate an organization's computers into a single, workable system. Sometimes called an IS manager, information technology manager, or IT manager. *Chapter 11.*

Information utility Multiuser commercial computer system that provides a variety of information services for users. *Chapter 7.*

Infrastructure The framework that is laid first so future economic activity can take advantage of it. *Chapter 14.*

Ink-jet printer A type of printer that sprays ink directly onto paper. *Chapter 2.*

Input Raw data put into a computer system for processing. *Chapter 2.*

Input device A computer *peripheral* accepts raw data and puts it in a machine-readable form for the computer. *Chapter 2.*

Insert To type text somewhere inside a document without overwriting any other text. *Chapter 4.*

Instruction set A vocabulary of instructions that can be executed by the *processor. Chapter 14.*

Integrated circuit A chip containing hundreds, thousands, or even millions of *transistors. Chapter 2.*

Integrated computing See *Enterprise computing.*

Integrated software A program that includes several applications designed to work well together. *Chapter 3.*

Intellectual property A legal category including the rights to the results of intellectual activity in the arts, science, and industry. *Chapter 13.*

Interactive fiction A type of story game with a natural-language or graphical interface that gives players some control over plot. *Chapter 12.*

Interactive movie Animated or video feature in which one or more of the characters are controlled by the viewers. *Chapter 12.*

Interactive multimedia Media that allow the viewer/listener to take an active part in the experience. *Chapter 8.*

Interactive processing A type of processing that allows users to interact with data through *terminals*, viewing and changing values in *real time*. Contrast with *Batch processing. Chapter 6.*

Interactive spelling checker A type of spelling checker that checks each word as it is typed. *Chapter 4.*

Interapplication communication Software feature that allows changes created in one document to be automatically reflected in other documents. *Chapter 3.*

Internet A massive interconnected group of networks linking academic, research, government, and commercial institutions. *Chapter 7.*

Interpreter A *translator program* that translates and transmits each program statement individually into *machine language. Chapter 9.*

ISDN (Integrated Services Digital Network) A type of network that links telephones, computers, fax machines, television, and even mail in a single digital system. *Chapter 7.*

IS manager See *Information systems manager.*

Italics A style of type used for emphasis, *like this. Chapter 4.*

IT manager See *Information systems manager.*

Jobless growth Occurs when productivity increases, not because of the work people do but because of the work of machines. *Chapter 11.*

Joystick A type of input device used mostly for video games. *Chapter 2.*

Justification The alignment of text on a line. Four justification choices are commonly available: *left justification*, *right justification*, *full justification*, and *centered justification. Chapter 4.*

K (kilobyte) 1024 bytes. *Chapter 2.*

Kerning The spacing between each pair of letters. *Chapter 4.*

Key field A *database field* that is used to tie information in different *files* together. *Chapter 6.*

Knowledge Information that incorporates the relationships between facts. *Chapter 10.*

Knowledge base A collection of information that includes facts and a system for determining and changing the relationship between those facts. *Chapter 10.*

Knowledge-based system A system like an *expert system* except that it draws on sources other than experts for its *knowledge base*. In practice the terms *expert system* and *knowledge-based system* are often used interchangeably. *Chapter 10.*

Knowledge engineer A specialist who interviews and observes experts and painstakingly converts their words and actions into a *knowledge base. Chapter 10.*

Label In a *spreadsheet*, a text entry that provides information for human readers. *Chapter 5.*

Laptop computer A lightweight battery-powered machine with fold-away screen that when closed, resembles a briefcase. *Chapter 1.*

Laser printer A type of printer that uses laser technology to produce high-quality printouts of text and graphics. *Chapters 2, 4.*

LCD (liquid crystal display) Flat-panel displays found in portable computers, calculators, and other electronic devices. *Chapter 2.*

Leading The spacing between lines of text. *Chapter 4.*

Left justification Having a smooth left margin and ragged right margin. *Chapter 4.*

License, software The agreement establishing the conditions under which a software user may use the software. *Chapter 3.*

Line chart The type of chart that uses a line or lines to show trends or relationships over time. *Chapter 5.*

Line printer The type of *impact printer* used to produce large printouts by rapidly hammering characters line by line onto a page. *Chapter 2.*

Links A connection between two documents (such as *spreadsheets*) so that a change in one affects the other. Also, a connection in a *hypermedia* document that allows users to rapidly move to another part of the document. *Chapters 5, 8.*

LISP (LISt Processing) A symbol-manipulation *programming language* used for *artificial intelligence* applications. *Chapter 9.*

Local area network (LAN) A *network* in which the computers are close to each other, usually in the same building. *Chapter 7.*

Logic bomb A program triggered to act when it detects some sequence of events or after a certain amount of time elapses. *Chapter 13.*

Logic error An error in the logical structure that cause differences between what the program is supposed to do and what it actually does. *Chapter 9.*

Login name A name assigned to a computer account to identify the user when logging on and communicating with others. *Chapter 7.*

LOGO A programming language designed for children. *Chapters 9, 12.*

Loop See *Repetition control structure.*

Low-level language *Machine language* or some other language that requires the programmer to use the extremely detailed logic of machine language. *Chapter 9.*

Machine language The language used by a computer to processes instructions. All computer programs must ultimately be translated into machine-language instructions made up of zeros and ones before they can be run. *Chapters 3, 9.*

Machine learning The ability of a computer program to learn from experience. *Chapter 10.*

Macintosh operating system The first widely available operating system to use a *graphical user interface. Chapter 3.*

Macro A custom-designed procedure that automates repetitive tasks. *Chapters 5, 9.*

Macro language A language, usually built into an application, utility, or operating system, that allows users to create programs, called *macros,* that automate repetitive tasks. Sometimes called a *scripting language. Chapters 5, 9.*

Magnetic ink character reader An input device that reads the magnetic characters printed on checks. *Chapter 2.*

Magnetic tape A magnetic medium for recording information sequentially. *Chapter 2.*

Mail merge Combining a *word processor* document with a *database file* to produce personalized form letters and similar documents. *Chapters 4, 6.*

Mainframe computer A room-sized machine designed to process large quantities of data quickly. *Chapter 1.*

Maintenance upgrade A software upgrade that corrects *bugs* and makes minor changes in the program. *Chapter 9.*

Management information systems (MIS) A system that includes, among other things, procedures for collecting data, a database for storing data, and software tools for analyzing data and producing a variety of reports for different levels of management. The term also applies to a branch of *computer science* that works with such systems. *Chapter 11.*

Master page In desktop publishing, a *template* that controls the general layout and includes common elements (margins, column guides, page numbers, graphic embellishments) for all left- and right-facing pages. *Chapter 4.*

Mathematics processing software Software designed to make it easier for mathematicians to create, manipulate, and solve equations. *Chapter 5.*

Megabyte (Mb) Approximately 1,000 K, or 1 million bytes. *Chapter 2.*

Megahertz One million cycles per second. A common measurement for a computer's *clock* speed. *Chapter 14.*

Memory Electronic circuitry for storing programs and data. *Chapter 2.*

Memory management The process of allocating memory and keeping programs in memory apart. *Chapter 3.*

Menu bar A bar at the top of the screen or *window* containing *pull-down menus. Chapter 3.*

Menu-driven interface An interface that allows users to choose commands from on-screen lists called *menus. Chapter 3.*

Micromachines Futuristic machines on the scale of a millionth of a meter. *Chapter 14.*

Microprocessor A computer housed on a silicon chip. *Chapter 1.*

Microsensor A microscopic device that can detect pressure, temperature, and other environmental qualities. *Chapter 14.*

Microsoft Windows Software that provides a consistent *graphical user interface* for IBM-compatible computers. Windows is a shell that adds a graphical user interface to *MS-DOS*, although it is gradually being converted into a full-blown operating system. *Chapter 3.*

Microtechnology Technology that allows researchers to develop *micromachines. Chapter 14.*

MIDI (Musical Instrument Digital Interface) A standard interface that allows electronic instruments and computers to communicate with each other and work together. *Chapter 8.*

Minicomputer A computer that is smaller and less expensive than a mainframe but larger and more powerful than a personal computer. *Chapter 1.*

MIPS (**millions of instructions per second)** A measure of *CPU* speed. *Chapter 14.*

Modeling, computer The use of computers to create abstract models of objects, organisms, organizations, and processes. *Chapter 5.*

Modem (short for **modulate/demodulate**) A hardware device that converts *digital* data into *analog signals* that can be transmitted over telephone lines and converts analog signals back into digital data. *Chapter 7.*

Modula-2 A powerful and complex programming language related to Pascal. *Chapter 9.*

Module A subprogram; a set of related statements that perform a task as part of a larger program. *Chapter 9.*

Monitor A computer display device that allows the user to view information on a screen. *Chapter 2.*

Monitoring, computer Using computer technology to track, record, and evaluate worker performance, often without the knowledge of the worker. *Chapter 11.*

Monochrome graphics A type of graphics in which each *pixel* can display one of two possible colors—commonly black or white. *Chapter 8.*

Monochrome monitor A *monitor* that can display a single color on a background of another color, such as white on black. *Chapter 2.*

Mouse A hand-held input device that, when moved around on a desktop or table, moves a pointer around the computer screen. *Chapter 2.*

MS-DOS (**Microsoft Disk Operating System,** sometimes called just **DOS**) The most widely used general-purpose operating system in the world; the standard operating system for the majority of IBM-compatible computers. *Chapter 3.*

Multimedia A combination of hardware and software that can produce output that combines several media, possibly including text, graphics, animation, video, music, voice, and sound effects. *Chapter 8.*

Music publishing software Software that can turn musical data into a printed score, ready for publishing. *Chapter 8.*

Nanomachines Future machines that, if they come to be, will be so small that they will have to be constructed atom by atom using processes drawn from particle physics, biophysics, and molecular biology. *Chapter 14.*

Nanotechnology The manufacture of *nanomachines*—machines on a scale of a few billionths of a meter. *Chapter 14.*

Narrowcasting The delivery of news, entertainment, and other information in customized packages aimed at narrow groups or individuals. *Chapters 12, 14.*

National Research and Education Network (NREN) A *network* championed by Vice President Gore and other leaders who see the need for a national data highway to replace and expand upon the *Internet. Chapter 7.*

Natural language An everyday human language like English or Japanese. *Chapters 9, 10.*

Navigate To move the cursor around in a document. *Chapters 4, 5, 6, 8.*

Network A computer system that links together two or more computers. *Chapter 7.*

Network administrator A computer professional whose job involves developing and maintaining a network. *Chapter 7.*

Network operating system Software that coordinates the details of network communication. *Chapter 7.*

Neural network (or **neural net**) *Distributed parallel* computing systems inspired by the structure of the human brain. A neural network uses thousands of processors called *neurons* to learn. *Chapter 10.*

Neuron A processor in a *neural network. Chapter 10.*

Nonimpact printer A type of printer that produces images without striking the page; includes *laser printers* and *ink-jet printers. Chapter 2.*

Nonprocedural language A language that allows programmers to program computers by stating the task to be accomplished rather than by listing the necessary steps to accomplish the task. *Chapter 9.*

Nonsequential A description of media (like *hypermedia*) that allow users to choose from many different paths through information. *Chapter 8.*

Nonvolatile memory Memory that can't be erased. *Chapter 2.*

Notebook computer A lightweight battery-operated computer that is about the size of a three-ring notebook. *Chapter 1.*

Numeric field A *database field* that can only contain numbers. *Chapter 6.*

Object-oriented database A database that stores software objects containing procedures (instructions) along with data. Object-oriented databases often are used in conjunction with *object-oriented programming* languages. *Chapter 6.*

Object-oriented graphics A type of graphics in which pictures are stored as collections of lines, shapes, and other objects, rather than as bit maps. Contrast with *Bit-mapped graphics*. *Chapter 8.*

Object-oriented programming (OOP) A type of programming in which a program is a collection of objects that contain both data and instructions, and these objects can interact with each other. *Chapter 9.*

On-line Connected to the computer system and ready to communicate. *Chapter 6.*

On-line database service A commercial, public, or private *database* that can be accessed through *telecommunication* lines. *Chapter 7.*

On-line documentation *Help screens* and tutorials that can be displayed on the computer screen. *Chapter 3.*

Open A command for loading a document, copying it from a disk into the computer's memory. *Chapter 3.*

Open system A computer system with *slots* and *ports* that can be customized. *Chapter 12.*

Operating system A system of continually running resource management programs that keep hardware running efficiently and make the process of communication with that hardware easier. *Chapter 3.*

Optical character recognition (OCR) The use of a special input device and software to read characters and convert them into electrical signals. *Chapters 2, 10.*

Optical computer A type of experimental computer that transmits information in light waves rather than electrical pulses. *Chapter 14.*

Optical disk High-capacity storage medium that uses laser beams to store read and write information on the disk surface. *Chapter 2.*

Optical-mark reader Input device that uses reflected light to determine the location of pencil marks on standardized test answer sheets and similar forms. *Chapter 2.*

Output Processed information sent from the computer through an *output device*. *Chapter 2.*

Output device A device like a *printer* or a *monitor* that makes processed information available for use outside the computer. *Chapter 2.*

Pad The name given by researchers to experimental flat-panel computers that are like smart note pads. *Chapter 14.*

Page-description language A language for describing text fonts, illustrations, and other elements of the printed page. *Chapter 8.*

Page-layout software *Desktop publishing* software used to combine the various source documents into a coherent, visually appealing publication. *Chapter 4.*

Painting software Software that allows the user to "paint" *pixels* on the screen with a pointing device; *bit-mapped graphics* software. *Chapter 8.*

Palette A small *window* that floats in front of a document window, providing quick access to tools. *Chapter 8.*

Paperless office A predicted office of the future in which magnetic and optical archives will replace reference books and file cabinets, electronic communication will replace letters and memos, and *information utilities* will replace newspapers and other periodicals. *Chapters 4, 11.*

Paradigm shift A change in thinking that results in a new way of seeing the world. *Chapter 11.*

Parallel port A socket on a computer chassis commonly used to connect printers and other external peripherals to a computer. *Bits* can pass through a parallel port in groups of 8, 16, or 32. *Chapter 7.*

Parallel processing Using multiple *processors* to divide jobs into pieces and work simultaneously on the pieces. *Chapters 2, 10, 14.*

Parsing program (or **parser**) Software that analyzes sentence structure and identifies parts of speech. *Chapter 10.*

Pascal A *high-level language* widely used for programming instruction. *Chapter 9.*

Password A secret string of letters and numbers that a user types to gain access to a computer system. *Chapters 7, 13.*

Path animation tool An *animation* tool that records the movement of visual objects as the artist drags them around the screen, and plays back motions on command. *Chapter 8.*

Path name A string of characters telling the computer where to find the *file* on the disk. *Chapter 3.*

Pattern recognition The branch of *artificial intelligence* that involves identifying recurring patterns in input data with the goal of understanding or categorizing that input. *Chapter 10.*

Pen-based computer A machine that accept input from a stylus applied directly to a flat-panel screen. *Chapter 2.*

Peripheral A device connected to a computer allowing it to communicate with the outside world or store information for later use. *Chapter 2.*

Personal communicator A portable device that typically combines a cellular phone, a fax modem, and other communication equipment in a lightweight, wireless box that resembles a *pen-based computer*. Similar to a *personal digital assistant (PDA)*. *Chapter 7.*

Personal computer (PC) A low-cost, typewriter-sized computer as powerful as many of the room-sized computers that had come before. *Chapter 1.*

Personal digital assistant (PDA) A portable (usually hand-held, pen-based) device designed to serve as an electronic organizer, notebook, appointment book, and communication device. Similar to a *personal communicator*. *Chapter 2.*

Personal information manager (PIM) A specialized *database* program designed to automate address book management, appointment calendars, to-do lists, and/or other personal record-keeping. Sometimes called an *electronic organizer*. *Chapter 6.*

Phototypesetting machine Expensive *output device* used in publishing to print documents at 1200 *dpi* or higher. *Chapter 4.*

Pie chart A type of chart designed to show the relative proportions of the parts to a whole. *Chapter 5.*

Pixel A picture element (dot) on a computer screen or printout. *Chapters 2, 8.*

Platform The hardware on which the software runs. Sometimes refers to the *hardware* and *operating system* together. *Chapter 3.*

Plotter An *output device* that draws by moving the pen and/or the paper in response to computer commands. *Chapter 2.*

Point-of-sale (POS) terminal A *terminal* in a store that accepts input from each sale and passes it on to a computer. *Chapter 2.*

Point size A measurement of type size; 1/72 inch. *Chapter 4.*

Port A socket on the outside of the computer chassis that allows information to pass in and out. *Chapters 2, 7.*

Portable computer A lightweight, battery-powered computer designed for mobility. *Chapter 1.*

Post industrial economy See *Information economy.*

PostScript A standard *page-description language* for describing text fonts, illustrations, and other elements of the printed page. *Chapter 8.*

Presentation graphics software Software designed to automate the creation of visual aids for lectures, workshops, training sessions, sales demonstrations, and other presentations. *Chapter 8.*

Primary storage Computer *memory. Chapter 2.*

Printer An *output device* that allows a computer user to print information on paper. Printers fall into two broad categories: *impact printers* and *nonimpact printers. Chapter 2.*

Procedural language A programming language that allows programmers to construct step-by-step procedures that tell the computer how to accomplish tasks. *Chapter 9.*

Processing Performing arithmetic or logical (decision-making) operations on information. *Chapters 1, 2, 3.*

Processor See *Central processing unit.*

Program A series of step-by-step instructions that directs a computer to perform specific tasks and solve specific problems. Also, to write programs. *Chapters 1, 3, 9.*

Programmer A person who writes *programs. Chapter 9.*

Programming The process of writing programs. *Chapter 9.*

Programming environment A programmer's software workspace, including a *text editor,* a *compiler,* a *debugger,* and a variety of other programming *utilities. Chapter 9.*

Programming language A set of rules that tells the computer what to do in response to program instructions. *Chapters 3, 9.*

Program verification The process of mathematically proving the correctness of a program; difficult for all but the simplest programs. *Chapter 9.*

Project management software Software to help coordinate, schedule, and track complex work projects. *Chapter 11.*

PROLOG (PROgramming LOGic) A popular language for *artificial intelligence* programming. *Chapter 9.*

Prompt A symbol on the screen signifying that the computer is waiting for the user to type a command. *Chapter 3.*

Proportionally spaced A description of *fonts* that allow more horizontal space for wide characters than for narrow characters. *Chapter 4.*

Protocol A set of rules for the exchange of data between a *terminal* and a computer or between two computers. *Chapter 7.*

Prototype A limited working system or subsystem to give users and management an idea of how the completed system will work. *Chapter 9.*

Pseudocode A cross between a computer language and plain English used to write *algorithms. Chapter 9.*

Public domain software Software that can legally be copied, used, and shared without being purchased. *Chapters 3, 12.*

Pull-down menu A *menu* that allows the user to select a command by "pulling down" the list of choices from the menu title using a pointing device like a *mouse. Chapter 3.*

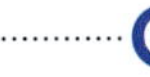

Quantitative graphics Charts and graphs generated from numbers. *Chapter 5.*

Query A request for information from a database. *Chapter 6.*

Query language A language that allows a user to request information from a database with carefully worded English-like questions. *Chapter 6.*

RAM (random access memory) A type of *primary storage* that can be used to store program instructions and data temporarily. The contents of RAM can be changed. *Chapter 2.*

Random access Immediate access to any information on a storage device, regardless of its location. Also called direct access. Contrast with *Sequential access. Chapter 2.*

Range A rectangular block of cells in a *spreadsheet. Chapter 5.*

Real-time teleconference A *teleconference* that allows each participant to view and respond to every contribution as it is entered. *Chapter 7.*

Record A collection of related information in a *database* file, typically the information relating to one person, product, or event. *Chapter 6.*

Record matching Using a common field, such as one containing Social Security Numbers, to combine information from two different data files. *Chapter 6.*

Recursion The ability of a program or procedure to call, or refer to, itself. *Chapter 12.*

Regional work center A shared office outside of a major urban center allowing workers to commute to a smaller office closer to their neighborhoods. *Chapter 11.*

Relational database Technically, a *database* whose data is organized in table form according to a particular set of rules. In popular usage, a database that allows files to be related to each other so that changes in one file can automatically be reflected in other files. *Chapter 6.*

Remote login The ability of a user on one system to access other host systems across a *network*. *Chapter 7.*

Repetition control structure A looping mechanism that allows a group of steps to be repeated several times, usually until some condition is satisfied. *Chapter 9.*

Repetitive-stress injuries Injuries resulting from repeating the same movements over long periods. *Chapter 11.*

Replication Duplication of data and formulas in a *spreadsheet* and adjustment of formulas to reflect new locations when necessary. *Chapter 5.*

Report An ordered list of selected *records* and *fields* in an easy-to-read form. *Chapter 6.*

Resolution The density of the *pixels*, usually described in *dots per inch*. *Chapter 8.*

Right justification Having both margins smooth. *Chapter 4.*

Right to privacy Freedom from interference into the private sphere of a person's affairs. *Chapters 6, 13.*

RISC (reduced instruction set computer) A computer whose processor works with only a small set of instructions and as a result can process information faster than a typical computer with a *CISC* design. *Chapter 14.*

Robot A computer-controlled machine designed to perform specific manual tasks. *Chapter 10.*

ROM cartridge A removable cartridge containing a permanent copy of software or data, often used in home video game machines and home computers. *Chapter 2.*

Sampler An electronic musical instrument that samples (digitizes) sounds from the real world and turns them into notes, that can be played iwth a keyboard or other device. *Chapter 8.*

Sampling rate The number of sound "snapshots" digital recording equipment takes each second. *Chapter 8.*

Sans serif font A *font* without serifs—fine lines at the ends of the main strokes of each character. Contrast with *Serif font*. *Chapter 4.*

Satellite office See *Regional work center.*

Save To make a disk *file* containing a document. *Chapter 4.*

Scanner An input device that can make a digital representation of any printed image. *Chapters 2, 8.*

Scanning tunneling microscope An experiment device that allows scientists to see and move individual atoms. *Chapter 14.*

Scatter chart A type of chart used to discover, rather than display, a relationship between two variables. *Chapter 5.*

Scientific visualization software Software that uses shape, location in space, color, brightness, and motion to make invisible relationships easier to understand. *Chapter 5.*

Script See *Macro*.

Scrolling A feature that allows the user of a program to move around in a document while the screen or window displays part of that document. *Chapters 4, 5.*

Search To issue a command to locate a particular piece of data. *Chapter 6.*

Search and replace A feature that allows selected words, phrases, or data to be changed throughout a document. *Chapter 4.*

Searching An *artificial intelligence* technique for looking ahead and comparing the results of different actions. *Chapter 10.*

Secondary storage A type of storage that allows the computer to record information semipermanently so it can be read later by the same computer or by another computer; includes disk and tape drives. *Chapter 2.*

Second-generation computers Computers based on *transistors*. *Chapter 1.*

Select To choose a command, object, or section of a document. Also, to locate a group of records from a database that match certain criteria. *Chapters 3, 4, 6.*

Selection (or decision) control structure A program *control structure* used to make logical decisions—to choose between alternate courses of action depending on certain conditions. It typically takes the form, "If (some condition is true) then (do something) else (do something else)." *Chapter 9.*

Semantics The underlying meaning of words and phrases. *Chapter 10.*

Sensing device An input device designed to monitor temperature, humidity, pressure, and other physical quantities. *Chapter 2.*

Sequence control structure A group of instructions followed in order from the first through the last. *Chapter 9.*

Sequencing software Software that allows a computer to be used as a tool for musical composition, recording, and editing. Sequencing software allows musical data to be recorded and manipulated by computer. *Chapter 8.*

Sequential access A medium, like *magnetic tape*, that requires information to be retrieved in the order in which it was recorded. *Chapter 2.*

Serial card Required by most IBM-compatible computers before they can be connected to a *network. Chapter 7.*

Serial port A *port* that requires *bits* to pass through one at a time. *Chapter 7.*

Serif font A font embellished with serifs—fine lines at the ends of the main strokes of each character. Contrast with *Sans serif font. Chapter 4.*

Service bureau In desktop publishing, a business that provides expertise, contract work, consulting, printing services, and/or public access to expensive output devices and other peripherals. *Chapter 4.*

SIG (special interest group) Part of a *bulletin board system, public information utility,* or *network. Chapter 7.*

SILK (speech, image, language, and knowledge) Four emerging *user interface* technologies. *Chapter 14.*

Simulation The use of computer models to test hypotheses and make decisions. *Chapter 5.*

Site licenses (or **network licenses**) A software license that allows for multiple copies or removes restrictions on software copying and use at a network site. *Chapter 7.*

Slot A socket for inserting a circuit board. *Chapters 2, 7.*

Smart card A credit-card-like card that contains embedded microprocessors and memory. *Chapter 12.*

Smart pill A pill that contains microelectronic circuitry allowing it to process information. *Chapter 14.*

Smart weapon A missile or other weapon that uses computerized guidance systems to locate its target. *Chapter 13.*

Software The instructions that tell the computer what to do. *Chapters 1, 3, 9.*

Software engineering A branch of *computer science* that attempts to apply engineering principles and techniques to the development of computer software. *Chapter 9.*

Software piracy The illegal duplication of copyrighted software. *Chapter 13.*

Solid-state storage device A storage device with no moving parts. *Chapter 14.*

Sort To arrange records in alphabetic or numeric order based on values in one or more *fields. Chapter 6.*

Source documents In *desktop publishing,* the documents containing articles, chapters, drawings, maps, charts, and photographs that are to appear in the publication. *Chapter 4.*

Speaker independence The ability of a computer to recognize words without being trained to an individual speaker. *Chapter 10.*

Special-purpose computer A computer dedicated to performing a specific task. *Chapter 10.*

Speech-recognition software Software designed to recognize human speech. *Chapter 10.*

Spelling checker Software that checks for and corrects spelling errors in a document. *Chapter 4.*

Spreadsheet Software designed to manipulate and analyze numbers and formulas in rows and columns. *Chapter 5.*

SQL (Structured Query Language) The standard *query language* for most *database* applications today. *Chapter 6.*

Stack A *HyperCard* document. *Chapter 8.*

Statistical analysis software Software designed to analyze numerical data and suggest answers to questions that can't be answered with certainty. *Chapter 5.*

Stepwise refinement The process of repeatedly subdividing a problem into smaller subproblems until a detailed *algorithm* for solving the problem emerges. *Chapter 9.*

Stored-program concept The concept of storing the computer's program instructions with the data in *memory. Chapter 3.*

Structured programming A set of techniques designed to make programming easier and less error prone, including the use of *modules* and the avoidance of the *GoTo statement. Chapter 9.*

Style sheet A set of characteristics that define formatting styles in a document. Many applications allow users to define their own customized style sheets. *Chapter 4.*

Subdirectory A collection of *files* that have been grouped together on a disk. *Chapter 3.*

Subsystem A system that is part of a larger system. *Chapter 5.*

Supercomputer One of the fastest, most powerful computers. *Chapter 1.*

Superconductor A substance that can transmit electricity without heat, offering potential for fantastic speed increases in computers. *Chapter 14.*

Syntax A set of rules associated with a language. Every *programming language* and *natural language* has a syntax. *Chapters 9, 10.*

Syntax error A violation of the rules of the "grammar" of the *programming language. Chapter 9.*

Synthesized Synthetically generated. *Chapter 8.*

Synthesizer An electronic instrument that can create *synthesized* sounds. *Chapter 8.*

Synthetic speech Artificially generated speech. *Chapter 10.*

System life cycle A sequence of steps or phases that a system passes through between the time it is conceived and the time it is phased out. *Chapter 9.*

Systems analysis The process of studying a system and analyzing, designing, developing, and maintaining a computer system. Performed by a *systems analyst. Chapter 9.*

Systems analyst The computer professional primarily responsible for developing and managing a system. *Chapter 9.*

System software A class of software that includes the *operating system* and *utility programs.* (By some definitions, system software also includes *programming language translators.*) *Chapter 3.*

Talkwriter A computer that can accept and reliably process speech input. *Chapters 4, 10.*

Tape drive A device that can store and retrieve information on *magnetic tape*. *Chapter 2.*

Tax preparation software Software to automate the process of filling out tax forms. *Chapter 5.*

Technophobia Fear of technology. *Chapter 12.*

Telecommunication Historically, long-distance communication; today, long-distance electronic communication. *Chapter 7.*

Telecommuting To use a home computer and, in many cases, *telecommunication* equipment, to work at home rather than commuting to an office. *Chapter 11.*

Teleconference An *on-line* "meeting" between two or more people. *Chapter 7.*

Terminal A device that consists of an input device (usually a keyboard), an output device (usually a *monitor*), and a link to a computer or network. *Chapters 2, 7.*

Terminal program (or **terminal emulator**) Software that allows a personal computer to function as a *terminal*. *Chapter 7.*

Tempest A U.S. military program to develop specially shielded machines that resist electronic spying. *Chapter 13.*

Template An "empty" or generic document that can be easily adapted to specific user needs. *Chapters 4, 5.*

Text editor A program similar to a word processor but lacking many advanced formatting features. *Chapter 9.*

Text field A *database field* that can contain only text. *Chapter 6.*

Third-generation computers Computers built around *integrated circuits*. *Chapter 1.*

3-D modeling software Software that allows graphic designers to create representations of three-dimensional objects with tools similar to those found in conventional drawing software. *Chapter 8.*

Timesharing An *operating system* technique allowing several users to use a computer concurrently. *Chapters 3, 7.*

Tool bar In some applications, a portion of the screen containing buttons for common commands. *Chapters 4, 5.*

Top-down design A technique for designing a program starting at the top—with the main ideas—and working down to the details. *Chapter 9.*

Touch tablet An input device that can detect movement (and sometimes pressure) of a stylus or finger on its surface. *Chapters 2, 8.*

Trackball An input device designed to move a pointer around in response to movements of an embedded ball. *Chapter 2.*

Transistor A small electronic device that transfers electricity across a tiny resistor. *Chapter 1.*

Translator program A program that translates a *high-level language* into *machine language* or some intermediate language. *Chapter 9.*

Transportable The quality of a program that allows it to be easily moved to another computer or *operating system*. *Chapter 9.*

Trojan horse A program that performs a useful task while at the same time carrying out some secret destructive act. *Chapter 13.*

True color Photo-quality color. *Chapter 8.*

Turing Machine A hypothetical machine that could read instructions from punched paper tape and perform all the critical operations of a computer. *Chapter 10.*

Turing test A proposed test for machine intelligence that involves fooling a human judge into believing that typed computer responses were produced by a human. *Chapter 10.*

Turtle graphics A type of graphics popularized by the *LOGO* language. *Chapter 12.*

Tutorial software Software that provides direct instruction in a clearly specified skill or subject. *Chapter 12.*

Tweening tools Animation tools that can automatically fill in a number of frames to smooth the movement between frames. *Chapter 8.*

Ubiquitous computers Computers everywhere, embedded in all kinds of tools. *Chapter 14.*

Undo A command that allows the user to take back the last operation. *Chapter 4.*

UNIX A multiuser *operating system* widely used on *mainframes*, *minicomputers*, and *workstations*. *Chapter 7.*

Upload To post software on a *bulletin board system*, *information utility*, or *network*. *Chapter 7.*

Up-skilled The transformation of a job into a more technically challenging job. *Chapter 11.*

User interface The look and feel of the computing experience from a human point of view. *Chapters 3, 14.*

User level The level of access a program allows a user. *Chapter 8.*

Utility program A software tool for doing system maintenance, repairs, and user interface enhancements that aren't automatically handled by the *operating system*. *Chapter 2.*

Vaccine (or **disinfectant program**) A program designed to search for *viruses*, notify users when they're found, and remove them from infected disks or files. *Chapter 13.*

Validator A likely addition to future *spreadsheets* that will check complex *worksheets* for consistency of entries and formula logic. *Chapter 5.*

Value A number in a *spreadsheet cell* or *database field*. *Chapters 5, 6.*

Variable A named portion of computer *memory* whose contents can be examined and changed by the program. *Chapter 9.*

Vertical-market application An application designed specifically for a particular business or industry. *Chapter 3.*

Videodisc An *optical disk* containing video information. *Chapter 8.*

Video digitizer A collection of circuits that can capture input from a video camera, video cassette recorder, television, or other video source and convert it to a digital signal that can be stored in memory and displayed on computer screens. *Chapters 2, 8.*

Video display terminal (VDT) See *Monitor.*

Video editing software Software that facilitates editing of video footage. *Chapter 8.*

Videophone A telephone with built-in video capability. *Chapter 14.*

Video teleconference A meeting in which people communicate face-to-face over long distances using video and computer technology. *Chapter 7.*

Virtual reality A *user interface* that looks to the user like an artificial world. *Chapters 3, 7, 14.*

Virus A program that spreads from program to program, or from disk to disk, and uses each infected program or disk to make more copies of itself. *Chapter 13.*

Visual programming To create programs by drawing pictures and pointing to on-screen objects. *Chapter 9.*

Voice annotation Sound messages attached to a document. *Chapter 5.*

Voice mail A telephone messaging system with many of the features of an *electronic mail* system. *Chapter 7.*

Volatile memory Memory that can be changed. *Chapter 2.*

Wand reader A wand used to read alphabetic and numeric characters written in a specially designed typeface found on many sales tags and credit card slips. *Chapter 2.*

Waveform audio Sound data stored in a computer's memory. *Chapter 8.*

Wide area network (WAN) A *network* that extends over a long distance. *Chapter 7.*

WIMP An acronym describing graphical user interfaces with windows, icons, menus, and pointing devices. *Chapter 14.*

Window A framed area on a computer screen that can be open, closed, and moved with a pointing device. *Chapter 3.*

Wireless network A *network* that transmits information through radio waves. *Chapter 7.*

Word processing A software *application* that allows text documents to be edited and formatted on screen before being printed. *Chapter 4.*

Word wrap A *word processing* feature that automatically transports any words that won't fit on the current line to the next line along with the cursor. *Chapter 4.*

Workgroup computing A style of work encouraged and facilitated by *groupware. Chapter 11.*

Worksheet A spreadsheet document. *Chapter 5.*

Workstation A high-end desktop computer with the computing power of a minicomputer at a fraction of the cost. *Chapter 1.*

Worm A virus-like program that travels over computer *networks,* seeking out uninfected *workstation*s to occupy. *Chapter 13.*

WYSIWYG (what you see is what you get) Pronounced "wizzy-wig." The arrangement of the words and pictures on the screen represents a close approximation of the way they will look on the printed page. *Chapter 4.*

CREDITS

Table of Contents

xii *top:* Courtesy of Apple Computer, Inc. *middle:* Courtesy of Microtouch. *bottom:* Courtesy of International Business Machines.
xiii Courtesy of Wordperfect Corporation.
xiv *top:* ©1992 Peter Menzek/Pacific Data Images.
xv *top:* Courtesy of Microsoft Corporation. *bottom:* ©1990 Peter Menzel/Courtesy of Evans & Sutherland.
xvi AT&T Archives.
xvii *top:* ©Dennis Hallinan/FPG. *bottom:* Courtsey of San Diego Supercomputer Center.
xviii Image Courtesy of Silicon Graphics, Inc./Created by Yonni Kinash of Art Center College of Design.
xix ©1993 Pacific Data Images/Peter Menzel.
xx *top:* ©David Graham/Black Star. *bottom:* ©Maggie Hallahan/Network Images.
xxi ©Tom Cushwa.

Part Openers

Part 1 ©Marc Yankus.
Part 2 Image courtesy of Silicon Graphics, Inc./Created by Bob Marcinka of Interprocess Service, Inc.
Part 3 ©Tom Cushwa.
Part 4 Gregory MacNicol ©1991.

Chapter 1

p.2 IBM Archives.
p.3 *bottom, top:* Culver Pictures, Inc.
p.4 *bottom:* ©Hank Morgan/Photo Researchers, Inc. *middle:* ©CNRI/PhotoTake, NYC *top:* ©Richard Nowitz/PhotoTake, NYC.
p.5 IBM Archives.
p.6 Courtesy of AT&T Archives.
p.7 *right top:* ©Jim Cornfield/Westlight. *right middle:* ©Lee F. Snyder/Photo Researchers, Inc. *right bottom:* ©HankMorgan/ Photo Researchers, Inc. *left:* ©Stephen Chenn/Westlight.
p.8 *top:* IBM Archives. *middle:* ©Van Bucher/Photo Researchers, Inc. *bottom:* Photo by Paul Shambroom, Courtesy of Cray Research, Inc.
p.9 *top:* Courtesy of International Business Machines. *bottom:* Courtesy of Hewlett-Packard Company. *middle:* Image provided courtesy of Silicon Graphics, Inc.
p.10 *middle:* Courtesy of Dell Computer Corporation. *top:* Photo courtesy of Jon Greenleigh/Apple Computer, Inc. *bottom:* Courtesy of Hewlett-Packard Company.
p.11 *top left:* ©Annie Griffiths/Westlight. *bottom left:* Courtesy of Solectria Corporation. *right:* ©Robin Riggs/Tony Stone World
p.14 *left:* ©1951 TIME, Inc. Reprinted by permission. *right:* ©1983 TIME, Inc. Reprinted by permission.
p.15 *top:* IBM Archives. *bottom:* Photo courtesy of Jon Greenleigh/Apple Computer, Inc.

Chapter 2

p.18 Courtesy of International Business Machines Corporation.
p.19 IBM Archives.
p.23 Courtesy of International Business Machines
p.24, 25 Jim Folts/Benjamin/Cummings.
p.28 *top left:* Courtesy of Appoint, Inc. *top right:* Courtesy of Suncom Technologies. *middle right:* ©Joseph Nettis/Photo Researchers, Inc. *middle left:* Courtesy of Microtouch Systems, Inc. *bottom:* Jim Folts/Benjamin Cummings.
p.29 *top:* Courtesy of John Greenleigh/Apple Computer, Inc. *bottom:* UPS and UPS in shield design are registered trademarks of United Parcel Service of America, Inc. Photo courtesy of United Parcel Service.
p.30 *left:* Courtesy of Logitech. *middle:* Canon U.S.A., Inc. *right:* Photo courtesy of Hewlett-Packard Company
p.31 ©1990 Peter Menzel
p.32 *top left:* Courtesy of Epson America, Inc. *middle left:* Courtesy of Hewlett-Packard Company. *bottom left:* Courtesy of Encad, Inc. *bottom right:* ©Charles Steiner/ Retna LTD.
p.33 *top:* NASA/Westlight. *middle:* Photo courtesy of Hewlett-Packard Company. *bottom:* ©Frederick D. Bodin.
p.35 Courtesy of John Greenleigh/ Apple Computer, Inc.
p.36 ©Joseph Nettis/Photo Researchers, Inc.

Chapter 3

p.38 The Computer Museum.
p.42 Courtesy of Comp U.S.A., The Nation's Largest Computer Superstore.
p.45 *top:* Courtesy of Claris Corporation. *bottom:* ©Peter Menzel.
p.47 Courtesy of Central Point Software.
p.57 *left, right:* ©Peter Menzel. *middle:* ©Ed Kashi.
p.58 ©Ed Kashi.

Chapter 4

p.62 Mark Twain Memorial, Hartford, CT.
p.63 The Bettmann Archive.
p.70 *left, right:* Courtesy of WordPerfect.
p.73 Reprinted with permission from Microsoft Corporation.
p.74 Peter Wiant/Benjamin/Cummings.
p.75 ©Frederik D. Bodin.
p.76 Artwork by Jan Dymond.

Chapter 5

p.84 Courtesy of Slate Corporation.
p.85 Courtesy of Kapor Enterprises, Inc.
p.89 Courtesy of Lotus Development Corporation.
p.90 Courtesy of Lotus Development Corporation.
p.96 *top:* Courtesy of Intuit. *bottom:* Courtesy of ChipSoft.
p.97 Courtesy of Wolfram Research, Inc.
p.98 ©James King-Holmes/Photo Researchers, Inc.
p.99 *left: © Tom Tracy/Tony Stone Images. right:* Courtesy of Microsoft Corporation.
p.100 *right:* Courtesy of Electronic Arts Sports, "Michael Jordan In Flight." *left:* Courtesy of Maxis.
p.102 Courtesy of Maxis.

Chapter 6

p.104 ©George Lange.
p.105 *top:* Courtesy of Microsoft Corporation. *bottom:* © Miro Vintoniv/ Stock Boston
p.108 *bottom, top:* Courtesy of Borland.
p.116 *left:* Courtesy of Lotus Development Corporation.
p.119 Jim Folts/Benjamin/Cummings.
p.122 ©David Graham/Black Star.
p.125 ©Miro Vintoniv/Stock Boston.

Chapter 7

p.128 Rocket Publishing Company LTD.
p.130 ©Lonnie Duka/Tony Stone Images.
p.131 *left:* Hayes Modem. *right:* Courtesy of Inmac.
p. 135 Courtesy of Lotus Development Corporation.
p.138 Courtesy of CompuServe Incorporated.
p.141 *bottom:* Courtesy of CompuServe Incorporated.
p.142 *top:* Courtesy of Prodigy. *bottom:* ©Thomas Craig/The Picture Cube.
p.146 *top:* Courtesy of Supra Corporation. *bottom:* Courtesy of Murata/ Muratec.
p.147 *top, middle:* AT&T Archives. *bottom:* Dave Martinez/Apple Computer Corp.
p.150 ©Thomas Craig/The Picture Cube.

Chapter 8
p.154 Reprinted with permission of SRI International.
p.156 ©Joseph Nettis/Stock Boston.
p.159 *top:* ©Frederick D. Bodin. *bottom:* ©1993 Pacific Data Images/Peter Menzel.
p.161 *a:* "Kim Reading" by Chelsea Sammel. *b:* Matti Kaarala/Courtesy of Corel Draw Corporation. *c:* ©Peter McCormick/Courtesy of Corel Draw Corporation. *d:* Van Gogh's Wheat Field with Cypresses by Elizabeth O'Rourke/Courtesy of Corel Draw Corporation.
p.166 *top:* Courtesy of Virtus Corporation. *bottom:* ©Boeing Computer Services.
p.172 *top:* Courtesy of Compton's NewMedia. *middle:* Courtesy of Presto Studios. *right:* Courtesy of Broderbund.
p.174 *top, bottom:* From Knicknack ©1989 Pixar.
p.175 *top:* ©Ed Kashi. *bottom:* Courtesy of ICOM Simulations.
p.176 *top:* Courtesy of Macromedia.
p.173 *bottom:* ©Claire Rydell.
p.177 *top, bottom:* Courtesy of Passport.
p.178 Cardiff University/Australian Information Service.
p.180 From Knicknack ©1989 Pixar.

Chapter 9
p.182 Department of the Navy.
p.195 Courtesy of 4GL.
p.200 *top:* ©Robert E. Daemmrich/Tony Stone Images. *middle, bottom:* Jim Folts/Benjamin Cummings.
p.201 Jim Folts/Benjamin Cummings.

Chapter 10
p.208 The Computer Museum.
p.212 The Bettman Archive.
p.215 Courtesy of Texas Instruments Incorporated.
p.218 Aion® Development System. Photo courtesy of Trinzic Corporation.
p.219 *bottom:* ©Becky Cohen *top:* Art by Harold Cohen. Photo © Becky Cohen.
p.221 *left:* ©Ed Kashi. *right:* Simon Fraser, Newcastle University, Robotics Group/SPL/ Photo Researchers, Inc.
p.224 ©Hank Morgan/Science Source 1988/Photo Researchers, Inc.
p.225 Courtesy of Xerox Imaging Systems, Inc.
p.226 ©Lawrence Ivy for the Merce Cunningham Dance Company.
p.228 *top, middle:* ©1991 Peter Menzel. *bottom:* ©T.J. Florian/Rainbow.
p.230 *top:* ©Ed Kashi. *bottom:* ©1991 Peter Menzel.

Chapter 11
p.234 ©Ed Kashi.
p.237 *top:* ©1993 Universal Studios/ Amblin Productions. Photo Provided Courtesy of Industrial Light & Magic.
p.238 *left:* ©Larry Mulvehill/Photo Researchers, Inc. *right:* Courtesy of Siemans Medical Systems. *bottom:* Courtesy of Aion® Development System.
p.239 *top:* Reprinted with permission of Compaq Computer Corporation. All rights reserved. *bottom:* ©Westlight.
p.241 Courtesy of Lotus Development Corporation.
p.242 Jim Folts/Benjamin/Cummings.
p.243 Courtesy of Microsoft.
p.244 *top left:* ©Charles Orrico/Superstock. *bottom left:* ©1986 Robert Rathe/FPG. *top right:* ©Jim Pickerell 1988/FPG. *middle right:* ©R. Chen/Superstock, Inc. *bottom right:* ©Rivear Collection/ Superstock, Inc.
p.246 ©Courtesy of Star System, Inc.
p.248 ©Catherine Ursillo/Photo Researchers, Inc.
p.249 ©David Graham/Black Star.
p.251 Courtesy of John Greenleigh/Apple Computer, Inc.
p.252 ©C.J. Howard 1990/FPG.
p.255 *bottom:* Reprinted with permission of Compaq Computer Corporation. All rights reserved. *top:* ©Westlight. *middle:* ©David Graham/Black Star.

Chapter 12
p.258 Photo courtesy of Apple Computer, Inc.
p.262 *top left:* Courtesy of Great Wave Software. *top right:* Courtesy of MECC. *middle:* Courtesy of Toolworks. *bottom:* Courtesy of International Business Machines Corporation.
p.264 ©Yoav Levy/PhotoTake, NYC.
p.265 *top right:* Courtesy of Knowledge Revolution. *top left:* Courtesy of Great Wave Software. *middle:* Courtesy of MECC. *bottom:* Courtesy of Broderbund.
p.267 ©Ed Kashi.
p.270 ©James D. Wilson/Newsweek/ Courtesy of Apple Computer, Inc.
p.273 Courtesy of Micro Card Technologies, Inc.
p.275 ©1991 LucasArts.
p.278 *right:* ©James D. Wilson/ Newsweek/Courtesy of Apple Computer, Inc.

Chapter 13
p.280 The Bettmann Archive.
p.282 ©Philippe Plailly/SPL/Photo Researchers, Inc.
p.287 ©Maggie Hallahan/Network Images.
p.288 Courtesy of Eyedentify, Inc.
p.291 Courtesy of Xerox Parc.
p.293 ©George Hall/Check Six.

Chapter 14
p.298 Photo courtesy of Apple Computer, Inc.
p.302 Brian Tramontaval/Permission of Xerox Corporation.
p.303 *top:* Courtesy Intel Corporation. *bottom:* Courtesy of Thinking Machines Corporation.
p.305 *top, bottom:* ©1990 Peter Menzel.
p.307 Courtesy of NCR Corporation.
p.309 LiveBoard from Xerox Corp., Photo courtesy of Niehaus, Ryan, Haller Public Relations.
p.311 ©Peter Menzel.
p.315 LiveBoard from Xerox Corp., Photo courtesy of Niehaus, Ryan, Haller Public Relations.

Text Acknowledgments
p. 149 John Perry Barlow, "Crime and Punishment on the Electronic Frontier," from The Whole Earth Review, and Newsletter of Computer Professionals for Social Responsibility.
p. 216 A Conversation with PC Therapist, AI Magazine, Summer 1992.
p. 234 Steven K. Roberts, Nomadness, Nomadic Research Labs, El Segundo, CA.
p. 260 Ludwig Braun, Vision: TEST (Technologically Enriched Schools of Tomorrow), International Society for Technology in Education.
p. 271-72 Luke T. Young et al., "Academic Computing in the Year 2000," Academic Computing, May/June 1988.
p. 310 From Mark Weiser, "The Computer for the 21st Century," Scientific American, September 1991. Copyright ©1991 by Scientific American, Inc. All rights reserved.

INDEX

NOTE: Page numbers in italics indicate illustrations or tables.

Microcomputer Applications

The Benjamin/Cummings Publishing Company, Inc.
Redwood City, California • Menlo Park, California
Reading, Massachusetts • New York • Don Mills, Ontario
Wokingham, U.K. • Amsterdam • Bonn • Sydney
Singapore • Tokyo • Madrid • San Juan

Sponsoring Editor: *Maureen A. Allaire*
Developmental Editors: *Nancy Canning, Sue Ewing, Rebecca Johnson, Shelly Langman, Evelyn Spire*
Associate Editor: *Nancy E. Davis*
Editorial Assistant: *MaryLynne Wrye*
Series Editor: *George Beekman*
Executive Editor: *Larry Alexander*
Production Editor: *Adam Ray*
Supplements Coordinator: *Teresa Thomas*
Senior Production Editor (Supplements): *Larry Olsen*
Production Manager: *Gwen Larson*
Associate Marketing Manager: *Melissa Baumwald*
Marketing Coordinator: *Michael Smith*
Senior Promotions Specialist: *Jim Fischer, Liane Shayer*
Executive Marketing Manager: *David Jackson*
Senior Manufacturing Coordinator: *Jenny Rossi*
Manufacturing Supervisor: *Casimira Kostecki*
V.P. Director of Manufacturing and
Inventory Management, West: *Diane MacIntosh*
Senior Microsystems Analyst: *Craig Johnson*
Production Technologist: *Ari Davidow*
Cover and Text Designer: *Mark Ong, Side-by-Side Studios*
Composition: *CR Waldman Graphics*
Film, Printing, and Binding: *R.R. Donnelley & Sons*

Ordering from the SELECT System

For more information on ordering and pricing policies for the SELECT System of microcomputer applications texts and their supplements, please contact your Addison-Wesley • Benjamin/Cummings sales representative or call our SELECT Hotline at 800/854-2595.

The Benjamin/Cummings Publishing Company, Inc.
390 Bridge Parkway
Redwood City, California 94065

Getting Started

Not too long ago computers were large, impersonal machines hidden away in glass-enclosed, climate-controlled rooms. To use one, you had to either prepare a deck of punched cards and hand them to a professional operator or type cryptic commands, line by line, on a terminal. Today, computers are as accessible and personal as you want them to be. So is the SELECT System.

The SELECT System allows your instructor to customize a group of modules on popular software packages, operating systems, and programming languages for you to learn. The modules themselves are organized around projects that reflect your world and how you will use computers. These projects help you master key concepts and problem-solving techniques while creating documents based on a mix of academic, business, and real-life situations. In the SELECT System, you will apply your computer knowledge in a variety of contexts, just as you will when you leave the classroom.

A Guided Tour

To facilitate the learning process, we have developed a consistent organizational structure for these modules.

You will begin using the software almost immediately. A brief *Overview* introduces the software package and the basic application functions. *Getting Help* covers the on-line Help feature in each package. *A Note to the Student* explains any special conventions observed in a particular module.

Each module contains six to eight *Projects*, an *Operations Reference* of commands covered in the module, an extensive *Glossary* of key terms, and an *Index*.

The following figures introduce the elements that you will encounter as you use a SELECT module.

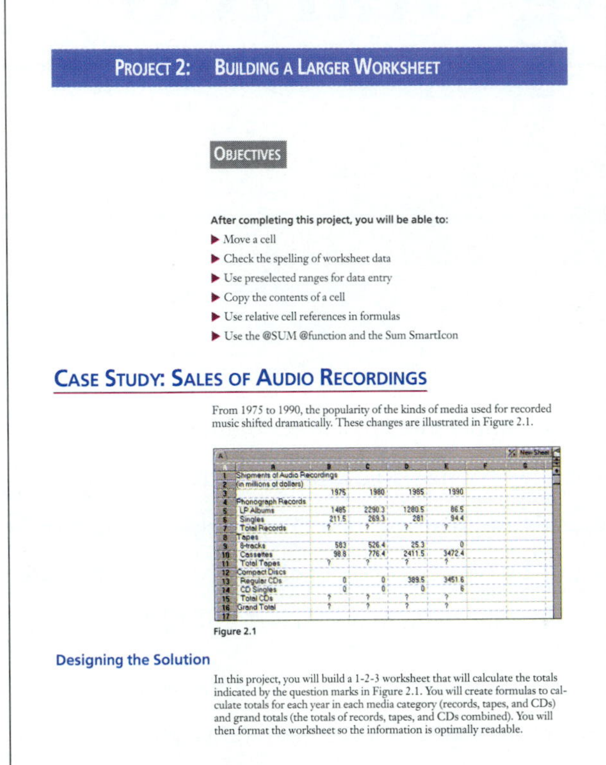

PROJECT 2: BUILDING A LARGER WORKSHEET

OBJECTIVES

After completing this project, you will be able to:

- Move a cell
- Check the spelling of worksheet data
- Use preselected ranges for data entry
- Copy the contents of a cell
- Use relative cell references in formulas
- Use the @SUM @function and the Sum SmartIcon

CASE STUDY: SALES OF AUDIO RECORDINGS

From 1975 to 1990, the popularity of the kinds of media used for recorded music shifted dramatically. These changes are illustrated in Figure 2.1.

	A	B	C	D	E	F	G
1	Shipments of Audio Recordings						
2	(in millions of dollars)						
3		1975	1980	1985	1990		
4	Phonograph Records						
5	LP Albums	1485	2290.3	1280.5	86.5		
6	Singles	211.5	269.3	281	94.4		
7	Total Records	?	?	?	?		
8	Tapes						
9	8-tracks	583	526.4	25.3	0		
10	Cassettes	98.8	776.4	2411.5	3472.4		
11	Total Tapes	?	?	?	?		
12	Compact Discs						
13	Regular CDs	0	0	389.5	3451.6		
14	CD Singles	0	0	0	6		
15	Total CDs	?	?	?	?		
16	Grand Total	?	?	?	?		
17							

Figure 2.1

Designing the Solution

In this project, you will build a 1-2-3 worksheet that will calculate the totals indicated by the question marks in Figure 2.1. You will create formulas to calculate totals for each year in each media category (records, tapes, and CDs) and grand totals (the totals of records, tapes, and CDs combined). You will then format the worksheet so the information is optimally readable.

- Each project begins with ***Learning Objectives*** that describe the skills and commands you will master.

- Projects revolve around ***Case Studies,*** real-world scenarios that allow you to learn an application in a broader context. Case studies give you a sense of when, how, and where an application can serve as an effective tool.

- ***Designing the Solution*** introduces you to important problem-solving techniques. You will see how to analyze the case study and design a solution before you sit down at the computer. Thinking through the problem before working with the application allows you to identify the larger issues that must be resolved in order to successfully complete the project.

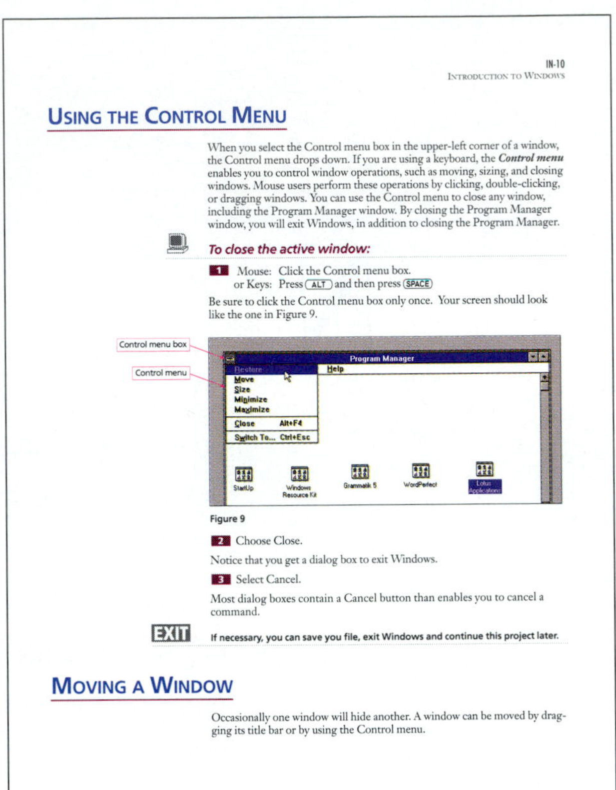

IN-10
INTRODUCTION TO WINDOWS

USING THE CONTROL MENU

When you select the Control menu box in the upper-left corner of a window, the Control menu drops down. If you are using a keyboard, the ***Control menu*** enables you to control window operations, such as moving, sizing, and closing windows. Mouse users perform these operations by clicking, double-clicking, or dragging windows. You can use the Control menu to close any window, including the Program Manager window. By closing the Program Manager window, you will exit Windows, in addition to closing the Program Manager.

To close the active window:

1 Mouse: Click the Control menu box.
or Keys: Press ALT and then press SPACE

Be sure to click the Control menu box only once. Your screen should look like the one in Figure 9.

Figure 9

2 Choose Close.

Notice that you get a dialog box to exit Windows.

3 Select Cancel.

Most dialog boxes contain a Cancel button than enables you to cancel a command.

EXIT If necessary, you can save you file, exit Windows and continue this project later.

MOVING A WINDOW

Occasionally one window will hide another. A window can be moved by dragging its title bar or by using the Control menu.

- Each topic begins with a brief explanation of concepts you will learn and the operations you will perform.

- The computer icon provides a cue that you should begin working at the computer. ***Numbered steps*** guide you step-by-step through each project, providing detailed instructions on how to perform operations. Instructions are provided for both mouse and keyboard where appropriate.

- Visual cues such as ***screen shots*** reinforce key concepts and help you check your work. Screen shots provide examples of what you will see on your own computer screen.

- ***Exit points*** identify good places in each project to take a break.

WRD-12
Word for Windows

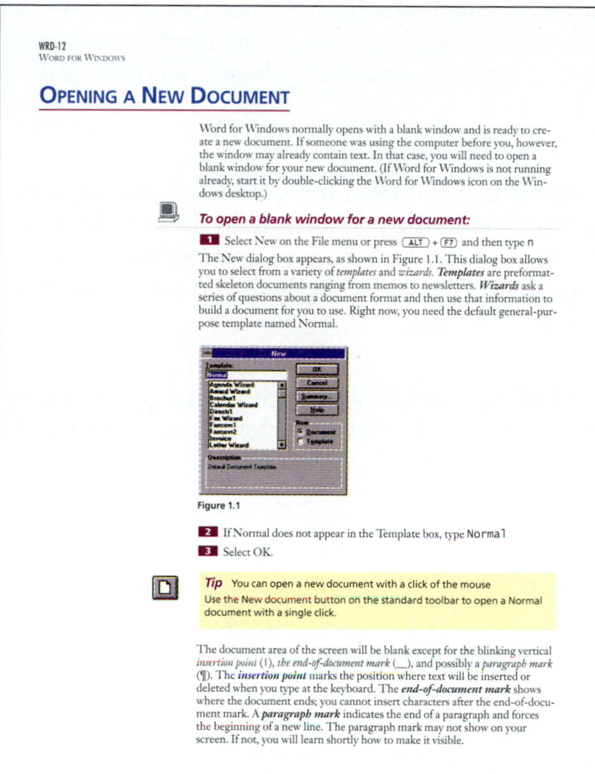

Opening a New Document

Word for Windows normally opens with a blank window and is ready to create a new document. If someone was using the computer before you, however, the window may already contain text. In that case, you will need to open a blank window for your new document. (If Word for Windows is not running already, start it by double-clicking the Word for Windows icon on the Windows desktop.)

To open a blank window for a new document:

1 Select New on the File menu or press ALT + F7 and then type n

The New dialog box appears, as shown in Figure 1.1. This dialog box allows you to select from a variety of *templates* and *wizards*. ***Templates*** are preformatted skeleton documents ranging from memos to newsletters. ***Wizards*** ask a series of questions about a document format and then use that information to build a document for you to use. Right now, you need the default general-purpose template named Normal.

Figure 1.1

2 If Normal does not appear in the Template box, type `Normal`

3 Select OK.

Tip You can open a new document with a click of the mouse

Use the New document button on the standard toolbar to open a Normal document with a single click.

The document area of the screen will be blank except for the blinking vertical *insertion point* (|), *the end-of-document mark* (__), and possibly a *paragraph mark* (¶). The ***insertion point*** marks the position where text will be inserted or deleted when you type at the keyboard. The ***end-of-document mark*** shows where the document ends; you cannot insert characters after the end-of-document mark. A ***paragraph mark*** indicates the end of a paragraph and forces the beginning of a new line. The paragraph mark may not show on your screen. If not, you will learn shortly how to make it visible.

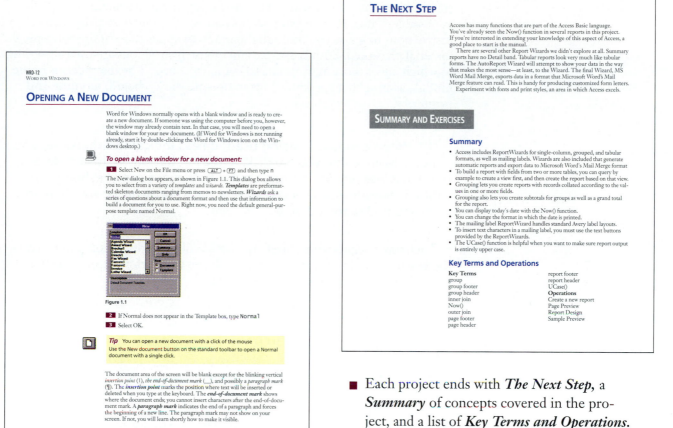

- ***Margin figures*** introduce tools from the computer interface. These tools are often convenient alternatives to the menu commands presented in the numbered steps.
- ***Tips, Reminders,*** and ***Quick Fixes*** appear throughout each project to highlight important, helpful, or pertinent information about each application. This extra level of support clearly identifies useful reference material that helps you work independently.
- ***Key Terms*** are boldfaced and italicized and appear throughout the module.

ACC-21
Access 2 for Windows

The Next Step

Access has many functions that are part of the Access Basic language. You've already seen the Now() function in several reports in this project. If you're interested in extending your knowledge of this aspect of Access, a good place to start is the manual.

There are several other Report Wizards we didn't explore at all. Summary reports have no Detail band. Tabular reports look very much like tabular forms. The AutoReport Wizard will attempt to show your data in the way that makes the most sense—at least, to the Wizard. The final Wizard, MS Word Mail Merge, exports data in a format that Microsoft Word's Mail Merge feature can read. This is handy for producing customized form letters.

Experiment with fonts and print styles, an area in which Access excels.

Summary and Exercises

Summary

- Access includes ReportWizards for single-column, grouped, and tabular formats, as well as mailing labels. Wizards are also included that generate automatic reports and export data to Microsoft Word's Mail Merge format
- To build a report with fields from two or more tables, you can query by example to create a view first, and then create the report based on that view.
- Grouping lets you create reports with records collated according to the values in one or more fields.
- Grouping also lets you create subtotals for groups as well as a grand total for the report.
- You can display today's date with the Now() function.
- You can change the format in which the date is printed.
- The mailing label ReportWizard handles standard Avery label layouts.
- To insert text characters in a mailing label, you must use the text buttons provided by the ReportWizards.
- The UCase() function is helpful when you want to make sure report output is entirely upper case.

Key Terms and Operations

Key Terms
group
group footer
group header
inner join
Now()
outer join
page footer
page header
report footer
report header
UCase()

Operations
Create a new report
Page Preview
Report Design
Sample Preview

- Each project ends with ***The Next Step,*** a ***Summary*** of concepts covered in the project, and a list of ***Key Terms and Operations.*** The Next Step discusses the concepts from the project and proposes other uses and applications for the skills you have learned.
- At the end of each project, you'll find ***Study Questions*** (multiple-choice, short answer, and discussion), which may be used as a self-test or as a homework assignment.
- ***Review Exercises*** present hands-on tasks with abbreviated instructions to help you build on skills acquired in the the project.
- ***Assignments*** draw on skills that have been introduced in the project. They encourage you to synthesize and integrate what you have learned through problems that require analysis and critical thinking to complete.

Following the Numbered Steps

To make the application modules easy to use in a lab setting, we have standardized the presentation of hands-on computer instructions as much as possible. The numbered step sections provide detailed, step-by-step instructions to guide you through the practical application of the conceptual material presented. Both keystroke and mouse instructions are used according to which one is more appropriate to complete a task. The instructions in the module assume that you know how to operate the keyboard, monitor, and printer.

> ***Tip*** **When a mouse is being used, unless indicated otherwise, you should assume that you are clicking the left button on the mouse. Several modules provide instructions for both mouse and keyboard users. When separate mouse and keyboard steps are given, be sure to follow one method or the other, but not both.**

Each topic begins with a brief explanation of concepts. A computer icon or the ▶symbol and a description of the task you will perform appear each time you are to begin working on the computer.

For Example:

To enter the address:

1 Type `123 Elm Street` and press (ENTER)

Notice that the keys you are to press and the text you are to type stand out. The text you will type appears in a special typface to distinguish it from regular text. The key that you are to press mimics the labels of the keys on your keyboard.

When you are to press two keys or a key and a character simultaneously, the steps show the keys connected either with a plus sign or a bar.

For Example:

(SHFT) + (TAB)
(CTRL) + C

When you are to press keys sequentially, the keys are not connected and a space separates them.

For Example:

(CTRL) (PGDN)
(HOME) (HOME) (↑)

Be sure to press each key firmly, but quickly, one after the other. Keys begin repeating if you hold them down too long.

In some instances margin figures of single icons or buttons will appear next to the numbered steps. Margin figures provide visual cues to important tools that you can select as an alternative to the menu command in the numbered step.

For typographical conventions and other information unique to the application, please see "A Note to the Student" in the Overview of each module.

AN OVERVIEW OF THE SELECT SERIES

Your instructor can choose any combination of concepts texts and applications modules listed below, and we bind them into one convenient, affordable text.

Concepts Texts

Essentials of Computing, Second Edition
by H.L. Capron

Computer Currents: Navigating Tomorrow's Technology
by George Beekman

Computers and Information Systems, Third Edition
by H.L. Capron and John D. Perron

Applications Modules

Each SELECT Edition that covers a Windows-based application includes a complimentary *Introduction to Windows* section.

Windows	DOS
Word Processing	
WordPerfect 6 Projects for Windows	WordPerfect 6.0 Projects for DOS
WordPerfect 5.2 Projects for Windows	Projects for WordPerfect 5.1
Word 6 Projects for Windows	
Spreadsheets	
Lotus 1-2-3 Rel. 4 Projects for Windows	Projects for Lotus 1-2-3, Rel. 2.3/2.4
Excel 5 Projects for Windows	Projects for Lotus 1-2-3, Rel. 2.2
Excel 4.0 Projects for Windows	Projects for Quattro Pro 4.0/5.0
Projects for Excel 3.0 (PC Version)	
Quattro Pro 1.0/5.0 Projects for Windows	
Database	
Access 2 Projects for Windows	Projects for dBASE IV
Paradox Projects for Windows	Projects for dBASE III PLUS
	Projects for Paradox 3.5
Integrated Packages	
Microsoft Works 3 Projects for Windows	Projects for Microsoft Works 3.0
	Projects for Microsoft Works 2.0

DOS/Windows Applications Modules

Projects for DOS 6.0 and Windows 3.1
Projects for DOS 5.0 and Windows 3.1
Projects for DOS 2.0/3.3 and Windows 3.0

Programming Modules

Structured Basic for Beginners
QBasic for Beginners

ACKNOWLEDGMENTS

The Benjamin/Cummings Publishing Company would like to thank George Beekman for his valuable contributions as the SELECT Series Editor. Equally important are the contributions of our reviewers:

Joseph Aieta
Babson College

Tom Ashby
Oklahoma CC

Bob Barber
Lane CC

Robert Caruso
Santa Rosa Junior College

Robert Chi
California State
Long Beach

Jill Davis
State University of
New York at Stony Brook

Fredia Dillard
Samford University

Peter Drexel
Plymouth State College

Ralph Duffy
North Seattle CC

David Egle
University of Texas,
Pan American

Jonathan Frank
Suffolk University

Patrick Gilbert
University of Hawaii

Maureen Greenbaum
Union County College

Sally Ann Hanson
Mercer County CC

Sunil Hazari
East Carolina University

Bruce Herniter
University of Hartford

Lisa Jackson
Henderson CC

Cynthia Kachik
Santa Fe CC

Bennett Kramer
Massasoit CC

Charles Lake
Faulkner State Junior College

Ron Leake
Johnson County CC

Randy Marak
Hill College

Charles Mattox, Jr.
St. Mary's University

Jim McCullough
Porter and Chester Institute

Gail Miles
Lenoir-Rhyne College

Steve Moore
University of
South Florida

Anthony Nowakowski
Buffalo State College

Gloria Oman
Portland State University

John Passafiume
Clemson University

Leonard Presby
William Paterson College

Louis Pryor
Garland County CC

Michael Reilly
University of Denver

Dick Ricketts
Lane CC

Dennis Santomauro
Kean College of
New Jersey

Pamela Schmidt
Oakton CC

Gary Schubert
Alderson-Broaddus College

T. Michael Smith
Austin CC

Cynthia Thompson
Carl Sandburg College

Marion Tucker
Northern Oklahoma
College

JoAnn Weatherwax
Saddleback College

David Whitney
San Francisco State
University

James Wood
Tri-County
Technical College

Minnie Yen
University of Alaska,
Anchorage

Allen Zilbert
Long Island University

SUPPLEMENTS

Each module has a corresponding Instructor's Manual with a Test Bank and Transparency Masters. For each project in the student text, the Instructor's Manual includes Expanded Student Objectives, Answers to Study Questions, and Additional Assessment Techniques. The Test Bank contains two separate tests (with answers) consisting of multiple choice, true/false, and fill-in questions that are referenced to pages in the student's text. Transparency Masters illustrate 25 to 30 key concepts and screen captures from the text.

The Instructor's Data Disk contains student data files, answers to selected Review Exercises, answers to selected Assignments, and the test files from the Instructor's Manual in ASCII format.

PROJECTS FOR WORDPERFECT 5.1

Marianne Fox, Butler University

Lawrence Metzelaar, Vincennes University

The Benjamin/Cummings Publishing Company, Inc.

Redwood City, California • Menlo Park, California
Reading, Massachusetts • New York • Don Mills, Ontario
Wokingham, U.K. • Amsterdam • Bonn • Sydney
Singapore • Tokyo • Madrid • San Juan

ISBN 0-8053-1096-7

Contents

WordPerfect 5.1

People have been processing words for centuries. Not that long ago, the typewriter dramatically changed the appearance of written business and personal communications. Now, *word processing* refers specifically to developing, storing, and managing documents using a word processing program on a computer. More recently, the phrase has expanded to include enhancing words by integrating data from many computer sources, including graphic art, and improving readability with formatting capabilities. If you examine documents all around you, you will notice how the graphics, columns, colors, and word size catch your eye and make the document more attractive. Word processing has forever changed the way we communicate.

Using a Word Processor

Word processing is the most widely used application for microcomputers. You can type text into a computer using a keyboard in much the same way as a typewriter. However, the similarity ends there. The basic purpose of word processing is to enter words into the computer to manipulate them into documents. Five essential actions make up this process: creating, saving, retrieving, editing, and printing documents. To help perform these basic tasks, a word processing program offers menus of various options, on-screen prompts, and help facilities.

Word Processing with WordPerfect 5.1

Word processing programs vary widely in what they can do and how easy they are to use. WordPerfect 5.1 is a powerful, well-established word processing program that provides a wide range of features.

You do not have to settle for less than perfection in your documents. Once you learn that making corrections and other changes to a document is very simple, your ideas will flow onto paper more easily. After you have entered the text, WordPerfect provides a variety of ways to improve the initial draft. Words can be inserted, deleted, and corrected. Blocks of text can be moved, copied, deleted, and enhanced. A specific word or phrase can be searched for and replaced automatically.

With WordPerfect 5.1 you can keep your documents safe from damage or loss by quickly making frequent copies on both disk and paper. New or edited text can be stored on disk with a few keystrokes and backup copies made quickly. Print commands give you control over the final document format.

WordPerfect 5.1 makes it easy to expand and enhance your documents. You can create custom documents by combining several files into a single file or extracting blocks of text for later use. Using an electronic dictionary to check spelling and looking up alternative words in a thesaurus make polishing your documents easy.

Desktop publishing features allow you to create high-quality, eye-catching documents. You can present data and perform calculations in tables you create yourself or import from spreadsheets and databases. WordPerfect 5.1 allows you to assemble complex documents that include headers and footers on each page, footnotes or endnotes, a table of contents, indexes, and lists. Text can be arranged in columns on the page and integrated with business graphics and clip art.

Using This Module

This WordPerfect 5.1 module is designed to make learning WordPerfect easy. You will learn to create, save, retrieve, edit, and print documents with a variety of enhancements. Seven hands-on projects will give you the practice you need to learn WordPerfect. Conceptual material is separate from numbered hands-on instructions to make using the module in a lab setting easy. You will get your hands on the keyboard immediately and learn to use WordPerfect's on-line Help facility so that you can get help when you need it.

The material in the Overview and in each project is reinforced with a Summary, a list of Key Terms, and Study Questions; each project also has Review Exercises. The module ends with Additional Projects, drawing on all the skills learned in the module; a Command Reference section; a Glossary, defining all the Key Terms; and an Index.

The screen examples shown in this module reflect WordPerfect's default display settings. Your WordPerfect software may be set up to display a horizontal ***menu bar*** and separator line across the top of your computer screen. If you follow the conventions outlined in "Setting Defaults," later in this section, and perform all the procedures correctly, your screen should look the same as the one in each figure. If you set features such as character pitch or margins in a way other than that outlined in this module, your screens will look slightly different.

System Requirements

To work through the projects in this module, you need the following:

- An IBM or IBM-compatible computer.
- One hard disk and one floppy disk drive, or two floppy disk drives.

- A monitor and a keyboard (a mouse is optional).
- An 80-column printer.
- MS-DOS or PC-DOS version 2.0 or higher.
- WordPerfect 5.1 installed on a hard disk or, for a dual-drive system, on a floppy disk. Versions of WordPerfect prior to 5.1 do not offer the option of executing commands through menu selections. Certain commands and options are also not available on earlier versions.
- One or more blank disks on which to store project files and review exercises. Even if you have a hard disk system, you should use floppy disks to store your files and make backups of your documents.

A Note to the Student

Here are some guidelines to help you understand the conventions used in this module:

- A special keycaps font indicates the keys you are to press.

  Example: Press (ENTER).

  Press (ENTER) (or (RETURN)) and then release it. Press the key firmly, but quickly. Keys begin repeating input if you hold them down too long.

- When you are to press two keys simultaneously, the instructions show two keys with a bar between them.

  Example: Press (ALT)-(F4).

- When you are to press keys sequentially, the keycaps are not connected.

  Example: Press (HOME) (ENTER).

- Single-character keys are shown in the bold text font.

  Examples: Press (CTRL)-**B**. Press **Y** to answer Yes in response to the prompt.

- When you are to type a string of text, the text string is shown in a bold monospaced font to distinguish it from regular text.

  Example: Type **`To: All WordPerfect Users`** and press (ENTER).

- Sometimes the module lists alternate ways to select from a full screen of options.

  Example: Press **4** for **I**nitial Settings.

  This instruction means you can press the number of the option or the highlighted letter (mnemonic) in the option name. In this case, you can press **4** or **I**.

- Some instructions offer two methods, menus or keys, with which to access a WordPerfect 5.1 feature.

  Menus: Press (ALT)-=, select File, and select Save.
  or Keys: Press (F10).

  In this case, follow one instruction or the other—not both. If you choose the menus approach, press (ALT)-= to access the menu bar at the top of the screen and use the arrow keys or the mnemonic to highlight the File option. Press ENTER or ↓ to activate the File pull-down menu, highlight the Save option, and press ENTER. If you choose the function keys approach, simply press F10.

Take some time to become familiar with the keyboard layout on your computer and the other components of your computer system. The instructions in this module assume that you know how to operate the keyboard, monitor, and printer.

Objectives

In this section, you will learn how to:

- Start the WordPerfect 5.1 program
- Get help
- Retrieve WordPerfect documents
- Save documents
- Print documents
- Use pull-down menus and keystrokes to invoke commands
- Use a mouse with WordPerfect's menus and commands
- Establish default settings
- Exit WordPerfect

Starting WordPerfect 5.1

In this module you will create, edit, save, and print several documents. Work all exercises in the order provided or your document content and screen displays may not coincide with those described. You can, however, interrupt your work at the end of any exercise and exit WordPerfect 5.1. If you wish to retrieve the document later and continue where you stopped, be sure to save your document (***file***) under a unique file name before exiting. You can print your document(s) at any point.

▶ To start WordPerfect 5.1 on a dual floppy-disk system:

1. Insert the WordPerfect 5.1 system disk into the A: disk drive.
2. Insert a blank formatted data disk into the B: disk drive.
3. At the A prompt, type **B:** and press ENTER.

Notice that the DOS prompt has changed from A to B indicating that B: is the default disk drive. When you enter WordPerfect 5.1, it automatically accesses the B: disk drive until you instruct it otherwise.

4. At the B prompt, type **A:WP** and press ENTER.

▶ To start WordPerfect 5.1 on a hard disk system and set drive A as the disk drive on which to store data files:

1. Follow the procedures that load the WordPerfect 5.1 software into your computer and present the blank document screen. Procedures differ according to the system setup.
2. Insert a blank formatted disk in the A: disk drive.
3. Press F5 for List, type **=A:**, press ENTER, and press F7 twice.

▶ To save the current document and exit WordPerfect 5.1:

1. Press F7 to initiate the exit process.
2. Press **Y** in response to the prompt "Save document? **Y**es (**N**o)."
3. Type a file name and press ENTER.
4. Press **Y** in response to the prompt "Exit WP? **N**o (**Y**es)."

When you name a file using WordPerfect 5.1, you must follow DOS naming conventions.

▶ To save the current document but remain in WordPerfect 5.1 and access a blank document screen:

1. Press F7 to initiate the exit process.
2. Press **Y** in response to the prompt "Save Document? **Y**es (**N**o)."
3. Type a file name and press ENTER.
4. Press **N** in response to the prompt "Exit WP? **N**o (**Y**es)."

You can elect not to save a document as you exit WordPerfect 5.1 or stay in WordPerfect 5.1 to work on another document by pressing **N** at the "Save Document?" prompt.

▶ To retrieve a WordPerfect 5.1 document from a list of files on disk:

1. Access a blank WordPerfect 5.1 document screen.
2. Press F5 for List, type the location (disk drive\directory) of the file, and press ENTER.
3. Highlight the file name on a list of file names and press **1** for Retrieve. (Do not press ENTER.)

▶ To retrieve a WordPerfect 5.1 document by typing its file name:

1. Access a blank WordPerfect 5.1 document screen.
2. Press SHIFT-F10.
3. Type the location and name (disk drive\directory\file name) of the file, and press ENTER.

▶ To print or view the current WordPerfect 5.1 document:

1. Press SHIFT-F7.
2. Press **1** for **F**ull Document or **2** for **P**age to send output to the printer.
3. Press **6** for **V**iew Document to see the page layout on the screen.

▶ To print a document from a list of files on disk:

1. Press F5, type the location (disk drive\directory) of the file, and press ENTER.
2. Highlight the file name on a list of file names and press **4** for **P**rint.
3. Respond to the prompt asking you to specify which pages to print.

Press ENTER at the prompt to print all pages. To print less than the full document, take one or both actions that follow before pressing ENTER: Type individual page numbers separated by a comma; or, type consecutive page numbers by typing the starting page number, a hyphen, and the ending page number.

The exercises in this module assume that you have started the WordPerfect 5.1 software. Refer to this section if you don't remember how to access or exit the word processing program, or for a quick review of procedures for saving, retrieving, and printing documents.

Getting Help

WordPerfect 5.1's Help facility is extensive and user friendly. In the steps that follow, you will use WordPerfect's menu system to access the initial Help screen. You could produce the same display by pressing the Help function key, F3. Your document is hidden from view until you exit the Help facility by following screen instructions to press ENTER.

▶ To access the Help facility using WordPerfect 5.1's menu system:

1. Press ALT-= to access the menu bar at the top of the screen.
2. Press **H**, or press → a sufficient number of times to highlight the Help option on the menu bar and press ENTER.

Check that your pull-down Help menu appears as shown in the next figure.

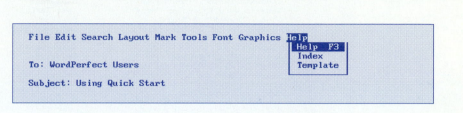

```
File Edit Search Layout Mark Tools Font Graphics Help
                                                 Help  F3
                                                 Index
To: WordPerfect Users                            Template

Subject: Using Quick Start
```

3. Press (ENTER) to select the highlighted Help (F3) option and study the initial Help screen shown in the following figure.

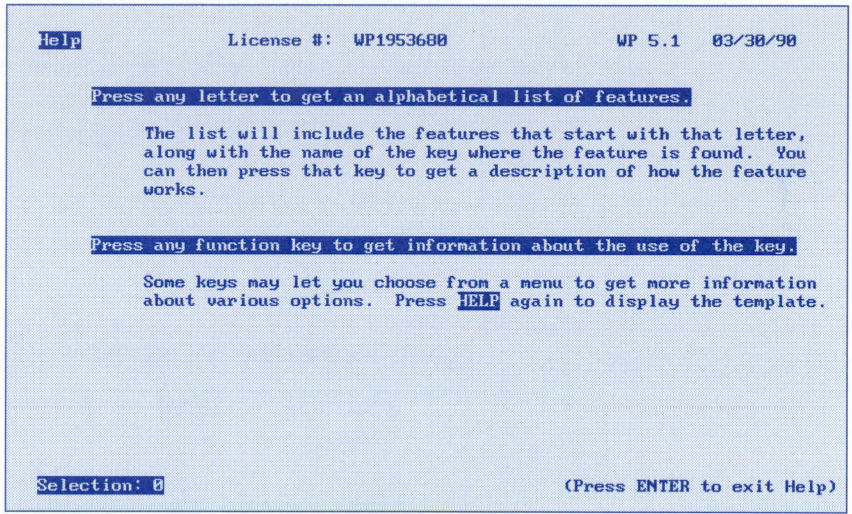

Help
License #: WP1953680
WP 5.1 03/30/90
Press any letter to get an alphabetical list of features.
The list will include the features that start with that letter, along with the name of the key where the feature is found. You can then press that key to get a description of how the feature works.
Press any function key to get information about the use of the key.
Some keys may let you choose from a menu to get more information about various options. Press HELP again to display the template.
Selection: 0
(Press ENTER to exit Help)

The version and release date of your software appear in the upper-right corner of the screen. Notice the two sets of instructions to get information about features and function keys. You will access information about the Go To command, look at two versions of the WordPerfect 5.1 template (function key layout), and press (ENTER) or the space bar to exit the Help facility.

▶ To view a list of commands beginning with the letter "G":

1. Press **G**.
2. Look for Go To on the list of features, and notice Ctrl-Home in the Keystrokes column, as shown in the next figure.

Features [G]	WordPerfect Key	Keystrokes
Generate Tables, Indexes, etc.	Mark Text	Alt-F5,6,5
Generic Word Processor Format	Text In/Out	Ctrl-F5,3,1
Global Search and Replace	Replace	Home,Alt-F2,Replace
Go To	GoTo	Ctrl-Home
Go to DOS/Shell	Shell	Ctrl-F1,1
Graphics	Graphics	Alt-F9
Graphics Box Options	Graphics	Alt-F9,1-4 or 6,4
Graphics Files Directory	Setup	Shft-F1,6,6
Graphics Quality	Print	Shft-F7,g
Graphics Quality (Default)	Setup	Shft-F1,4,8,3
Graphics Screen Type	Setup	Shft-F1,2,2

▶ To view detailed information about the Go To command:

1. Press CTRL-HOME.

▶ To view two versions of the template showing function key assignments:

1. Press F3 to view the template for a 12-function key enhanced keyboard layout.
2. Follow the screen instructions to press **1** to view the PC/XT keyboard template shown next.

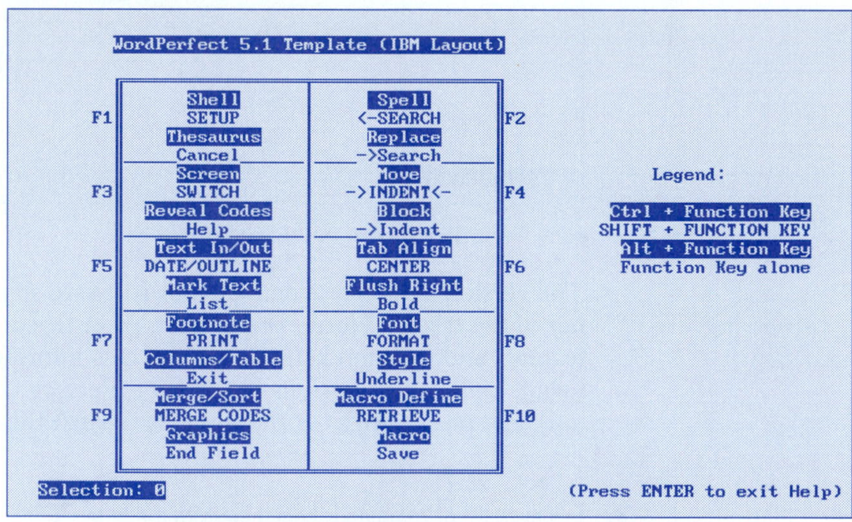

3. Press ENTER or the space bar to exit the Help facility.

▶ To practice using the Help facility on your own:

1. Press F3 to access the Help facility.
2. Look up the function of END.
3. Look up the functions of PGUP and PGDN.
4. Randomly press keys to view other Help screens.
5. Press ENTER to exit the Help facility.

USING THE STATUS LINE

Creating a new document is as easy as typing on the blank screen that appears on the monitor after you access WordPerfect 5.1. The ***status line*** appears at the bottom of the screen. This line contains valuable information about the document you are editing.

Four items on the right side of the status line indicate the current position of the cursor (the WordPerfect 5.1 cursor is usually a flashing dash within a document). The components of the current status line are:

Doc 1	The document that you are currently editing on the screen. WordPerfect 5.1 allows you to have two documents open at one time. You may switch between the documents or have two windows open on the screen and view both documents at once.
Pg 1	Current page number being edited.
Ln 1"	Current line number being edited.
Pos 1"	Current position of the cursor within the line indicated as Ln.

The status line indicates that the cursor is located in document 1, page 1, on a line 1 inch from the top of the page and 1 inch from the left margin of the page. These margin settings are automatically set by WordPerfect 5.1 (***default settings***) but can be changed, as can the method of measuring (***unit of measure***).

The screen examples in this module display cursor status, margins, and tab positions in inches, and they initially reflect default settings. The placements of text on your screen may vary somewhat from those shown in this module if different settings have been established for your system.

WordPerfect 5.1 initially displays the line number (Ln) and current position of the cursor (Pos) as inches, indicated by the inches symbol (") or the small letter "i" next to the number. The unit of measure can be changed to centimeters or points, or to WordPerfect 4.2 format, which states the number of lines from the top of the page and the number of characters (columns) from the left margin. There are normally six lines per inch down the page and ten characters per inch across a line. Your display is usually easier to read if inches are displayed when you use fonts that have other than the standard 10 pitch (characters per inch).

EXPLORING WORDPERFECT 5.1'S MENUS

Prior to WordPerfect's version 5.1, command sequences were initiated only by pressing function keys alone or in combination with (CTRL), (ALT), and (SHIFT). WordPerfect 5.1 provides an extensive menu system as an alternative to pressing function key combinations. For example, you can press the function key combination (SHIFT)-(F1) to access a full-screen display of six setup areas: **M**ouse, **D**isplay, **E**nvironment, **I**nitial Settings, **K**eyboard Layout, and **Loc**ation of Files. As an alternative, you can use the series of menus shown in the next figure to access the same six options.

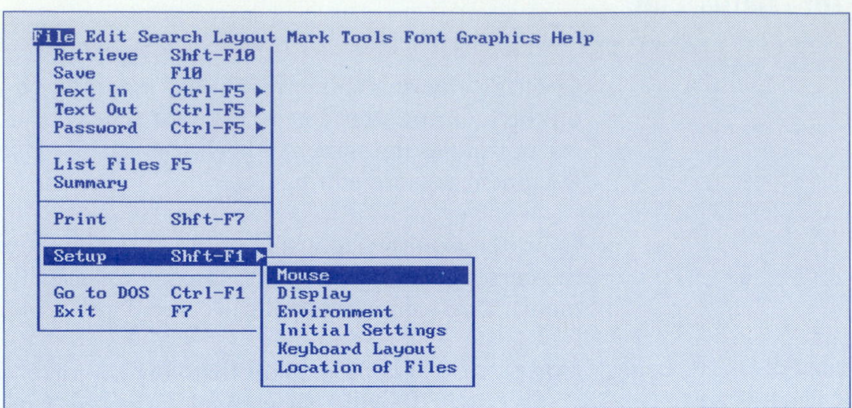

Press (ALT)-= to access the WordPerfect 5.1 menu system and the horizontal menu that first appears across the top of the screen. To select an option on the horizontal menu bar and display the associated pull-down menu, press (←) or (→) to highlight the option and then press (ENTER) or (↓).

To select an option from a pull-down menu, such as the File pull-down menu in the previous figure, press (↓) or (↑) to highlight the desired option and press (ENTER). A ▶ symbol at the right end of an option indicates an additional pull-down menu. Starting with the 3/30/90 release of WordPerfect 5.1, the comparable function key combinations appear next to each menu option.

If you want to abort a command sequence initiated by menus or function keys, simply press (ESC) or (F1) for Cancel. Press the key a sufficient number of times to back out of previous selections.

Working with a Mouse

A ***mouse*** is a piece of equipment used to execute operations otherwise specified through a keyboard. WordPerfect 5.1 supports the use of most two- or three-button mice to perform three tasks: to move the WordPerfect cursor, to make menu selections, and to mark (highlight) text as a block. This alternate input device requires that you position the mouse cursor on the screen and "click," "double-click," or "drag" the mouse.

Do not confuse the WordPerfect 5.1 cursor—usually a flashing dash (_)—with the ***mouse cursor.*** The mouse cursor is usually displayed as a reverse-video box that appears when you move the mouse. To ***click*** a mouse means to press a button, then release it. To ***double-click*** a mouse, execute two clicks in rapid succession. To ***drag*** a mouse, press and hold down a button, then move the mouse.

To distinguish between two separate single clicks and a double-click, WordPerfect 5.1 assesses the time interval between clicks. If you want an action to be interpreted as a double-click, be sure the second click falls within the established time interval (which you can alter using the Mouse Setup menu options).

The WordPerfect 5.1 Cursor

Position the mouse cursor at the target location within the document and click the left mouse button. If the mouse cursor is positioned on text or codes that control the document, the WordPerfect 5.1 cursor moves to that location. If the mouse cursor is located in a blank area of the screen, the WordPerfect cursor moves to the closest text.

Menu Selections

Click the right mouse button to display the menu bar. Either move the mouse pointer to a pull-down menu option and click the left mouse button (or click the left button, drag the mouse to the desired option, and release the button). Click the right button to exit from a menu.

The method to abort a menu sequence varies with the number of buttons on the mouse. To cancel with a three-button mouse, simply click the middle mouse button. To cancel with a two-button mouse, press and hold either button, click the other button, and then release the initial button.

Text Blocks

Move the mouse cursor to the beginning of the text you want to mark as a ***block***, press and hold down the left button, drag the pointer to the end of the text, and release the left button.

If you have the mouse correctly installed and set up to run with WordPerfect 5.1, practice until you become adept at clicking, double-clicking, and dragging.

Setting Defaults

WordPerfect 5.1 comes with defaults set automatically. You can adjust how your display looks or mouse behaves, where your files will be saved, and the initial page layout for every document.

Using an option on the Initial Settings menu, you can establish codes to set ***margins***, ***fonts*** (print styles), and the ***alignment*** of text along left and right margins (***justification***). In Project 3, you will learn how to enter and view codes that control that current document only. In this section, you will use the Setup menu to establish initial codes that will be automatically in effect for every new document.

To illustrate the concept, you will establish an initial left-justification code, which causes all text to align along the left margin but not the right margin (the default setting in WordPerfect 5.1 is full justification, which spaces words within a line to align text along both left and right margins). After you complete the appropriate Setup command sequence, the code [Just:Left] controls each new document.

▶ To access the screen on which to enter initial codes:

1. Load WordPerfect 5.1 and access a blank document screen (refer to "Starting WordPerfect 5.1" if you do not remember the steps).
2. Press SHIFT-F1 to access the Setup screen.

3. Press **4** for **I**nitial Settings.

   To select from a full screen of options, type the number of the option or the highlighted letter in the option name. In this case, press **4** or **I**.

4. Press **5** for Initial **C**odes and check that your screen display resembles the following figure.

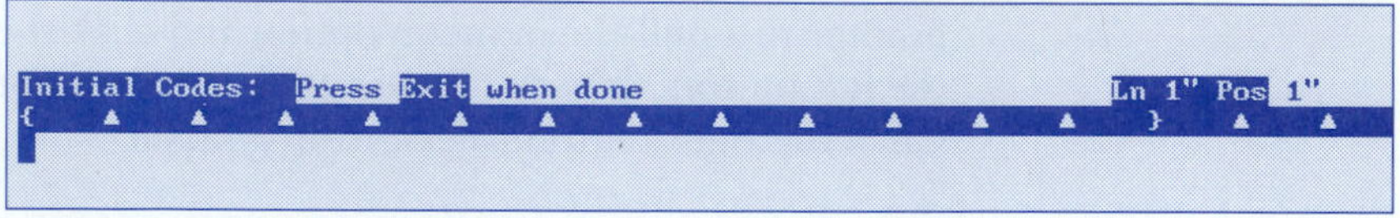

▶ To place a left-justification code on the Initial Codes screen:

Do not complete these instructions if you have been advised by your instructor or supervisor not to change initial settings.

1. Press (SHIFT)-(F8) to access **F**ormat options.
2. Press **1** for **L**ine and then **3** for **J**ustification.
3. Press **1** for **L**eft and press (F7) to return to the Initial Codes screen.

   Check for the addition of the left-justification code, shown next.

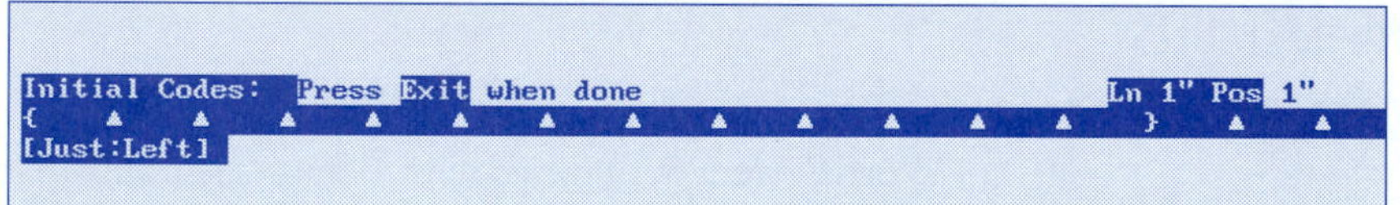

4. Press (F7) twice to restore the blank document screen.

Figures representing printouts of documents developed in this module reflect the left-justification setting. To remove an initial code, repeat the steps to access the Initial Codes screen, use arrow keys to highlight the code to be removed, and press (DEL).

Summary

- Word Perfect 5.1 is a popular word processing program that is easy to install and begin using on a computer.
- You can either accept or customize WordPerfect's defaults for screen display, mouse movement, file storage, and document layout.

- To invoke commands and manipulate text, you can select pull-down menu options with a keyboard or a mouse or you can press function key combinations.
- Whenever you get stuck with menus, commands, or concepts, you can use WordPerfect's on-screen Help facility instead of having to page through a manual.
- You can create new or retrieve previously saved documents. Once a document is open, the status line at the bottom of the screen supplies important information.
- Before printing, you can make changes and corrections easily using WordPerfect's extensive editing features.
- WordPerfect allows you to set up how all your documents will look when printed. You can establish layout settings for margins, tabs, and text justification that will automatically apply to all the documents you create, or you can customize settings for each individual document.

Key Terms

alignment	file	on-screen help
block	font	point
click	justification	pull-down menu
cursor	margin	status line
default setting	menu bar	type
double-click	mouse	unit of measure
drag	mouse cursor	

Study Questions

True/False

1. Pressing (F1) activates the Help feature. T F
2. WordPerfect 5.1 can automatically search for words or phrases you specify. T F
3. You exit WordPerfect by pressing (F10). T F
4. Pressing (F7) activates the Print feature. T F
5. You can choose to print all or part of a document. T F
6. The mouse cursor is the same as WordPerfect's flashing underline text cursor. T F
7. A triangle at the right of a menu option indicates an additional pull-down menu. T F
8. You remove initial codes by exiting WordPerfect. T F
9. Both (ESC) and (F1) cancel command sequences. T F
10. You can see how your final document will look on screen by selecting View Document. T F

Fill in the Blanks

1. You start WordPerfect 5.1 on a dual floppy system by typing the command __________.
2. To tell WordPerfect to store your data on a disk in drive A:, press (F5) for List, type __________ and press (ENTER).
3. Pressing (SHIFT)-(F10) __________ a document from your disk.
4. The __________ shows you where you are located in your document.
5. The standard keyboard has __________ function keys, and the enhanced keyboard has __________ function keys.
6. The default unit of measure for WordPerfect's status line is inches, but you can change it to __________ or __________.
7. Press __________ to exit the Help facility.
8. Making changes to a document is usually called __________.
9. All documents are saved as files whose names must follow __________ naming conventions.
10. You activate the menu bar by typing __________.

For Discussion

1. Name the five components of word processing.
2. What are the four items displayed in WordPerfect 5.1's status line?
3. What is a default setting?
4. What are the three keys used in combination with WordPerfect's function keys to initiate command sequences?
5. What does Initial Codes establish for new documents?

Project 1: Creating and Editing a Memo

After completing this project, you should be able to:

- Enter text into a WordPerfect 5.1 document
- Move the cursor
- Insert and delete blank lines
- Insert and delete text
- Save a document

ENTERING TEXT

Entering text into WordPerfect 5.1 involves nearly the same procedure as entering it on a typewriter, with one exception. Press ENTER, the equivalent of the ***carriage return*** on a typewriter, at the end of the paragraph instead of at the end of every line within the paragraph. If a single line of text is shorter than the width of the page, such as the title of a document, press ENTER at the end of the line. The cursor moves to the next line. To enter a blank line, press ENTER without entering text. In this project, you will create and edit the following document.

```
MEMO

To: WordPerfect Users

Subject: Using Quick Start

Welcome to our new employees and interns. We are pleased to
enroll you in our accelerated word processing training program.

This Quick Start program is designed to introduce you to the
documents most commonly produced by all departments of the
newspaper.

The highlight of this accelerated program will be your work with
the Advertising Department. The targeted custom promotional
brochures they create using WordPerfect will amaze you.

You will find all of us eager to help you. Quick Start has been
one of the most successful programs at the newspaper.

P.S. You will not believe how much better you will type using
WordPerfect.
                                  Doc 1 Pg 1 Ln 4.83" Pos 2.2"
```

▶ To enter a single line of text and two blank lines:

1. Position the cursor so the status line reads Doc 1 Pg 1 Ln 1" Pos 1".
2. Type **`MEMO`** and press ENTER.
3. Press ENTER twice to insert two blank lines.

   The newly typed line appears on the screen, and the cursor is now on the fourth line (the status line reads Doc 1 Pg 1 Ln 1.5" Pos 1"). Pressing ENTER the first time ended line 1; pressing ENTER twice inserted two blank lines.

▶ To enter the "To:" line at line 1.5 inches:

1. Position the cursor so the status line reads Ln 1.5".
2. Type **`To: WordPerfect Users`** and press ENTER.
3. Press ENTER to insert one blank line.

▶ To enter the "Subject" line:

1. Position the cursor two lines below the "To:" line.
2. Type **`Subject: Using Quick Start`** and press ENTER.

3. Press ENTER twice to insert two blank lines.

   Your status line should now read Doc 1 Pg 1 Ln 2.33" Pos 1". The line (Ln) and position (Pos) may vary depending on typing errors or alternate margin settings on your system. Check the screen frequently against the figures in this module to ensure that your document is generally correct.

A document is beginning to take shape on the screen. Single-line sentences were formed by using words, punctuation, the space bar, and ENTER. Pressing ENTER inserts a ***hard carriage return***, forcing the line to end and moving the cursor to the next line.

```
MEMO

To:  WordPerfect Users

Subject:  Using Quick Start





                                   Doc 1 Pg 1 Ln 2.33" Pos 1"
```

Your Ln and Pos may vary from those shown in illustrations, depending on where the cursor is located at the time.

Next you will learn techniques to move the cursor through the document. Then you will create the rest of the memo.

Moving the Cursor

Always think of a document in WordPerfect 5.1 as you think of a paper document. There may be one or more pages. The WordPerfect screen is a window through which portions of the document may be viewed.

The cursor points to a specific ***character*** position in a document—a position where some action might take place, such as changing the character or inserting and deleting text.

Several keys move the cursor around in the document. Most keyboards have ***cursor keys*** on the numeric keypad. Enhanced keyboards also have an extra set of cursor keys on their own keypads. The keys are shown in the figure that follows, and the table after the figure describes the function of each key.

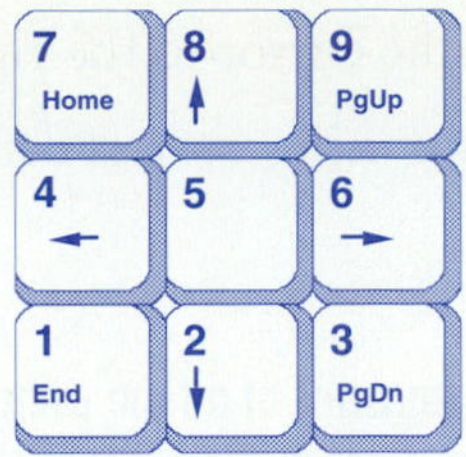

(↑), (↓), (←), or (→)	Moves the cursor up or down one line, respectively, and left or right one character.
(HOME) (←) (or (→) (↑) (↓))	Moves the cursor in the direction of the arrow, to the edge of the screen.
(HOME) (HOME) (←) (or (→) (↑) (↓))	Moves the cursor in the direction of the arrow, to the left, right, top, or bottom of the document.
(END)	Moves the cursor to the end of the line.
(CTRL)-(HOME)	This combination, referred to as Go To, moves the cursor to a defined character, to the top of a specified page, and to other locations in the text.

In the exercises that follow, be sure that (NUM LOCK) is turned *off* if your keyboard has both arrow keys and number keys on the same pad. Also, watch the changes in the status line.

▶ To move the cursor one line or one character at a time using the arrow keys:

1. Press (↑) until the cursor reaches the top of the page.
2. Press (↓) until the cursor reaches the bottom of the current document (line 2.33").
3. Move the cursor up to the "Subject" line.
4. Press (→) until the cursor reaches the end of the line.
5. Press (←) until the cursor reaches the beginning of the line.
6. Practice moving the cursor with the arrow keys until you are comfortable using them.

▶ To move the cursor more than one line or one character at a time using (HOME):

1. Press (HOME) (↑) to move the cursor to the top of the screen (not necessarily the top of the document) in one movement.
2. Press (HOME) (↓) to move the cursor to the bottom of the screen in one movement.
3. Move the cursor to the beginning of the "Subject" line using the arrow keys.

4. Press HOME → to move the cursor to the right edge of the screen.
5. Practice moving the cursor using various combinations of the HOME and arrow keys.

▶ To move the cursor more than one character at a time using END:

1. Move the cursor to the beginning of the "Subject" line.
2. Press END.

   Notice that the cursor moved to the end of the current line.

▶ To move the cursor using the Go To feature, CTRL-HOME, and send the cursor to the next place that an uppercase "Q" is found:

1. Move the cursor to the upper-left corner of the page. The status line should read Doc 1 Pg 1 Ln 1" Pos 1".
2. Press CTRL-HOME.

   Check that the words "Go to" are in the lower-left corner of the screen.
3. Press **Q**.

   Check that the cursor moved to the first character position to the right of the "Q" in "Quick" on the "Subject" line of the memo.

If you type a lowercase "q," the operation terminates with a beep, since no lowercase "q" exists in the document. When the Go To fails to find the target you defined, no message appears on the screen. If you are working with a multiple-page document, you can press CTRL-HOME and type a specific page number.

Composing Paragraphs

As you type, text fills the line and continues on to the next line automatically; WordPerfect 5.1 automatically moves the cursor to the beginning of the next line. Also, the program moves the last word of one line to the next line if the word does not fit. This automatic positioning of text, which happens if you do not press ENTER at the end of a line, is called ***word wrap***. Do not worry if you type faster than the words appear on the screen. WordPerfect stores the words for a moment until it can catch up with you. The device that allows this is called a keyboard buffer.

At the end of a ***paragraph***, press ENTER. Only the last line should end with a hard carriage return. By pressing ENTER, in this case, you signal WordPerfect 5.1 to place codes within the document to end the line of text before the end of the line. Other codes cue other operations. You cannot see the codes except by using a special "reveal" command illustrated later in the module.

Check that the MEMO document shown in the following figure is on the screen.

```
MEMO

To:  WordPerfect Users

Subject:  Using Quick Start







                                        Doc 1 Pg 1 Ln 2.33" Pos 1"
```

▶ To enter the body of the memo:

1. Position the cursor three lines below the "Subject" line and type the text shown in the next figure.
2. If you make a mistake, keep typing. You will be able to correct it in a few minutes, when you edit the document.
3. Do not press ENTER at the end of a line unless it is the end of a paragraph or the end of a short line or unless you want to insert a blank line.

```
Welcome to our new employees and interns. We are pleased to
enroll you in our accelerated word processing training program.

This Quick Start program is designed to introduce you to the
documents most commonly produced by all departments of the
newspaper.

The highlight of this accelerated program will be your work with
the Advertising Department. The targeted custom promotional
brochures they create using WordPerfect will amaze you.

You will find all of us eager to help you. Quick Start has been
one of the most successful programs at the newspaper.
```

The *content* of your document should be the same as that of the document just shown. However, the *distribution* of the text on each line may be different. For example, alternate margin settings could be in effect or a special type font (print style and number of characters per inch) may be active for your printer.

Inserting and Deleting Text

Everyone makes mistakes. WordPerfect 5.1 makes correcting, or ***editing***, a document easy. Using the cursor keys, simply move the cursor to the text that needs changing. Replace incorrect text by typing over the error(s) or by inserting correct text and deleting errors.

WordPerfect 5.1 has been programmed to insert a character in an existing document if that character is typed where another character already exists. When you are typing a character where another exists, the default action will insert the new character, pushing the existing character to the right. You may, however, turn ***Insert*** mode off and replace an existing character with a new one (by using ***Typeover*** mode).

▶ To input additional text:

1. Move the cursor two lines below the last typed line.
2. Type the following text exactly as shown below; do not correct any errors yet.

   P.S. You wood knot believe how more better you will type using WordPerfect.

▶ To use the overtyping technique to change the word "more" to "much" in the line you just typed:

1. Turn on Typeover mode by pressing the (INS) key until the word "Typeover" appears at the left end of the status line at the bottom of the screen.
2. Move the cursor to the letter "m" in the word "more" in the last typed line.
3. Type **much** over the word "more."
4. Turn off Typeover mode by pressing the (INS) key until the word "Typeover" disappears at the left end of the status line at the bottom of the screen.

   The phrase should read "how much better."

You can also correct errors in text by inserting correct text and deleting errors. The following keys are often used in editing operations:

(INS)	Toggles between Insert (the default) and Typeover mode.
(DEL)	Deletes a single character *at the current cursor position*.
(BACKSPACE)	Deletes a single character *to the left of the current cursor position*.

(BACKSPACE) is usually located above (ENTER). The final screen display after pressing (BACKSPACE) is dependent on the mode in use at the time the key is pressed.

- *In Insert mode*, pressing (BACKSPACE) removes the character to the left of the cursor and packs in text from the right, removing blank spaces.

- *In Typeover mode*, pressing (BACKSPACE) removes the character to the left of the cursor but does not pack in text from the right, leaving blank spaces.

Generally, you use (BACKSPACE) when Insert mode (the default) is on.

▶ To correct the word "wood" to read "will" in the last sentence of the current document:

1. Position the cursor on the word "wood" in the last sentence of the document.
2. Press (INS) until the message "Typeover" disappears from the status line at the bottom left side of the screen.
3. Move the cursor to the space *immediately following* the word "wood" (between the words "wood" and "knot").
4. Press (BACKSPACE) four times to erase the word "wood."
5. Type **`will`**

   Notice how everything moves over to make room for the new text when Typeover mode is off (Insert is on). There are other ways to make this change, such as to type the letters "ill" over the letters "ood" (with Typeover mode turned on) to form the word "will." As you continue, there are plenty of opportunities to discover what works best for you.

▶ To correct the word "knot" to read "not" in the last line:

1. Move the cursor to the "k" in "knot."
2. Press (DEL) one time to remove the "k."

   The "k" above the cursor disappeared, and everything moved left one character. You just learned another way to delete text. The first way was to back up over it using (BACKSPACE).

   Check that your revisions result in the display shown next.

```
MEMO

To: WordPerfect Users

Subject: Using Quick Start


Welcome to our new employees and interns. We are pleased to
enroll you in our accelerated word processing training program.

This Quick Start program is designed to introduce you to the
documents most commonly produced by all departments of the
newspaper.

The highlight of this accelerated program will be your work with
the Advertising Department. The targeted custom promotional
brochures they create using WordPerfect will amaze you.

You will find all of us eager to help you. Quick Start has been
one of the most successful programs at the newspaper.

P.S. You will not believe how much better you will type using
WordPerfect.
                                    Doc 1 Pg 1 Ln 4.67" Pos 2"
```

Do *not* make any other corrections in your document yet. You will have an opportunity to do so in the next section.

The ability to make changes easily allows you to work efficiently and creatively. In part, this is because you know that you do not have to compromise your final output because of the labor of retyping large portions of a document to make small changes.

Saving the Document

Normally, you want to save your work, with all changes, on disk. The ability to save a document on disk is the real power of word processing or any computer program. Once saved on disk, it may be called back on the screen, changed, and saved again.

WordPerfect 5.1 provides a Save option on its File pull-down menu. You can also use two function keys to save your documents. Press F10 to initiate a save operation that returns you to the current document for additional input or editing; press F7 to exit your current document—saving the document or not saving the document—and then either exit WordPerfect or access a blank document screen.

You must provide a storage location and file name for any document you wish to save. The name may contain one to eight characters, optionally followed by a period and three additional characters. Do not use blank spaces. The instructions in this module assume you are saving your documents on a floppy disk in the A: disk drive. Modify the location specification from A: to the appropriate disk drive and directory as necessary for your computer system.

▶ To save your document and continue editing:

1. Menus: Press ALT-=, select File, then select Save.
   or Keys: Press F10.

   Check that the following message appears in the status line at the bottom of your screen.

   ```
   Document to be saved:
   ```

   In this module, all disk access will be to the A: disk drive. If you use a disk drive or path other than A:, make the necessary changes to the directions in the remainder of this module.

2. Insert a blank formatted disk in disk drive A:.

3. Type **A:QUICK** to designate the A: disk drive and the file called QUICK.

   The preceding steps store the current document on the A: disk drive under the name QUICK. If you are using a hard disk, you may prefer to store documents on the hard disk. If so, change the disk drive designator and path to the appropriate directory on the hard disk. If you are using a dual floppy-disk system, store documents on the B: disk drive. The A: drive designator is not required if you set the default disk drive and directory as suggested in "Starting WordPerfect 5.1," earlier in this module.

Check that your screen display resembles the following figure.

```
Document to be saved: A:QUICK
```

4. Press (ENTER).

   The current memo named QUICK is saved on disk and is also still available on the screen for editing. Notice that the file name now appears in the lower-left corner of the screen. The file name appears whenever you are editing the named document.

```
A:\QUICK                                         Doc 1 Pg 1 Ln 6.5" Pos 1"
```

To correct any other errors in your QUICK document, compare the document on your screen with the memo shown at the beginning of the project, and make the necessary changes in content to make them the same.

Printing the Document

WordPerfect 5.1 provides three general methods to print all or a portion of a document. Two methods apply to the current document. A third alternative allows you to print a document stored on disk (Project 2).

If you want to print a single page or the entire document currently in memory, press (SHIFT)-(F7) to access the Print menu. You can also print a marked block of text (Project 4).

▶ To view how printed output will appear:

1. Menus: Press (ALT)-=, select File, and select Print.
   or Keys: Press (SHIFT)-(F7).
2. Press **6** for View Document.
3. Press **3** for Full Page.
4. Press the space bar to restore the Print menu.

▶ **To print the current document QUICK:**

1. Check that your printer is turned on.
2. Press **2** for Page.

Exiting the Current Document

In the previous save, you accessed the Save option on the File pull-down menu or pressed (F10) to initiate a command to save your document and continue working on the same document. Access the Exit option on the File pull-down menu or press (F7) when you wish to exit the current document—saving or not saving the file. Now you have the choice of exiting WordPerfect 5.1, accessing a blank document screen, or accessing a document stored on disk.

▶ **To save the on-screen document on disk and exit that document:**

1. Menus: Press (ALT)-=, select File, and then select Exit.
   or Keys: Press (F7).

   Check that the following message appears in the status line at the bottom of the screen.

```
Save document? Yes (No)
```

If you have not made any changes to the document since the last save operation, an additional message ("Text was not modified") appears on the right side of the status line.

2. Press **Y** or (ENTER).

   Check that the following message appears in the status line at the bottom of the screen.

```
Document to be saved: A:\QUICK
```

3. Press (ENTER) to save the file under the old name, QUICK.
4. Press **Y** to replace the old file.

   The current version of the memo named QUICK is saved on disk.

   Check that the following message appears in the status line at the bottom of the screen.

```
Exit WP? No (Yes)                                    (Cancel to return to document)
```

Pressing **N** returns you to a blank screen, where you may begin a new document or retrieve an existing document to continue. Pressing **Y** returns you to DOS.

5. Press **N** to stay in WordPerfect 5.1, or press **Y** to exit WordPerfect.

This project has introduced you to the basics of creating a WordPerfect document. You can continue with the Review Exercises, go on the the next project, or exit WordPerfect.

Summary

- In WordPerfect, text automatically "wraps" from the end of one line to the next. You only need to press ENTER (the equivalent of a carriage return on a typewriter) at the end of a paragraph.
- You can move the cursor one or more character spaces at a time using different combinations of arrow keys and command keys or clicking and dragging with your mouse.
- WordPerfect's status line lets you know where the cursor is located in the document. It always reports which document window is active, and what page, line, and position you are working in.
- Depending upon how you have used Setup to configure margins, font, and size defaults, your status line and screen may look slightly different from those shown in the figures.
- To insert a blank line, press ENTER at the beginning of a line. To delete a blank line, position the cursor at the beginning of the blank line and press DEL. To insert text, position the cursor at the point of insertion, press INS if the word Typeover appears in the lower-left corner of the screen, and type the new text.
- To type over existing text, position the cursor at the text to be edited, press INS until the word Typeover appears in the lower-left corner of the screen, and type the new text.
- Press BACKSPACE to delete a character preceding the cursor; press DEL to delete the character at the cursor.
- When you save your document, you can choose the drive and directory where you want to store it. WordPerfect uses the same conventions as DOS for naming files. Remember to save your files frequently.
- WordPerfect allows you to print the current document or a document stored on disk.

Key Terms

carriage return
character
cursor key
editing
hard carriage return
Insert
paragraph
Typeover
word wrap

Study Questions

True/False

1. You can move the cursor without inserting text with either the arrow keys or a mouse. T F
2. Press SCROLL LOCK to switch between Insert and Typeover modes. T F
3. Pressing BACKSPACE deletes one character to the right of the cursor. T F
4. If you are currently working with a document on the screen, you must save the text before you can access a blank document screen. T F
5. The top of the screen is always the top of the document. T F
6. WordPerfect 5.1 automatically saves your text as you type. T F
7. When the cursor rests at the first character position on a line, press ENTER without typing in text to create a blank line. T F
8. When using the Go To command to position the cursor at the first occurrence of a specified character, it doesn't matter whether you type your specification in upper- or lowercase letters. T F
9. You can access WordPerfect's on-line Help facility by pressing F3. T F
10. Pressing HOME HOME ↓ moves the cursor to the bottom of the screen. T F

Fill in the Blanks

1. To end a paragraph or insert a blank line, press __________.
2. To save a document and continue editing the document, press __________.
3. Press __________ to initiate exiting from WordPerfect.
4. The automatic positioning of text, which happens if you do not press ENTER at the end of a line, is called __________ .
5. In the status line on the bottom right of the screen, "Ln" means __________ .
6. When Insert mode is off, the word __________ appears in the status line at the bottom of the screen.
7. Press __________ to go to a specific position in your document.
8. If you have NUM LOCK turned on, when pressing END, you will insert a __________ into your document instead of moving your cursor to the end of the line.
9. Pressing SHIFT-F1 accesses the __________ menu.
10. To remove the character at the current cursor position, press __________ .

For Discussion

1. What happens when you press (HOME) (→)?
2. Describe what word wrap is and where you encounter it.
3. How is a paragraph on a word processor different from one typed on a typewriter?
4. List three ways to insert a character into text.

REVIEW EXERCISES

Review the concepts presented in Project 1 by completing the following tasks. If necessary, review the material.

Prepare the first part of a memo to the president of a company. You will add a table and additional text in later review exercises.

1. Access a blank document screen in WordPerfect 5.1 and enter the following memo.

```
To: Linda Wiest, Vice President

From: Jeff Kelner, Supervisor-Finishing Department

Date: August 15, 1992

Re: Request for payroll data and promotion recommendations


The following table contains the information you requested. I am
also recommending that two employees receive pay increases based
on the performance evaluations which I have included below the
table.
```

2. Edit the memo to read as shown below (correct spelling of names, titles, the subject line, and the content of the memo).
3. Save the new memo to the diskette in the A: drive under the name **8_15WAGE.MEM**. You will use this document in a subsequent review exercise.

```
To: Linda Weist, President

From: Jeff Keller, Foreman-Finishing Department

Date: August 15, 1992

Re: Departmental payroll data

The following table contains the information you requested by
phone this morning. I suggest that two employees receive pay
increases based on performance evaluations summarized below the
table.
```

Project 2: Managing Your Files

After completing this project, you should be able to:

- Specify the drive on which to store a document
- List the files on a disk
- Retrieve a document file from disk
- Rename a file
- Look at a file without retrieving it
- Copy files
- Delete files

Using the List Files Feature

WordPerfect 5.1's ***List Files*** feature offers a menu of commands to help you manage your files on disk while remaining in WordPerfect. To access List Files, select the List Files option on the File pull-down menu or press F5. Type a new disk drive\directory path or accept the current path and press ENTER. A menu appears at the bottom of the screen.

```
1 Retrieve; 2 Delete; 3 Move/Rename; 4 Print; 5 Short/Long Display;
6 Look; 7 Other Directory; 8 Copy; 9 Find; N Name Search: 6
```

Keystroke/Command	Result
1 for **R**etrieve	Loads the highlighted document into memory, ready for editing.
2 for **D**elete	Removes a file from disk. Is similar to the DOS DELETE and ERASE commands.
3 for **M**ove/Rename	Changes the name of a file in the current directory or moves a file to another directory.
4 for **P**rint	Prints a file from disk. The advantage of the Print option is that you can print all or part of a file. For example, to print page 1 of a document and then pages 5 through 9, at the prompt "Page(s): (ALL)" type `1,5-9` and press ENTER. To print the document currently on-screen does not require using List Files.

5 for **S**hort/Long Display	Allows you to switch between a short display of file names (the default: two columns, file names only) and a long display of file names (one file name to a line, including file description, file name, file size, and last revision date).
6 for **L**ook	Allows you to see the contents of a file, without retrieving the file into WordPerfect 5.1. In ***Look*** mode you cannot edit the document; you can only scroll up and down.
7 for **O**ther Directory	Changes the disk drive and directory currently accessed by List Files. You can access any disk or directory on your computer.
8 for **C**opy	Duplicates a file from a hard disk to a floppy disk or to another subdirectory on the hard disk. If you duplicate a file on the same disk or subdirectory, you must give the duplicate file a different name.
9 for Find	Searches file names or file contents for words or phrases and marks the file names with an asterisk if the word or phrase is found.
N for **N**ame Search	Locates a file name in a long list of names when you press **N** and the first letter of the file name. The highlight moves to the first file that begins with that letter. Pressing a second letter causes the highlight to move to the first file name beginning with the two letters just typed.

CHANGING DISK DRIVES

If you are like most WordPerfect 5.1 users, you will probably store data in several subdirectories on a hard disk and on floppy disks. There are several methods of changing disk drives and subdirectories. The change can be temporary (affecting only the current operation) or permanent (staying in effect until you specify a different drive).

Method 1: You can make a temporary change by preceding a file name with a subdirectory any time you store or retrieve a file to disk, as you did when you saved the QUICK document in Project 1.

Method 2: You can specify a disk drive and subdirectory at the time you access the List Files feature. Select List Files from the File pull-down menu or press (F5). You then see the current disk drive and subdirectory, which may vary from the following figure.

```
Dir C:\WP51\DATA51\*.*                    (Type = to change default Dir)
```

To change the current disk drive and directory, enter the name of the new disk drive and directory after accessing List Files. This change is temporary. The next time you access List Files or save a new document on disk, the old default disk drive is used. To make this change permanent, follow the screen instructions to precede the new disk drive and directory designation with an equals (=) sign.

Method 3: You can also establish a permanent change of directory after accessing the List Files feature by pressing **7** for **O**ther Directory from the List Files menu.

Note: The instructions in this project reflect A: as the disk drive containing the disk on which to store WordPerfect 5.1 files. Modify the instructions as necessary if you are storing documents in a different disk drive or directory.

▶ To temporarily change the disk drive and list files on the disk containing the project files:

1. Access a blank WordPerfect 5.1 document screen.
2. Menus: Press (ALT)-=, select File, and select List Files.
   or Keys: Press (F5).
3. Type `A:` and press (ENTER).

   Substitute another disk drive\directory for A: if you are storing your files in another location.

   To view only selected files, include the DOS wildcard * when you specify location. For example, if you want to see only files that begin with the letters WP, type `A:\WP*.*` and then press (ENTER).

   Check that the designation of the new disk drive you specified appears at the top of your screen display of files. The information on your screen may vary from that shown in the following example.

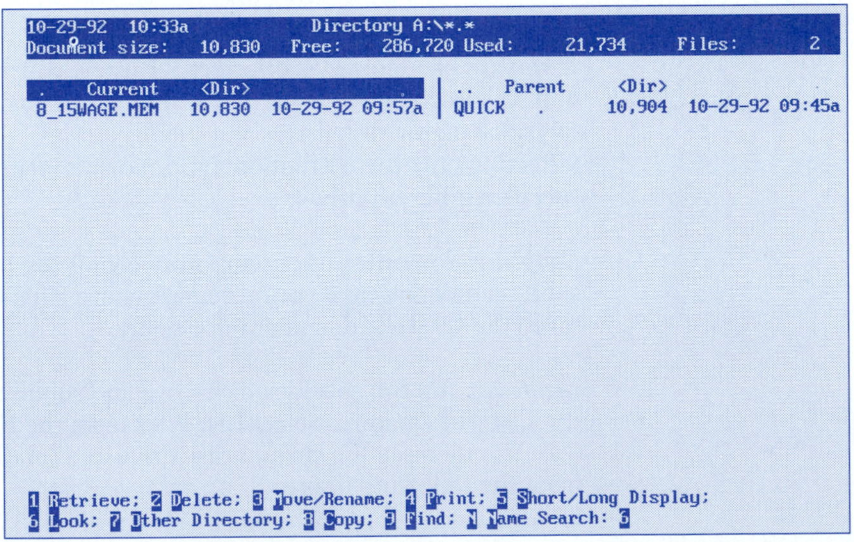

The first two lines are highlighted and display the date, time, document directory path, document size, the amount of remaining space on the disk in use, the amount of space used, and the number of files.

The next lines display information about files stored on the disk. File names are listed in alphabetical order in two columns divided by a center line. If files are too numerous to be displayed on a single screen, an arrowhead (▲▼) appears at the top or bottom of the line dividing the rows of file names. The arrowhead indicates that you can ***scroll*** the display up or down to view all files.

The ten-option List Files menu appears at the bottom of the screen. The number 6 appears at the end of the menu, indicating that Look (option 6) is the default menu choice. If you press (ENTER) without pressing a key from **1** to **9** or pressing **N**, WordPerfect 5.1 looks at the current directory.

RETRIEVING A DOCUMENT

A major feature of a word processing program is the ability to store documents on disk and ***retrieve*** them for editing and printing. To retrieve a document using the List Files feature, access the list of file names, highlight the name of the file to be retrieved, and press **1** to select the **R**etrieve option from the menu.

▶ To retrieve the document QUICK:

1. Use the arrow keys to highlight QUICK on the List Files screen shown in the previous figure.
2. Press **1** to **R**etrieve the highlighted document (do not press (ENTER)!).

   A short delay occurs while the file is being loaded from disk. Do not press keys while the file is being loaded. WordPerfect 5.1 will "remember" the keys you pressed, then apply them to the document once it is loaded.

   Check that the upper portion of the document QUICK has been retrieved and is now designated as DOC 1 in the status line at the bottom of the screen.

   To ***view*** (but not edit) the contents of a document, press (F5) to get a listing of files. Then position the cursor on the desired file name and press (ENTER) or **6** for **L**ook.

Caution: In many software programs, such as Lotus 1-2-3, pressing (ENTER) after highlighting a file name retrieves that file for editing. If you see a WordPerfect 5.1 document (file) on screen but you cannot make a change in the document, you probably pressed (ENTER) after highlighting a file name instead of pressing **1** to **R**etrieve a file for editing.

▶ To exit the current document without making changes and remain in WordPerfect 5.1:

1. Press (F7).
2. Press **N** in response to the prompt about saving the document.
3. Press **N** in response to the prompt about exiting WordPerfect 5.1.

Renaming a Document

Frequently, you ***rename*** files to make their names easier to remember. Using the rename option is as easy as accessing List Files, highlighting the file name to be changed, pressing **3** for **M**ove/Rename, and entering the new name. WordPerfect 5.1 places the disk drive designator, path, and file name at the bottom of the screen. If you change the file path, the file will be moved to the new subdirectory. If you change only the file name, the file is renamed but not moved.

▶ To access the rename option:

1. Menus: Press (ALT)-=, select File, and select List Files.
   or Keys: Press (F5).
2. Type **A:** and press (ENTER).
3. Highlight QUICK, press **3** for **M**ove/Rename, and check that the file name appears at the bottom of the screen.

New name: A:\QUICK

▶ To rename the file:

1. Press (END) to move the cursor to the end of the line.
2. Type **.MEM** and press (ENTER) to add the extension to the end of the name; check that the file name QUICK has been changed to QUICK.MEM.

3. Press (F7) to exit the List Files display.

Looking at Documents

Often, you cannot remember which file you want to access from disk until you look at the document. The Look option provides a quick and easy way to view a document.

► To access List Files and look at the QUICK.MEM file without retrieving it:

1. Menus: Press (ALT)-=, select File, and select List Files.
   or Keys: Press (F5).
2. Type `A:` and press (ENTER).
3. Highlight QUICK.MEM and press **6** for **L**ook or press (ENTER).

   Check that the QUICK.MEM document, a memo to WordPerfect users about the benefits of using Quick Start, is displayed on the screen.

   To access the contents of QUICK.MEM while in Look mode, press the arrow keys. You can move the cursor up and down to view the entire document, but you cannot move the cursor left and right to access words within the document.
4. Press (F7) twice to restore and then exit the List Files display.

Copying a Document

Often, it is necessary to make a second copy of a document. For example, before making extensive changes to a document, you can use the Copy option to make a duplicate copy of the original file. Then, if it is necessary to undo your changes, you can delete the changed file and use the original (unchanged) version.

You can also use Copy to transfer files from one disk drive to another. To copy more than one file at a time, highlight each file name and press * to ***mark*** the file before you press **8** for **C**opy.

► To access List Files, copy the QUICK.MEM file to QUICK.BAK, and exit List Files:

1. Menus: Press (ALT)-=, select File, and select List Files.
   or Keys: Press (F5).
2. Type `A:` and press (ENTER).
3. Highlight the name of the QUICK.MEM file and press **8** for **C**opy.
4. Type `QUICK.BAK` at the "Copy this file to:" prompt and press (ENTER).

   Check that your screen displays QUICK.MEM and QUICK.BAK files.

```
10-29-92  10:48a              Directory A:\*.*
Document size:    10,830   Free:    275,456 Used:       32,638      Files:        3

 .    Current      <Dir>                         |  ..     Parent       <Dir>
 8_15WAGE.MEM     10,830   10-29-92 09:57a       |  QUICK    .BAK      10,904   10-29-92 09:45a
 QUICK   .MEM     10,904   10-29-92 09:45a
```

5. Press (F7) to exit the List Files display.

Deleting a Document

Often, it is desirable to expand available disk memory by removing files that are no longer needed. You can use the Delete option to remove one or more files. To remove one file, access the List Files screen, highlight the file name to be deleted, and press **2** for **D**elete. WordPerfect 5.1 displays the file name and the prompt "Delete drive\directory\filename? **N**o (**Y**es)." Press **Y** to complete the removal of the file.

In the exercises that follow, you will delete the QUICK.BAK document you created using the List Files Copy option.

▶ To access the List Files display and the Delete option:

1. Menus: Press (ALT)-**=**, select File, and select List Files.
   or Keys: Press (F5).
2. Type **A:** and press (ENTER).
3. Highlight the name of the QUICK.BAK file and press **2** for **D**elete.

▶ To delete QUICK.BAK and exit the List Files screen:

1. Press **Y** in response to the prompt "Delete A:QUICK.BAK? **N**o (**Y**es)."
2. Press (F7).

Exercise caution when using the Delete function. You can delete more than one file at a time by first marking the files you want to remove with an asterisk (*), and then following the same procedure for single files. Instead of asking you to confirm a specific file name to be deleted, WordPerfect 5.1 will prompt you with "Delete marked files? **N**o (**Y**es)." If you Press **Y,** it asks you to confirm your first response with "Marked files will be deleted. Continue? **N**o (**Y**es)."

If you press **Y** you will lose the files that are marked or highlighted. If your current directory is highlighted, you will delete all the files in that directory.

This concludes Project 2 on managing your files. You can stay in WordPerfect 5.1 and continue with the Review Exercises, work Project 3, or press (F7) to exit WordPerfect.

SUMMARY

- By using your computer regularly, you will create many files. WordPerfect 5.1's List Files feature helps you manage the storage and retrieval of your WordPerfect documents.
- By using List Files, you can display a list of WordPerfect documents stored on the disk.
- If you want to modify a document, you must first retrieve your file from disk. If you want only to examine the contents of a file, you can use the Look feature to view your document without making changes.
- Always make backup copies of files you created. You can either make a copy with the same name on another disk or directory or you can make a copy on the same disk or directory by changing the name.
- Use the Move/Rename option on the List Files screen to change the location or name of a file.
- Saving copies of your work is always a good idea, but once you're certain you no longer need them, you can delete the files.

KEY TERMS

List Files	rename	view
Look	retrieve	
mark	scroll	

STUDY QUESTIONS

True/False

1. Two files on a floppy disk or in the same directory on a hard disk cannot have the same name. T F
2. When you retrieve a file, the document loads from memory to disk for editing. T F
3. Moving and renaming a file are two options on the List Files menu. T F
4. You can print all or part of a file from disk using the List Files command. T F
5. Renaming a file makes a copy of it. T F
6. The Short file display lists file names in two columns. T F
7. Name Search locates a file name in a list when you press the first letter of the file name. T F
8. You can delete more than one file at a time. T F
9. Pressing command keys while the document is being loaded makes it run faster. T F
10. You can store files on drive A: only. T F

Fill in the Blanks

1. Pressing (F5) accesses the __________ command.
2. To duplicate a file, use the __________ option of List Files.
3. Press __________ to exit the List Files screen.
4. To change the directory you are using to store or view files, use the __________ option of List Files.
5. To view a list of all the files in the WP subdirectory on drive C: that begin with "P," specify __________.
6. The __________ consists of the drive letter followed by a __________, subdirectory name(s) followed by a __________, and the file name.
7. "Document to be saved?" appears when you press __________.
8. You can view the contents of a file without retrieving it using the __________ option of List Files.
9. By selecting Find you can mark file names with an __________ if the word or phrase you specified is found.
10. Files are listed in __________ order.

For Discussion

1. What is the difference between a directory and a subdirectory?
2. How do you change the disk drive where files will be saved temporarily? How do you change it permanently?
3. What information about files is available on the List Files screen?
4. Discuss the purposes of the List Files options for which hands-on activities were not provided.
5. How is viewing a document different from editing it?

Review Exercises

Review the concepts presented in Project 2 by completing the following tasks. If necessary, review the material.

1. Access a blank document screen in WordPerfect 5.1.
2. Use List Files to retrieve the QUICK.MEM document.
3. Immediately exit the document screen, saving the file as BACKUP1.MEM.
4. Use the Look option on the List Files screen to view the newly created BACKUP1.MEM document.
5. Use the Copy option to copy BACKUP1.MEM to BACKUP2.MEM on the same disk drive.
6. Mark the BACKUP1.MEM and BACKUP2.MEM files with asterisks and use the Delete option to remove the files.
7. Exit the List Files screen.

PROJECT 3: FORMATTING THE MEMO

After completing this project, you should be able to:

- Set and change margins
- Use the tab ruler
- Reveal formatting codes
- Delete formatting codes
- Indent paragraphs

USING FORMATTING OPTIONS

WordPerfect 5.1 offers a variety of options for formatting documents. Format options control the general layout, or appearance, of a document. Several more commonly used format functions include setting tabs and margins, specifying page numbers, and creating page ***headers*** and ***footers*** that appear at the tops and bottoms of all pages.

You can initially access format features by menus or the function key combination (SHIFT)-(F8). WordPerfect 5.1 divides the format functions into four groups (Line, Page, Document, and Other) according to their applications, as shown by the following figure, which WordPerfect displays after you press (SHIFT)-(F8).

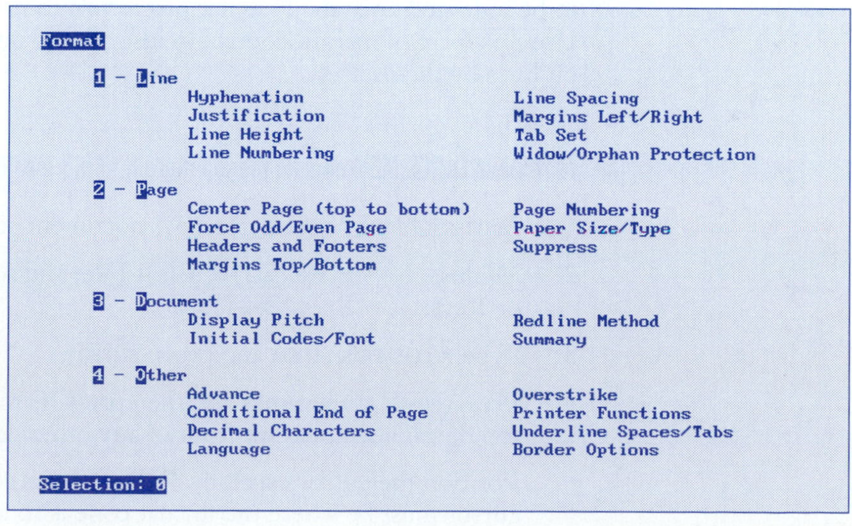

After selecting one of the four groups of format options, you are presented with the next menu from which to select the option you want to invoke. For example, to insert a new ***tab ruler*** in the current document, you access the Format screen, select Line, and then select Tab Set from the next menu. Once you specify the desired tab settings, press (F7) to exit the Format menu; WordPerfect 5.1 inserts the new tab ruler into the text.

Formatting codes are inserted in the text at the points where the Format menu was accessed. The codes are generally hidden from view. However, pressing (ALT)-(F3) for **R**eveal Codes causes the text to be displayed in the upper half of the screen and the same text with codes revealed to be displayed in the lower half of the screen. In the following exercises, you will set the left, right, top, and bottom margins; set a new tab ruler; and explore the ***hidden codes*** inserted by WordPerfect 5.1.

Setting Margins

Margins are the space between the primary text area and the top, bottom, and side edges of the paper or a screen that represents the paper. Margin settings control the distance that printing begins from the top and left edges and the distance printing ends at the bottom and right edges. WordPerfect 5.1, by default, sets 1-inch margins on all sides. You may reset these margins at any point in the document by using the Format menu. Once you establish new margin settings, the margins remain set until changed or the end of the document is encountered.

The left margin can be temporarily altered by pressing (F4) to access the ***→Indent*** function. The margin is indented one tab each time you press (F4). The left tab returns to the original margin when you press (ENTER). Pressing (SHIFT)-(F4) to access the ***→Indent←*** function causes the left and right margins to be indented one tab. The margins return to normal when you press (ENTER). Use this form of margin control to insert large quotations that are to appear on lines by themselves.

▶ To retrieve QUICK.MEM and set the top margin to 0.5 inch and the bottom margin to 1 inch:

1. Access a blank WordPerfect 5.1 document screen.
2. Menus: Press (ALT)-=, select File, and select Retrieve.
   or Keys: Press (SHIFT)-(F10).
3. Type **`A:QUICK.MEM`** and press (ENTER).
4. Press (HOME) three times and then press (↑) to position the cursor at the top of the document, in front of any other codes.

   Position the cursor carefully. Before you access the Format menu, the cursor must be where the format code is to take effect.

5. Menus: Press ALT-=, select Layout, and select Page.
   or Keys: Press SHIFT-F8 **2**.

   Check that the Format: Page menu shown next appears on your screen.

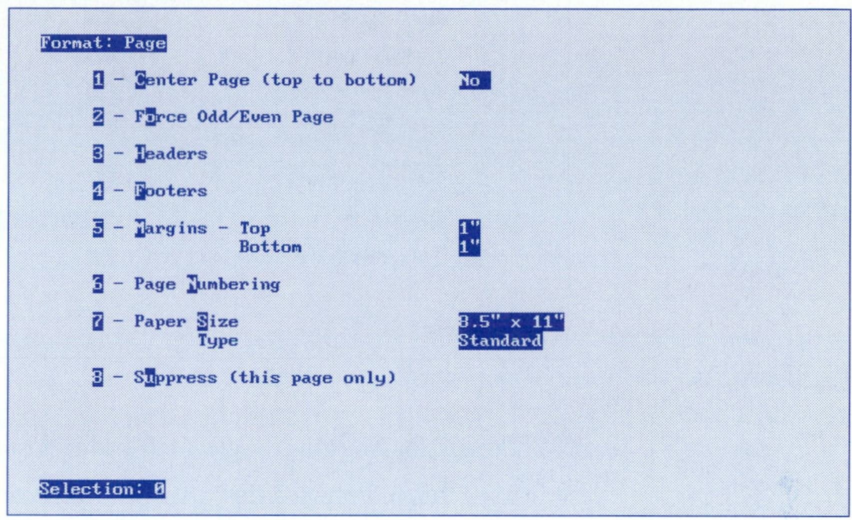

```
Format: Page

     1 - Center Page (top to bottom)          No

     2 - Force Odd/Even Page

     3 - Headers

     4 - Footers

     5 - Margins - Top                        1"
                   Bottom                     1"

     6 - Page Numbering

     7 - Paper Size                           8.5" x 11"
               Type                           Standard

     8 - Suppress (this page only)



Selection: 0
```

6. Press **5** for **M**argins.
7. Type **.5** and press ENTER to set the top margin to 0.5 inch.
8. Type **1** and press ENTER to set the bottom margin to 1 inch.

   Check that the top and bottom margins are defined as shown in the following figure.

```
     5 - Margins - Top                        0.5"
                   Bottom                     1"
```

9. Press F7 to exit the Format menu.

   With the cursor at the top of the page, the line number (Ln) in the status line should read 0.5" instead of 1". When typing measurements, such as margins, *do not* type the inches symbol ("). The symbol is added when you type the number and press ENTER.

▶ To set the left and right margins:

1. Menus: Press ALT-=, select Layout, and select Line.
   or Keys: Press SHIFT-F8 **1**.

   Check that the following Format: Line menu appears on your screen.

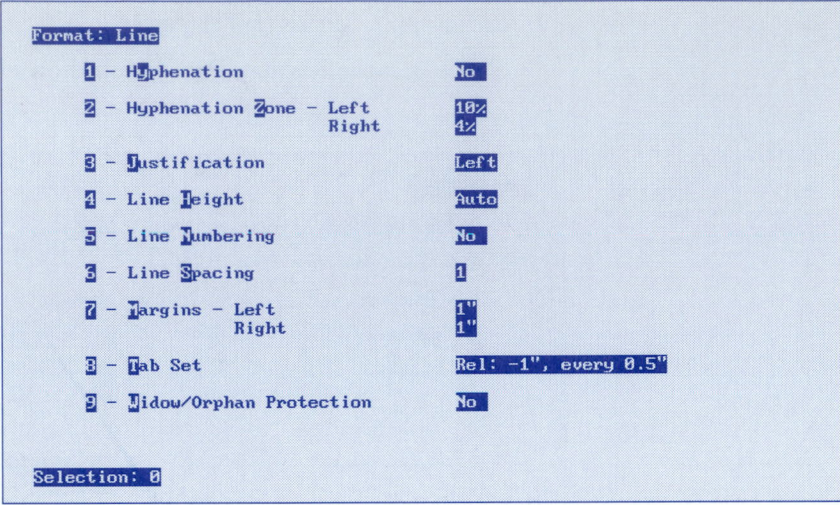
```
Format: Line

     1 - Hyphenation                          No

     2 - Hyphenation Zone - Left              10%
                            Right             4%

     3 - Justification                        Left

     4 - Line Height                          Auto

     5 - Line Numbering                       No

     6 - Line Spacing                         1

     7 - Margins - Left                       1"
                   Right                      1"

     8 - Tab Set                              Rel: -1", every 0.5"

     9 - Widow/Orphan Protection              No

Selection: 0
```

2. Press **7** for **M**argins to select left and right margins.
3. Type **1.5** and press (ENTER) to set the left margin.
4. Type **1** and press (ENTER) to set the right margin.
5. Press (F7) to exit the Format menu.
6. Press (HOME) twice and then press (↓) to reformat the document.
7. Press (HOME) twice and then press (↑) to return to the top of the document.

   Check that your document has been reformatted as shown in the following figure.

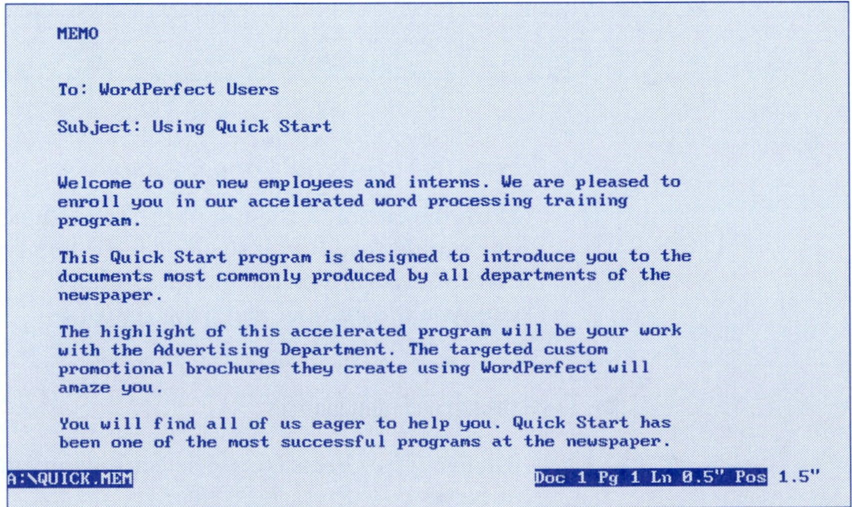
```
MEMO

To: WordPerfect Users

Subject: Using Quick Start

Welcome to our new employees and interns. We are pleased to
enroll you in our accelerated word processing training
program.

This Quick Start program is designed to introduce you to the
documents most commonly produced by all departments of the
newspaper.

The highlight of this accelerated program will be your work
with the Advertising Department. The targeted custom
promotional brochures they create using WordPerfect will
amaze you.

You will find all of us eager to help you. Quick Start has
been one of the most successful programs at the newspaper.
A:\QUICK.MEM                          Doc 1 Pg 1 Ln 0.5" Pos 1.5"
```

Notice the effect of changing margin settings. The narrower margins shorten the lines so that text is redistributed on all lines. However, the content of the lines has not changed. Also, note the effect on the status line. With the cursor at the top of the document, the line status (Ln) indicates the top margin is set at 0.5 inch. The position status (Pos) indicates that the left margin is set at 1.5 inches.

SETTING TABS

Tab settings are used to control paragraph indentations, temporary margins, columns of text, headings, and the alignment of decimal points in ***columns*** of numbers. They are set by inserting a tab ruler into the text at the place that you wish to change tab settings. The default tab ruler contains tab stops every 0.5 inch.

Tabs may be set at any location on the tab ruler. WordPerfect 5.1 offers four types of tab settings: left, right, center, and decimal. Each of the types may be preceded by a series of periods called ***dot leaders***. These tab settings control how text is positioned around the tab setting. For example, while typing, if you set a centered tab, the text you type disperses evenly on each side of the tab. A left tab causes text to align at the left of the tab setting, and a right tab causes text to align at the right. A ***decimal tab*** causes typed numbers to extend to the left until a period (.) is typed; then the numbers begin extending to the right. The dot leader setting causes periods to precede typed text from the last tab setting.

Using WordPerfect 5.1, you can establish settings for ***relative tabs*** (the default), tabs that are defined in relation to the left margin in the document, or ***absolute tabs***, those that are defined in terms of the left side of the paper. For example, assume that you set a relative 1.5-inch left tab. If the current document has a 1-inch left margin, the first tab position is 2.5 inches from the left side of the page. If the current document has a 1.5-inch left margin, the first tab position is 3 inches from the left side of the page, but still only 1.5 inches from the left margin.

If you set an absolute 1.5-inch tab setting (the only tab type in WordPerfect versions prior to 5.1), the first tab position is 1.5 inches from the left edge of the paper regardless of the left margin setting. In the exercises that follow, you will set a tab at the beginning of each paragraph in the QUICK.MEM document, eliminate the default left tab settings every 0.5 inch, and set a single relative left tab stop.

▶ To start each paragraph in the current QUICK.MEM document with one tab:

1. Position the cursor at the beginning of the first paragraph on the letter "W" in "Welcome . . . ."
2. Press (TAB).

   The first paragraph is properly indented one tab stop, and all text on the line has shifted to the right.
3. Position the cursor at the beginning of the second paragraph.
4. Press (TAB).
5. Position the cursor at the beginning of the third paragraph.

6. Press TAB.
7. Position the cursor at the beginning of the fourth paragraph.
8. Press TAB.

   Each paragraph in the memo should now begin with a traditional paragraph indentation.

▶ To access the Tab Set option on the Format: Line menu:

1. Press HOME twice and then press ↑ to position the cursor at the top of the document.
2. Menus: Press ALT-=, select Layout, and select Line.
   or Keys: Press SHIFT-F8 **1**.

   The following figure illustrates the default Tab Set option.

```
8 - Tab Set                          Rel: -1", every 0.5"
```

▶ To insert a new tab ruler at the beginning of the memo:

1. Press **8** to access the **T**ab Set facility and check that the tab ruler appears at the bottom of the screen.
2. Press HOME twice and then press ← to move the cursor to the left edge

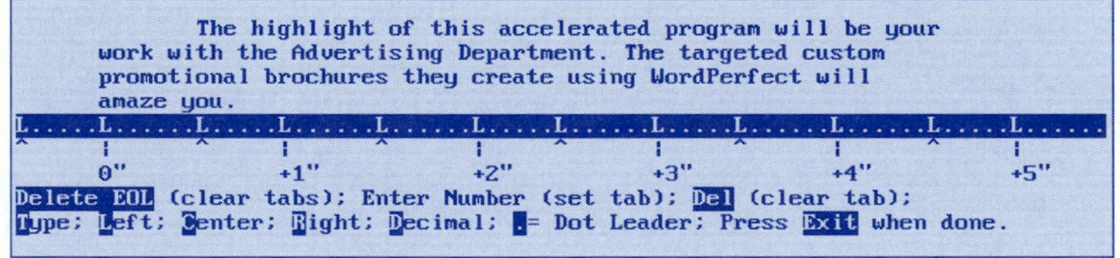

   of the tab ruler.

3. Press CTRL-END to clear all current tabs.
4. Position the cursor at the vertical mark (|) indicating 1 inch.
5. Press **L** to insert a left tab.

   Another method for entering tab settings is to type the tab position and press ENTER. For example, you can accomplish the preceding two actions by typing **1** and pressing ENTER.

   Check that your new tab ruler matches the one in the following figure.

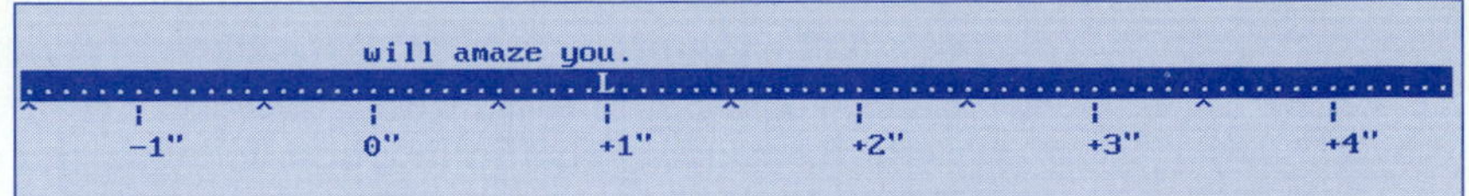

6. Press (F7) twice to return to editing the memo.

   Check that the paragraph indentations in your memo have changed to reflect the new tab setting. The indentations should be wider.

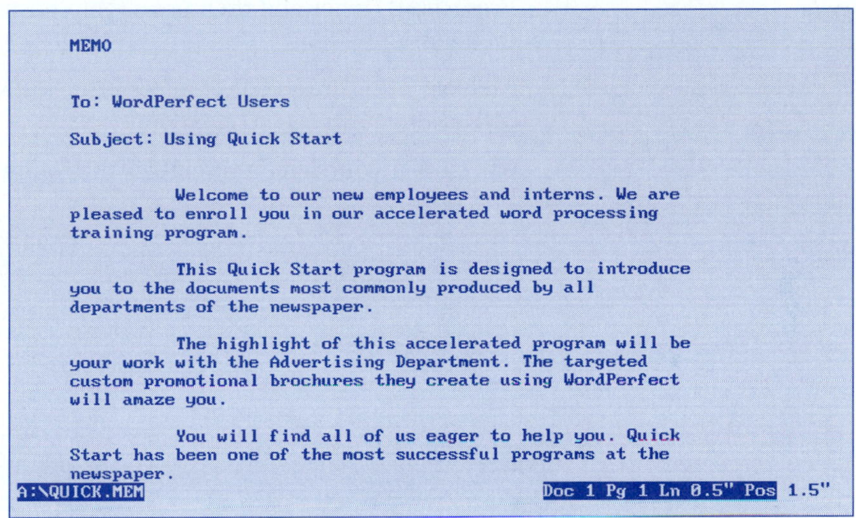

REVEALING FORMATTING CODES

To produce the results of formatting features, both on the screen and in printed copy, WordPerfect 5.1 embeds hidden codes within the document. You see only the results of the codes, such as a centered heading or the indentations resulting from setting tabs.

To use menus to display the hidden codes, select Reveal Codes from the Edit pull-down menu. Otherwise, press (ALT)-(F3) or (F11). The resulting screen display contains three sections:

- A status line splits the screen horizontally and indicates the current disk drive and document name as well as information about the position of the cursor.
- Above the status line, text from the current document is displayed as it is normally viewed on the screen.
- Below the status line, corresponding text from the current document is displayed with the formatting codes visible.

To delete an unwanted code, highlight the code in ***Reveal Codes*** mode and press DEL. Or, press BACKSPACE to delete a hidden code. When not in Reveal Codes, you are prompted with a question that must be answered with a **Y** or **N**. In the exercises that follow, you will view the embedded codes in the QUICK.MEM document and, at the top of the document, delete the code that sets a 1-inch tab. For a complete listing of codes and for information concerning the editing of codes displayed using the Reveal Codes mode, consult the WordPerfect 5.1 documentation.

▶ To reveal the codes in the QUICK.MEM document currently on the screen:

1. Press HOME twice and then press ↑ to position the cursor at the top of the memo.
2. Menus: Press ALT-=, select Edit, and select Reveal Codes.
   or Keys: Press ALT-F3 or F11.

   Check that your screen resembles the following figure.

```
     MEMO

     To: WordPerfect Users

     Subject: Using Quick Start

               Welcome to our new employees and interns. We are
A:\QUICK.MEM                                     Doc 1 Pg 1 Ln 0.5" Pos 1.5"
     [           ▲                                                   ]
[T/B Mar:0.5",1"][L/R Mar:1.5",1"][Tab Set:Rel; +1"]MEMO[HRt]
[HRt]
[HRt]
To: WordPerfect Users[HRt]
[HRt]
Subject: Using Quick Start[HRt]
[HRt]
[HRt]
[Tab]Welcome to our new employees and interns. We are[SRt]
pleased to enroll you in our accelerated word processing[SRt]
training program.[HRt]
[HRt]

Press Reveal Codes to restore screen
```

Three symbols usually appear beneath the status line if the Reveal Codes mode is active. Each ▲ symbol is a tab-setting indicator. The [symbol marks the location of the left margin. The right margin is indicated by a] symbol. If the original tab settings have not been changed, { } braces appear in place of [ ] braces.

The right-margin indicator may not appear in the figure if the margins have been changed in the current editing session. Once the document is saved and then retrieved, the margin indicators on a Reveal Codes screen will accurately reflect the current settings.

Six embedded codes appear in the bottom half of the screen:

[T/B Mar:0.5",1"]	Indicates the 0.5-inch top margin setting and the 1-inch bottom margin setting.
[L/R Mar:1.5",1"]	Indicates the 1.5-inch left margin setting and the 1-inch right margin setting.

[Tab Set:Rel: +1"]	Indicates the relative tab that is 1 inch from the current left margin.
[HRt]	Hard return code—that is, movement to the next line after pressing (ENTER).
[Tab]	Tab code—that is, temporarily moving the left margin to the next tab. Subsequent lines return to the original left margin.
[SRt]	Soft return code—that is, movement to the next line without pressing (ENTER).

▶ To delete the [Tab Set:Rel: +1"] code:

1. Press (HOME) twice and then press (↑) to position the cursor on the "M" in "MEMO" at the top of the QUICK.MEM document.
2. Press (←) to position the cursor on the [Tab Set:Rel: +1"] code.
3. Press (DEL).

   The code setting wider indentations for all paragraphs in the memo is removed and the indentations revert to the original 0.5-inch tab settings.

If a document does not print with the layout and appearance you desire, use the Reveal Codes mode to check the codes that are controlling the document, then delete unwanted codes.

▶ To return to document display without embedded codes:

1. Menus: Press (ALT)-=, select Edit, and select Reveal Codes.
   or Keys: Press (ALT)-(F3) or (F11).

Most users of WordPerfect 5.1 do not activate the Reveal Codes mode while creating or editing, preferring instead the full-screen display of the document without codes. However, if you encounter undesirable document formatting, activate Reveal Codes and check for unwanted codes.

▶ To exit the current document without saving changes to margins and tabs:

1. Menus: Press (ALT)-=, select File, and select Exit.
   or Keys: Press (F7).
2. Press **N** in response to the prompt "Save document? **Y**es (**N**o)."
3. Press **N** in response to the prompt "Exit WP? **N**o (**Y**es)."

INDENTING TEXT

In a previous exercise you pressed (TAB) to shift text to the right one tab for the first line of a paragraph. Subsequent lines within the paragraph aligned at the original left margin. Use (F4) for ***Indent→*** instead of (TAB) if you prefer that all lines—as opposed to just the first line—within the paragraph indent to align at the left. To indent text from both left and right margins, use SHIFT-F4 for →Indent←.

▶ To retrieve the original QUICK.MEM document and save it for an indent exercise to follow:

1. Menus: Press ALT-=, select File, and select Retrieve.
   or Keys: Press SHIFT-F10.
2. Type **A:QUICK.MEM** and press ENTER.
3. Menus: Press ALT-=, select File, and select Save.
   or Keys: Press F10.
4. Type **A:INDENT.MEM** as the new file name, and press ENTER.

▶ To indent the first paragraph one tab stop from the left margin in the INDENT.MEM document currently on the screen:

1. Position the cursor on the "W" in the first word of the first paragraph beginning with "Welcome . . . ."
2. Menus: Press ALT-=, select Layout, select Align, and select Indent→.
   or Keys: Press F4.

▶ To indent the second paragraph three tab stops from both margins in the INDENT.MEM document:

1. Position the cursor on the "T" in the first word of the second paragraph beginning with "This Quick Start . . . ."
2. Menus: Press ALT-=, select Layout, select Align, and select →Indent←.
   or Keys: Press SHIFT-F4.
3. Press SHIFT-F4 twice.

   Check that your document reflects the alignment shown in the following figure.

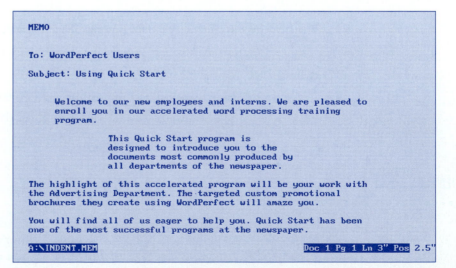

```
MEMO

To: WordPerfect Users

Subject: Using Quick Start

     Welcome to our new employees and interns. We are pleased to
     enroll you in our accelerated word processing training
     program.

               This Quick Start program is
               designed to introduce you to the
               documents most commonly produced by
               all departments of the newspaper.

The highlight of this accelerated program will be your work with
the Advertising Department. The targeted custom promotional
brochures they create using WordPerfect will amaze you.

You will find all of us eager to help you. Quick Start has been
one of the most successful programs at the newspaper.

A:\INDENT.MEM                                Doc 1 Pg 1 Ln 3" Pos 2.5"
```

▶ To exit the current document without saving indent settings:

1. Menus: Press ALT-=, select File, and select Exit.
   or Keys: Press F7.
2. Press **N** in response to the prompt "Save document? **Y**es (**N**o)."
3. Press **N** to stay in WordPerfect 5.1 and continue with the review exercises, or press **Y** to exit.

The original version of the memo should still be stored on disk as QUICK.MEM because you worked with a document named INDENT.MEM to avoid accidentally changing the main file used in the projects. The Review Exercises contain instructions to copy the QUICK.MEM version of the memo and to edit the 8_15WAGE.MEM document created in a previous Review Exercise.

SUMMARY

- Before or after you type the text of a document, a word processing program makes it easy to adjust the appearance of the document. Using WordPerfect 5.1's powerful formatting features, you can specify how to arrange single lines or paragraphs, whole pages, or entire documents.
- You can set unique margins and tabs for each document or for sections within a document. Margin settings control how far from the edge of the paper your text begins to be printed. Tabs are considered *absolute* when they are measured just like margins, but *relative* when they are measured beginning from the margin setting instead of the edge of the paper. The default setting is for relative tabs.
- You can set a temporary left margin by using the indent function. An indent sets the left margin one tab to the right for each time you press F4.
- As you make changes to the default settings of your document, WordPerfect inserts invisible formatting codes wherever a feature is to begin or end. Once you reveal the formatting codes, you can delete an unwanted code.

KEY TERMS

absolute tab
column
decimal tab
dot leader
footer
formatting code
header
hidden code
→Indent←
→Indent
margin
relative tab
Reveal Codes
tab ruler
tab setting

Study Questions

True/False

1. Pressing (F8) accesses Format features. T F
2. The size of WordPerfect 5.1's default Tab setting is five spaces. T F
3. Margin changes must be specified in a document before typing in the text. T F
4. Margin settings remain set until changed. T F
5. WordPerfect inserts codes to mark where you made spelling mistakes. T F
6. The default tab settings are relative to the left margin. T F
7. The →Indent← function causes the left and right margins to be indented one tab. T F
8. Use the inches symbol (") when specifying margins. T F
9. You are limited to setting one tab ruler for each document. T F
10. Formatting codes are invisible until you reveal them. T F

Fill in the Blanks

1. Press __________ to change line spacing.
2. The four groups of WordPerfect 5.1 Format functions are: __________.
3. WordPerfect's default margin settings are __________, for the left and right, and __________ for the top and bottom.
4. A way to temporarily set the left margin is to press __________ for __________.
5. To fit more text on a page, set the margins __________.
6. A(n) __________ tab setting measures from the left side of the paper.
7. To delete an unwanted formatting code, access Reveal codes, highlight the unwanted code, and press __________.
8. The code for a hard carriage return is __________.
9. The series of dots that may precede a tab are called __________.
10. The [T/B Mar:0.5",1"] code specifies __________.

For Discussion

1. Explain the two ways to measure tab settings.
2. When should you use an indent function instead of Tab?
3. What are the three symbols that usually appear beneath the status line if the Reveal Codes mode is active and what do they represent?
4. Why might you use a decimal tab? What are the other three kinds of tabs?
5. How would you set your left margin to 2 inches and right margin to 0.75 inch?

REVIEW EXERCISES

Review the concepts presented in Project 3 by completing the following tasks. If necessary, review the material.

1. Access the List Files screen, and copy the QUICK.MEM file to the same directory under the name PRACTICE.MEM.
2. Retrieve the PRACTICE.MEM document.
3. Set top and bottom margins of 0.5 inch in the PRACTICE.MEM document.
4. Set left and right margins of 2 inches in the PRACTICE.MEM document.
5. Establish three tab settings at 0.5-inch intervals starting at +1" on the tab ruler.
6. Press (TAB) twice at the beginning of each paragraph.
7. Access the Reveal Codes mode, and look for all hidden codes.
8. Delete one of the two tab codes at the beginning of each paragraph.
9. Exit the Reveal Codes mode.
10. Save the PRACTICE.MEM document and access a blank document screen.
11. Retrieve the 8_15WAGE.MEM document created in a previous review exercise, and use the indent feature to align the headings as shown below.

```
To:    Linda Weist, President

From:  Jeff Keller, Foreman-Finishing Department

Date:  August 15, 1992

Re:    Departmental payroll data
```

12. Save the 8_15WAGE.MEM document and access a blank document screen.

Project 4: Revising the Memo

After completing this project, you should be able to:

- Manipulate large chunks of text
- Mark blocks of text
- Copy and move blocks within a document
- Delete and undelete blocks
- Correct typing and spelling errors
- Use WordPerfect 5.1's Thesaurus
- Search for words and phrases
- Easily replace all occurrences of specific text
- Add print codes to enhance the appearance of your document

Manipulating Blocks of Text

Many WordPerfect 5.1 commands act on a ***block*** of text. Before invoking commands that act on a block of text, you must first mark that text by using the Block command. For example, if you want to delete a block of text, you must first mark that text by:

- Positioning the cursor at the beginning of the block
- Activating the Block feature
- Highlighting the block using the cursor keys

You can use menus to activate the Block feature by selecting Block from the Edit pull-down menu. As an alternative, press (ALT)-(F4) or (F12). Once the block of text is highlighted, invoke the Delete command by pressing (DEL) and pressing **Y** in response to the prompt "Delete Block? **N**o (**Y**es)."

Several WordPerfect 5.1 commands that manipulate text require that you first mark the text. Other commands that enhance text also require that you first mark the text. For example, if you want to underline a block of text that has already been typed, follow the block instructions outlined above. Once you have marked the block of text, press (F8) for Underline, and WordPerfect underlines the block.

The following is a list of the most common features that may be used after the text has been marked as a block.

Manipulate text	Enhance text
Copy	Bold
Delete	Center
Mark Text	Italics
Move	Underline
Print	
Search and Replace	
Sort	
Spell	
Switch	

Several of the features listed are discussed next. Once you know how to use the Block command, applying the other features is easy.

COPYING AND MOVING BLOCKS

The procedures for copying and moving text are identical. However, the results are different. ***Copying text***, as the name implies, means to duplicate a block of text in another location. ***Moving text***, on the other hand, means to transfer the text to a new location from its original location. To copy or move a block of text:

- Mark the text to be copied or moved using the Block command.
- Initiate the Copy or Move command.
- Indicate where the text is to be copied or moved, and complete the procedure.

► To retrieve QUICK.MEM and immediately save the document as BLOCK.MEM:

1. Access a blank WordPerfect 5.1 document screen.
2. Menus: Press (ALT)-=, select File, and select Retrieve.
   or Keys: Press (SHIFT)-(F10).
3. Type `A:QUICK.MEM` and press (ENTER).
4. Menus: Press (ALT)-=, select File, and select Save.
   or Keys: Press (F10).
5. Type `A:BLOCK.MEM` as the new file name, and press (ENTER).

   If you are not saving your document files to the A: disk drive during retrieve and save operations, substitute the appropriate drive and directory for your system.

► To insert a new block of text:

1. Position the cursor on the second line below the "Subject" line (that is, one line above the first full line of text).

2. Type

   In conclusion, we hope this program will be one of the most enjoyable experiences of your career.

3. Press ENTER.

   For illustrative purposes, the new paragraph is in the wrong position in the document. In the exercise that follows, you will position the new text at the bottom of the memo.

▶ To mark the new block of text for copying:

1. Position the cursor at the beginning of the new paragraph, on the "I" of "In conclusion . . . ."

2. Menus: Press ALT-=, select Edit, and select Block.
   or Keys: Press ALT-F4 or F12.

3. Press **.** (period) to move the cursor to the period at the end of the paragraph.

   Check that the first paragraph is highlighted as shown in the following figure.

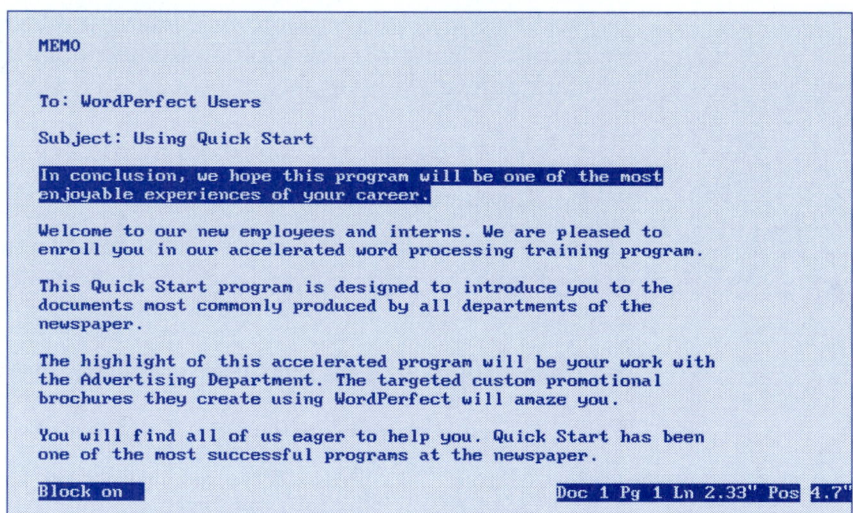

MEMO

To: WordPerfect Users

Subject: Using Quick Start

In conclusion, we hope this program will be one of the most
enjoyable experiences of your career.

Welcome to our new employees and interns. We are pleased to
enroll you in our accelerated word processing training program.

This Quick Start program is designed to introduce you to the
documents most commonly produced by all departments of the
newspaper.

The highlight of this accelerated program will be your work with
the Advertising Department. The targeted custom promotional
brochures they create using WordPerfect will amaze you.

You will find all of us eager to help you. Quick Start has been
one of the most successful programs at the newspaper.

Block on Doc 1 Pg 1 Ln 2.33" Pos 4.7"

▶ To complete copying:

1. Menus: Press ALT-=, select Edit, and select Copy.
   or Keys: Press CTRL-INS.

   The highlight on the paragraph to be copied has been turned off, and you see the following message at the lower-left corner of the screen. If you had selected Move, the entire paragraph would have disappeared.

Move cursor; press Enter to retrieve. Doc 1 Pg 1 Ln 2.33" Pos 6.6"

2. Position the cursor at the end of the last paragraph (after "newspaper") and press (ENTER) to transfer the block of text.

   If necessary, adjust spacing so that one blank space appears before the copied paragraph.

   Check that your document resembles the partial display shown next.

```
You will find all of us eager to help you. Quick Start has been
one of the most successful programs at the newspaper. In
conclusion, we hope this program will be one of the most
enjoyable experiences of your career.

P.S. You will not believe how much better you will type using
A:\BLOCK.MEM                                Doc 1 Pg 1 Ln 5.17" Pos 1"
```

If you want to change the position of a block of text within a document, execute a Move operation. Substitute (CTRL)-(DEL) for (CTRL)-(INS) in the previous directions.

An alternative to moving or copying a sentence, paragraph, or page is to position the cursor on the material to be moved; press (CTRL)-(F4); press **1** for **S**entence, **2** for **P**aragraph, or **3** for **P**age; and then press **1** for **M**ove or **2** for **C**opy. WordPerfect 5.1 highlights the selected material automatically.

You just completed a Copy operation to create duplicate text. In the next exercise, you will delete the original block of duplicate text.

DELETING AND UNDELETING BLOCKS

Earlier, you learned to delete text, one character at a time, by positioning the cursor on the text to be deleted and pressing (DEL). This method is impractical and time-consuming when deleting large blocks of text. Instead, mark the block of text to be deleted and press (DEL). WordPerfect 5.1 deletes the entire block at one time. If text is accidentally deleted, press (F1) for Cancel to display the most recent deletion. Press **1** to restore the highlighted text or press **2** to view the previous deletion. WordPerfect allows you to recall the three most recent deletions.

▶ To delete the first paragraph of the memo:

1. Position the cursor on the first character of the first paragraph, the "I" in "In conclusion, we . . . ."

2. Menus: Press (ALT)-=, select Edit, and select Block.
   or Keys: Press (ALT)-(F4) or (F12).

3. Press (ENTER) to move the cursor to the next hard return code, which indicates the end of the paragraph.

4. Press (DEL) and check that you see the following prompt on the status line.

```
Delete Block? No (Yes)
```

5. Press **Y** for Yes.

   The marked paragraph is deleted, and the remaining text has moved up to fill the space.

▶ To undelete the last text deleted:

1. Position the cursor two lines below the "Subject" line, where the deleted paragraph was located.
2. Press (F1) to Cancel the last deletion.

   The text reappears and remains highlighted until you restore or cancel the action.

   Check that the Undelete menu appears at the bottom of the screen.

```
Undelete: 1 Restore; 2 Previous Deletion: 0
```

3. Press **1** to **R**estore the highlighted text to the screen.

   The paragraph is restored.

▶ To delete the first paragraph again using an alternate method:

1. Position the cursor on any character within the first paragraph that begins with "In conclusion, we . . . ."
2. Menus: Press (ALT)-=, select Edit, and select Select.
   or Keys: Press (CTRL)-(F4).
3. Menus: Select Paragraph.
   or Keys: Press **2** for **P**aragraph.

   Check that the paragraph containing the cursor is highlighted and that the following menu appears at the bottom of your screen.

```
1 Move; 2 Copy; 3 Delete; 4 Append: 0
```

4. Press **3** for **D**elete to remove the highlighted paragraph and check that your memo appears without the "In conclusion" paragraph, as shown next.

```
MEMO

To: WordPerfect Users

Subject: Using Quick Start

Welcome to our new employees and interns. We are pleased to
enroll you in our accelerated word processing training program.
```

5. Press F7 to exit your document without saving it.

Checking Spelling and Using the Thesaurus

WordPerfect 5.1's ***Speller*** and ***Thesaurus*** are two important tools that help you develop effective documents. You can spell-check a word, a block, a page, or an entire document. When you invoke the spell-checking feature, WordPerfect accesses a dictionary with more than 100,000 words and "looks up" each word in your document. If a word is not found in the dictionary, the word is highlighted and a window on the bottom half of the screen appears with a list of possible correct spellings and a menu of actions you can take.

If a correct spelling appears on the list, simply press the letter that appears next to it, and the correct word replaces the misspelled word in the document. If the correct word does not appear on the list of possible spellings, one option is to leave the word as it is. The term may be correct; the Speller has failed to recognize it because it is an acronym, abbreviation, slang, or simply not in the dictionary. You can add the word to the dictionary, and the Speller will accept the term the next time it encounters the word. Also, you can change the spelling of the word, and the Speller will check the new spelling.

Other Speller features include the ***Look Up*** and ***Count*** options. Select the Speller and then the Look Up option, and WordPerfect 5.1 prompts you to input a word pattern. Enter the approximate spelling of the word you are interested in and a list of possible spellings appears. The word cannot be selected and inserted into the text. To do this, you must type the word into the document and then spell-check it as described above. Selecting the Count option returns a count of the number of words contained in the block, page, or document. You also see this count when you finish spell-checking a document.

When you invoke the Speller feature, you can select from the following options:

Word	Spell-checks the word at the cursor.
Page	Spell-checks the page on which the cursor is located.
Document	Spell-checks the whole document.
New Sup. Dictionary	Selects a new dictionary in which to look up words.

Look Up	Allows you to type a word pattern for the Speller to look up.
Count	Counts the number of words in the document.

When the Speller cannot find a word, you can select from the following options:

Skip Once	Skips the word and continues spell-checking the document.
Skip	Skips the word every time it is encountered.
Add	Adds the word to a supplemental dictionary; the word will not be checked again. Later you can add the word to the main dictionary.
Edit	Allows you to change the spelling of the word in the document.
Look Up	Allows you to type a word pattern for the Speller to look up.
Ignore Numbers	Ignores words that contain numbers in the rest of the document.

Invoking the Thesaurus causes WordPerfect 5.1 to look up the word at the cursor and return a list of words with a similar meaning (synonyms) and words that have the opposite meaning (antonyms). Use the Thesaurus to look up alternative words that may better express what you are trying to say. For example, suppose you are writing an evaluation about the new sales trainee who is assigned to you. In your report you write ". . . the new salesperson displays a great attitude." You want to use a stronger word to express "great." Place the cursor anywhere within the word "great" and select Thesaurus. On the screen appears a list of 26 similar words, including "magnificent," "superb," "outstanding," "excellent," and "exceptional."

To help you learn the process for using the Speller and Thesaurus, complete the following exercises. You will access a blank screen and begin typing notes from a recent sales meeting. As you type, spell-check your work and use the Thesaurus to enhance your notes.

▶ To create a new document with spelling errors:

1. Access a blank WordPerfect document if one does not appear on your screen.
2. At the first line, press (SHIFT)-(F6) to center the text that follows.
3. Type **WPC MEETING NOTES** and press (ENTER).
4. At the second line, press (SHIFT)-(F6).

5. Type **Western Region Sales Conference** and press ENTER.
6. At the third line, press SHIFT-F6.
7. Type **August 2, 1992** and press ENTER.
8. Press ENTER to position the cursor two lines below the date.
9. Type **1.** and then press F4 to indent the left margin.
10. Type

    Linda Weist, Oregon. Indikates telefone follow-up calls within three daze of a sales visit increased orders 40 percent, compared to visits without a follow-up call.

    Check that your document matches the one displayed next.

```
                    WPC MEETING NOTES
             Western Region Sales Conference
                     August 2, 1992

1.    Linda Weist, Oregon. Indikates telefone follow-up calls
      within three daze of a sales visit increased orders 40
      percent, compared to visits without a follow-up call.
```

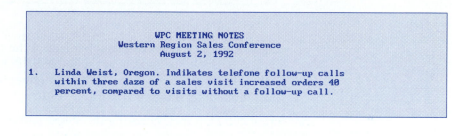

► To access the Speller:

1. Menus: Press ALT-=, select Tools, and select Spell.
   or Keys: Press CTRL-F2.

   Check that the Speller menu appears at the bottom of your screen as shown in the next example.

```
Check: 1 Word; 2 Page; 3 Document; 4 New Sup. Dictionary; 5 Look Up; 6 Count: 3
```

2. Using the menu at the bottom of the screen, you can press **1** for **W**ord to spell-check the word under the cursor, **2** for **P**age to spell-check the current page of text, or **3** for **D**ocument to spell-check the entire document. To spell-check a block of text, first mark the block of text to be checked and then press CTRL-F2 to start the spell-check.

► To initiate a spell-check of the current page:

1. Press **2** for **P**age to spell-check the current page.

   Check that your screen matches the display shown next.

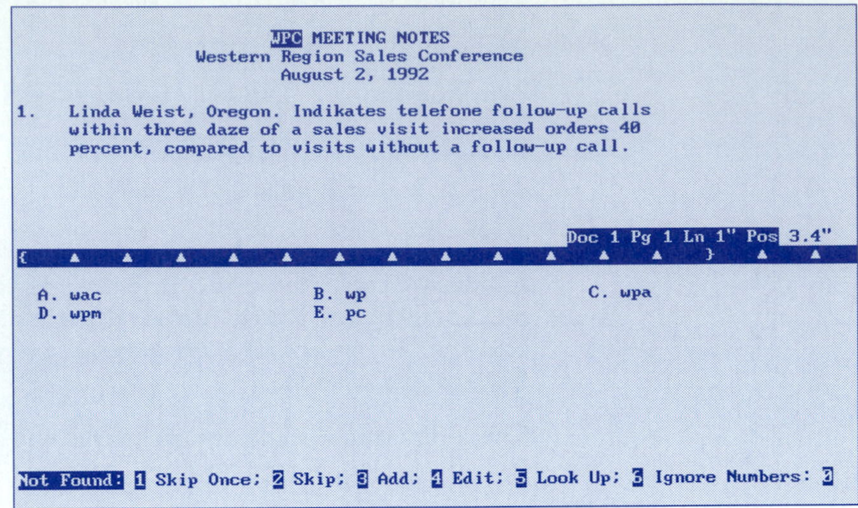

The document appears in the upper half of the screen, and a list of possible correct spellings appears in the lower half of the screen along with the spell-check Not Found menu. The highlighted word, "WPC," is an abbreviation, not a misspelled word.

2. Press **2** to **S**kip spell-checking the abbreviation "WPC."

3. Press **2** to **S**kip spell-checking the name "Weist."

▶ To correct misspelled words:

1. Check that the word "Indikates" is highlighted as being misspelled and that a list of five possible correct spellings is displayed as shown in the following figure.

2. Press **A** to select the word "indicates" from the list of possible correct spellings.

   The word "Indikates" changes to "Indicates"; the highlight rests on the next spelling error, "telefone."

3. Press **A** to select the word "telephone."

   Check that your screen matches the following figure.

```
                    WPC MEETING NOTES
              Western Region Sales Conference
                    August 2, 1992

1.   Linda Weist, Oregon. Indicates telephone follow-up calls
     within three daze of a sales visit increased orders 40
     percent, compared to visits without a follow-up call.






Word count: 32          Press any key to continue
```

The document has been spell-checked, and a message indicates that there are 32 words in the document. Notice that the word "daze" has not been corrected. The word "daze" is in the dictionary, so the Speller accepts the word as correct. Although you have spell-checked your document, it is important that you proofread the document for words that are spelled correctly but used inappropriately.

4. Press ENTER twice to exit the Speller.

▶ To expand the document and spell-check a single word:

1. Position the cursor two lines below the end of note 1.
2. Type **`2.`** and press F4 to indent the left margin.
3. Type

   `Arthur Morley, Washington. Prognistication for FY 1993 is a dramatic 300 percent increase in new sales.`

4. Position the cursor anywhere in the misspelled word "Prognistication."
5. Menus: Press ALT-=, select Tools, and select Spell.
   or Keys: Press CTRL-F2.
6. Press **1** for **W**ord to spell-check the word at the cursor.
7. Press **A** to select the first (and only) choice on the list.

   Check that your screen matches the following figure.

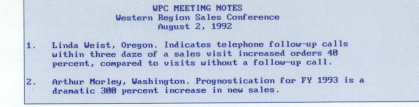

```
                    WPC MEETING NOTES
             Western Region Sales Conference
                     August 2, 1992

1.   Linda Weist, Oregon. Indicates telephone follow-up calls
     within three daze of a sales visit increased orders 40
     percent, compared to visits without a follow-up call.

2.   Arthur Morley, Washington. Prognostication for FY 1993 is a
     dramatic 300 percent increase in new sales.
```

▶ To exit the Spell feature and correct the word "daze" in note 1:

1. Press (F7) to Exit the Speller.
2. Change the word "daze" to "days" in note 1.

▶ To use the Thesaurus to change the word "dramatic":

1. Position the cursor anywhere in the word "dramatic" in note 2.
2. Menus: Press (ALT)-=, select Tools, and select Thesaurus.
   or Keys: Press (ALT)-(F1).

   Check that your screen matches the Thesaurus screen shown next.

   Two lines of the document appear at the top of the screen so that you can see, in context, the word marked for replacement. A list of 11 synonyms and one antonym for "dramatic" appears below the text. Notice that a period appears in front of several words. You can look at Thesaurus listings for these words, called ***headwords***, by pressing **3** for Look Up Word from the menu at the bottom of the screen.

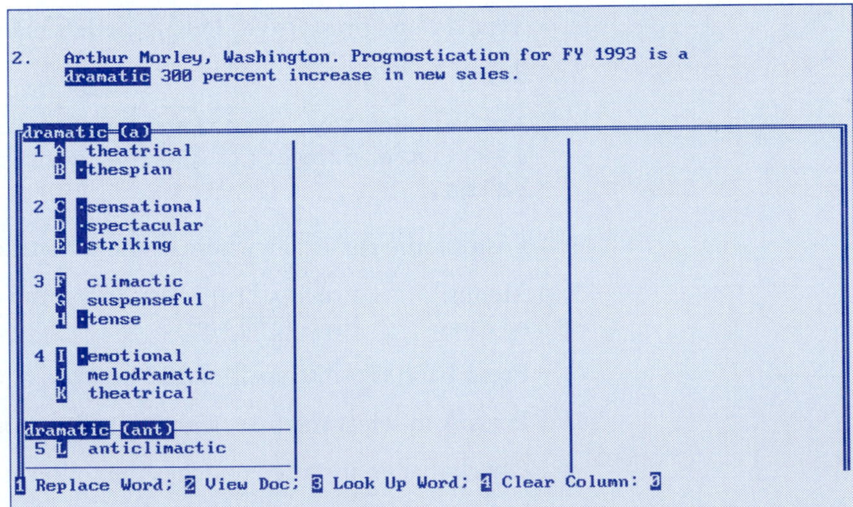

3. Press **1** for **W**ord to activate the Replace Word menu option.
4. Press **D** at the prompt "Press letter for word."

   Check that your screen matches the following figure. The word "dramatic" has been replaced by the word "spectacular."

```
2.   Arthur Morley, Washington. Prognostication for FY 1993 is a
     spectacular 300 percent increase in new sales.
```

5. Press F7 to exit without saving changes.

SEARCHING AND REPLACING TEXT

In the preceding sections, most of your efforts were directed toward improving the effectiveness of a single word or phrase. You changed type style, corrected spelling, and found appropriate substitutions. There are likely to be times, however, when you need to find—and perhaps change—some element of a document that appears in multiple places. For example, imagine typing a name such as "Theresa" several places in a long document, only to find the correct name is "Teresa.

" It would be tedious and time-consuming to proofread each page, looking for the name. Although a spell-check would eventually stop at each location if the name in question was not in the dictionary, you would still have to edit each occurrence individually.

Search commands make it easy to locate words and phrases or to ***replace*** text throughout an entire document. You can also remove excessive spacing, edit hidden codes, expand abbreviations, abbreviate words, and put the commands to a long list of other uses.

To use WordPerfect 5.1's powerful Search and Replace commands, take two initial steps: press ALT-= to access the Search pull-down menu and then select among the options shown in the following figure.

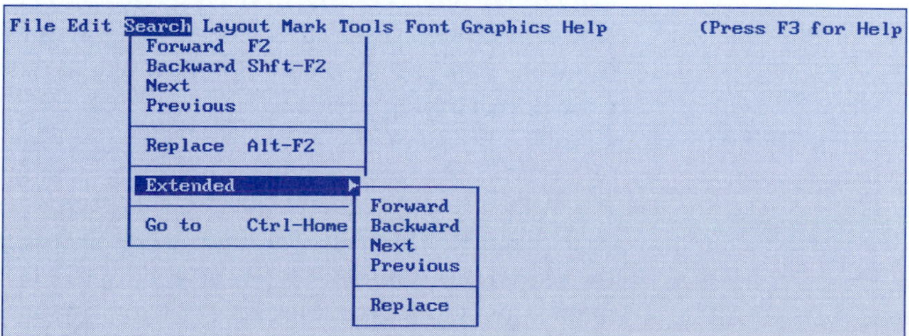

You can bypass the menu-related steps for the four Search options (Forward, Backward, Replace, and Go To) using the associated shortcut key(s) shown in the previous figure. For example, press F2 to initiate a Forward search, press SHIFT-F2 for a Backward search, press ALT-F2 to initiate a Replace operation, or press CTRL-HOME twice for Go To. The following table describes the actions associated with each option in the Search pull-down menu.

Option	Action
Forward	Searches forward from the position of the cursor to the end of the file. Pressing ↑ reverses the search direction.
Backward	Searches backward from the position of the cursor to the beginning of the file. Pressing ↓ reverses the search direction.
Next	Continues the search, locating the next occurrence of the designated text by searching forward from the current cursor position to the end of the document. Pressing F2 twice performs the same action.
Previous	Continues the search, locating the next occurrence of the designated text by searching backward from the current cursor position to the beginning of the document. Pressing F2 ↑ F2 performs the same action.
Replace	Performs the search function and gives you the added option of replacing each occurrence of the designated text with specified text or codes. When you select this option, you can confirm or not confirm each replacement. If you choose to confirm, you must select Yes or No at each occurrence.
Extended	Includes headers, footers, and graphic boxes in the Search and Replace operations.
Go To	Positions the cursor at the top of the specified page.

When you invoke the Search or Replace command, you are asked to enter a search condition. You can search for and replace nontext or hidden codes by including them in your search and replace condition. Include hidden codes like [INDENT], [TAB], [BOLD], [HRt] and [UND] by pressing the keys when prompted. Codes that are set using menu selections must be specified using the appropriate menu. For example, to enter a search condition for the code [Open Style], press ALT-F8 to access the Styles menu and press **3** for **C**reate.

If you specify a text search and enter the search condition in all lowercase characters, WordPerfect 5.1 finds every occurrence of the condition. To make the search ***case-sensitive***, type the condition exactly as it appears in the document—including capital letters. The search condition "the" directs WordPerfect to find every occurrence of the word "the"; the condition "The" directs WordPerfect to find only those occurrences beginning with the capital letter "T."

The following figure represents a printout of a document that includes several common errors and editing situations that are easily corrected using Search and Replace.

TO: All Supervisors

FROM: Mary Choy, Director
Software Acquisition and Installation

DATE: July 19, 1993

SUBJECT: Distribution of Lotus 1-2-3

Replace all "Lotus 1-2-3" with "WordPerfect 5.1"

We have obtained a site license to install 30 copies of Lotus 1-2-3. Installation will be scheduled over the next three weeks on a first-come, first-served basis. Requests for Lotus 1-2-3 installation should be submitted before close of business Friday.

There

Their are several actions you must take before the installation team members make their first visit.

1. Schedule your work so that the computer will be free for a minimum of three hours beginning promptly when the installation team arrives.

2. Prepare 12 blank low-density 5.25" (or six 3.5" disks) for use in backing up the new software.

there

3. Have hot coffee ready in the event that their is a problem installing the new software on your system.

Indent

Remove and check all use of "the"

If you have any questions or comments about scheduling or the preparing for the installation team's visit, please call. Schedule your installation early so that the work can be done at the most convenient time for you.

The memo announces plans for distribution of Lotus 1-2-3 software. You can easily modify the standard memo to reflect a different software program by changing every occurrence of "Lotus 1-2-3" to "WordPerfect 5.1." The Replace option without confirm allows you to make the change automatically. The word "their" is used incorrectly in two of three places, errors that can be corrected using options within the Replace command that allow you to be selective.

Items 1, 2, and 3 in the sample document can be indented automatically by searching for each occurrence of a tab preceded by a period and replacing each occurrence with an indent preceded by a period. In the next three sections, you will learn how to write search conditions to find or find and replace text and text control symbols.

Searches

WordPerfect 5.1's Search option locates the first occurrence of text that matches the search condition you specify. After you select the Forward option from the Search pull-down menu (or press F2 for Search) the "→Srch:" prompt appears in the status line. Type the word, phrase, character string, or control code to be located and press F2.

Unless you specify otherwise, the search begins at the current cursor position and proceeds forward to the end of the document until reaching the first occurrence of the search condition. You can edit the text at the cursor, search for the next occurrence of the search condition, or perform any other word processing activity. To find the next occurrence of the search condition, select Next from the Search pull-down menu or press (F2) twice.

When searching for a complete word that contains a collection of letters often found within other words or phrases, include a space at the beginning and end of the word. If you do not include the space before and after the word "the," for example, Search locates words such as "lathe," "there," and "either" as well as "the."

▶ To create a practice document for search and replace exercises:

1. Type the memo shown in the last figure (do not implement the handwritten corrections).
2. Proofread your version of the memo, and make any changes necessary to make yours match the one in the preceding figure.
3. Menus: Press (ALT)-=, select File, and select Save.
   or Keys: Press (F10).
4. At the "Document to be saved:" prompt, type A: **SEARCH** and press (ENTER).

▶ To check every occurrence of the word "the" and correct the mistyped word:

1. Position the cursor at the top of the current document.
2. Menus: Press (ALT)-=, select Search, and select Forward.
   or Keys: Press (F2).
3. At the "→Srch:" prompt that appears in the status line, type **the** and include a space before and after the word.
4. Press (F2) to start the search.

   The cursor stops immediately following the first occurrence of " the " in paragraph 1. If the cursor stops at "the" that is part of another word, repeat the search and be sure to specify the search criteria *[space]***the***[space]*.
5. Repeat the search until the cursor stops after " the " in the phrase "scheduling or the preparing" in the last paragraph.
6. Delete the word "the" so the phrase reads "scheduling or preparing."

The search condition " the " finds *THE*, *the*, and *The* because all lowercase characters indicate a non–case-sensitive search. To create a case-sensitive search, simply type, when you define the search condition, the exact combination of upper- and lowercase characters you need to find.

Selective Replacement

The Replace feature is similar to the Search forward and backward feature, with one powerful addition. After WordPerfect 5.1 finds the specified word, phrase, or hidden code, you can replace one or more occurrences with a word, phrase, or hidden code that you designate. If a replaced word or phrase appears at the beginning of a sentence, WordPerfect automatically capitalizes the first letter.

The incorrect use of "Their" in the practice document provides an opportunity to use the Replace feature. The first occurrence of "Their" should be replaced with "There," and the third occurrence should be replaced with "there." In the sample document, you could search and then edit each occurrence because the document is short. However, a search and replace operation using the confirm option is more efficient for long documents. Responding Yes to the "w/Confirm? **No** (**Y**es)" message allows you to decide if each occurrence of a word or phrase should be replaced.

First, you will practice the process that uses verification (that is, the process that asks for instructions after finding each occurrence of the search condition). In this exercise you will change "their" to "there" when appropriate.

▶ To initiate a selective search and replace using confirmation:

1. Position the cursor at the top of the current document.
2. Menus: Press ALT-=, select Search, and select Replace.
   or Keys: Press ALT-F2.
3. At the "w/Confirm? **N**o (**Y**es)" prompt, press **Y**.
4. At the "→Srch:" prompt that appears in the status line, type `their` and press F2.
5. At the "Replace with:" prompt, type `there` and press F2 to begin the search.

   The cursor stops on the first occurrence of "their"; the prompt "Confirm? **N**o (**Y**es)" appears on the status line.

▶ To complete the search, selectively replacing "their" with the correct "there":

1. Press **Y** to replace the first occurrence of "Their."

   Notice that WordPerfect 5.1 capitalizes the search condition, inserting "There." The cursor moves to the next word automatically.
2. At the second "w/Confirm? **N**o (**Y**es)" prompt, press **N** to bypass the second occurrence of "their"; this usage is correct.
3. At the third "w/Confirm? **N**o (**Y**es)" prompt, press **Y** to replace the third occurrence of "their"; this usage is incorrect.

Replacement of Text and Hidden Codes

Answer No to use the "w/Confirm?" prompt during a Replace operation to replace all occurrences of specified text or codes without waiting for verification. This option has the potential for making unintended changes; save your document on disk before initiating the Replace.

To practice the process, you will make changes to the current document so that it will look like the one shown in the following figure.

```
TO:        All Supervisors

FROM:      Mary Choy, Director
           Software Acquisition and Installation

DATE:      July 19, 1993

SUBJECT:   Distribution of WordPerfect 5.1

We have obtained a site license to install 30 copies of
WordPerfect 5.1.  Installation will be scheduled over the next
three weeks on a first-come, first-served basis.  Requests for
WordPerfect 5.1 installation should be submitted before close of
business Friday.

There are several actions you must take before the installation
team members make their first visit.

     1.   Schedule your work so that the computer will be free
          for a minimum of three hours beginning promptly when
          the installation team arrives.

     2.   Prepare 12 blank low-density 5.25" (or six 3.5" disks)
          for use in backing up the new software.

     3.   Have hot coffee ready in the event that there is a
          problem installing the new software on your system.

If you have questions or comments about scheduling or preparing
for the installation team's visit, please call. Schedule your
installation early so that the work can be done at the most
convenient time for you.
```

▶ To initiate a Replace operation without confirming each replacement:

1. Position the cursor at the top of the document.
2. Menus: Press ALT-=, select Search, and select Replace.
   or Keys: Press ALT-F2.
3. At the "w/Confirm? **N**o (**Y**es)" prompt, press **N**.
4. At the "→Srch:" prompt that appears in the status line, type **`Lotus 1-2-3`** and press F2.
5. At the "Replace with:" prompt, type **`WordPerfect 5.1`** and press F2 to execute the replace operation.
6. Use cursor keys to view the document and verify that all occurrences of Lotus 1-2-3 have been replaced with WordPerfect 5.1.

► **To initiate a Replace operation to replace hidden codes:**

1. Position the cursor at the top of the document.
2. Menus: Press ALT-=, select Search, and select Replace.
   or Keys: Press ALT-F2.
3. At the "w/Confirm? No (Yes)" prompt, press **N**.
4. At the "→Srch:" prompt that appears in the status line, type **.** (period), press TAB, and press F2.
5. At the "Replace with:" prompt, type **.** and press F4.
6. Press F2 to execute the replacement.
7. Use cursor keys to view the document and verify that indents have replaced tabs for three numbered sentences.
8. Press F10 to save your changes to the Search document and continue editing the document.

You have applied WordPerfect 5.1's Search options to make a number of changes to a short memo. Imagine the power at your disposal to edit a very long document.

EMPHASIZING TEXT

Many commands that enhance text use paired codes to mark the text. For example, text that is marked for bold printing begins with the hidden code [BOLD] and ends with the hidden code [bold]. If you know at the time you type the text that you want it to print bold, you can press F6 and begin typing. At the end of the bold text, press F6 again to turn off bold, or press → once to move past the hidden code. If the text is already typed, mark the block to be printed bold and press F6. The marked text will be surrounded by the reveal codes [BOLD] and [bold].

Text marked for enhancement appears highlighted on your screen. Depending on the type of monitor installed on your computer and your specific display setup, this highlighting may be in different colors or, if you have a monochrome monitor, in shades of black and white. The actual enhancements are seen only when they are viewed using WordPerfect 5.1's View Document feature or printed.

► **To center a word on the first line of your document:**

1. Press HOME twice and then press ↑ to position the cursor on the "T" in "To:".
2. Make sure Insert mode is on, and press ENTER twice to insert two blank lines.
3. Press HOME twice and then press ↑ to position the cursor on the first line.
4. Type **MEMO**
5. Position the cursor on the "M" in "MEMO."

6. Menus: Press ALT-=, select Layout, select Align, and select Center.
   or Keys: Press SHIFT-F6.

   Check that "MEMO" is centered.

You can also mark as a block the text to be centered, and then press SHIFT-F6. You will see the prompt "[Just:Center]? **N**o (**Y**es)." Pressing **Y** centers the text. Blocking and centering text requires more keystrokes and is necessary only if the text being centered is not the only text on the line.

▶ To have "WordPerfect 5.1" print in bold in the SUBJECT: line:

1. Position the cursor on the "W" in "WordPerfect 5.1."
2. Menus: Press ALT-=, select Edit, and select Block.
   or Keys: Press ALT-F4 or F12.
3. Highlight "WordPerfect 5.1."
4. Menus: Press ALT-=, select Font, select Appearance, and select Bold.
   or Keys: Press F6.

   Repeat these instructions to have "WordPerfect 5.1" print in bold both times in the first paragraph.

▶ To underline "before close of business Friday":

1. Position the cursor at the beginning of the text "before close of business Friday."
2. Menus: Press ALT-=, select Edit, and select Block.
   or Keys: Press ALT-F4 or F12.
3. Press **y** to highlight text through the first occurrence of a "y."
4. Menus: Press ALT-=, select Font, select Appearance, and select Underline.
   or Keys: Press F8.

Depending on your monitor and the specific setup of your screen display, you may or may not see enhancements, such as underlined text on the screen. If your monitor does not support underlining on the screen, underlined text will remain highlighted according to your specific display setup.

▶ To view the bold and underline codes:

1. Press HOME twice, and then press ↑.
2. Press ALT-F3 or F11 to access Reveal Codes mode.

   Check that your screen matches the next figure and notice the [Center] and [BOLD] . . . [bold] codes.

```
                              MEMO
To:        All Supervisors

FROM:      Mary Choy, Director
           Software Acquisition and Installation

DATE:      July 19, 1993

A:\SEARCH                                      Doc 1 Pg 1 Ln 1" Pos 1"
{   ▲    ▲    ▲    ▲    ▲    ▲    ▲    ▲    ▲    ▲    ▲    ▲    }    ▲    ▲
[Center]MEMO[HRt]
[HRt]
To:[→Indent][→Indent]All Supervisors[HRt]
[HRt]
FROM:[→Indent]Mary Choy, Director[HRt]
[→Indent][→Indent]Software Acquisition and Installation[HRt]
[HRt]
DATE:[→Indent]July 19, 1993[HRt]
[HRt]
SUBJECT:[→Indent]Distribution of [BOLD]WordPerfect 5.1[bold][HRt]
[HRt]
[HRt]

Press Reveal Codes to restore screen
```

3. Use cursor keys to view additional codes including [UND] . . . [und].
4. Press (ALT)-(F3) or (F11) to exit Reveal Codes mode.

Printing a Block

WordPerfect 5.1 provides a ***View Document*** option on the Print menu that enables you to look at full ***page layouts*** and to see the results of formatting changes, such as right justification or underlining, that do not appear on the document-editing screen. To reach the main Print menu, select Print from the File pull-down menu or press (SHIFT)-(F7). Press **6** for **V**iew Document mode.

The quality of the results you see depends on the quality of your monitor. The first two menu options, 100% and 200%, are readable. Options 3, for Full Page, and 4, for Facing Pages, are used mostly to see the page layout, not to read the contents.

▶ To view the finished document on your screen:

1. Menus: Press (ALT)-=, select File, and select Print.
   or Keys: Press (SHIFT)-(F7).
2. Press **6** for **V**iew Document.

   The screen display you see is determined by what option you last used.
3. Press **3** for Full Page.
4. Press **1** for 100% to see a magnified half-page view.
5. Press **2** for 200% to see a magnified quarter-page view.
6. Press (F7) to exit the View Document mode.

▶ To save the enhanced memo and remain in the document:

1. Menus: Press (ALT)-=, select File, and select Save.
   or Keys: Press (F10).

2. Type **A:ENHANCE.MEM** and press (ENTER).

As you develop a document, you may want to print a portion of it to check how the final results will look. To print a portion of a document that is less than a full page, block the text to be printed, then access the Print feature by pressing (SHIFT)-(F7) or selecting Print from the File pull-down menu.

▶ To mark a block that extends from the third paragraph to the end of the enhanced memo:

1. Position the cursor at the beginning of the third paragraph, on the "I" in "If you have questions."
2. Menus: Press (ALT)-=, select Edit, and select Block.
   or Keys: Press (ALT)-(F4) or (F12).
3. Press (HOME) twice, and then press (↓) to highlight to the end of the current document.

▶ To print the block of text (print this block only if a printer is attached to your computer and the printer is in Ready mode):

1. Menus: Press (ALT)-=, select File, and select Print.
   or Keys: Press (SHIFT)-(F7).

   Check that the following message appears at the bottom of your screen.

```
Print block? No (Yes)
```

2. Press **Y** for Yes and check that the printed output contains all of the formatting and enhancements that you applied.

   If you want to print a page within the current document or print the entire current document, press (SHIFT)-(F7) to access the Print menu, and then press **1** to print the **F**ull Document or **2** to print the current **P**age.

3. Press (F7) to exit the document without saving it and either exit WordPerfect or access a blank document screen.

   This concludes Project 4. You can continue with the Review Exercises, go on to the next project, or exit WordPerfect.

Summary

- In this project you learned some of the more advanced skills needed to create professional-looking documents.
- Mark blocks to define larger chunks of text on which you want to perform some action. You can copy, delete and undelete, or move blocks of text within the same document or between documents.
- You may not always want to print an entire document. After marking a block, you can print it as a sample for proofing before printing the whole document.

- By marking a group of characters as a block, you can make changes quickly, instead of having to define the formatting characteristics for every character or word. Blocks of text can be emphasized with bold, italic, or underlining to enhance the final appearance of your document.
- The Speller can check one word in a document or every word in a document, and it reports any questionable entries for your correction or verification.
- The Thesaurus helps you write more effectively by suggesting alternatives to words you indicate.
- The Search and Replace functions can help you make consistent editing and formatting changes. Rather than having to skim your document to make changes, WordPerfect can locate and change text and formatting codes.

KEY TERMS

block
case-sensitive
copying text
Count
headword
Look Up
moving text
page layout
Ready
replace
search
Speller
Thesaurus
View Document

STUDY QUESTIONS

True/False

1. The best way to delete a block of text is with BACKSPACE. T F
2. You can restore text that is accidentally deleted by pressing F1. T F
3. To find out how many words are in a document, count the number of words in the first line and multiply by 66 lines. T F
4. You can check a single word, page, or document with the Speller. T F
5. Selecting Next in Search locates the next word to be replaced. T F
6. Answering No to the "w/Confirm?" prompt in Replace might result in unintended changes. T F
7. Many commands to enhance text use paired codes to mark the text. T F
8. The only way to see how your final document will look is to use the Print command. T F
9. Use SHIFT-F4 to mark a block of text. T F
10. You can undelete one or two preceding actions. T F

Fill in the Blanks

1. To underline a word, you must first __________, and then press __________.
2. __________ a block of text transfers it to a new location, whereas __________ a block of text duplicates the original text in another location.

3. Both __________ and __________ access the Block feature.
4. If a the Speller does not recognize a word, it is either __________ or __________.
5. The Thesaurus suggests both __________ and __________.
6. The four Search options are: __________, __________, __________, and __________.
7. Answering Yes to the "w/Confirm?" prompt while searching and replacing lets you __________.
8. To view where you have placed codes for bold and underlining, press __________ to access __________.
9. You can examine your formatted document as a __________ % half-page view or a __________ % quarter-page view.
10. When a block of text is highlighted, it means it is __________.

For Discussion

1. Name five text manipulation features that require that the text be marked as a block.
2. List five tasks that the Search and Replace features can make more efficient.
3. What steps would you take to try to locate the spelling of a word?
4. What are the two ways you could instruct WordPerfect 5.1 to check the spelling of only page 2 of your document?
5. Why would you use the Full Page or Facing Page selections in View Document?

Review Exercises

Review the concepts presented in Project 4 by completing the following tasks. If necessary, review the material.

1. Access WordPerfect 5.1 and retrieve the ENHANCE.MEM document.
2. Access the Reveal Codes mode and delete existing codes to center, print bold, and underline text.
3. Mark the third numbered action about coffee as a block; delete the block.
4. Center the phrase "Happy word processing!" at the bottom of the memo.
5. Add the codes needed to specify that "before close of business Friday" prints bold.
6. Underline the phrase "at the most convenient time for you."
7. Use the View Document feature to see page layout and formatting enhancements on the screen.
8. Print only the first paragraph of the memo.
9. Print the entire memo.
10. Save the memo as ENHANCE.ALT.

Project 5: Building a Table

After completing this project, you should be able to:

- Create a new table
- Define the shape and size of the table
- Move the cursor within a table
- Add column headings
- Add and change information in tables
- Format individual cells or blocks of cells
- Enter and copy formulas for automatic calculations
- Recalculate the table after making changes
- Lock out data entry in specific cells
- Print the table

Defining a Table

A ***spreadsheet***, one of the most powerful software tools used on a microcomputer, is included in WordPerfect 5.1. The ***table*** you will create in this project stores data in columns and rows as it is in the traditional spreadsheet used in accounting. The following figure shows a table that presents data about a company's stock investments.

Clearwater Manufacturing, Inc. Stock Value Report As of: August 2, 1992			
Stock Name	# of Shares	Market per Share	Total Market
StdPrd	200	23.75	4,750.00
Itel pf	150	40.00	6,000.00
GTE pf	950	27.50	26,125.00
GM	800	36.50	29,200.00
Chevrn	500	74.00	37,000.00
			103,075.00

Rows are identified by numbers, and ***columns*** by letters. A ***cell***, which can contain numeric or text data, is formed by the intersection of a row and column. Each cell can be referenced by its row and column numbers. For example, the cell in the upper-left corner of the table is referred to as A1 because it is in the first row of column A. Numeric cells can contain a specific ***value*** (such as 200) or a ***formula*** (such as B3*C3), which can contain ***cell references*** as well as numbers. A cell can also contain a ***function,*** such as +, which indicates that the numbers in the column above the function are to be added and the result is to be placed in the cell where the function appears.

In the previous figure, row 1 contains one large cell, referred to as A1, which displays the table heading. Row 1 originally contained four cells, like the other rows, but the four cells were joined into one big cell. Row 2 contains four cells, referred to as A2 through D2, which are used for the column headings. Rows 3 through 7 contain data. Column A (A3 through A7) contains the names of stocks acquired by Clearwater Manufacturing, Inc. Columns B and C contain the specific values displayed. Column D displays results based on formulas. The value in row 8 was generated using a function that adds the contents in the column above and displays the result. Tables retain their automatic calculating ability when inserted into documents.

Creating a table requires six tasks:

1. Defining the table
2. Entering the table and column headings
3. Setting the cell attributes
4. Entering and validating formulas and functions
5. Entering the data
6. Changing lines and making final adjustments

The first step in defining a WordPerfect 5.1 table is specifying the number of rows and columns. If you are not sure how many are needed, estimate the number. You can add and delete rows and columns as you need them. For the Clearwater Manufacturing table, you will initially specify six rows by four columns.

Once the table is created and the cursor is positioned within the borders of the table, the status line at the bottom of the screen displays the current cell location of the cursor. A variety of keys are used to move around in the table.

Key	Action
(ALT) (→) (or (←), (↑), (↓))	Moves cursor one cell in the direction of the arrow
(←) or (→)	Moves cursor one character left or right within a cell*
(↑) or (↓)	Moves cursor one line up or down within a cell*
(SHIFT)-(TAB)	Moves cursor one cell to the left
(TAB)	Moves cursor one cell to the right
(CTRL)-(HOME) (↑)	Moves cursor to the beginning of text in a cell

CTRL-HOME ↓	Moves cursor to the end of text in a cell
ALT-HOME → (or ←, ↑, ↓)	Moves cursor in the direction of the arrow to the beginning or end of a row or column
ALT-HOME HOME ↑ (or ↓)	Moves cursor to the first or last cell of the table

*If no text is in a cell, the cursor moves one cell, rather than one line or character, in the direction of the arrow.

Note: Alt-key combinations work only with enhanced keyboards.

▶ To access the table definition command:

1. Access a blank WordPerfect 5.1 document screen.
2. Menus: Press ALT-=, select Layout, and select Tables.
   or Keys: Press ALT-F7 and press **2** for Tables.
3. Menus: Select Create.
   or Keys: Press **1** for **C**reate.

▶ To define the table:

1. Type **4** at the "Number of Columns: 3" prompt and press ENTER.
2. Type **6** at the "Number of Rows: 1" prompt and press ENTER.
3. Press F7 to exit Table Edit mode and restore the normal Edit mode.

▶ To practice moving the cursor:

1. If your cursor is outside the table, use the arrow keys to move it inside the table.
2. Press ↓ until the cursor is in row 5.
3. Press TAB until the cursor is in column D.
4. Press SHIFT-TAB until the cursor is in column B.
5. Practice moving the cursor with different keys.

SPECIFYING HEADINGS

Headings add valuable information to any table. There are two headings in the Clearwater Manufacturing table. The ***table heading*** (row 1) joins all of the row 1 cells into one large cell. The ***column headings*** in row 2 display a brief description about the contents of each column.

You will work with your table in the ***normal edit*** mode or the ***Table Edit*** mode. The normal edit mode allows you to enter and edit data in cells. The Table Edit mode causes an Edit menu to appear at the bottom of the screen. Use this mode to make changes to size, appearance, and format of cells. You cannot change cell contents while in the Table Edit mode.

To add headings, you will first insert two new rows at the top of the table. Once the rows are inserted, you will identify them as headings and specify that the cells will contain text. Failure to identify the contents as text may cause any numbers typed in those cells to be included in table calculations. Last, you will enter the headings and center the contents of row 1 in cell A1.

▶ To insert two rows at the top of the table:

1. Position the cursor in cell A1.
2. Menus: Press ALT-=, select Layout, select Tables, and select Edit.
   or Keys: Press ALT-F7.

   When the cursor is positioned within a table, pressing ALT-F7 automatically activates Table Edit mode. Subsequent instructions will use the ALT-F7 key combination to access Table Edit mode instead of the more time-consuming menu approach. The figure that follows shows the result.

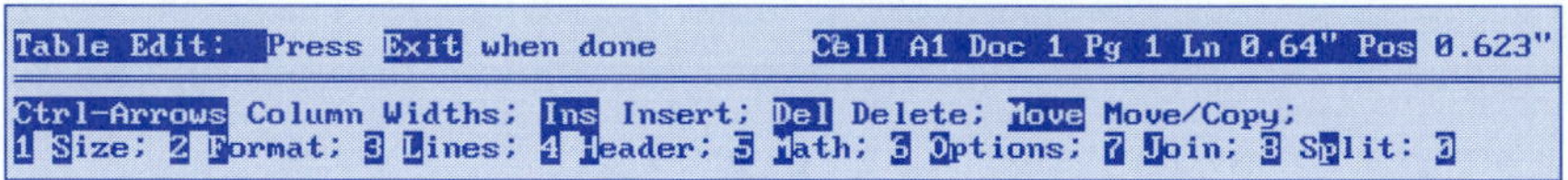

3. Press INS.
4. Type **1** at the prompt "Insert 1 **R**ows; 2 **C**olumns: 0."
5. Type **2** at the prompt "Number of Rows 1" and press ENTER.

   Double lines appear around the inserted rows.

▶ To join cells and thereby create one cell:

1. Make sure you are still in the Table Edit mode. You can add and delete a row or column while you are in either the normal edit mode or Table Edit mode.
2. Position the cursor in cell A1.
3. Press ALT-F4 or F12.
4. Press END to mark all cells in row 1 as a block.
5. Press **7** for **J**oin and type **Y** at "Join cells? **N**o (**Y**es)".

   Row 1 has been changed to one large cell.

▶ To specify the cell data type in rows 1 and 2:

1. Press ALT-F4 or F12.

2. Press ⓓ to highlight all the cells in rows 1 and 2.
3. Press **2** for **F**ormat.
4. Press **1** for **C**ell.
5. Press **1** for **T**ype to specify the data options.
6. Press **2** for **T**ext to specify that the data in rows 1 and 2 are text.

▶ To specify data justification within cell A1:

1. Position the cursor in cell A1.
2. Press **2** for **F**ormat.
3. Press **1** for **C**ell.
4. Press **3** for **J**ustify.
5. Press **2** for **C**enter to specify that the contents of cell A1 are to be centered.

▶ To designate rows 1 and 2 as headers:

1. Press **4** for **H**eader.
2. Type **2** at the prompt "Number of header rows: 0" and press (ENTER).
3. Press (F7) for Exit to return to the normal edit mode.

If the table becomes too long and extends to more than one page, rows 1 and 2 will print at the top of each page.

▶ To enter a report heading in cell A1:

1. Position the cursor at cell A1.
2. Type **`Clearwater Manufacturing, Inc.`** and press (ENTER).
3. Type **`Stock Value Report`** and press (ENTER).
4. Type **`As of: August 2, 1992`**

   Check that your cell A1 matches the following figure.

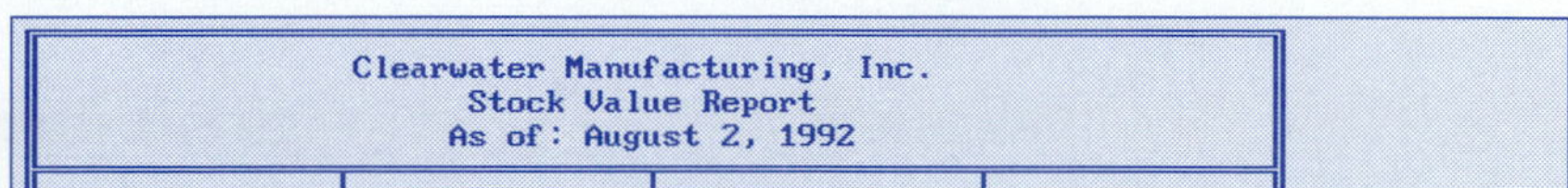

▶ To enter the column heading in cell A2:

1. Position the cursor in cell A2, type **`Stock`** and press (ENTER).
2. Type **`Name`** and press (TAB) to position the cursor at cell B2.

To position the cursor in the next cell, press (TAB). Pressing (ENTER) would cause WordPerfect 5.1 to enter an extra line in the cell. If you press (ENTER) by mistake, press (BACKSPACE) until the extra line disappears.

▶ To enter the column heading in cell B2:

1. Type **`# of`** and press (ENTER).
2. Type **`Shares`** and press (TAB) to position the cursor at cell C2.

▶ To enter the column heading in cell C2:

1. Type **`Market`** and press (ENTER).
2. Type **`per Share`** and press (TAB) to position the cursor at cell D2.

▶ To enter the column heading in cell D2:

1. Type **`Total`** and press (ENTER).
2. Type **`Market`**

   Check that your table resembles the following figure.

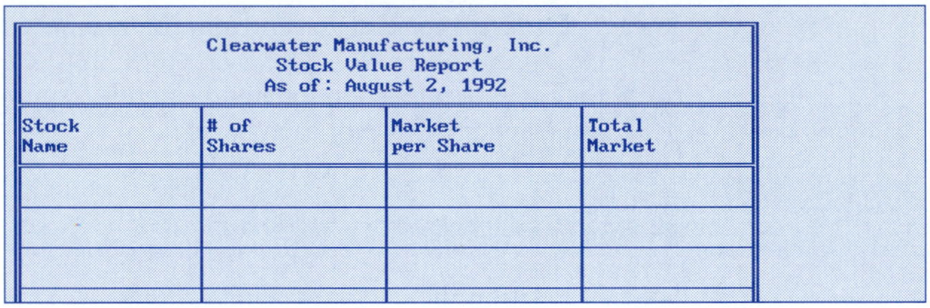

Clearwater Manufacturing, Inc. Stock Value Report As of: August 2, 1992			
Stock Name	# of Shares	Market per Share	Total Market

In the status line the names of cells marked as headings are followed by an asterisk (*). The names of cells marked as text are preceded by a double quotation mark. Cell A1 is a heading that contains text. So, as the following figure shows, the name of the cell is accompanied by a double quotation mark and an asterisk.

```
A:\STOCK.TBL                              Cell "A1* Doc 1 Pg 1 Ln 1.31" Pos 3.35"
```

SETTING CELL ATTRIBUTES

The size, style, and alignment of data in a cell are known as ***cell attributes.*** By default, all data within a WordPerfect 5.1 table are left-justified. Even numeric data are initially set up to be aligned to the left in the cell. Select from Left, Center, Right, Full, and Decimal Align to position cell contents. Recall that the heading in cell A1 was centered.

Numeric data should be right-justified or aligned at the decimal place. For example, data about the number of shares, which is in column B (B3 through B7), should appear with the rightmost digits in alignment. In columns C and D, the decimal points should align.

▶ To specify that the contents of cells B3 through B7 be aligned at the right:

1. Position the cursor at cell B3.
2. Press ALT-F7 to access the Table Edit mode.
3. Press ALT-F4 or F12.
4. Position the cursor at cell B7.
5. Press **2** for **F**ormat.
6. Press **1** for **C**ell.
7. Press **3** for **J**ustify.
8. Press **3** for **R**ight to cause the data in cells B3 through B7 to be right-aligned.

   As characters are typed into a cell defined as right- or decimal-aligned, each entry appears beginning at the right side of the cell. Cell contents shift left as each new character is typed. This shifting format is similar to how numbers appear on a calculator display.

▶ To specify that decimal points in cells C3 through D8 align:

1. Position the cursor at cell C3.
2. Press ALT-F4 or F12.
3. Position the cursor at cell D8 to highlight the remaining cells in columns C and D.
4. Press **2** for **F**ormat.
5. Press **1** for **C**ell.
6. Press **3** for **J**ustify.
7. Press **5** for **D**ecimal Align to cause the data in marked cells to align on their decimal points.

In normal edit mode, the words “Align Char = .” appear at the left side of the status line, at the bottom of the screen.

8. Press (F7) for Exit to return to the normal edit mode.

► **To save the table and continue to edit:**

1. Menus: Press (ALT)-=, select File, and select Save.
   or Keys: Press (F10).
2. Type **`A:STOCK.TBL`** and press (ENTER).

   If you have elected to store files on a disk that is not in the A: disk drive, replace the “A:” with the correct disk drive and path information.

Entering Formulas and Functions

In cells D3 through D7 are formulas that compute the total market value of each stock holding. The cell D8 contains a function that totals the results in the column above the cell and displays the result. Once formulas are entered into their respective cells and before you enter data in the table, test the formulas to ensure that they work properly.

In this project you will enter a formula in cell D3 of the spreadsheet for Clearwater Manufacturing. After you test (validate) the formula, you will copy it into cells D4 through D7. The table that follows explains the formula.

Column	Computation
Total Market (column D)	Multiplies the contents of column B times the contents of column C

Formulas contain values and cell references to cells containing values and formulas. Formulas combine values and cell references by using the ***math operators*** for addition, subtraction, multiplication, and division, as shown in the following table.

Operator	Operation	Example
+	Addition	10+5+C1 (10 plus 5 plus the contents of cell C1)
–	Subtraction	F3–D3 (the contents of cell F3 minus the contents of cell D3)

*	Multiplication	B3*C3 (the contents of cell B3 times the contents of cell C3)
/	Division	G3/2 (the contents of cell G3 divided by 2)

When more than one operator is used in a formula, the formula is solved from left to right. Enclosing portions of the formula in parentheses alters the sequence in which WordPerfect 5.1 evaluates the formula. For example, 5+10/2 yields the result 7.5, but 5+(10/2) yields the result 10 because the contents inside the parentheses are computed first.

Three functions are available for totaling, subtotaling, and grand totaling the contents of a column. The plus (+) function subtotals the numbers in the column above the cell containing the function. The equals (=) function totals all subtotals in the column above the cell containing the function. The asterisk (*) function adds all totals (=) in the column above the cell containing the function.

▶ To enter, in cell D3, the formula that computes the value for Total Market:

1. Position the cursor at cell D3 and press ALT-F7 to access Table Edit mode.
2. Press **5** for **M**ath.
3. Press **2** for **F**ormula.
4. Type `B3*C3` at the "Enter Formula:" prompt and press ENTER.

▶ To enter, in cell D8, the function that adds the values in Total Market:

1. Position the cursor at cell D8.
2. Press **5** for **M**ath.
3. Press **4** or press **+**.

   Each cell where you entered a formula or function now displays "0.00," which indicates that a calculation is stored in that cell and the result is zero.
4. Press F7 to exit Table Edit mode.

▶ To enter test values in cells B3 and C3:

1. Position the cursor at cell B3 and type `1`
2. Position the cursor at cell C3 and type `1.00`

▶ To recalculate the values:

1. Press ALT-F7 to enter the Table Edit mode.
2. Press **5** for **M**ath.

3. Press **1** for **C**alculate.

   The notation "Please wait" appears in the lower-left corner of the screen. There may be a slight delay while WordPerfect 5.1 performs the calculations. The delay depends on the size of the table and the speed of your computer and disk drives.

4. Press F7 for Exit to return to normal edit mode, and check that your table appears as shown in the following figure.

Clearwater Manufacturing, Inc. Stock Value Report As of: August 2, 1992			
Stock Name	# of Shares	Market per Share	Total Market
	1	1.00	1.00
			1.00

▶ To copy the formula in D3 to D4 through D7:

1. Position the cursor at cell D3.
2. Press ALT-F7 to access the Table Edit mode.
3. Press **5** for **M**ath.
4. Press **3** for Cop**y** Formula.
5. Press **2** for **D**own, press **4**, and press ENTER.

   Check that zeros appear in cells D4 through D7 and press F7 for Exit.

▶ To save the table on disk:

1. Menus: Press ALT-=, select File, and select Save.
   or Keys: Press F10.
2. Press ENTER to accept the file name A:STOCK.TBL. Press **Y** for Yes when prompted to replace the existing file on disk.

Entering Data

Entering data involves the simple process of positioning the cursor in the appropriate cells and typing the data. However, before entering data, it is wise to protect the cells containing headings, formulas, and functions so that their contents cannot be inadvertently overtyped and destroyed. Protecting cells requires the use of the Lock command, which is a selection in the Formula menu. Once the data is entered, it may be necessary to widen or narrow the columns to accommodate it.

▶ To lock the cells in rows 1 and 2:

1. Position the cursor at cell A1.
2. Press ALT-F7 to access the Table Edit mode.
3. Press ALT-F4 or F12.
4. Position the cursor at row 2, highlighting all cells in rows 1 and 2.
5. Press **2** for **F**ormat.
6. Press **1** for **C**ell.
7. Press **5** for **L**ock and then press **1** for **O**n.

▶ To lock the cells D3 through D8:

1. Position the cursor at cell D3.
2. Press ALT-F4 or F12.
3. Position the cursor at cell D8, highlighting the remaining cells in column D.
4. Press **2** for **F**ormat.
5. Press **1** for **C**ell.
6. Press **5** for **L**ock and then press **1** for **O**n.
7. Press F7 to exit Table Edit mode.

▶ To enter data in column A (A3 through A7):

1. At cell A3 type **`StdPrd`**
2. At cell A4 type **`Itel pf`**
3. At cell A5 type **`GTE pf`**
4. At cell A6 type **`GM`**
5. At cell A7 type **`Chevrn`**

▶ To enter data in column B (B3 through B7):

1. Press (INS) to activate Typeover mode in order to overwrite the test figures.
2. At cell B3 type **200**
3. At cell B4 type **150**
4. At cell B5 type **950**
5. At cell B6 type **800**
6. At cell B7 type **500**

▶ To enter data in column C (C3 through C7):

1. Make sure Typeover mode is still active.
2. At cell C3 type **23,** press (→) and type **.75**
3. At cell C4 type **40.00**
4. At cell C5 type **27.50**
5. At cell C6 type **36.50**
6. At cell C7 type **74.00**
7. Press (INS) to restore Insert mode.

▶ To recalculate the values in the table:

1. Press (ALT)-(F7) to enter Table Edit mode.
2. Press **5** for **M**ath.
3. Press **1** for **C**alculate.

   To widen or narrow a column, move the cursor to the column and press (CTRL)-(←) or (CTRL)-(→) in Table Edit mode.

4. Press (F7) to exit Table Edit mode..

   Check that your table results resemble those shown in the following figure.

Clearwater Manufacturing, Inc. Stock Value Report As of: August 2, 1992			
Stock Name	# of Shares	Market per Share	Total Market
StdPrd	200	23.75	4,750.00
Itel pf	150	40.00	6,000.00
GTE pf	950	27.50	26,125.00
GM	800	36.50	29,200.00
Chevrn	500	74.00	37,000.00
			103,075.00

▶ **To save the table on disk and then print the table:**

1. Menus or Keys: Press ALT-=, select File, and select Save.
   Press F10.
2. Press ENTER and then type **Y** for Yes when prompted to replace the existing file on disk.
3. Menus or Keys: Press ALT-=, select File, and select Print.
   Press SHIFT-F7.
4. Press **2** for **P**age to print the page containing the table.
5. Press F7 to exit the current document.

   You can stay in WordPerfect 5.1 and continue with the Review Exercises, or exit WordPerfect.

SUMMARY

- Tables can greatly enhance the appearance of your reports. WordPerfect 5.1 has a spreadsheet feature that stores and manipulates information in rows and columns like those in traditional spreadsheets used in accounting.
- Cells are formed by the intersection of a row and column. Starting in the upper-left corner of a table, rows are identified by consecutive numbers beginning with 1, and columns with letters beginning with A. The cell in the upper-left corner of a table is referred to as A1. Cells can contain either numeric or text data.
- The steps in creating a table are defining its dimensions, entering column headings, and setting attributes to define how the data should be formatted in each cell or block of cells. You can add optional enhancements before or after you enter the data.
- You do not have to type information into every cell. You can embed formulas that automatically calculate values and write the results in a specific cell. When you change the data, WordPerfect recalculates the results after you access Table Edit mode and select the Calculate option from the Math menu.
- To make sure you do not accidentally damage the headings, data, or formulas, you can lock any cell to prevent changes.

KEY TERMS

cell
cell attribute
cell reference
column
column heading
formula
function
math operator
normal edit
table
row
spreadsheet
table
Table Edit
table heading
value

Study Questions

True/False

1. A cell in a WordPerfect table can contain numeric data only. T F
2. The cell in the upper-left corner of the table is referred to as A1. T F
3. Pressing (CTRL)-(HOME) (↑) moves the cursor to the top of the table. T F
4. Table Heading mode joins all the cells in row 1 into one large cell. T F
5. Cells marked as headings display a $ after the cell reference in the status line. T F
6. The default alignment for all data within a WordPerfect 5.1 table is right-justified. T F
7. Decimal alignment of numeric data makes columns of numbers line up on their decimal points. T F
8. If the value in cell A3 is 63, the result of the formula A3/7 is 9. T F
9. Enclosing portions of a formula in parentheses makes no difference in how WordPerfect evaluates the formula. T F
10. Locking a cell protects it from unwanted changes. T F

Fill in the Blanks

1. A spreadsheet is organized into __________ and __________.
2. The operator for multiplication is __________.
3. Pressing (TAB) moves the cursor __________ in a table.
4. Press the key combination __________ to access Table Edit mode if the cursor is positioned within the table.
5. Press __________ to insert a line into the table. Use __________ to remove it.
6. Press __________ to exit Table Edit mode.
7. Like a calculator display, numbers in cells shift __________ as each new character is typed.
8. The __________ function subtotals the numbers in the column above it, the __________ function totals all subtotals, and the __________ function adds all totals in the column above the cell containing the function.
9. The formula to add the contents of cell B3 with H6 is __________.
10. A __________ is formed by the intersection of a row and column.

For Discussion

1. List the four kinds of numeric data a cell can contain.
2. What are the different uses of the normal edit mode and Table Edit mode?
3. Data within a cell can be justified (aligned) in five ways. List them.

4. Name the four math operations and their operators in WordPerfect 5.1 tables.
5. Which two key combinations adjust the width of columns? Which edit mode must you be in?

Review Exercises

Review the concepts presented in Project 5 by completing the following tasks. If necessary, review the material.

The president of the company has asked to see a list of wages for the six employees in the Finishing Department for the week beginning August 3, 1992. Prepare a table using WordPerfect 5.1 to create this list. Use a formula to compute each employee's wage and total that column so that the table can be used again.

1. Access a blank WordPerfect 5.1 document screen.
2. Create a table with five columns and nine rows.
3. Combine the cells in row 1 into one large cell.
4. Designate rows 1 and 2 as headings that contain text.
5. At cell A1 type: **Employee Wages**
Finishing Department
Week of: August 3, 1992
6. At cell A2 type **First Name** on two lines.

   At cell B2 type **Last Name** on two lines.

   At cell C2 type **Hours Worked** on two lines.

   At cell D2 type **Rate of Pay** on two lines.

   At cell E2 type **Wages**
7. Enter the formula in the wages column (E) and the function to total the wages in cell E9.
8. Enter dummy data in row 3, calculate the table values, and validate that the formula and function compute properly. When they work properly, lock the cells in rows 1 and 2 and column E to protect what you have entered.
9. Enter data for six employees, then print the table.
10. Save the table on the diskette in the A: drive; call the file WAGES.TBL. You will use this table in the review exercises in Project 6.

Project 6: Inserting a Table in a Letter

After completing this project, you should be able to:

- View more than one document at a time
- Move between documents
- Combine documents
- Specify page breaks
- Add or suppress headers and footers
- Position page numbers
- Create and move footnotes and endnotes
- Print the final document

Working with Multiple-Page Documents

Most documents contain two or more pages. WordPerfect 5.1 offers many features that accommodate multiple-page documents. For example, WordPerfect's ***Page Numbering*** facility permits you to place page numbers anywhere on a page and control the numbering sequence of even the most complex documents. Use ***headers*** and ***footers*** to place repeating text and/or graphics at the top or bottom of every page. With WordPerfect you can use footnotes or endnotes to annotate your text and credit your sources of information.

As you type, WordPerfect 5.1 automatically breaks every page with a ***soft page break*** after a specified number of lines. When a page should terminate prematurely, for example at the end of a chapter, use a ***hard page break*** to end that page. If your document has been created in pieces, as separate documents, use the Retrieve option to ***combine documents***.

Viewing Documents with Windows

It is often necessary to create a ***split screen*** to view two documents on the same screen. WordPerfect 5.1 permits users to open a ***window***—that is, to use different parts of the same screen to display more than one file. Documents may then be created in or loaded into both windows for editing. WordPerfect allows you to move or copy text within a single document or between the documents in both windows. To create a window, select Window from the Edit pull-down menu or press CTRL-F3 and then **1** for **W**indow.

You can also view two documents on two alternating screens, shifting between them by selecting Switch Document from the Edit pull-down menu or pressing SHIFT-F3. You will practice moving between two documents in the following hands-on exercises.

▶ To retrieve QUICK.MEM and immediately save the document as a new practice file called UTILITY.MEM:

1. Access a blank WordPerfect 5.1 document screen.
2. Menus: Press ALT-=, select File, and select Retrieve.
   or Keys: Press SHIFT-F10.
3. Type **A:QUICK.MEM** and press ENTER.
4. Menus: Press ALT-=, select File, and select Save.
   or Keys: Press F10.
5. Type **A:UTILITY.MEM** as the new file name and press ENTER.

▶ To open the window:

1. Press HOME twice and then press ↑ to position the document on the screen.
2. Menus: Press ALT-=, select Edit, and select Window.
   or Keys: Press CTRL-F3 and then **1** for **W**indow.

   Check that the following message appears on your screen.

```
Number of lines in this window: 24
```

   A total of 24 lines of text may be viewed on the screen. You can specify how many lines you want in the top (document 1) window, thereby determining the number of lines remaining in the bottom window.
3. Type **12** and press ENTER to split the screen into halves.

   Check that your screen resembles the following figure.

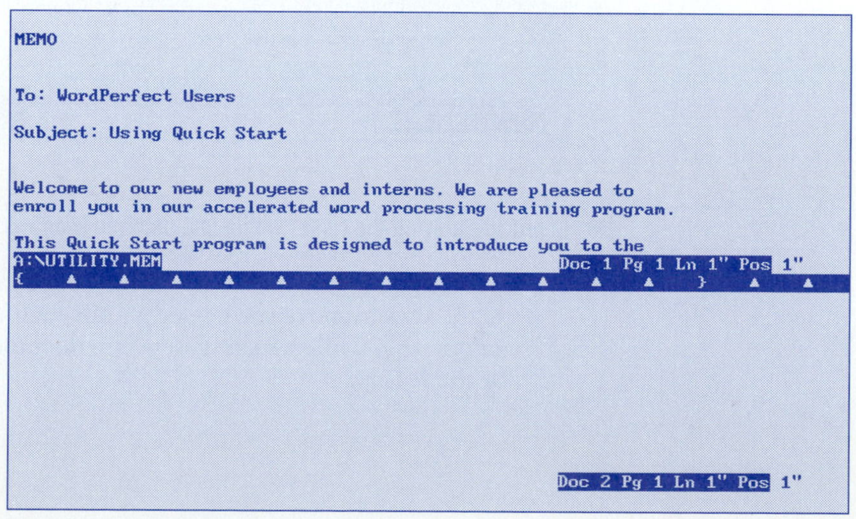

A highlighted tab bar has appeared in the center of the screen. The window in the top half of the screen contains Doc 1, as indicated by the status line at the bottom of the window. The window at the bottom of the screen is empty but is labeled Doc 2. The ***active window*** (where the cursor is) is indicated by the arrowheads pointing upward in the tab bar at the center of the screen.

▶ To move the cursor to the bottom window:

1. Menus: Press ALT-=, select Edit, and select Switch Document.
   or Keys: Press SHIFT-F3.

   Notice that the arrows in the status line are now pointing down. Window 2 is now active. The arrows in the tab bar indicate the current tab settings. The symbols { } indicate left and right margins, respectively. Your screen may not display the right-margin indicator.

▶ To retrieve the 8_15WAGE.MEM memo and place it in the window as the second document:

1. Menus: Press ALT-=, select File, and select Retrieve.
   or Keys: Press SHIFT-F10.
2. Type **A:8_15WAGE.MEM** and press ENTER.

   Check that your screen resembles the following figure.

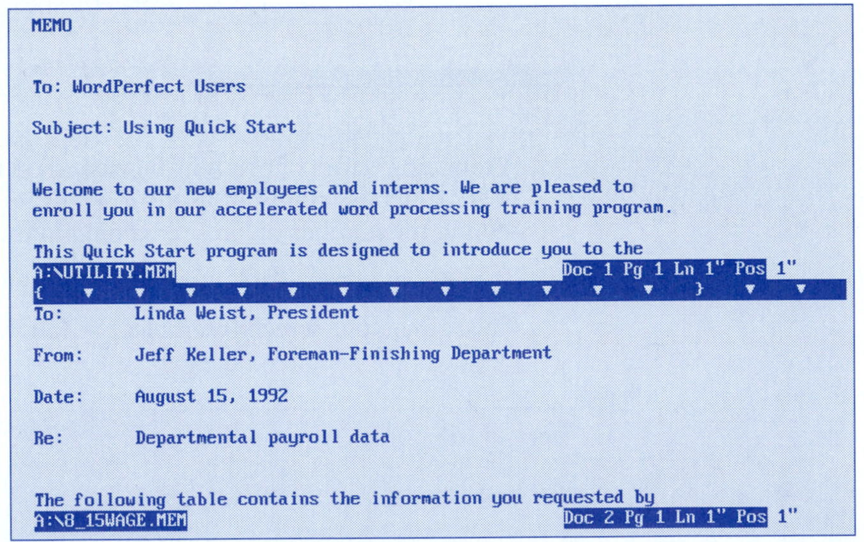

```
MEMO

To: WordPerfect Users

Subject: Using Quick Start

Welcome to our new employees and interns. We are pleased to
enroll you in our accelerated word processing training program.

This Quick Start program is designed to introduce you to the
A:\UTILITY.MEM                                 Doc 1 Pg 1 Ln 1" Pos 1"
{  ▼   ▼   ▼   ▼   ▼   ▼   ▼   ▼   ▼   ▼   ▼   ▼   }   ▼   ▼
To:        Linda Weist, President

From:      Jeff Keller, Foreman-Finishing Department

Date:      August 15, 1992

Re:        Departmental payroll data

The following table contains the information you requested by
A:\8_15WAGE.MEM                                Doc 2 Pg 1 Ln 1" Pos 1"
```

▶ To practice moving the cursor within and between windows:

1. Press SHIFT-F3 to move the cursor between windows. Press a variety of cursor keys to move the cursor within each document. Once you are comfortable with switching between documents, you may find many uses for the feature.

You can easily copy or move text from one document to another. Simply follow the usual procedures to mark the text block, and initiate a Move or Copy command. When prompted to "Move cursor; press Enter to retrieve," press (SHIFT)-(F3) to access the target document, position the cursor on the appropriate location within the target document, and then press (ENTER).

▶ To restore the window to 24 lines:

1. Menus: Press (ALT)-=, select Edit, and select Window.
   or Keys: Press (CTRL)-(F3) and then **1** for **W**indow.

   Check that the message "Number of lines in this window:" appears at the bottom of your screen.

2. Type **24** and press (ENTER) to eliminate the display of two documents.

▶ To view a full-screen display of the alternate document:

1. Menus: Press (ALT)-=, select Edit, and select Switch Document.
   or Keys: Press (SHIFT)-(F3).

▶ To exit both documents without saving and access a blank document/screen:

1. Press (SHIFT)-(F3) until "Doc 2" appears in the status line.
2. Menus: Press (ALT)-=, select File, and select Exit.
   or Keys: Press (F7).
3. Press **N** in response to the prompt "Save document? **Y**es (**N**o)."
4. Press **Y** in response to the prompt "Exit Doc 2? **N**o (**Y**es)."

   Only the UTILITY.MEM document remains on the screen, where it is displayed as Doc 1.

5. Menus: Press (ALT)-=, select File, and select Exit.
   or Keys: Press (F7).
6. Press **N** in response to the prompt "Save Document? **Y**es (**N**o).
7. Press **N** in response to the prompt "Exit WP? **N**o (**Y**es).

COMBINING DOCUMENTS

Documents are often created in pieces, as separate documents, and then combined into one large document. This is particularly true if more than one person works on a document. Combining documents involves retrieving a document from disk, placing it into one already in memory, and then saving the result.

In the following exercises, you will create a letter in reply to a person who has just written Clearwater Manufacturing, Inc., to request information about the company's stock investments. You will then copy the table that you created in the previous project into the letter you just created.

▶ To create the beginning of a letter to a stockholder:

1. Access a blank WordPerfect 5.1 document screen.
2. Type the letter shown in the following figure, and include several blank lines after the opening paragraph.

```
                   Clearwater Manufacturing, Inc.
                           14 Gulf Drive
                        Clearwater, FL  34630

August 15, 1992


Mr. Marcus Jimenez
2825 N. Cape Drive
Chicago, IL  60283

Dear Mr. Jimenez:

Thank you for your inquiry about the value of Clearwater
Manufacturing's stock investments. The table below represents all
stock holdings by the firm at the end of July 1992.
```

▶ To combine the table created in Project 5 with the current document:

1. Position the cursor two lines below the last line of the letter.
2. Menus: Press ALT-=, select File, and select List Files.
   or Keys: Press F5.
3. Type **A:** and press ENTER.
4. Highlight STOCK.TBL and press **1** for **R**etrieve.
5. Press **Y** in response to the prompt "Retrieve into current document? **N**o (**Y**es)."

   Check that your combined document includes the letter and table as shown in the following figure.

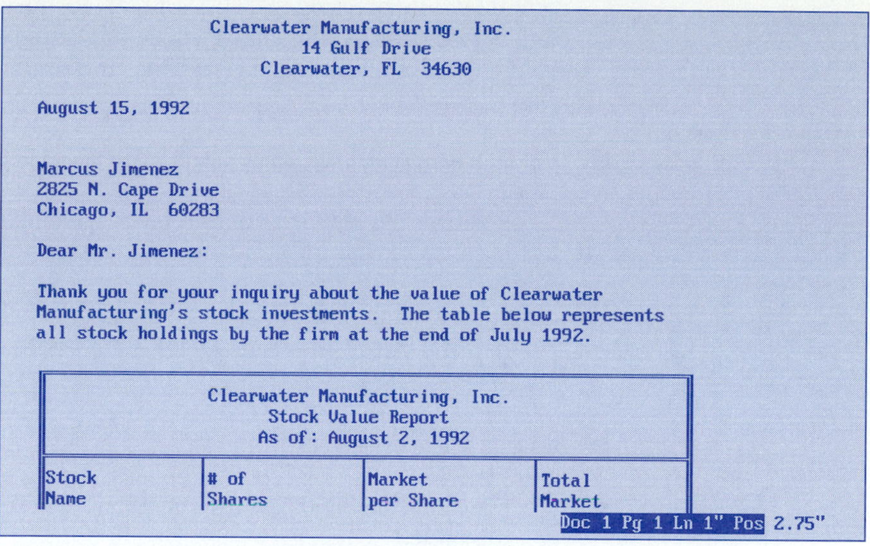

```
                Clearwater Manufacturing, Inc.
                       14 Gulf Drive
                   Clearwater, FL  34630

August 15, 1992


Marcus Jimenez
2825 N. Cape Drive
Chicago, IL  60283

Dear Mr. Jimenez:

Thank you for your inquiry about the value of Clearwater
Manufacturing's stock investments.  The table below represents
all stock holdings by the firm at the end of July 1992.
```

Clearwater Manufacturing, Inc. Stock Value Report As of: August 2, 1992			
Stock Name	# of Shares	Market per Share	Total Market

```
                                          Doc 1 Pg 1 Ln 1" Pos 2.75"
```

▶ **To save the combined letter and table and continue to edit:**

1. Menus: Press (ALT)-=, select File, and select Save.
   or Keys: Press (F10).
2. Type **A:REPLY.LTR** and press (ENTER).

INSERTING PAGE BREAKS

Normally, a standard typing page is 8.5 by 11 inches, and a printer types six lines per inch, or 66 lines per page. In WordPerfect 5.1 the default margin setting for both the tops and bottoms of pages is 1 inch. If you use the default settings, WordPerfect automatically "knows" that you can print only 9 inches (or 54 lines) per page. When the line counter in the status line at the bottom of the screen displays 10" (or 54 lines), a page break is automatically inserted in the document. The line counter returns to 1" (or 7 lines) and a single dashed line appears across the screen. At this point you begin typing a new page.

If you insert text in or delete text from a document, all text is adjusted to fill each page. However, if it is necessary to terminate a page before it is full, insert a hard page break by pressing (CTRL)-(ENTER). You will see a double dashed line appear on the screen and a new page. If you insert or delete text, that page will always terminate at the hard page break. You can view a hard page code [HPg] by pressing (ALT)-(F3) or (F11) for Reveal Codes. To delete a hard page break, position the cursor at the unwanted hard page break, access Reveal Codes, highlight the [HPg] code, and press (DEL).

▶ To insert a hard page break immediately below the table in the document:

1. Position the cursor two lines below the table.
2. Press (CTRL)-(ENTER).

   Check that a double dashed line appears below the table on the page and that the status line reads Doc 1 Pg 2 Ln 1".

▶ To delete a hard page break:

1. Position the cursor just below the double dashed line that appears below the table.
2. Menus: Press (ALT)-=, select Edit, and select Reveal Codes.
   or Keys: Press (ALT)-(F3) or (F11).

   Check that the revealed codes include those in the following figure.

```
| GM     |   800 | 36.50 |  29,200.00 |
| Chevrn |   500 | 74.00 |  37,000.00 |
|        |       |       | 103,075.00 |

==========================================================================
A:\REPLY.LTR                                   Doc 1 Pg 2 Ln 1" Pos 1"
[Row][Cell]Chevrn[Cell]500[Cell]74.00[Cell]37,000.00
[Row][Cell][Cell][Cell][Cell]103,075.00
[Tbl Off][HRt]
[HPg]
```

3. Highlight [HPg] and press (DEL).
4. Menus: Press (ALT)-=, select Edit, and select Reveal Codes.
   or Keys: Press (ALT)-(F3) or (F11).

▶ **To insert a hard page break immediately below the table in the document:**

1. Position the cursor two lines below the table.
2. Press CTRL-ENTER.

   Check that a double dashed line appears below the table on your screen and that the status line indicates Doc 1 Pg 2 Ln 1".

▶ **To save the combined letter and table and remain in the current document:**

1. Menus: Press ALT-=, select File, and select Save.
   or Keys: Press F10.
2. Press ENTER at the prompt "Document to be saved: A:\REPLY.LTR."
3. Press **Y** for Yes at the prompt to replace the document on disk.

Adding Headers and Footers

Multiple-page documents often have repeating text or graphics at the top or bottom of each page. For example, a letter might have the subject line and date at the tops of all pages after page 1 and a page number and perhaps the company name or logo at the bottom of each page. Books often have the book title and chapter titles alternating at the tops of odd and even pages. Term papers might contain the writer's name, title of the paper, and course number at the top of all pages.

Typing the headers and footers at the top or bottom of every page would be cumbersome. Another problem with typing headers and footers on every page is that typing errors or variations in format can result. Also, if text is inserted in or deleted from the document, the positioning of headers and footers can shift; they may no longer fall at the tops or bottoms of the pages.

Using WordPerfect 5.1's Header and Footer options on the Format menu allows you to type headers and footers on a screen similar to the document screen. After you exit the Header or Footer edit screen, the headers and footers cannot be seen on the document screen. However, the line counter (Ln) in the status line includes the header and footer in the line count, and so does the display that reports the position of the cursor. The headings are stored until the document is printed or viewed using the View Document option on the Print menu.

Specify the headers and footers at the beginning of the document so the codes will be easy to find if they need to be accessed or deleted. However, headers and footers do not normally appear on the first page. Press **2** for **P**age under Format to suppress headers and footers on a specified page.

In the following exercise, you will add a header that displays the date and subject line of the letter.

▶ To access the Header menu:

1. Press (HOME) twice and then press (↑) to position the cursor at the top of the document.
2. Menus: Press (ALT)-=, select Layout, and select Page.
   or Keys: Press (SHIFT)-(F8) and then **2** for **P**age.
3. Press **3** for **H**eaders.
4. Press **1** to select Header A at the prompt "1 Header **A**: 2 Headers **B**: 0."

   Check that the Header menu shown in the following figure appears at the bottom of the screen.

```
1 Discontinue; 2 Every Page; 3 Odd Pages; 4 Even Pages; 5 Edit: 0
```

5. Press **2** for Every **P**age.

   A blank document screen has appeared with the prompt "Header A: Press Exit when done" at the left side of the status line. Type header information, along with format codes, font codes, and graphics as you would type them into any document. A header can be any length not exceeding one page.

▶ To enter heading information:

1. Type `Subject: Stock Investments, Clearwater Manufacturing, Inc.` and press (ENTER).
2. Press (ENTER) twice to add two blank lines.
3. Press (F7) for Exit until you have returned to the document.

▶ To suppress the heading on page 1:

1. Menus: Press (ALT)-=, select Layout, and select Page.
   or Keys: Press (SHIFT)-(F8) and then **2** for **P**age.
2. Press **8** for S**u**ppress (this page only).

   Check that your screen matches the one shown in the next figure.

   You can suppress any combination of headers and footers or page numbering. Or, you can suppress them all. The selected action applies only to the current page.
3. Press **1** for Suppress **A**ll Page Numbering, Headers and Footers.
4. Press (F7) for Exit until you return to the document screen.

```
Format: Suppress (this page only)

     1 - Suppress All Page Numbering, Headers and Footers

     2 - Suppress Headers and Footers

     3 - Print Page Number at Bottom Center      No

     4 - Suppress Page Numbering                 No

     5 - Suppress Header A                       No

     6 - Suppress Header B                       No

     7 - Suppress Footer A                       No

     8 - Suppress Footer B                       No
```

► To add a concluding paragraph and signature to the second page:

1. Press (PGDN) to position the cursor at the top of the second page. Check that the status line indicates "Doc 1 Pg 2 Ln 1.94."

   Your Ln number may vary depending on the print font or pitch selected for your computer. However, notice that the Ln number now takes into account the extra space used by the header. To see the difference, move the cursor to the top of page 1, then to the top of page 2.

2. On page 2, type the concluding paragraph and signature, as shown in the following figure.

```
The Stock Value Report, shown on page 1, indicates a gain of 6.9
percent in market value over cost. However, we are projecting
that the stock portfolio will close the year with a gain of 8.5
percent. At this time the company has no planned changes to the
portfolio.

Thank you for your interest in Clearwater Manufacturing, Inc. If
I can provide further information about the company, please
write.


Sincerely,



Donald Choy
Controller
```

► To view page 2 of the document in the View Document mode:

1. Position the cursor on page 2.
2. Menus: Press (ALT)-=, select File, and select Print.
   or Keys: Press (SHIFT)-(F7).
3. Press **6** for **V**iew Document.

   Check that the heading on your View Document screen matches the heading in the following figure.

```
Subject: Stock Investments, Clearwater Manufacturing, Inc.


The Stock Value Report, shown on page 1, indicates a gain of 6.9
percent in market value over cost.  However, we are projecting
that the stock portfolio will close the year with a gain of 8.5
percent.  At this time the company has no planned changes to the
portfolio.

Thank you for your interest in Clearwater Manufacturing, Inc. If
I can provide further information about the company, please write.


Sincerely,



Donald Choy
Controller
```

When the document prints or is displayed in the View Document mode, the heading is added to the output. While editing the document on screen, you cannot see the headers or footers. To change a header or footer, repeat the steps to create a header or footer, but in step 5 press **5** for **E**dit instead of **2** for Every **P**age; then make changes.

▶ **To save the document and continue editing:**

1. Menus: Press ALT-=, select File, and select Save.
   or Keys: Press F10.
2. Press ENTER at the prompt "Document to be saved: A:\REPLY.LTR."
3. Type **Y** for Yes at the prompt about replacing the document on disk.

Numbering Pages

One of the most important formatting features on a page is the page number. Page numbers are often taken for granted until it becomes necessary to look something up in the table of contents or index, refer to a fact on a page, or make notes. There are two methods of page numbering in WordPerfect 5.1.

The Page Numbering option in the Format menu determines the starting page number and the placement of the page number on the page. By selecting the starting page number, you can create very large documents, such as books, in separate and manageable files, such as chapters. You can center a page number at the top or bottom of the page or place a number in one of the four corners. The page number is placed on the first print line after the top margin or before the bottom margin. If a header or footer is specified, the page number prints on the first line after the header or before the footer. The line counter in the status line automatically accounts for this line usage.

However, if you have specified a header or footer and it will conflict with the page number, put the page number in the header or footer. Though the Page Numbering option in the Format menu specifies the starting page number, it does not position the page number. Instead, when you create the header or footer, you will position the cursor where you want the page number to print and press CTRL-**B**. The symbol ^B will appear, indicating automatic page numbering at that location.

► To access the Page Numbering menu:

1. Press HOME twice, and then press ↑ to position the cursor at the top of the first page.
2. Menus: Press ALT-=, select Layout, and select Page.
   or Keys: Press SHIFT-F8 and then **2** for **P**age.
3. Press **6** for Page **N**umbering.

   Check that the Format: Page Numbering menu, shown in the next figure, appears on your screen.

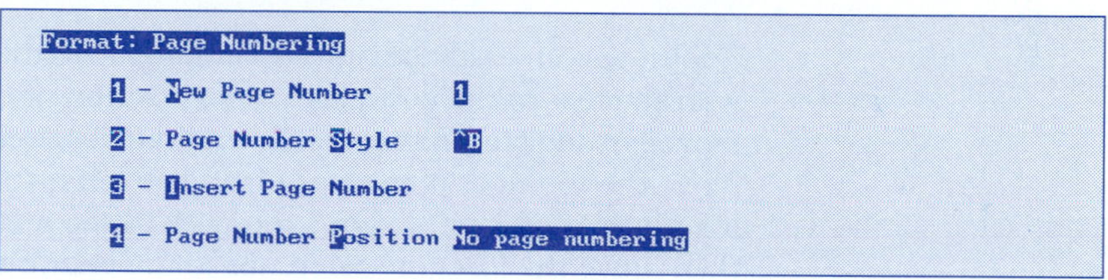

   Press **1** for **N**ew Page Number to set the starting number. Press **2** for Page Number **S**tyle to change how the page number prints. The default is ^B. To print the word "Page" in front of the page number, change this setting to "Page ^B." To insert the page number at the position of the cursor, press **3** for **I**nsert Page Number.

► To position the page number and view the document:

1. Press **4** for Page Number **P**osition.

   Check that your screen appears as shown in the following figure.

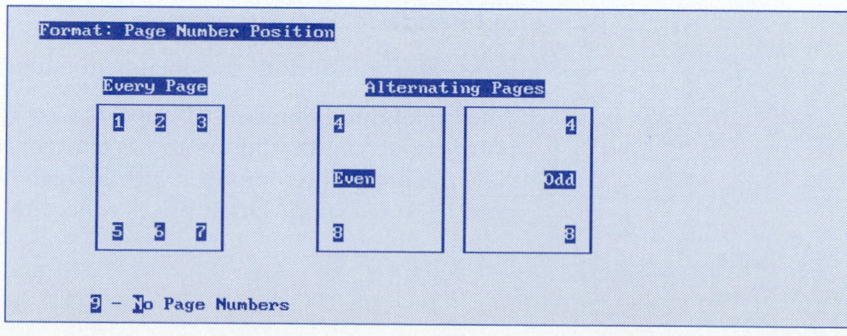

2. Type **6** to center the page number at the bottom of every page.
3. Press F7 for Exit until your document appears on the screen and press PGDN until the cursor is at the top of the second page.
4. Menus: Press ALT-=, select File, and select Print.
   or Keys: Press SHIFT-F7.
5. Press **6** for **V**iew Document, adjust the document until you see the bottom of the page and the page number ("2"), and press F7 to exit the Print menu options.

Using Footnotes and Endnotes

Footnotes amplify information in a document or credit other sources. Footnotes are numbered sequentially and placed at the bottom of a page. Their numbers correspond to a number in the text, next to the item being footnoted. ***Endnotes*** serve the same function and are referenced in the same way. However, some writing conventions call for notations to be placed at the end of the document rather than at the bottom of the page.

Footnotes can easily be moved. Simply move the text; the footnotes move with the text to the new pages. The position of other footnotes affected by the move are adjusted appropriately and renumbered automatically. You can also move the footnote number itself and attach it to different text. In the following exercise you will assign a footnote to the text "Stock Value Report" and then move the footnote reference to the end of the sentence.

▶ To create a footnote attached to the words "Stock Value Report" on page 2:

1. Position the cursor just after the comma following the words "Stock Value Report" on the first line of page 2.
2. Menus: Press ALT-=, select Layout, select Footnote, and select Create.
   or Keys: Press CTRL-F7 and then press **1** twice.

   Check that your monitor displays a blank document screen with the message "Footnote: Press Exit when done" on the left side of the status line. The footnote number should appear in the upper-left corner of the screen.
3. Type `Market prices reflect July 31, 1992, stock exchange closing prices.`
4. Press F7 for Exit until the document appears on the screen.

   The highlighted number "1" appears next to the text "Stock Value Report," indicating that footnote 1 is electronically linked to the text. If you view the highlighted number with Reveal Codes, you see "[Footnote:1;[Note Num]Market prices reflect July 31, . . .]."

▶ To view page 2 of the document in View Document mode:

1. Position the cursor on page 2, if necessary.
2. Menus: Press ALT-=, select File, and select Print.
   or Keys: Press SHIFT-F7.
3. Press **6** for **V**iew Document.

   Check that the bottom of page 2 on your View Document screen matches the footnote displayed in the following figure.

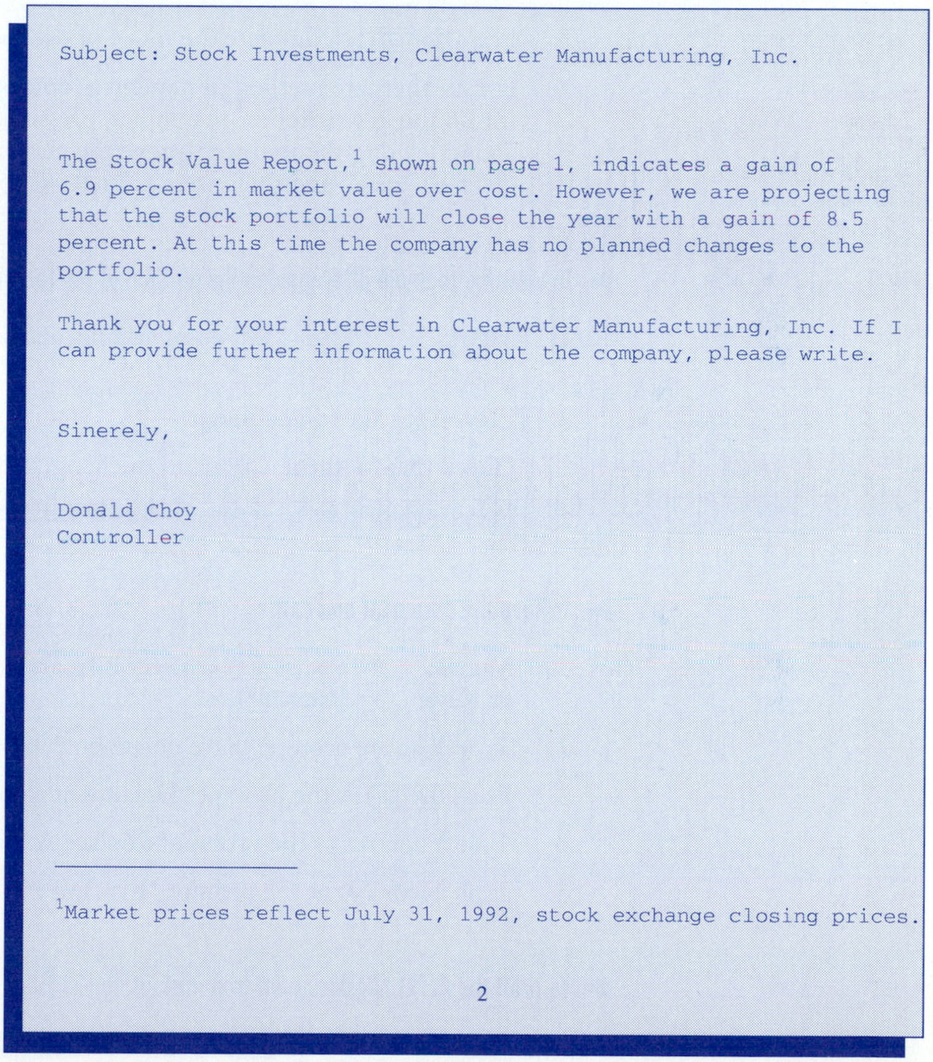

```
Subject: Stock Investments, Clearwater Manufacturing, Inc.


The Stock Value Report,[1] shown on page 1, indicates a gain of
6.9 percent in market value over cost. However, we are projecting
that the stock portfolio will close the year with a gain of 8.5
percent. At this time the company has no planned changes to the
portfolio.

Thank you for your interest in Clearwater Manufacturing, Inc. If I
can provide further information about the company, please write.


Sinerely,


Donald Choy
Controller



______________

[1]Market prices reflect July 31, 1992, stock exchange closing prices.

                                2
```

Your page may vary slightly in the number of characters per line, depending on the print font or pitch selected for your printer. Also, notice that a small superscripted 1 appears both in the text and next to the footnote. The matching superscripts indicate the association of the text and the footnote.

▶ To move the reference to footnote 1 to the end of the sentence:

1. Press (F7) for Exit.
2. Position the cursor on the superscripted 1 in the text.
3. Menus: Press (ALT)-=, select Edit, and select Block.
   or Keys: Press (ALT)-(F4) or .
4. Press (→) to mark the block.
5. Press (CTRL)-(DEL) to remove the block.
6. Position the cursor on the period (.) at the end of the sentence.
7. Press (ENTER) to complete the move of the footnote reference.

   For an alternate method of moving a footnote reference, position the cursor on the in-text footnote number, press (DEL), respond Y to the prompt about deleting the footnote, move the cursor to the new position, press (F1) for Cancel, and then press **1** for **R**estore.

▶ To view the footnote after moving the position of the footnote reference:

1. Menus: Press (ALT)-=, select File, and select Print.
   or Keys: Press (SHIFT)-(F7).
2. Press **6** for **V**iew Document.

   Check that footnote 1 remains unchanged at the bottom of the page.
3. Press (F7) for Exit to return to the document Edit screen.

▶ To save the document and exit:

1. Menus: Press (ALT)-=, select File, and select Exit.
   or Keys: Press (F7).
2. Type **Y** at the prompt "Save document? **Y**es (**N**o)."
3. Press (ENTER) at the prompt "Document to be saved: A:\REPLY.LTR."
4. Type **Y** for Yes at the prompt "Replace A:\REPLY.LTR? **N**o (**Y**es)."
5. Type **N** for No at the prompt "Exit WP? **N**o (**Y**es)."

▶ To print the REPLY.LTR document from disk using List Files:

1. Menus: Press (ALT)-=, select File, and select List Files.
   or Keys: Press (F5).
2. Type **A:** and press (ENTER).

3. Highlight REPLY.LTR.
4. Press **4** for **P**rint.
5. Press ENTER at the prompt "Page(s):(All)."

   To print selected pages instead of all pages, list consecutive page numbers by placing a dash between the beginning and ending pages in the sequence and list individual page numbers separated by commas. For example, to print pages 1 through 3, 5, and 7, you would enter 1-3, 5, 7 at the prompt "Page(s):(All)."

6. Press F7 to restore the blank document screen.

   This concludes Project 6. You can work the Review Exercises, go on to the last project, or exit WordPerfect.

SUMMARY

- Rather than being typed in from start to finish, many documents are pieced together from blocks of text that have been created as separate documents. You can view several documents at once in different windows to make it easier to move and copy data to a new document.
- Many layout and formatting features not required for single-page documents become necessary once you start to create longer documents or combine several documents to create a new document.
- Before printing, a document must contain codes that tell the printer where to end one page and begin the next and how and where the pages should be numbered. You have to decide whether to add descriptions—headers or footers—to each page at the top or bottom.
- WordPerfect 5.1 makes it easy to link in-text references to footnotes to the footnotes themselves. If you move the reference to a new page, WordPerfect moves the footnote to the new page automatically.

KEY TERMS

active window
combine documents
endnote
footer
footnote
hard page break
header
page numbering
soft page break
split screen
window

Study Questions

True/False

1. Only one document can be viewed on the screen at a time. T F
2. You can specify how many lines of a document you want to view at a time by setting the size of the window. T F
3. Pressing (F3) allows you to switch between documents. T F
4. Reveal Codes must be used to delete unwanted page breaks. T F
5. A double dashed line across the screen means you are out of disk space. T F
6. Headers and footers appear on the document screen. T F
7. A header can be of any length. T F
8. The status line incorporates the header and footer in the line counter (Ln) reference. T F
9. To print several pages instead of all pages, list individual page numbers separated by spaces. T F
10. The number of lines you specify for the top window determines how many lines remain to form the bottom window. T F

Fill in the Blanks

1. Moving or copying blocks of text can be done within _________ or between _________ documents.
2. To create a window, press _________.
3. The normal typewritten page prints _________ lines. Because of its default margin settings, the default WordPerfect 5.1 page prints _________ lines.
4. Pressing (CTRL)-(ENTER) inserts _________.
5. Text or graphics that is repeated at the top of each page is called a _________; when text or graphics is repeated at the bottom of each page, it is called a _________.
6. When you _________ any combination of headers, footers, or page numbering, the selected action applies to that page only.
7. When automatic page numbering is active, the _________ symbol appears at that location.
8. Combining documents requires that one document already be _________ while another is retrieved from _________.
9. When the line counter in the status line at the bottom of the page says 10" (or 54 lines), WordPerfect automatically _________, the line counter returns to _________, and a _________ dashed line appears across the screen.

For Discussion

1. List five features you would use only in multipage documents.
2. How does WordPerfect 5.1 show which window is active? How does it label the documents in the windows?

3. What are the two procedures for numbering pages in WordPerfect?
4. What are footnotes used for? Where are they placed?
5. What are the three ways WordPerfect provides to print all or a portion of a document?

REVIEW EXERCISES

Review the concepts presented in Project 6 by completing the following tasks. If necessary, review the material.

The foreman, Jeff Keller, has asked you to access and finish his memo to the president about wages for workers in the Finishing Department. Jeff would like you to add the wages table WAGES.TBL, created in Project 5's review exercises, to the end of the memo 8_15WAGE.MEM, created in the exercises in Project 1. In addition, break to a new page and finish the memo for his signature.

1. Access a blank WordPerfect 5.1 document screen.
2. Retrieve the memo 8_15WAGE.MEM.
3. Position the cursor at the end of the text, add a blank line for spacing, and retrieve WAGES.TBL, combining the table and the memo.
4. Enter a hard page break two lines below the table.
5. At the top of page 1, enter the code to suppress all headers, footers, and page numbers.
6. At the top of page 1, enter the header **`Subject: Department Wages; August 5, 1992`** and, using View Document mode, check that the header appears correctly on page 2. Use the Header Edit option to make necessary corrections.
7. Specify page numbering to begin at the bottom right corner of the second page and verify that page numbering is suppressed on page 1 and appears on page 2.
8. Type a concluding paragraph on page 2. The paragraph should recommend pay increases for two of the employees mentioned in the table.
9. Place a footnote at the end of the first sentence in the first paragraph on page 1. Type the following footnote text:

   `Paid travel and training reimbursements are not included in these figures.`
10. Verify the format of the document using View Document, then print a copy.
11. Save the final wages memo on disk. Retain the current name of the memo, 8_15WAGE.MEM.

Project 7: Creating a Custom Document with Merge

After completing this project, you should be able to:

- Merge data from two documents to form a custom document
- Name and code the fields in the database
- Create a WordPerfect 5.1 database to use as a secondary merge file
- Insert the database field names into your primary merge file
- Merge data from the keyboard into your primary merge file

Merging Data

One of WordPerfect 5.1's most powerful and useful features is the capability to create documents by ***merging*** data from one document (or the keyboard) into another document. Imagine that you are responsible for sending hundreds of similar letters every month. The following figure illustrates a standard letter reminding customers to have their cars serviced.

```
                     18-Minute Car Care
                   2001 Corporation Drive
                    Santa Fe, NM  87639
                      (505) 321-CARE

August 2, 1993

Carla Castelli
23943 Sunset Dr.
Santa Fe, NM  87643

Dear Carla,

Our records indicate that it is time for your Ford Econoline van
to be serviced.  The vehicle was last serviced at 57,821 miles.

If you bring your car in for our $19.95 lubrication package any
time during the next 7 days, you will receive these valuable
additional services and products:

     *    Car wash and hot wax
     *    Tire and exhaust inspection
     *    18-Minute Car Care tee shirt
     *    A chance to win $1,000

At 18-Minute Car Care, trained mechanics and name-brand products
provide you with driving confidence.

Sincerely,


Jeff Keller, Owner
```

Variable data

If you had only a typewriter to work with, you would have to retype the letter and change the car model and odometer reading for each customer. Using a word processing program on a computer, you could type and print one letter and then, to print the next letter, change the text related to a specific customer name, address, make and model of car, and odometer reading. Use this approach when only a few similar documents must be prepared.

WordPerfect 5.1 provides the Merge facility to produce the same letter, with personalized touches, for a large number of recipients. You must create two files before a merge can take place: a primary and a secondary merge document. A ***primary merge document*** contains both the text that does not change and codes that refer to fields of data in the secondary merge document. These fields contain the data that does change from letter to letter. The ***secondary merge document*** serves as the database of separate records that contain the different fields.

During a merge, WordPerfect 5.1 replaces the ***merge codes*** in the primary document with the corresponding data from the first record in the secondary file to create the ***custom document***. The process continues until a custom document has been produced for each record in the secondary file. A special form of merge allows users to merge input from the keyboard.

Merge function applications are endless. You can use the feature to merge names and addresses into letters and labels, stock inventory information into purchase orders and invoices, standard specifications into proposals, and personnel information into special forms and letters.

Creating a Primary Merge File

The primary merge file controls how the finished document looks and the position of data inserted from the fields in the secondary merge file. The following figure shows a screen view of a primary document with merge codes.

```
                    18-Minute Car Care
                  2001 Corporation Drive
                    Santa Fe, NM  87639
                      (505) 321-CARE


August 2, 1993


{FIELD}FIRSTNAME~ {FIELD}LASTNAME~
{FIELD}STREET~
{FIELD}CITY~, {FIELD}STATE~  {FIELD}ZIP~

Dear {FIELD}FIRSTNAME~,

Our records indicate that it is time for your {FIELD}CAR~ to be
serviced.  The vehicle was last serviced at {FIELD}ODOMETER~ miles.

If you bring your car in for our $19.95 lubrication package any
time during the next 7 days, you will receive these valuable
additional services and products:
```

Notice that the document looks like any ordinary document except for {FIELD} codes. To create a primary merge document, you will access a blank document screen and begin typing as you would type any document. At the places where data from the secondary merge file should be inserted, you will enter a {FIELD} code and type the name of the data field to be inserted. When the document is complete, you will save it on disk so it can be used as part of the merge process.

▶ To enter standard text at the top of the document:

1. Access a blank document screen.
2. Type in and center the company name, address, and phone number data shown in the previous figure.
3. Insert two blank lines, enter **`August 2, 1993`** and insert another blank line.

▶ To enter two merge codes to access name data in the secondary merge file:

1. Press (SHIFT)-(F9) and then **1** for **F**ield.
2. At the "Enter field:" prompt, type **`FIRSTNAME`** and press (ENTER) to create the first variable field.
3. Press the space bar to insert a space between the first name and the last name.
4. Press (SHIFT)-(F9) and then **1** for **F**ield.
5. At the "Enter field:" prompt, type **`LASTNAME`** and press (ENTER).
6. Complete the top of the letter and the first paragraph by typing the text and entering the remaining field name codes shown in the previous figure.
7. Type in the rest of the primary document that reminds customers to have their cars serviced.
8. Verify that the typing and coding are correct. When they are, save the document under the name **`CUSTOMER.PRI`**.

   Use the extensions PRI and SEC when naming primary and secondary files, respectively. These designations are not required to merge data, but they will help you to remember the purpose of each file.

Creating a Secondary Merge File

With WordPerfect 5.1, you can set up a database as a secondary merge file. A ***database*** is a collection of ***records***. Each record contains standard pieces of data called ***fields***. The following figure illustrates the organization of a WordPerfect 5.1 database.

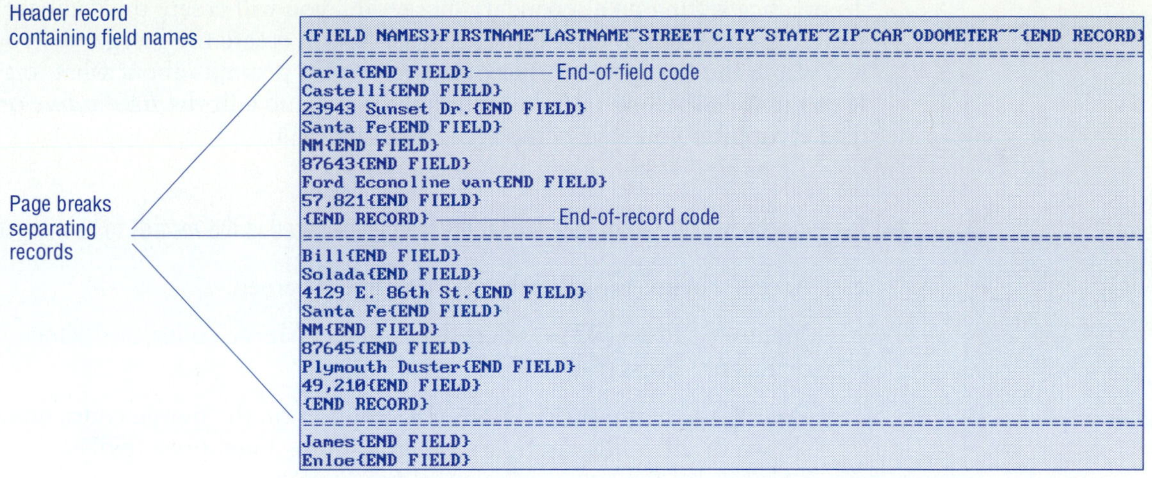

The sample database contains eight fields of data: first name, last name, street, city, state, zip code, make of car, and odometer reading. Since field names cannot contain spaces, you will name the first name field FIRSTNAME, the last name field LASTNAME, and so on. If you need to sort and search on individual last names, states, and zip codes, you would create a separate field for each item. Use the following field names in the database for this project: FIRSTNAME, LASTNAME, STREET, CITY, STATE, ZIP, CAR, and ODOMETER.

The first record of the database document is a special ***header record,*** which lists the names of the data fields. Note that WordPerfect 5.1 inserts a tilde (~) to separate each field, and the entire statement ends with two tildes (~~). Each field within a data record appears on a separate line and ends with an {END FIELD} code. Each record in the database ends with an {END RECORD} code.

Note: As you enter data, a field indicator in the lower-left corner of the screen displays the name of the data field. In the Merge function, "Pg" refers to individual records, not pages.

The following figure shows menu options related to Merge operations. Selections allow you to create a secondary file, to set up a primary file containing merge codes, and to activate the merge.

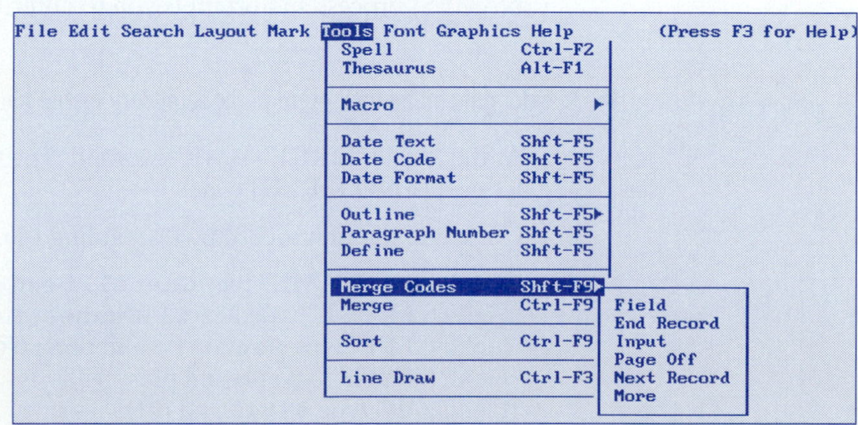

To practice setting up a secondary merge file, you will create the database structure and enter at least three records. As you create the merge file, you will watch the lower-left corner of the screen for prompts about what to type. If you make a spelling mistake, continue typing and edit the ***field name*** or data error after you have completed the instructions.

▶ To create the header record that defines the field names used in the records to be merged:

1. Access a blank WordPerfect 5.1 document screen.
2. Menus: Press ALT-=, select Tools, select Merge codes, and select More.
   or Keys: Press SHIFT-F9 **6**.
3. Press ↓ until the {FIELD NAMES} option on the merge codes menu shown in the following figure is highlighted. Then press ENTER.

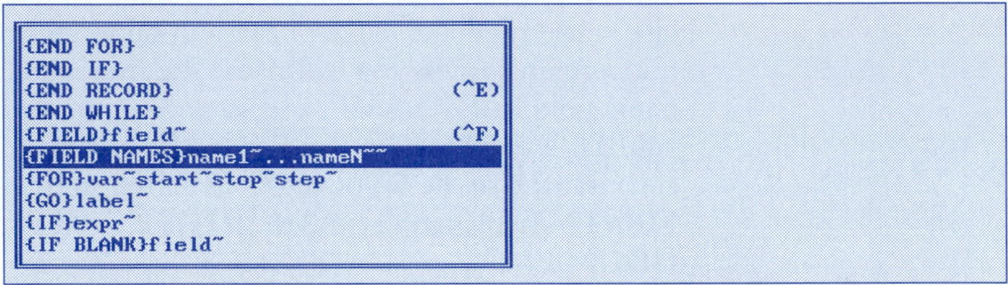

4. At the "Enter Field 1:" prompt, type **`FIRSTNAME`** and press ENTER.

▶ To complete the header record, respond to the prompts as follows:

"Enter Field 2:" type **`LASTNAME`** and press ENTER.
"Enter Field 3:" type **`STREET`** and press ENTER.
"Enter Field 4:" type **`CITY`** and press ENTER.
"Enter Field 5:" type **`STATE`** and press ENTER.
"Enter Field 6:" type **`ZIP`** and press ENTER.
"Enter Field 7:" type **`CAR`** and press ENTER.
"Enter Field 8:" type **`ODOMETER`** and press ENTER.
"Enter Field 9:" press ENTER.

Pressing ENTER without entering a field name ends the {FIELD NAMES} process and prompts you to enter the first field of data.

▶ To enter data in the first record of the secondary merge file:

1. At the "Field: FIRSTNAME" prompt, type **`Carla`** and press F9 to insert a {END FIELD} code.
2. Complete the first record by responding to the prompts as follows:

   "Field: LASTNAME" type **`Castelli`** and press F9.
   "Field: STREET" type **`23943 Sunset Dr.`** and press F9.
   "Field: CITY" type **`Santa Fe`** and press F9.
   "Field: STATE" type **`NM`** and press F9.
   "Field: ZIP" type **`87643`** and press F9.

"Field: CAR" type **Ford Econoline van** and press (F9).
"Field: ODOMETER" type **57,821** and press (F9).

3. Press (SHIFT)-(F9) and then **2** for End Record to enter an {END RECORD} code. Your screen should look like the following figure.

```
{FIELD NAMES}FIRSTNAME~LASTNAME~STREET~CITY~STATE~ZIP~CAR~ODOMETE
R~~{END RECORD}
=================================================================
Carla{END FIELD}
Castelli{END FIELD}
23943 Sunset Dr.{END FIELD}
Santa Fe{END FIELD}
NM{END FIELD}
87643{END FIELD}
Ford Econoline van{END FIELD}
57,821{END FIELD}
{END RECORD}
=================================================================

Field: FIRSTNAME                              Doc 1 Pg 3 Ln 1" Pos 1"
```

4. Enter records containing the data shown below. Remember to press (F9) at the end of each field, then (SHIFT)-(F9), and then **2** for End Record to complete each record.

Prompt	Record 2	Record 3
FIRSTNAME	**Bill**	**James**
LASTNAME	**Solada**	**Enloe**
STREET	**4129 E. 86th St.**	**9018 Twesbury**
CITY	**Santa Fe**	**Santa Fe**
STATE	**NM**	**NM**
ZIP	**87645**	**87631**
CAR	**Plymouth Duster**	**Buick Park Avenue**
ODOMETER	**49,210**	**32,834**

Verify that the data you have entered is correct and make any necessary changes.

▶ To save the secondary merge file:

1. Menus: Press (ALT)-=, select File, and select Exit.
   or Keys: Press (F7).
2. Press **Y** in response to the "Save document?" prompt.
3. At the "Document to be saved:" prompt, type **CUSTOMER.SEC** and press (ENTER).
4. In response to the "Exit WP?" prompt, press **N**.

Merging Two Documents

To execute a merge, you select Merge from the Tools pull-down menu. The merge begins automatically after you respond to prompts for the names of the primary and secondary files.

During the Merge process, WordPerfect 5.1 inputs the primary merge document into a document screen and inserts data from the first record in the secondary merge file each time a {FIELD} code is encountered. The process is repeated, creating one custom letter for each record in the secondary file. A new document is formed on the screen, and you can save, edit, or print it just as you would any other document. This method has the advantage of letting you edit the resulting document before printing it.

You will merge two files stored on disk by merging a primary document, which notifies customers of a lubrication promotion, with the customer records in the secondary merge file. Then you will print the results.

▶ To initiate the merge process:

1. Access a blank WordPerfect 5.1 document screen.
2. Menus: Press ALT-=, select Tools, and select Merge.
   or Keys: Press CTRL-F9 **1**.
3. At the "Primary file:" prompt, type **`CUSTOMER.PRI`** and press ENTER.
4. At the "Secondary file:" prompt, type **`CUSTOMER.SEC`** and press ENTER.

   The status message "* Merging *" appears in the lower-left corner of the screen while the merge file is being created.

▶ To view and verify the custom letters:

1. Use the cursor keys to view the merge file.
2. Check that three custom letters, one for each record in the CUSTOMER.SEC file, have been created.
3. Check that the correct data about customer names, addresses, car types, and odometer readings have replaced the merge field names.

   If a field does not contain any data, check that the correct field name was specified in the CUSTOMER.PRI document.

▶ To print the custom letters:

1. Menus: Press ALT-=, select File, and select Print.
   or Keys: Press SHIFT-F7.
2. Check that your printer is on and in Ready mode.
3. Press **1** for **F**ull Document to print three custom letters.

You have seen how easy it is to create three custom letters. Just imagine the ease with which you can produce hundreds of personalized documents after entering appropriate data in a secondary database file and then crafting a primary document that points to fields in the database.

Merging from the Keyboard

A secondary merge file is useful only if the data will be used more than once. Examples of such data include the names and addresses of customers, clients, or friends. If variable data will not be used more than once, you can create a standard primary document and use the keyboard to enter the text that changes.

For example, cover letters usually accompany resumes that are sent to prospective employers. You could send the same cover letter with each resume that you submit and change only the variable information, such as the name and address of the personnel contact and the source of the newspaper advertisement announcing a job opening.

The process for merging keyboard entry with a primary document is basically the same as merging data from a secondary merge file. The first step is to create a primary document containing the standard text but use merge codes at the positions where the data from the keyboard is to be placed. The next step is to initiate the Merge process and enter the primary merge file name. When prompted for a secondary file, pressing (ENTER) allows you to bypass the prompt without specifying a name. As the custom merge document is created, a prompt requests input for each field.

To practice the process, you will create and save the resume cover letter shown in the following figure and execute a keyboard merge. The cover letter is a primary document containing two merge codes. The {DATE} code causes the computer's system date to be inserted at print time. The {INPUT}message~ code causes the Merge process to stop, display the user-specified message, and accept user input from the keyboard.

```
                        Scott Brown
                     33 Rangeline Road
                  Indianapolis, IN 46315
                      (317)849-9876

{DATE}

{INPUT}Type full contact name~
{INPUT}Type company name~
{INPUT}Type company street~
{INPUT}Type company city, state and zip code~

Dear {INPUT}Type contact's last name~

     Your ad in the {INPUT}Type source~ caught my attention. I am
interested in the challenging position you described. Enclosed is
my resume. I will be in town next week and would like to set up
an interview at the earliest possible time.

Sincerely,


Scott Brown, MBA, CPA
```

You can substitute a {KEYBOARD} code for an {INPUT}message code when you do not want to display a message.

▶ To enter standard text at the top of the document and enter a current date code:

1. Access a blank WordPerfect 5.1 document screen.
2. Center the name, address, and phone number data as shown in the previous figure, and insert one blank line.
3. Press SHIFT-F9 and then **6** for **M**ore.
4. Highlight {DATE} in the pop-up window displaying merge codes (see the following figure), press ENTER, and insert one blank line.

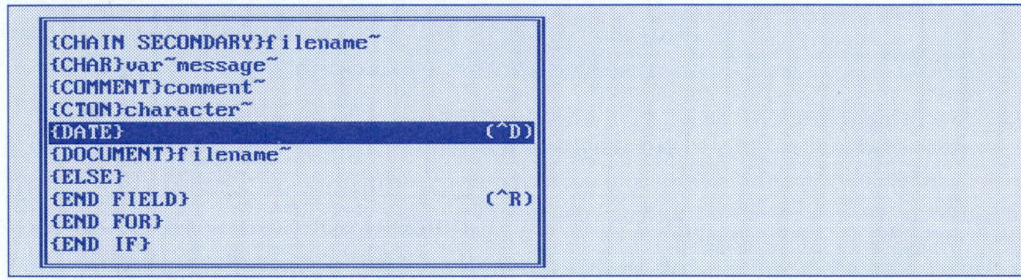

▶ To enter the first {INPUT}message code:

1. Press SHIFT-F9 and then **6** for **M**ore.
2. Highlight {INPUT}message~ in the pop-up window displaying merge codes and press ENTER.
3. At the "Enter Message:" prompt, type `Type full contact name` and press ENTER to complete the prompt.
4. Enter the remaining text, merge codes, and messages.
5. Verify that the data you entered is correct, and save the document under the name `JOBS.PRI`.

▶ To initiate a keyboard merge and enter the contact name:

1. Menus: Press ALT-=, select Tools, and select Merge.
   or Keys: Press CTRL-F9 **1**.
2. At the "Primary file:" prompt, type `JOBS.PRI` and press ENTER.
3. At the "Secondary file:" prompt, press ENTER.

   The primary file should appear on screen with the cursor positioned at the first {INPUT} code. The prompt "Type full contact name" should appear in the lower-left corner of the screen.
4. Type `Mr. Albert Coe` and press F9 to display the prompt for the company name shown in the following figure.

Cursor marking position for data entry

{INPUT} code has been removed

Message prompts user for specific data

```
                    Scott Brown
                 33 Rangeline Road
               Indianapolis, IN 46315
                   (317)849-9876

July 24, 1991

Mr. Albert Coe
_
{INPUT}Type company street~
{INPUT}Type company city, state and zip code~

Dear {INPUT}Type contact's last name~

     Your ad in the {INPUT}Type source~ caught my attention. I am
interested in the challenging position you described. Enclosed is
my resume. I will be in town next week and would like to set up
an interview at the earliest possible time.

Sincerely,


Scott Brown, MBA, CPA

Type company name                          Doc 1 Pg 1 Ln 1.83" Pos 1"
```

▶ To complete additional data entry from the keyboard:

1. At the "Type company name" prompt, type **`Electronics 2001`** and press F9.
2. At the "Type company street" prompt, type **`300 Duplex Road`** and press F9.
3. At the "Type company city, state, and zip code" prompt, type **`Indianapolis, IN 46250`** and press F9.
4. At the "Type contact's last name" prompt, type **`Mr. Coe`** and press F9.
5. At the "Type source" prompt, type **`Indianapolis Star`** and press F9 to complete the custom letter shown in the following figure.

```
                    Scott Brown
                 33 Rangeline Road
               Indianapolis, IN 46315
                   (317)849-9876

July 24, 1991

Mr. Albert Coe
Electronics 2001
300 Duplex Road
Indianapolis, IN 46250

Dear Mr. Coe,

     Your ad in the Indianapolis Star caught my attention. I am
interested in the challenging position you described. Enclosed is
my resume. I will be in town next week and would like to set up
an interview at the earliest possible time.

Sincerely,


Scott Brown, MBA, CPA
```

After the Merge process is complete, you can make additional editing changes and print the results. Ordinarily, you will not save a one-time letter to disk. To create a second letter, access a blank WordPerfect 5.1 screen and start the keyboard Merge process again.

This concludes the projects in the WordPerfect 5.1 module. You can exit the current document and exit WordPerfect or remain in the program and work the Review Exercises and Additional Projects.

Summary

- When you need to send out the same or very similar information to several people, WordPerfect 5.1's Merge facility can help you get the job done.
- By setting up a primary merge document that contains the data that is to be sent to all recipients and then inserting codes to indicate where the variable data goes, you can type in the text once and produce many documents.
- The codes that you insert in your form letter point to the names of fields you create in the secondary document that serves as your database. These {FIELD NAMES} are separated from one another in the database header record and in your form with a tilde (~).
- Once you have proofed your primary document, checked it with the Speller, verified that all the data in your secondary document is accurate and that the names and number of the fields in the primary document match the corresponding names in the secondary document, you can perform the merge.
- For smaller merge projects, an alternative to creating a secondary document file is to input the variable data directly from the keyboard during the merge.

Key Terms

custom document
database
field
field name
header record
merge code
merging
primary merge document
record
secondary merge document

Study Questions

True/False

1. You can merge no more than 100 names and addresses into a form letter. T F
2. Field names may not contain spaces. T F
3. WordPerfect 5.1 inserts a ^ (caret) between fields in a header record. T F
4. In the Merge function, "Pg" in the status line refers to records, not pages. T F
5. SHIFT-F9 inserts an {END FIELD} code. T F
6. The secondary document controls how the finished document looks. T F
7. The merge begins automatically when you select Merge from the Tools menu. T F
8. Each custom document created by Merge is saved as a separate file. T F

9. You use a primary file when merging data from a secondary file, not when merging from the keyboard. T F
10. The {DATE} code prompts you to enter the date from the keyboard. T F

Fill in the Blanks

1. You can merge data into a document from __________ or __________.
2. Pieces of information in the secondary document are organized as separate __________ of data.
3. For each custom document, one __________ from the secondary file is merged with a copy of the primary document.
4. Each data field within a record ends with an __________ code.
5. Another name for a secondary document is a __________.
6. A header record contains __________.
7. To define the field names in your header record, press __________.
8. During the merge process, you are prompted first for the name of a __________ file.
9. __________ prompts appear in the lower-left corner of the screen to notify you when to enter information from the keyboard.
10. Press __________ to initiate a merge operation.

For Discussion

1. What purpose do merge codes serve?
2. How does the primary document "know" where to insert the data from the secondary merge file?
3. If you merge data from the keyboard instead of a file, what two codes can you insert to prompt you to type in the information at the appropriate time?
4. Provide your own example for using WordPerfect's Merge feature.
5. Why would you choose to input variable data from the keyboard instead of from a file?

REVIEW EXERCISES

Review the concepts presented in Project 7 by completing the following tasks. If necessary, review the material.

The president of the company has asked you to send a memo to each employee to remind him or her of the upcoming annual review and to verify each person's current rate of pay and annual salary. She is not sure yet what the cost-of-living increase or range of merit raises will be, so she asks that you leave these fields to input when you are ready to print the memos. You will modify the 8_15WAGE.MEM document you have used in previous projects and create a new document to use as the secondary merge file.

1. Access a blank WordPerfect 5.1 document screen.
2. Retrieve the memo 8_15WAGE.MEM.
3. Change the memo so it looks like the figure that follows.

```
To:       {FIELD}FIRSTNAME~ {FIELD}LASTNAME~
          {FIELD}TITLE~, {FIELD}DEPARTMENT~

From:     Linda Wiest, President

Date:     August 15, 1992

Re:       Annual Review and Pay Increases

Employee annual reviews are quickly approaching.  I am taking
this opportunity to remind you of your current payroll status.  I
also want to give you a general idea of the (across-the-board)
pay increases that will be forthcoming, independent of individual
merit increases.

Our records show that your current rate of pay is {FIELD}PAYRATE~ per
hour and that your annual salary (not including overtime
compensation and bonuses) is {FIELD}SALARY~.  The company-wide
cost-of-living increases will remain at 7 percent.  Your merit
increase may include up to an additional 3 percent.  Final
figures will be available after all annual reviews are completed.
```

4. Save and exit the edited memo, giving it the new name **9_1WAGE.PRI**
5. Access a blank WordPerfect document screen and create the header record of your secondary merge document; it should look like the header that follows.

```
{FIELDNAMES}FIRSTNAME~LASTNAME~TITLE~DEPARTMENT~PAYRATE
~SALARY~~{END RECORD}
=========================================================
```

6. Enter the following data after the header record. Remember to press F9 at the end of each field, and SHIFT-F9 to file each employee record.

FIRSTNAME	Kerri	Jacob	Abdul	Sofia
LASTNAME	Chen	Wasserman	Hassan	Petral
TITLE	Technician	Assembler 1	Clerk 2	Driver
DEPARTMENT	Drafting	Production	Accounting	Facilities
PAYRATE	8.36	5.87	7.48	6.55
SALARY	17,388	12,209	15,558	13,624

7. Save the secondary document on the diskette in drive A:, giving the file the name **WAGEDATA.SEC.**

8. Access a blank document screen and execute the merge.
9. Check that all the field codes have been replaced correctly with the corresponding data from WAGEDATA.SEC.
10. Save the merged document to the disk in drive A:. Call the file **`WAGEMERG.9_1`**
11. Print the first two pages of WAGEMERG.9_1.
12. Exit the current document and either exit WordPerfect or continue to work through Additional Projects.

Additional Projects

Developing Documents for a Job Search

1. Using your own letterhead, write a letter to your state's legislative board to request copies of the appropriate forms and materials necessary for you to apply for a summer internship position.
2. In addition to sending you several forms, the Secretary of the Legislature directs you to send your resume to each of your district's three representatives. Create a general cover letter to accompany your resume.
3. Create your resume. Limit it to one page. Be sure to include your address and contact information, education and job history, personal and/or professional references, career objectives, and interests. Use indent and tab settings, margins, and text emphasis to create a professional layout.
4. Use the WordPerfect 5.1 Speller to help you proofread your documents.
5. Using the Merge feature, create a document listing the names and contact information for each resume you send out, including the date you mailed each packet. Include the various codes Merge requires.
6. Create a follow-up letter addressed to each representative's office. Ask the status of your application and when you might be able to schedule an interview. Use either a copy of your original cover letter or copy the block of the address needed to form a new document.
7. After your interview, send a follow-up letter to the person who conducted your interview. Thank him or her for the time spent with you, and reiterate why you believe you are the best candidate for the position.
8. Make a copy of the original cover letter you sent to the representatives. Using WordPerfect 5.1's capacities for searching, replacing, copying blocks, moving, and deleting and by using the INS and DEL keys, modify your text to send a similar letter to assembly and council members.

Creating a Monthly Status Report

1. After you begin your job with Representative X, one of your first projects is to send out a monthly status report to all the district managers. In addition to a brief paragraph for each topic, the first page should contain the general address information, an introductory paragraph on what the report covers, and when the next meeting to discuss the information will be held. The second page should contain a table summarizing the finances of the district.

Developing a Newspaper Review

1. One of the first ways a budding journalist can get a byline is to write restaurant, movie, music, or book reviews for a local newspaper. Write a review of anything from a new fast-food chain, the latest blockbuster film, your favorite performer's new CD, or a new novel.
2. Format your review as follows: Create two pages of text in 12-point type, double-spaced, with 2-inch left and right margins. Indent one tab at the beginning of each paragraph. The title of your review should be centered on the first line and underlined. The header should contain your name and phone number. The footer should include the date, the word "MORE" on page 1, and the "-30-" on page 2 to signal the end.

COMMAND REFERENCE

Function Key Applications

The ten function keys have been assigned four separate applications, depending on whether the key is pressed alone or in combination with the CTRL, SHIFT, or ALT key. For example, pressing F3 accesses Help. However, pressing the combination of keys SHIFT-F2 accesses Search Backward. Pressing a combination of keys, such as SHIFT-F3, means to press and hold the first key down, press the second key, and then release both keys. The following is a summary of the function keys.

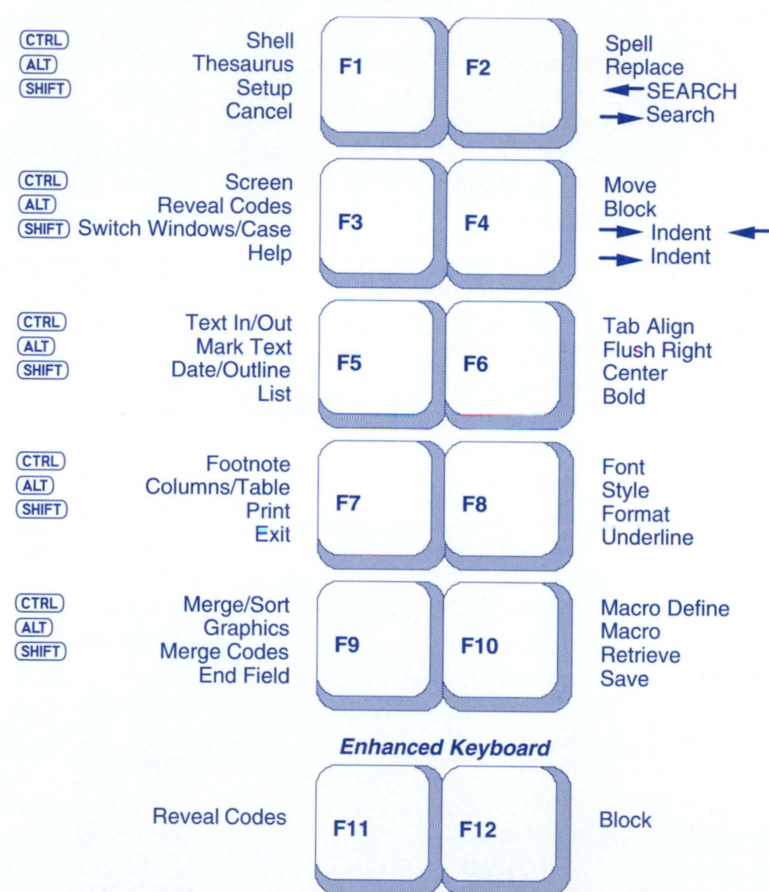

Alphabetical Listing of Function Key Operations

The function key applications shown on the previous page are listed alphabetically below by function to assist you in locating the desired key sequence.

Function	Keys
Block	ALT-F4 or F12
Bold	F6
Cancel	F1
Center	SHIFT-F6
Columns/Table	ALT-F7
Date/Outline	SHIFT-F5
End Field	F9
Exit	F7
Flush Right	ALT-F6
Font	CTRL-F8
Footnote	CTRL-F7
Format	SHIFT-F8
Graphics	ALT-F9
Help	F3
→Indent←	SHIFT-F4
→Indent	F4
List Files	F5
Macro	ALT-F10
Macro Define	CTRL-F10
Mark Text	ALT-F5
Merge/Sort	CTRL-F9
Merge Codes	SHIFT-F9
Move	CTRL-F4
Print	SHIFT-F7
Replace	ALT-F2
Retrieve	SHIFT-F10
Reveal Codes	ALT-F3 or F11
Save	F10
Screen	CTRL-F3
←Search	SHIFT-F2
→Search	F2
Setup	SHIFT-F1
Shell	CTRL-F1
Spell	CTRL-F2
Style	ALT-F8
Switch	SHIFT-F3
Tab Align	CTRL-F6
Text In/Out	CTRL-F5
Thesaurus	ALT-F1
Underline	F8

Glossary for WordPerfect 5.1

alignment Text spaced to always begin or end evenly at the left or right margin or to be arranged in a column at a tab stop.

absolute tab A tab positioned relative to the left edge of the paper. Text aligned on an absolute tab does not shift when the left margin changes. *See also* relative tab.

active window The screen displaying the document currently being edited. Two documents can be open for editing at the same time. If the screen is split to display part of each document, the active window is the portion where the cursor is located.

(ALT)-= The two-key combination that activates the WordPerfect 5.1 menu system.

block WordPerfect 5.1 text to which a command will apply. For example, by marking text as a block and entering the appropriate command, you can move, copy, or delete the block; unmarked text remains unchanged.

case-sensitive A search condition that finds words or phrases with specific capitalization.

cell The intersection of a row and a column in a WordPerfect 5.1 table.

cell attribute The size, style, and alignment of data displayed in the cell of a table.

cell reference A symbol in one cell of a table that refers to the contents of another cell in the table.

character A symbol from the standard keyboard (a...z, A...Z, 0...9, and special symbols) and over 1700 other symbols that must be composed or selected using the combination (CTRL)-**V** or (CTRL)-**2**.

click To press a mouse button to make a selection.

column Text between a right and left margin. Up to 24 text columns can appear across a page; text can appear in "newspaper" format, flowing from column to column, or in "parallel" format, in which copy is independent of text in adjacent columns.

column heading Text placed at the top of a column indicating what information appears in the column.

column table A group of cells arranged vertically in a table. Columns of cells are referenced alphabetically (i.e., the letters A...IV).

combine documents Retrieve a document from disk into a document already in memory.

control code A keystroke combination produced by pressing (CTRL) and a letter key. In WordPerfect 5.1 control codes control macros and merges (for example, (CTRL)-**N**).

copying text To duplicate a block of text at another location in a document.

cursor A flashing prompt on-screen that indicates where the next character is to be inserted.

cursor movement key A key that controls movement of the cursor: (→), (←), (↑), (↓), (PGUP), (PGDN), (HOME), and (END).

custom document A document formed by merging a document that stays the same with a file that contains data that changes for each record.

database A collection of records containing related information. An example is a name and address file used by Merge to create custom documents.

decimal tab A tab used to place numeric data in a column so the decimal points align.

default setting A WordPerfect 5.1 specification used automatically until changed by the user.

dot leader A series of dots (....) that precede tabbed data or page numbers in a table of contents. Dot leaders can be inserted automatically by several WordPerfect 5.1 features.

double-click To press a mouse button twice to make a selection.

drag To move or copy a block of text by using a mouse.

editing The process of adding, changing, or deleting the contents of a document.

endnote Credits, citations, and explanatory remarks that are organized and placed at the end of a chapter or document.

field A group of related characters in a record—for example, a person's first name.

field name A name assigned to a field in a database so that data in that field can be accessed.

file A collection of related records stored in a file on disk—for example, a file of stock records containing inventory information.

font The attributes of printed characters—for example, 12-pitch Courier font refers to the style and size of the characters being printed.

footer A standard annotation that appears at the bottom of each page of a printed document. The footers on odd and even pages are often different.

footnote A credit, citation, or explanatory remark at the end of a page.

format text To make text readable by setting margins and tabs, centering text, changing print fonts, and enhancing the page by specifying bold, italic, and other features.

formatted disk A disk that has been prepared for use—that is, to read and write files.

formatting code Code used to improve the attractiveness and readibility of text by controlling margins and tabs; centering text; changing print fonts; and specifying bold, italic, and other enhancing features.

formula A math operation entered in a cell of a table.

function Symbol (+, t, =, T, and N) used in the Math mode to control totaling and subtotaling actions.

hard carriage return Hard carriage returns are inserted in text (by pressing (ENTER)) to indicate the end of a paragraph or block of text and to insert blank lines. Soft carriage returns are inserted by WordPerfect 5.1 to indicate the end of a print line and cause text to wrap around to the next line.

hard page break A code entered in text (by pressing (CTRL)-(ENTER)) to cause a page break prior to the normal end of a page.

header A standard annotation that appears at the top of each page of a printed document.

header record The first record of a secondary merge file. The header record describes and names the fields used in merge records.

headword A word in the Thesaurus that has additional synonyms and antonyms.

hidden code A code inserted in a document by WordPerfect 5.1 when you press certain keys. Some codes, such as the codes that represent tabs and indents, control text. Other codes, such as those that represent headers and footers, contain data used in the document. *See also* Reveal Codes.

indent Temporarily moves the left margin in one tab until ENTER is pressed.

Insert Causes newly input characters entered from the keyboard to shift existing text to the right of the current cursor position.

justification Alignment of text with the left and/or right margins.

List Files The WordPerfect 5.1 file management facility.

Look An option in the List Files facility. Look mode lets you see the contents of a file on disk, without retrieving the file into random-access memory.

Look Up An option in the List Files facility that lets you search the contents of files in a directory for a character, word, or phrase.

margin The top, bottom, left, and right boundaries on a page that limit the area in which text and graphics can appear.

mark To identify text as copy subject to a command.

math operator An arithmetic symbol that performs addition, subtraction, multiplication, or division in tables.

menu bar A menu in which options appear horizontally across a line at the top of the screen; choosing an option causes a pull-down menu to appear.

merge code A code inserted in a primary merge document and secondary merge file. A merge code controls how data is merged from the secondary merge file or keyboard into the primary merge file.

merging Combining text entry from the keyboard or data in a document with another document stored on disk.

mouse A hand-held device used to control the cursor on the screen and make menu selections.

mouse cursor A reverse-video box that appears when you move the mouse.

moving text To transfer a block of text from one location to another.

on-screen help Documentation that can be viewed on the monitor by pressing the F3 Help function key.

page layout The general organization of a page. Elements in the layout include margins, tab settings, headers and footers, and usable text area.

paragraph A block of text typed continuously and ended by pressing ENTER.

point To make a menu selection by highlighting the choice and pressing ENTER.

primary merge document A document containing unchanging text and merge codes that control how data from a secondary merge file or keyboard is combined with the unchanging text to create a custom document.

print A List Files option to print files from disk.

pull-down menu A menu in which options appear vertically in a column when you highlight a choice in the menu bar.

Ready The mode on a printer that indicates that the printer is ready to print.

record A group of related fields—for example, a stock record containing fields of data about an item of furniture in an inventory.

relative tab A tab positioned relative to the left margin. Text aligned on a relative tab shifts when the left margin changes. *See also* absolute tab.

rename To give a file or document a new name.

replace To scan a document electronically for a character, word, phrase, or hidden code and replace it with another character, word, phrase, or hidden code.

retrieve To load a document from disk onto a WordPerfect 5.1 screen.

Reveal Codes The mode in which WordPerfect 5.1's hidden codes are made visible. The hidden codes control, format, and enhance text.

row A group of cells arranged horizontally across a table. Rows of cells are numbered sequentially beginning with 1. An individual cell is referenced by its column and row placement within a table.

save To store a document on a disk.

scroll To move a document up and down to view other parts of it.

search To scan a document electronically for a character, word, phrase, or hidden code.

secondary merge document A document containing a header record and database records. The database records can be merged into a primary merge document.

soft page break A hidden code [SPg] indicating that text continues on the next page automatically.

software Computer instructions, written by people, which cause the computer to complete specified tasks.

Speller A feature in WordPerfect 5.1 that checks the spelling of each word in a block, page, or document against an electronic dictionary. If a word is not found in the dictionary, the Speller offers several possible correct spellings and the chance to add the word to the dictionary.

split screen A WordPerfect 5.1 screen display divided into two parts (windows). Different documents can be displayed in each part.

spreadsheet Data in a row-and-column format from programs such as PlanPerfect, Lotus 1-2-3, and Excel. Many spreadsheets can be imported into a WordPerfect 5.1 table.

status line On the WordPerfect 5.1 screen, the line that displays information about the current document, including the location of the cursor.

tab ruler A bar that displays the current tab settings and margins. The tab ruler can be displayed at the bottom of the screen and is visible when using a split screen.

tab setting Controls the position of text from the left margin when the TAB, <←INDENT→>, or <←Indent> is pressed.

table Data displayed in cells arranged in rows and columns. *Table* is the term used in WordPerfect 5.1 to describe its spreadsheet capabilities.

Table Edit The mode in WordPerfect 5.1 that allows you to make changes to the size, appearance, and format of cells in a table. You cannot change cell contents in this mode.

table heading Cells in a table at the top of the table or the top of a new page of a table.

Thesaurus An electronic tool that accesses a list of synonyms and antonyms from which a substitute word may be selected and inserted into the document in place of the original word.

Typeover The mode in which characters entered from the keyboard type over existing characters.

unit of measure The standard by which distance or size is calculated—for example, inches, centimeters, point size, characters, or lines.

value The numeric contents of a cell in a table, expressed as a number or a formula.

view To look at a document on disk using F5 for List Look or F7 for Print View options.

View Document A print option used to view a document and its graphics as they will appear when printed.

window The screen displaying a document. Two documents, thus two windows, can be in use at one time. Users can switch between the two windows to edit. *See also* split screen.

word wrap The facility that automatically shifts text that extends beyond the right margin to the next line.

INDEX

Note: All page numbers refer to the WordPerfect 5.1 (WP) module only.